Caitlin
Thompson!

French
Universal Dictionary

French – English
Anglais – Français

Berlitz Publishing
New York · Munich · Singapore

Original edition edited by the
Langenscheidt editorial staff

Compiled by LEXUS

Book in cover photo: © Punchstock/MedioImages

© 2010 Berlitz Publishing/APA Publications GmbH & Co.
Verlag KG, Singapore Branch, Singapore

Trademark Reg. U.S. Patent Office and other countries.
Marca Registrada.
Used under license from
Berlitz Investment Corporation.

Printed in Germany
ISBN 978-981-268-354-0

(73282)

10010

Contents / Table des matières

Abbreviations / Abréviations 4

La prononciation / Pronunciation 7

French – English / Français – Anglais 9

English – French / Anglais – Français 265

Verbes irréguliers anglais 571

Numbers / Les nombres 574

Abbreviations / Abréviations

and	&	et
see	→	voir
registered trademark	®	marque déposée
adjective	*adj*	adjectif
adverb	*adv*	adverbe
agriculture	AGR	agriculture
anatomy	ANAT	anatomie
architecture	ARCH	architecture
astronomy	ASTR	astronomie
astrology	ASTROL	astrologie
attributive	*atr*	devant le nom
motoring	AUTO	automobiles
aviation	AVIAT	aviation
biology	BIOL	biologie
botany	BOT	botanique
British English	*Br*	anglais britannique
chemistry	CHIM	chimie
commerce, business	COMM	commerce
computers, IT term	COMPUT	informatique
conjunction	*conj*	conjonction
cooking	CUIS	cuisine
economics	ÉCON	économie
education	EDU	éducation
education	ÉDU	éducation
electricity	ÉL	électricité
electricity	ELEC	électricité
especially	*esp*	surtout
euphemism	*euph*	euphémisme
familiar, colloquial	F	familier
feminine	*f*	féminin
figurative	*fig*	figuré

finance	FIN	finance
formal	*fml*	langage formel
feminine plural	*fpl*	féminin pluriel
geography	GEOG	géographie
geography	GÉOGR	géographie
geology	GÉOL	géologie
geometry	GÉOM	géométrie
grammar	GRAM	grammaire
historical	HIST	historique
IT term	INFORM	informatique
interjection	*int*	interjection
invariable	*inv*	invariable
law	JUR	juridique
law	LAW	juridique
linguistics	LING	linguistique
literary	*litt*	littéraire
masculine	*m*	masculin
nautical	MAR	marine
mathematics	MATH	mathématiques
medicine	MED	médecine
medicine	MÉD	médecine
masculine and feminine	*m/f*	masculin et féminin
military	MIL	militaire
motoring	MOT	automobiles
masculine plural	*mpl*	masculin pluriel
music	MUS	musique
noun	*n*	nom
nautical	NAUT	marine
plural noun	*npl*	nom pluriel
singular noun	*nsg*	nom singulier
oneself	o.s.	se, soi
popular, slang	P	populaire
pejorative	*pej*	péjoratif

pejorative	*péj*	péjoratif
pharmacy	PHARM	pharmacie
photography	PHOT	photographie
physics	PHYS	physique
plural	*pl*	pluriel
politics	POL	politique
preposition	*prep*	préposition
preposition	*prép*	préposition
pronoun	*pron*	pronom
psychology	PSYCH	psychologie
something	*qch*	quelque chose
someone	*qn*	quelqu'un
radio	RAD	radio
railroad	RAIL	chemin de fer
religion	REL	religion
singular	*sg*	singulier
someone	s.o.	quelqu'un
sports	SP	sport
something	*sth*	quelque chose
subjunctive	*subj*	subjonctif
noun	*subst*	substantif
theater	THEA	théâtre
theater	THÉÁT	théâtre
technology	TECH	technique
telecommunications	TÉL	télécommunications
telecommunications	TELEC	télécommunications
typography, typesetting	TYP	typographie
television	TV	télévision
vulgar	V	vulgaire
auxiliary verb	*v/aux*	verbe auxiliaire
intransitive verb	*v/i*	verbe intransitif
transitive verb	*v/t*	verbe transitif
zoology	ZO	zoologie

La Prononciation / Pronunciation

Les consonnes / Consonants

[b]	*bag*	*bouche*
[d]	*dear*	*dans*
[f]	*fall*	*foule*
[g]	*give*	*gai*
[h]	*hole*	*et hop*
[j]	*yes*	*radio*
[k]	*come*	*qui*
[l]	*land*	*la*
[m]	*mean*	*mon*
[n]	*night*	*nuit*
[p]	*pot*	*pot*
[r]	*right (la langue vers le haut)*	*reine*
[s]	*sun*	*sauf*
[t]	*take*	*table*
[v]	*vain*	*vain*
[w]	*wait*	*oui*
[z]	*rose*	*rose*
[ŋ]	*bring*	*feeling*
[ʃ]	*she*	*chat*
[tʃ]	*chair*	*cha-cha-cha*
[dʒ]	*join*	*adjuger*
[ʒ]	*leisure*	*juge*
[θ]	*think*	langue entres les dents
[ð]	*the*	langue derrière les dents du haut

Les voyelles anglaises / English vowels

[ɑː]	far	âme
[æ]	man	salle
[e]	get	sec
[ə]	utter	le
[ɜː]	absurd	beurre
[ɪ]	stick	i très court
[iː]	need	si
[ɒ]	in-laws	phase
[ɔː]	more	essor
[ʌ]	mother	entre à et eux
[ʊ]	book	bouquin (très court)
[uː]	hoot	sous

Les diphtongues anglaises / English diphthongs

[aɪ]	time	aïe
[aʊ]	cloud	ciao
[eɪ]	name	nez suivi d'un y court
[ɔɪ]	point	cow-boy
[oʊ]	so	eau

['] indique que la syllabe suivante est accentuée: *ability* [ə'bɪlətɪ]

Some French words starting with h have ' before the h. This ' is not part of the French word. It shows i) that a preceding vowel does not become an apostrophe and ii) that no elision takes place. (This is called an aspirated h).

'hanche	la hanche, les hanches [no z sound between *les* and *hanches*]
habit	l'habit, les habits [a z sound between *les* and *habits*]

French – English
Français – Anglais

A

à *lieu* in; *direction* to; **au bout de la rue** at/to the end of the street; **~ 2 heures d'ici** 2 hours from here; **~ cinq heures** at five o'clock; **~ Noël** at Christmas; **~ demain** until tomorrow; **c'est ~ moi** it's mine, it belongs to me; **aux cheveux blonds** with blonde hair; **~ pied** on foot; **~ dix euros** at *ou* for ten euros

abaissement *m* lowering; (*humiliation*) abasement; **abaisser** lower; *fig* (*humilier*) humble; **s'~** drop; *fig* demean o.s.

abandonner abandon; *pouvoir* give up; SP withdraw from; **s'~** (*se confier*) open up; **s'~ à** give way to

abasourdi amazed

abat-jour *m* (lamp)shade

abattre *arbre* fell; AVIAT shoot down; *animal* slaughter; *péj* (*tuer*) kill; *fig* (*épuiser*) exhaust; (*décourager*) dishearten; **s'~** collapse

abbaye *f* abbey

abcès *m* abscess

abdomen *m* abdomen

abeille *f* bee

aberrant F absurd

abêtir make stupid

abîmer spoil, ruin; **s'~** be ruined; *d'aliments* spoil

aboiement *m* barking

abolir abolish; **abolition** *f* abolition

abominable appalling

abondance *f* abundance

abonné, ~e *m/f* subscriber; **abonnement** *m* subscription; *de transport, de spectacles* season ticket; **abonner: s'~ à** subscribe to

abord *m*: **d'~** first; **au premier ~** at first sight; **~s** surroundings; **aborder 1** *v/t* (*prendre d'assaut*) board; (*heurter*) collide with; *fig: question* tackle; *personne* approach **2** *v/i* land (**à** at)

aboutir *d'un projet* succeed; **~ à** end at; *fig* lead to; **aboutissement** *m* (*résultat*) result

aboyer bark

abréger abridge

abréviation *f* abbreviation

abri *m* shelter; **être sans ~** be homeless

abricot *m* apricot; **abricotier** *m* apricot (tree)

abriter (*loger*) take in, shelter; **~ de** (*protéger*) shelter from; **s'~** take shelter

abrupt abrupt; *pente* steep

abruti stupid; **abrutir: ~ qn** be bad for s.o.'s brain; (*surmener*) exhaust s.o.

absence *f* absence; **absent** absent; *air* absent-minded; **absenter: s'~** leave, go away

absolu absolute; **absolument** absolutely

absorber absorb; *nourriture* eat; *boisson* drink; **s'~ dans** be absorbed in

abstenir: s'~ POL abstain; **s'~ de faire qc** refrain from doing sth; **abstention** *f* POL abstention

abstrait abstract

absurdité *f* absurdity; **~(s)** nonsense

abus *m* abuse; **~ de confiance** breach of trust; **abuser** overstep the mark; **~ de qc** misuse ou abuse sth; **s'~** be mistaken; **abusif, -ive** excessive; *emploi d'un mot* incorrect

académie *f* academy

acajou *m* mahogany

accabler: être accablé de be weighed down by; **~ qn de qc** heap sth on s.o.

accalmie *f aussi fig* lull

accaparer ÉCON, *fig* monopolize

accéder: ~ à reach, get to; INFORM access; *à l'indépendance, au pouvoir* gain; *d'un chemin* lead to

accélérateur *m* AUTO gas pedal, *Br* accelerator; **accélérer** *aussi* AUTO accelerate

accent *m* accent; (*intonation*) stress; **mettre l'~ sur qc** *fig* put the emphasis on sth; **accentuer** *syllabe* stress, accentuate

acceptable acceptable; **accepter** accept; (*reconnaître*) agree; **~ de faire** agree to do

accès *m aussi* INFORM access; MÉD fit

accessoire 1 *adj* incidental **2** *m* detail; **~s** accessories; THÉÂT props

accident *m* accident; *événement fortuit* mishap; **par ~** by accident, accidentally; **accidentel, ~le** accidental

acclamation *f* acclamation; **~s** cheers, cheering; **acclamer** cheer

acclimater: s'~ become acclimatized

accolade *f* embrace; *signe* brace, *Br* curly bracket

accommodation *f* adaptation; **accommoder** adapt; CUIS prepare; **~ à** adapt to; **s'~ de** make do with

accompagnateur, -trice *m/f* guide; MUS accompanist; **accompagner** accompany

accomplir accomplish; *souhait* realize

accord *m* agreement; MUS chord; **d'~** OK, alright; **être d'~** agree; **tomber d'~** come to an agreement; **accordé:**

(**bien**) ~ in tune

accordéon accordion

accorder *crédit* grant; GRAM make agree; MUS tune; **s'~** get on; GRAM agree; **s'~ qc** allow o.s. sth

accouchement *m* birth; **accoucher** give birth (**de** to)

accouder: **s'~** lean (one's elbows); **accoudoir** *m* armrest

accoupler connect; **s'~** BIOL mate

accourir come running

accoutumance *f* MÉD dependence; **accoutumer**: ~ **qn à qc** get s.o. used to sth; **s'~ à qc** get used to sth

accrocher *manteau* hang up; AUTO collide with; **s'~ à** hang on to; *fig* cling to

accroître increase; **s'~** grow

accroupir: **s'~** crouch, squat

accueil *m* reception, welcome; **accueillir** greet, welcome

accumulation *f* accumulation; **accumuler** accumulate; **s'~** accumulate

accusation *f* accusation; JUR prosecution; *plainte* charge; **accusé, ~e** *m* 1 JUR: **l'~** the accused 2 COMM: **accusé** *m* **de réception** acknowledgement (of receipt); **accuser** (*incriminer*) accuse (**de** of); (*faire ressortir*) emphasize

acerbe caustic

acéré sharp

acharnement *m* grim deter-

mination; **acharner**: **s'~ à faire qc** be bent on doing sth; **s'~ sur** *ou* **contre qn** pick on s.o.

achat *m* purchase; **faire des ~s** go shopping

acheter buy

achever finish; **s'~** finish

acide 1 *adj* sour; CHIM acidic 2 *m* CHIM acid

acier *m* steel

acné *f* acne

à-coup *m* jerk; **par ~s** in fits and starts

acoustique acoustic

acquéreur *m* purchaser; **acquérir** acquire; *droit* win

acquiescer: ~ **à** agree to

acquis acquired; *résultats* achieved

acquisition *f* acquisition

acquitter *facture* pay; JUR acquit; **s'~ de** carry out; *dette* pay

âcre acrid; *goût, fig* bitter; **âcreté** *f* bitterness

acrobate *m/f* acrobat; **acrobatie** *f* acrobatics *pl*

acte *m* (*action*) action, deed; (*document officiel*) deed; THÉÂT act; ~ **de mariage** marriage certificate

acteur, -trice *m/f* actor; actress

actif, -ive 1 *adj* active 2 *m* COMM assets *pl*

action *f* action; COMM share; **~s** stock, shares *pl*; **actionnaire** *m/f* shareholder

actionner operate; *alarme etc*

activate
activer (*accélérer*) speed up
activité *f* activity
actualiser update
actualité *f* current events *pl*; **~s** TV news *sg*
actuel, **~le** current, present; (*d'actualité*) topical; **actuellement** currently, at present
adaptation *f* adaptation; **adapter** adapt; **s'~ à** adapt to
addition *f* addition; *au restaurant* check, *Br* bill; **additionner** add
adéquat suitable; *montant* adequate
adhérent, **~e** *m/f* member; **adhérer** stick, adhere (**à** to)
adhésif, **-ive 1** *adj* sticky, adhesive **2** *m* adhesive
adieu *m* goodbye; **faire ses ~x** say one's goodbyes (**à qn** to s.o.)
adjectif *m* GRAM adjective
adjoint, **~e** *m/f & adj* assistant, deputy
admettre (*autoriser*) allow; (*accueillir*) admit, allow in; (*reconnaître*) admit
administrateur, **-trice** *m/f* administrator; **administratif**, **-ive** administrative; **administration** *f* administration; (*direction*) management, running
admirateur, **-trice 1** *adj* admiring **2** *m/f* admirer; **admiration** *f* admiration; **admirer** admire

admissible *candidat* eligible; **ce n'est pas ~** that's unacceptable
admission *f* admission
adolescence *f* adolescence; **adolescent**, **~e** *m/f* adolescent, teenager
adopter adopt; **adoption** *f* adoption
adorable adorable; **adorer** REL worship; *fig* (*aimer*) adore
adosser lean; **s'~ contre** *ou* **à** lean against ou on
adoucir soften; **s'~ du temps** become milder
adrénaline *f* adrenalin
adresse *f* address; (*habileté*) skill; **~ électronique** email address
adresser *lettre* address (**à** to); *remarque* direct (**à** at); **~ la parole à** address, speak to; **s'~ à qn** apply to s.o.; (*être destiné à*) be aimed at s.o.
adroit skillful, *Br* skilful
adulte 1 *adj* adult; *plante* mature **2** *m/f* adult, grown-up
adultère 1 *adj* adulterous **2** *m* adultery
adverbe *m* GRAM adverb
adversaire *m/f* opponent, adversary
adversité *f* adversity
aération *f* ventilation; **aérer** ventilate; *literie*, *pièce* air
aérien, **~ne** *atr*; *vue* aerial
aérobic *f* aerobics
aérodynamique aerodynamic

aéronautique aeronautical

aéroport *m* airport

aérosol *m* aerosol

affable affable

affaiblir weaken; **s'~** weaken

affaire *f* (*question*) matter, business; (*entreprise*) business; *marché* deal; (*bonne occasion*) bargain; JUR case; (*scandale*) affair, business; **~s biens personnels** things, belongings; **les ~s étrangères** foreign affairs; **affairer: s'~** busy o.s.

affaisser: s'~ *du terrain* subside; *d'une personne* collapse

affamé hungry (*de* for)

affectation *f* *d'une chose* allocation; *d'un employé* assignment; MIL posting; (*pose*) affectation; **affecter** (*destiner*) allocate; *employé* assign; MIL post; (*émouvoir*) affect

affectif, -ive emotional

affection *f* affection; MÉD complaint

affectueux, -euse affectionate

affermir strengthen

affichage *m* billposting; INFORM display; **affiche** *f* poster; **afficher** *affiche* stick up; *attitude*, INFORM display

affilier: s'~ à *club* join; **être affilié à** be a member of

affiner refine

affinité *f* affinity

affirmatif, -ive affirmative;

personne assertive; **affirmation** *f* statement; **affirmer** (*prétendre*) maintain; *autorité* assert

affligeant distressing, painful; **affliger** distress

affluence *f*: **heures d'~** rush hour *sg*; **affluent** *m* tributary; **affluer** come together

affolement *m* panic; **affoler** (*bouleverser*) madden, drive to distraction; *d'une foule, d'un cheval* panic; **s'~** panic

affranchir free; *lettre* meter, *Br* frank

affreux, -euse horrible; *peur, mal de tête* terrible

affront *m* insult, affront; **affronter** confront, face; SP meet; **s'~** confront ou face each other; SP meet

afin: **~ de faire** in order to do, so as to do; **~ que** (+ *subj*) so that

africain, ~e African; **Africain, ~e** *m/f* African; **Afrique** *f*: **l'~** Africa

agaçant annoying; **agacement** *m* annoyance; **agacer** annoy; (*taquiner*) tease

âge *m* age; **Moyen-Âge** Middle Ages *pl*; **personnes fpl du troisième ~** senior citizens; **quel ~ a-t-il?** how old is he?, what age is he?; **âgé** elderly; **~ de deux ans** aged two, two years old

agence *f* agency; *d'une banque* branch; **~ immobilière**

realtor's, *Br* estate agent's; **~ *matrimoniale*** marriage bureau

agenda *m* diary; **~ *électronique*** (personal) organizer

agenouiller: s'~ kneel (down)

agent *m* agent; **~ *de change*** stockbroker; **~ *immobilier*** realtor, *Br* real estate agent; **~ *de police*** police officer

agglomération *f* built-up area; *concentration de villes* conurbation

aggraver make worse; **s'~** worsen

agile agile; **agilité** *f* agility

agios *mpl* ÉCON bank charges

agir act; **~ *sur qn*** affect s.o.; *il s'agit de* it's about

agitation *f* hustle and bustle; POL unrest; (*nervosité*) agitation; **agiter** *bouteille* shake; *mouchoir*, *main* wave; (*préoccuper*, *énerver*) upset; **s'~** *d'un enfant* fidget; (*s'énerver*) get upset

agneau *m* lamb

agonie *f* death throes *pl*

agrafer *vêtements* fasten; *papier* staple; **agrafeuse** *f* stapler

agrandir enlarge; **agrandissement** *m* enlargement; *d'une ville* expansion

agréable pleasant (*à* to)

agrément *m* approval, consent; **les ~s** (*attraits*) the delights

agresser attack; **agresseur** *m* attacker; *pays* aggressor;

agressif, **-ive** aggressive; **agression** *f* attack; PSYCH stress

agriculteur *m* farmer; **agriculture** *f* agriculture, farming

agrumes *mpl* citrus fruit

ahuri astounded; **ahurissant** astounding

aide 1 *f* help, assistance; **à l'~ *de qc*** with the help of sth; **avec l'~ *de qn*** with s.o.'s help **2** *m/f* (*assistant*) assistant; **s'~ *de qc*** use sth **2** *v/i* help; **~ *à qc*** contribute to sth

aïeul, **~e** *m/f* ancestor; **aïeux** ancestors

aigle *m* eagle

aigre sour; *vent* bitter; *critique* sharp; *voix* shrill

aigu, **~ë** sharp; *son* high-pitched; *conflit* bitter; *intelligence* keen; MÉD, GÉOM, GRAM acute

aiguille *f* needle; *d'une montre* hand; *tour* spire

aiguiser sharpen; *fig: appétit* whet

ail *m* garlic

aile *f* wing; AUTO fender, *Br* wing

ailier *m* SP wing, winger

ailleurs somewhere else, elsewhere; **d'~** besides; **par ~** moreover

aimable kind

aimant *m* magnet

aimer like; *parent*, *enfant*, *mari etc* love; **~ *mieux*** prefer

aine f groin

aîné, ~e 1 adj elder; de trois ou plus eldest 2 m/f elder/eldest; il est mon ~ de deux ans he is two years older than me

ainsi this way, thus fml; ~ que and, as well as

air m air; aspect look; MUS tune; se donner des ~s give o.s. airs; airbag m airbag

aire f area; ~ de jeu playground

aisance f ease; (richesse) wealth

aise f ease; être à l'~ be comfortable; être mal à l'~ be uncomfortable; prendre ses ~s make o.s. at home

aisselle f armpit

ajourner postpone (de for); JUR adjourn

ajouter add; s'~ à be added to

ajuster adjust; vêtement alter; (viser) aim at; (joindre) fit (à to)

alarme f alarm; donner l'~ raise the alarm; ~ antivol burglar alarm; alarmer alarm; s'~ de be alarmed by

album m album

alcool m alcohol; alcoolique adj & m/f alcoholic; alcoolisme alcoholism; alco(o)test m Breathalyzer®, Br Breathalyser®

aléatoire uncertain; INFORM, MATH random

alentour ~s mpl surroundings pl; aux ~s de in the vicinity of; (autour de) about

alerte 1 adj alert 2 f alarm; ~ à la bombe bomb scare; alerter alert

algèbre f algebra

Algérie f: l'~ Algeria; algérien, ~ne Algerian; Algérien, ~ne m/f Algerian

algue f BOT seaweed

aligner TECH align (sur with); (mettre sur une ligne) line up; s'~ line up; s'~ sur qc align o.s. with sth

aliment m foodstuff; ~s food; alimentation f food; en eau, en électricité supply; ~ de base staple diet; alimenter feed; en eau, en électricité supply (en with); conversation keep going

alinéa m paragraph

allaiter breast-feed

allécher tempt

allée f (avenue) path; ~s et venues comings and goings

allégé yaourt low-fat; confiture low-sugar; alléger lighten; impôt, tension reduce

allègre cheerful

Allemagne f: l'~ Germany; allemand, ~e 1 adj German 2 m langue German; Allemand, ~e m/f German

aller 1 v/i go; ~ en voiture go by car; ~ chercher go for, fetch; comment allez-vous? how are you?; je vais bien I'm fine; ça va? is that OK?; (comment te portes-tu?) how are you?; ça va

bien merci fine, thanks; **~ bien avec** go well with; **on y va!** F let's go!; **allez!** go on!; **allons!** come on!; **allons donc!** come now!; **s'en ~** leave; *d'une tâche* disappear; **cette couleur te va bien** that color really suits you **2** *v/aux*: **je vais partir demain** I'm going to leave tomorrow, I'm leaving tomorrow **3** *m*: **~ et retour** round trip, *Br* return trip; **billet** round-trip ticket, *Br* return (ticket); **~ simple** one-way ticket, *Br* single; **match** *m* **~** away game

allergie *f* allergy; **allergique** allergic (**à** to)

alliance *f* POL alliance; *(mariage)* marriage; *(anneau)* wedding ring; **allié, ~e 1** *adj* allied; *famille* related by marriage **2** *m/f* ally; *famille* relative by marriage

allô hello

allocation *f* allowance; **~ chômage** workers' compensation, *Br* unemployment benefit

allonger lengthen, make longer; *jambes* stretch out; **s'~** get longer; *(s'étendre)* lie down

allumage *m* AUTO ignition; **allumer 1** *v/t* light; *chauffage, télévision etc* turn on **2** *v/i* turn the lights on; **allumette** *f* match

allure *f* *(démarche)* walk; *(vi-*

tesse) speed; *(air)* appearance; **avoir de l'~** have style

allusion *f* allusion

alors then; *(par conséquence)* so; **~ que** *temps* when; *opposition* while

alouette *f* lark

alourdir make heavy

Alpes *fpl*: **les ~** the Alps

alphabet *m* alphabet

alpinisme *m* mountaineering; **alpiniste** *m/f* mountaineer

altercation *f* argument

altérer *denrées* spoil; *couleur* fade; *vérité* distort; *texte* alter

alternance *f* alternation; *de cultures* rotation; **alternative** *f* alternative; **alterner** alternate

altitude *f* altitude

alto *m* alto; **à cordes** viola

altruisme *m* altruism

aluminium *m* aluminum, *Br* aluminium

amabilité *f* kindness

amadouer softsoap

amaigri thinner; **amaigrir**: **~ qn** cause s.o. to lose weight; **s'~** lose weight, get thinner

amalgame *m* mixture, amalgamation

amande *f* almond

amant *m* lover

amarrer MAR moor

amas *m* pile; **amasser** amass

amateur *m* lover; *non professionnel* amateur; **en ~** as a hobby ambassade *f* embassy; **ambassadeur, -drice** *m/f* ambassador

ambiance *f* (*atmosphère*) atmosphere

ambigu, ~ë ambiguous; **ambiguité** *f* ambiguity

ambitieux, -euse 1 *adj* ambitious 2 *m/f* ambitious person; **ambition** *f* ambition

ambivalence *f* ambivalence

ambulance *f* ambulance; **ambulancier** *m* paramedic, *Br* ambulance man

ambulant traveling, *Br* travelling

âme *f* soul; **état** *m* **d'~** state of mind; **~ charitable** do-gooder

amélioration *f* improvement; **améliorer** improve; **s'~** improve, get better

aménager *appartement* arrange, lay out; *terrain* develop; *vieille maison* convert

amende *f* fine

amender improve; *projet de loi* amend

amener bring; (*causer*) cause; **s'~** turn up

amer, -ère bitter

américain, ~e 1 *adj* American 2 *m* LING American English; **Américain, ~e** *m/f* American; **américaniser** Americanize

amérindien, ~ne Native American; **Amérindien, ~ne** *m/f* Native American

Amérique *f*: *l'~* America; *l'~* **centrale** Central America; *l'~* **latine** Latin America; *l'~* **du Nord** North America; *l'~* **du Sud** South America

amertume *f* bitterness

ameublement *m* (*meubles*) furniture

ameuter rouse

ami, ~e 1 *m/f* friend; (*amant*) boyfriend; (*maîtresse*) girlfriend; **devenir ~ avec qn** make friends with s.o. 2 *adj* friendly; amiable: **à l'~** amicably; JUR out of court; *arrangement* amicable, friendly; JUR out-of-court

amical, ~e 1 *adj* friendly 2 *f* association

amincir 1 *v/t* make thinner; *d'une robe* make look thinner 2 *v/i* get thinner

amiral *m* admiral

amitié *f* friendship; **~s** best wishes

amnésie *f* amnesia

amnistie *f* amnesty

amoindrir diminish, lessen; **s'~** diminish

amollir soften

amonceler pile up

amont *m*: **en ~** upstream (**de** from)

amoral amoral

amorcer begin; INFORM boot up

amorphe *sans énergie* listless

amortir *choc* cushion; *bruit* muffle; *douleur* dull; *dettes* pay off; **amortisseur** *m* AUTO shock absorber

amour *m* love; **~s** love life; **faire l'~** make love; **amoureux, -euse** *regard* loving; *vie* love *atr*; *personne* in love (**de** with); **tomber ~** fall in love; **amour-propre** *m* pride

amphithéâtre *m* amphitheater, *Br* amphitheatre; *d'université* lecture hall

ample *vêtements* loose; *sujet* broad; *ressources* ample; **ampleur** *f d'un désastre etc* scale

amplification *f* TECH amplification; *fig* growth; **amplifier** TECH amplify; *fig: problème* magnify; *idée* expand

ampoule *f sur la peau* blister; *de médicament* ampoule; *lampe* bulb

amputer amputate; *fig* cut

amusant funny, amusing

amuse-gueule *m* appetizer

amuser amuse; **s'~** have a good time, enjoy o.s.; **s'~ à faire qc** have fun doing sth, enjoy doing sth; **faire qch pour s'~** do sth for fun

amygdale *f* ANAT tonsil; **amygdalite** *f* tonsillitis

an *m* year; **le jour** *ou* **le premier de l'~** New Year's Day; **elle a 15 ~s** she's 15 (years old)

analogie *f* analogy; **analogique** INFORM analog; **analogue** analogous (**à** with)

analphabète illiterate; **analphabétisme** *m* illiteracy

analyse *f* analysis; *de sang* test; **analyser** analyze; *Br* analyse; *sang* test; **analytique** analytical

ananas *m* BOT pineapple

anarchie *f* anarchy; **anarchiste** *m* anarchist

anatomie *f* anatomy

ancêtres *mpl* ancestors

anchois *m* anchovy

ancien, ~ne old; *de l'Antiquité* ancient; **anciennement** formerly

ancre *f* anchor

Andorre *f: l'~* Andorra

âne *m* donkey; *fig* ass

anéantir annihilate

anecdote *f* anecdote

anémie *f* MÉD anemia, *Br* anaemia

anesthésie *f* MÉD anesthesia, *Br* anaesthesia

ange *m* angel

angine *f* MÉD throat infection; **~ de poitrine** angina

anglais, ~e 1 *adj* English **2** *m* langue English; **Anglais, ~e** *m/f* Englishman; Englishwoman; **les ~** the English

angle *m* angle; *(coin)* corner; **~ mort** blind spot

Angleterre *f: l'~* England

anglophone English-speaking

angoisse *f* anguish; **angoisser** distress

anguille *f* eel

anguleux, -euse angular

animal 1 *m* animal; **~ domestique** pet **2** *adj* animal *atr*

animateur, -trice *m/f d'une*

émission host, presenter; *d'une discussion* moderator; *d'activités culturelles, d'une entreprise* leader; *de dessin animé* animator; **animation** *f* (*vivacité*) liveliness; *de mouvements* hustle and bustle; *de dessin animé* animation; **animé** *rue, quartier* busy; *conversation* lively, animated; **animer** *fête* liven up; (*stimuler*) animate; *discussion, émission* host; **s'~** come to life; *d'une personne, discussion* become animated

animosité *f* animosity

anneau *m* ring

année *f* year; **les ~s 90** the 90s; **bonne ~!** happy New Year!

annexe *f d'un bâtiment* annex; *d'un document* appendix; *d'une lettre* enclosure

anniversaire *m* birthday; *d'un événement* anniversary

annonce *f* announcement; *dans journal* ad (vertisement); (*présage*) sign; **petites ~s** classified ads; **annoncer** announce; **s'~ bien/mal** be off to a good/bad start

annotation *f* annotation

annuaire *m*: **~ du téléphone** phone book

annuel, **~le** annual, yearly

annulaire *m* ring finger

annulation *f* cancellation; *d'un mariage* annulment; **annuler** cancel; *mariage an-*

nul

anodin harmless; *personne* insignificant; *blessure* slight

anomalie *f* anomaly

anonyme anonymous; **société** *f* **~** incorporated *ou Br* limited company

anorak *m* anorak

anorexie *f* anorexia; **anorexique** anorexic

anormal abnormal

anse *f d'un panier etc* handle; GÉOGR cove

antagonisme *m* antagonism

antarctique 1 *adj* Antarctic **2** *m* l'Antarctique Antarctica, the Antarctic

antécédents *mpl* history

antenne *f* ZO antenna, feeler; TV, *d'une radio* antenna, *Br* aerial

antérieur (*de devant*) front; (*d'avant*) previous, earlier; **~ à** prior to, before

anthropologie *f* anthropology

antibiotique *m* antibiotic

antibrouillard *m* fog lamp

anticipation *f* anticipation; **payer par ~** pay in advance; **d'~** *roman* science-fiction

anticiper anticipate; **~ un paiement** pay in advance

anticonstitutionnel, **~le** unconstitutional

antidater backdate

antidérapant *m* AUTO non--skid tire *ou Br* tyre

antidote *m* MÉD antidote

antigel *m* antifreeze

antipathie *f* antipathy

antipelliculaire: *shampoing* *m* ~ dandruff shampoo

antiquaire *m* antique dealer; **antique** ancient; *meuble* antique; *péj* antiquated; **antiquités** *fpl* antiques

antisémite 1 *adj* anti-Semitic **2** *m/f* anti-Semite

antiseptique *m & adj* antiseptic

antisocial antisocial

antiterroriste anti-terrorist

antivol *m* anti-theft device

anxiété *f* anxiety; **anxieux, -euse** anxious

août *m* August

apaiser *personne* calm down; *douleur* soothe; *soif, faim* satisfy

apathie *f* apathy

apercevoir see; **s'~ de qc** notice sth

apéritif *m* aperitif

à-peu-près *m* approximation

apitoyer: ~ *qn* move s.o. to pity; **s'~ sur qn** feel sorry for s.o.

aplanir flatten, level; *fig:* *différend* smooth over

aplatir flatten; **s'~** *(s'écraser)* be flattened; **s'~ devant** kowtow to

aplomb *m* self-confidence; *(audace)* nerve; **d'~** vertical, plumb; **je ne suis pas d'~** *fig* I don't feel a hundred percent

apostrophe *f* *(interpellation)* rude remark; *signe* apostrophe

apparaître appear; **faire ~** bring to light

appareil *m* device; AVIAT plane; **qui est à l'~?** TÉL who's speaking?; **~ ménager** household appliance; **~ photo** camera

apparemment apparently

apparence *f* appearance; **en** ~ on the face of things; **sauver les ~s** save face; **apparent** visible; *(illusoire)* apparent

apparenté related (à to)

apparition *f* appearance

appartement *m* apartment, *Br* flat

appartenir belong (à to); **il ne m'appartient pas d'en décider** it's not up to me to decide

appauvrir impoverish; **s'~** become impoverished; **appauvrissement** *m* impoverishment

appel *m* call; MIL *(recrutement)* draft, *Br* call-up; JUR appeal; ÉDU roll-call; **faire ~ à qc** *(nécessiter)* require; **faire ~ à qn** appeal to s.o.; **appeler** call; *(nécessiter)* call for; **en ~ à qn** approach s.o.; **comment t'appelles-tu?** what's your name?, what are you called?

appendice *m* appendix; **appendicite** *f* MÉD appendicitis

appétissant appetizing; **appétit** *m* appetite; **bon ~!** enjoy (your meal)!

applaudir applaud, clap; **applaudissements** *mpl* applause, clapping

applicateur *m* applicator; **application** *f* application; **appliquer** apply; **s'~** *d'une personne* work hard; **~ Y sur X** smear X with Y

apport *m* contribution; **apporter** bring

appréciation *f* estimate; (*jugement*) opinion; COMM appreciation; **apprécier** estimate; *personne, musique, la bonne cuisine* appreciate

appréhender: **~ qc** be apprehensive about sth; **~ qn** JUR arrest s.o.; **appréhension** *f* apprehension

apprendre learn; *nouvelle aussi* hear (**par qn** from s.o.); **~ qc à qn** (*enseigner*) teach s.o. sth; (*raconter*) tell s.o. sth

apprenti, **~e** *m/f* apprentice; *fig* beginner; **apprentissage** *m* learning; *d'un métier* apprenticeship

apprivoiser tame

approbateur, **-trice** approving; **approbation** *f* approval

approcher 1 *v/t* bring closer (**de** to) **2** *v/i* approach; **s'~ de** approach

approfondir deepen; (*étudier*) go into in detail

approprié appropriate, suitable (**à** for); **approprier**: **s'~ qc** appropriate sth

approuver *loi* approve; *personne, manières* approve of

approvisionnement *m* supply (**en** of)

approximatif, **-ive** approximate; **approximation** *f* approximation

appui *m* support; *d'une fenêtre* sill; **prendre ~ sur** lean on; **appuyer 1** *v/t* lean; (*tenir debout*) support; *fig candidat, idée* support, back **2** *v/i*: **~ sur** bouton press, push; *fig* stress; **s'~ sur** lean on; *fig* rely on

après 1 *prép* after; **d'~ les journaux** going by what the papers say **2** *adv* afterward **3** *conj*: **~ que** after

après-demain the day after tomorrow

après-midi *m ou f* afternoon

apr. J.-C. (= **après Jésus--Christ**) AD (= anno Domini)

aptitude *f* aptitude

aquarelle *f* watercolor, *Br* watercolour

aquarium *m* aquarium

arabe 1 *adj* Arab **2** *m langue* Arabic; **Arabe** *m/f* Arab; **Arabie** *f*: **l'~ Saoudite** Saudi (Arabia)

araignée *f* spider

arbitrage *m* arbitration

arbitre *m* referee; **libre ~** *m* free will; **arbitrer** arbitrate

arbre *m* tree; TECH shaft

arbuste *m* shrub

arc *m* ARCH arch; GÉOM arc

arc-en-ciel *m* rainbow

arche *f* arch; *Bible* Ark

archéologie *f* archeology, *Br* archaeology; **archéologue** *m/f* archeologist, *Br* archaeologist

archet *m* archer; MUS bow

archevêque *m* archbishop

architecte *m/f* architect; **architecture** *f* architecture

arctique **1** *adj* Arctic **2** *m* **l'Arctique** the Arctic

ardent *soleil* blazing; *désir* burning; *défenseur* fervent; **ardeur** *f fig* ardor, *Br* ardour

ardoise *f* slate

ardu arduous

arène *f* arena; **~s** arena

arête *f d'un poisson* bone; *d'une montagne* ridge

argent *m* silver; *(monnaie)* money; **~ liquide** *ou* **comptant** cash

argot *m* slang

argument *m* argument; **argumenter** argue

aride arid, dry

aristocrate *m/f* aristocrat; **aristocratie** *f* aristocracy

armateur *m* shipowner

arme *f* weapon *(aussi fig)*; **~ à feu** firearm; **armée** *f* army; **~ de l'air** airforce; **armement** *m* arming; **~s** armaments; **armer** arm *(de* with); *fig* equip *(de* with)

armistice *m* armistice

armoire *f* cupboard; *pour les vêtements* closet, *Br* wardrobe

arnaque *f* F rip-off F; **arnaquer** F rip off F

aromate *m* herb; *(épice)* spice; **arome, arôme** *m* flavor, *Br* flavour; *(odeur)* aroma

arracher pull out; *pommes de terre* pull up; **~ qc à qn** snatch sth from s.o.; **s'~ à** *ou* **de qc** free o.s. from sth; **s'~ qc** fight over sth

arrangement *m* arrangement; **arranger** arrange; *objet* fix; *différend* settle; **cela m'arrange** that suits me; **s'~ avec qn pour faire qch** come to an arrangement with s.o. about sth; **s'~ pour faire qch** manage to do sth

arrestation *f* arrest; **en état d'~** under arrest

arrêt *m (interruption)* stopping; *d'autobus* stop; JUR judgment; **sans ~** constantly; **arrêter 1** *v/i* stop **2** *v/t* stop; *moteur* turn off; *voleur* arrest; *jour, date* set; **~ de faire qch** stop doing sth; **s'~** stop

arrière 1 *adv* back; **en ~** backward; *regarder* back; *(à une certaine distance)* behind; **en~ de** behind **2** *adj inv* rear **3** *m* AUTO, SP back; **à l'~** in back, at the back

arrière-goût *m* aftertaste; **arrière-grand-mère** *f* great-grandmother; **arrière-grand-père** *m* great-grandfather; **arrière-pensée** *f* ulterior motive; **arrière-petit-fils** *m* great-grandson

arrivée *f* arrival; SP finish line; **arriver** arrive; *d'un événement* happen; **~ à faire qch** manage to do sth; **~ à qn** happen to s.o.; **j'arrive!** (I'm) coming!

arrogance *f* arrogance; **arrogant** arrogant

arrondir *vers le haut* round up; *vers le bas* round down; **arrondissement** *m d'une ville* district

arroser water; **~ qch** *fig* have a drink to celebrate sth; **arrosoir** *m* watering can

art *m* art; **avoir l'~ de faire qch** have a knack for doing sth

artère *f* ANAT artery; *(route)* main road

arthrite *f* arthritis

artichaut *m* artichoke

article *m* article, item; JUR article, clause; *de presse*, GRAM article; **~s de luxe** luxury goods

articulation *f* ANAT joint; *d'un son* articulation; **articuler** *son* articulate

artificiel, **~le** artificial

artisan *m* craftsman; **artisanal** hand-made; *fromage, pain etc* traditional

artiste 1 *m/f* artist; *comédien, chanteur* performer **2** *adj* artistic

as *m* ace

ascenseur *m* elevator, Br lift

ascension *f* ascent; *fig (progrès)* rise; **l'Ascension** REL Ascension

asiatique Asian; **Asiatique** *m/f* Asian; **Asie** *f:* **l'~** Asia

asile *m* shelter; POL asylum; **~ de vieillards** old people's home; **demandeur** *m* **d'~** asylum seeker

aspect *m (vue)* look; *(point de vue)* angle, point of view; *d'un problème* aspect; *(air)* appearance; **à l'~ de** at the sight of

asperge *f* BOT stalk of asparagus; **~s** asparagus

asperger sprinkle; **~ qn de qch** spray s.o. with sth

asphyxie *f* asphyxiate

aspirateur *m* vacuum (cleaner); **aspirer** *de l'air* breathe in, inhale; *liquide* suck up; **~ à (faire) qch** aspire to (doing) sth

aspirine *f* aspirin

assagir: **s'~** settle down

assaillir *vedette* mob; **être assailli de** be assailed by; *de coups de téléphone* be bombarded by

assainir *(nettoyer)* clean up; *eau* purify

assaisonnement *m* seasoning

assassin *m* murderer; *d'un président* assassin; **assassinat** *m* assassination; **assassiner** murder; *un président* assassinate

assemblée *f* gathering; *(réu-*

nion) meeting; **~ générale** annual general meeting; **assembler** assemble; **s'~** assemble, gather

asseoir: **s'~** sit down

assez enough; (*plutôt*) quite; **~ d'argent** enough money; **~ grand** big enough

assidu *élève* hard-working

assiette *f* plate; **ne pas être dans son ~** *fig* be under the weather

assigner assign

assimiler (*comparer*) compare; *connaissances, étrangers* assimilate

assis: **être~** be sitting; **assise** *f fig* basis

assistance *f* (*public*) audience; (*aide*) assistance; **assistant**, **~e** *m/f* assistant; **~e sociale** social worker; **assister 1** *v/i*: **~ à qc** attend sth, be (present) at sth **2** *v/t*: **~ qn** assist s.o

association *f* association; **associé**, **~e** *m/f* partner; **associer** associate (**à** with); **s'~** join forces; COMM go into partnership; **s'~ à** *douleur* share in

assoiffé thirsty

assombrir: **s'~** darken

assommant F deadly boring; **assommer** stun; F bore to death

Assomption *f* REL Assumption

assorti matching; **~ de** accompanied by; **assortiment**

m assortment

assoupir send to sleep; *fig*: *douleur, sens* dull; **s'~** doze off; *fig* die down

assourdir deafen; *bruit* muffle

assumer take on, assume

assurance *f* assurance; (*contrat*) insurance

assuré, **~e 1** (*sûr*) confident **2** *m/f* insured party; **assurément** certainly; **assurer** *succès* ensure; *par une assurance* insure; **s'~** take out insurance; **s'~ de qc** (*vérifier*) make sure of sth, check sth

asthme *m* asthma

astiquer *meuble* polish; *casserole* scour

astre *m* star

astrologie astrology

astronaute *m/f* astronaut

astronomie *f* astronomie; **astronomique** astronomical (*aussi fig*)

astuce *f* (*ingéniosité*) astuteness; (*truc*) trick; **astucieux**, **-euse** astute

atelier *m* workshop; *d'un artiste* studio

athée *m/f* atheist; **athéisme** *m* atheism

athlète *m/f* athlete; **athlétisme** *m* athletics *sg*

Atlantique *m*: **l'~** the Atlantic

atlas *m* atlas

atmosphère *f* atmosphere

atome *m* atom

atout *m fig* asset

atroce dreadful, atrocious;

atrocité f atrocity

attachant captivating

attaché-case m executive briefcase

attacher 1 v/t attach, fasten; *animal* tie up; *prisonnier* secure; *chaussures* do up 2 v/i CUIS *(coller)* stick; *s'~ à* become attached to

attaquant, ~e m/f SP striker; *attaque f* attack; *~ à la bombe* bomb attack; **attaquer** attack; *travail, sujet* tackle; *s'~ à* attack; *problème* tackle

attarder: *s'~* linger

atteindre v/t *d'un projectile* strike, hit; *d'une maladie* affect

atteinte f fig attack; *porter ~ à qc* undermine sth; *hors d'~* out of reach

attendant: *en ~* in the meantime; *en ~ qu'il arrive (subj)* while waiting for him to arrive; **attendre** wait; *~ qn* wait for s.o.; *s'~ à qc* expect sth; *~ un enfant* be expecting a baby

attendrir fig: *personne* move; *cœur* soften; *s'~* be moved *(sur* by); **attendrissement** m tenderness

attentat m attack; *~ à la bombe* bombing, bomb attack; *~ à la pudeur* indecent assault

attente f wait; *(espoir)* expectation

attentif, -ive attentive *(à* to); **attention** f attention; *(fais) ~!* look out!, (be) careful!;

faire ~ à qc pay attention to sth

atténuer reduce; *propos, termes* tone down

atterrir AVIAT land; *~ en catastrophe* crash-land

attestation f certificate; **attester** certify; *(prouver)* confirm

attirance f attraction; **attirer** attract; *s'~ des critiques* come in for criticism

attitude f attitude; *d'un corps* pose

attraction f attraction

attrait m attraction

attraper catch; *(duper)* take in

attrayant attractive

attribuer attribute; *prix* award; *part, rôle* allot; *valeur* attach; *s'~* take; **attribution** f allocation; *d'un prix* award; *~s (compétence)* competence

attrister sadden

attroupement m crowd; **attrouper**: *s'~* gather

aube f dawn; *à l'~* at dawn

auberge f inn; *~ de jeunesse* youth hostel

aubergine f BOT eggplant, *Br* aubergine

aucun, ~e 1 adj avec négatif no, not ...any; *avec positif, interrogatif* any 2 pron avec négatif none; *~ des deux* neither of the two; *avec positif, interrogatif* anyone, anybody

audace f daring, audacity; *péj* audacity; **audacieux, -euse** (*courageux*) daring, audacious; (*insolent*) insolent

au-delà beyond; **~ de** above; **au-dessous: ~ (de)** below; **au-dessus: ~ (de)** above; **au-devant: aller ~ de** meet; *désirs* anticipate

audible audible

audience f d'un tribunal hearing

audiovisuel, ~le audiovisual

auditeur, -trice m/f listener; FIN auditor; **audition** f audition; (*ouïe*) hearing; de témoins examination

augmentation f increase; de salaire raise, *Br* rise; **augmenter 1** v/t increase; salarié give a raise ou *Br* rise to **2** v/i increase, rise

aujourd'hui today

auparavant beforehand; **deux mois ~** two months earlier

auprès: ~ de beside, near

auquel → **lequel**

auriculaire m little finger

aurore f dawn

ausculter MÉD sound

aussi 1 adv too, also; **il est ~ grand que moi** he's as tall as me **2** conj therefore

aussitôt immediately; **~ que** as soon as

austère austere

Australie f: **l'~** Australia; **australien, ~ne** Australian; **Australien, ~ne** m/f Australian

autant (*tant*) as much (*que* as); **avec pluriel** as many (*que* as); **comparatif: ~ de ... que ...** as much ... as ...; **avec pluriel** as many ... as ...; **(pour) que je sache** (*subj*) as far as I know; **en faire ~** do the same

auteur m/f author; d'un crime perpetrator

authenticité f authenticity; **authentique** authentic

autiste autistic

auto f car, automobile

autobiographie f autobiography

autocollant 1 adj adhesive **2** m sticker

autodéfense f self-defense, *Br* self-defence

autodidacte self-taught

auto-école f driving school

autographe m autograph

automatique adj & m automatic; **automatiquement** automatically; **automatiser** automate

automne m fall, *Br* autumn

automobile f car, automobile; **automobiliste** m/f driver

autonomie f independence; POL autonomy

autoradio m car radio

autorisation f authorization, permission; **autoriser** authorize, allow; **autoritaire** authoritarian; **autorité** f authority

27

aversion

autoroute *f* highway, *Br* motorway

auto-stop *m*: **faire de l'~** hitchhike

autour: **~ (de)** around

autre 1 *adj* other; *un/une* **~ ...** another ...; *nous* **~s Américains** we Americans; *rien d'~* nothing else; **~ part** somewhere else; *d'~ part* on the other hand **2** *pron*: *un/une* **~** another (one); *l'~* the other (one); *les* **~s** the others; *(autrui)* other people; *l'un l'~*, *les uns les* **~** each other, one another

autrefois in the past

autrement *(différemment)* differently; *(sinon)* otherwise

Autriche *f*: *l'~* Austria; **autrichien**, **~ne** Austrian; **Autrichien**, **~ne** *m/f* Austrian

autrui other people *pl*, others *pl*

auxquelles, **auxquels** → **lequel**

av. (= **avenue**) Ave (= avenue)

aval 1 *adv*: *en* **~** downstream *(de* from) **2** *m* FIN guarantee

avalanche *f* avalanche

avaler swallow

avance *f* advance; *d'une course* lead; *d'~* in advance; *en* **~** ahead of time; **avancement** *m* progress; *(promotion)* promotion; **avancer 1** *v/t chaise*, *date* bring forward; *main* put out; *argent* advance; *thèse* put forward **2** *v/i* make progress; MIL advance; *d'une montre* be fast; **s'~ vers** come up to

avant 1 *prép* before; **~ tout** above all; **~ de faire qch** before doing sth **2** *adv temps* before; *espace* in front of; *en* **~** forward **3** *conj*: **~ que** (+ *subj*) before **4** *adj*: *roue* *f* **~** front wheel **5** *m* front; *d'un navire* bow; SP forward

avantage *m* advantage; **~s sociaux** fringe benefits; **avantager** suit; *(favoriser)* favor, *Br* favour

avant-dernier, **-ère** last but one

avant-hier the day before yesterday

avant-première *f* preview

avant-propos *m* foreword

avant-veille *f*: *l'~* two days before

avare 1 *adj* miserly **2** *m* miser; **avarice** *f* miserliness

avarié *nourriture* bad

avec with

avenir *m* future; *à l'~* in future; *d'~* promising

Avent *m* Advent

aventure *f* adventure; *(liaison)* affair; **aventurer**: **s'~** venture *(dans* into)

avenue *f* avenue

avérer: **s'~** (+ *adj*) prove

averse *f* shower

aversion *f* aversion *(pour ou contre* to); *prendre qn en* **~** take a dislike to s.o.

avertir inform (*de* of); (*mettre en garde*) warn (*de* of); **avertissement** *m* warning; **avertisseur** *m* AUTO horn

aveu *m* confession

aveuglant blinding; **aveugle 1** *adj* blind **2** *m/f* blind man; blind woman; **aveugler** blind

aviateur, -trice *m/f* pilot; **aviation** *f* aviation, flying

avide greedy, avid (*de* for); **avidité** *f* greed

avilissant degrading

avion *m* (air)plane, *Br* (aero-)plane; **aller en ~** fly, go by plane; **par ~** (by) airmail

aviron *m* oar; SP rowing

avis *m* opinion; (*information*) notice; **à mon ~** in my opinion; **changer d'~** change one's mind; **sauf ~ contraire** unless otherwise stated

aviser: ~ qn de qc advise *ou* inform s.o. of sth; **s'~ de qc** notice sth; **s'~ de faire qch** take it into one's head to do sth

av. J.-C. (= *avant Jésus-*

-Christ) BC (= before Christ)

avocat, ~e 1 *m/f* lawyer; (*défenseur*) advocate **2** *m* BOT avocado

avoir 1 *v/t* (*posséder*) have, have got; (*obtenir*) get; **j'ai froid/chaud** I am cold/hot; **~ 20 ans** be 20; **il y a** there is; *avec pluriel* there are; **qu'est-ce qu'il y a?** what's the matter?; **il y a un an a** year ago **2** *v/aux* have; **j'ai déjà parlé** I have *ou* I've already spoken; **je lui ai parlé hier** I spoke to him yesterday **3** *m* COMM credit; (*possessions*) possessions *pl*

avoisiner: ~ qc border on sth

avortement *m* miscarriage; *provoqué* abortion; **avorter 1** *v/t femme* terminate the pregnancy of; **se faire ~** have an abortion **2** *v/i* miscarry; *fig* fail

avouer (*avoir fait qc*) confess (to having done sth)

avril *m* April

axe *m* axle; GÉOM axis; *fig* basis

B

babiller babble

bâbord *m* MAR: **à ~** to port

bac[1] *m bateau* ferry; *récipient* container

bac[2] *m* F, **baccalauréat** *m* exam that is a prerequisite for university entrance

bâche *f* tarpaulin

bâcler F botch F

badaud *m* onlooker

badiner joke

baffe *f* F slap

bafouiller 1 *v/t* stammer **2** *v/i* F talk nonsense

bagages *mpl* baggage, luggage; *fig* (*connaissances*) knowledge; **faire ses ~** pack

bagarre *f* fight; **bagarrer** F: **se ~** fight

bagnole *f* F car

bague *f* ring; **~ de fiançailles** engagement ring

baguette *f* stick; MUS baton; *pain* French stick; **~s pour manger** chopsticks

baie[1] *f* BOT berry

baie[2] *f* (*golfe*) bay; **Baie d'Hudson** Hudson Bay

baigner *enfant* bathe, *Br* bath; **se ~** go for a swim; **baignoire** *f* (bath) tub

bail *m* lease

bâiller yawn; *d'un trou* gape; *d'une porte* be ajar

bain *m* bath; **salle** *f* **de ~s** bathroom; **être dans le ~** *fig* (*au courant*) be up to speed; **~ de bouche** mouthwash; **bain-marie** *m* CUIS double boiler

baiser 1 *m* kiss **2** *v/t* kiss; V screw

baisse *f* fall; **être en ~** be falling; **baisser 1** *v/t* lower; *radio, chauffage* turn down **2** *v/i de forces* fail; *de lumière* fade; *d'une température, d'un prix* drop, fall; *de vue* deteriorate; **se ~** bend down

bal *m* dance; *formel* ball

balade *f* walk, stroll; **balader** walk; **se ~** go for a walk *ou* stroll

baladeur *m* Walkman®

balai *m* broom; **donner un coup de ~ à qch** give sth a sweep

balance *f* scales *pl*; COMM balance; ASTROL **Balance** Libra;

balancer *jambes* swing; F (*lancer*) chuck F; F (*jeter*) chuck out F; **se ~** swing; **balançoire** *f* swing

balayer sweep; *fig: gouvernement* sweep from power; *soucis* sweep away

balbutier stammer

balcon *m* balcony

baleine *f* whale

ballade *f* ballad

balle *f* ball; *d'un fusil* bullet; *de marchandises* bale

ballet *m* ballet

ballon *m* ball; *pour enfants,* AVIAT balloon

ballotter 1 *v/t buffet* **2** *v/i* bounce up and down

balnéaire: **station** *f* **~** seaside resort

balourd clumsy

balte Baltic; **Baltique**: **la (mer) ~** the Baltic (Sea)

balustrade *f* balustrade

bambou *m* bamboo

banal (*mpl* -als) banal; **banalité** *f* banality

banane *f* banana; **bananier** *m* banana tree

banc *m* bench, seat; **~ de sable** sandbank

bancaire bank *atr*

bancal (*mpl* -als) *table* wobbly

bandage *m* MÉD bandage

bande f de terrain, de tissu strip; MÉD bandage; (rayure) stripe; (groupe) group; péj gang, band; bander MÉD bandage; ~ les yeux à qn blindfold s.o.

bandit m bandit; (escroc) crook

banlieue f suburbs pl; de ~ suburban

bannière f banner

bannir banish

banque f bank; ~ du sang blood bank

banquet m banquet

banquette f seat

banquier m banker

baptême m baptism; baptiser baptize

bar m bar; meuble cocktail cabinet

baraque f shack

barbant F boring

barbare 1 adj barbaric **2** m/f barbarian

barbe f beard; ~ à papa cotton candy, Br candy floss

barbecue m barbecue

barber F bore rigid F

barbu bearded

barder F: ça va~ there's going to be trouble

baromètre m barometer

barque f MAR boat

barrage m dam; (barrière) barrier

barre f bar; MAR helm; (trait) line; ~ des témoins JUR witness stand

barreau m bar; d'échelle rung

barrer (obstruer) block, bar; mot cross out; se ~ F leave

barrette f barrette, Br hairslide

barrière f barrier; (clôture) fence; ~s douanières customs barriers

bar-tabac m bar-cum-tobacco store

bas, ~se 1 adj low; GÉOGR lower; instrument bass; voix deep **2** adv low; parler in a low voice, quietly; en ~ downstairs; là~ there **3** m bottom; (vêtement) stocking; au ~ de at the bottom of

basané weatherbeaten; naturellement swarthy

bas-côté m d'une route shoulder

basculer topple over

base f base; d'un édifice foundation; fig: d'une science basis; de ~ basic; à ~ de lait milk-based

base f de données database

base-ball m baseball

baser base (sur on); se ~ sur draw on; d'une idée be based on

basilic m BOT basil

basket(-ball) m basketball; **baskets** fpl sneakers, Br trainers

basque 1 adj Basque **2** m langue Basque; **Basque** m/f Basque

basse-cour f AGR farmyard; animaux poultry

bassine f bowl

bataille f battle; **livrer ~** give battle; **batailler** fig battle

bâtard m bastard; *chien* mongrel

bateau m boat; **faire du ~** go sailing; **mener qn en ~** fig put s.o. on, Br have s.o. on

bâti 1 adj built on; **bien ~** well-built **2** m frame

bâtiment m building; *secteur* construction industry; MAR ship

bâtir build

bâton m stick; **parler à ~s rompus** make small talk; **~ de rouge** lipstick; **~ de ski** ski pole ou stick

battant 1 adj *pluie* driving **2** m *d'une porte* leaf; *personne* fighter

batte f de base-ball bat

battement m de cœur beat; *de temps* interval

batterie f ÉL battery; MUS drums pl; *dans un orchestre* percussion; **batteur** m CUIS whisk; *électrique* mixer; MUS drummer; *en base-ball* batter; **battre 1** v/t beat; *cartes* shuffle **2** v/i beat; *d'un volet* bang; **se ~** fight

bavard, **~e 1** adj talkative **2** m/f chatterbox; **bavarder** chatter; *(divulguer un secret)* talk

baver drool, slobber; **bavure** f fig blunder, blooper F; **sans ~** impeccable

Bd (= *boulevard*) Blvd (= Boulevard)

B.D. f (= **bande dessinée**) comic strip

béant gaping

béat péj: *sourire* silly

beau, bel, belle (*mpl* **beaux**) beautiful, lovely; *homme* handsome; **il fait beau** (*temps*) it's lovely weather; **il a beau dire …** it's no good him saying …

beaucoup a lot; **~ de** lots of, a lot of; **~ de gens** lots ou a lot of people, many people; **je n'ai pas ~ d'argent** I don't have a lot of ou much money; **~ trop cher** much too expensive

beau-fils m son-in-law; *d'un remariage* stepson; **beau- -frère** m brother-in-law; **beau-père** m father-in-law; *d'un remariage* stepfather

beauté f beauty

beaux-arts mpl: **les ~** fine art

beaux-parents mpl parents- -in-law

bébé m baby

bec m *d'un oiseau* beak; *d'un récipient* spout; MUS mouthpiece; F mouth

bedaine f (beer) belly

bégayer stutter, stammer

béguin m fig F: **avoir le ~ pour** have a crush on

beige beige

beignet m CUIS fritter

belge Belgian; **Belge** m/f Belgian; **Belgique: la ~** Belgium

bélier m ZO ram; ASTROL **Bé-**

lier Aries

belle → *beau*

belle-famille *f* in-laws *pl*

belle-fille *f* daughter-in-law; *d'un remariage* stepdaughter; belle-mère *f* mother-in-law; *d'un remariage* stepmother; belle-sœur *f* sister-in-law

belliqueux, -euse warlike

bémol *m* MUS flat

bénédiction *f* blessing

bénéfice *m* benefit; COMM profit; bénéficier: ~ *de* benefit from; bénéfique beneficial

Bénélux: *le* ~ the Benelux countries *pl*

bénévolat voluntary work; bénévole 1 *adj travail* voluntary 2 *m/f* volunteer

bénin, -igne *tumeur* benign; *accident* minor

bénir bless; bénit consecrated; *eau f ~e* holy water

béquille *f* crutch; *d'une moto* stand

berceau *m* cradle; bercer rock; *se ~ d'illusions* delude o.s.

béret *m* beret

berger *m* shepherd; *chien* German shepherd, *Br aussi* Alsatian

berline *f* AUTO sedan, *Br* saloon

bermuda(s) *m* (*pl*) Bermuda shorts *pl*

berner fool

besogne *f* job, task

besoin *m* need; *avoir* ~ *de* (*faire*) *qch* need (to do) sth; *au* ~ if need be

bestial bestial

bétail *m* (*sans pl*) livestock

bête 1 *adj* stupid 2 *f* animal; (*insecte*) insect; *chercher la petite* ~ nitpick; bêtement stupidly; bêtise *f* stupidity; *dire des* ~s talk nonsense; *une* ~ a stupid thing to do/say

béton *m* concrete

betterave *f* beet, *Br* beetroot

beugler *de bœuf* low; F *d'une personne* shout

beurre *m* butter; ~ *de cacahuètes* peanut butter

bévue *f* blunder

biais 1 *adv:* *en* ~ diagonally; *de* ~ *regarder* sideways 2 *m fig* (*aspect*) angle; *par le* ~ *de* through

biberon *m* (baby's) bottle

Bible *f* bible

bibliothèque *f* library; *meuble* bookcase

bic® *m* ballpoint (pen)

bicentenaire *m* bicentennial, *Br* bicentenary

biceps *m* biceps

biche *f* ZO doe

bicyclette *f* bicycle; *aller en ou* à ~ cycle

bidon *m:* ~ à *essence* gas *ou Br* petrol can

bidonville *m* shanty town

bidule *m* F gizmo F

bien 1 *m* good; (*possession*) possession; *le* ~ *ce qui est juste* good; **faire le ~** do good; **faire du ~ à qn** do s.o. good; **~s** (*possessions*) property; (*produits*) goods **2** *adj* good; (*beau, belle*) good-looking; **être ~** feel well; (*à l'aise*) be comfortable; **ce sera très ~ comme ça** that will do very nicely; **se sentir ~** feel well; **avoir l'air ~** look good; **des gens ~** respectable people **3** *adv* well; (*très*) very; **~ des fois** lots of times; **eh ~** well; **oui, je veux ~** yes please **4** *conj* **~ que** (+ *subj*) although

bien-être *m* welfare; *sensation agréable* well-being

bienfait *m* benefit

bien-fondé *m* legitimacy

bienheureux, -euse happy; REL blessed

bienséance *f* propriety

bientôt soon; **à ~!** see you (soon)!

bienveillance *f* benevolence

bienvenu, ~e 1 *adj* welcome **2** *m/f* **être le/la ~(e)** be welcome **3** *f* **souhaiter la ~e à** welcome

bière *f* beer; **~ blanche** wheat beer; **~ brune** dark beer, *Br* bitter; **~ pression** draft (beer), *Br* draught (beer)

bifteck *m* steak

bifurquer: ~ (*vers*) fork (off onto); *fig* branch out (into)

bigame 1 *adj* bigamous **2** *m/f* bigamist; **bigamie** *f* bigamy

bijou *m* jewel; **~x** jewelry, *Br* jewellery; **bijouterie** *f* jewelry store, *Br* jeweller's; **bijoutier, -ère** *m/f* jeweler, *Br* jeweller

bikini *m* bikini

bilan *m* balance sheet; *fig* (*résultat*) outcome; **faire le ~ de** take stock of

bilingue bilingual

billard *m* billiards *sg*; *table* billiard table; **~ américain** pool

bille *f* marble; *billard* (billiard) ball; **stylo** *m* (**à**) **~** ball-point (pen)

billet *m* ticket; (*petite lettre*) note; **~** (**de banque**) bill, *Br* (bank)note; **billetterie** *f* ticket office; *automatique* ticket machine; FIN ATM, *Br aussi* cash dispenser

biochimie *f* biochemistry

biodégradable biodegradable

biodiversité *f* biodiversity

biographie *f* biography

biologie *f* biology; **biologique** biological; *aliments* organic

biotechnologie *f* biotechnology

bis 1 *adj*: **24** $\sim$ 24A **2** *m* encore

biscornu *fig* weird

biscotte *f* rusk

biscuit *m* cookie, *Br* biscuit

bise *f*: **faire la ~ à** kiss

bisexuel, ~le bisexual

bisou *m* F kiss

bissextile: année *f* **~** leap year

bistro(t) *m* bistro
bit *m* INFORM bit
bitume *m* asphalt
bizarre strange, bizarre
blafard wan
blague *f* joke; **sans ~!** no kidding!; **blaguer** joke
blaireau *m* badger; *pour se raser* shaving brush
blâme *m* blame; (*sanction*) reprimand
blanc, blanche **1** *adj* white; *page* blank; **nuit** *f* **blanche** sleepless night **2** *m* white; *textile* (household) linen; *par opposé aux couleurs* whites *pl*; *dans un texte* blank **3** *m/f* **Blanc, Blanche** white, White
blancheur *f* whiteness; blanchir **1** *v/t* whiten; *mur* whitewash; *linge* launder, wash; *du soleil* bleach; *fig: innocenter* clear **2** *v/i* go white
blasé blasé
blasphème *m* blasphemy; blasphémer blaspheme
blé *m* wheat, *Br* corn
blêmir turn pale
blesser hurt (*aussi fig*); *dans un accident* injure; *à la guerre* wound; **se ~** injure *ou* hurt o.s.; **blessure** *f* *d'accident* injury; *d'arme* wound
bleu **1** *adj* blue; *viande* very rare **2** *m* blue; *fromage* blue cheese; *sur la peau* bruise; *fig* (*novice*) rookie F
blindage *m* armor, *Br* armour; blinder armor, *Br* ar-

mour; *fig* F harden
bloc *m* block; POL bloc; *de papier* pad; **faire ~** join forces
bloc-notes *m* notepad
blocus *m* blockade
blond, ~e **1** *adj* blonde; *tabac* Virginian; *sable* golden **2** *m/f* blonde **3** *f bière* beer, *Br aussi* lager
bloquer block; *mécanisme* jam; *roues* lock; *compte* freeze
blouson *m* jacket, blouson
bluff *m* bluff; **bluffer** bluff
bobard *m* F tall tale *ou Br* story
bocal *m* (glass) jar
bock *m:* **un ~** a (glass of) beer
bœuf *m* steer; *viande* beef
bohémien, ~ne *m/f* gipsy
boire drink; (*absorber*) soak up
bois *m* matière, forêt* wood; **en ~** wooden
boisson *f* drink; **~s alcoolisées** alcohol
boîte *f* box; *en tôle* can, *Br aussi* tin; F (*entreprise*) company; **~ (de nuit)** nightclub; **en ~** canned, *Br aussi* tinned; **~ à gants** glove compartment; **~ aux lettres** mailbox, *Br* letterbox
boiter limp; *fig: de raisonnement* be shaky; **boiteux, -euse** *table etc* wobbly; *fig: raisonnement* shaky; **être ~** *d'une personne* have a limp
boîtier *m* case, housing
bol *m* bowl

bombardement *m* bombing; *avec obus* bombardment; **bombarder** bomb; *avec obus*, *questions* bombard; **bombe** *f* bomb; (*atomiseur*) spray; *~ à retardement* time bomb; **bombé** bulging

bon, ~ne 1 *adj* good; *route*, *moment* right; *de ~ne foi personne* sincere; *être ~ en qch* be good at sth; *à quoi ~?* what's the use?; wittcism; *~ anniversaire!* happy birthday!; *~ voyage!* have a good trip!, bon voyage!; *~ne chance!* good luck!; *~ne année!* Happy New Year!; *~ne nuit!* good night!; *ah ~* really **2** *adv*: *sentir ~* smell good; *tenir ~* not give in; *trouver ~ de faire qch* think it right to do sth **3** *m* COMM voucher; *avoir du ~* have its good points; *~ d'achat* gift voucher; *~ du Trésor* Treasury bond

bonbon *m* candy, *Br* sweet; *~s* candy, *Br* sweets

bond *m* leap; *d'une balle* bounce

bondé packed

bondir jump, leap (*de* with)

bonheur *m* happiness; (*chance*) luck; *par ~* luckily; *au petit ~* at random

bonhomme *m* F (*type*) guy F

boniment *m battage* spiel F, sales talk; F (*mensonge*) fairy story

bonjour *m* hello

bonne *f* maid

bonnet *m* hat; *gros ~* fig F big shot F; *~ de douche* shower cap

bonsoir *m* hello, good evening

bonté *f* goodness

bonus *m* no-claims bonus

bord *m* edge; (*rive*) bank; *d'une route* side; *d'un verre* brim; *au ~ de la mer* at the seaside; *être au ~ des larmes* be on the verge of tears; *monter à ~* go on board

bordel *m* F brothel; (*désordre*) mess F

bordélique F chaotic

border (*garnir*) edge (*de* with); (*être le long de*) border; *enfant* tuck in

bordure *f* border, edging; *en ~ de forêt*, *ville* on the edge of

borne *f* boundary marker; ÉL terminal; *~s* *fig* limits; *dépasser les ~s* go too far; **borné** narrow-minded; **borner**: *se ~ à* (*faire*) restrict o.s. to (doing)

bosse *f* (*enflure*) lump; *d'un bossu*, *d'un chameau* hump; *du sol* bump

bosser F work hard

bossu, ~e *m/f* hunchback

botanique 1 *adj* botanical **2** *f* botany

botte *f chaussure* boot

bouc *m* goat; *~ émissaire* *fig* scapegoat

bouche

bouche *f* mouth; *de métro* entrance; ~ **d'aération** vent; ~ **d'incendie** (fire) hydrant
bouché blocked; *temps* overcast
bouche-à-bouche *m* MÉD mouth-to-mouth resuscitation
bouchée *f* mouthful
boucher[1] *v/t* block; *trou* fill (in); **se** ~ *d'un évier* get blocked; **se** ~ **le nez** hold one's nose
boucher[2], **-ère** *m/f* butcher (*aussi fig*)
boucherie *f magasin* butcher's; *fig* slaughter
bouchon *m* top; *de liège* cork; *fig: trafic* hold-up
boucle *f* loop; *de ceinture* buckle; *de cheveux* curl; ~ **d'oreille** earring; **bouclé** *cheveux* curly; **boucler** *ceinture* fasten; *porte* lock; MIL surround; *en prison* lock away
bouddhisme *m* Buddhism; **bouddhiste** *m* Buddhist
bouder **1** *v/i* sulk **2** *v/t:* ~ **qn/qc** give s.o./sth the cold shoulder
boudin *m:* ~ (**noir**) blood sausage, *Br* black pudding
boue *f* mud
bouée *f* MAR buoy
bouffée *f de fumée, vent* puff; *de parfum* whiff
bouffer F eat
bouffi bloated
bouger move; *de prix* change

bougie *f* candle; AUTO spark plug
bouillie *f* baby food
bouillir boil; *fig* be boiling (with rage); **faire** ~ boil; **bouilloire** *f* kettle
bouillon *m* (*bulle*) bubble; CUIS stock; **bouillonner** bubble; *fig: d'idées* seethe
bouillotte *f* hot water bottle
boulanger, **-ère** *m/f* baker; **boulangerie** *f* bakery
boule *f* ball; **jeu** *m* **de** ~**s** bowls *sg*
bouleau *m* BOT birch (tree)
boulevard *m* boulevard
bouleversement *m* upheaval; **bouleverser** (*mettre en désordre*) turn upside down; *traditions* overturn; *émotionnellement* shatter
boulimie *f* bulimia
boulot *m* F work
bouquet *m* bouquet
bouquin *m* F book; **bouquiner** read
bourde *f* blunder, blooper F
bourdon *m* ZO bumblebee; **bourdonner** *d'insectes* buzz; *de moteur* hum; *d'oreilles* ring
bourgeois, ~**e** **1** *adj* middle-class **2** *m/f* member of the middle classes
bourgeoisie *f* middle classes *pl*
bourgeon *m* BOT bud
bourrasque *f* gust
bourratif, **-ive** stodgy
bourré crammed (**de** with); F

(ivre) drunk, sozzled F

bourrer *coussin* stuff; *pipe* fill; **se ~ de qc** F stuff o.s. with sth

bourru surly

bourse *f d'études* grant; *(porte-monnaie)* coin purse, *Br* purse; **Bourse (des valeurs)** Stock Exchange

boursouf(f)lé swollen

bousculer *(heurter)* jostle; *(presser)* rush; *fig: traditions* overturn

bousiller F *travail* screw up F; *(détruire)* wreck

boussole *f* compass

bout *m* end; *(morceau)* piece; **au ~ de** at the end of; **d'un ~ à l'autre** right the way through; **être à ~** be at an end; **venir à ~ de** overcome

bouteille *f* bottle; *de butane* cylinder

boutique *f* store, *Br* shop; *de mode* boutique

bouton *m* button; *de porte* handle; ANAT spot, zit F; BOT bud; **bouton-d'or** *m* BOT buttercup; **boutonner** button; BOT bud; **boutonneux, -euse** spotty

bovin 1 *adj* cattle *atr* **2** *mpl* **~s** cattle *pl*

bowling *m* bowling, *Br* tenpin bowling; *lieu* bowling alley

boxe *f* boxing; **boxer** box; **boxeur** *m* boxer

boycott *m* boycott; **boycotter** boycott

B.P. (= **boîte postale**) PO Box (= Post Office Box)

bracelet *m* bracelet

braconnier *m* poacher

braguette *f* fly

brailler bawl

braiser CUIS braise

brancard *m* *(civière)* stretcher

branche *f* branch; *de céleri* stick

brancher connect up **(sur)**; *à une prise* plug in; **branché** F *(informé)* clued up; *(en vogue)* trendy

brandir brandish

braquer *v/t:* **~ sur** aim *ou* point at **2** *v/i* AUTO turn the wheel; **se ~ contre** *fig* turn against

bras *m* arm; **avoir le ~ long** *fig* have influence

brasse *f* stroke

brasser *bière* brew; **brasserie** *f usine* brewery; *établissement* restaurant

brave 1 *adj* brave; *(before the noun)* good **2** *m:* **un ~** a brave man; **braver** *(défier)* defy; **bravoure** *f* bravery

break *m* AUTO station wagon, *Br* estate (car)

brebis *f* ewe

bredouiller mumble

bref, -ève 1 *adj* brief, short **2** *adv* briefly, in short

Brésil: le ~ Brazil; **brésilien, ~ne** Brazilian; **Brésilien, ~ne** *m/f* Brazilian

Bretagne: la ~ Britanny

bretelle *f de lingerie* strap;

d'autoroute ramp, *Br* slip road; *~s de pantalon* suspenders, *Br* braces

brevet *m* diploma; *pour invention* patent; **breveter** patent

bric-à-brac *m inv* bric-à-brac

bricolage *m* do-it-yourself, DIY; **bricole** *f* little thing; **bricoler** do odd jobs

brièvement briefly; **brièveté** *f* briefness, brevity

brigade *f* MIL brigade; *de police* squad; *d'ouvriers* gang

brillamment brilliantly; **brillant** shiny; *couleur* bright; *fig* brilliant; **briller** shine (*aussi fig*); **faire ~ meuble** polish

brin *m d'herbe* blade; *de corde* strand

brindille *f* twig

brioche *f* CUIS brioche; F (*ventre*) paunch

brique *f* brick

briquet *m* lighter

brise *f* breeze

brisé broken

briser 1 *v/t* break; *vie, bonheur* destroy; *(fatiguer)* wear out **2** *v/i de la mer* break; **se ~ de verre etc** break; *des espoirs* be shattered

britannique British; **Britannique** *m/f* Briton, Britisher, Brit F; **les ~s** the British

broc *m* pitcher

brocante *f magasin* second-hand store

broche *f* CUIS spit; *bijou* brooch

brochet *m* pike

brochette *f* CUIS skewer; *plat* shish kebab

brochure *f* brochure

brocolis *mpl* broccoli *sg*

broncher: **sans ~** without batting an eyelid

bronches *fpl* ANAT bronchial tubes

bronchite *f* MÉD bronchitis

bronze *m* bronze

bronzé tanned; **bronzer 1** *v/t peau* tan **2** *v/i* get a tan; **se ~** sunbathe

brosse *f* brush; *coiffure* crew-cut; **~ à dents/cheveux** toothbrush/hairbrush; **brosser** brush; **se ~ les dents** brush one's teeth

brouhaha *m* hubbub

brouillard *m* fog; **il y a du ~** it's foggy

brouille *f* quarrel; **brouiller** *œufs* scramble; *cartes* shuffle; *papiers* muddle; *radio* jam; *involontairement* cause interference to; *amis* cause to fall out; **se ~ du ciel** cloud over; *de vitres* mist up; *d'idées* get muddled; *d'amis* fall out

brouillon *m* draft; *papier m ~* scratch paper, *Br* scrap paper

broussailles *fpl* undergrowth

broyer grind; **~ du noir** *fig* be down

bru *f* daughter-in-law

brugnon *m* BOT nectarine

bruine *f* drizzle

bruit *m* sound; *qui dérange* noise; *(rumeur)* rumor, *Br* rumour; **faire du ~** make a noise; *fig* cause a sensation

brûlant burning *(aussi fig)*; *(chaud)* burning hot; *liquide* scalding; **brûlé** burnt; **brûler 1** *v/t* burn; **se ~** burn o.s.; *d'eau bouillante* scald; *électricité* use; **~ un feu rouge** go through a red light **2** *v/i* burn; **se ~** burn o.s.; *d'eau bouillante* scald o.s.; **brûleur** *m* burner; **brûlure** *f* sensation burning; *lésion* burn; **~s d'estomac** heartburn

brume *f* mist

brun, ~e 1 *adj* brown; *cheveux, peau* dark **2** *m/f* dark-haired man/woman; **une ~e** a brunette **3** *m* couleur brown

brushing® *m* blow-dry

brusque abrupt, brusque; *(soudain)* abrupt, sudden; **brusquement** abruptly, suddenly; **brusquer** rush

brut, ~e 1 *adj* raw; *poids, revenu* gross; *pétrole* crude; *sucre* unrefined; *champagne* very dry **2** *m* crude (petroleum) **3** *f* brute; **brutal** brutal; **brutalement** brutally; **brutaliser** ill-treat; **brutalité** *f* brutality

Bruxelles Brussels

bruyant noisy

buanderie *f* laundry room

bûcher[1] *m* woodpile; *(échafaud)* stake

bûcher[2] *v/i* work hard; ÉDU F hit the books, *Br* swot

budget *m* budget

buée *f* steam, condensation

buffet *m* buffet; *meuble* sideboard

buisson *m* shrub, bush

bulbe *f* BOT bulb

bulgare 1 *adj* Bulgarian **2** *m* langue Bulgarian; **Bulgare** *m/f* Bulgarian; **Bulgarie: la ~** Bulgaria

bulle *f* bubble

bulletin *m* *(formulaire)* form; *(rapport)* bulletin; *à l'école* report card; **~ (de vote)** ballot (paper); **~ de salaire** paystub, *Br* payslip

bureau *m* office; *meuble* desk; **~ de change** exchange office, *Br* bureau de change; **~ de poste** post office; **~ de tabac** tobacco store, *Br* tobacconist's

bureaucratie *f* bureaucracy; **bureautique** *f* office automation

bus *m* bus

buste *m* bust

but *m* *(cible)* target; *(objectif)* aim, goal; *d'un voyage* purpose; SP goal; **sans ~** aimlessly; **buteur** *m* goalscorer

buté stubborn

buter: ~ contre qch bump into sth; **~ sur un problème** hit a problem; **se ~** *fig* dig one's heels in

butin *m* booty; *de voleurs* haul

butte *f* (*colline*) hillock; *être*
en ~ à be exposed to

buvable drinkable; **buvette** *f*
bar; **buveur, -euse** *m/f*
drinker

C

c' → **ce**

ça that; **~ va?** how are things?; (*d'accord?*) ok?; **~ y est** that's it; **c'est ~!** that's right

cabale *f* (*intrigue*) plot

cabane *f* (*baraque*) hut

cabaret *m* (*boîte*) night club

cabine *f* cabin; *d'un camion* cab; **~ téléphonique** phone booth

cabinet *m* petite pièce small room; *d'avocat* office; *de médecin* office, *Br* surgery; (*clientèle*) practice; POL Cabinet

câble *m* cable

cabosser dent

cabrer: se ~ *d'un animal* rear

cabriolet *m* AUTO convertible

cacah(o)uète *f* BOT peanut

cacao *m* cocoa; BOT cocoa bean

cache-cache *m*: **jouer à ~** play hide-and-seek; **cache-nez** *m* scarf; **cacher** hide; **se ~ de** hide from

cachet *m* seal; *fig* (*caractère*) style; PHARM tablet; (*rétribution*) fee; **~ de la poste** postmark

cachette *f* hiding place; **en ~** secretly

cachotterie *f*: **faire des ~s** be secretive; **cachottier, -ère** secretive

cactus *m* cactus

cadavre *m* (dead) body, corpse; *d'un animal* carcass

caddie® *m* cart, *Br* trolley

cadeau *m* present, gift; **faire un ~ à qn** give s.o. a present

cadenas *m* padlock

cadence *f* tempo rhythm; *de travail* rate

cadet, -te *m/f* younger; *de plus de deux* youngest; *il est mon ~ de trois ans* he's three years younger than me

cadran *m* dial; **~ solaire** sundial

cadre *m* frame; *fig* framework; *d'une entreprise* executive; (*environnement*) surroundings *pl*

cafard *m* ZO cockroach; **avoir le ~** F be feeling down

café *m* coffee; *établissement* café; **~ crème** coffee with milk, *Br* white coffee

cafeteria *f* cafeteria

cafetière *f* coffee pot; **~ électrique** coffee maker

cage f cage

cagibi m F box room

cagneux, -euse knock-kneed

cagoule f hood; (*passe-montagne*) balaclava

cahier m notebook; ÉDU exercise book

cahoter jolt

cahoteux, -euse bumpy

caille f quail

cailler *du lait* curdle; *du sang* clot

caillou m pebble, stone

caisse f chest; *pour le transport* crate; *de champagne, vin* case; (*argent*) cash; (*guichet*) cashdesk; *dans un supermarché* checkout; **caissier, -ère** m/f cashier

cajoler (*câliner*) cuddle

calamité f disaster, calamity

calcium m calcium

calcul[1] m calculation

calcul[2] m MÉD stone; **~ rénal** kidney stone

calculatrice f: **~ (de poche)** (pocket) calculator; **calculer** calculate; **calculette** f pocket calculator

calé F: **être ~ en qch** be good at sth

caleçon m *d'homme* boxer shorts pl; *de femme* leggings pl

calembour m pun

calendrier m calendar; *emploi du temps* schedule, Br timetable

caler *moteur* stall; TECH wedge

califourchon: à ~ astride

câlin 1 adj affectionate **2** m (*caresse*) cuddle

calmant 1 adj soothing; *contre douleur* painkilling **2** m tranquilizer, Br tranquillizer; *contre douleur* painkiller

calme 1 adj calm; *Bourse, vie* quiet **2** m calmness; MAR calm; (*silence*) peace and quiet; **calmement** calmly; **calmer** *personne* calm down; *douleur* relieve; **se ~** calm down

calomnie f slander; *écrite* libel; **calomnier** insult; *par écrit* libel

calorie f calorie

calquer trace

calvitie f baldness

camarade m/f friend; POL comrade

cambriolage m break-in, burglary; **cambrioler** burglarize, Br burgle

cambrioleur, -euse m/f house-breaker, burglar

camelote f F junk

caméra f camera

caméscope m camcorder

camion m truck, Br aussi lorry

camionnette f van

camomille f BOT camomile

camoufler camouflage; *fig: intention* hide; *faute* cover up

camp m camp (*aussi* MIL, POL); **ficher le ~** F get lost F

campagne f country, coun-

tryside; MIL, *fig* campaign; **à
la ~** in the country
camper camp; **se ~ devant**
plant o.s. in front of; campeur, -euse *m/f* camper
camping *m*: (**terrain** *m* **de**) **~**
campground, campsite; **fai-
re du ~** go camping
Canada **le ~** Canada; canadien, ~ne Canadian; Cana-
dien, ~ne *m/f* Canadian
canal *m* channel; (*tuyau*)
pipe; (*bras d'eau*) canal
canalisation *f* (*tuyauterie*)
pipes *pl*, piping; **canaliser**
fig channel
canapé *m* sofa; GASTR canapé
canapé-lit *m* sofa-bed
canard *m* duck; F newspaper
canari *m* canary
cancans *mpl* gossip
cancer *m* MÉD cancer; ASTROL
Cancer Cancer
candeur *f* ingenuousness
candidat, ~e *m/f* candidate;
candidature *f* candidacy; **à
un poste** application
candide ingenuous
cane *f* (*female*) duck; **cane-
ton** *m* duckling
canette *f* (*bouteille*) bottle
caniche *m* poodle
canicule *f* heatwave
canif *m* pocket knife
canin dog *atr*, canine
canine *f* canine
canne *f* cane, stick; **~ à pêche**
fishing rod
cannelle *f* cinnamon
canoë *m* canoe; *activité* ca-

noeing
canon *m* MIL gun; HIST cannon; *de fusil* barrel
canot *m* small boat; **~ pneumatique** rubber dinghy; **~
de sauvetage** lifeboat
cantine *f* canteen
canular *m* hoax
caoutchouc *m* rubber; (*bande élastique*) rubber band
cap *m* GÉOGR cape; AVIAT, NAUT
course
capable capable (**de faire** of
doing)
capacité *f* (*compétence*) ability; (*contenance*) capacity
cape *f* cape
capitaine *m* captain
capital 1 *adj* essential **2** *m*
capital; **capitaux** capital **3** *f
ville* capital (city); *lettre* capital (letter)
capitalisme *m* capitalism
capituler capitulate
capot *m* AUTO hood, Br bonnet
capote *f* vêtement greatcoat;
AUTO top, Br hood; **~ (anglaise)** F condom
caprice *m* whim; capricieux,
-euse capricious
Capricorne *m* ASTROL Capri-
corn
capter *regard* catch; RAD, TV
pick up
capteur *m*: **~ solaire** solar
panel
captif, -ive *m/f & adj* captive;
captivant *personne* captivating; *lecture* gripping;

captiver *fig* captivate; captivité *f* captivity

capture *f* capture; (*proie*) catch; capturer capture

capuche *f* hood

car[1] *m* bus, *Br aussi* coach

car[2] *conj* for

carabine *f* rifle

carabiné F: *un … carabiné* one hell of a … F

caractère *m* character; *avoir bon ~* be good-natured; caractériel *troubles* emotional; *personne* emotionally disturbed

caractériser be characteristic of; caractéristique *f & adj* characteristic

carambolage *m* AUTO pile-up

caramel *m* caramel

caravane *f* AUTO trailer, *Br* caravan

carboniser burn

carburant *m* fuel

carburateur *m* TECH carburet(t)or

cardiaque MÉD 1 *adj* cardiac, heart *atr* 2 *m/f* heart patient

cardinal: *les quatre points mpl cardinaux* the four points of the compass

cardiologue *m/f* cardiologist, heart specialist

carême *m* REL Lent

carence *f* (*incompétence*) inadequacy; (*manque*) deficiency

caresse *f* caress; caresser caress; *idée* play with; *espoir* cherish

cargaison *f* cargo; *fig* load

caricature *f* caricature

carie *f* MÉD: *une ~* a cavity

carié *dent* bad

caritatif, *~ive* charitable

carnage *m* carnage

carnassier, *-ère* carnivorous

carnaval *m* carnival

carnet *m* notebook; *de tickets, timbres* book

carnivore 1 *adj* carnivorous 2 *m* carnivore

carotte *f* carrot; *poil de ~* ginger

carpe *f* ZO carp

carpette *f* rug

carré 1 *adj* square; *fig: réponse* straightforward 2 *m* square

carreau *m de fenêtre* pane; *cartes* diamonds; *à ~x* checked

carrefour *m* crossroads *sg* (*aussi fig*)

carrelage *m* (*carreaux*) tiles *pl*

carrément bluntly, straight out

carrière *f* quarry; *profession* career; *militaire m de ~* professional soldier

carrosserie *f* AUTO bodywork

carrure *f* build

cartable *m* schoolbag; *à bretelles* satchel

carte *f* card; *dans un restaurant* menu; GÉOGR map; NAUT, *du ciel* chart; *~ bancaire* debit card, banker's card; *~ de crédit* credit card;

~ d'embarquement boarding pass; **~ d'identité** identity card; **~ postale** postcard; **~ téléphonique** phonecard

carton *m* cardboard; *boîte* cardboard box; **~ jaune/rouge** *en football* yellow/red card

cartouche *f* cartridge; *de cigarettes* carton

cas *m* case; **en aucun ~** under no circumstances; **dans ce ~-là** in that case; **en tout ~** in any case; **en ~ de** in the event of

casanier, -ère *m/f* stay-at-home

cascade *f* waterfall

case *f* (*hutte*) hut; (*compartiment*) compartment; *dans formulaire* box; *dans mots-croisés, échiquier* square

caser put; (*loger*) put up; **se ~** (*se marier*) settle down

caserne *f* barracks; **~ de pompiers** fire station

casier *m courrier* pigeonholes *pl*; *bouteilles, livres* rack; **~ judiciaire** criminal record

casino *m* casino

casque *m* helmet; *de radio* headphones *pl*; **casquette** *f* cap

cassable breakable

casse-cou *m inv* daredevil; **casse-croûte** *m* snack; **casse-noisettes** *m* nutcrackers *pl*; **casse-pieds** *m/f inv* F pain in the neck F

casser 1 *v/t* break; *noix* crack; JUR quash; **~ les pieds à qn** F (*embêter*) get on s.o.'s nerves F; **se ~** break **2** *v/i* break

casserole *f* (sauce)pan

casse-tête *m fig: problème* headache

cassette *f* cassette; **~ vidéo** video

cassis *m* BOT blackcurrant; (*crème f de*) **~** blackcurrant liqueur

castrer castrate

cataclysme *m* disaster

catalogue *m* catalog, *Br* catalogue; **cataloguer** catalog, *Br* catalogue; F *péj* label

catalytique AUTO: **pot** *m* **~** catalytic converter

cataracte *f* waterfall; MÉD cataract

catastrophe *f* disaster, catastrophe; **en ~** in a rush; **catastrophique** disastrous, catastrophic

catch *m* wrestling

catéchisme *m* catechism

catégorie *f* category; **catégorique** categorical

cathédrale *f* cathedral

catholique 1 *adj* (Roman) Catholic **2** *m/f* Roman Catholic

cauchemar *m* nightmare (*aussi fig*)

cause *f* cause; JUR case; **à ~ de** because of; **être en ~** d'honnêteté be in question

causer 1 *v/t* (*provoquer*) cause **2** *v/i* (*s'entretenir*) chat

(*avec qn de* with s.o. about);
causette *f* chat; **faire la ~**
have a chat

caustique CHIM, *fig* caustic

caution *f* security; *pour logement* deposit; JUR bail; *fig
(appui)* backing; **cautionner**
stand surety for; JUR bail; *fig
(se porter garant de)* vouch
for; *(appuyer)* back

cavaler F: **~ après qn** chase
after s.o.

cavalier, -ère 1 *m/f pour cheval* rider; *pour bal* partner 2
m aux échecs knight 3 *adj*
offhand, cavalier

cave *f* cellar; **~ (à vin)** wine
cellar

caverne *f* cave

caviar *m* caviar

cavité *f* cavity

CD *m* (= *compact disc*) CD;
CD-Rom *m* CD-Rom

ce *m* (cet *m*, cette *f*, ces *pl*) 1
adj this, *pl* these; **~ livre-ci**
this book; **~ livre-là** that
book; **ces jours-ci** these
days 2 *pron* **c'est pourquoi**
that is *ou* that's why; **c'est
triste** it's sad; **~ sont mes
enfants** these are my children; **c'est un acteur** he is
ou he's an actor; **c'est que
tu as grandi!** how you've
grown!; **ce que tu fais** what
you're doing; **ce qui me
plaît** what I like; **ce qu'il
est gentil!** isn't he nice!;
sur ~ with that

ceci this

cécité *f* blindness

céder 1 *v/t* give up; **cédez le
passage** AUTO yield, *Br* give
way 2 *v/i* give in (**à** to); *(se
casser)* give way

cédille *f* cedilla

cèdre *m* BOT cedar

ceinture *f* belt; ANAT waist; **~
de sécurité** seatbelt

cela that; **à ~ près** apart from
that

célèbre famous

célébrer celebrate

célébrité *f* fame; *personne* celebrity

céleri *m* BOT: **~ (en branche)**
celery; **~(-rave)** celeriac

célibat *m* single life; *d'un prêtre* celibacy; **célibataire 1**
adj single, unmarried **2** *m*
bachelor **3** *f* single woman

celle, celles → **celui**

cellophane *f* cellophane

cellule *f* cell

cellulose *f* cellulose

Celsius *m* Celsius

celui *m* (celle *f*, ceux *mpl*,
celles *fpl*) the one, *pl* those;
~ qui ... *personne* he who ...;
chose the one which; **celle
de Claude** Claude's; **celui-
-ci** this one; **celui-là** that one

cendre *f* ash; **~s de cigarette**
cigarette ash; **cendrier** *m*
ashtray

cène *f* REL: **la ~** (Holy) Communion; **la Cène** *peinture*
the Last Supper

censé: **il est ~ être malade**
he's supposed to be sick

censure f censorship; *organe* board of censors; **censurer** censor

cent 1 adj hundred **2** m a hundred, one hundred; *monnaie* cent; *pour* ~ per cent; *centaine* f: *une* ~ *de* a hundred or so; *des* ~*s de* hundreds of; **centenaire 1** adj hundred-year-old **2** m fête centennial, Br centenary; **centième** hundredth; **centilitre** m centiliter, Br centilitre; **centimètre** m centimeter, Br centimetre; *ruban* tape measure

central, ~**e 1** adj central **2** m TÉL telephone exchange **3** f power station; **centraliser** centralize

centre m center, Br centre; ~ *d'accueil* temporary accommodations pl; **centrer** center, Br centre

centre-ville m downtown area, Br town centre

cep m vine stock

cèpe m BOT cèpe, boletus

cependant yet, however

cercle m circle; ~ *vicieux* vicious circle

cercueil m casket, Br coffin

céréales fpl (breakfast) cereal

cérébral cerebral

cérémonie f ceremony; *sans* ~ *repas* etc informal; *se présenter* etc informally; *mettre à la porte* unceremoniously

cerf m deer

cerf-volant m kite

cerise f cherry; **cerisier** m cherry (-tree)

cerne m: *avoir des* ~*s* have bags under one's eyes; **cerner** (*encercler*) surround; *fig: problème* define

certain 1 adj certain; *être* ~ *de qc* be certain of sth; *d'un* ~ *âge* middle-aged **2** pron: *certains,* -*aines* some (people)

certainement certainly; (*sûrement*) probably

certes certainly

certificat m certificate; ~ *de mariage* marriage certificate; **certifier** guarantee; ~ *qc à qn* assure s.o. of sth

certitude f certainty

cerveau m brain

cervelle f brains pl; *se brûler la* ~ fig blow one's brains out

ces → *ce*

cesser stop; ~ *de faire qch* stop doing sth; **cessez-le--feu** m ceasefire

cession f disposal

c'est-à-dire that is, that is to say

cet, cette → *ce*

ceux → *celui*

chacun, ~*e* each (one); *c'est* ~ *pour soi* it's every man for himself

chagrin m grief; *faire du* ~ *à* upset

chahut m F racket, din; **chahuter** heckle

chaîne f chain; *radio,* TV

channel; **~s** AUTO snow chains; **~ hi-fi** hi-fi

chair f flesh; **avoir la ~ de poule** have goosebumps

chaise f chair; **~ longue** (*transatlantique*) deck chair

chalet m chalet

chaleur f heat; *plus modérée* warmth (*aussi fig*); **chaleureusement** warmly

chamailler F: **se ~** bicker

chambre f (bed)room; JUR, POL chamber; **~ à air** de pneu inner tube; **~ à coucher** bedroom; **~ à un lit** single (room); **~ à deux lits** twin-bedded room; **~ d'amis** spare room

chambré vin at room temperature

chameau m camel

champ m field (*aussi fig*); **~ de courses** racecourse

champagne m champagne

champêtre country atr

champignon m fungus; *nourriture* mushroom

champion, -ne m/f champion; **championnat** m championship

chance f luck; (*occasion*) chance; **bonne ~!** good luck!; **avoir de la ~** be lucky; **c'est une ~ que** (+ subj) it's lucky that

chanceler stagger; *d'un gouvernement* totter

chanceux, -euse lucky

chandail m sweater

change m exchange; **taux m de ~** exchange rate; **donner le ~ à qn** deceive s.o.; **changeant** changeable; **changement** m change; **~ de vitesse** AUTO gear shift; **changer 1** v/t change (**en** into); (*échanger*) exchange (**contre** for) **2** v/i change; **~ d'avis** change one's mind; **se ~** change

chanson f song

chant m song; *action de chanter* singing; *d'église* hymn

chantage m blackmail

chanter sing; *d'un coq* crow; **faire ~ qn** blackmail s.o.

chanteur, -euse m/f singer

chantier m building site; **~ naval** shipyard

chaos m chaos; **chaotique** chaotic

chaparder F pinch F

chapeau m hat; **chapeauter** fig head up

chapelet m REL rosary

chapelle f chapel

chapelure f CUIS breadcrumbs pl

chapitre m chapter; *division de budget* heading; fig subject

chaque each

charbon m coal; **~ de bois** charcoal

charcuterie f CUIS cold cuts pl, Br cold meat; *magasin* pork butcher's; **charcutier** m pork butcher

charge f load; fig burden; ÉL, JUR, MIL charge; (*responsa-*

bilité) responsibility; ***avoir des enfants à* ~** have dependent children; **~s** charges; (*impôts*) costs; **~s fiscales** taxation

chargement *m* loading; *ce qui est chargé* load; **charger 1** *v/t navire, arme* load; *batterie,* JUR charge; (*exagérer*) exaggerate; **~ qn de qc** put s.o. in charge of sth; **se ~ de** look after **2** *v/i* charge

chariot *m pour bagages, achats* cart, *Br* trolley; (*charrette*) cart

charisme *m* charisma

charitable charitable; **charité** *f* charity; **faire la ~ à qn** give s.o. money

charmant charming, delightful; **charme** *m* charm; **charmer** charm

charnière *f* hinge

charnu fleshy

charognard *m* scavenger

charpente *f* framework; **charpentier** *m* carpenter

charte *f* charter

charter *m* charter

chasse[1] *f* hunting; (*poursuite*) chase; **prendre en ~** chase (after); **~ privée** private game reserve

chasse[2] *f*: **~ d'eau** flush

chasser *gibier* hunt; (*expulser*) drive away; *employé* dismiss; **chasseur** *m* hunter; AVIAT fighter; *dans un hôtel* bellhop, *Br* bellboy

châssis *m* frame; AUTO chas-

sis

chaste chaste

chat[1] *m* cat

chat[2] *m* INFORM chatroom; *conversation* (online) chat

châtaigne *f* chestnut; **châtaignier** *m* chestnut (tree); **châtain** *inv* chestnut

château *m* castle; **~ fort** (fortified) castle; **~ d'eau** water tower

châtier punish; **châtiment** *m* punishment

chaton *m* kitten

chatouiller tickle

chatte *f* cat

chatter INFORM chat (online)

chaud 1 *adj* hot; *plus modéré* warm; *il fait ~* it's hot/warm **2** *m* heat; *plus modéré* warmth; *j'ai ~* I'm hot/warm; **chaudière** *f* boiler

chauffage *m* heating; **~ central** central heating

chauffard *m* F roadhog

chauffer 1 *v/t* heat (up), warm (up); *maison* heat; **se ~** warm o.s.; *d'un sportif* warm up **2** *v/i* warm *ou* heat up; *d'un moteur* overheat

chauffeur *m* driver; *privé aussi* chauffeur; **~ de taxi** taxi *ou* cab driver

chaussée *f* pavement, *Br* roadway

chausser *bottes* put on; **se ~** put one's shoes on; **chaussette** *f* sock; **chausson** *m* slipper; **chaussure** *f* shoe; **~s de marche** hiking boots;

49 **chien**

~s de ski ski boots

chauve bald; **chauve-souris** f bat

chauvinisme m chauvinism

chef m (*meneur*), POL leader; (*patron*) boss; *d'une entreprise* head; *d'une tribu* chief; CUIS chef; **au premier ~** first and foremost; **de propre mon ~** on my own initiative

chef-d'œuvre m masterpiece

chemin m way; (*route*) road; (*allée*) path; **~ de fer** railroad, *Br* railway

cheminée f chimney; (*âtre*) fireplace; (*encadrement*) mantelpiece; *de bateau* funnel

cheminot m rail worker

chemise f shirt; (*dossier*) folder; **~ de nuit** *de femme* nightdress; **chemisier** m blouse

chêne m BOT oak (tree)

chenil m kennels pl

chenille f ZO caterpillar

chèque m COMM check, *Br* cheque; **~ de voyage** traveler's check, *Br* traveller's cheque; **chéquier** m checkbook, *Br* chequebook

cher, -ère 1 adj dear (**à qn** to s.o.); *coûteux* dear, expensive **2** adv: **payer qch ~** pay a high price for sth **3** m/f **mon cher, ma chère** my dear

chercher look for; **~ à faire qch** try to do sth; **aller ~** fetch, go for; **venir ~** collect,

come for; **envoyer ~** send for

chéri darling

chétif, -ive puny

cheval m horse; AUTO horsepower; **aller à ~** ride; **être à ~ sur qch** straddle sth; **chevalier** m HIST knight; **chevalière** f signet ring

chevelu *personne* long-haired; **chevelure** f hair

chevet m bedhead; **table** f **de ~** nightstand, *Br aussi* bedside table

cheveu m hair; **~x** hair; **aux ~x courts** short-haired

cheville f ANAT ankle; TECH peg

chèvre f goat

chevreau m kid

chevreuil m deer; CUIS venison

chez: ~ lui at his place; *direction* to his place; **~ Marcel** at Marcel's; **quand nous sommes ~ nous** when we are at home; **rentrer ~ soi** go home; **aller ~ le coiffeur** go to the hairdresser *ou Br* hairdresser's; **~ Molière** in Molière

chez-soi m home

chiant F boring

chic 1 m style **2** adj chic; (*sympathique*) decent

chicaner quibble (**sur** over)

chicorée f BOT chicory

chien m dog; **temps de ~** fig F filthy weather; **~ d'aveugle** seeing-eye dog, *Br* guide dog; **chienne** f dog; **le chien et la** ~ the dog and the bitch

chier V shit; **ça me fait** ~ P it pisses me off P

chiffon m rag; ~ (**à poussière**) duster; **chiffonner** crumple; *fig* F bother

chiffre m number; (**code**) cipher

Chili: le ~ Chili; **chilien, ~ne** Chilean; **Chilien, ~ne** m/f Chilean

chimie f chemistry

chimiothérapie f chemotherapy

chimique chemical

Chine: la ~ China; **chinois, ~e 1** *adj* Chinese **2** m *langue* Chinese; **Chinois, ~e** m/f Chinese

chiot m pup

chips *mpl* chips, *Br* crisps

chirurgie f surgery; ~ **esthétique** plastic surgery; **chirurgien, ~ne** m/f surgeon; ~ **dentiste** dental surgeon

choc m shock; *d'opinions, intérêts* clash

chocolat m chocolate

chœur m choir **en** ~ in chorus

choisir choose; ~ **de faire** decide to do; **choix** m choice; (*assortiment*) range; **de** (**premier**) ~ choice

cholestérol m cholesterol

chômage m unemployment; **être au** ~ be unemployed; ~ **partiel** short time; **chômeur, -euse** m/f unemployed person; **les** ~**s** the

unemployed *pl*

chope f beer mug

choquant shocking; **choquer:** ~ **qc** knock sth; ~ **qn** shock s.o.

chorale f choir

chose f thing; **autre** ~ something else; **c'est** ~ **faite** it's done

chou m BOT cabbage; ~**x de Bruxelles** Brussels sprouts

chouette 1 f owl **2** *adj* F great

chou-fleur m cauliflower

chrétien, ~ne *adj* & m/f Christian

christianisme m Christianity

chrome m chrome

chronique 1 *adj* chronic **2** f *d'un journal* column; *reportage* report; **chroniqueur** m *pour un journal* columnist

chronologique chronological

chronométrer time

chuchoter whisper

chut: ~**!** hush

chute f fall; ~ **des cheveux** hair loss

ci: à cette heure-~ at this time; **comme** ~ **comme ça** F so-so; **par-**~ **par-là** here and there

cible f target; **cibler** target

ciboulette f BOT chives *pl*

cicatrice f scar (*aussi fig*); **cicatriser:** (**se**) ~ heal

ci-contre opposite; **ci-dessous** below; **ci-dessus** above

cidre m cider

ciel *m* sky; REL heaven
cigale *f* cicada
cigare *m* cigar
cigarette *f* cigarette
ci-inclus enclosed; ci-joint enclosed, attached
cil *m* eyelash
ciment *m* cement
cimetière *m* cemetery
ciné *m* F movie theater, *Br* cinema; cinéma *m* movie theater, *Br* cinema; *art* cinema, movies *pl*
cinglé F mad, crazy
cinq five; *le ~ mai* May fifth, *Br* the fifth of May; cinquantaine *f* about fifty; *elle approche la ~* she's getting on for fifty; cinquante fifty; cinquantième fiftieth cinquième fifth
cintre *m* arch; *pour vêtements* coathanger
cirage *m* *pour parquet* wax, polish; *pour chaussures* polish
circonférence *f* circumference
circonspect circumspect
circonstance *f* circumstance
circuit *m* circuit; *de voyage* tour; SP track
circulaire *adj* & *f* circular
circulation *f* circulation; *voitures* traffic; *circuler* circulate; *faire ~ nouvelles* spread
cire *f* wax; cirer polish; *parquet aussi* wax
cirque *m* circus
cirrhose *f*: *~ du foie* cirrhosis

of the liver
ciseaux *mpl* scissors *pl*
citadin, *~e* **1** *adj* town *atr*, city *atr* **2** *m/f* town-dweller, city-dweller
citation *f* quotation; JUR summons *sg*
cité *f* city; *~ universitaire* fraternity house, *Br* hall of residence
citoyen, *~ne* *m/f* citizen; citoyenneté *f* citizenship
citron *m* lemon; *~ vert* lime; citronnier *m* lemon (tree)
civière *f* stretcher
civil **1** *adj* civil; *non militaire* civilian; *état m ~* marital status **2** *m* civilian; *en ~* in civilian clothes; *policier* in plain clothes; civilisation *f* civilization
civique civic
civisme *m* public-spiritedness
clair **1** *adj* clear; *couleur* light; *chambre* bright **2** *adv* voir clearly; *dire, parler* plainly **3** *m*: *~ de lune* moonlight
clairière *f* clearing
clairvoyant perceptive
clandestin secret, clandestine; *passager m ~* stowaway
claque *f* slap; claquer **1** *v/t porte* slam; *~ des doigts* snap one's fingers **2** *v/i d'un fouet* crack; *des dents* chatter; *d'un volet* slam
clarifier clarify

clarinette f clarinet
clarté f (lumière) brightness; (transparence) clarity
classe f class; il a de la ~ he's got class; ~ économique economy class
classement m position, place; BOT, ZO classification; de lettres filing; classer classify; actes, dossiers file; ~ une affaire consider a matter closed
classique 1 adj classical; (traditionnel) classic 2 m en littérature classical author; MUS classical music; film, livre classic
clause f clause; ~ pénale penalty clause
clavicule f collarbone
clavier m keyboard
clé f key; TECH wrench; ~ de fa MUS bass clef; fermer à ~ lock; sous ~ under lock and key
clef f → clé
clément merciful
clergé m clergy
clic m bruit, INFORM click
client, ~e m/f (acheteur) customer; d'un médecin patient; d'un avocat client; clientèle f customers pl, clientèle; d'un médecin patients pl; d'un avocat clients pl
cligner: ~ (des yeux) blink; ~ de l'œil à qn wink at s.o.
clignotant m turn signal, Br indicator; clignoter d'une

lumière flicker
climat m climate (aussi fig)
climatisation f air conditioning; climatisé air conditioned
clin m: ~ d'œil wink; en un ~ d'œil in a flash
clinique 1 adj clinical 2 f clinic
cliquer INFORM click (sur on)
clochard, ~e m/f hobo, Br tramp
cloche f bell f; F (idiot) nitwit F; clocher 1 m steeple 2 v/i F: ça cloche something's not right
cloison f partition
cloîtrer fig: se ~ shut o.s. away
clonage m cloning; clone m clone; cloner clone
clope m ou f F cigarette, Br F fag; (mégot) cigarette end
cloque f blister
clôture f d'un débat closure; d'un compte closing; (barrière) fence
clou m nail; fig main attraction; MÉD boil; clouer nail; être cloué au lit be confined to bed
clown m clown
club m club; ~ de gym gym
coaguler du lait curdle; du sang coagulate
cobaye m ZO, fig guinea pig
coca m Coke®
coccinelle f ladybug, Br ladybird; F AUTO Volkswagen® beetle
cocher sur une liste check, Br

aussi tick off

cochon 1 *m* zo, *fig* pig **2** *adj*
cochon, ⁓ne F dirty; **co-
chonnerie** *f* F: **des ⁓s** filth;
nourriture junk food

coco *m*: **noix f de** ⁓ coconut

cocotte *f* CUIS casserole; F
darling; *péj* tart; ⁓ **minute**
pressure cooker

code *m* code; ⁓ **confidentiel**
PIN number; ⁓ **pénal** penal
code; **se mettre en** ⁓ switch
to low beams; ⁓ **postal** zip-
code, *Br* postcode

cœur *m* heart; **de bon** ⁓ gladly; **par** ⁓ by heart; **j'ai mal au**
⁓ I feel nauseous

coffre *m meuble* chest; FIN
safe; AUTO trunk, *Br* boot;
coffre-fort *m* safe

cogérer co-manage

cognac *m* brandy, cognac

cogner *d'un moteur* knock; ⁓
à *ou* **contre qc** bang against
sth; **se** ⁓ **à** *ou* **contre qc**
bump into sth

cohabiter cohabit

cohérent *théorie* consistent,
coherent

cohue *f* crowd, rabble

coiffer: ⁓ **qn** do s.o.'s hair; **se**
⁓ do one's hair; **coiffeur** *m*
hairdresser, hair stylist; **coiffeuse** *f* hairdresser, hair stylist; *meuble* dressing table;
coiffure *f* **de cheveux** hairstyle

coin *m* corner; **cale** wedge

coincer squeeze; *porte, tiroir*
jam; **coincé dans un em-**

bouteillage stuck in a traffic
jam

coïncidence *f* coincidence

col *m* collar; *d'une bouteille,
d'un pull* neck; GÉOGR col;
⁓ **blanc/bleu** white-collar/
/blue-collar worker

colère *f* anger; **se mettre en** ⁓
get angry

colique *f* colic; (*diarrhée*) diarrhea, *Br* diarrhoea

colis *m* parcel, package

collaborateur, -trice *m/f* collaborator ((*aussi* POL *péj*);
collaboration *f* collaboration, cooperation; POL *péj*
collaboration; **collaborer**
collaborate, cooperate
(**avec** with; **à** on); POL *péj*
collaborate

collant 1 *adj* sticky; *vêtement*
close-fitting; F *personne*
clingy **2** *m* pantyhose *pl*,
Br tights *pl*

colle *f* glue; *fig* P *question*
tough question; (*retenue*)
detention

collecte *f* collection; **collectif, -ive** collective; **voyage**
m ⁓ group tour

collection *f* collection; **collectionner** collect; **collec-
tionneur, -euse** *m/f* collector

collège *m école* junior high,
Br secondary school; **collé-
gien, ⁓ne** *m/f* junior high
student, *Br* secondary
school pupil

collègue *m/f* colleague, co-worker

coller 1 *v/t* stick, glue **2** *v/i* stick (*à* to); **se ~ contre mur** press o.s against; *personne* cling to

collier *m bijou* necklace; *de chien* collar

colline *f* hill

collision *f* collision; **entrer en ~ avec** collide with

colocataire *m/f* roommate, *Br* flatmate

colombe *f* dove (*aussi fig*)

Colombie: la~ Colombia; **colombien, ~ne** Colombian; **Colombien, ~ne** *m/f* Colombian

colonie *f* colony; **~ de vacances** summer camp

colonne *f* column

colorant 1 *adj shampoing* color *atr, Br* colour *atr* **2** *m* dye; *dans la nourriture* coloring, *Br* colouring; **colorer** color, *Br* colour

coma *m* coma

combat *m* fight; MIL *aussi* battle; **mettre hors de ~** put out of action; combattant **1** *adj* fighting **2** *m* combatant; **combattre** fight

combien 1 *adv quantité* how much; *avec* pl how many **2** *m*: **tous les ~** how often; **on est le ~ aujourd'hui?** what date is it today?

combinaison *f* combination; (*astuce*) scheme; *de mécanicien* coveralls *pl, Br* boiler suit; *lingerie* (full-length)

slip; **~ de plongée** wet suit

combiner combine; *voyage, projet* plan

comble 1 *m fig*: **sommet** height; **~s** *pl* attic; **de fond en ~** from top to bottom **2** *adj* full (to capacity); **combler** *trou* fill in; *déficit* make good; *personne* overwhelm; **~ qn de qch** shower s.o. with sth

combustible 1 *adj* combustible **2** *m* fuel

comédie *f* comedy; **~ musicale** musical; **comédien, ~ne** *m/f* actor; *qui joue le genre comique* comic actor

comestible 1 *adj* edible **2** *mpl* **~s** food

comique 1 *adj* THÉÂT comic; (*drôle*) funny, comical **2** *m* comedian; *acteur* comic (actor); *genre* comedy

comité *m* committee

commande *f* COMM order; TECH control; INFORM command; **commander 1** *v/t* COMM order; (*ordonner*) command, order; MIL be in command of; TECH control **2** *v/i* (*diriger*) be in charge; COMM order

comme 1 *adv* like; **noir ~ la nuit** as black as night; **~ ci ~ ça** F so-so; **~ vous voulez** as you like; **~ si** as if; **il travaillait ~ ...** he was working as a ...; **moi, ~ les autres, je ...** like the others, I ... **2** *conj* as

commencement *m* beginning, start; **commencer** begin, start; ~ **qc par qc** start sth with sth; ~ **par faire qc** start by doing sth

comment how; ~**?** (qu'avez-vous dit?) pardon me?, *Br* sorry?; ~**!** surpris what!

commentaire *m* comment; RAD, TV commentary; **commenter** comment on; RAD, TV commentate on

commerçant, ~**e 1** *adj*: **rue f** ~**e** shopping street **2** *m/f* merchant, trader

commerce *m* trade, commerce; (*magasin*) store, *Br* shop; *fig* (*rapports*) dealings *pl*;**commercial** commercial; **commercialiser** market

commettre commit; *erreur* make

commis *m*: ~ **voyageur** commercial traveler *ou Br* traveller

commissaire *m* commission member; *de l'UE* Commissioner; *SP* steward; **commissariat** *m* commissionership; ~ **(de police)** police station

commission *f* commission; (*message*) message

commode 1 *adj* handy; *arrangement* convenient; **pas** ~ *personne* awkward **2** *f* chest of drawers; **commodité** *f* convenience

commotion *f* MÉD: ~ **cérébrale** stroke

commun 1 *adj* common; *œu-*

vre joint; **mettre en** ~ *argent* pool **2** *m*: **hors du** ~ out of the ordinary

communal (*de la commune*) local

communauté *f* community; *de hippies* commune

communication *f* communication; (*message*) message; ~ **téléphonique** telephone call

communion *f* REL Communion

communiquer 1 *v/t* communicate; *maladie* pass on, give (**à qn** to s.o.) **2** *v/i* communicate

communisme *m* communism; **communiste** *m/f* & *adj* Communist

commutateur *m* switch

compact compact

compagne *f* companion; *dans couple* wife

compagnie *f* company; ~ **aérienne** airline

compagnon *m* companion; *dans couple* husband; *employé* journeyman

comparaison *f* comparison; **par** ~ **à** compared with; **comparer** compare (**à** to, **avec** with)

compartiment *m* compartment; *de train* car, *Br* compartment

compas *m* compass

compassion *f* compassion

compatible compatible

compatir: ~ **à** sympathize

with

compatriote *m/f* compatriot

compenser compensate for

compétence *f* (*connaissances*) ability, competence; JUR jurisdiction; **compétent** competent, skillful; *Br* skilful; JUR competent

compétitif, -ive competitive; **compétition** *f* competition

compiler compile

complaire: *se ~ dans/à faire* delight in/in doing

complet, -ète 1 *adj* complete; *hôtel, description, jeu de cartes* full; *pain* whole wheat, *Br* wholemeal **2** *m* suit; **complètement** completely; **compléter** complete; **se ~** complement each other

complexe *adj & m* complex

complication *f* complication

complice 1 *adj* JUR: *être ~ de* be an accessory to **2** *m/f* accomplice

compliment *m* compliment; *mes ~s* congratulations

compliqué complicated; **compliquer** complicate; **se ~** become complicated

comporter (*comprendre*) comprise; (*impliquer*) involve; **se ~** behave (o.s)

composer 1 *v/t* (*former*) make up; MUS compose; *livre, poème* write; *numéro* dial **2** *v/i transiger* come to terms (*avec* with); **se ~ de** be consist of

compositeur, -trice *m/f* com-

poser

composter *billet* punch

compote *f: ~ de pommes* stewed apples

compréhension *f* understanding

comprendre understand; (*inclure*) include; (*comporter*) comprise

compresse *f* MÉD compress

comprimé *m* tablet

compris (*inclus*) included; *y ~* including

compromettre compromise

comptabilité *f* accountancy; (*comptes*) accounts *pl*; **comptable** *m/f* accountant

comptant: *au ~* cash

compte *m* account; (*calcul*) calculation; *~s* accounts; *en fin de ~* when all's said and done; *se rendre ~ de* realize; *tenir ~ de qc* take sth into account; *~ courant* checking account, *Br* current account; *~ rendu* report; *de réunion* minutes *pl*; **compter 1** *v/t* count; (*prévoir*) allow; (*inclure*) include; *~ faire* plan on doing **2** *v/i* count; *~ sur* rely on; *à ~ de* starting (from); **compteur** *m* meter

comptoir *m d'un café* bar; *d'un magasin* counter

con, ~ne P 1 *adj* damn stupid F **2** *m/f* damn idiot F

concentration *f* concentration; **concentrer** concentrate; **se ~** concentrate

(**sur** on)

concept *m* concept

conception *f* (*idée*) concept; (*planification*) design; BIOL conception

concernant concerning, about; concerner concern

concert *m* MUS concert; **de ~ avec** together with

concession *f* concession; AUTO dealership

concevable conceivable; concevoir (*comprendre*) understand, conceive; (*inventer*) design; BIOL, plan, idée conceive

concierge *m/f* superintendent, *Br* caretaker; *d'école* janitor, *Br aussi* caretaker; *d'un hôtel* concierge

concis concise

concitoyen, ~ne *m/f* fellow citizen

conclure conclude; ~ **de** conclude from; conclusion *f* conclusion

concombre *m* cucumber

concours *m* competition; (*assistance*) help

concret, -ète concrete

concurrence *f* competition; **faire ~ à** compete with; concurrent, ~e **1** *adj* rival **2** *m/f* competitor

condamnation *f* sentence; *action* sentencing; *fig* condemnation

condamner JUR sentence; *malade* give up; (*réprouver*) condemn; *porte* block up

condescendance *f péj* condescension

condition *f* condition; ~ **préalable** prerequisite; **à** (**la**) ~ **que** (+ *subj*) on condition that; conditionner (*emballer*) package; PSYCH condition

condoléances *fpl* condoléances

conducteur, -trice **1** *m/f* driver **2** *m* PHYS conductor

conduire **1** *v/t* take; (*mener*) lead; *voiture* drive; EL conduct; **se ~** behave **2** *v/i* AUTO drive; (*mener*) lead

conduit *m d'eau, de gaz* pipe; ~ **d'aération** ventilation shaft

conduite *f* (*comportement*) behavior, *Br* behaviour; *direction* management; *d'eau, de gaz* pipe; AUTO driving

cône *m* cone

confection *f* making; *industrie* clothing industry

conférence *f* conference; (*exposé*) lecture; **être en ~** be in a meeting

confesser confess; ~ **qn** REL hear s.o.'s confession; **se ~** REL go to confession; confession *f* confession; (*croyance*) faith

confiance *f* confidence; **faire ~ à** trust; confiant confident; (*crédule*) trusting

confidence *f* confidence; **faire une ~ à** confide in; confident, ~e *m/f* confidant; confidentiel, ~le confidential

confier: ~ *qc à qn* (*laisser*) entrust s.o. (with sth); *se ~ à* confide in

confirmation *f* confirmation (*aussi* REL); **confirmer** confirm (*aussi* REL)

confiserie *f* confectionery; *magasin* confectioner's; ~**s** candy , *Br* sweets

confisquer confiscate (*à* from)

confiture *f* jelly, *Br* jam

conflit *m* conflict; *d'idées* clash

confondre confuse; (*déconcerter*) take aback; *se ~* (*se mêler*) merge

conforme: ~ *à* in accordance with; **conformiste** *m/f* conformist

confort *m* comfort; **confortable** comfortable; *somme* sizeable

confronter confront; (*comparer*) compare

confusion *f* confusion; (*embarras*) embarrassment

congé *m* vacation, *Br* holiday; *MIL* leave; *avis de départ* notice; **prendre** ~ *de* take one's leave of; ~ *de maladie* sick leave

congélateur *m* freezer; **congelé** *aliment* frozen; **congeler** freeze

congénital congenital

congestion *f* MÉD congestion; ~ *cérébrale* stroke; **congestionné** *visage*

flushed

congrès *m* convention, conference; **Congrès** *aux États-Unis* Congress

conique conical

conjecture *f* conjecture

conjoint, ~**e 1** *adj* joint **2** *m/f* spouse

conjonctivite *f* MÉD conjunctivitis

conjugaison *f* GRAM conjugation

conjugal conjugal; *vie* married

conjuguer *efforts* combine; GRAM conjugate

connaissance *f* knowledge; (*conscience*) consciousness; *personne connue* acquaintance; ~**s** *d'un sujet* knowledge; **connaisseur** *m* connoisseur; **connaître** know; (*rencontrer*) meet; **s'y ~ en** be an expert on

connecter TECH connect; *se~* INFORM log on

connerie *f* V: *une* ~ a damn stupid thing to do/say

connexion *f* connection; *hors* ~ INFORM off-line

connu well-known

conquérir conquer

conquête *f* conquest

consacrer REL consecrate; (*dédier*) dedicate; *temps, argent* spend; *se ~ à* dedicate *ou* devote o.s. to

conscience *f moral* conscience; *physique,* PSYCH consciousness; **prendre** ~

de become aware of
consécutif, -ive consecutive;
 ~ à resulting from
conseil *m* advice; *(conseiller)*
 adviser; *(assemblée)* council;
 un ~ a piece of advice; **~**
 d'administration board of
 directors
conseiller *personne* advise; **~**
 qc à qn recommend sth to
 s.o.
consentir 1 *v/i* consent, agree
 (à to) **2** *v/t prêt, délai* agree
conséquence *f* conse-
 quence; **en ~** consequently
conservation *f* preservation;
 des aliments preserving
conserve *f* preserve; *en boîte*
 canned food, *Br aussi* tinned
 food; **conserver** keep; *ali-*
 ments preserve
considérable considerable;
 considération *f* consideration; **considérer** consider
consigne *f* orders *pl*; *d'une*
 gare baggage checkroom,
 Br left luggage office; *pour*
 bouteilles deposit; ÉDU detention
consistance *f* consistency;
 consistant *liquide, potage*
 thick; *mets* substantial; **con-**
 sister: ~ en/dans consist of;
 ~ à faire consist in doing
consolation *f* consolation
console *f* console; ***jouer à la***
 ~ play computer games
consoler consolet; **se ~ de**
 get over
consolider consolidate

consommateur, -trice *m/f*
 consumer; *dans un café* customer; **consommation** *f*
 consumption; *dans un café*
 drink; **consommer 1** *v/t*
 consume, use **2** *v/i dans un*
 café drink
consonne *f* consonant
conspiration *f* conspiracy;
 conspirer conspire
constamment constantly
constance *f* *(persévérance)*
 perseverance; *en amour*
 constancy
constant constant; *ami*
 staunch; *efforts* persistent
constater observe
consternation *f* consternation; **consterner** fill with
 consternation, dismay
constipation *f* MÉD constipation
constituer constitute; *comi-*
 té, société form; *rente* settle
 (à on); **se ~** *fortune* build up
constitution *f* *(composition)*
 composition; ANAT, POL constitution; *d'un comité, d'une*
 société formation
construction *f* construction,
 building; **construire** construct, build; *théorie, roman*
 construct
consul *m* consul; **consulat** *m*
 consulate
consultation *f* consultation;
 consulter 1 *v/t* consult **2**
 v/i be available for consultation
contact *m* contact; ***se mettre***

en ~ avec contact; **mettre/ couper le ~** AUTO switch the engine on/off

contagieux, -euse contagious; *rire* infectious

contaminer contaminate; MÉD *personne* infect

conte *m* story, tale

contempler contemplate

contemporain *m & adj* contemporary

contenir contain; *foule* control; *larmes* hold back; *peine* suppress; **se ~** contain o.s.

content pleased, content (**de** with)

contenu *m* content

contestation *f* discussion; *(opposition)* protest; contester challenge

contexte *m* context

continent *m* continent

contingent *m (part)* quota

continu continuous; EL *courant* direct; continuer 1 *v/t* continue; *rue, ligne* extend 2 *v/i* continue, go on; *de route* extend; **~ à ou de faire** continue to do, go on doing; continuité *f* continuity; *d'une tradition* continuation

contorsion *f* contorsion

contour *m* contour; *d'une fenêtre, d'un visage* outline; **~s** *(courbes)* twists and turns

contourner get around

contraceptif, -ive contraceptive; contraception *f* contraception

contracter *dette* incur; *mala-*

die aussi contract; *obligation, engagement* enter into; *assurance* take out; *habitude* acquire

contradiction *f* contradiction

contraindre: **~ qn à faire qc** force s.o. to do sth; contrainte *f* constraint; **sans ~** freely, without restraint

contraire 1 *adj sens* opposite; *principes* conflicting; *vent* contrary 2 *m*: **le ~ de** the opposite *ou* contrary of; **au ~** on the contrary

contrarier *personne* annoy; *projet* thwart

contraster contrast

contrat *m* contract

contravention *f* infringement; *(procès-verbal)* ticket

contre 1 *prép* against; *(en échange)* (in exchange) for; **tout ~ qch** right next to sth; **par ~** on the contrary; **quelque chose ~ la diarrhée** something for diarrhea 2 *m*: **le pour et le ~** the pros and the cons *pl*

contrebande *f* smuggling; *marchandises* contraband; contrebandier *m* smuggler

contrebasse *f* double bass

contrecœur: **à ~** reluctantly

contrecoup *m* after-effect

contredire contradict

contrée *f* country

contrefaire counterfeit; *signature* forge; *personne, gestes* imitate; *voix* disguise

contre-nature unnatural

contrepartie f compensation; **en ~** in return

contre-plaqué m plywood

contrer counter

contresens m misinterpretation; **prendre une route à ~** go down a road the wrong way

contretemps m hitch

contribuable m taxpayer; contribuer contribute (**à** to); **~ à faire** help to do

contrôle m MÉD (*vérification*) check; (*domination*) control; (*maîtrise de soi*) self-control; **~ douanier** customs inspection; **~ radar** radar speed check; contrôler *identité, billets etc* check; (*maîtriser, dominer*) control; **se ~** control o.s.

controversé controversial

contusion f MÉD bruise

convaincre (*persuader*) convince; **~ qn de faire qch** persuade s.o. to do sth

convalescent, **~e** m/f convalescent

convenable suitable; (*correct*) personne respectable; *salaire* adequate; convenance f: **les ~s** the proprieties

convenir: **~ à qn** suit s.o.; **~à qc** be suitable for sth; **~ de qc** (*décider*) agree on sth; **~ que** (*reconnaître que*) admit that; **comme convenu** as agreed

convention f convention

converger converge

conversation f conversation; **~ téléphonique** telephone conversation, phonecall

conversion f conversion

convertir convert

conviction f conviction

convive m/f guest; convivialité f conviviality, friendliness; INFORM user-friendliness

convocation f d'une assemblée convening; JUR summons sg

convoi m convoy

convoquer *assemblée* convene; JUR summons; *candidat* notify; *employé, écolier* call in

convoyer MIL escort

convulsion f convulsion

coopération f cooperation; coopérer cooperate (**à** in)

coordination f coordination

coordonnées fpl MATH coordinates pl; *de personne* contact details

copain m F pal

copie f copy; ÉDU paper; copier copy (**sur qn** from s.o.)

copieux, -euse copious

copine f F pal

copropriétaire m/f co-owner, part owner

coq m rooster

coquelicot m BOT poppy

coquetier m eggcup

coquetterie f flirtatiousness; (*élégance*) stylishness

coquillage m shell; **des ~s**

shellfish

coquille f shell; *erreur* misprint, typo

coquin, ~e **1** *adj enfant* naughty **2** *m/f* rascal

corbeau *m* zo crow

corbeille f basket; *au théâtre* circle

corbillard *m* hearse

corde f rope; MUS, *de tennis* string

cordialité f cordiality

cordon *m* cord; **~ littoral** offshore sand bar

cordonnier *m* shoe repairer

Corée: **la ~** Korea; **coréen**, ~ne **1** *adj* Korean **2** *m langue* Korean; **Coréen**, ~ne *m/f* Korean

corne f horn

cornée f cornea

corneille f crow

corner *m en football* corner

cornet *m sachet* (paper) cone; MUS cornet

cornichon *m* gherkin

corporation f body; HIST guild

corporel, ~le *hygiène* personal; *châtiment* corporal; *art* body *atr*

corps *m* body; *mort aussi* corpse; MIL corps; **prendre ~** take shape

corpulence f stoutness, corpulence

correct correct; *tenue* suitable; F *(convenable)* acceptable, ok F

correcteur *m*: **~ orthographique** spellchecker

correction f *qualité* correctness; *(modification)* correction; *(punition)* beating

correspondance f correspondence; *de train etc* connection; **correspondre** correspond; *de salles* communicate; **~ à réalité** correspond with; *preuves* tally with; *idées* fit in with

corridor *m* corridor

corriger correct; *épreuve* proof-read; *(battre)* beat

corrompre corrupt; *(soudoyer)* bribe

corrosion f corrosion

corruption f corruption; *(pot-de-vin)* bribery

corsage *m* blouse

corse Corsican; **Corse 1** *m/f* Corsican **2** f **la Corse** Corsica

corsé *vin* full-bodied; *sauce* spicy; *café* strong; *facture* stiff; *problème* tough

cortège *m* cortège; *(défilé)* procession

cortisone f cortisone

corvée f chore; MIL fatigue

cosmétique *m & adj* cosmetic

cosmopolite *m & adj* cosmopolitan

costaud F sturdy

costume *m* costume; *pour homme* suit

cote f *en Bourse* quotation; *d'un document* identification code

côte f ANAT rib; (*pente*) slope; **à la mer** coast; *viande* chop; **~ à ~** side by side

côté m side; **à ~** (*près*) nearby; **à ~ de** next to; **de ~** aside; **de l'autre~** on the other side of; **du~ de** in the direction of; **sur le ~** on one's/its side; **mettre de ~** put aside

côtelette f CUIS cutlet

cotisation f contribution; *à une organisation* subscription

coton m coton

côtoyer rub shoulders with; **~ qc** border sth

cottage m cottage

cou m neck

couchant 1 m west **2** adj: **soleil** m **~** setting sun

couche f layer; *de peinture aussi* coat; *de bébé* diaper, Br nappy

coucher 1 v/t (*mettre au lit*) put to bed; (*héberger*) put up; (*étendre*) put ou lay down **2** v/i sleep; **se ~** go to bed; (*s'étendre*) lie down; *du soleil* set, go down **3** m: **du soleil** sunset

coucou m cuckoo; (*pendule*) cuckoo clock

coude m ANAT elbow; *d'une route* turn

coudre sew; *bouton* sew on; *plaie* sew up

couette f comforter, Br quilt

couler 1 v/i flow, run; *d'eau de bain* run; *d'un bateau* sink **2** v/t *liquide* pour; (*mouler*) cast; *bateau* sink

couleur f color, Br colour

coulisse f: **~s** THÉÂT wings; **dans les ~s** fig behind the scenes

couloir m passage, corridor; *d'un bus, avion* aisle

coup m blow; *dans jeu* move; **boire un ~** F have a drink; **du ~** and so; **après ~** after the event; **tout d'un ~, tout à ~** suddenly, all at once; *de couteau* stab; **coup de foudre: ce fut le~** it was love at first sight; **coup de main: donner un ~ à qn** give s.o. a hand; **coup d'œil: au premier ~** at first glance; **coup de pied** kick; **coup de poing** punch; **donner un ~ à** punch; **coup de téléphone** (phone) call; **coup de soleil: avoir un ~** have sun stroke

coupable 1 adj guilty **2** m/f culprit, guilty party

coupe¹ f *de cheveux, d'une robe* cut

coupe² f (*verre*) glass; SP cup; *de fruits, glace* dish

coupe-ongles m inv nail clippers pl

couper 1 v/t cut; *morceau, eau* cut off; *robe, chemise* cut out; *vin* dilute; *animal* castrate **2** v/i cut; **se ~** cut o.s.; (*se trahir*) give o.s. away

couple m couple

coupon m *de tissu* remnant; COMM coupon; (*ticket*) ticket

coupure f cut; *de journal* cutting; (*billet de banque*) bill, *Br* note; **~ de courant** power outage, *Br* power cut

cour f court; ARCH courtyard; **Cour internationale de justice** International Court of Justice

courage m courage, bravery; **courageux, -euse** brave, courageous

couramment fluently

courant 1 *adj* current; *eau* running; *langage* everyday **2** m current (*aussi* ÉL); **~ d'air** draft, *Br* draught; **être au ~ de qch** know about sth

courbature f stiffness; **avoir des ~s** be stiff

courbe 1 *adj* curved **2** f curve; **courber** bend; **se ~** (*se baisser*) stoop, bend down

coureur m runner; *péj* skirt-chaser

courge f BOT squash, *Br* marrow

courgette f BOT zucchini, *Br* courgette

courir 1 *v/i* run (*aussi d'eau*); *d'un bruit* go around **2** *v/t risque, danger* run; **~ les magasins** go around the stores

couronne f crown; *de fleurs* wreath; **couronnement** m coronation

courrier m mail, *Br aussi* post; (*messager*) courier; **~ électronique** electronic mail, e-mail

courroie f belt

cours m course; ÉCON price; *de devises* rate; (*leçon*) lesson; *à l'université* class, *Br aussi* lecture; **donner libre ~ à** give free rein to; **en ~ de route** on the way

course f à pied running; SP race; *en taxi* ride; (*commission*) errand; **~s** (*achats*) shopping; **faire des ~s** go shopping

court¹ m (*aussi* **~ de tennis**) (tennis) court

court² *adj* short; **à ~ de** short of

court-circuit m ÉL short circuit

courtier m broker

courtiser *femme* court

courtoisie f courtesy

cousin, ~e m/f cousin

coussin m cushion

coût m cost; **coûter 1** *v/t* cost; **combien ça coûte?** how much is it?, how much does it cost? **2** *v/i* cost; **~ cher** be expensive

couteau m knife

coûteux, -euse expensive, costly

coutume f custom; **avoir ~ de faire** be in the habit of doing

couture f sewing; *d'un vêtement, bas etc* seam

couvée f clutch; *fig* brood

couvent m convent

couver 1 *v/t* hatch; *personne* pamper **2** *v/i d'un feu* smolder, *Br* smoulder; *d'une révolution* be brewing

couvercle *m* cover

couvert 1 *adj ciel* overcast; ~ **de** covered with *ou* in **2** *m* à *table* place setting; ~**s** flatware, *Br* cutlery; **mettre le** ~ set the table; **couverture** *f* cover; *sur un lit* blanket

couvrir cover (**de** with *ou* in); ~ **qn** *fig* (*protéger*) cover (up) for s.o.; **se~** (*s'habiller*) cover o.s. up; *du ciel* cloud over

covoiturage *m* carpooling; **faire du** ~ carpool

crabe *m* crab

cracher spit

crachin *m* drizzle

craie *f* chalk

craindre fear, be frightened of; ~ **de faire** be afraid of doing; ~ **que** (**ne**) (+ *subj*) be afraid that

crainte *f* fear; **de~ de** for fear of

craintif, -ive timid

cramoisi crimson

crampe *f* MÉD cramp

crampon *m* crampon

cran *m* notch; **il a du** ~ F he's got guts

crâne *m* skull

crâner F (*pavaner*) show off

crapaud *m* ZO toad

crapule *f* villain

craquelé cracked

craquement *m* crackle; **craquer** crack; *d'un parquet* creak; *de feuilles* crackle; *d'une couture* split; *d'une personne* (*s'effondrer*) crack

up

crasse 1 *adj ignorance* crass **2** *f* dirt

cravate *f* necktie, *Br* tie

crayon *m* pencil; ~ **à bille** ballpoint pen; ~ **de couleur** crayon

créance *f* COMM debt; **créancier, -ère** *m/f* creditor

création *f* creation; *de mode, design* design; **créativité** *f* creativity

créature *f* creature

crèche *f* day nursery; *de Noël* crèche, *Br* crib

crédibilité *f* credibility; **crédit** *m* credit; (*prêt*) loan; (*influence*) influence; **acheter à** ~ buy on credit; **faire** ~ **à qn** give s.o. credit

créditeur, -trice 1 *m/f* creditor **2** *adj solde* credit *atr*; **être** ~ be in credit

crédule credulous

créer create; *institution* set up; COMM *produit* design

crématorium *m* crematorium

crème 1 *f* cream; ~ **anglaise** custard; ~ **dépilatoire** hair remover; ~ **solaire** suntan cream **2** *m* coffee with milk, *Br* white coffee **3** *adj inv* cream

créneau *m* AUTO space; COMM niche

crêpe *f* CUIS pancake

crépiter crackle

crépu frizzy

crépuscule *m* twilight

crétin, ~e *m/f* idiot, cretin

creuser hollow out; *trou* dig; *fig* look into

creux, -euse 1 *adj* hollow; *assiette f creuse* soup plate **2** *adv*: *sonner* ~ ring hollow **3** *m* hollow

crevaison *f* puncture

crevant F (*épuisant*) exhausting; (*drôle*) hilarious

crevasse crack; *se* ~ crack

crever 1 *v/t ballon* burst; *pneu* puncture **2** *v/i* burst; F (*mourir*) kick the bucket F; F AUTO have a flat *ou* Br puncture

crevette *f* shrimp

cri *m* shout, cry; *c'est le dernier* ~ *fig* it's all the rage

cribler sieve; *criblé de fig* riddled with

cric *m* jack

crier 1 *v/i* shout; ~ *au scandale* protest **2** *v/t* shout

crime *m* crime; (*assassinat*) murder; *criminel, ~le 1* *adj* criminal **2** *m/f* criminal; (*assassin*) murderer

crinière *f* mane

criquet *m* ZO cricket

crise *f* MÉD attack; ~ *cardiaque* heart attack

crisper *muscles* tense; *visage* contort; *fig* F irritate; *se* ~ tense up

crisser squeak

cristal *m* crystal

critère *m* criterion

critique 1 *adj* critical **2** *m* critic **3** *f* criticism; *d'un film etc* review; **critiquer** criticize;

(*analyser*) look at critically

croc *m* (*dent*) fang; *de boucherie* hook

crochet *m* hook; *ouvrage* crochet; *d'une route* sharp turn; *~s en typographie* square brackets

crochu *nez* hooked

crocodile *m* crocodile

croire 1 *v/t* believe; (*penser*) think; ~ *qc de qn* believe sth about s.o. **2** *v/i*: ~ *à qc* believe in sth; ~ *en Dieu* believe in God **3**: *il se croit intelligent* he thinks he's intelligent

croisade *f* crusade

croisement *m* crossing (*aussi* BIOL); *animal* cross; **croiser 1** *v/t* cross (*aussi* BIOL); ~ *qn dans la rue* pass s.o. in the street **2** *v/i* MAR cruise; *se* ~ *de routes* cross; *de personnes* meet

croisière *f* MAR cruise

croissance *f* growth

croissant *m de lune* crescent; CUIS croissant

croître grow

croix *f* cross; *mettre une* ~ *sur qc fig* give sth up

croquer 1 *v/t* crunch; (*dessiner*) sketch **2** *v/i* be crunchy

croquis *m* sketch

crotte *f* droppings *pl*

crouler collapse (*aussi fig*)

croupir stagnate (*aussi fig*)

croustillant crusty

croûte *f de pain* crust; *de fromage* rind; MÉD scab

croûton m crouton

croyance f belief; **croyant, ~e** m/f REL believer

cru 1 adj raw; *lumière, vérité* harsh; *paroles* blunt **2** m (*domaine*) vineyard; *de vin* wine

cruauté f cruelty

cruche f pitcher

crucial crucial

crucifier crucify; **crucifix** m crucifix

crudité f crudeness; *de paroles* bluntness; *de lumière* harshness; *de couleur* garishness; **~s** CUIS raw vegetables

cruel, ~le cruel

crustacés mpl shellfish pl

Cuba f Cuba; **cubain, ~e** Cuban; **Cubain, ~e** m/f Cuban

cube MATH **1** m cube **2** adj cubic; **cubisme** m ART cubism

cueillir pick

cuiller, cuillère f spoon; **cuillerée** f spoonful

cuir m leather; **~ chevelu** scalp

cuirasse f armor, Br armour

cuire cook; *au four* bake; *rôti* roast

cuisine f cooking; *pièce* kitchen; **la ~ italienne** Italian cooking *ou* cuisine; **cuisiner** cook; **cuisinière** f cook; (*fourneau*) stove

cuisse f ANAT thigh; CUIS *de poulet* leg

cuisson f cooking; *du pain* baking; *d'un rôti* roasting

cuit cooked, done; *rôti, pain*

done

cuivre m copper; **~ jaune** brass; **~s** brasses

cul m V ass P, Br arse P

cul-de-sac m blind alley; *fig* dead end

culminer *fig* peak

culotte f short pants pl, Br short trousers pl; *de femme* panties pl

culpabilité f guilt, culpability

culte m worship; (*religion*) religion; (*service*) church service; *fig* cult

cultivateur, -trice m/f farmer; **cultiver** cultivate (*aussi fig*); *légumes, tabac* grow; **se ~** improve one's mind

culture f culture; AGR cultivation; *de légumes, fruits etc* growing

culturel, ~le cultural

cumuler: **~ des fonctions** have more than one position

cupidité f greed, cupidity

cure f MÉD course of treatment; **~ de repos** rest cure

curé m curate

cure-dent m tooth pick

curiosité f curiosity; *objet rare* curio

curry m curry

curseur m INFORM cursor

cuvée f *de vin* vatful; *vin* wine, vintage; **cuver 1** v/i mature **2** v/t: **~ son vin** *fig* sleep it off

cuvette f (*bac*) basin; *de cabinet* bowl

CV m (= *curriculum vitae*) ré-

sumé, *Br* CV (= curriculum
vitae)
cybercafé *m* Internet café
cycle *m* cycle; **cyclisme** *m* cycling; **cycliste** *m/f* cyclist
cyclone *m* cyclone

cygne *m* swan
cylindre *m* cylinder
cynique 1 *adj* cynical **2** *m/f* cynic
cystite *f* MÉD cystitis

D

dactylo *f* typing; *personne* typist
daigner: ~ **faire qch** deign to do sth
daim *m* ZO deer; *peau* suede
dalle *f* flagstone
daltonien, ~**ne** colorblind, *Br* colourblind
dame *f* lady; *aux échecs, cartes* queen; *jeu* *m* **de ~s** checkers *sg*, *Br* draughts *sg*
damner damn
Danemark: **le ~** Denmark
danger *m* danger; **courir un ~** be in danger
dangereux, -**euse** dangerous
danois, ~**e 1** *adj* Danish **2** *m langue* Danish; **Danois**, ~**e** *m/f* Dane
dans in; **boire** ~ **un verre** drink from a glass
danse *f* dance; *action* dancing; ~ **folklorique** folk dance; **danser** dance; **danseur**, -**euse** *m/f* dancer
dard *m d'une abeille* sting
date *f* date; **de longue ~** amitié long-standing; ~ **limite** deadline; ~ **limite de conservation** use-by date; da-

ter **1** *v/t* date **2** *v/i* ~ **de** date from; **à ~ de ce jour** from today
datte *f* date
davantage more
de 1 *prép origine* from; *possession* of; **il vient ~ Paris** he comes from Paris **la maison ~ mon père** my father's house; **un film ~ Godard** a movie by Godard; ~ **jour** by day; **trembler ~ peur** shake with fear; **cesser ~ travailler** stop working **2** *partitif*: **du pain** (some) bread; **des petits pains** (some) rolls; **je n'ai pas d'argent** I don't have any money; **est-ce qu'il y a des disquettes?** are there any diskettes?
dé *m jeu* dice; ~ **(à coudre)** thimble
dealer *m* dealer
déambuler stroll
débâcle *f de troupes* rout; *d'une entreprise* collapse
déballer unpack
débandade *f* stampede
débarbouiller: ~ **un enfant**

wash a child's face

débardeur *m vêtement* tank top

débarquement *m de marchandises* unloading; *de passagers* landing, disembarkation; **débarquer 1** *v/t marchandises* unload; *passagers* land, disembark **2** *v/i* land, disembark; **~ chez qn** *fig* F turn up at s.o.'s place

débarrasser *table etc* clear; **~ qn de qc** take sth off s.o.; **se ~ de** get rid of

débat *m* debate; *(polémique)* argument

débattre: **~ qc** discuss *ou* debate sth; **se ~** struggle

débauche *f* debauchery; **débaucher** *(licencier)* lay off; F lead astray

débile 1 *adj* weak; F idiotic **2** *m*: **~ mental** mental defective

débit *m (vente)* sale; *d'un stock* turnover; *d'une usine* output; *(élocution)* delivery; FIN debit; **débiter** *marchandises* sell (retail); *péj: fadaises* talk; *texte étudié* deliver, *péj* recite; *d'une pompe* deliver; *d'une usine, de produits* output; *bois, viande* cut up; FIN debit **(de** with); **débiteur, -trice 1** *m/f* debtor **2** *adj compte* overdrawn; *solde* debit

déblayer *endroit* clear; *débris* clear (away)

débloquer 1 *v/t* TECH release;

prix, compte unfreeze; *fonds* release **2** *v/i* F go crazy; **se ~ d'une situation** get sorted out

déboguer debug

déboires *mpl* disappointments

déboisement *m* deforestation

déboîter 1 *v/t* MÉD dislocate **2** *v/i* AUTO pull out; **se ~ l'épaule** dislocate one's shoulder

débonnaire kindly

débordé snowed under **(de** with); **~ par les événements** overwhelmed by events; **déborder** *d'une rivière* overflow its banks; *du lait, de l'eau* overflow

débouché *m d'une vallée* entrance; COMM outlet; **~s d'une profession** prospects; **déboucher 1** *v/t tuyau* unblock; *bouteille* uncork **2** *v/i*: **~ emerge from; ~ sur** lead to *(aussi fig)*

débourser *(dépenser)* spend

debout standing; *objet* upright, on end; **être ~** stand; *(levé)* be up, be out of bed; **se mettre ~** stand up, get up

déboutonner unbutton

débraillé untidy

débrancher ÉL unplug

débrayer AUTO declutch; *fig* down tools

débris *mpl* debris *sg*; *fig* remains

débrouillard resourceful; **débrouiller** disentangle; *fig:* *affaire* clear up; **se ~** cope

début *m* beginning, start; **~s** THÉÂT, POL debut; **débutant**, **~e** *m/f* beginner

décacheter *lettre* open

décadent decadent

décaféiné: *café m* **~** decaffeinated coffee, decaff F

décalage *m dans l'espace* moving; *(différence)* difference; *fig* gap; **décaler** *rendez-vous* change the time of; *dans l'espace* move

décamper F clear out

décaper *surface* clean; *meuble vernis* strip

décapiter decapitate

décapotable *f* (**voiture** *f*) **~** convertible

décapsuleur *m* bottle opener

décarcasser: **se ~** F bust a gut F

décéder die

déceler *(découvrir)* detect; *(montrer)* point to

décembre *m* December

décemment decently; *(raisonnablement)* reasonably

décennie *f* decade

décent decent,

décentralisation *f* decentralization

déception *f* disappointment

décerner *prix* award

décès *m* death

décevoir disappoint

déchaîner *fig* provoke; **se ~**

d'une tempête break; *d'une personne* fly into a rage

décharge *f* JUR acquittal; *dans fusillade* discharge; **~ électrique** electric shock; **décharger** unload; *batterie* discharge; *arme* fire; *accusé* acquit; *colère* vent (**contre** on); **~ qn de qch** relieve s.o. of sth

décharné skeletal

déchausser: **se ~** take one's shoes off

déchéance *f* decline; JUR forfeiture

déchets *mpl* waste

déchiffrer decipher

déchiqueté *côte* jagged; **déchiqueter** *corps, papier* tear to pieces

déchirant heart-breaking; **déchirer** *tissu* tear; *papier* tear up; *fig:* silence pierce; **se ~** *d'une robe* tear; **se ~ un muscle** tear a muscle

décidé *(résolu)* determined (**à faire qc** to do sth); **décidément** really; **décider 1** *v/t* decide on; *question* settle, decide; **~ qn à faire qc** convince s.o. to do sth; **~ de faire qch** decide to do sth **2** *v/i* decide; **se ~** make one's mind up, decide (**à faire qch** to do sth)

décimal decimal

décimer decimate

décimètre *m:* **double ~** ruler

décisif, -ive decisive; **décision** *f* decision; *(fermeté)* determination

déclaration f declaration, statement; d'une naissance registration; d'un vol, perte report; **déclarer** declare; naissance register; **se ~** declare o.s.; en amour declare one's love; d'un feu, d'une épidémie break out

déclencher trigger; **se ~** be triggered

déclic m bruit click

déclin m decline

décliner 1 v/i du soleil go down; du jour, des forces, du prestige wane; de la santé decline **2** v/t offre decline

décoder decode; **décodeur** m decoder

décoiffer cheveux ruffle

décollage m AVIAT take-off; **décoller 1** v/t peel off **2** v/i AVIAT take off; **se ~** peel off

décolleté 1 adj robe low-cut **2** m neckline

décolorer tissu, cheveux bleach; **se ~** fade

décombres mpl rubble

décommander cancel; **se ~** cancel

décomposer produit break down (**en** into); CHIM decompose; **se ~** d'un cadavre decompose; d'un visage become contorted

décompresser F unwind, chill out F

décompte m deduction; d'une facture breakdown

déconcentrer: **~ qn** make it

hard for s.o. to concentrate

déconcertant disconcerting

déconfit disheartened

déconfiture f collapse

décongeler aliment thaw out

décongestionner route decongest; nez clear

déconnecter unplug, disconnect; **se ~** INFORM log off, log out

déconner P actions fool around; paroles talk crap P

déconseiller advise against

décontenancer disconcert

décontracter relax; **se ~** relax

décor m decor; fig (cadre) setting; **~s** de théâtre sets, scenery; **décorateur**, **-trice** m/f decorator; THÉÂT set designer; **décorer** decorate (**de** with)

découler **~** de arise from

découper cut up; photo cut out (**dans** from); **se ~ sur** fig stand out against

décourager discourage (**de faire qc** from doing sth); **se ~** lose heart, become discouraged

découvert, **~e 1** adj tête, épaules bare, uncovered; **à ~** FIN overdrawn **2** m overdraft **3** f discovery; **découvrir** uncover; (trouver) discover; ses intentions reveal; (comprendre) find (**que** that); **se ~** d'une personne take off a couple of layers; (enlever son chapeau) take

off one's hat; *du ciel* clear
décret *m* decree
décrire describe; **~ une orbite autour de** orbit
décrocher *tableau* take
down; *fig* F *prix, bonne situation* land F; **~ le téléphone** pick up the receiver;
pour ne pas être dérangé
take the phone off the hook
décroître decrease, decline
déçu disappointed
décupler increase tenfold
dédaigner 1 *v/t* scorn; *personne* treat with scorn **2**
v/i: **~ de faire qc** disdain
to do sth; **dédaigneux, -eu-
se** disdainful; **dédain** *m* disdain
dedans inside
dédicace *f* dedication; **dédier** dedicate
dédommager compensate
(**de** for)
dédouanement *m* customs
clearance; **dédouaner: ~
qch** clear sth through customs; **~ qn** *fig* clear s.o.
dédoublement *m:* **~ de personnalité** split personality;
dédoubler split in two; **se
~** split
dédramatiser play down,
downplay
déduction *f* deduction; **déduire** COMM deduct; (*conclure*) deduce (**de** from)
déesse *f* goddess
défaillance *f* weakness; *fig*
shortcoming; *technique* fail-

ure; **défaillir** weaken; (*se
trouver mal*) feel faint
défaire undo; (*démonter*)
take down, dismantle; *valise*
unpack; **se ~** come undone;
se ~ de qn/qc get rid of s.o./
sth; **défait** *visage* drawn;
chemise, valise undone; *armée, personne* defeated; **défaite** *f* defeat; **défaitisme** *m*
defeatism
défaut *m* (*imperfection*) defect; *morale* shortcoming,
failing; (*manque*) lack; JUR
default; **faire ~** be lacking;
par ~ INFORM default atr
défavorable unfavorable, *Br*
unfavourable; **défavorisé**
disadvantaged; **les milieux
~s** the underprivileged
classes
défectueux, -euse defective
défendre defend; **~ à qn de
faire qc** forbid s.o. to do sth
défense *f* defense, *Br* defence *f*; *d'un éléphant* tusk;
~ de fumer no smoking; **défenseur** *m* defender; *d'une
cause* supporter; JUR de-
fense attorney, *Br* counsel
for the defence; **défensif,
-ive** *adj & f* defensive
déférent deferential; **déférer:
~ qn à la justice** prosecute
s.o.
défi *m* challenge; (*bravade*)
defiance
défiance *f* distrust, mistrust
déficience *f* deficiency; **~ immunitaire** immune deficien-

cy

déficit *m* deficit; **déficitaire** *balance* showing a deficit; *compte* in debit

défier (*provoquer*) challenge; (*braver*) defy; ~ **qn de faire qch** dare s.o. to do sth

défigurer disfigure; *fig: réalité* misrepresent

défilé *m* parade; GÉOGR pass; ~ **de mode** fashion show; *défiler* parade, march

défini definite; **bien** ~ well defined; *définir* define; *définitif, -ive* definitive; **en définitive** in the end; *définition* definition; *définitivement* definitely; (*pour de bon*) for good

déflagration *f* explosion

défoncer *voiture* smash up, total; *porte* break down; *terrain* break up

déformer deform; *chaussures* stretch (out of shape); *visage, fait* distort; *idée* misrepresent; **se** ~ **de chaussures** lose their shape

défouler: **se** ~ give vent to one's feelings

défroisser *vêtement* crumple

défunt, ~e 1 *adj* late **2** *m/f*: **le** ~ the deceased

dégagement *m* *d'une route* clearing; *de chaleur* release; *dégager* (*délivrer*) free; *route* clear; *odeur, chaleur* give off; **se** ~ *d'une route, du ciel* clear

dégât *m* damage; **~s** damage

dégel *m* thaw (*aussi* POL)

dégeler 1 *v/t frigidaire* defrost; *crédits* unfreeze **2** *v/i d'un lac* thaw

dégénérer degenerate (**en** into)

dégivrer defrost; TECH de-ice

déglutir swallow

dégonfler let the air out of, deflate; **se** ~ deflate; *fig* F lose one's nerve

dégourdi resourceful; *dégourdir membres* loosen up; **se** ~ **les jambes** stretch one's legs

dégoût *m* disgust; *dégoûtant* disgusting; *dégoûter* disgust; ~ **qn de qc** put s.o. off sth; **se** ~ **de qc** take a dislike to sth

dégrader MIL demote; *édifice* damage; (*avilir*) degrade; **se** ~ deteriorate; *d'un édifice* fall into disrepair

degré *m* degree; (*échelon*) level

dégressif, -ive *tarif* tapering

dégringoler fall

dégriser sober up

déguerpir clear off

dégueulasse P disgusting

dégueuler F vomit

déguisement *m* disguise; *pour bal masqué etc* costume; *déguiser* disguise; *enfant* dress up (**en** as); **se** ~ disguise o.s.; *pour bal masqué etc* dress up

dégustation *f* tasting; *déguster* taste

dehors 1 *adv* outside **2** *prép*: **en ~ de** outside **3** *m* exterior

déjà already; **c'est qui déjà?** F who's he again?

déjeuner 1 *v/i midi* (have) lunch; *matin* (have) breakfast **2** *m* lunch; **petit ~** breakfast

déjouer thwart

DEL *f* (= **diode électroluminescente**) LED (= light-emitting diode)

délabré dilapidated

délacer loosen, unlace

délai *m* (*temps imparti*) time allowed; (*date limite*) deadline; (*prolongation*) extension; **sans ~** without delay

délaisser (*abandonner*) leave; (*négliger*) neglect

délassement *m* relaxation; **délasser** relax; **se ~** relax

délateur, -trice *m/f* informer; **délation** *f* denunciation

délayer dilute, water down; *fig*: *discours* pad out

délecter: **se ~ de** take delight in

délégué, ~e *m/f* delegate; **déléguer** delegate

délibération *f* deliberation; (*décision*) resolution; **délibéré** deliberate; **délibérer** deliberate

délicat delicate; *problème* tricky; (*plein de tact*) tactful; **délicatesse** *f* delicacy; (*tact*) tact; **délicatement** delicately

délicieux, -euse delicious

délier loosen, untie; **~ la langue à qn** loosen s.o.'s tongue

délimiter delimit

délinquance *f* crime, delinquency

délire *m* delirium; *enthousiasme* frenzy; **foule en ~** ecstatic crowd; **délirer** be delirious; F *être fou* be stark raving mad

délit *m* offense, *Br* offence; **commettre un ~ de fuite** leave the scene of an accident

délivrance *f* release; (*soulagement*) relief; (*livraison*) delivery; *certificat* issue

délivrer release; (*livrer*) deliver; *certificat* issue

délocaliser relocate

déloyal disloyal; **concurrence** *f* **~e** unfair competition

deltaplane *m* hang-glider; **faire du ~** go hang-gliding

déluge *m* flood

demain tomorrow; **à ~!** see you tomorrow!

demande *f* (*requête*) request; *écrite* application; ÉCON demand; **sur** *ou* **à la ~ de** at the request of; **demandé** popular, in demand; **demander** ask for; *somme d'argent* ask; (*nécessiter*) call for; **~ qch à qn** ask s.o. for sth; (*vouloir savoir*) ask s.o. sth; **~ à qn de faire qc** ask s.o. to do sth; **se ~ si** wonder if

démanger: *le dos me dé-mange* my back itches; *ça me démange depuis longtemps* I've been itching to do it for ages

démanteler dismantle

démaquillant *m* cleanser; *lait m ~* cleansing milk; démaquiller: *se ~* take off one's make-up

démarcation *f* demarcation

démarchage *m* selling

démarche *f* step (*aussi fig*); *faire des ~s* take steps

démarquer: *se ~* stand out (*de* from)

démarrage *m* start; démarrer start (up)

démasquer unmask

démêlé *m* argument; *avoir des ~s avec la justice* have problems with the law; démêler disentangle; *fig* clear up

déménager move; déménageurs *mpl* movers, removal men

démence *f* dementia; dément demented; *c'est ~ fig* F it's unbelievable

démener: *se ~* struggle; (*s'efforcer*) make an effort

démenti *m* denial

démentir (*nier*) deny; (*infirmer*) belie

démerder: *se ~* F manage, sort things out

démesuré enormous; *orgueil* excessive

démettre *poignet* dislocate;

se ~ *de ses fonctions* resign one's office

demeure *f* residence; demeurer (*habiter*) live; (*rester*) stay, remain; demeuré retarded

demi 1 *adj* half; *une heure et ~e* an hour and a half; *il est quatre heures et ~* it's four thirty, it's half past four 2 *adv* half; *à ~* half 3 *m* half; *bière* half a pint; *en football, rugby* halfback

demi-cercle *m* semi-circle

demi-finale *f* semi-final

demi-frère *m* half-brother

demi-heure *f* half-hour

démilitariser demilitarize

demi-litre *m* half liter *ou Br* litre

demi-mot: *il nous l'a dit à ~* he hinted at it to us

demi-pension *f* American plan, *Br* half board

demi-pression *f* half-pint of draft *ou Br* draught beer

demi-sel *m* slightly salted butter

demi-sœur *f* half-sister

démission *f* resignation; *fig* renunciation; démissionner 1 *v/i* resign; *fig* give up 2 *v/t* sack

demi-tarif *m* half price

demi-tour *m* AUTO U-turn; *faire ~ fig* turn back

démocrate democrat; démocratie *f* democracy

démodé old-fashioned

démographique demographic; **poussée** f ~ population growth

demoiselle f (*jeune fille*) young lady; ~ **d'honneur** bridesmaid

démolir demolish (*aussi fig*); **démolition** f demolition

démon m demon

démonstration f demonstration

démonter dismantle; *fig* disconcert

démontrer demonstrate, prove; (*faire ressortir*) show

démoraliser demoralize

démotiver demotivate

démuni penniless

dénaturer distort

dénicher find

dénier deny

dénigrer denigrate

dénivellation f difference in height

dénombrer count

dénomination f name

dénoncer denounce; à la police report; *contrat* terminate; **se** ~ **à la police** give o.s. up to the police; **dénonciateur, -trice** m/f informer; **dénonciation** f denunciation

dénoter indicate, denote

dénouement m ending; **dénouer** loosen; **se** ~ *fig* d'une scène end; d'un mystère be cleared up

denrée f: ~**s** (**alimentaires**) foodstuffs

dense dense; **densité** f density; du brouillard, d'une forêt denseness

dent f tooth; **j'ai mal aux** ~**s** I've got toothache; **avoir une** ~ **contre qn** have a grudge against s.o.; **dentaire** dental

dentelle f lace

dentier m false teeth pl; **dentifrice** m toothpaste; **dentiste** m/f dentist

dénuder strip

dénué devoid of sth; ~ **de tout** deprived of everything; **dénuement** m destitution

déodorant m deodorant

dépannage m AUTO etc repairs pl; (*remorquage*) recovery; **dépanner** repair; (*remorquer*) recover; ~ **qn** fig F help s.o. out; **dépanneur** m repairman; pour voitures mechanic; **dépanneuse** f wrecker, Br tow truck

départ m departure; SP, fig start; **au** ~ at first

départager decide between

départemental departmental; **route** ~**e** secondary road

dépassé out of date, old-fashioned; **dépasser** personne pass; AUTO pass, Br overtake; but etc overshoot; fig exceed; **se** ~ surpass o.s.

dépaysement m disorienta-

tion; *changement agréable*
change of scene
dépêcher dispatch; *se ~ de
faire qch* hurry to do sth;
dépêche-toi! hurry up!
dépendance f dependence;
~s bâtiments outbuildings;
entraîner une (forte) ~ be
(highly) addictive; **dépendre:** *~ de* depend on; *mora-
lement* be dependent on
dépens *mpl: aux ~ de* at the
expense of
dépense f expenditure; *d'essence, d'électricité* consumption, use; **dépenser** spend;
son énergie, ses forces use
up; *essence* consume, use;
se ~ exert o.s., be physically
active; **dépensier, -ère 1** *adj*
extravagant **2** *m/f* spendthrift
dépérir waste away; *fig d'une
entreprise* go downhill
dépeuplement *m* depopula-
tion
dépilatoire: crème f *~* hair remover, depilatory cream
dépistage *m d'un criminel*
tracking down; MÉD screen-
ing
dépit *m* spite; *en ~ de* in spite
of
dépité crestfallen
déplacé out of place; *(incon-
venant)* uncalled for; POL
displaced; **déplacer** move;
personnel transfer; *problème* shift the focus of; *se ~*
move; *(voyager)* travel

déplaire: *~ à qn (fâcher)* offend s.o.; *cela lui déplaît
de faire ...* he dislikes doing
...
déplaisant unpleasant
dépliant *m* leaflet; **déplier**
unfold
déploiement *m* MIL deploy-
ment; *de forces, courage* display
déplorable deplorable
déporter POL deport; *se ~
d'un véhicule* swing
déposer 1 *v/t* put down; *armes* lay down; *passager*
drop; *roi* depose; *argent,
boue* deposit; *projet de loi*
table; *ordures* dump; *plainte*
lodge **2** *v/i d'un liquide* settle; JUR testify; *se ~ de la
boue* settle; **dépôt** *m* deposit; *chez le notaire* lodging;
d'un projet de loi tabling;
des ordures dumping; *(entrepôt)* depot
dépouiller *animal* skin; *(voler)* rob *(de* of); *(examiner)*
go through; *~ le scrutin* ou
les votes count the votes
dépourvu: *~ de* devoid of;
prendre qn au ~ take s.o.
by surprise
dépoussiérer dust; *fig* modernize
dépraver deprave
déprécier *chose* decrease the
value of; *personne* belittle;
se ~ depreciate, lose value;
d'une personne belittle o.s.
dépression f depression; **fai-**

re une ~ be depressed

déprime f depression; **déprimer** depress

dépuceler deflower

depuis 1 *prép* since; *espace* from; **j'attends** ~ **une heure** I have been waiting for an hour; ~ **quand permettent-ils que …?** since when do they allow …? **2** *adv* since **3** *conj*: ~ **que** since

député *m* POL MP, Member of Parliament; ~ **européen** *m* Euro MP

déraciner uproot; (*extirper*) root out, eradicate

dérailler go off the rails; *fig* F: *d'un mécanisme* go on the blink; (*déraisonner*) talk nonsense; **dérailleur** *m* *d'un vélo* derailleur

déraisonnable unreasonable

dérangement *m* disturbance; **déranger** disturb

déraper AUTO skid

déréglé *vie* wild

déréglementer deregulate

dérégler *mécanisme* upset

dérision *f* derision; **tourner en** ~ deride

dérisoire derisory, laughable

dérivatif *m* diversion; **dériver 1** *v/t* MATH derive; *cours d'eau* divert **2** *v/i* MAR, AVIAT drift; ~ **de** *d'un mot* be derived from

dermatologue *m/f* dermatologist

dernier, -ère last; (*le plus récent*) *mode, roman etc* latest;

extrême utmost; **ce** ~ the latter; **dernièrement** recently, lately

dérobée: à la ~ furtively; **dérober** steal; ~ **qch à qn** rob s.o. of sth, steal sth from s.o.; **se** ~ **à** *discussion* shy away from; *obligations* shirk

déroger JUR: ~ **à** make an exception to, depart from

déroulement *m* unfolding; **le** ~ **du projet** the running of the project; **dérouler** unroll; *bobine, câble* unwind; **se** ~ take place; *d'une cérémonie* go (off)

dérouter (*déconcerter*) disconcert

derrière 1 *adv* behind **2** *prép* behind **3** *m* back; ANAT bottom; **de** ~ *patte etc* back *atr*

dès from, since; ~ **lors** from then on; (*par conséquent*) consequently; ~ **lundi** as of Monday; ~ **que** as soon as

désabuser disillusion

désaccord *m* disagreement

désaffecté disused; *église* deconsecrated

désagréable unpleasant, disagreeable

désappointement *m* disappointment

désapprobateur, -trice disapproving

désapprouver disapprove of

désarmement *m* MIL disarmament; **désarmer** disarm (*aussi fig*)

désarroi *m* disarray

désastre *m* disaster

désavantage *m* disadvantage; **désavantager** put at a disadvantage

désaveu *m* disowning; *d'un propos* retraction; **désavouer** disown; *propos* retract

descendance *f* descendants *pl*; **descendant**, **~e** *m/f* descendant

descendre 1 *v/i* go/come down; *d'un bus* get off; *d'une voiture* get out; *de température, prix* go down; *d'un chemin* drop; AVIAT descend; **~ chez qn** stay with s.o.; **~ de qn** be descended from s.o. **2** *v/t* (*porter vers le bas*) bring down; (*emporter*) take down; *passager* drop off; F (*abattre*) shoot down; *vallée, rivière* descend; **~ les escaliers** come/go downstairs; **descente** *f* descent; (*pente*) slope; *en parachute* jump; **~ de lit** bedside rug

description *f* description

désemparé at a loss

déséquilibré PSYCH unbalanced

désert 1 *adj* deserted; *une île* **~e** a desert island **2** *m* desert; **déserter** desert; **déserteur** *m* MIL deserter

désertification *f* desertification

désertion *f* desertion

désespérant depressing

désespérer 1 *v/t* drive to despair **2** *v/i* despair

désespoir *m* despair; **en ~ de cause** in desperation

déshabillé *m* negligee; **déshabiller** undress; **se ~** get undressed

déshériter disinherit

déshonorer disgrace, bring dishonor *ou* Br dishonour on

déshydraté *aliments* desiccated; *personne* dehydrated; **déshydrater: se ~** become dehydrated

design *m*: **~ d'intérieurs** interior design

désigner (*montrer*) point to, point out; (*appeler*) call; (*nommer*) appoint (*pour* to), designate

désillusion *f* disillusionment

désinfectant *m* disinfectant

désintéressé disinterested, impartial; *personne* selfless; **désintéresser: se ~ de** lose interest in

désintoxication *f*: **faire une cure de ~** go into detox

désinvolture *f* casualness

désir *m* desire; (*souhait*) wish

désirer want; *sexuellement* desire; **~ faire qch** want to do sth; **désireux, -euse** eager (**de faire** to do)

désister POL: **se ~** withdraw, stand down

désobéir disobey; **~ à** disobey; **désobéissant** disobedient

désobligeant disagreeable
désodorisant *m* deodorant
désolé upset (*de* about, over); **je suis~** I am so sorry
désopilant hilarious
désordre *m* untidiness; **en~** untidy
désorganisé disorganized
désormais now; *à partir de maintenant* from now on
désosser remove the bones from
despote *m* despot; despotique despotic
dessécher dry out; *de fruits* dry
dessein *m* intention; **à~** intentionally; *dans le~ de faire qc* with the intention of doing sth
desserrer loosen
dessert *m* dessert
desservir *des transport publics* serve; (*s'arrêter à*) stop at; *table* clear; **~ qn** do s.o. a disservice
dessin *m* drawing; (*motif*) design; dessiner draw
dessouler F sober up
dessous **1** *adv* underneath; **en~** underneath **2** *m* underside; **ci-~** below; **les voisins du~** the downstairs neighbors
dessous-de-plat m inv table mat
dessus **1** *adv* on top; **sens~ dessous** upside down; **en~** on top; **par~** over; **ci-~** above **2** *m* top; **les voisins**

du~ the upstairs neighbors; **avoir le~** *fig* have the upper hand; **dessus-de-lit** *m inv* bedspread
déstabilisant unnerving; déstabiliser destabilize
destin *m* destiny, fate
destinataire *m* addressee; destination *f* destination; destinée *f* destiny; destiner mean, intend (*à* for)
destituer dismiss; MIL discharge
destructeur, -trice destructive; destruction *f* destruction
désuet, -ète obsolete; *mode* out of date
détachable detachable; détacher detach; *ceinture* undo; *chien* release; *employé* second; (*nettoyer*) clean; **se ~ sur** stand out against
détail *m* detail; COMM retail trade; *vendre au~* sell retail; *prix m de~* retail price; **en~** detailed
détaillant *m* retailer
détartrage *m* descaling
détecteur *m* sensor
détective *m* detective
déteindre fade; **~ sur** come off on; *fig* rub off on
détendre slacken; *se~ d'une corde* slacken; *fig* relax
détenir hold; JUR detain, hold
détente *f d'une arme* trigger; *fig* relaxation; POL détente
détention *f* holding; JUR detention

détenu, **~e** *m/f* inmate

détergent *m* detergent

détériorer damage; **se~** deteriorate

déterminant decisive; **déterminer** establish, determine

déterrer dig up

détester detest, hate

détonation *f* detonation

détour *m* detour; *d'un chemin, fleuve* bend; **sans ~** *fig*: *dire qch* straight out

détourné *fig* indirect; **détourner** *trafic* divert; *avion* hijack; *tête, yeux* turn away; *de l'argent* embezzle; **se ~** turn away

détresse *f* distress

détriment *m*: **au ~ de** to the detriment of

détritus *m* garbage, *Br* rubbish

détroit *m* strait

détromper put right

détruire destroy; *(tuer)* kill

dette *f* debt

deuil *m* mourning; **il y a eu un ~ dans sa famille** there's been a bereavement in his family

deux 1 *adj* two; **les ~** both; **nous ~** the two of us, both of us; **~ fois** twice **2** *m* two; **en ~** in two, in half; **~ à ou par ~** in twos, two by two; **deuxième** second; *étage* third, *Br* second; **deux-pièces** *m inv* bikini two-piece swimsuit; *appartement* two-room apartment; **deux-**

-points *m inv* colon

dévaliser *banque* rob, raid; *maison* burglarize, *Br* burgle; *personne* rob; *fig: frigo* raid

dévalorisant demeaning; **dévalorisation** *f* drop in value; *fig* belittlement; **dévaloriser** devalue; *fig* belittle

dévaluation *f* devaluation; **dévaluer** devalue

devancer be ahead of; *désir, objection* anticipate

devant 1 *adv* in front; **droit ~** straight ahead **2** *prép* in front of; **passer ~ l'église** go past the church; **~ Dieu** before God **3** *m* front

devanture *f* shop window

dévaster devastate

développement *m* development; **développer** develop; **se ~** develop

devenir become; **il devient vieux** he's getting old; **que va-t-il ~?** what's going to become of him?

dévergondé *sexuellement* promiscuous

déverser *ordures* dump; *passagers* disgorge

dévêtir undress

déviation *f d'une route* detour; *(écart)* deviation

dévier 1 *v/t* divert, reroute **2** *v/i* deviate **(de** from)

deviner guess

devis *m* estimate

dévisager stare at

devise *f* FIN currency; *(moto,*

règle de vie motto; **~s étrangères** foreign currency

dévisser unscrew

dévoiler unveil; *secret* reveal, disclose

devoir 1 *v/t de l'argent* owe **2** *v/aux:* **il doit le faire** he has to do it, he must do it; **il aurait dû me le dire** he should have told me; **tu devrais l'acheter** you should buy it; **ça doit être cuit** it should be done **3** *m* duty; *pour l'école* homework

dévorer devour

dévouement *m* devotion; **dévouer: se ~ pour** dedicate one's life to

dextérité *f* dexterity, skill

diabète *m* diabetes *sg*

diable *m* devil; **diabolique** diabolical

diagnostic *m* MÉD diagnosis; **diagnostiquer** MÉD diagnose

diagonal, ~e 1 *adj* diagonal **2** *f* diagonal (line); **en ~e** diagonally

diagramme *m* diagram

dialogue *m* dialog, *Br* dialogue

diamant *m* diamond

diamètre *m* diameter

diapositive *f* slide

diarrhée *f* diarrhea, *Br* diarrhoea

dictateur *m* dictator; **dictature** *f* dictatorship

dictée *f* dictation

dictionnaire *m* dictionary

diesel *m* diesel

diète *f* diet

Dieu *m* God; **~ merci!** thank God!

diffamer slander

différence *f* difference; **différencier** differentiate

différend *m* dispute

difficile difficult; (*exigeant*) hard to please; **difficulté** *f* difficulty

difformité *f* deformity

diffusion *f* spread; RAD, TV broadcast; *de chaleur etc* diffusion

digérer digest

digestion *f* digestion

digital digital; **empreinte *f* ~e** fingerprint

dignité (*plein de dignité*) dignified; **~ de** worthy of; **dignité** *f* dignity; (*charge*) office

digue *f* dyke

dilapider squander

dilater expand; *pupille* dilate

dilemme *m* dilemma

diluer dilute

dimanche *m* Sunday

dimension *f* dimension; (*taille*) size; *d'une faute* magnitude

diminuer 1 *v/t nombre, prix* reduce; *joie, forces* diminish; *mérites* detract from; *souffrances* lessen, decrease **2** *v/i* decrease

diminutif *m* diminutive; **diminution** *f* decrease, decline; *d'un nombre, prix* reduction

dinde *f* turkey; **dindon** *m* turkey

dîner 1 *v/i* dine **2** *m* dinner

dingue F crazy, nuts F

diplomate *m* diplomat; **diplomatie** *f* diplomacy

diplôme *m* diploma; *universitaire* degree; **diplômé** diploma holder; *de l'université* graduate

dire say; *(informer, révéler, ordonner)* tell; **~ à qn de faire qch** tell s.o. to do sth; **à vrai ~** to tell the truth; **cela va sans ~** that goes without saying

direct direct; **en ~** *émission* live; **directement** directly; **directeur, -trice 1** *adj comité* management **2** *m/f* manager; *plus haut dans la hiérarchie* director; ÉDU principal, Br head teacher; **direction** *f* *(sens)* direction; *(gestion, directeurs)* management; AUTO steering; **~ assistée** power steering; **directive** *f* instruction; *de l'UE* directive

dirigeant *m* leader; **diriger** manage, run; *pays* lead; *orchestre* conduct; *voiture* steer; *arme, critique* aim **(contre** at); *regard, yeux* turn **(vers** to); *personne* direct; **se ~ vers** head for

discerner make out; **~ le bon du mauvais** tell good from bad

discipline *f* discipline

disc-jockey *m* disc jockey, DJ

discontinu *ligne* broken; *effort* intermittent

discorde *f* discord

discothèque *f* *(boîte)* discotheque, disco; *collection* record library

discours *m* speech

discréditer discredit

discret, -ète *(qui n'attire pas l'attention)* unobtrusive; *couleur* quiet; *robe* simple; *(qui garde le secret)* discreet; **discrétion** *f* discretion

discrimination *f* discrimination

disculper clear, exonerate; **se ~** clear o.s.

discussion *f* discussion; *(altercation)* argument; **discuter** discuss; *(contester)* question

disjoncter 1 *v/t* ÉL break **2** *v/i* F be crazy; **disjoncteur** *m* circuit breaker

disparaître disappear; *(mourir)* die; *d'une espèce* die out; **faire ~** get rid of

disparition *f* disappearance; *(mort)* death; **espèce en voie de ~** endangered species

dispenser: ~ qn de (faire) qc excuse s.o. from (doing) sth

disperser disperse; **se ~** *(faire trop de choses)* spread o.s. too thin

disponibilité *f* availability; **disponible** available

disposer *(arranger)* arrange;

~ de qn/qc have s.o./sth at
one's disposal; **se ~ à faire
qc** get ready to do sth
dispositif *m* device
disposition *f* (*arrangement*)
arrangement; *d'une loi* provision; (*humeur*) mood;
(*tendance*) tendency; **être à
la ~ de qn** be at s.o.'s disposal; **avoir des ~s pour qch**
have an aptitude for sth
disputer *match* play; **~ qc à
qn** compete with s.o for
sth.; **se ~** quarrel, fight
disqualifier disqualify
disque *m* disk; SP discus; **~
compact** compact disc; dis-
quette *f* diskette, disk; **~ de
sauvegarde** backup disk
dissertation *f* ÉDU essay
dissimuler conceal, hide (*à*
from)
dissiper dispel; *brouillard*
disperse; *fortune* squander;
se ~ *du brouillard* clear
dissoudre dissolve
dissuader: ~ qn de faire qc
dissuade s.o. from doing
sth, persuade s.o. not to do
sth; **dissuasion** *f* dissuasion
distance *f* distance; **prendre
ses ~s avec qn** distance
o.s. from s.o.; **distancer** out-
distance
distiller distill; **distillerie** *f*
distillery
distinct distinct; **~ de** different from; **distinctif**, *-ive* distinctive; **distinguer** (*percevoir*) make out; (*différen-*

cier) distinguish (*de* from);
se ~ (*être différent*) differ
(*de* from); (*ressortir*) stand
out (*de* from)
distraction *f* (*passe-temps*)
amusement; (*inattention*)
distraction
distraire *du travail, des soucis*
distract (*de* from); (*divertir*)
amuse, entertain; **se ~**
amuse o.s.; **distrait** absent-
-minded
distribuer distribute; *courrier* deliver; **distributeur** *m*
distributor; **~ automatique**
vending machine
dit (*surnommé*) referred to as;
(*fixé*) appointed
divaguer talk nonsense
divan *m* couch
diverger diverge; *d'opinions*
differ
divers (*différent*) different,
varied; *au pl* (*plusieurs*) various
diversifier diversify
diversion *f* diversion
diversité *f* diversity
divertir amuse, entertain; **divertissement** *m* amuse-
ment, entertainment
divin divine; **divinité** *f* divin-
ity
diviser divide; **se ~** be divid-
ed (*en* into); **division** *f* division
divorce *m* divorce; **demander le ~** ask for a divorce; di-
vorcé, ~e *m/f* (*plusieurs*); di-
vorcer get a divorce (*d'avec*
from)

85

double

dix ten; dix-huit eighteen; dixième tenth; dix-neuf nineteen; dix-sept seventeen; dizaine f: **une ~ de** about ten, ten or so

D.J. m/f (= **disc-jockey**) DJ, deejay (= disc jockey)

docile docile

docteur m doctor; doctorat m doctorate, PhD

doctrine f doctrine

document m document; documentation f documentation; documenter: **se ~** collect information

dodu chubby

dogmatique dogmatic

doigt m finger; **~ de pied** toe; **croiser les ~s** keep one's fingers crossed

dollar m dollar

domaine m estate; fig domain

dôme m dome

domestique **1** adj domestic **2** m servant

domicile m place of residence; domicilié: **~ à** resident at

domination f domination; dominer **1** v/t dominate **2** v/i (prédominer) be predominant; **se ~** control o.s.

dommage m: (**quel ~!** what a pity!; **c'est ~ que** (+ subj) it's a pity (that); **~s et intérêts** JUR damages

dompter animal tame; rebelle subdue; dompteur m trainer

DOM-TOM mpl (= départe-

ments et territoires d'outre-mer) overseas departments and territories of France

don m donation; (cadeau, aptitude) gift; **~ du ciel** godsend; donation f donation

donc conclusion so; écoutez **~!** do listen!; **comment ~?** how (so)?; **allons ~!** come on!

données fpl data sg (aussi INFORM), information; donner **1** v/t give **2** v/i: **~ sur la mer** look onto the sea

dont whose; **le film ~ elle parlait** the movie she was talking about; **la manière ~ elle me regardait** the way (in which) she was looking at me

doré bijou gilded; couleur golden

dorénavant from now on

dorer gild

dormeur, -euse m/f sleeper; dormir sleep

dortoir m dormitory

dos m back; **~ d'âne** m speed bump; pont hump-backed bridge

dose f MÉD dose; PHARM proportion; doser measure out

dossier m d'une chaise back f; de documents file, dossier; **~ médical** medical record(s)

douane f customs pl; douanier, -ère **1** adj customs atr **2** m/f customs officer

double **1** adj double **2** m

doubler

deuxième exemplaire duplicate; *au tennis* doubles (match); **le ~** double, twice as much; **doubler 1** *v/t* double; AUTO pass, *Br* overtake; *film* dub; *vêtement* line **2** *v/i* double; **doublure** *f d'un vêtement* lining

doucement gently; (*bas*) softly; (*lentement*) slowly; **douceur** *f d'une personne* gentleness; **~s** (*jouissance*) pleasures; (*sucreries*) sweet things

douche *f* shower; **prendre une ~** shower, take a shower

doué gifted; **~ de qc** endowed with sth

douleur *f* pain

douloureux, -euse painful

doute *m* doubt; **sans ~** without doubt; **sans aucun ~** undoubtedly; **douter: ~ de qn/qch** doubt s.o./sth; **se ~ de qc** suspect sth; **se ~ que** suspect that; **douteux, -euse** doubtful

doux, douce sweet; *temps* mild; *personne* gentle; *au toucher* soft

douzaine *f* dozen; **douze** twelve; **douzième** twelfth

dragée *f* sugared almond

draguer *rivière* dredge; F *femmes* try to pick up; **dragueur** *m* F ladies' man

dramatique dramatic; **dramatiser** dramatize; **drame** *m* drama

drap *m de lit* sheet

drapeau *m* flag

drap-housse *m* fitted sheet

dresser put up; *contrat* draw up; *animal* train; **~ qn contre qn** set s.o. against s.o.; **se ~** straighten up; *d'une tour* rise up; *d'un obstacle* arise

drogue *f* drug; **~ douce** soft drug; **~ récréative** recreational drug; **drogué, ~e** *m/f* drug addict; **droguer** drug; MÉD (*traiter*) give medication to; **se ~** take drugs; MÉD *péj* pop pills; **droguerie** *f* hardware store

droit 1 *adj côté* right; *ligne* straight; (*debout*) erect; (*honnête*) upright **2** *adv tout* **~** straight ahead **3** *m* right; (*taxe*) fee; JUR law; **être en ~ de faire qch** be entitled to do sth; **~s d'auteur** royalties

droite *f* right; *côté* right-hand side; **à ~** on the right(-hand side)

drôle funny; **une ~ d'idée** a funny idea

dubitatif, -ive doubtful

duc *m* duke

duchesse *f* duchess

duel *m* duel

dûment duly

dune *f* (sand) dune

Dunkerque Dunkirk

duper dupe

duplex *m* duplex

duquel → **lequel**

dur 1 *adj* hard; *climat* harsh;

viande tough **2** *adv travailler, frapper* hard
durable durable, lasting; *croissance, utilisation de matières premières* sustainable
durant during; *des années ~* for years
durcir 1 *v/t* harden **2** *v/i*: *se ~* harden
durée *f* duration; *~ de vie* life; *d'une personne* life expectancy

durement harshly; *être frappé ~ par* be hard hit by
durer last
duvet *m* down; (*sac de couchage*) sleeping bag
DVD *m* DVD (= digitally versatile disk)
dynamique 1 *adj* dynamic **2** *f* dynamics
dynamo *f* dynamo
dyslexique dyslexic

E

eau *f* water; **tomber à l'~** fall in the water; *fig* fall through; *~ courante* running water; *~ gazeuse* carbonated water, *Br* fizzy water; *~ de Javel* bleach
eau-de-vie *f* brandy
ébahi dumbfounded
ébaucher *tableau, roman* rough out; *texte* draft; *~ un sourire* smile faintly
ébéniste *m* cabinetmaker
éblouir dazzle (*aussi fig*)
éboueur *m* garbageman, *Br* dustman
éboulement *m* landslide
ébouriffé tousled; **ébouriffer** *cheveux* ruffle
ébranler shake; **s'~** move off
ébriété *f* inebriation
ébruiter *nouvelle* spread
ébullition *f* boiling point; **être en ~** be boiling
écaille *f* de *coquillage, tortue*

shell; *de poisson* scale; *de peinture, plâtre* flake; *matière* tortoiseshell; **écailler** *poisson* scale; *huître* open; **s'~** de *peinture* flake (off); *de vernis à ongles* chip
écart *m* (*intervalle*) gap; (*différence*) difference; *moral* indiscretion; **à l'~** at a distance (*de* from)
écarter *jambes* spread; *fig: idée* reject; *danger* avert; **s'~** de (*s'éloigner*) stray from
écervelé scatterbrained
échafaudage *m* scaffolding
échancré low-cut
échange *m* exchange; *~s extérieurs* foreign trade; *en ~* in exchange (*de* for); **échanger** exchange (*contre* for); **échangeur** *m* interchange
échantillon *m* COMM sample
échappement *m* AUTO exhaust; *tuyau m d'~* tail pipe;

échapper *d'une personne* ~ **à qn** escape from s.o.; ~ **à qc** escape sth; *l'~* **belle** have a narrow escape; **s'~** escape

écharde *f* splinter

écharpe *f* scarf; *de maire* sash; **en** ~ MÉD in a sling

échauffer heat; **s'~** SP warm up; ~ **les esprits** get people excited

échéance *f d'un contrat* expiration date, *Br* expiry date; *de police* maturity

échec *m* failure; **essuyer un** ~ meet with failure

échecs *mpl* chess; **jouer aux** ~ play chess

échelle *f* ladder; *d'une carte, des salaires* scale; **à l'~ mondiale** on a global scale

échelonner space out; *paiements* spread, stagger (**sur un an** over a year)

échevelé disheveled, *Br* dishevelled

échiner F: **s'~ à faire qch** go to great lengths to do sth

échiquier *m* chessboard

écho *m* echo

échotier, -ère *m/f* gossip columnist

échouer fail; (**s'**)~ *d'un bateau* run aground

éclabousser spatter

éclair *m* flash of lightning; CUIS eclair; **comme un** ~ in a flash; **éclairage** *m* lighting

éclaircie *f* clear spell; éclaircir lighten; *fig: mystère* clear up; **s'~** *du ciel* clear

éclairer light; ~ **qn** light the way for s.o.; *fig* enlighten s.o.

éclat *m de verre* splinter; *de métal* gleam; *des yeux* sparkle; *de couleurs, fleurs* vividness; ~ **de rire** peal of laughter; **un** ~ **d'obus** a piece of shrapnel; éclatant dazzling; *couleur* vivid; *rire* loud; éclater *d'une bombe* blow up, explode; *d'un ballon, pneu* burst; *d'un coup de feu* ring out; *d'une guerre, d'un incendie* break out; *fig: d'un groupe, parti* break up; ~ **en sanglots** burst into tears

éclipser eclipse (*aussi fig*); **s'~** F vanish, disappear

éclore *d'un oiseau* hatch out; *de fleurs* open

écluse *f* lock

écœurement *m* disgust; (*découragement*) discouragement; écœurer disgust, sicken; (*décourager*) dishearten; ~ **qn** *d'un aliment* make s.o. feel nauseous

école *f* school; ~ **maternelle** nursery school; ~ **primaire** elementary school, *Br* primary school ~ **publique** state school; écolier *m* schoolboy; écolière *f* schoolgirl

écologie *f* ecology; écologique ecological

économe economical, thrifty

économie *f* economy; *science*

economics *sg*; ~ **souterraine** black economy; **~s** savings; **économiser** save; ~ **sur qc** save on sth; **économiseur** *m* d'écran INFORM screen saver

écorce *f* d'un arbre bark; d'un fruit rind

écorcher animal skin; (égratigner) scrape; fig: nom, mot murder

écossais, ~e Scottish; **Écossais, ~e** m/f Scot; **Écosse** f: **l'~** Scotland

écoulement *m* flow; COMM sale; **écouler** COMM sell; **s'~** flow; du temps pass; COMM sell

écourter shorten; vacances cut short

écoute f: **être à l'~** be always listening out; **aux heures de grande ~** RAD at peak listening times; TV at peak viewing times; **écouter 1** v/t listen to **2** v/i listen; **écouteur** m TÉL receiver; **~s** RAD headphones

écran m screen; **porter à l'~** TV adapt for television; ~ **tactile** touch screen; ~ **total** sunblock

écrasant overwhelming; **écraser** crush; cigarette stub out; (renverser) run over; **s'~ au sol** d'un avion crash

écrémé: lait m ~ skimmed milk

écrevisse f crayfish

écrier: s'~ cry out

écrire write; **comment est-ce que ça s'écrit?** how do you spell it?; **écrit** m document; **l'~ examen** the written exam; **par ~** in writing; **écriteau** m notice; **écriture** f writing; COMM entry; **les (Saintes) Écritures** Holy Scripture

écrivain m writer

écrou m nut

écrouler: s'~ collapse

écru couleur natural

écueil m reef; fig pitfall

éculé chaussure worn-out; fig hackneyed

écume f foam

écureuil m squirrel

écurie f stable

édenté toothless

édifice m building; **édifier** erect; fig build up

éditer livre publish; texte edit; **éditeur, -trice** m/f publisher; (commentateur) editor; **édition** f publishing; action de commenter editing; (tirage) edition; **maison** f **d'~** publishing house; **éditorial** m editorial

édredon m eiderdown

éducatif, -ive educational; **éducation** f education; (culture) upbringing

éduquer educate; (élever) bring up

effacer erase; **s'~** d'une inscription wear away; d'une personne fade into the background

effarement m fear; **effarer**

frighten

effectif, -ive 1 *adj* effective **2** *m* manpower, personnel; **effectivement** true enough

effectuer carry out

efféminé *péj* effeminate

effervescent effervescent; *fig: foule* excited

effet *m* effect; COMM bill; **en ~** sure enough; **faire de l'~** have an effect; **~s** (personal) effects

efficace *remède* effective; *personne* efficient; **efficacité** *f* effectiveness; *d'une personne* efficiency

effleurer brush against; (*aborder*) touch on

effondrement *m* collapse; **effondrer: s'~** collapse

efforcer: s'~ de faire qch try very hard to do sth

effort *m* effort; **faire un ~** make an effort, try a bit harder

effraction *f* JUR breaking and entering

effrayant frightening; **effrayer** frighten; **s'~** be frightened (**de** at)

effroi *m* fear

effronterie *f* impertinence, effrontery

effroyable terrible, dreadful

égal 1 *adj* equal; *surface* even; *vitesse* steady; **ça lui est ~** it's all the same to him **2** *m* equal; **sans ~** unequaled, *Br* unequalled; **également** (*pareillement*) equally; (*aus-*

si) as well, too; **égaler** equal; **égaliser** *v/t* haies, cheveux even up; *sol* level **2** *v/i* SP tie the game, *Br* equalize; **égalité** *f* equality; *en tennis* deuce; **être à ~** be level; *en tennis* be at deuce

égard *m*: **à cet ~** in that respect; **à l'~ de qn** to(ward) s.o.; **par ~ pour** out of consideration for; **~s** respect

égarer *personne* lead astray; *chose* lose; **s'~** get lost; *du sujet* stray from the point

égayer cheer up

église *f* church

égocentrique egocentric

égoïsme *m* selfishness, egoism; **égoïste 1** *adj* selfish **2** *m/f* egoist

égorger: ~ qn cut s.o.'s throat

égout *m* sewer

égoutter drain

égratignure *f* scratch

Égypte *f*: **l'~** Egypt; **égyptien, ~ne** Egyptian; **Égyptien, ~ne** *m/f* Egyptian

éjecter eject; F *personne* kick out

élaborer *projet* draw up

élan *m* momentum; SP run--up; *de tendresse* upsurge; *de générosité* fit; (*vivacité*) enthusiasm

élancer *v/i*: **ma jambe m'élance** I've got shooting pains in my leg; **s'~** dash; SP take a run-up

élargir widen, broaden; *vêtement* let out; *débat* widen

élastique 1 adj elastic **2** m elastic; de bureau rubber band

électeur, -trice m/f voter; **élection** f election; **électorat** m droit franchise; per-sonnes electorate

électricien, ~ne m/f electrician; **électricité** f electricity; **~ statique** static (electricity); **électrique** electric; **électriser** electrify

électrocuter electrocute

électroménager: appareils mpl **~s** household appliances

électronique 1 adj electronic; **livre ~** e-book, electronic book **2** f electronics

élégance f elegance; **élégant** elegant

élément m element; (compo-sante) component; d'un puz-zle piece; **~s** (rudiments) ru-diments; **élémentaire** ele-mentary

éléphant m elephant

élevage m breeding; **~ (du bétail)** cattle farming

élève m/f pupil

élevé high; esprit noble; style elevated; **bien/mal ~** well/badly brought up; **élever** raise; prix, température raise, increase; statue put up, erect; enfants bring up, raise; animaux breed; **s'~** rise; d'une tour rise up; d'un cri go up; **s'~ contre** rise up against; **s'~ à** amount

to; **éleveur, -euse** m/f breeder

élimination f elimination; des déchets disposal; **éliminatoi-re** f qualifying round; **élimi-ner** eliminate; difficultés get rid of

élire elect

elle f she; après prép her; cho-se it

elle-même herself; chose it-self

elles fpl they; après prép them

elles-mêmes themselves

éloigné remote

éloigner move away; soup-çon remove; **s'~** move away (de from); **s'~ de qn** distance o.s. from s.o.

éloquence f eloquence; **élo-quent** eloquent

élu, ~e 1 adj: **le président ~** the President elect **2** m/f POL (elected) representative

élucider mystère clear up; question clarify

émacié emaciated

e-mail m e-mail

émanciper emancipate; **s'~** become emancipated

emballage m packaging; em-baller package; fig F thrill; **s'~** d'un moteur race; fig F get excited; **emballé sous vide** vacuum packed

embargo m embargo

embarquer 1 v/t load **2** v/i ou **s'~** embark; **s'~ dans** F get involved in

embarras *m* difficulty; (*gêne*) embarrassment; **être dans l'~** be in an embarrassing position; *sans argent* be short of money; **embarrassant** embarrassing; (*encombrant*) cumbersome; **embarrasser** embarrass; (*encombrer*) *escaliers* clutter up

embaucher take on, hire

embellir **1** *v/t* make more attractive; *fig* embellish **2** *v/i* become more attractive

embêtant F annoying; **embêter** F (*ennuyer*) bore; (*contrarier*) annoy; **s'~** be bored

emblème *m* emblem

emboîter insert; **~ le pas à qn** fall into step with s.o. (*aussi fig*); **s'~** fit together

embolie *f* embolism

embonpoint *m* stoutness

embouchure *f* GÉOGR mouth; MUS mouthpiece

embouteillage *m* traffic jam

emboutir crash into

embranchement *m* branch; (*carrefour*) intersection, Br junction

embrasser kiss; *période, thème* take in, embrace; *métier* take up; **~ du regard** take in at a glance

embrayage *m* AUTO clutch; *action* letting in the clutch

embrouiller muddle; **s'~** get muddled

embryon *m* embryo

éméché F tipsy

émeraude *f* & *adj* emerald

émerger emerge

émerveiller amaze; **s'~** be amazed (*de* by)

émetteur *m* RAD, TV transmitter

émettre *radiations etc* give off, emit; RAD, TV broadcast, transmit; *opinion* voice; *action, nouveau billet* issue; *emprunt* float

émeute *f* riot

émietter crumble

émigration *f* emigration; **émigré, ~e** *m/f* emigré; **émigrer** emigrate

émincer cut into thin slices

éminent eminent

émission *f* emission; RAD, TV program, Br programme; COMM, FIN issue

emmagasiner store

emmêler *fils* tangle; *fig* muddle

emménager: **~ dans** move into

emmener take

emmerder F: **~ qn** get on s.o.'s nerves; **s'~** be bored rigid

emmitoufler wrap up; **s'~** wrap up

émotion *f* emotion; F (*frayeur*) fright

émouvant moving; **émouvoir** (*toucher*) move; **s'~** be moved

emparer: **s'~ de** seize; *clés, héritage* grab; *des doutes, de la peur* overcome

empâter: **s'~** thicken

empêchement *m*: *j'ai eu un~* something has come up; empêcher prevent; *~ qn de faire qc* prevent *ou* stop s.o. doing sth; (*il*) *n'empêche que* nevertheless
empereur *m* emperor
empiéter: *~ sur* encroach on
empiffrer F: *s'~* stuff o.s.
empiler pile (up)
empire *m* empire; *fig* (*maîtrise*) control
empirer get worse, deteriorate
emplacement *m* site
emplette *f* purchase; *faire des ~s* go shopping
emplir fill; *s'~* fill (*de* with)
emploi *m* (*utilisation*) use; ÉCON employment; *~ du temps* schedule, *Br* timetable; *chercher un ~* be looking for work *ou* for a job
employé, ~e *m/f* employee; **employer** use; *personnel* employ; *s'~ à faire qc* strive to do sth; **employeur, -euse** *m/f* employer
empocher pocket
empoigner grab, seize
empoisonner poison
emporter take; *prisonnier* take away; (*entraîner, arracher*) carry away; *du courant* sweep away; *d'une maladie* carry off; *l'~ sur qn/qc* get the better of s.o./sth.; *s'~* fly into a rage
empreinte *f* impression; *fig* stamp; *~ génétique* genetic

fingerprint
empresser: *s'~ de faire qc* rush to do sth; *s'~ auprès de qn* be attentive to s.o.
emprise *f* hold
emprisonnement *m* imprisonment; **emprisonner** imprison
emprunt *m* loan; **emprunter** borrow (*à* from); *chemin, escalier* take
ému moved, touched
en[1] *prép* in; *direction* to; *agir ~ ami* act as a friend; *~ voiture* by car; *~ or* of gold; *en même temps* while, when; *mode* by
en[2] *pron*: *qu'~ pensez-vous?* what do you think about it?; *il y ~ a deux* there are two (of them); *j'~ ai* I have some; *j'~ ai cinq* I have five; *je n'~ ai pas* I don't have any; *il ~ est mort* he died of it
encadrer *tableau* frame; *encadré de deux gendarmes* *fig* flanked by gendarmes
encaisser COMM take; *chèque* cash; *fig* take
en-cas *m* CUIS snack
encastrer build in
enceinte[1] *adj* pregnant
enceinte[2] *f* enclosure; *~ (acoustique)* speaker
encens *m* incense
encercler encircle
enchaîner chain up; *fig: pensées, faits* link (up)
enchanté enchanted; *~!* how do you do?; **enchanter** (*ra*

vir) delight; (*ensorceler*) enchant

enchère f bid; ***vente f aux ～s*** auction

enchevêtrer tangle; *fig*: *situation* confuse; **s'～** *de fils* get tangled up; *d'une situation* get muddled

enclin: *être ～ à faire qch* be inclined to do sth

encoche f notch

encolure f neck; *tour de cou* neck (size)

encombrant cumbersome; *être ～ d'une personne* be in the way; **encombrer** *maison* clutter up; *rue, passage* block; **s'～** *de* load o.s. down with

encore *de nouveau* again; (*toujours*) still; *pas ～* not yet; *～ une bière?* another beer?; *～ plus rapide* even faster

encourageant encouraging; **encourager** encourage; *projet, entreprise* foster

encrasser dirty; **s'～** get dirty

encre f ink

encyclopédie f encyclopedia

endetter: **s'～** get into debt

endeuillé bereaved

endive f chicory

endolori painful

endommager damage

endormi asleep; *fig* sleepy; **endormir** send to sleep; *douleur* dull; **s'～** fall asleep

endosser *vêtement* put on; *responsabilité* shoulder; *chè-*

que endorse

endroit m (*lieu*) place; *d'une étoffe* right side

enduire: *～ de* cover with; **enduit** m *de peinture* coat

endurance f endurance

endurcir harden

endurer endure

énergie f energy; **énergique** energetic; *protestation* strenuous

énervant irritating; **énerver**: *～ qn* (*agacer*) get on s.o.'s nerves; (*agiter*) make s.o. edgy; **s'～** get excited

enfance f childhood

enfant m ou f child

enfer m hell (*aussi fig*)

enfermer shut ou lock up; *champ* enclose; **s'～** shut o.s. up

enfiler *aiguille* thread; *perles* string; *vêtement* slip on; *rue* turn into

enfin (*finalement*) at last; (*en dernier lieu*) lastly, last; (*bref*) in a word

enflammer set light to; *allumette* strike; MÉD inflame; *fig*: *imagination* fire; **s'～** catch; MÉD become inflamed; *fig*: *de l'imagination* take flight

enfler swell; **enflure** f swelling

enfoncer 1 *v/t clou, pieu* drive in; *couteau* thrust, plunge (*dans* into); *porte* break down **2** *v/i dans sable etc* sink (*dans* into); **s'～** sink

enfreindre infringe
enfuir: *s'~* run away
engagement *m* (*obligation*) commitment; *personnel* recruitment; THÉAT booking; (*mise en gage*) pawning
engager (*lier*) commit (*à* to); *personnel* hire; TECH (*faire entrer*) insert; *discussion* begin; (*entraîner*) involve (*dans* in); THÉAT book; (*mettre en gage*) pawn; *s'~* (*se lier*) commit o.s. (*à faire qc* to doing sth); (*commencer*) begin; MIL enlist
engelure *f* chilblain
engendrer *fig* engender
engin *m* machine; MIL missile; F *péj* thing
englober include
engloutir (*dévorer*) devour, wolf down, *fig* engulf
engouffrer devour, wolf down; *s'~ dans de l'eau* pour in; *fig*: *dans un bâtiment* rush into; *dans une foule* be swallowed up by
engourdir numb; *s'~* go numb
engraisser fatten
engrenage *m* gear
engueuler F bawl out; *s'~* have an argument
énigme *f* enigma, (*devinette*) riddle
enivrer intoxicate; *fig* exhilarate
enjamber step across; *d'un pont* span
enjeu *m* stake

enjoliveur *m* AUTO wheel trim, hub cap
enjoué cheerful, good humored, *Br* good-humoured
enlèvement *m* (*rapt*) abduction, kidnap; **enlever** take away, remove; *vêtement* take off, remove; (*kidnapper*) abduct, kidnap; *~ qc à qn* take sth away from s.o.
enneigé *route* blocked by snow; *sommet* snow-capped
ennemi *m* **1** *m/f* enemy **2** *adj* enemy *atr*
ennui *m* boredom; *~s* problems; **ennuyer** (*contrarier, agacer*) annoy; (*lasser*) bore; *s'~* be bored; **ennuyeux, -euse** (*contrariant*) annoying; (*lassant*) boring
énoncé *m* statement; *d'une question* wording; **énoncer** state; *~ des vérités* state the obvious
énorme enormous; **énormément** enormously; *~ de* F an enormous amount of
énormité *f* enormity
enquête *f* inquiry; *policière aussi* investigation; (*sondage d'opinion*) survey; **enquêter**: *~ sur* investigate
enraciné deep-rooted
enregistrement *m* registration; *de disques* recording; AVIAT check-in; **enregistrer** register; *disques* record; *bagages* check in
enrhumer: *s'~* catch (a) cold
enrichir enrich; *s'~* get richer

enrouer: **s'~** get hoarse

enrouler *tapis* roll up; **~ qc
autour de qch** wind sth
around sth

enseignant, **~e** *m/f* teacher

enseignement *m* education;
d'un sujet teaching; enseigner teach (**qc à qn** s.o. sth)

ensemble **1** *adv* (*simultanément*) together **2** *m* (*totalité*)
whole; (*groupe*) group, set;
MUS, *vêtement* ensemble;
MATH set; **dans l'~** on the
whole

ensevelir bury

ensoleillé sunny

ensommeillé sleepy

ensuite then; (*plus tard*) after

entacher smear

entaille *f* cut; (*encoche*)
notch; entailler notch; **s'~
la main** cut one's hand

entamer start; *économies*
make

entasser *choses* pile up; *personnes* cram

entendre hear; (*comprendre*)
understand; (*vouloir dire*)
mean; **~ faire qc** intend to
do sth; **s'~** (*avec qn*) get on (with
s.o.); (*se mettre d'accord*)
come to an agreement (with
s.o.); entendu *regard* knowing; **bien ~** of course; enten-
te *f* agreement

enterrement *m* burial; *cérémonie* funeral; enterrer
bury

en-tête *m* heading; INFORM

header; COMM letterhead;
d'un journal headline

entêtement *m* stubbornness;
entêter: **s'~** persist (**dans**
in; **à faire qc** in doing sth)

enthousiasme *m* enthusi-
asm; enthousiasmer: **s'~
pour** be enthusiastic about

enticher: **s'~ de** *personne* become infatuated with; *activité* develop a craze for

entier, -ère whole, entire; (*intégral*) intact; *confiance, satisfaction* full

entonnoir *m* funnel

entorse *f* MÉD sprain

entortiller (*envelopper*) wrap

entourage *m* entourage;
(*bordure*) surround; entourer: **~** de surround with;
s'~ de surround o.s. with

entraide *f* mutual assistance;
entraider: **s'~** help each other

entrailles *fpl* intestines

entrain *m* liveliness; entraînement *m* training; TECH
drive; entraîner (*charrier,
emporter*) sweep along; SP
train; *fig* result in; *frais* entail; *personne* drag; TECH
drive; **s'~** train

entrave *f* fig hindrance; entraver hinder

entre between; **le meilleur d'~
nous** the best of us; **~ autres**
among other things

entrebâiller half open

entrechoquer: **s'~** knock
against one another

entrecôte f rib steak

entrée f entrance, way in; *accès au théâtre, cinéma* admission; (*billet*) ticket; (*vestibule*) entry(way); CUIS starter; INFORM *touche* enter (key); *de dames* input; *~ interdite* no admittance

entrejambe m crotch

entrelacer interlace

entremets m CUIS dessert

entremise f: *par l'~ de* through (the good offices of)

entreposer store; **entrepôt** m warehouse

entreprenant enterprising; **entreprendre** undertake; **entrepreneur, -euse** m/f entrepreneur; **entreprise** f enterprise; (*firme*) company, business

entrer 1 v/i come/go in, enter; *~ dans* come/go into, enter; *voiture* get into; *pays* enter; *catégorie* fall into; *l'armée, le parti etc* join **2** v/t bring in; INFORM input, enter

entre-temps in the meantime

entretenir *maison, machine etc* maintain; *famille* keep, support; *amitié* keep up; *s'~ de qc* talk to each other about sth

entretien m maintenance, upkeep; (*conversation*) conversation

entrevoir glimpse; *fig* foresee

entrevue f interview

entrouvrir half open

énumérer list, enumerate

envahir invade; *d'un sentiment* overwhelm; **envahissant** *personne* intrusive; *sentiments* overwhelming

enveloppe f *d'une lettre* envelope; **envelopper** wrap; **enveloppé de brume**, *mystère* enveloped in

envenimer poison (*aussi fig*)

envergure f *d'un oiseau, avion* wingspan; *fig* scope; *d'une personne* caliber, *Br* calibre

envers 1 *prép* toward, *Br* towards **2** m *d'une feuille* reverse; *d'une étoffe*: wrong side; *à l'~* pull inside out; (*en désordre*) upside down

envie f (*convoitise*) envy; (*désir*) desire (**de** for); **avoir ~ de (faire) qc** want (to do) sth; **envier** envy; **~ qc à qn** envy s.o. sth

environ 1 *adv* about **2** *mpl*: *~s* surrounding area; **dans les *~s*** in the vicinity

environnement m environment

envisager (*considérer*) think about; (*imaginer*) envisage

envoi m shipment; *d'un fax* sending

envoler: *s'~* fly away; *d'un avion* take off; *fig*: *du temps* fly

envoyé m envoy; *d'un journal* correspondent; **envoyer** send; *gifle* give

éolienne f wind turbine
épais, ~se thick; *foule* dense;
épaisseur f thickness;
épaissir thicken
épancher: s'~ pour out one's
heart (**auprès de** to)
épanouir: s'~ blossom
épargne f saving; **~s** (*écono-*
mies) savings; **épargner 1**
v/t save; *personne* spare; **~**
qc à qn spare s.o. sth **2** v/i
save
éparpiller scatter
épars sparse
épatant F great, terrific; **épa-**
ter astonish
épaule f shoulder
épave f wreck (*aussi fig*)
épée f sword
épeler spell
éperdu *besoin* desperate; **~**
de beside o.s. with
épi m ear
épice f spice; **épicer** spice;
épicerie f grocery store, *Br*
grocer's; **épicier, -ère** m/f
grocer
épidémie f epidemic
épier spy on; *occasion* watch
for
épilepsie f epilepsy; **crise** f
d'~ epileptic fit
épiler remove the hair from
épinards mpl spinach
épine f d'une rose thorn; d'un
hérisson spine, prickle; **épi-**
neux, -euse *problème*
thorny
épingle f pin; **~ de sûreté**
safety pin; *tiré à quatre* **~s**

fig well turned-out
Épiphanie f Epiphany
épisode m episode
éploré tearful
éplucher peel; *fig* scrutinize;
épluchures fpl peelings
éponge f sponge; **éponger**
sponge down; *flaque* sponge
up; *déficit* mop up
époque f age, epoch; **meu-**
bles mpl **d'~** period *ou* antique furniture
époumoner: s'~ F shout o.s.
hoarse
épouse f wife; **épouser** marry; *principe etc* espouse
épousseter dust
époustouflant F breathtaking
épouvantable dreadful
épouvantail m scarecrow
épouvanter horrify; *fig* terrify
époux m husband; **les ~** the
married couple
éprendre: s'~ de fall in love
with
épreuve f trial; *SP* event; *im-*
primerie proof; *photogra-*
phie print; **à toute ~** *confian-*
ce etc never-failing; **à l'~ du**
feu fireproof
éprouver test, try out; (*res-*
sentir) experience
épuisé exhausted; *livre* out of
print; **épuiser** exhaust; **~ les**
ressources be a drain on resources; **s'~** tire o.s. out (**à**
faire qch doing sth); *d'une*
source dry up

épurer purify

équateur *m* equator

équilibre *m* balance, equilibrium; **équilibrer** balance

équipage *m* crew

équipe *f* team; *d'ouvriers* gang; **~ de nuit** night shift; **~ de secours** rescue party;

équipement *m* equipment;
équiper equip (**de** with)

équitable *f* just, equitable

équitation *f* riding

équivalent **1** *adj* equivalent (**à** to) **2** *m* equivalent

équivoque **1** *adj* equivocal, ambiguous **2** *f* ambiguity; (*malentendu*) misunderstanding

érable *m* BOT maple

érafler scratch; **éraflure** *f* scratch

ère *f* era

érection *f* erection

éreinter exhaust; **s'~** exhaust o.s. (**à faire qch** doing sth)

ériger erect; **s'~ en** set o.s. up as

érosion *f* erosion

érotisme *m* eroticism

errer roam; *des pensées* stray

erreur *f* mistake, error; **~ de calcul** miscalculation

érudit erudite; **érudition** *f* erudition

éruption *f* eruption; MÉD rash

escabeau *m* (*tabouret*) stool; (*marchepied*) stepladder

escalade *f* climbing; **~ de violence** etc escalation in; **escalader** climb

escalator *m* escalator

escale *f* stopover; **faire ~ à** MAR call at; AVIAT stop over in

escalier *m* stairs *pl*, staircase; **dans l'~** on the stairs; **~ de secours** fire escape

escalope *f* escalope

escamoter (*dérober*) make disappear; *antenne* retract; *fig*: *difficulté* get around

escapade *f*: **faire une ~** get away from it all

escargot *m* snail

escarpement *m* slope

esclaffer: **s'~** guffaw, laugh out loud

esclavage *m* slavery; **esclave** *m/f* slave

escompte *m* discount; **escompter** discount; *fig* expect

escorter escort

escrime *f* fencing; **escrimer**: **s'~** fight, struggle (**à** to)

escroc *m* crook

espace *m* space; **espacer** space out; **s'~ en** become more and more infrequent

Espagne *f* Spain; **espagnol**, **~e 1** *adj* Spanish **2** *m langue* Spanish; **Espagnol**, **~e** *m/f* Spaniard

espèce *f* kind, sort (**de** of); BIOL species; **~ d'abruti!** *péj* idiot!; **en ~s** COMM cash

espérer **1** *v/t* hope for; **~ que** hope that; **~ faire qc** hope to do sth **2** *v/i* hope; **~ en** trust in

espiègle mischievous

espion

espion, **~ne** *m/f* spy; **espionnage** *m* espionage, spying; **espionner** spy on

espoir *m* hope

esprit *m* spirit; (*intellect*) mind; (*humour*) wit

esquisse *f* sketch; *fig*: *d'un roman* outline; **esquisser** sketch; *fig*: *projet* outline

esquiver dodge; **s'~** slip away

essai *m* (*test*) test, trial; (*tentative*) attempt; *en rugby* try; *en littérature* essay; **à l'~** on trial

essaim *m* swarm

essayage *m*: **cabine** *f* **d'~** changing cubicle; **essayer** try; (*mettre à l'épreuve, évaluer*) test; *vêtement* try on; **~ de faire qc** try to do sth; **s'~ à qc** try one's hand at sth

essence *f* essence; *carburant* gas, *Br* petrol; BOT species *sg*

essentiel, **~le 1** *adj* essential **2** *m*: **l'~** the main thing; *de sa vie* the main part

essieu *m* axle

essor *m fig* expansion

essorer wring out; *d'une machine à laver* spin

essoufflé out of breath

essuie-glace *m* (windshield) wiper, *Br* (windscreen) wiper; **essuie-mains** *m* handtowel; **essuyer** wipe; *fig* suffer

est 1 *m* east **à l'~ de** (to the) east of **2** *adj* east, eastern

est-ce que: **~ c'est vrai?** is it true?; **est-ce qu'ils se por-**

tent bien? are they well?

esthéticienne *f* beautician

esthétique esthetic, *Br* aesthetic

estimatif, **-ive** estimated; **devis** *m* **~** estimate; **estimation** *f* estimation; *des coûts* estimate

estime *f* esteem; **estimer** *valeur* estimate; (*respecter*) have esteem for; (*croire*) feel, think; **s'~ heureux** consider o.s. lucky

estival summer *atr*

estomac *m* stomach

Estonie *f* Estonia

estrade *f* podium

estropier cripple

estuaire *m* estuary

et and; **~ ... ~** both ... and ...

étable *f* cowshed

établi *m* workbench

établir *entreprise* establish, set up; , *contact, ordre* establish; *salaires, prix* set, fix; *facture, liste* draw up; *record* set; *culpabilité* establish, prove; *raisonnement, réputation* base (**sur** on); **s'~** (*s'installer*) settle; **établissement** *m* establishment; *de salaires, prix* setting; *d'une facture, liste* drawing up; *d'un record* setting; *d'une loi, d'un impôt* introduction

étage *m* floor, story, *Br* storey; *d'une fusée* stage

étagère *f meuble* bookcase,

shelves *pl*; *planche* shelf

étain *m* pewter

étalage *m* display; **faire ~ de qch** show sth off; *étaler carte* spread out; *peinture, paiements* spread (**sur** over); *vacances* stagger; *marchandises* display; *fig* (*exhiber*) show off; **s'~ de peinture** spread; *de paiements* be spread out (**sur** over); (*se vautrer*) sprawl; *par terre* fall flat

étanche watertight; **étancher** make watertight

étang *m* pond

étape *f lieu* stopover, stopping place; *d'un parcours* stage, leg; *fig* stage

état *m* state; (*liste*) statement, list; **en tout ~ de cause** in any case, anyway; **hors d'~** out of order

États-Unis *mpl*: **les ~** the United States

été *m* summer

éteindre *incendie, cigarette* put out; *électricité, radio, chauffage* turn off; **s'~ de feu, lumière* go out; *de télé etc* go off; *euph* (*mourir*) pass away

étendre *malade, enfant* lay (down); *beurre, enduit* spread; *peinture* apply; *bras* stretch out; *linge* hang up; *vin* dilute; *sauce* thin; *influence* extend; **s'~** extend, stretch (**jusqu'à** as far as, to); *d'une personne* lie

down; *d'un incendie, d'une maladie* spread; *d'un tissu* stretch; **étendue** *f* extent; *d'eau* expanse; *de connaissances, d'une catastrophe* extent

éternel, ~le eternal; **éternité** *f* eternity

éternuer sneeze

éthique 1 *adj* ethical **2** *f* ethics

étinceler sparkle; **étincelle** *f* spark

étiqueter label (*aussi fig*)

étiquette *f* label; (*protocole*) etiquette

étirer: **s'~** stretch

étoffe *f* material; **étoffer** *fig* flesh out

étoile *f* star (*aussi fig*); **~ filante** falling star, *Br* shooting star; **~ de mer** starfish

étonnement *m* astonishment, surprise; **étonner** astonish, surprise; **s'~ de** be astonished *ou* surprised at; **s'~ que** (+ *subj*) be surprised that

étouffant stifling, suffocating; **étouffée** CUIS: **à l'~** braised; **étouffer** suffocate; *avec un oreiller* smother, suffocate; *fig: bruit* quash; *révolte* put down, suppress; *cri* smother; *scandale* hush up

étourderie *f* foolishness; *action* foolish thing to do

étourdi foolish, thoughtless; **étourdir** daze; **~ qn** *d'alcool, de succès* go to s.o.'s head;

étourdissement *m* (*vertige*) dizziness, giddiness

étrange strange

étranger, -ère 1 *adj* strange; de l'étranger foreign 2 *m/f* stranger; de l'étranger foreigner 3 *m*: **à l'~** abroad; *investissement* foreign, outward

étrangler strangle; *fig*: critique, liberté stifle

être 1 *v/i* be; **nous sommes lundi** it's Monday; **nous avons été éliminé** we were eliminated; **~ à qn** appartenir à belong to s.o. 2 *v/aux* have; **elle n'est pas encore arrivée** she hasn't arrived yet; **elle est arrivée hier** she arrived yesterday 3 *m* being; *personne* person

étreindre grasp; *ami* embrace, hug; *de sentiments* grip; **étreinte** *f* hug, embrace; *de la main* grip

étrenner use for the first time

étrennes *fpl* New Year's gift

étroit narrow; *tricot* tight, small; *amitié* close; **être ~ d'esprit** be narrow-minded

étroitesse *f* narrowness

étude *f* study; *salle à l'école* study room; *de notaire* office; *activité* practice; **faire des ~s** study; **~ de marché** market research; **étudiant**, **~e** *m/f* student; **étudier** study

étui *m* case

étuvée CUIS: **à l'~** braised

euphorique euphoric

euro *m* euro

Europe *f*: **l'~** Europe; **européen**, **~ne** European; **Européen**, **~ne** *m/f* European

eux *mpl* they; *après prép* them

eux-mêmes *mpl* themselves

évacuation *f* evacuation

évadé *m* escaped prisoner; **évader**: **s'~** escape

évaluer (*estimer*) evaluate; *tableau, meuble* value; *coût, nombre* estimate

évanouir: **s'~** faint; *fig* vanish, disappear

évaporer: **s'~** evaporate

évasif, -ive evasive; **évasion** *f* escape

éveil *m* awakening; **en ~** alert; **éveiller** wake up; *fig* arouse; **s'~** wake up; *fig* be aroused

événement *m* event

éventail *m* fan; *fig: de marchandises* range

éventé *boisson* flat; **éventer** fan; *fig: secret* reveal

éventualité *f* eventuality, possibility; **éventuel**, **~le** possible

évêque *m* bishop

évertuer: **s'~ à faire qc** try one's hardest to do sth

évident obvious

évier *m* sink

éviter avoid; **~ qc à qn** spare s.o. sth; **~ de faire qc** avoid doing sth

évoluer develop, evolve; **évolution** *f* development; BIOL evolution

évoquer *esprits* conjure up; ~ **un problème** bring up a problem

exact *nombre, poids* exact, precise; *reportage* accurate; *calcul, date, solution* right, correct; *personne* punctual; **exactitude** *f* accuracy; (*ponctualité*) punctuality

ex æquo: **être** ~ tie, draw

exagération *f* exaggeration; **exagérer** exaggerate

exalter excite; (*vanter*) exalt

examen *m* exam; MÉD examination; **passer un** ~ take an exam; **être reçu à un** ~ pass an exam; **examiner** examine

exaspérer exasperate

excédent *m* excess; *budgétaire, de trésorerie* surplus; ~ **de bagages** excess baggage; **excéder** exceed; (*énerver*) irritate

excellence *f* excellence; **Excellence** Excellency; **excellent** excellent; **exceller** excel (*dans* in; *en* in, at; *à faire qch* at doing sth)

excepté 1 *adj*: **la Chine ~e** except for China **2** *prép* except; ~ **que** except for the fact that; ~ **si** unless, except if; **excepter** exclude, except; **exception** *f* exception; **à l'~ de** with the exception of; **exceptionnel, ~le** exceptional; **~le** exceptional

excès *m* excess; **à l'~** to excess, excessively; ~ **de vitesse** speeding; **excessif, -ive**

excessive

excitation *f* excitement; (*provocation*) incitement (**à** to); *sexuelle* arousal; **exciter** excite; (*provoquer*) incite (**à** to); *sexuellement* arouse; *appétit* whet; *imagination* stir

exclamation *f* exclamation; **exclamer**: **s'~** exclaim

exclure exclude

exclusion *f* expulsion; **à l'~ de** to the exclusion of; (*à l'exception de*) with the exception of

exclusivité *f* COMM exclusivity, sole rights *pl*; **en** ~ exclusively

excursion *f* trip, excursion

excuse *f* excuse; **~s** apology; **excuser** excuse; **s'~** apologize (**de** for); **excusez-moi** excuse me

exécuter *ordre, projet* carry out; MUS perform; *loi, jugement* enforce; *condamné* execute; **exécution** *f d'un ordre, projet* carrying out; MUS performance; *d'une loi, un jugement* enforcement; *d'un condamné* execution

exemplaire 1 *adj* exemplary **2** *m* copy; (*échantillon*) sample; **en deux ~s** in duplicate

exemple *m* example; **par** ~ for example; **donner l'~** set a good example

exempt exempt (**de** from); *souci* free (**de** from); **exempter** exempt (**de** from);

exemption *f* exemption

exercer *corps* exercise; *influence* exert, use; *pouvoir* use; *profession* practise, *Br* practise; *mémoire* train; MIL drill; **s'~** (*s'entraîner*) practice, *Br* practise; **exercice** *m* exercise (*aussi* ÉDU); *d'une profession* practice; COMM fiscal year, *Br* financial year; MIL drill

exhiber exhibit; *document* produce; **s'~** make an exhibition of o.s.; **exhibitionniste** *m* exhibitionist

exigeant demanding; **exigence** *f* demand; **exiger** demand

exigu, ~ë tiny

exil *m* exile; **exilé**, ~e *m/f* exile; **exiler** exile; **s'~** go into exile

existence *f* existence; **exister** exist

exonérer exempt

exorbitant exorbitant

exotique exotic

expansion *f* expansion

expatrier *argent* move abroad *ou* out of the country; **s'~** settle abroad

expédier send; COMM ship, send; *travail* do quickly

expéditeur, -trice *m/f* sender; COMM shipper, sender; **expédition** *f* sending; COMM shipment; (*voyage*) expedition

expérience *f* experience; *scientifique* experiment

expérimenté experienced;

expérimenter (*tester*) test

expert, ~e *adj* & *m/f* expert; **expertise** *f* (*estimation*) valuation; JUR expert testimony

expier expiate

expiration *f d'un délai* expiration, *Br* expiry; *de souffle* exhalation; **expirer** *d'un contrat, délai* expire; (*respirer*) exhale; (*mourir*) die, expire *fml*

explication *f* explanation; **expliquer** explain; **s'~** explain o.s.; **s'~ avec qn** talk things over with s.o.

exploit *m* sportif, médical feat; *amoureux* exploit

exploitant, ~e *m/f* agricole farmer

exploitation *f d'une ferme, ligne aérienne* running; *du sol* farming; *de richesses naturelles péj*: *des ouvriers* exploitation; (*entreprise*) operation

exploiter *ferme, ligne aérienne* run; *sol* farm; *richesses naturelles* exploit (*aussi péj*)

explorateur, -trice *m/f* explorer; **explorer** explore

exploser explode (*aussi fig*); **~ de rire** F crack up F; **explosif**, -ive *adj* & *m* explosive; **explosion** *f* explosion (*aussi fig*)

exportateur, -trice **1** *adj* exporting **2** *m* exporter; **exportation** *f* export; **exporter** export

exposé *m* account, report; ÉDU presentation; **exposer** *art*, *marchandise* exhibit, show; *problème*, *programme* explain; *à l'air*, *à la chaleur* expose (*aussi* PHOT); **exposition** *f d'art, de marchandise* exhibition; *d'un problème* explanation; *au soleil* exposure (*aussi* PHOT)

exprès¹ *adv* (*intentionnellement*) deliberately, on purpose; (*spécialement*) expressly

exprès², **-esse 1** *adj* express **2** *adj inv* **lettre** *f* **exprès** express letter

express 1 *adj inv* express **2** *m* train express; *café* espresso

expressément expressly

expression *f* expression

exprimer express; **s'~** express o.s.

expulser expel; *d'un pays* deport; **expulsion** *f* expulsion; *d'un pays* deportation

exquis exquisite

extase *f* ecstasy

extension *f des bras, jambes* stretching; (*prolongement*) extension; *d'une épidémie* spread; INFORM expansion

exténuer exhaust

extérieur 1 *adj* external; *mur aussi* outside **2** *m* (*partie externe*) outside, exterior; **à l'~ de** outside; **extérioriser** express, let out; **s'~** *d'un senti-*

ment find expression; *d'une personne* express one's emotions

exterminer exterminate

externaliser COM outsource

externe external

extincteur *m* extinguisher

extinction *f* extinction (*aussi* fig)

extirper *mauvaise herbe* pull up; MÉD remove; *fig renseignement* drag out

extorquer extort

extorsion *f* extortion

extraction *f* extraction

extrader extradite

extraire extract

extrait *m* extract

extraordinaire extraordinary

extraterrestre *m/f* extraterrestrial, alien

extravagance *f* extravagance; *d'une personne, d'une idée* eccentricity

extraverti extrovert

extrême 1 *adj* extreme **2** *m* extreme; **à l'~** to extremes

Extrême-Orient *m*: **l'~** the Far East

extrémiste *m/f* POL extremist; **extrémité** *f d'une rue* (very) end; *d'un doigt* tip; (*situation désespérée*) extremity; **~s** ANAT extremities

exubérant exuberant

exulter exult

eye-liner *m* eyeliner

F

fable *f* fable

fabricant, ~e *m/f* manufacturer, maker; **fabrication** *f* making; *industrielle* manufacture; **fabriquer** make; *industriellement aussi* manufacture; *histoire* fabricate

fabuleux, -euse fabulous

fac *f* (= **faculté**) uni, university

façade *f* façade

face *f* face; *d'une pièce* head; **en ~ (de)** opposite; **faire ~ à** face up to; **face-à-face** *m inv* face-to-face (debate)

fâché annoyed; **fâcher** annoy; **se ~** get annoyed; **se ~ avec qn** fall out with s.o.; **fâcheux, -euse** annoying; *(déplorable)* unfortunate

facile easy; *personne* easy-going; **facilement** easily; **facilité** *f* easiness; *à faire qch* ease; **~s de paiement** easy terms; **faciliter** make easier, facilitate

façon *f* (*manière*) way, method; *de* **(à ce) que** (+*subj*) so that; **de toute ~** anyway, anyhow; **de cette ~** in that way; **à la ~ de** like, in the style of

facteur *m* mailman, *Br* postman; MATH, *fig* factor

factrice *f* mailwoman, *Br* postwoman

facture *f* bill; COMM invoice; **facturer** invoice

facultatif, -ive optional

faculté *f* faculty

fade insipid

faible 1 *adj* weak; *bruit, lumière, espoir* faint; *avantage* slight **2** *m* *pour personne* soft spot; *pour chocolat etc* weakness; **faiblesse** *f* weakness; **faiblir** weaken

faille *f* GÉOL fault; *dans théorie* flaw

faillible fallible; **faillir**: **il a failli gagner** he almost won

faim *f* hunger; **avoir ~** be hungry; **mourir de ~** starve (*aussi fig*)

fainéant, ~e 1 *adj* idle, lazy **2** *m/f* idler

faire 1 *v/t* do; *robe, meuble, repas, liste* make; **~ de la natation/du ski** swim/ski, go swimming/skiing; **cinq plus cinq font dix** five and five are *ou* make ten; **ça ne fait rien** it doesn't matter; **~ rire qn** make s.o. laugh; **~ peindre la salle de bain** have the bathroom painted **2** *v/i*: **~ vite** hurry up, be quick **3** *impersonnel*: **il fait chaud/froid** it is *ou* it's warm/cold **4**: **ça ne se fait pas** it's not done; **se ~ rare** become rarer; **se ~ à qc** get used to sth; **je ne m'en fais pas** I'm not worrried

faisable feasible

faisan *m* pheasant

faisceau *m* bundle; *de lumière* beam

fait[1] *m* fact; *(action)* act; *(événement)* development; **au ~** by the way; **de ce ~** consequently; **en ~** in fact; **tout à ~** absolutely; **un ~ divers** a brief news item

fait[2] *adj*: **être ~ pour qn/qch** be made for s.o./sth; **c'est bien ~ pour lui** serves him right!

falaise *f* cliff

falloir: **il faut un visa** you need a visa, you must have a visa; **il faut l'avertir** we have to warn him; **il me faut sortir, il faut que je sorte** *(subj)* I have to go out, I must go out; **s'il le faut** if necessary; **il aurait fallu prendre le train** we should have taken the train; **comme il faut** respectable; **il ne faut pas que je sorte** *(subj)* I mustn't go out

falsifier *argent* forge; *document* falsify; *vérité* misrepresent

famélique starving

fameux, -euse *(célèbre)* famous; *(excellent)* wonderful

familiariser familiarize; **se ~** familiarité *f* familiarity; familier, -ère familiar

famille *f* family

famine *f* famine

fanatique 1 *adj* fanatical **2** *m/f* fanatic; **fanatisme** *m* fanaticism

faner: **se ~** fade

fanfare *f* *(orchestre)* brass band; *(musique)* fanfare; **fanfaron, ~ne 1** *adj* boastful **2** *m* boaster

fantaisie *f* imagination; *(caprice)* whim

fantasme *m* fantasy; **fantasmer** fantasize

fantasque strange, weird

fantastique 1 *adj* fantastic; *(imaginaire)* imaginary **2** *m*: **le ~** fantasy

fantôme *m* ghost

farce *f* *au théâtre* farce; *(tour)* joke; CUIS stuffing; **farceur, -euse** *m/f* joker; **farcir** CUIS stuff; *fig* cram

fard *m* make-up; **~ à paupières** eye shadow

fardeau *m* burden *(aussi fig)*

farder: **se ~** make up

farine *f* flour; **~ de maïs** corn starch, *Br* cornflour

farouche *(timide)* shy; *volonté, haine* fierce

fascination *f* fascination; **fasciner** fascinate

faste *m* pomp

fast-food *m* fast food restaurant

fastidieux, -euse tedious

fastueux, -euse lavish

fatal fatal; *(inévitable)* inevitable; **fatalisme** *m* fatalism;

fataliste 1 *adj* fatalistic **2** *m/f* fatalist; **fatalité** *f* fate

fatigant tiring; *(agaçant)* tiresome; **fatigue** *f* tiredness; **fatiguer** tire; *(importuner)* annoy; *se* **~** get tired

faubourg *m* (working-class) suburb

fauché F broke F; **faucher** *fig* mow down; F *(voler)* pinch F

faufiler: *se* **~ dans une pièce** slip into a room

faune *f* wildlife, fauna

faussaire *m* forger; **fausser** *calcul*, *vérité* distort; *clef* bend

faute *f* mistake; *(responsabilité)* fault; **par sa ~** because of him; **~ de** for lack of; **sans ~** without fail

fauteuil *m* armchair; **~ roulant** wheelchair

fauve 1 *adj* tawny **2** *m* félin big cat

faux, fausse 1 *adj* false; *incorrect aussi* wrong; *bijoux* imitation, fake; **fausse couche** *f* miscarriage; **~ témoignage** perjury **2** *adv*: *chanter* **~** sing out of tune **3** *m* *copie* forgery, fake

faux-filet *m* CUIS sirloin

faux-monnayeur *m* counterfeiter, forger

faux-semblant *m* pretense, *Br* pretence

faveur *f* favor, *Br* favour; **de ~** *traitement* preferential; *prix* special; **en ~ de** in favor of

favorable favorable, *Br* fa-

vourable; **favori, ~te** *m/f* & *adj* favorite, *Br* favourite; **favoriser** favor, *Br* favour; *faciliter, avantager* promote; **favoritisme** *m* favoritism, *Br* favouritism

fax *m* fax; **faxer** fax

féconder fertilize; **fécondité** *f* fertility

fécule *f* starch

fédéral federal; **fédération** *f* federation

feeling *m* feeling; **avoir un bon ~ pour qc** have a good feeling about sth

feindre: **~ l'étonnement** pretend to be astonished, feign astonishment; **~ de faire qch** pretend to do sth; **feinte** *f* feint

fêler: *se* **~** crack

félicitations *fpl* congratulations; **féliciter** congratulate (*de* on)

fêlure *f* crack

femelle *f* & *adj* female

féminin 1 *adj* feminine; *sexe* female; *problèmes, magazines, mode* women's **2** *m* GRAM feminine; **féministe** *m/f* & *adj* feminist; **féminité** *f* femininity

femme *f* woman; *(épouse)* wife; **~ battue** battered wife; **~ au foyer** homemaker, *Br* housewife

fendre split; *(fissurer)* crack; *cœur* break; *se* **~** split; *(se fissurer)* crack

fenêtre f window

fenouil m BOT fennel

fente f crack; *d'une boîte à lettres, jupe* slit; *pour pièces de monnaie* slot

fer m iron; **~ à cheval** horseshoe; **~ à repasser** iron

férié: jour m **~** (public) holiday

ferme[1] *adj* firm; **terre f ~** dry land, terra firma **2** *adv* travailler hard; **s'ennuyer ~** be bored stiff

ferme[2] f farm

fermé closed, shut; *robinet* off; *club* exclusive

fermenter ferment

fermer 1 v/t close, shut; *eau, gaz, robinet* turn off; *manteau* fasten; **ferme-la!** shut up! **2** v/i close, shut; *d'un manteau* fasten; **se ~** close, shut

fermeté f firmness

fermeture f closing; *définitive* closure; *mécanisme* fastener; **~ éclair** zipper, Br zip (fastener)

fermier 1 *adj* œufs, poulet free-range **2** m farmer

féroce fierce, ferocious; **férocité** f fierceness, ferocity

ferré, ~e: voie f **~e** (railroad *ou* Br railway) track

ferroviaire railroad *atr*, Br railway *atr*

fertile fertile; **~ en** full of; **fertilité** f fertility

fervent fervent

fesse f buttock; **~s** butt, Br bottom; **fessée** f spanking

festin m feast

festival m festival

festivités fpl festivities

fêtard m F reveler; fête f festival; (*soirée*) party; *publique* holiday; REL feast (day), festival; *jour d'un saint* name day; **les ~s (de fin d'année)** the holidays, Christmas and New Year; **faire la ~** party; **~ foraine** fun fair; **Fête des mères** Mother's Day; **Fête nationale** Bastille Day; **fêter** celebrate; (*accueillir*) fête

feu m fire; AUTO, MAR light; *de circulation* (traffic) light, Br (traffic) lights *pl*; *d'une cuisinière* burner; *fig* (*enthousiasme*) passion; **coup** m **de ~** shot; **prendre ~** catch fire; **vous avez du ~?** got a light?; **~ arrière** AUTO taillight

feuillage m foliage; **feuille** f leaf; *de papier* sheet; **~ d'impôt** tax return; **~ de paie** payslip; **feuilleter** livre etc leaf through

feuilleton m serial; TV soap opera

feutre m felt; *stylo* felt-tipped pen; *chapeau* fedora

février m February

fiable reliable

fiançailles fpl engagement; **fiancé, ~e** m/f fiancé; **fiancer: se ~ avec** get engaged to

fibre

110

fibre f fiber, Br fibre; **avoir la ~ paternelle** fig be a born father; **la ~ patriotique** patriotic feelings

ficeler tie up; ficelle f string; pain thin French stick

fiche f pour classement index card; formulaire form; ÉL plug

ficher F (faire) do; (donner) give; (mettre) stick; **fiche-moi la paix!** leave me alone!; **je m'en fiche** I don't give a damn

fichier m INFORM file; ~ joint attachment

fichu (inutilisable) kaput F; (sale) filthy; **être mal ~** santé be feeling rotten

fictif, -ive fictitious; fiction f fiction

fidèle 1 adj faithful 2 m/f REL, fig: **les fidèles** the faithful pl; fidélité f faithfulness

fier¹: **se ~ à** trust

fier², -ère adj proud (de) of; fierté f pride

fièvre f fever; **avoir de la ~** have a fever; fiévreux, -euse feverish

figer congeal; **se ~** fig: d'un sourire become fixed

figue f fig; figuier m fig tree

figurant, ~e m/f de théâtre walk-on; de cinéma extra; figure f figure; (visage) face; figuré figurative; figurer figure; **se ~ qc** imagine sth

fil m thread; de métal, ÉL, TÉL wire; **coup m de ~** TÉL

(phone) call

filature f spinning; usine mill; **prendre qn en ~** fig tail s.o.

file f line; d'une route lane; ~ (d'attente) line, Br queue

filer 1 v/t spin; F (donner) give; (épier) tail F 2 v/i F (partir vite) race off; du temps fly past

filet m d'eau trickle; de pêche, tennis net; CUIS fillet

filial, ~e 1 adj filial 2 f COMM subsidiary

fille f girl; parenté daughter; **vieille ~** old maid; fillette f little girl

filleul m godson; filleule f goddaughter

film m movie, Br aussi; couche film; ~ policier detective movie ou Br aussi film; filmer film

fils m son; ~ à papa (spoilt) rich kid

filtre m filter; filtrer 1 v/t filter; fig screen 2 v/i filter through; fig leak

fin¹ f end; **à la ~** in the end; **mettre ~ à qc** put an end to sth; **sans ~** endless; parler endlessly

fin² 1 adj fine; (mince) thin; taille, cheville slender; esprit refined; (rusé, malin) sharp 2 adv fine(ly)

final, ~e 1 adj final 2 m: ~e MUS finale 3 f SP final; finale 1 m MUS finale 2 f SP final; finaliser finalize; finaliste m/f finalist finance f finance; financer fund, finance; financier, -ère **1** adj financial **2** m financier

finesse f (délicatesse) fineness

fini **1** adj finished **2** m finish; finir **1** v/t finish **2** v/i finish; ~ **de faire qc** finish doing sth; ~ **par faire qc** finish up doing sth

finlandais, ~e **1** adj Finnish **2** m langue Finnish; Finlandais, ~e m/f Finn; Finlande f: **la ~** Finland

firme f firm

fisc m tax authorities pl

fissure f crack

fixe **1** adj fixed; adresse, personnel permanent **2** m basic salary; fixer fasten; (déterminer) fix, set; PHOT fix; (regarder) stare at; **se ~** (s'établir) settle down

flageolet m flageolet bean

flagrant flagrant; **en ~ délit** red-handed

flair m sense of smell; fig intuition; flairer smell (aussi fig)

flambant: **~ neuf** brand new; flamber **1** v/i blaze **2** v/t CUIS flambé

flamme f flame; fig fervor, Br fervour

flan m flan

flancher quail

flâner stroll

flanquer flank; F (jeter) fling; coup give

flaque f puddle

flasque flabby

flatter flatter; **se ~ de qc** congratulate o.s. on sth; flatterie f flattery; flatteur, -euse **1** adj flattering **2** m/f flatterer

flèche f arrow; d'un clocher spire; **monter en ~** de prix skyrocket

fléchir **1** v/t bend; (faire céder) sway **2** v/i d'une matière bend; fig (céder) give in; (faiblir) weaken; d'un prix, de ventes fall

flegmatique phlegmatic

flemme f F laziness; **j'ai la ~ de le faire** I can't be bothered

flétrir: **se ~** wither

fleur f flower; d'un arbre blossom; fleurir flower, bloom; fig flourish; fleuriste m/f florist

fleuve m river

flexibilité f flexibility; flexible flexible

flic m F cop F

flinguer F gun down

flipper **1** m pinball machine; jeu pinball **2** v/i F freak out F

flirter flirt

flocon m flake; ~ **de neige** snowflake

Floride f Florida

florissant fig flourishing

flot m flood (aussi fig); ~**s** waves; **remettre à ~** refloat (aussi fig)

flottant floating; vêtements baggy

flotte f fleet; F (*eau*) water; F (*pluie*) rain; **flotter** *d'un bateau* float; *d'un drapeau* flutter; *d'un sourire, air* hover; *fig* waver

flou blurred, fuzzy; *robe* loose-fitting

fluctuation f fluctuation; **fluctuer** COMM fluctuate

fluide 1 *adj* fluid; *circulation* moving freely **2** *m* PHYS fluid; **fluidité** f fluidity

fluorescent fluorescent

flûte f MUS, *verre* flute; *pain* thin French stick

fluvial river *atr*

flux *m* MAR flow

fœtus *m* fetus, Br foetus

foi f faith; **être de bonne/mauvaise ~** be sincere/insincere

foie *m* liver; **une crise de ~** a stomach upset

foire f fair

fois f time; **une ~** once; **deux ~** twice; **trois ~** three times; **il était une ~ ...** once upon a time there was ...; **quatre ~ six** four times six; **à la ~** at the same time

foisonner be abundant

folie f madness; **faire des ~s** achats go on a spending spree

folk *m* folk (music)

folklore folklore

follement madly

fomenter foment

foncé *couleur* dark; **foncer** de *couleurs* darken; AUTO speed

along; **~ sur** rush at

foncier, **-ère** COMM land

foncièrement fundamentally

fonction f function; (*poste*) office; **faire ~ de** act as; **en ~ de** according to; **prendre ses ~s** take up office

fonctionnaire *m/f* public servant

fonctionnement *m* functioning; **fonctionner** work; *du système* function

fond *m* bottom; *d'une salle, armoire* back; *d'une peinture* background; (*contenu*) content; *d'un problème* heart; *d'un pantalon* seat; **à ~** thoroughly; **au ~, dans le ~** basically

fondamental fundamental

fondateur, **-trice** *m/f* founder; **fondation** f foundation; **fondé 1** *adj* well-founded **2** *m*: **~ de pouvoir** authorized representative; **fondement** *m* fig basis; **sans ~** groundless; **fonder** found; **~ qch sur** base sth on; **se ~ sur** *d'une personne* base o.s. on; *d'une idée* be based on

fondre *v/t* neige melt; *dans l'eau* dissolve; *métal* melt down **2** *v/i* de la neige melt; *dans l'eau* dissolve; **~ sur** proie pounce on

fonds *m* **1** sg fund; *d'une bibliothèque* collection; **~ de commerce** business **2** *pl* (*argent*) funds

fondu melted

fondue *f* CUIS fondue; **~ bourguignonne** beef fondue

fontaine *f* fountain; (*source*) spring

fonte *f métal* cast iron; **~ des neiges** spring thaw

football *m* soccer, *Br aussi* football; **~ américain** football, *Br* American football; **footballeur, -euse** *m/f* soccer player, *Br aussi* footballer

footing *m* jogging; **faire du ~** jog, go jogging

force *f* strength; (*violence*) force; **à ~ de travailler** by working; **de ~** by force; **~s armées** armed forces

forcené, -e *m/f* maniac

forcer force; **se ~** force o.s.

forestier, -ère 1 *adj* forest *atr* **2** *m* ranger, *Br* forest warden

forêt *f* forest

forfait *m* COMM package; (*prix*) all-in price; **déclarer ~** withdraw

formaliser: se ~ de take offense *ou Br* offence at; **formalité** *f* formality

format *m* format; **formater** format

formation *f* formation; (*éducation*) training; **~ continue** continuing education

forme *f* form; **en ~ de** in the shape of; **être en ~** be in form, be in good shape; **formel, ~le** formal; (*explicite*) categorical; **formellement** *adv*: **~ interdit** strictly for-

bidden; former form; (*instruire*) train; **se ~** form

formidable enormous; F great F

formulaire *m* form

formulation *f* wording

formule *f* formula; **formuler** formulate; **vœux, jugement** express

fort 1 *adj* strong; (*gros*) stout; *coup, pluie* heavy; *somme* big; **être ~ en qch** be good at sth **2** *adv parler* loudly; *pousser, frapper* hard; (*très*) extremely; (*beaucoup*) a lot **3** *m* strong point; MIL fort; **fortement** *pousser* hard; (*beaucoup*) greatly

fortifier strengthen

fortuit chance

fortune *f* luck; **de ~** makeshift

fosse *f* pit; (*tombe*) grave; **fossé** *m* ditch; *fig* gulf; **fossette** *f* dimple

fossile *m & adj* fossil

fou, folle 1 *adj* mad; (*incroyable*) incredible; **être ~ de qn/qc** be mad *ou* crazy about s.o./sth.; **~ de joie** *etc* beside o.s. with **2** *m/f* madman; madwoman

foudre *f* lightning; **coup m de ~** *fig* love at first sight

foudroyer strike down; **~ qn du regard** give s.o. a withering look

fouet *m* whip; CUIS whisk

fougueux, -euse fiery

fouiller 1 *v/i* dig; (*chercher*) search **2** *v/t de police* search;

en archéologie excavate

fouiner nose around

foulard *m* scarf

foule *f* crowd; *une ~ de* masses of

fouler trample; *sol* set foot on; *se ~ la cheville* twist one's ankle; *foulure f* sprain

four *m* oven; TECH kiln; *fig* F (*insuccès*) flop F

fourchette *f* fork; (*éventail*) bracket; **fourchu** forked; *cheveux mpl ~s* split ends

fourgon *m* baggage car, *Br* luggage van; *camion* van; **fourgonnette** *f* small van

fourmi *f* ant

fourmillements *mpl* pins and needles; **fourmiller** swarm (*de* with)

fournaise *f* *fig* oven; **fourneau** *m* furnace; CUIS stove

fourni: bien ~ well stocked; **fournir** supply (*de, en* with); *occasion* provide; *effort* make; *~ qc à qn* provide s.o. with sth; **fournisseur** *m* supplier; *~ d'accès (Internet)* Internet service provider, ISP; **fourniture** *f* supply; *~s scolaires* school stationery and books

fourré[1] *m* thicket

fourré[2] *adj* CUIS filled; *vêtement* lined

fourrer stick, shove; (*remplir*) fill; *se ~ dans* get into

fourrière *f* pound

fourrure *f* fur

fourvoyer: se ~ go astray

foutre F do; (*mettre*) stick; *coup* give; *se ~ de qn* make fun of s.o.; *indifférence* not give a damn about s.o.; *je m'en fous!* I don't give a damn!

foyer *m* fireplace; *d'une famille* home; *de jeunes* club; (*pension*) hostel; *d'un théâtre* foyer; *d'un incendie* seat; *d'une infection* source

fracas *m* crash; **fracasser** shatter

fractionner divide (up) (*en* into)

fracture *f* MÉD *m* fracture; **fracturer** *coffre* break open; *jambe* fracture

fragile fragile; *santé* frail; *cœur* weak; **fragiliser** weaken; **fragilité** *f* fragility

fragment *m* fragment

fraîcheur *f* freshness; (*froideur*) coolness (*aussi fig*); **fraîchir** *du vent* freshen; *du temps* get cooler

frais[1], **fraîche 1** *adj* fresh; (*froid*) cool; *peinture* wet; *nouvelles* recent; *servir ~* serve chilled; *il fait~* it's cool **2** *adv* freshly, newly **3** *m*: *prendre le ~* get a breath of fresh air

frais[2] *mpl* expenses *pl*; COMM costs *pl*; *faire des ~* incur costs; *à mes ~* at my (own) expense; *~ bancaires* bank charges; *~ généraux* overhead, *Br* overheads

fraise *f* strawberry

framboise f raspberry

franc[1], **franche** adj frank; regard open; COMM free

franc[2] m franc

français, ~e 1 adj French **2** m
langue French; **Français, ~e**
m/f Frenchman; French-
woman; **les ~** the French
pl; **France** f: **la ~** France

franchir cross; obstacle negotiate

franchise f caractère frankness; (exemption) exemp-
tion; COMM franchise; d'une
assurance deductible, Br excess

franco adv: **~ (de port)** carriage free; **y aller ~** fig F
go right ahead

francophone 1 adj French-
-speaking **2** m/f French
speaker

franc-parler m outspoken-
ness

frange f bangs pl, Br fringe

frappant striking; **frappe** f
INFORM keying; **faute** f **de ~**
typo, typing error; **frapper**
1 v/t hit, strike; (impressionner) strike **2** v/i (agir) strike;
à la porte knock (à at); **~**
dans ses mains clap (one's
hands)

fraternel, ~le brotherly, fraternal; **fraternité** f brother-
hood

fraude f fraud; ÉDU cheating;
passer en ~ smuggle; frauduleux, -euse fraudulent

frayer: **se ~** chemin clear

frayeur f fright

fredonner hum

frein m brake; **sans ~** fig un-
bridled; **~ à main** parking
brake, Br hand brake; **frei-**
ner 1 v/i brake **2** v/t fig curb,
check

frêle frail

frelon m hornet

frémir shake; de feuilles quiver; de l'eau simmer; **frémis-**
sement m shiver; de feuilles
quivering

frénésie f frenzy; **avec ~** fre-
netically

fréquemment frequently;
fréquence f frequency;
quelle est la ~ des bus?
how often do the buses
go?; **fréquent** frequent; situation common

fréquentation f d'un théâtre
etc attendance; **tes ~s** (amis)
the company you keep; **fré-**
quenter endroit go to regularly, frequent; personne
see; groupe go around with

frère m brother

fret m freight

frétiller wriggle

friable crumbly

friand: **être ~ de qc** be fond of
sth; **friandises** fpl sweet
things

fric m F money, dosh F

friche f AGR: **en ~** (lying) fal-
low

friction f friction; de la tête
scalp massage; **frictionner**
massage

frigidaire *m* refrigerator

frigide frigid

frigo *m* F icebox, fridge; **frigorifier** refrigerate

frileux, -euse: *être ~* feel the cold

frimer show off; **frimeur, -euse** show-off

fringues *fpl* F clothes, gear F

frire 1 *v/i* fry **2** *v/t:* **faire ~** fry

frisé curly; **friser** *cheveux* curl; *fig: le ridicule* verge on

frissonner shiver

frit fried; **(pommes) frites** *fpl* (French) fries, *Br aussi* chips; **friteuse** *f* deep fryer; **friture** *f* *poissons Br* whitebait, *small fried fish;* *huile* oil; *à la radio,* TÉL interference

frivole frivolous; **frivolité** *f* frivolity

froid 1 *adj* cold *(aussi fig);* **j'ai ~** I'm cold; **prendre ~** catch (a) cold *m* cold; **humour** *m* **à ~** dry humor; **froidement** *fig* coldly; *(calmement)* coolly; *tuer* in cold blood; **froideur** *f* coldness

froissement *m* *bruit* rustle; **froisser** crumple; *fig* offend; **se ~** crumple; *fig* take offense *ou Br* offence

fromage *m* cheese; **~ blanc** fromage frais; **~ à tartiner** cheese spread

froncer gather; **~ les sourcils** frown

front *m* front; ANAT forehead; **de ~** from the front; *fig*

head-on; **marcher de ~** walk side by side

frontière *f* frontier, border

frotter 1 *v/i* rub **2** *v/t* rub **(de** with); *meuble* polish; *sol* scrub; *allumette* strike

frousse *f* F fear; **avoir la ~** be scared

fructifier BOT bear fruit; *d'un placement* yield a profit

fructueux, -euse fruitful

fruit *m* fruit; **~s** fruit; **~s de mer** seafood

frustrant frustrating; **frustration** *f* frustration

fugitif, -ive 1 *adj* runaway; *fig* fleeting **2** *m/f* fugitive

fugue *f* *d'un enfant* escapade; MUS fugue; **faire une ~** run away

fuir 1 *v/i* flee; *du temps* fly; *d'un tuyau* leak; *d'un robinet* drip; *d'un liquide* leak out **2** *v/t* shun; *question* avoid; *fuite f* flight **(devant** from); *d'un tuyau etc* leak; **prendre la ~** take flight

fulgurant dazzling; *vitesse* lightning

fumé smoked; *verre* tinted

fumée *f* smoke; **fumer** smoke; **fumeur, -euse** *m/f* smoker

funèbre funeral *atr;* *(lugubre)* gloomy

funérailles *fpl* funeral

funeste fatal

fur: *au ~ et à mesure* as I/you *etc* go along; *au ~ et à mesure que* as

fureter ferret around
fureur f fury; **faire ~** be all the rage
furie (*colère*) fury; *femme* shrew; **furieux, -euse** furious (**contre qn** with s.o.; **de qch** with *ou* at sth)
furtif, -ive furtive, stealthy
fuseau m: **~ horaire** time zone
fusée f rocket
fusible m ÉL fuse

fusil m rifle; **~ de chasse** shotgun; **fusiller** execute by firing squad
fusion f COMM merger; PHYS fusion; **fusionner** COMM merge
futé cunning, clever
futile futile; *personne* frivolous
futur m & adj future
fuyant *menton* receding; *regard* evasive

G

gabarit m size; TECH template
gâcher *fig* spoil; *travail* bungle; *temps, argent* waste
gâchis m (*désordre*) mess; (*gaspillage*) waste
gadget m gadget
gaffe f F blooper F, blunder; **faire ~ à** F be careful of
gaffer F make a gaffe *ou* blooper F
gage *fig* forfeit; (*preuve*) token; **tueur** m **à ~s** hitman; **mettre en ~** pawn
gagnant, ~e 1 adj winning **2** m/f winner
gagne-pain m livelihood
gagner win; *salaire, amitié etc* earn; *place, temps* gain; *endroit* reach; *de peur etc* overcome; **~ sa vie** earn one's living
gai cheerful; *un peu ivre* tipsy; **gaieté** f cheerfulness
gain m gain; (*avantage*) bene-

fit; **~s** profits; *d'un employé* earnings
gaine f sheath
galant galant; **homme ~** gentleman
galaxie f galaxy
galère f: **il est dans la ~** *fig* F he's in a mess; **galérer** F sweat
galerie f gallery; AUTO roofrack; **~ d'art** art gallery; **~ marchande** mall
galet m pebble
Galles fpl: **le pays m de ~** Wales; **gallois, ~e 1** adj Welsh **2** m langue Welsh; **Gallois, ~e** m/f Welshman; Welsh woman
galop m gallop; **galoper** gallop
galopin m urchin
galvaniser galvanize
gambader gambol, leap
gamin, ~e 1 m/f kid **2** adj

childlike

gamme f MUS scale; *fig* range; **bas de ~** downscale, Br downmarket

gang m gang

gangster m gangster

gant m glove; **~ de toilette** washcloth, Br facecloth

garage m garage; **garagiste** m auto mechanic; *propriétaire* garage owner

garant, **~e** m/f guarantor; **garantie** f guarantee; **garantir** guarantee

garce f F bitch

garçon m boy; (*serveur*) waiter; **~ d'honneur** best man; **~ manqué** tomboy; **garçonnière** f bachelor apartment *ou* Br flat

garde[1] f care (*de* of); MIL guard; **prendre ~** be careful; **être de ~** be on duty; **mettre qn en ~** put s.o. on their guard; **~ à vue** police custody

garde[2] m guard; **~ forestier** (forest) ranger

garde-boue m AUTO fender, Br wing

garde-fou m railing

garde-malade m/f nurse

garder *objet* keep; *vêtement* keep on; (*surveiller*) guard; *malade, enfant* look after; **se ~ de faire qch** be careful not to do sth

garderie f daycare center, Br daycare centre

gardien, **~ne** m/f *de prison* guard, Br warder; *d'un musée* attendant; *d'immeuble, d'école* janitor; *fig* guardian; **~ (de but)** goalkeeper **~ de la paix** police officer

gare[1] f station; **~ routière** bus station

gare[2]: **~ à toi!** watch out!; *ça va mal se passer* you'll be for it!

garer park; **se ~** park; *pour laisser passer* move aside

gargariser: **se ~** gargle

gargouiller gurgle; *de l'estomac* rumble

garnement m rascal

garnir (*fournir*) fit (*de* with); (*orner*) trim (*de* with); **garniture** f *légumes* vegetables pl

gars m F guy F

gasoil m gas oil, Br diesel

gaspillage m waste; **gaspiller** waste; **gaspilleur**, **-euse 1** *adj* wasteful **2** m/f waster

gastroentérite f gastroenteritis

gastronome m/f gourmet; **gastronomie** f gastronomy

gâteau m cake; **~ sec** cookie, Br biscuit

gâter spoil; **se ~** *d'un aliment* spoil; *du temps* deteriorate

gauche 1 *adj* left; *manières* gauche **2** f left; **à ~** on the left (*de* of); **gaucher**, **-ère 1** *adj* left-handed **2** m/f left-hander

gaufre f waffle; **gaufrette** f wafer

gaver *oie* force-feed; **~ qn de qch** *fig* stuff s.o. full of sth

gaz *m* gas; **mettre les ~** step on the gas; **~ à effet de serre** greenhouse gas

gaze *f* gauze

gazeux, -euse *boisson* carbonated, *Br* fizzy

gazinière *f* gas cooker

gazole *m* gas oil, *Br* diesel

gazon *m* grass

gazouiller twitter

géant, ~e 1 *adj* gigantic, giant *atr* **2** *m/f* giant

geindre groan

gel *m* frost; *fig: des prix* freeze; *cosmétique* gel

gélatine *f* gelatine

gelée *f* frost; CUIS aspic; *confiture* jelly, *Br* jam; **geler 1** *v/t* freeze **2** *v/i d'une personne* freeze; **il gèle** there's a frost

Gémeaux *mpl* ASTROL Gemini

gémir groan; **gémissement** *m* groan

gênant (*embarrassant*) embarrassing

gencive *f* gum

gendarme *m* policeman; **gendarmerie** *f* police force; *lieu* police station

gendre *m* son-in-law

gêne *f* (*embarras*) embarrassment; (*dérangement*) inconvenience; *physique* difficulty; **sans ~** shameless; **gêner** bother; (*embarrasser*) embarrass; (*encombrer*) be in

the way

général, ~e 1 *adj* general; **en ~** generally **2** *m* MIL general **3** *f* THÉÂT dress rehearsal; **généraliser** generalize; **se ~** spread; **généraliste** *m* MÉD generalist; **généralités** *fpl* generalities

générateur *m* generator; **générer** generate

généreux, -euse generous; **générosité** *f* generosity

génétique genetic; **génétiquement** genetically; **~ modifié** genetically modified, GM

génétiquement genetically; **~ modifié** genetically modified, GM

Genève Geneva

génial of genius; (*formidable*) terrific; **génie** *m* genius; TECH engineering; **avoir du ~** be a genius; **~ civil** civil engineering

genou *m* knee; **à ~x** on one's knees

genre *m* kind, sort; GRAM gender; **bon chic, bon ~** preppie *atr*

gens *mpl* people *pl*

gentil, ~le nice; *enfant* good; **gentillesse** *f* (*amabilité*) kindness

géographie *f* geography

géologie *f* geology; **géologue** *m/f* geologist

géomètre *m/f* geometrician; **géométrie** *f* geometry

gérance *f* management; **gé-**

rant, ~e *m/f* manager

gerbe *f de blé* sheaf

gercé *lèvres* chapped

gérer manage

gériatrie *f* geriatrics

germain: **cousin** *m* **~, cousine** *f* **~e** (first) cousin

germe *m* germ (*aussi fig*); germiner germinate

gestation *f* gestation

geste *m* gesture; gesticuler gesticulate

gestion *f* management; gestionnaire *m/f* manager

ghetto *m* ghetto

gibier *m* game

giboulée *f* wintry shower

gicler spurt

gifle *f* slap (in the face); gifler slap (in the face)

gigantesque gigantic

gigaoctet *m* gigabyte

gigot *m d'agneau* leg

gigoter F fidget

gilet *m* vest, *Br* waistcoat; (*chandail*) cardigan; **~ de sauvetage** lifejacket

gin *m* gin; **~ tonic** gin and tonic

gingembre *m* BOT ginger

girafe *f* giraffe

giratoire: **sens** *m* **~** traffic circle, *Br* roundabout

gisement *m* GÉOL deposit; **~ pétrolifère** *ou* **de pétrole** oilfield

gitan, ~e *m/f* gypsy

gîte *m* holiday home

givre *m* frost; givré covered with frost; *avec du sucre*

frosted; F (*fou*) crazy

glace *f* ice; (*miroir*) mirror; AUTO window; (*crème glacée*) ice cream; *d'un gâteau* frosting, *Br* icing; *d'une tarte* glaze; glacer freeze; (*intimider*) petrify; *gâteau* frost, *Br* ice; *tarte* glaze; **se ~** freeze; *du sang* run cold; glacial icy (*aussi fig*); glacière *f* cool bag; *fig* icebox; glaçon *m* icicle; *artificiel* icecube

glaise *f* (*aussi* **terre** *f* **~**) clay

gland *m* acorn

glande *f* gland

glander F hang around F

glaner *fig* glean

glapir shriek

glauque *eau* murky; *couleur* blue-green

glissade *f* slide; *accidentelle* slip; glissant slippery; glissement *m* **~ de terrain** landslide; glisser **1** *v/t* slip (**dans** into) **2** *v/i* slide; *sur l'eau* glide (**sur** over); (*déraper*) slip; *être glissant* be slippery; **se ~ dans** slip into

global global; *prix, somme* total, overall; globalisation *f* globalization; globe *m* globe; **~ oculaire** eyeball

gloire *f* glory; glorieux, -euse glorious; glorifier glorify

glousser cluck; *rire* giggle

gluant sticky

glycine *f* wisteria

gnangnan F *film, livre* sloppy F

goal *m* goalkeeper

gobelet *m* tumbler; *en carton, plastique* cup

gober gobble; F *mensonge* swallow

godet *m récipient* pot; *de vêtements* flare

gogo F: **à ~** galore

goinfrer: se ~ *péj* stuff o.s.

golf *m* SP golf; *terrain* golf course

golfe *m* GÉOGR gulf

gomme *f* gum; *pour effacer* eraser; **gommer** (*effacer*) erase

gond *m* hinge; **sortir de ses ~s** fly off the handle

gondole *f* gondola

gonflable inflatable; **gonfler 1** *v/i* swell **2** *v/t* blow up; (*exagérer*) exaggerate

gonzesse *f* F *péj* chick F

gorge *f* throat; (*poitrine*) bosom; GÉOGR gorge; **avoir mal à la ~** have a sore throat; **gorgée** *f* mouthful; **gorger: se ~** gorge o.s. (**de** with)

gosier *m* throat

gosse *m/f* F kid F

goudron *m* tar

gouffre *m* abyss; *fig* depths *pl*

goujat *m* boor

goulot *m* neck; **boire au ~** drink from the bottle

goulu greedy

gourd numb (with the cold)

gourde *f récipient* water bottle; *fig* F moron F

gourer F: **se ~** goof F, *Br* boob F

gourmand, ~e 1 *adj* greedy **2** *m/f* gourmand; **gourmandi-** se *f* greediness; **~s** *mets* delicacies; **gourmet** *m* gourmet

gourmette *f* chain

gourou *m* guru

gousse *f* pod; **~ d'ail** clove of garlic

goût *m* taste; **de bon ~** tasteful, in good taste; **de mauvais ~** tasteless, in bad taste; **avoir du ~** have taste; **goûter 1** *v/t* taste; *fig* enjoy **2** *v/i* prendre un goûter have an afternoon snack **3** *m* afternoon snack

goutte *f* drop; **~ de pluie** raindrop; **goutte-à-goutte** *m* MÉD drip; **goutter** drip; **gouttière** *f* gutter

gouvernement *m* government; **gouverner** *pays* govern; *passions* master, control; MAR steer; **gouverneur** *m* governor

grâce *f* grace; (*bienveillance*) favor, *Br* favour; JUR pardon; **faire ~ à qn de qc** spare s.o. sth; **~ à** thanks to; **gracier** reprieve; **gracieux, -euse** graceful; **à titre ~** free

grade *m* rank; **gradé** *m* MIL noncommissioned officer

gradins *mpl* SP bleachers, *Br* terraces

graduellement gradually

graduer (*augmenter*) gradually increase; *instrument* graduate

graffitis *mpl* graffiti *sg ou pl*

grain *m* grain; MAR squall; **~ de**

beauté mole, beauty spot; ~ *de raisin* grape

graine f seed

graissage m lubrication, greasing; **graisse** f fat; TECH grease; **graisser** grease, lubricate; (*salir*) get grease on; **graisseux, -euse** greasy

grammaire f grammar; **grammatical** grammatical

gramme m gram

grand 1 adj big; (*haut*) tall; (*adulte*) grown-up; (*long*) long; (*important, glorieux*) great; *il est ~ temps* it's high time; **~e surface** f supermarket; **les ~es vacances** fpl the summer vacation, Br the summer holidays; ~ **ensemble** new development, Br (*housing*) estate **2** adv ouvrir wide **3** m giant, great man

grand-chose: *pas* ~ not much

Grande-Bretagne: *la* ~ Great Britain

grandeur f (*taille*) size; **~ nature** lifesize

grandiose magnificent

grandir 1 v/i grow **2** v/t: ~ **qn** make s.o. look taller; *de l'expérience* strengthen s.o.

grand-mère f grandmother

grand-père m grandfather

grands-parents mpl grandparents pl

granit(e) m granite

granuleux, -euse granular

graphique 1 adj graphic **2** m

chart; MATH graph; INFORM graphic

grappe f cluster; ~ **de raisin** bunch of grapes

grappin m: *mettre le* ~ *sur qn* get one's hands on s.o.

gras, ~se 1 adj fatty, fat; *personne* fat; *cheveux, peau* greasy; *faire la* ~se *matinée* sleep late **2** m CUIS fat

gratification f (*prime*) bonus; PSYCH gratification; **gratifier:** ~ **qn de qc** present s.o. with sth

gratiné CUIS with a sprinkling of cheese; *fig* F *addition* colossal

gratitude f gratitude

gratte-ciel m skyscraper; **gratter** scrape; (*griffer, piquer*) scratch; (*enlever*) scrape off; *mot* scratch out; *se* ~ scratch; **grattoir** m scraper

gratuit free; *fig* gratuitous

gravats mpl rubble

grave serious; *son* deep; *ce n'est pas* ~ it's not a problem

graver engrave; *disque* cut

gravier m gravel

gravillon m grit; **~s** gravel, Br loose chippings pl

gravir climb

gravité f seriousness; PHYS gravity

gravure f ART engraving; (*reproduction*) print

gré m: *bon* ~, *mal* ~ like it or not; *contre mon* ~ against my will; **de bon ~** willingly; **de son plein ~** of one's own free will

grec, **~que 1** *adj* Greek **2** *m langue* Greek; **Grec**, **~que** *m/f* Greek; **Grèce:** *la* **~** Greece

greffe *f* graft; **~ du cœur** MÉD heart transplant; **greffer** graft; **cœur**, **poumon** transplant

greffier *m* clerk of the court

grêle[1] *adj jambes* skinny; *voix* shrill

grêle[2] *f* hail; **grêler:** *il grêle* it's hailing; **grêlon** *m* hailstone

grelotter shiver

grenade *f* BOT pomegranate; MIL grenade

grenadine *f* grenadine, pomegranate syrup

grenier *m* attic

grenouille *f* frog

grès *m* sandstone; *poterie* stoneware

grésiller sizzle; RAD crackle

grève[1] *f* strike; **être en ~, faire ~** be on strike; **se mettre en ~** go on strike; **~ de la faim** hunger strike

grève[2] *f* (*plage*) shore

gréviste *m/f* striker

gribouillage *m* scribble; (*dessin*) doodle; **gribouillis** scribble; (*dessiner*) doodle

grief *m* grievance

grièvement *blessé* seriously

griffe *f* claw; COMM label; *fig* (*empreinte*) stamp; **griffer**

scratch

griffonner scribble

grignoter 1 *v/t* nibble on; *économies* nibble away at **2** *v/i* nibble

grill *m* broiler, *Br* grill; **grillade** *f* broil, *Br* grill

grillage *m* wire mesh; (*clôture*) fence

grille *f d'une fenêtre* grille; (*clôture*) railings *pl*; *d'un four* rack; (*tableau*) grid;

grille-pain *m inv* toaster;

griller 1 *v/t viande* broil, *Br* grill; *pain* toast; *café*, *marrons* roast **2** *v/i d'une ampoule* burn out; **~ un feu rouge** go through a red light

grillon *m* cricket

grimace *f* grimace; **faire des ~s** pull faces

grimper climb

grincement *m de porte* squeaking; **grincer** *d'une porte* squeak; **~ des dents** grind one's teeth

grincheux, **-euse** grouchy

grippe *f* MÉD flu; **prendre qn en ~** take a dislike to s.o.;

grippé: MÉD: **être ~** have flu

gris *adj* gray, *Br* grey; *temps*, *vie* dull; (*ivre*) tipsy

grisant exhilarating

grisâtre grayish, *Br* greyish

griser: **~ qn** go to s.o.'s head; **se laisser ~ par** get carried away by

grisonner go gray *ou Br* grey

grognement *m* (*plainte*)

grumbling; *d'un cochon etc*
grunt; **grogner** (*se plaindre*)
grumble; *d'un cochon*
grunt; **grognon**, **-ne**: **être ~** be grumpy

grommeler mutter

gronder 1 *v/i* growl; *du tonnerre* rumble; *d'une révolte* brew **2** *v/t* scold

gros, **~se 1** *adj* big; (*corpulent*) fat; *lèvres* thick; *rhume*, *souliers* heavy; *chaussettes* thick; *plaisanterie* coarse; *vin* rough; **~ mots** *mpl* bad language **2** *adv*: **gagner ~** win a lot; **en ~** (*globalement*) on the whole; COMM wholesale **3** *m personne* fat man; COMM wholesale trade

groseille *f* BOT currant; **~ à maquereau** gooseberry

grossesse *f* pregnancy

grosseur *f* (*corpulence*) fatness; (*volume*) size; (*tumeur*) growth

grossier, **-ère** (*rudimentaire*) crude; (*indélicat*) coarse; (*impoli*) rude; *erreur* bad

grossir 1 *v/t au microscope* magnify; *rivière* swell; (*exagérer*) exaggerate; **~** *qn d'une robe etc* make s.o. look fatter **2** *v/i d'une personne* put on weight

grotesque grotesque

grotte *f* cave

grouiller: **~ de** be swarming with; **se ~** F get a move on

groupe *m* group; **~ sanguin** blood group; **grouper** group; **se ~ autour de qn** gather around s.o.

grue *f* ZO, TECH crane

grumeleux, **-euse** lumpy

gué *m* ford

guenilles *fpl* rags

guêpe *f* wasp

guère: **ne ... ~** hardly

guéridon *m* round table

guérir 1 *v/t* cure (**de** of) **2** *v/i* heal; *d'un malade* get better; **guérison** *f* (*rétablissement*) recovery

guerre *f* war; **en ~** at war; **faire la ~** be at war (**à** with); **~ civile** civil war; **~ des gangs** gang warfare; **guerrier**, **-ère 1** *adj* warlike **2** *m* warrior

guet *m*: **faire le ~** keep watch; **guet-apens** *m* ambush; **guetter** keep an eye open for; (*épier*) watch

gueule *f* F mouth; (*visage*) face; **ta ~!** F shut it! F; **~ de bois** hangover; **gueuler** F yell

gueuleton *m* F enormous meal

guichet *m de banque, poste* wicket, Br window; *de théâtre* box office; **~ automatique** ATM, Br aussi cash dispenser

guide 1 *m* guide **2** *f* girl scout, Br guide **3**: **~s** *fpl* guiding reins; **guider** guide

guidon *m de vélo* handlebars *pl*

guillemets *mpl* quote marks

guindé stiff

guirlande f garland; **~s de Noël** tinsel

guise f: **agir à sa ~** do as one likes; **en ~ de** as, by way of

guitare f guitar; **guitariste** m/f guitarist

guttural guttural

Guyane: **la ~** Guyana

gym f gym; **gymnase** m SP gym; **gymnaste** m/f gymnast; **gymnastique** f gymnastics sg; corrective, matinale exercises pl

gynécologue m/f MÉD gynecologist, Br gynaecologist

gyrophare m flashing light

H

habile skillful, Br skilful; **habileté** f skill; **habilité** JUR authorized

habillé (élégant) dressy; **habiller** dress; **s'~** get dressed, dress; **élégamment** get dressed up

habit m: **~s** clothes

habitable inhabitable; **habitant**, **~e** m/f inhabitant; **habitation** f living; (domicile) residence; **habiter 1** v/t live in **2** v/i live

habitude f habit, custom; **d'~** usually; **par ~** out of habit; **habitué**, **~e** m/f regular; **habituel**, **~le** usual; **habituer**: **~ qn à qch** get s.o. used to sth; **s'~ à** get used to

'**hache** f ax, Br axe; '**hacher** chop; **viande f hachée** ground beef, Br mince

'**hachisch** m hashish

'**hachoir** m appareil meat grinder, Br mincer; couteau cleaver; planche chopping board

haddock m smoked haddock

'**haie** f hedge; SP hurdle; pour chevaux fence, jump; **une ~ de policiers** fig a line of police

'**haillons** mpl rags

'**haine** f hatred; '**haineux**, -euse full of hatred

'**haïr** hate

'**hâle** m (sun)tan

haleine f breath; **hors d'~** out of breath

'**haleter** pant

'**hall** m d'hôtel, immeuble foyer; de gare concourse

'**halle** f market

halloween f Halloween

hallucination f hallucination

halogène m: (lampe f) **~** halogen light

'**halte** f stop; **faire ~** halt, make a stop

haltère m dumbbell; **faire des ~s** do weightlifting

haltérophilie f weightlifting

'**hamac** m hammock

'**hameau** m hamlet

hameçon m hook

'**hamster** m hamster

'hanche f hip
'handicap m handicap; 'handicapé, ~e **1** adj disabled, handicapped **2** m/f disabled ou handicapped person
'hangar m shed; AVIAT hangar
'hanter haunt
'hantise f fear, dread
'happer catch; fig: de train, bus hit
'haras m stud farm
'harassant travail exhausting
'harceler harass
'hard m hardcore; MUS hard rock
'hardi bold
'hareng m herring
'hargne f bad temper; 'hargneux, -euse venomous; chien vicious
'haricot m BOT bean; **c'est la fin des ~s** F that's the end
harmonie f harmony; harmoniser match (up); MUS harmonize; **s'~ de couleurs** go together; **s'~ avec** go with
'harpe f MUS harp
'harpon m harpoon
'hasard m chance; **au ~** at random; **par ~** by chance; 'hasarder hazard; **se ~ à faire qc** venture to do sth
'hâte f hurry, haste; **en ~** in haste; **avoir ~ de faire qc** be eager to do sth; 'hâter hasten; **se ~** hurry
'hausse f increase, rise; 'hausser increase; **~ les épaules** shrug (one's shoulders)

'haut **1** adj high; immeuble tall, high; cri, voix loud; fonctionnaire high-level **2** adv high; **de ~** from above; **de ~ en bas** from top to bottom; regarder qn up and down; **en ~** above; **en ~ de** at the top of **3** m top; **du ~ de** from the top of; **des ~s et des bas** ups and downs
'hautain haughty
'hauteur f height; fig haughtiness; **être à la ~ de qc** be up to sth
hebdomadaire m & adj weekly
hébergement m accommodations pl, Br accommodation; héberger: **~ qn** put s.o. up; fig take s.o. in
hébreu m: l'~ Hebrew
hectare m hectare (approx 2.5 acres)
'hein F eh?; **c'est joli, ~?** it's pretty, isn't it?
'hélas alas
'héler hail
hélice f MAR, AVIAT propeller; **escalier m en ~** spiral staircase
hélicoptère m helicopter
hémisphère m hemisphere
hémorragie f hemorrhage, Br haemorrhage
'hennir neigh
hépatite f hepatitis
herbe f grass; CUIS herb; **mauvaise ~** weed; **fines ~s** herbs
héréditaire hereditary; hérédité f heredity

hérésie f heresy; **hérétique 1** adj heretical **2** m/f heretic

'hérissé ruffled

'hérisson m hedgehog

héritage m inheritance; **hériter 1** v/t inherit **2** v/i: **~ de qc** inherit sth; **~ de qn** receive an inheritance from s.o.; **héritier, -ère** m/f heir

'hernie f MÉD hernia; **~ discale** slipped disc

héroïne[1] f drogue heroin

héroïne[2] f heroine

héroïque heroic

héroïsme m heroism

'héron m heron

'héros m hero

herpès m herpes

hésitation f hesitation; **hésiter** hesitate

hétérogène heterogeneous

hétérosexuel, ~le heterosexual

heure f hour; **arriver à l'~** arrive on time; **de bonne ~** early; **à tout à l'~!** see you soon!; **quelle ~ est-il?** what time is it?; **il est six ~s** it's six (o'clock); **~ locale** local time; **~s d'ouverture** opening hours

heureusement luckily, fortunately; **heureux, -euse** happy; (chanceux) fortunate

'heurt m de deux véhicules collision; fig (friction) clash; **'heurter** collide with; fig offend; **se ~** collide (à with); fig (s'affronter) clash (**sur** over)

hiberner hibernate

'hibou m owl

'hideux, -euse hideous

hier yesterday

'hiérarchie f hierarchy

high-tech inv high tech, hi-tech

hilare grinning

hippique SP equestrian; **concours** m **~** horse show; **hippodrome** m race course

hirondelle f swallow

hirsute hairy

hispanique Hispanic

'hisser drapeau, voile hoist; (monter) lift, raise; **se ~** pull o.s. up

histoire f history; (récit, conte) story; **faire des ~s** make a fuss

historique 1 adj historic **2** m chronicle

hiver m winter

H.L.M. m ou f (= **habitation à loyer modéré**) low cost housing

'hocher: **~ la tête** approbation nod (one's head); désapprobation shake one's head

'hockey m sur gazon field hockey, Br hockey; sur glace hockey, Br ice hockey

'holding m holding company

'hold-up m holdup

'hollandais, ~e 1 adj Dutch **2** m langue Dutch; **'Hollandais, ~e** m/f Dutchman; Dutchwoman; **'Hollande: la ~** Holland

'homard m lobster

homéopathie f homeopathy
homicide m homicide; ~ **in-volontaire** manslaughter; ~ **volontaire** murder
hommage m homage; *rendre* ~ *à* pay homage to
homme m man; ~ *d'affaires* businessman; ~ *d'État* statesman
homologue m counterpart, opposite number; homologuer *record* ratify; *tarif* authorize
homophobe homophobic
homosexuel, ~le m/f & adj homosexual
'Hongrie f: *la* ~ Hungary; 'hongrois, ~e 1 *adj* Hungarian 2 m *langue* Hungarian; Hongrois, ~e m/f Hungarian
honnête honest; (*convenable*) decent; (*passable*) reasonable; honnêteté honesty
honneur m honor, *Br* honour; *en l'~ de* in honor of; *faire~à qc* honor sth; honorable honorable, *Br* honourable; honoraire 1 *adj* honorary 2 *~s mpl* fees; *honorer* honor, *Br* honour; honorifique honorific
'honte f shame; *avoir~ de* be ashamed of; 'honteux, -euse (*déshonorant*) shameful; (*déconfit*) ashamed
'hooligan m hooligan
hôpital m hospital; *à l'~* in the hospital, *Br* in hospital
'hoquet m hiccup; *avoir le* ~ have (the) hiccups
horaire 1 *adj* hourly 2 m *emploi du temps* timetable, schedule; *des avions, trains etc* schedule, *Br* timetable
horizon m horizon
horizontal horizontal
horloge f clock
'hormis but
hormonal hormonal; hormone f hormone
horodateur m *dans parking* pay and display machine
horoscope m horoscope
horreur f horror; (*monstruosité*) monstrosity; *avoir ~ de qc* detest sth; (*quelle*) ~*!* how awful!
horrible horrible
horrifiant horrifying
'hors: ~ *de* (*à l'extérieur de*) outside; ~ *de danger* out of danger; ~ *sujet* beside the point; *être ~ de soi* be beside o.s.
'hors-bord m outboard
'hors-d'œuvre m cuis appetizer, starter
'hors-jeu offside
horticulture f horticulture
hospice m rel hospice; (*asile*) home
hospitalier, -ère hospitable; méd hospital *atr*
hospitaliser hospitalize
hospitalité f hospitality
hostile hostile; hostilité f hostility
'hot-dog m hot dog
hôte m host; (*invité*) guest

hôtel *m* hotel; **~ de ville** town hall

hôtellerie *f*: **l'~** the hotel business

hôtesse *f* hostess; **~ de l'air** air hostess

'houblon *m* BOT hop

'houille *f* coal

'houle *f* MAR swell; 'houleux, -euse *fig* stormy

'housse *f* protective cover

'houx *m* BOT holly

'hublot *m* NAUT porthole; AVIAT window

'huer boo, jeer

huile *f* oil; **~ solaire** suntan oil; huiler oil

'huis *m*: **à ~ clos** behind closed doors; JUR in camera; huissier *m* JUR bailiff

'huit eight; **~ jours** a week; **demain en ~** a week tomorrow; 'huitaine *f*: **une ~ de une ~ (de jours)** a week; 'huitième eighth

huître *f* oyster

humain human; *traitement* humane; humaniser humanize; humanitaire humanitarian; humanité *f* humanity

humble humble

humecter moisten

'humer breathe in

humeur *f* mood; (*tempérament*) temperament; **être de bonne/mauvaise ~** be in a good/bad mood

humide damp; (*chaud et ~*)

humid; humidifier moisten; *atmosphère* humidify; humidité *f* dampness; humidity

humiliation *f* humiliation; humiliant humiliating; humilier humiliate

humour *m* humor, *Br* humour; **avoir de l'~** have a (good) sense of humor

'huppé exclusive

'hurlement *m d'un loup* howl; *d'une personne* scream; 'hurler *d'un loup* howl; *d'une personne* scream; **~ de rire** roar with laughter

hydratant *cosmétique* moisturizing

hydraulique hydraulic

hydroélectrique hydroelectric

hydrogène *m* CHIM hydrogen

hydroglisseur *m* jetfoil

hygiène *f* hygiene; **avoir une bonne ~ de vie** have a healthy lifestyle; hygiénique hygienic; **papier ~** toilet paper; **serviette ~** sanitary napkin, *Br* sanitary towel

hymne *m* hymn; **~ national** national anthem

hyperactif, -ive hyperactive

hypersensible hypersensitive

hypertension *f* MÉD high blood pressure

hypertexte: **lien** *m* **~** hypertext link

hypnotiser hypnotize

hypocrisie *f* hypocrisy; hypocrite **1** *adj* hypocritical **2** *m/f* hypocrite

hypothèque *f* COMM mortgage

hypothèse *f* hypothesis; **hypothétique** hypothetical

hystérie *f* hysteria; **hystérique** hysterical

I

ici here; **jusqu'~** to here; (*jusqu'à maintenant*) so far; **par ~** this way; (*dans le coin*) around about here; **d'~ là** by then, by that time

icône *f* icon

idéal *m & adj* ideal; **idéaliser** idealize; **idéalisme** *m* idealism; **idéaliste 1** *adj* idealistic **2** *m/f* idealist

idée *f* idea; (*opinion*) view; **avoir dans l'~ de faire qch** be thinking of doing sth; **tu te fais des ~s** (*tu te trompes*) you're imagining things; **~ fixe** obsession

identifier identify (**avec, à** with); **s'~ avec** ou **à** identify with

identique identical (**à** to)

identité *f* identity; **pièce** *f* **d'~** identity, ID

idéologie *f* ideology

idiomatique idiomatic

idiot, ~e 1 *adj* idiotic **2** *m/f* idiot; **idiotie** *f* idiocy; **dire des ~s** talk nonsense

idole *f* idol

idylle *f* romance

ignare *péj* **1** *adj* ignorant **2** *m/f* ignoramus

ignoble vile

ignorance *f* ignorance; **ignorant** ignorant; **ignorer** not know; *personne, talent* ignore

il he; *chose* it; *impersonnel* it; **~ va pleuvoir** it is ou it's going to rain

île *f* island; **les ~s britanniques** the British Isles

illégal illegal

illégitime *enfant* illegitimate

illettré illiterate

illicite illicit

illimité unlimited

illisible illegible; *mauvaise littérature* unreadable

illogique illogical

illuminer light up, illuminate; *par projecteur* floodlight

illusion *f* illusion; **se faire des ~s** delude o.s.; **illusoire** illusory

illustration *f* illustration; illustrer illustrate; **s'~** distinguish o.s. (**par** by)

îlot *m* (small) island; *de maisons* block

ils *mpl* they

image *f* picture; *dans un miroir* reflection, image; (*ressemblance*) image

imaginaire imaginary; imagination *f* imagination; imaginer imagine; (*inventer*) devise; **s'~ que** imagine that

imbattable unbeatable

imbécile **1** *adj* idiotic **2** *m/f* idiot, imbecile

imbiber soak (**de** with)

imbu: **~ de** *fig* full of

imitation *f* imitation; THÉÂT impersonation; imiter imitate; THÉÂT impersonate

immaculé immaculate

immangeable inedible

immatriculation *f* registration; **plaque** *f* **d'~** AUTO license plate, *Br* number plate; immatriculer register

immature immature

immédiat **1** *adj* immediate **2** *m*: **dans l'~** for the moment; immédiatement immediately

immense immense

immerger immerse; **s'~ d'un** *sous-marin* submerge

immeuble *m* building

immigrant, **~e** *m/f* immigrant; immigration *f* immigration; immigrer immigrate

imminent imminent

immiscer: **s'~ dans qc** interfere in sth

immobile immobile

immobilier, **~ère 1** *adj*: **biens** *mpl* **~s** real estate **2** *m* property

immoblliser immobilize; *train*, *circulation* bring to a standstill; *capital* tie up; **s'~**

(*s'arrêter*) come to a standstill

immonde foul

immoral immoral; immoralité *f* immorality

immortaliser immortalize; immortalité *f* immortality; immortel, **~le** immortal

immuniser immunize; **immunisé contre** *fig* immune to; immunité *f* JUR, MÉD immunity

impact *m* impact

impair **1** *adj* odd **2** *m* blunder

impardonnable unforgiveable

imparfait imperfect

impartial impartial

impasse *f* dead end; *fig* deadlock, impasse

impassible impassive

impatience *f* impatience; impatient impatient; impatienter: **s'~** get impatient

impayé unpaid

impeccable impeccable

impénétrable impenetrable

impératif, **-ive 1** *adj* imperative **2** *m* (*exigence*) requirement; GRAM imperative

impératrice *f* empress

imperceptible inperceptible

imperfection *f* imperfection

impérieux, **-euse** *personne* imperious; *besoin* urgent

impérissable immortal; *souvenir* unforgettable

imperméabiliser waterproof; imperméable **1** *adj* *tissu* waterproof **2** *m* raincoat

impersonnel, ~le impersonal

impertinence f impertinence; **impertinent** impertinent

imperturbable imperturbable

impétueux, -euse impetuous

impitoyable pitiless

implacable implacable

implanter *fig* introduce; *usine* set up; **s'~** become established; *d'une industrie* set up

implicite implicit

impliquer *personne* implicate; *(entraîner)* mean, involve; *(supposer)* imply

implorer *aide* beg for; **~ qn de faire qch** implore *ou* beg s.o. to do sth

impoli rude, impolite

impopulaire unpopular

importance f importance; *d'une ville* size; *d'une somme, catastrophe* magnitude; **important 1** *adj* important; *ville, somme* large, sizeable **2** m: **l'~, c'est que ...** the important thing is that ...

importateur, -trice 1 *adj* importing **2** m importer; **importation** f import; **importer 1** *v/t* import; *mode, musique* introduce **2** *v/i* matter, be important (**à** to); **n'importe quand** any time; **n'importe quoi!** nonsense!

importun troublesome; **importuner** bother

imposable taxable

imposant imposing; **imposer** impose; *marchandise* tax; **s'~** *(être nécessaire)* be essential; *(se faire admettre)* gain recognition

impossible 1 *adj* impossible **2** m: **faire l'~ pour faire qch** do one's utmost to do sth

imposteur m imposter

impôt m tax; **déclaration** f **d'~s** tax return

impotent crippled

impraticable *projet* impractical; *rue* impassable

imprécis vague, imprecise

imprégner impregnate (**de** with); **imprégné de** *fig* full of

impression f impression; *imprimerie* printing; **impressionnant** impressive; *(troublant)* upsetting; **impressionner** impress; *(troubler)* upset; **impressionniste** m/f & *adj* impressionist

imprévisible unpredictable

imprévu 1 *adj* unexpected **2** m: **sauf ~** all being well

imprimante f INFORM printer; **~ laser** laser printer; **~ à jet d'encre** ink-jet (printer); **imprimé** m *(formulaire)* form; *tissu* print; *poste* **~s** printed matter; **imprimer** print; INFORM print out; *édition* publish

improbable unlikely, improbable

improductif, -ive unproductive

impropre *mot, outil* inappropriate; **~ à la consommation** unfit for human consumption

improviste: **à l'~** unexpectedly

imprudence *f* imprudence; **imprudent** imprudent

impudence *f* impudence; **impudent** impudent

impudique shameless

impuissance *f* powerlessness; **MÉD** impotence; **impuissant** powerless; **MÉD** impotent

impulsif, **-ive** impulsive; **impulsion** *f* impulse; **à l'économie** boost

impuni unpunished

impur *eau* dirty, polluted; *(impudique)* impure

imputer attribute (**à** to); **FIN** charge (**sur** to)

inabordable *prix* unaffordable

inacceptable unacceptable

inaccessible inaccessible; *personne* unapproachable; *objectif* unattainable

inachevé unfinished

inactif, **-ive** idle; *population* non-working; *remède, méthode* ineffective; *marché* slack

inadéquat inadequate; *méthode* unsuitable

inadmissible unacceptable

inadvertance *f*: **par ~** inadvertently

inanimé inanimate; *(mort)* lifeless; *(inconscient)* unconscious

inaperçu: **passer ~** pass unnoticed

inapproprié inappropriate

inapte: **~ à** unsuited to; **MÉD**, **MIL** unfit for

inattendu unexpected

inattention *f* inattentiveness; **erreur d'~** careless mistake

inaudible inaudible

inaugurer inaugurate

inavouable shameful

incapable incapable (**de faire** of doing)

incapacité *f* *(inaptitude)* incompetence; *de faire qch* inability

incarcérer imprison

incassable unbreakable

incendiaire incendiary; *discours* inflammatory; **incendie** *m* fire; **~ criminel** arson; **incendier** set fire to

incertain uncertain; *temps* unsettled; *(hésitant)* indecisive; **incertitude** *f* uncertainty

incessamment any minute now

inchangé unchanged

incident *m* incident; **~ de parcours** mishap

incinérer incinerate; *cadavre* cremate

incisif, **-ive** incisive; **incision** *f* incision

inciter encourage (**à faire qch** to do sth); *péj* egg on, incite

inclinable tilting; **inclinaison** *f* slope

inclination *f fig* inclination (*pour* for); ~ **de tête** (*salut*) nod; **incliner** tilt; **s'~** bend; *pour saluer* bow; **s'~ devant qc** (*céder*) yield to sth; **s'~ devant qn** *aussi fig* bow to s.o.

inclure include; *dans une lettre* enclose; *inclus*: **ci-inclus** enclosed; *jusqu'au 30 juin* ~ to 30th June inclusive

incohérence *f de comportement* inconsistency; *de discours* incoherence

incolore colorless, *Br* colourless

incomber: **il vous incombe de le lui dire** it is your duty to tell him

incommoder bother

incomparable incomparable

incompatibilité *f* incompatibility; **incompatible** incompatible

incompétence *f* incompetence; **incompétent** incompetent

incomplet, -ète incomplete

incompréhensible incomprehensible; **incompréhension** *f* lack of understanding

incompris misunderstood (**de** by)

inconcevable inconceivable

inconditionnel, ~le 1 *adj* unconditional **2** *m/f* fan, fanatic

inconfortable uncomfortable

ble

inconnu, ~e 1 *adj* (*ignoré*) unknown; (*étranger*) strange **2** *m/f* stranger

inconscient unconscious; (*irréfléchi*) irresponsible

inconsidéré rash, thoughtless

inconsistant inconsistent; *fig: raisonnement* flimsy

inconsolable inconsolable

incontestable indisputable

incontesté outright

incontournable: **être** ~ be a must

inconvénient *m* disadvantage *m*; **si vous n'y voyez aucun** ~ if you have no objection

incorporer incorporate (**à** with, into); MIL draft

incorrect wrong, incorrect; *tenue, langage* improper

incorrigible incorrigible

incrédule (*sceptique*) incredulous; **incrédulité** *f* incredulity

incriminer *personne* blame; JUR accuse; *paroles, actions* condemn

incroyable incredible, unbelievable

inculpé, ~e *m/f*: **l'~** the accused, the defendant; **inculper** JUR charge, indict (**de, pour** with)

inculquer: ~ **qc à qn** instill *ou Br* instil sth into s.o.

inculte *terre* waste *atr*, uncultivated; (*ignorant*) uneducated

incurable incurable

incursion f MIL raid, incursion; *fig*: *dans la politique etc* venture (**dans** into)

Inde f: *l'~* India

indécent indecent; (*incorrect*) inappropriate, improper

indécis undecided; *personne, caractère* indecisive

indéfini indefinite; (*imprécis*) undefined

indéfinissable indefinable

indélicat *personne, action* tactless

indemne unhurt; **indemniser** compensate (**de** for); **indemnité** f (*dédommagement*) compensation; (*allocation*) allowance

indéniable undeniable

indépendance f independence; **indépendant** independent (**de** of); *travailleur* freelance; **indépendantiste** (pro-)independence *atr*

indescriptible indescribable

indésirable undesirable

indéterminé unspecified

index m index; *doigt* index finger

indicateur, -trice m (*espion*) informer; TECH gauge, indicator

indicatif m TÉL code

indication f indication; (*information*) piece of information; **~s** instructions

indice m (*signe*) sign, indica-

tion; JUR clue

indien, ~ne Indian; *d'Amérique aussi* native American; **Indien** m/f Indian; *d'Amérique aussi* native American

indifférence f indifference; **indifférent** indifferent

indigène *adj & m/f* native

indigeste indigestible; **indigestion** f MÉD indigestion

indignation f indignation

indigne unworthy; *parents* unfit

indigner make indignant; **s'~ de qc/contre qn** be indignant about sth/with s.o.

indiqué appropriate; *ce n'est pas ~* it's not advisable; **indiquer** indicate, show; *d'une pendule* show; (*recommander*) recommend

indirect indirect

indiscipline f indiscipline; **indiscipliné** undisciplined; *cheveux* unmanageable

indiscret, -ète indiscreet; **indiscrétion** f indiscretion

indispensable indispensable

indistinct indistinct

individu m individual; **individualisme** m individualism; **individuel, ~le** individual; *secrétaire* private, personal; *liberté* personal; *chambre* single; *maison* detached

indivisible indivisible

indolent lazy, indolent

indolore painless

indomptable *fig* indomitable

indu: *à une heure ~e* at some

ungodly hour
indubitable indisputable
induire: ~ qn en erreur mislead s.o.
indulgence f indulgence;
d'un juge leniency; indulgent indulgent; juge lenient
industrialisé industrialized;
industrialiser industrialize;
industrie f industry; industriel, ~le 1 adj industrial 2 m
industrialist
inébranlable solid (as a rock)
inédit (pas édité) unpub-
lished; (nouveau) original,
unique
inégal unequal; surface uneven; rythme irregular; inégalité f inequality; d'une
surface unevenness
inepte inept; ineptie f inepti-
tude; ~s nonsense
inépuisable inexhaustible
inerte corps lifeless, inert;
PHYS inert; inertie f inertia
inespéré unexpected, un-
hoped-for
inestimable tableau priceless; aide invaluable
inévitable inevitable; accident unavoidable
inexact inaccurate
inexcusable inexcusable, unforgiveable
inexistant non-existent
inexplicable inexplicable
inexprimable inexpressible
infaillible infallible
infantile mortalité infant atr;
péj infantile; maladie chil-

dren's
infarctus m MÉD: ~ du myocarde coronary (thrombo-
sis)
infatigable tireless, indefati-
gable
infect disgusting; temps foul;
infecter infect; air, eau pollute; s'~ become infected;
infectieux, -euse infectious;
infection f MÉD infection
inférieur, ~e 1 adj lower; qualité inferior 2 m/f inferior;
infériorité f inferiority
infernal infernal
infidèle unfaithful; REL pagan
atr; infidélité f infidelity
infiltrer: s'~ dans get into; fig
infiltrate
infime tiny, infinitesimal
infini 1 adj infinite 2 m infinity
infirme 1 adj disabled 2 m/f
disabled person; infirmerie
f infirmary; ÉDU sickbay; infirmier, -ère m/f nurse; infirmité f disability
inflammation f MÉD inflammation
inflation f inflation
inflexible inflexible
infliger peine inflict (à on);
défaite impose
influence f influence; influencer influence; influent
influential
influer: ~ sur affect
info f F RAD, TV news item; les
~s the news sg
informaticien, ~ne m/f com-

puter scientist

information f information; JUR inquiry; **une ~** a piece of information; **les ~s** RAD, TV the news sg; **traitement** *m* **de l'~** data processing

informatique 1 *adj* computer *atr* **2** f information technology, IT; **informatiser** computerize

informe shapeless

informer inform; **s'~** find out (**de qc auprès de qn** about sth from s.o.)

infraction f infringement (**à** of)

infranchissable impossible to cross; *obstacle* insurmountable

infrarouge infrared

infrastructure f infrastructure

infroissable crease-resistant

infructueux, -euse unsuccessful

infusion f herb tea

ingénierie f engineering; **ingénieur** *m* engineer

ingéniosité f ingeniousness

ingrat ungrateful; *tâche* thankless; **ingratitude** f ingratitude

ingrédient *m* ingredient

ingurgiter gulp down

inhabitable uninhabitable; **inhabité** uninhabited

inhalateur *m* MÉD inhaler; **inhaler** inhale

inhérent inherent (**à** in)

inhibé inhibited; **inhibition** f

PSYCH inhibition

inhospitalier, -ère inhospitable

inhumain inhuman

ininflammable non-flammable

ininterrompu uninterrupted; *pluie, musique* non-stop

initial, ~e 1 *adj* initial **2** f initial (letter)

initiation f initiation; **~ à** *fig* introduction to

inimitié f enmity

initiative f initiative

initié, ~e *m/f* insider; **initier** initiate (**à** in); *fig* introduce (**à** to)

injecté: ~ (de sang) blood-shot; **injecter** inject; **injection** f injection

injoignable unreachable, uncontactable

injure f insult; **~s** abuse; **injurier** insult, abuse

injuste unfair, unjust; **injustice** f injustice; **d'une décision** *aussi* unfairness

inlassable tireless

inné innate

innocence f innocence; **innocent** innocent; **innocenter** clear

innombrable countless; *auditoire, foule* vast

innovant innovative; **innovation** f innovation

inoccupé *personne* idle; *maison* unoccupied

inodore odorless, *Br* odourless

inoffensif, **-ive** harmless; *humour* inoffensive

inondation *f* flood; **inonder** flood; ~ *de fig* inundate with

inopiné unexpected

inopportun ill-timed

inorganique inorganic

inoubliable unforgettable

inouï unheard-of

inoxydable stainless

inquiet, **-ète** anxious, worried (*de* about); **inquiéter** worry; **s'~** worry (*de* about); **inquiétude** *f* anxiety

insaisissable elusive; *différence* imperceptible

insatiable insatiable

insatisfaisant unsatisfactory; **insatisfait** unsatisfied; *mécontent* dissatisfied

inscription *f* inscription; (*immatriculation*) registration; **inscrire** (*noter*) write down, note; *dans registre* enter; *à examen* register; (*graver*) inscribe; **s'~** put one's name down; *à l'université* register; *à un cours* enroll, *Br* enrol (*à* for)

insecte *m* insect; **insecticide** *m* insecticide

insécurité *f* insecurity; POL security problem

insensé mad, insane

insensibiliser numb; **insensible** ANAT numb; *personne* insensitive (*à* to)

insérer insert; *annonce* put; **insertion** *f* insertion

insigne *m* (*emblème*) insig-

nia; (*badge*) badge

insignifiant insignificant

insinuer insinuate; **s'~ dans** worm one's way into

insipide insipid

insistance *f* insistence; **insistant** insistent; **insister** insist; F (*persévérer*) persevere; ~ **pour faire qch** insist on doing sth; ~ **sur qc** (*souligner*) stress sth

insolation *f* sunstroke

insolence *f* insolence; **insolent** insolent

insolite unusual

insoluble insolvent

insomnie *f* insomnia

insonoriser soundproof

insouciant carefree

insoumis rebellious

insoutenable (*insupportable*) unbearable; *argument* untenable

inspecter inspect; **inspecteur**, **-trice** *m/f* inspector; **inspection** *f* inspection

inspiration *f fig* inspiration; **inspirer 1** *v/i* breathe in, inhale **2** *v/t* inspire; **s'~ de** be inspired by

installation *f* installation; ~ **électrique** wiring; **~s** facilities; **installer** install; *appartement*: fit out; (*loger*, *placer*) put; **s'~** (*s'établir*) settle down; *à la campagne etc* settle; *d'un médecin, dentiste* set up

instant *m* instant, moment; **à l'~** just this minute; **dans un**

~ in a minute; **pour l'~** for the moment; instantané **1** *adj* immediate; *café* instant; *mort* instantaneous **2** *m* PHOT snap(shot)

instaurer establish

instinct *m* instinct; **instinctif, -ive** instinctive

instituer introduce; **institut** *m* institute; ~ **de beauté** beauty salon; **instituteur, -trice** *m/f* (primary) school teacher; **institution** *f* institution

instructeur *m* MIL instructor; **instructif, -ive** instructive; **instruction** *f* (*enseignement, culture*) education; MIL training; JUR preliminary investigation; INFORM instruction; **~s** instructions; **instruire** ÉDU educate, teach; MIL train; JUR investigate; **instruit** (well-)educated

instrument *m* instrument

insu *m*: **à l'~ de** unbeknownst to

insubordination *f* insubordination

insuffisance *f* deficiency; ~ **respiratoire** respiratory problem; **insuffisant** *quantité* insufficient; *qualité* inadequate

insulaire 1 *adj* island *atr* **2** *m/f* islander

insuline *f* insulin

insulte *f* insult; **insulter** insult

insupportable unbearable

insurger: **s'~ contre** rise up against

insurrection *f* insurrection

intact intact

intégral full, complete; *texte* unabridged

intégration *f* (*assimilation*) integration

intègre of integrity

intégrer (*assimiler*) integrate; (*incorporer*) incorporate; **intégriste** *m/f* & *adj* fundamentalist

intégrité *f* (*honnêteté*) integrity

intellectuel, ~le *m/f* & *adj* intellectual

intelligence *f* intelligence; **intelligent** intelligent

intempéries *fpl* bad weather

intempestif, -ive untimely

intenable *situation*, *froid* unbearable

intense intense; **intensif, -ive** intensive; **intensification** *f* intensification; *d'un conflit* escalation; **intensifier** intensify; **s'~** intensify; *d'un conflit* escalate; **intensité** *f* intensity

intenter: ~ **un procès contre** start proceedings against

intention *f* intention; **avoir l'~ de faire qch** intend to do sth; **à l'~ de** for; **intentionné**: **bien ~** well-meaning; **mal ~** ill-intentioned; **intentionnel, ~le** intentional

interactif, -ive interactive

intercéder: ~ **pour qn** intercede for s.o.

intercepter intercept; *soleil* shut out

interchangeable interchangeable

interdiction f ban; interdire ban; ~ **à qn de faire qc** forbid s.o. to do sth; interdit forbidden; (*très étonné*) taken aback

intéressant interesting; (*avide*) selfish; *prix* good; *situation* well-paid; intéréssé interested; (*concerné*) concerned; intéresser interest; (*concerner*) concern; **s'~ à** be interested in; intérêt m interest; (*égoïsme*) self-interest; **~s** COMM interest

interface f interface

intérieur 1 *adj poche* inside; *porte, vie* inner; *politique, vol* domestic; *mer* inland 2 m inside; *d'une auto etc* interior; **à l'~ (de)** inside

intérim m interim; *travail* temporary work; intérimaire 1 *adj travail* temporary 2 m/f temp

interlocuteur, -trice m/f: **mon/son ~** the person I/ she was talking to

intermédiaire 1 *adj* intermediate 2 m/f intermediary; COMM middleman

interminable interminable

intermittence f: **par ~** intermittently

international, ~e m/f & adj international

interne 1 *adj* internal; *oreille* inner; *d'une société* in-house 2 m/f *élève* boarder; *médecin* intern, Br houseman; interner intern

Internet m Internet; **sur ~** on the Internet

interpeller call out to; *de la police*, POL question

interphone m intercom; *d'un immeuble* entry phone

interposer interpose; **s'~** (*intervenir*) intervene

interprète m/f interpreter; (*porte-parole*) spokesperson; interpréter interpret; *rôle*, MUS play

interrogation f question; *d'un suspect* questioning, interrogation; interrogatoire m *par police* questioning; *par juge* cross-examination; interroger question; *de la police* question, interrogate; *d'un juge* cross-examine

interrompre interrupt; **s'~** break off

interrupteur m switch; interruption f interruption; **sans ~** without stopping

intersection f intersection

intervalle m space, gap; *de temps* interval

intervenir intervene; *d'une rencontre* take place; intervention f intervention; MÉD operation; (*discours*) speech

interview f interview; interviewer interview

intestin 1 *adj* internal 2 m intestin

intime 1 *adj* intimate; *ami* close; *pièce* cozy, *Br* cosy; *vie* private **2** *m/f* close friend

intimider intimidate

intimité *f* intimacy; *vie privée* privacy

intituler call; **s'~** be called

intolérable intolerable; **intolérance** *f* intolerance; **intolérant** intolerant

intoxication *f* food poisoning; **~ alimentaire** food poisoning; **intoxiquer** poison; *fig* brainwash

intransigeant intransigent

intrépide intrepid

intrigue *f* plot; **~s** scheming, plotting; **intriguer 1** *v/i* scheme, plot **2** *v/t* intrigue

introduction *f* introduction; **introduire** introduce; *visiteur* show in; *(engager)* insert; **s'~ dans** gain entry to

introuvable impossible to find

introverti, **~e** *m/f* introvert

intrus, **~e** *m/f* intruder

intuitif, **-ive** intuitive; **intuition** *f* intuition; *(pressentiment)* premonition

inusable hard-wearing

inutile *qui ne sert pas* useless; *(superflu)* pointless, unnecessary; **inutilisable** unuseable

invalide 1 *adj (infirme)* disabled **2** *m/f* disabled person; **invalider** JUR, POL invalidate; **invalidité** *f* disability

invariable invariable

invasion *f* invasion

invendable unsellable

inventaire *m* inventory; COMM *opération* stocktaking

inventer invent; *histoire* make up; **inventeur**, **-trice** *m/f* inventor; **invention** *f* invention

inverse 1 *adj* MATH inverse; *sens* opposite; **dans l'ordre ~** in reverse order **2** *m* opposite, reverse; **inverser** invert; *rôles* reverse

investigation *f* investigation

investir FIN invest; *(cerner)* surround; **investissement** *m* FIN investment

invétéré inveterate

investisseur, **-euse** *m* investor

invincible invincible; *obstacle* insuperable

invisible invisible

invitation *f* invitation; **invité**, **~e** *m/f* guest; **inviter** invite; **~ qn à faire qch** urge s.o. to do sth

inviable unbearable

involontaire unintentional; *témoin* unwilling; *mouvement* involuntary

invoquer *Dieu* call on, invoke; *aide* call on; *texte, loi* refer to; *solution* put forward

invraisemblable unlikely, improbable

Iran *m*: **l'~** Iran; **iranien**, **~ne** Iranian; **Iranien**, **~ne** *m/f* Iranian

Iraq *m:* *l'~* Iraq; **iraquien**, **~ne** Iraqi; **Iraquien**; **~ne** *m/f* Iraqi

irascible irascible

irlandais, **~e 1** *adj* Irish **2** *m langue* Irish (Gaelic); **Irlandais**, **~e** *m/f* Irishman; Irishwoman; **Irlande** *f:* *l'~* Ireland

ironie *f* irony; **ironiser** be ironic

irraisonné irrational

irrationnel, **~le** irrational

irréalisable *projet* impracticable; *rêve* unrealizable

irréaliste unrealistic

irréconciliable irreconcilable

irrécupérable beyond repair; *personne* beyond redemption; *données* irretrievable

irréductible indomitable; *ennemi* implacable

irréel, **~le** unreal

irréfléchi thoughtless, reckless

irréfutable irrefutable

irrégulier, **-ère** irregular; *surface*, *terrain* uneven; *étudiant*, *sportif* erratic

irrémédiable *maladie* incurable; *erreur* irreparable

irremplaçable irreplaceable

irréparable *faute*, *perte* irreparable; *vélo* beyond repair

irréprochable irreproachable

irrésistible irresistible

irrésolu *personne* indecisive; *problème* unresolved

irrespirable unbreathable

irresponsable irresponsible

irrigation *f* AGR irrigation

irritable irritable; **irritation** *f* irritation; **irriter** irritate; **s'~** get irritated

islam, **Islam** *m* REL Islam; **islamique** Islamic; **islamiste** Islamic fundamentalist

islandais, **~e 1** *adj* Icelandic **2** *m langue* Icelandic; **Islandais**, **~e** *m/f* Icelander; **Islande** *f:* *l'~* Iceland

isolation *f* insulation; *contre le bruit* soundproofing; **isolé** isolated; TECH insulated; **isolement** *m* isolation; **isoler** isolate; *prisonnier* place in solitary confinement; ÉL insulate

Israël *m* Israel; **israélien**, **~ne** Israeli; **Israélien**, **~ne** *m/f* Israeli

issu: **être ~ de** *parenté* come from; *résultat* stem from

issue *f* way out (*aussi fig*), exit; (*fin*) outcome; **à l'~ de** at the end of

Italie *f:* *l'~* Italy; **italien**, **~ne 1** *adj* Italian **2** *m langue* Italian; **Italien**, **~ne** *m/f* Italian

itinéraire *m* itinerary

IVG *f* (= **interruption volontaire de grossesse**) termination, abortion

ivoire *m* ivory

ivre drunk; **~ de** *joie*, *colère* wild with; **ivresse** *f* drunkenness; **ivrogne** *m/f* drunk

J

jacasser chatter
jacinthe *f* BOT hyacinth
jade *m* jade
jaillir shoot out (*de* from)
jalousie *f* jealousy; (*store*) Venetian blind; **jaloux, -ouse** jealous
jamais ◇ *positif* ever; **à ~** for ever, for good; ◇ *négatif* never; **ne ... ~** never; **je ne lui ai ~ parlé** I've never spoken to him
jambe *f* leg
jambon *m* ham
jante *f* rim
janvier *m* January
Japon: **le ~** Japan; **japonais, ~e 1** *adj* Japanese **2** *m langue* Japanese; **Japonais, ~e** *m/f* Japanese
jappement *m* yap
jaquette *f d'un livre* dust jacket
jardin *m* garden; **~ botanique** botanical gardens *pl*; **~ public** park; **jardinage** *m* gardening; **jardiner** garden; **jardinier** *m* gardener; **jardinière** *f à fleurs* window box; **femme** gardener
jargon *m* jargon; *péj* (*charabia*) gibberish
jarret *m* back of the knee; CUIS shin
jaser gossip
jatte *f* bowl

jauge *f* gauge; **jauger** gauge
jaunâtre yellowish; **jaune 1** *adj* yellow **2** *m*: **~ d'œuf** egg yolk; **jaunir** go yellow; **jaunisse** *f* MÉD jaundice
jazz *m* jazz; **jazzman** *m* jazz musician
je I
jean *m* jeans *pl*; **veste** *f* **en ~** denim jacket
jeep *f* jeep
Jésus-Christ Jesus (Christ)
jet *m* (*lancer*) throw; (*jaillissement*) jet; *de sang* spurt; **~ d'eau** fountain
jetable disposable
jetée *f* MAR jetty
jeter throw; (*se défaire de*) throw away; **~ un coup d'œil à qch** glance at sth
jeton *m* token; *de jeu* chip
jeu *m* play (*aussi* TECH); *activité, en tennis* game; (*série, ensemble*) set; *de cartes* deck, *Br* pack; MUS playing; THÉÂT acting; **le ~** gambling; **être en ~** be at stake; **~ de mots** play on words
jeudi *m* Thursday
jeun: **à ~** on an empty stomach
jeune 1 *adj* young; **~s mariés** newly-weds *pl*; **un ~ a** young man; **les ~s** young people *pl*, the young *pl*
jeûne *m* fast; **jeûner** fast

jeunesse *f* youth; *caractère jeune* youthfulness

J.O. *mpl* (= *Jeux Olympiques*) Olympic Games

joaillerie *f magasin* jewelry store, *Br* jeweller's; *articles* jewelry, *Br* jewellery; **joaillier, -ère** *m/f* jeweler, *Br* jeweller

jogging *m* jogging; (*survêtement*) sweats *pl*, *Br* tracksuit; *faire du* ~ go jogging

joie *f* joy; *débordant de* ~ jubilant

joindre join; *efforts* combine; *à un courrier* enclose (*à* with); *personne* contact, get in touch with; *mains* clasp; *se* ~ *à qn pour faire qch* join s.o. in doing sth

joint *m* joint; *d'étanchéité* seal, gasket; *de robinet* washer

joli pretty

joncher strew (*de* with)

jonction *f* junction

jongler juggle; **jongleur** *m* juggler

joue *f* cheek

jouer 1 *v/t* play; *argent, réputation* gamble; THÉÂT *pièce* perform; *film* show; ~ *la comédie* put on an act **2** *v/i* play; *d'un acteur* act; *parier* gamble; ~ *au football* play football; ~ *d'un instrument* play an instrument; ~ *sur cheval etc* put money on

jouet *m* toy

joueur, -euse *m/f* player; *de*

jeux d'argent gambler; *être beau/mauvais* ~ be a good/bad loser

jouir have an orgasm, come; ~ *de qc* enjoy sth; (*posséder*) have sth; **jouissance** *f* enjoyment; JUR possession

jour *m* day; (*lumière*) daylight; (*ouverture*) opening; *au grand* ~ in broad daylight; *de nos* ~s these days; *du* ~ *au lendemain* overnight; *être à* ~ be up to date; *se faire* ~ *de problèmes* come to light; *deux ans* ~ *pour* ~ two years to the day; *il fait* ~ it's (getting) light; *au petit* ~ at first light

journal *m* (news)paper; *intime* diary; TV, *à la radio* news *sg*; **journalisme** *m* journalism; **journaliste** *m/f* journalist

journée *f* day

jovial jovial

joyeux, -euse joyful; ~ *Noël!* Merry Christmas!

jubilation *f* jubilation; **jubiler** be jubilant; *péj* gloat

jucher perch

judiciaire legal

judicieux, -euse sensible, judicious

judo *m* judo

juge *m* judge; ~ *d'instruction* examining magistrate; ~ *de touche* SP linesman; **jugement** *m* judg(e)ment; *en matière criminelle* sentence; *porter un* ~ *sur* pass judg(e)-

ment on; **juger 1** *v/t* JUR try;
(*évaluer*) judge; **~ qc/qn intéressant** consider sth/s.o.
interesting; **~ que** think that;
~ de qn/qc judge s.o./sth **2**
v/i judge

juif, -ive *adj* Jewish; **Juif, -ive**
m/f Jew

juillet *m* July

juin *m* June

jumeau, jumelle *m/f & adj*
twin; **jumeler** *villes* twin; **jumelles** *fpl* binoculars

jument *f* mare

jungle *f* jungle

jupe *f* skirt

juré *m* JUR juror; **jurer** swear
(**de qch** to sth)

juridiction *f* jurisdiction

juridique legal

juron *m* curse

jury *m* JUR jury; *d'un concours* panel, judges *pl*; ÉDU
board of examiners

jus *m* juice

jusque 1 *prép*: **jusqu'à** *lieu* as
far as, up to; *temps* until;
jusqu'où vous allez? how
far are you going? **2** *adv*
even, including **3** *conj*: **jusqu'à ce qu'il s'endorme**
(*subj*) until he falls asleep

juste 1 *adj* fair, just; *salaire,
récompense* fair; (*précis*)
right, correct; *vêtement* tight
2 *adv* just; *viser, tirer* accurately; **chanter ~** sing in
tune; **justesse** *f* accuracy;
de ~ only just; **justice** *f* fairness, justice; JUR justice; **la ~**
the law; **faire ~ à qn** do s.o.
justice

justification *f* justification;
justifier justify; **~ de qc**
prove sth

juteux, -euse juicy

juvénile youthful; **délinquance ~** juvenile delinquency

juxtaposer juxtapose

K

kaki khaki

kamikaze *m/f* suicide bomber

kangourou *m* kangaroo

kébab *m* kabob, *Br* kebab

kermesse *f* fair

kérosène *m* kerosene

ketchup *m* ketchup

kg (= **kilogramme**) kg (= kilogram)

kidnapping *m* kidnapping;
kidnapper kidnap

kilo(gramme) *m* kilo(gram);
kilométrage *m* mileage; **kilomètre** *m* kilometer, *Br* kilometre; **kilo-octet** *m* kilobyte, k

kinésithérapeute *m/f* physiotherapist

kiosque *m* pavilion; COMM
kiosk; **~ à journaux** newsstand

kit *m*: **en ~** kit

klaxon *m* AUTO horn; **klaxon- ner** sound one's horn, hoot km (= *kilomètre*) km (= kilo- meter)

knock-out *m* knockout K-O *m* (= *knock-out*) KO Ko *m* (= *kilo-octet m*) k (= kil- obyte)

L

la¹ → *le*
la² *pron personnel* her; *chose* it
là here; *dans un autre lieu qu'ici* there; *causal* hence; *par~* that way; *là-bas* (over) there
laboratoire *m* laboratory, lab
laborieux, -euse laborious; *personne* hardworking
labourer plow, Br plough
labyrinthe *m* labyrinth, maze
lac *m* lake
lacer tie
lacérer lacerate
lacet *m de chaussures* lace; *de la route* sharp turn
lâche **1** *adj* loose; *personne* cowardly **2** *m* coward
lâcher **1** *v/t* let go of; (*laisser tomber*) drop; (*libérer*) re- lease; *ceinture* loosen; *juron, vérité* let out; SP leave be- hind **2** *v/i de freins* fail; *d'une corde* break
lâcheté *f* cowardice
lacrymogène *gaz* tear *atr*; *grenade* tear-gas *atr*
lacune *f* gap
là-dedans inside; là-des- sous underneath; *derrière* behind it; là-dessus on it,

on top; *à ce moment* at that instant; *sur ce point* about it; là-haut up there
laid ugly; laideur *f* ugliness; (*bassesse*) meanness
lainage *m étoffe* woolen *ou* Br woollen fabric; *vêtement* woolen, Br woollen; laine *f* wool; laineux, -euse fleecy
laïque **1** *adj* REL secular; (*sans confession*) State *atr* **2** *m/f* lay person
laisse *f* leash
laisser leave; (*permettre*) let; *se ~ aller* let o.s. go
laisser-aller *m* casualness
laissez-passer *m* pass
lait *m* milk; laitage *m* dairy product; laitier, -ère dairy *atr*
laiton *m* brass
laitue *f* BOT lettuce
lambin, ~e *m/f* F slowpoke F, Br slowcoach F
lambris *m* paneling, Br panel- ling
lame *f* blade; (*plaque*) strip; (*vague*) wave
lamentable deplorable; la- menter: *se ~* complain
lampadaire *m* floor lamp; *dans la rue* street light

lampe *f* lamp; **~ de poche** flashlight, *Br* torch

lancé established; **lancement** *m* launch; **lancer** throw; *avec force* hurl; *injure* shout, hurl (**à** at); *cri* give; *fusée*, COMM launch; INFORM *programme* run; *moteur* start; **se ~ sur** *marché* enter; *piste de danse* step out onto; **se ~ dans** *des activités* take up; *des explications* launch into; *des discussions* get involved in

langage *m* language

langouste *f* spiny lobster

langue *f* tongue; LING language; **mauvaise ~** gossip; **~ maternelle** mother tongue

languette *f d'une chaussure* tongue

languir languish; *d'une conversation* flag

lanière *f* strap

laper lap up

lapider stone

lapin *m* rabbit

laps *m:* **~ de temps** period of time

laque *f* lacquer

larcin *m* petty theft

lard *m* bacon

lardon *m* lardon, diced bacon

large 1 *adj* wide; *épaules, hanches* broad; *mesure, rôle* large; (*généreux*) generous **2** *adv:* **voir ~** think big **3** *m* MAR open sea; **prendre le ~** *fig* take off; **largesse** *f* generosity; **largeur** *f* width; **~ d'es-**

prit broad-mindedness

larme *f* tear; **une ~ de** a drop of; **larmoyer** *des yeux* water; (*se plaindre*) complain

laryngite *f* laryngitis

las, ~se weary

laser *m* laser

lasser weary, tire; **se ~ de** tire *ou* weary of

latent latent

latéral lateral, side *atr*

latitude *f* latitude

latte *f* lath; *de plancher* board

lauréat, ~e *m/f* prizewinner

laurier *m* laurel; **feuille f de ~** CUIS bayleaf

lavabo *m* (wash)basin; **~s** toilets

lavage *m* washing

lavande *f* lavender

laver wash; *tâche* wash away; **laverie** *f:* **~ automatique** laundromat, *Br* laundrette; **lavette** *f* dishcloth; *fig péj* spineless individual

lave-vaisselle *m* dishwasher

laxatif, -ive *adj & m* laxative

laxisme *m* laxness

le *complément d'objet direct* him; *chose* it; **oui, je ~ sais** yes, I know

le, f la, pl les *article défini* the; **le garçon/les garçons** the boy/the boys; **je me suis cassé la jambe** I broke my leg; **j'aime le vin** I like wine; **les dinosaures avaient ...** dinosaurs had ...; **le premier mai** May first, *Br* the first of May; **ouvert le samedi**

open (on) Saturdays; *10 euros les 5* 10 euros for 5; *tu connais la France?* do you know France; *le printemps est là* spring is here; *je ne parle pas l'italien* I don't speak Italian

leader *m* POL leader

lécher lick

leçon *f* lesson

lecteur, -trice *m/f* reader; *à l'université* foreign language assistant **2** *m* INFORM drive; *~ de CDs* CD player; **lecture** *f* reading

ledit, ladite the said

légal legal; **légaliser** *signature* authenticate; *(rendre légal)* legalize; **légalité** *f* legality

légende *f* legend; *sous image* caption; *d'une carte* key

léger, -ère light; *erreur, retard* slight; *mœurs* loose; *(frivole, irréfléchi)* thoughtless; *à la légère* lightly; **légèrement** lightly; *(un peu)* slightly; **légèreté** *f* lightness; *(frivolité, irréflexion)* thoughtlessness

légion *f* legion; *~ étrangère* Foreign Legion; **légionnaire** *m* legionnaire

législation *f* legislation

légitime legitimate

legs *m* legacy

léguer bequeath

légume *m* vegetable

lendemain *m*: *le ~* the next *ou* following day; *le ~ de son*

élection the day after he was elected

lent slow; **lentement** slowly; **lenteur** *f* slowness

lentille *f* TECH lens; *légume sec* lentil

léopard *m* leopard

lequel, laquelle (*pl* lesquels, lesquelles) *interrogatif* which (one); *relatif, avec personne* who; *avec chose* which

les¹ → **le**

les² *pron personnel* them

lesbien, ~ne *adj & f* lesbian

léser injure; *intérêts* damage; *droits* infringe

lésion *f* MÉD lesion

lessive *f produit* laundry detergent, *Br* washing powder; *liquide* detergent; *linge* laundry; *faire la ~* do the laundry

leste agile; *propos* crude

léthargie *f* lethargy

lettre *f* letter; *à la ~, au pied de la ~* literally; *en toutes ~s* in full; *fig* in black and white; *~s* literature; *études* arts; **lettré** well-read

leucémie *f* MÉD leukemia, *Br* leukaemia

leur 1 *adj possessif* their **2** *pron personnel*: *le/la ~, les ~s* theirs **3** *complément d'objet indirect* (to) them

leurrer *fig* deceive

levé: *être ~* be up; **levée** *f* lifting; *d'une séance* adjournment; *du courrier* collection; *aux cartes* trick; lever **1** *v/t* raise, lift; *poids, interdiction* lift; *impôts* collect **2** *v/i de la pâte* rise; *se* ~ get up; *du soleil* rise; *du jour* break **3** *m*: ~ *du jour* daybreak; ~ *du soleil* sunrise

levier *m* lever; ~ *de vitesse* gear shift, *surtout Br* gear lever

lèvre *f* lip

levure *f* yeast; ~ *chimique* baking powder

lézard *m* lizard

lézarde *f* crack

liaison *f* connection; *amoureuse* affair; *de train* link; LING liaison

liant sociable

libellule *f* dragonfly

libéral liberal; *profession f* ~*e* profession; libéralisme *m* liberalism

libérateur, -trice *I adj* liberating **2** *m/f* liberator; libération *f* liberation; *d'un prisonnier* release; ~ *conditionnelle* parole; libérer liberate; *prisonnier* release, free (*de* from); *gaz, d'un engagement* release

liberté *f* freedom, liberty; *mettre en* ~ set free, release

librairie *f* bookstore, *Br* bookshop

libre free (*de faire* to do); libre-service *m* self-service; *magasin* self-service shop

Libye *f* Libya; libyen, ~ne Libyan; Libyen, ~ne *m/f* Libyan

licence *f* license, *Br* licence; *diplôme* degree

licenciement *m* layoff; (*renvoi*) dismissal; licencier lay off; (*renvoyer*) dismiss

lié: *être* ~ *par* be bound by; *être très* ~ *avec qn* be very close to s.o.

lien *m* tie, bond; (*rapport*) connection; *avoir un* ~ *de parenté* be related

lier tie (up); *d'un contrat* be binding on; CUIS thicken; *pensées, personnes* connect; ~ *amitié avec qn* make friends with s.o.

lierre *m* BOT ivy

lieu *m* place; ~*x* premises; JUR scene; *au* ~ *de (faire) qch* instead of (doing) sth; *avoir* ~ take place; *donner* ~ *à* give rise to; *en premier* ~ in the first place; *s'il y a* ~ if necessary

lièvre *m* hare

ligne *f* line; *d'autobus* number; *garder la* ~ keep one's figure; *entrer en* ~ *de compte* be taken into consideration; *pêcher à la* ~ go angling; *en* ~ INFORM on line; *achats en* ~ on line shopping

liguer: *se* ~ join forces (*pour faire* to do)

lilas *m & adj inv* lilac

limace *f* slug

lime *f* file; ~ *à ongles* nail file; limer file

limitation *f* limitation; ~ *de*

vitesse speed limit; **limite** *f* limit; (*frontière*) boundary; **à la ~** if absolutely necessary; **date** *f* **~** deadline; **vitesse** *f* **~** speed limit; **limiter** limit (**à** to)

limoger POL dismiss

limonade *f* lemonade

limousine *f* limousine

lin *m* BOT flax; *toile* linen

linéaire linear

linge *m* linen; (*lessive*) washing

lingerie *f* lingerie

linguiste *m/f* linguist

lion *m* lion; ASTROL **Lion** Leo; **lionne** *f* lioness

liposuccion *f* liposuction

liqueur *f* liqueur

liquidation *f* liquidation; *vente au rabais* sale

liquide 1 *adj* liquid; *argent m* **~** cash **2** *m* liquid; **~ de freins** brake fluid; **liquider** liquidate; *stock* sell off; *problème* dispose of

lire read

lis *m* BOT lily

lisible legible

lisse smooth; **lisser** smooth

liste *f* list; **~ d'attente** waiting list; **~ de commissions** shopping list; **lister** list; **listing** *m* printout

lit *m* bed; **aller au ~** go to bed; **~ de camp** cot, *Br* camp bed; **literie** *f* bedding

litige *m* dispute

litre *m* liter, *Br* litre

littéraire literary; **littérature** *f* literature

littoral 1 *adj* coastal **2** *m* coastline

livraison *f* delivery

livre[1] *m* book; **~ de poche** paperback

livre[2] *f poids, monnaie* pound

livrer *marchandises* deliver; *prisonnier* hand over; *secret* divulge; **se ~** (*se confier*) open up; (*se soumettre*) give o.s. up; **se ~ à** (*se confier*) confide in; *activité* indulge in; *l'abattement* give way to

livret *m* booklet; *d'opéra* libretto

livreur *m* delivery man; **~ de journaux** paper boy

lobby *m* lobby

lobe *m*: **~ de l'oreille** earlobe

local 1 *adj* local **2** *m* (*salle*) premises *pl*; **locaux** premises; **localisation** *f* location; *de software etc* localization; **localiser** locate; (*limiter*), *de software* localize

locataire *m/f* tenant; **location** *f par propriétaire* renting out; *par locataire* renting; (*loyer*) rent; *au théâtre* reservation

logement *m* accommodations, *Br* accommodation, *pl*; (*appartement*) apartment, *Br aussi* flat; **loger 1** *v/t* accommodate **2** *v/i* live; **logeur** *m* landlord; **logeuse** *f* landlady

logiciel *m* INFORM software

logique 1 *adj* logical **2** *f* logic

loi f law

loin far (**de** from); *dans le passé* long ago; *dans l'avenir* a long way off; **au ~** in the distance

lointain 1 adj distant **2** m distance

loisir m leisure; **~s** leisure activities

Londres London

long, longue 1 adj long; **à ~ terme** in the long term; **à la longue** in time; **être ~ (à faire qch)** take a long time (doing sth) **2** adv: **en dire ~** speak volumes **3** m: **de deux mètres de ~** two meters long; **le ~ de** along

longer follow

longitude f longitude

longtemps a long time

longuement for a long time; *parler* at length

longueur f length; **sur la même ~ d'onde** on the same wavelength

loquace talkative

loque f rag

loquet m latch

lorgner eye; *héritage, poste* have one's eye on

lors: dès ~ from then on; **~ de** during

lorsque when

lot m (*destin*) fate; *à la loterie* prize; (*portion*) share; COMM batch

loterie f lottery

loti: bien/mal ~ well/badly off

lotion f lotion

lotissement m (*parcelle*) plot; *terrain loti* housing development

louable praiseworthy; **louange** f praise

louche¹ adj sleazy

louche² f ladle

loucher squint

louer¹ rent

louer² (*vanter*) praise (**de, pour** for)

loup m wolf

loupe f magnifying glass

louper F *travail* botch; *bus* miss

lourd heavy; *plaisanterie* clumsy; *temps* oppressive; **lourdaud, ~e 1** adj clumsy **2** m/f oaf; **lourdement** heavily

loyal honest; *adversaire* fair-minded; *ami* loyal

loyer m rent

lubie f whim

lubrifiant m lubricant; **lubrifier** lubricate

lucarne f skylight

lucide lucid; (*conscient*) conscious; **lucidité** f lucidity

lucratif, -ive lucrative

lueur f faint light; **une ~ d'espoir** a glimmer of hope

luge f toboggan; **faire de la ~** go tobogganing

lugubre gloomy, lugubrious

lui *complément d'objet indirect, masculin* (to) him; *féminin* (to) her; *chose, animal* (to) it; *après prép, masculin* him; *animal* it lui-même himself; *de chose* itself

luire glint, glisten

lumière *f* light; *à la ~ de* in the light of

lumineux, -euse luminous; *ciel, couleur* bright; *affiche* illuminated; *idée* brilliant

lunaire lunar

lunatique lunatic

lundi *m* Monday

lune *f* moon; *~ de miel* honeymoon

lunette *f*: *~s* glasses; *~s de soleil* sunglasses; *~s de ski* ski goggles

lustre *m* (*lampe*) chandelier; *fig* luster, *Br* lustre; lustrer polish

lutte *f* fight, struggle; SP wrestling; lutter fight, struggle; SP wrestle

luxe *m* luxury; *de ~* luxury *atr*

Luxembourg: *le ~* Luxemburg; luxembourgeois, *~e* of/from Luxemburg, Luxemburg *atr*; Luxembourgeois, *~e m/f* Luxemburger

luxer: *se ~ l'épaule* dislocate one's shoulder

luxueux, -euse luxurious

luxuriant luxuriant

lycée *m* senior high, *Br* grammar school; lycéen, *~ne m/f* student (at a lycée)

lyophilisé freeze-dried

lyrique lyric; *qui a du lyrisme* lyrical; *artiste ~* opera singer

M

M. (= *monsieur*) Mr

ma → *mon*

macabre macabre

macédoine *f*: *~ de légumes* mixed vegetables *pl*; *~ de fruits* fruit salad

macérer CUIS: *faire ~* marinate

mâcher chew

machin *m* F thing

machinal mechanical

machine *f* machine; NAUT engine; *fig* machinery; *~ à laver* washing machine; *~ à sous* slot machine

machisme *m* machismo; macho **1** *adj* male chauvinist **2**

m macho type

mâchoire *f* jaw; mâchonner chew (on); (*marmonner*) mutter

maçon *m* bricklayer; *avec des pierres* mason; maçonnerie *f* masonry

maculer spatter

madame *f*: *Madame Durand* Mrs Durand; *mesdames et messieurs* ladies and gentlemen

mademoiselle *f*: *Mademoiselle Durand* Miss Durand

madone *f* Madonna

magasin *m* (*boutique*) store, *surtout Br* shop; (*dépôt*) store room; **grand** ~ department store; magasinier *m* storeman

magazine *m* magazine

mage *m*: **les Rois** ~**s** the Three Wise Men, the Magi

magicien, ~ne *m/f* magician; magie *f* magic; magique magic, magical

magistral *ton* magisterial; *fig* masterly; **cours** *m* ~ lecture

magistrat *m* JUR magistrate

magnanime magnanimous

magner: **se** ~ F move it F

magnétique magnetic

magnétophone *m* tape recorder

magnétoscope *m* video (recorder)

magnifique magnificent

magouille *f* F scheming; ~**s électorales** election shenanigans F

mai *m* May

maigre thin; *résultat, salaire* meager, *Br* meagre; maigrir get thin, lose weight

mailing *m* mailshot

maille *f* stitch

maillet *m* mallet

maillot *m* SP shirt, jersey; *de coureur* vest; ~ **(de bain)** swimsuit

main *f* hand; **fait à la** ~ handmade; **prendre qc en** ~ take sth in hand; **perdre la** ~ *fig* lose one's touch; **sous la** ~ to hand, within reach

main-d'œuvre *f inv* manpower, labor, *Br* labour

maint *fml* many; **à** ~**es reprises** time and again

maintenance *f* maintenance

maintenant now; ~ **que** now that

maintenir keep; *tradition* uphold; *(tenir fermement)* hold; *d'une poutre* hold up; *(soutenir)* maintain; **se** ~ *d'un prix* hold steady; *d'une tradition, de la paix* last; **se** ~ **au pouvoir** stay in power; **maintien** *m* maintenance; ~ **de la paix** peace keeping

maire *m* mayor; **mairie** *f* town hall

mais **1** *conj* but **2** *adv*: ~ **bien sûr!** of course!; ~ **non!** no!

maïs *m* BOT corn, *Br aussi* maize; *en boîte* sweet corn

maison *f* house; *(chez-soi)* home; COMM company; **à la** ~ at home; **pâté** *m* ~ homemade pâté; ~ **de campagne** country house

maître *m* master; *(professeur)* school teacher; *(peintre, écrivain)* maestro; ~ **chanteur** blackmailer; ~ **d'hôtel** maître d', *Br* head waiter; ~ **nageur** swimming instructor

maîtresse **1** *f* mistress *(aussi amante)*; *(professeur)* schoolteacher **2** *adj*: **idée** *f* ~ main idea

maîtrise *f* mastery; *diplôme* MA, master's (degree); ~ **de soi** self-control; maîtriser master; *cheval* gain control of; *incendie* bring under control

majestueux, -euse majestic

majeur 1 *adj* major; **être ~** JUR be of age **2** *m* middle finger; **majorité** *f* majority

majuscule *f & adj*: (*lettre f*) ~ capital (letter)

mal 1 *m* evil; (*maladie*) illness; (*difficulté*) difficulty; **faire ~** hurt; *avoir ~ aux dents* have toothache; *se donner du ~* go to a lot of trouble; *faire du ~ à qn* hurt s.o.; *~ de mer* seasickness **2** *adv* badly; *pas ~* not bad; *se sentir ~* feel ill **3** *adj*: *faire/dire qc de ~* do/say sth bad

malade ill, sick; *tomber ~* fall ill; *~ mental* mentally ill; **maladie** *f* illness

maladresse *f* clumsiness; **maladroit** clumsy

malaise *m* discomfort; POL malaise; *faire un ~* faint

malavisé ill-advised

malchance *f* bad luck

mâle *m & adj* male

malédiction *f* curse

malencontreux, -euse unfortunate

malentendant hard of hearing

malfaiteur *m* malefactor

malgré in spite of

malheur *m* misfortune; (*malchance*) bad luck; *par ~* unfortunately; **malheureusement** unfortunately;

malheureux, -euse unfortunate; (*triste*) unhappy; (*insignifiant*) silly little

malhonnête dishonest; **malhonnêteté** *f* dishonesty

malice *f* malice; (*espièglerie*) mischief; **malicieux, -euse** malicious; (*coquin*) mischievous

malin, -igne (*rusé*) crafty, cunning; (*méchant*) malicious; MÉD malignant

malle *f* trunk; **mallette** *f* little bag

malodorant foul-smelling

malpoli impolite

malpropre dirty

malsain unhealthy

malt *m* malt

Malte *f* Malta; **maltais, ~e** Maltese; **Maltais, ~e** *m/f* Maltese

maltraiter mistreat, maltreat

malveillant malevolent

malvoyant, ~e 1 *adj* visually impaired **2** *m/f* visually impaired person

maman *f* Mom, Br Mum

mamelle *f* de vache udder; *de chienne* teat

mamie *f* F granny

mammifère *m* mammal

manager *m* manager

manche¹ *m* d'outils handle; *d'un violon* neck

manche² *f* sleeve; SP round; **la Manche** the English Channel

manchette *f* cuff; *d'un journal* headline

mandarine f mandarin (orange)

mandat m POL term of office, mandate; *(procuration)* proxy; *de la poste* postal order; **~ d'arrêt** arrest warrant; **mandataire** m/f *à une réunion* proxy

manège m riding school; *(carrousel)* carousel; *Br* roundabout; *fig* game

mangeable edible, eatable

mangeoire f manger

manger eat; *argent, temps* eat up; *mots* swallow

maniable *voiture* easy to handle

maniaque fussy; **manie** f mania

manier handle

manière f way, manner; **~s** manners; *affectées* airs and graces; **à la ~ de** in the style of; **de cette ~** (in) that way; **de toute ~** anyway; **d'une ~ générale** generally speaking; **de ~ à faire qch** so as to do sth; **maniéré** affected

manifestant, ~e m/f demonstrator; **manifestation** f *de joie etc* expression; POL demonstration; *culturelle, sportive* event

manifeste 1 adj obvious **2** m POL manifesto; **manifester** 1 v/t show; **se ~** *de maladie, problèmes* manifest itself/themselves **2** v/i demonstrate

manipulateur, -trice manipulative; **manipulation** f *d'un appareil* handling; *d'une personne* manipulation; **~ génétique** genetic engineering; **manipuler** handle; *personne* manipulate

mannequin m *dans magasin* dummy; *personne* model

manœuvre 1 f maneuver, *Br* manoeuvre; *d'un outil, une machine etc* operation **2** m unskilled laborer *ou Br* labourer; **manœuvrer** maneuver, *Br* manoeuvre

manoir m manor (house)

manque m lack; **par ~ de** for lack of; **manqué** unsuccessful; *rendez-vous* missed; **manquer 1** v/i *(être absent)* be missing; *(faire défaut)* be lacking; *(échouer)* fail; **tu me manques** I miss you; **~ à** *promesse* fail to keep; *devoir* fail in **2** v/t *(être absent à)* miss; *examen* fail; **elle a manqué (de) se faire écraser** she was almost run over **3** *impersonnel* **il manque des preuves** there's a lack of evidence

manteau m coat; *de neige* blanket; **~ de cheminée** mantelpiece

manucure f manicure

manuel, -le adj & m manual; **~ d'utilisation** instruction manual

manufacturé: produits mpl **~s** manufactured goods

manuscrit 1 adj handwritten

2 *m* manuscript

maquereau *m* zo mackerel; F (*souteneur*) pimp

maquette *f* model

maquillage *m* make-up; **maquiller** make up; *crime, vérité* conceal; **se ~** put one's make-up on

marais *m* swamp

marathon *m* marathon

marbre *m* marble

marc *m*: **~ de café** coffee grounds *pl*

marchand, ~e 1 *adj valeur* market *atr*; *rue* shopping *atr*; *marine* merchant *atr* **2** *m/f* merchant, storekeeper, *Br* shopkeeper; **marchander** haggle, bargain; **marchandise** *f*: **~s** merchandise; **train ~ de ~s** freight train

marche *f* walking; *d'escalier* step; MUS, MIL march; *des événements* course; (*démarche*) walk; **~ arrière** AUTO reverse; **mettre en ~** start (up)

marché *m* market; (*accord*) deal; (*à*) **bon ~** cheap; **par-dessus le ~** into the bargain; **~ boursier** stock market; **le Marché Commun** POL the Common Market; **~ noir** black market

marcher walk; MIL march; *d'une machine* run, work; F (*réussir*) work; *d'un bus, train* run; **faire ~ qn** pull s.o.'s leg

mardi *m* Tuesday; **Mardi gras**

Mardi Gras, *Br* Shrove Tuesday

mare *f* pond; **~ de sang** pool of blood

marécage *m* swamp; **marécageux, -euse** swampy

marée *f* tide; **~ basse/haute** low/high tide; **~ noire** oil slick

margarine *f* margarine

marge *f* margin; **en ~ de** on the fringes of

marguerite *f* daisy

mari *m* husband

mariage *m* *fête* wedding; *état* marriage

marié 1 *adj* married **2** *m* (bride)groom; **mariée** *f* bride; **marier** marry; **se ~** get married; **se ~ avec** marry, get married to

marijuana *f* marijuana

marin 1 *adj* sea *atr*; *animaux* marine **2** *m* sailor

marine *f* MIL navy; (**bleu**) **~** navy (blue)

marionnette *f* puppet; *avec des ficelles aussi* marionnette

marmelade *f* marmalade

marmite *f* (large) pot

marmonner mutter

maroquinerie *f* leather goods shop; *articles* leather goods *pl*

marquant remarkable

marque *f* mark; COMM brand; *de voiture* make; COMM (*signe*) trademark; **~ déposée** registered trademark; **de ~**

COMM branded; *fig: personne* distinguished; **marquer** mark; (*noter*) write down; *personnalité* leave its mark on; *d'un baromètre etc* show; (*accentuer*) *taille* emphasize; ~ **un but** score (a goal); **marqueur** *m* marker pen

marraine *f* godmother

marrant F funny

marre F: **j'en ai** ~ I've had enough

marrer F: **se** ~ have a good laugh

marron 1 *m* chestnut **2** *adj inv* brown; **marronnier** *m* chestnut tree

mars *m* March

marteau *m* hammer; ~ **piqueur** pneumatic drill; **marteler** hammer

martyr, ~**e**[1] *m/f* martyr; **martyre**[2] *m* martyrdom; **martyriser** abuse; *petit frère*, *camarade de classe* bully

masculin male; GRAM masculine

masque *m* mask; **masquer** mask

massacre *m* massacre; **massacrer** massacre

massage *m* massage

masse *f* masse; ÉL ground, *Br* earth,; **en** ~ in large numbers, en masse; *manifestation* massive; **une** ~ **de choses à faire** masses *pl* (of things) to do

massif, **-ive 1** *adj* massif; *or*, *chêne* solid **2** *m* massif; ~

de fleurs flowerbed

massue *f* club

mastiquer *nourriture* chew

mat[1] matt; *son* dull

mat[2] *inv aux échecs* checkmated

mât *m* mast

match *m* game, *Br aussi* match; ~ **nul** tied game, *Br* draw

matelas *m* mattress; ~ **pneumatique** air bed

matelot *m* sailor

matérialiser: **se** ~ materialize; **matériau** *m* material; **matériel**, ~**le 1** *adj* material **2** *m de camping*, SP equipment; INFORM hardware

maternel, ~**le 1** *adj* maternal; **langue** *f* ~**le** mother tongue **2** *f* nursery school; **maternité** *f* motherhood; *établissement* maternity hospital; (*enfantement*) pregnancy

mathématicien, ~**ne** *m/f* mathematician; **mathématique 1** *adj* mathematical **2** *fpl*: ~**s** mathematics

matière *f* material; PHYS, PHIL matter; (*sujet*) subject; **entrée en** ~ introduction; **en** ~ **de** when it comes to; ~ **première** raw material

matin *m* morning; **le** ~ in the morning; **tous les lundis** ~**s** every Monday morning; **matinal** morning *atr*; **être** ~ be an early riser; **matinée** *f* morning; (*spectacle*) matinée; **faire la grasse** ~ sleep

late
matou *m* tom cat
matricule *m* number
matrimonial matrimonial
maturité *f* maturity
maudire curse; **maudit** F
damn F
mauvais 1 *adj* bad; *(erroné)*
wrong **2** *adv* bad; **il fait ~**
the weather is bad
mauve mauve
maximum *adj & m* maximum; **au ~** at most, at the
maximum
mayonnaise *f* mayonnaise,
mayo F
me me; *complément d'objet
indirect* to me; **je ~ suis
coupé** I've cut myself; **je ~
lève à ...** I get up at ...
mec *m* F guy F
mécanicien *m* mechanic;
mécanique 1 *adj* mechanical **2** *f* mechanics; **mécanisme** *m* mechanism
méchanceté *f* nastiness; *action, parole* nasty thing to
do/say; **méchant, ~e 1** *adj*
nasty; *enfant* naughty **2** *m/f*
F: **les gentils et les ~s** the
goodies and the baddies
mèche *f de bougie* wick; *d'explosif* fuse; *de perceuse* bit;
de cheveux strand
méconnaissable unrecog-
nizable
mécontent unhappy, dis-
pleased (**de** with); **mécon-
tenter** displease
médaille *f* medal; **médaillon**

m medallion
médecin *m* doctor
médecine *f* medicine; **les ~s
douces** alternative medicines
média *m* media *pl*
médiateur, -trice *m/f* mediator
médiatique media *atr*
médical medical
médicament *m* medicine,
drug
médiéval medieval, *Br* medi-
aeval
médiocre mediocre; **~ en**
ÉDU poor at
médire: ~ de qn run s.o. down
méditation *f* meditation; **méditer 1** *v/t* think about, reflect on **2** *v/i* meditate (**sur**
on)
Méditerranée: la ~ the Mediterranean; **méditerranéen,
~ne** Mediterranean; **Méditerranéen, ~ne** *m/f* Mediterranean *atr*
méduse *f* ZO jellyfish
meeting *m* meeting
méfait *m* JUR misdemeanor,
Br misdemeanour; **~s de la
drogue** harmful effects
méfiance *f* mistrust, suspicion; **méfiant** suspicious;
méfier: se ~ de mistrust,
be suspicious of; *(se tenir
en garde)* be wary of
mégaoctet *m* INFORM megabyte
mégarde *f*: **par ~** inadvertently

mégot *m* cigarette butt

meilleur 1 *adj* better; *le ~ ...* the best ... *2 m: le ~* the best

mél *m* email

mélancolie *f* gloom, melancholy

mélange *m* mixture; *de thés* blend; *action* mixing; *de thés* blending; **mélanger** mix; *thés* blend; (*brouiller*) jumble up, mix up

mêlée *f* fray, melee; *en rugby* scrum; **mêler** mix; (*réunir*) combine; (*brouiller*) jumble up, mix up; *~ qn à qc* *fig* involve s.o. in sth; *se ~ à qc* get involved with sth; *se ~ de qc* interfere in sth

mélodie *f* tune, melody; **mélodieux, -euse** tuneful, melodious; *voix* melodious

mélodramatique melodramatic; **mélodrame** *m* melodrama

melon *m* BOT melon

membre *m* ANAT limb; *fig* member

même 1 *adj*: *le/la ~, les ~s* the same; *la bonté ~* kindness itself *2 pron*: *le/la ~* the same one; *les ~s* the same ones; *cela revient au ~* it comes to the same thing *3 adv even*; *~ pas* not even; *faire de ~* do the same; *de ~!* likewise!; *être à ~ de faire* be able to do; *tout de ~* all the same; *quand ~* all the same; *moi de ~* me too

mémoire 1 *f* memory; *à la ~*

de in memory of *2 m* (*exposé*) report; (*dissertation*) thesis; *~s* memoirs; **mémorable** memorable; **mémoriser** memorize

menace *f* threat; **menacer** threaten (*de* with; *de faire* to do)

ménage *m* (*famille*) household; (*couple*) (married) couple; *faire le ~* clean house, *Br* do the housework; **ménagement** *m* consideration; **ménager**[1] *v/t* treat with consideration; *temps, argent* use sparingly; (*arranger*) arrange; **ménager**[2], *-ère 2 f* household atr *2 f* home-maker, housewife

mendiant, *~e m/f* beggar; **mendier 1** *v/i* beg *2 v/t* beg for

mener 1 *v/t* lead; (*amener, transporter*) take *2 v/i*: *~ à d'un chemin* lead to; *ne ~ à rien des efforts* come to nothing; **meneur** *m* leader; *péj* ringleader

mensonge *m* lie; **mensonger**, *-ère* false

mensualité *f* *somme à payer* monthly payment; **mensuel**, *~le* monthly

mental mental; *calcul m ~* mental arithmetic; **mentalité** *f* mentality

menteur, -euse *m/f* liar

menthe *f* BOT mint

mention *f* mention; *à un examen* grade, *Br aussi* mark;

mentionner mention

mentir lie (**à** to)

menton *m* chin

menu **1** *adj* slight; *morceaux* small **2** *adv* finely, fine **3** *m* menu (*aussi* INFORM); (*repas*) set meal; *par le* ~ in minute detail

menuisier *m* carpenter

méprendre: *se* ~ be mistaken (*sur* about)

mépris *m* (*indifférence*) disdain; (*dégoût*) scorn; méprisable despicable; méprisant scornful; mépriser *argent, ennemi* despise; *conseil, danger* scorn

mer *f* sea; *en* ~ at sea; *la Mer du Nord* the North Sea

mercenaire *m* mercenary

mercerie *f magasin* notions store, *Br* haberdashery; *articles* notions, *Br* haberdashery *pl*

merci **1** *int* thanks, thank you (*de, pour* for); ~ *bien* thanks a lot, thank you very much **2** *f* mercy

mercredi *m* Wednesday

merde *f* P shit P; merder P screw up P

mère *f* mother

méridional southern

mérite *m* merit; mériter deserve; ~ *le détour* be worth a visit

merle *m* blackbird

merveille *f* wonder, marvel; *à* ~ wonderfully well; merveilleux, -euse wonderful

mes → *mon*

mésaventure *f* mishap

mesquin mean

message *m* message; messager, -ère *m/f* messenger, courier; messagerie *f* parcels service; *électronique* electronic mail; ~ *vocale* voicemail

messe *f* REL mass

mesure *f* measurement; *disposition* measure, step; MUS (*rythme*) time; *à* ~ *que* as; *être en* ~ *de faire qch* be in a position to do sth; *outre* ~ excessive; *sur* ~ *fig* tailor-made; mesurer measure; *risque, importance* gauge; *paroles* weigh; *se* ~ *avec qn* pit o.s. against s.o.

métal *m* metal; métallique metallic

métamorphoser: *se* ~ metamorphose

météo *f* weather forecast

météore *m* meteor

météorologie *f* meteorology; *service* weather office

méthode *f* method

méticuleux, -euse meticulous

métier *m* profession; *manuel* trade; (*expérience*) experience; *machine* loom

métrage *m d'un film* footage; *court* ~ short

mètre *m* meter, *Br* metre; (*règle*) tape measure

métrique metric

métro *m* subway, *Br* underground; *à Paris* metro

métropole *f* metropolis; *de colonie* mother country

mettre put; *vêtements, lunettes, chauffage* put on; *réveil* set; *argent dans entreprise* put in; **~ *deux heures à faire qc*** take two hours to do sth; **se ~ *à faire*** start to do

meuble *m* piece of furniture; **~s** furniture; **meubler** furnish

meurtre *m* murder; **meurtrier, -ère 1** *adj* deadly **2** *m/f* murderer

meurtrir bruise; **meurtrissure** *f* bruise

meute *f* pack; *fig* mob

mexicain, ~e Mexican; **Mexicain, ~e** *m/f* Mexican; **Mexique:** *le* **~** Mexico

mi-... half; **à mi-chemin** half-way; **(à la) mi-janvier** mid--January

mi-bas *mpl* knee-highs, pop socks

miche *f* large round loaf

micro *m* mike; INFORM computer, PC; *d'espionnage* bug

microbe *m* microbe

microfilm *m* microfilm

micro-ondes *m* microwave

microphone *m* microphone

microscope *m* microscope

midi *m* noon, twelve o'clock; *(sud)* south; **le Midi** the South of France

mie *f de pain* crumb

miel *m* honey

mien: *le mien, la mienne, les*

miens, les miennes mine

miette *f* crumb

mieux 1 *adv comparatif de bien* better; *superlatif de bien* best; *le* **~** best; *de* **~** *en* **~** better and better; *tant* **~** so much the better; *vous feriez* **~** *de* ... you would *ou* you'd do best to ... **2** *m: (progrès)* progress; **j'ai fait de mon ~** I did my best; *le* **~**, *c'est de* ... the best thing is to ...

mièvre insipid

mignon, ~ne *(charmant)* cute; *(gentil)* nice

migraine *f* migraine

migration *f* migration; **migrer** migrate

mijoter CUIS simmer; *fig* hatch

milieu *m (centre)* middle; *biologique, social* environment; *au* **~** *de* in the middle of; *le* **~** the underworld

militaire 1 *adj* military **2** *m* soldier; *les* **~s** the military *sg ou pl*

militant active

militer: **~** *dans* be an active member of; **~** *pour/contre* *fig* militate for/against

mille 1 (a) thousand **2** *m mesure* mile; **~** *marin* nautical mile

millénaire 1 *adj* thousand--year old **2** *m* millennium

milliard *m* billion; **milliardaire** *m* billionaire

millième thousandth

millier *m* thousand

milligramme *m* milligram

millimètre millimeter, *Br* millimetre

million *m* million; millionnaire *m/f* millionaire

minable mean, shabby; *un salaire ~* a pittance

mince thin; *personne* slim; *espoir* slight; *somme, profit* small; *argument* flimsy

mine¹ *f* appearance, look; *avoir bonne/mauvaise ~* look/not look well

mine² *f* mine (*aussi* MIL); *de crayon* lead; *miner* undermine; MIL mine

minéral *adj* & *m* mineral

minéralogique AUTO: *plaque f ~* license plate, *Br* number plate

mineur¹ *adj* JUR, MUS minor

mineur² *m* (*ouvrier*) miner

miniature *f* miniature

minimal minimum; *minime* minimal; *salaire* tiny; *minimiser* minimize; *minimum adj* & *m* minimum; *au ~* at the very least; *un ~ de* the least little bit of

ministère *m* department; (*gouvernement*) government; REL ministry; *ministre m* minister; *~ des Affaires étrangères* Secretary of State, *Br* Foreign Secretary; *~ de l'Intérieur* Secretary of the Interior, *Br* Home Secretary

minitel *m* small home terminal connected to a number of data banks

minorité *f* JUR, POL minority

minuit *m* midnight

minuscule **1** *adj* tiny, minuscule; *lettre* small, lower case **2** *f* small *ou* lower-case letter

minute *f* minute

minuterie *f* time switch

minutie *f* meticulousness; minutieux, -euse meticulous

miracle *m* miracle; miraculeux, -euse miraculous

mirage *m* mirage; *fig* illusion

miroir *m* mirror

miroiter sparkle

mise *f au jeu* stake; *de ~* acceptable; *~ en bouteilles* bottling; *~ en marche ou route* start-up; *miser* stake (*sur* on)

misérable wretched; *misère f* destitution; (*chose pénible*) misfortune

miséricordieux, -euse merciful

misogyne *m* misogynist

missile *m* MIL missile

mission *f* mission; (*tâche*) task

mite *f* ZO (clothes) moth

mi-temps **1** *f* SP half-time **2** *m* part-time job; *à ~ travail* part-time

mitigé moderate; *sentiments* mixed

mi-voix: *à ~* under one's breath

mixer, mixeur *m* CUIS blender; mixte mixed; mixture *f*

péj vile concoction

MM (= *Messieurs*) Messrs.

Mme (= *Madame*) Mrs

Mo *m* (= *mégaoctet*) Mb (= megabyte)

mobile 1 *adj* mobile; *(amovible)* movable; *feuilles* loose; *ombres* moving **2** *m* motive; ART mobile

mobilier, -ère 1 *adj* JUR movable, personal **2** *m* furniture

mobilisation *f* mobilization; **mobilité** *f* mobility

mobylette® *f* moped

moche F ugly; *(méprisable)* mean

mode[1] *m* method; ~ *d'emploi* instructions (for use); ~ *de vie* life-style

mode[2] *f* fashion; *être à la* ~ be fashionable, be in fashion

modèle *m* model; *tricot* pattern; **modeler** model

modem *m* INFORM modem

modération *f* moderation; **modéré** moderate; **modérer** moderate; *se* ~ control o.s.

moderne modern; **modernisation** *f* modernization; **moderniser** modernize

modeste modest; **modestie** *f* modesty

modification *f* modification; **modifier** modify

modique modest

module *m* TECH module; **moduler** modulate

moelle *f* marrow; ~ *épinière* spinal cord; **moelleux, -euse** *lit* soft; *chocolat, vin*

smooth

mœurs *fpl* morals; *(coutumes)* customs

moi me; *avec* ~ with me

moi-même myself

moindre lesser; *prix* lower; *quantité* smaller; *le/la* ~ the least

moine *m* monk

moineau *m* sparrow

moins 1 *adv* less; *au ou du* ~ at least; *à* ~ *que ... ne* (+ *subj*) unless; *de* ~ *en* ~ less and less; *20 euros de* ~ 20 euros less **2** *m*: *le* ~ the least **3** *prép* MATH minus; *dix heures* ~ *cinq* it's five of ten , Br it's five to ten; *il fait* ~ *deux* it's 2 below zero

mois *m* month

moisi 1 *adj* moldy, Br mouldy **2** *m* BOT mold, Br mould; **moisir** go moldy *ou* Br mouldy; **moisissure** *f* BOT mold, Br mould

moisson *f* harvest; **moissonner** harvest

moite damp, moist

moitié *f* half; *à* ~ *vide/endormi* half-empty/-asleep; ~ ~ fifty-fifty

molaire *f* molar

molécule *f* molecule

molester rough up

molette *f de réglage* knob

mollesse *f* softness; *d'une personne, d'actions* lethargy

mollet[1], **-te** *adj* soft; *œuf* soft-boiled

mollet[2] *m* calf

môme *m/f* F kid F

moment *m* moment; ***d'un ~ à l'autre*** at any moment; ***par ~s*** at times, sometimes; ***pour le ~*** for the moment

momentané temporary; **momentanément** for a short while

mon *m*, **ma** *f*, **mes** *pl* my

monarchie *f* monarchy; **monarque** *m* monarch

monastère *m* monastery

monceau *m* mound

mondain *vie* society *atr*; **mondanités** *fpl* social niceties

monde *m* world; *gens* people *pl*; ***tout le ~*** everybody, everyone; ***mettre au ~*** bring into the world

mondial world *atr*, global; **mondialisation** *f* globalization

monétaire monetary; *marché* money *atr*

moniteur, -trice 1 *m/f* instructor **2** *m* INFORM monitor

monnaie *f* money; *(pièces)* change; *(unité monétaire)* currency

monologue *m* monolog, *Br* monologue

monopole *m* monopoly; **monopoliser** monopolize

monospace *m* people carrier, MPV

monotone monotonous; **monotonie** *f* monotony

monsieur *m* *(pl* **messieurs)** *dans lettre* Dear Sir; **Mon-**

sieur Durand Mr Durand; ***bonjour ~*** good morning

monstre 1 *m* monster **2** *adj* colossal

mont *m* mountain

montage *m* TECH assembly; *d'un film* editing; *d'une photographie* montage; ÉL connecting

montagnard, ~e 1 *adj* mountain *atr* **2** *m/f* mountain dweller; **montagne** *f* mountain; ***à la ~*** in the mountains; ***~s russes*** roller coaster; **montagneux, -euse** mountainous

montant 1 *adj robe* high-necked; *mouvement* upward **2** *m somme* amount

montée *f sur montagne* ascent; *(pente)* slope; *de prix, de température* rise; **monter 1** *v/t* climb, go/come up; *valise* take/bring up; *machine* assemble; *tente* put up; THÉÂT put on; *film* edit; *entreprise* set up; *cheval* ride **2** *v/i* come/go upstairs; *d'avion, de route* climb; *des prix* rise, go up; *de baromètre, fleuve* rise; ***~ dans avion, train* get on; *voiture* get in(to) **3**: ***se ~ à* de frais** amount to

montre *f* (wrist)watch

montrer show; ***~ qn/qc du doigt*** point at s.o./sth

monture *f (cheval)* mount; *de lunettes* frame; *d'un diamant* setting

monument *m* monument; **monumental** monumental

moquer: se ~ de (*railler*) make fun of; (*dédaigner*) not care about; (*tromper*) fool; **moquerie** *f* mockery

moquette *f* wall-to-wall carpet

moqueur, -euse 1 *adj* mocking **2** *m/f* mocker

moral, ~e 1 *adj* moral; *souffrance, santé* spiritual **2** *m* morale **3** *f* morality, morals *pl*; *d'une histoire* moral

morbide morbid

morceau *m* piece; *d'un livre* passage

morceler divide up

mordant biting; **mordre** bite; *d'un acide* eat into

morfondre: se ~ mope; (*s'ennuyer*) be bored

morgue *f lieu* mortuary, morgue

moribond dying

morne gloomy

morose morose

mors *m* bit

morsure *f* bite

mort[1] *f* death

mort[2], **~e 1** *adj* dead; *eau* stagnant; *yeux* lifeless; *membre* numb; **ivre ~** dead drunk; **être ~ de rire** F die laughing **2** *m/f* dead man; dead woman; **les ~s** the dead *pl*

mortalité *f* mortality; **taux** *m* **de ~** death rate, mortality; **mortel, ~le** mortal; *blessure,*

dose, maladie fatal; *péché* deadly

morue *f* cod

morveux, -euse *m/f* F squirt F

mosaïque *f* mosaic

Moscou Moscow

mosquée *f* mosque

mot *m* word; (*court message*) note; **bon ~** witticism; **~ clé** key word; **~ de passe** password; **gros ~** rude word, swearword; **~ à ~** word for word

motard *m* motorcyclist, biker; *de la gendarmerie* motorcycle policeman

moteur, -trice 1 *m* engine, motor; *fig: personne* driving force (**de** behind) **2** *adj arbre* drive; **force** driving

motif *m* motive, reason; (*forme*) pattern; MUS theme, motif; *en peinture* motif

motion *f* POL motion

motivation *f* motivation; **motiver** motivate; (*expliquer*) be the reason for, prompt; (*justifier par des motifs*) give a reason for

moto *f* motorbike, motorcycle; **faire de la ~** ride one's motorbike; **motocycliste** *m/f* motorcyclist

motoriser mechanize; **je suis motorisé** F I have a car

mou, molle soft; *caractère, résistance* weak

mouche *f* fly

moucher: se ~ blow one's nose

moucheron m gnat

mouchoir m handkerchief

moudre grind

moue f pout; **faire la ~** pout

mouette f seagull

moufle f mitten

mouillé wet; **mouiller 1** v/t wet; (*humecter*) dampen; *liquide* water down **2** v/i MAR anchor

moule 1 m mold, *Br* mould; CUIS tin **2** f ZO mussel

mouler mold, *Br* mould

moulin m mill; **~** (**à vent**) windmill; **~ à café** coffee grinder

mourir die (**de** of); **~ de froid** freeze to death

mousse f foam; BOT moss; CUIS mousse; **mousser** lather; **mousseux, -euse 1** adj foamy **2** m sparkling wine

moustache f mustache, *Br* moustache

moustique m mosquito

moutarde f mustard

mouton m sheep; *viande* mutton; *fourrure* sheepskin

mouvement m movement; *trafic* traffic; **en ~** moving; **mouvementé** eventful; *débat* lively

mouvoir: **se ~** move

moyen, ~ne 1 adj average; *classe* middle; **Moyen Âge** m Middle Ages pl; **Moyen-Orient** m Middle East **2** m (*façon, méthode*) means sg; **~s** (*argent*) means pl; *intellectuelles* faculties; **au ~ de,**

par le ~ de by means of **3** f average; *statistique* mean; **en~ne** on average; **moyenâgeux, -euse** medieval

moyennant for

Mt (= **Mont**) Mt (= Mount)

muer *d'oiseau* molt, *Br* moult; *de voix* break

muet, ~te dumb; *fig* silent

mufle m muzzle; *fig* F boor

mugir moo; *du vent* moan

muguet m BOT lily of the valley

mule f mule

multicolore multicolored, *Br* multicoloured

multimédia m & adj multimedia

multinational, ~e 1 adj multinational **2** f: **multinationale** multinational

multiplication f multiplication; **la ~ de** (*augmentation*) the increase in the number of; **multiplier** multiply; **se ~** d'une espèce multiply

multitude f: **une ~ de** a host of; **la ~** péj the masses pl

multiusages versatile

municipal town *atr*, municipal; **municipalité** f (*commune*) municipality; *conseil* town council

munir: **~ de** fit with; *personne* provide with; **se ~ de qc** d'un parapluie, de son passeport take sth

mur m wall

mûr ripe

muraille f wall

national

mûre *f* BOT mulberry; *des ron-
ces* blackberry
murer *enclos* wall in; *porte*
wall up
mûrier *m* mulberry (tree)
mûrir ripen
murmure *m* murmur; mur-
murer murmur; (*médire*)
talk
muscle *m* muscle; musclé
muscular; musculation *f*
body-building
museau *m* muzzle
musée *m* museum
museler muzzle (*aussi fig*);
muselière *f* muzzle
musical musical; musicien,
~ne 1 *adj* musical 2 *m/f* musician; musique *f* music; ~
de fond piped music

must *m* must
musulman, ~e *m/f* & *adj*
Muslim
mutation *f* change; BIOL mutation; *de fonctionnaire*
transfer
mutiler mutilate
mutuel, ~le mutual
myope shortsighted
myrtille *f* bilberry
mystère *m* mystery; mystérieux, -euse mysterious
mystifier fool, take in
mystique 1 *adj* mystical 2 *m/f*
mystic 3 *f* mystique
mythe *m* myth; mythologie *f*
mythology
mythomane *m/f* pathological
liar

N

nabot *m* péj midget
nacre *f* mother-of-pearl
nage *f* swimming; *style*
stroke; *être en ~ fig* be drip-
ping with sweat
nageoire *f* fin
nager 1 *v/i* swim 2 *v/t*: ~ la
brasse do the breaststroke
naïf, naïve naive
nain, ~e *m/f* & *adj* dwarf
naissance *f* birth (*aussi fig*)
naître be born (*aussi fig*); faire ~ sentiment give rise to
naïveté *f* naivety
nana *f* F chick F, girl
nantir provide (*de* with)

nappe *f* tablecloth; *de gaz,
pétrole* layer
narcotique *m* & *adj* narcotic
narguer taunt
narine *f* nostril
narquois taunting
narrateur, -trice *m/f* narrator;
narration *f* narration
nasal nasal
natal *pays etc* of one's birth,
native; natalité *f*: (taux *m
de*) ~ birth rate
natation *f* swimming
natif, -ive native
nation *f* nation; national, ~e 1
adj national 2 *mpl*: natio-

naux nationals **3** *f highway;* **nationaliser** nationalize; **nationaliste 1** *adj* nationalist; *péj* nationalistic **2** *m/f* nationalist; **nationalité** *f* nationality

natte *f* (*tapis*) mat; *de cheveux* braid, plait

naturalisation *f* naturalization

nature 1 *adj yaourt* plain; *thé, café* without milk or sugar; *personne* natural **2** *f* nature; **~ morte** ART still life; naturel, ~le **1** *adj* natural **2** *m* (*caractère*) nature; (*spontanéité*) naturalness; **naturellement** naturally

naufrage *m* shipwreck; *faire* ~ be shipwrecked

nausée *f* nausea; *j'ai la* ~ I'm nauseous, *Br* I feel sick; **nauséeux, -euse** nauseous

nautique nautical; *ski* water *atr*

nautisme *m* water sports and sailing

naval naval; *construction* ship *atr*

navet *m* rutabaga, *Br* swede; *fig* turkey F, *Br* flop

navette *f* shuttle; *faire la* ~ shuttle

navigable navigable; **navigation** *f* sailing; (*pilotage*) navigation; **~ aérienne** air travel; **~ spatiale** space travel; **naviguer** *d'un navire, marin* sail; *d'un avion* fly; (*conduire*), INFORM navigate; **~ sur**

Internet surf the Net

navire *m* ship

navrant upsetting; **navré:** *je suis* ~ I am so sorry

ne: *je* ~ *comprends pas* I don't understand, I do not understand; *ne ... guère* hardly; *ne ... jamais* never; *ne ... personne* nobody; *ne ... plus* no longer; not any more; *ne ... que* only; *ne ... rien* nothing, not anything; → *aussi* **guère, jamais** etc

né born; **~e Lepic** nee Lepic

néanmoins nevertheless

néant *m* nothingness

nécessaire 1 *adj* necessary **2** *m* necessary; *le strict* ~ the bare minimum; **~ de toilette** toiletries *pl;* **nécessité** *f* necessity; **nécessiter** require, necessitate

néerlandais, ~e 1 *adj* Dutch **2** *m langue* Dutch; **Néerlandais, ~e** *m/f* Dutchman; Dutchwoman

néfaste harmful

négatif, -ive *adj & m* negative; **négation** *f* negation; GRAM negative

négligé 1 *adj travail* careless; *tenue* untidy; *épouse, enfant* neglected **2** *m* negligee; **négligence** *f* negligence, carelessness; *d'une épouse, d'un enfant* neglect; (*nonchalance*) casualness; **négligent** careless, negligent; *parent* negligent; *geste* casual; négliger neglect; *occasion* miss; *avis* disregard; **~ de faire** fail to do

négoce *m* trade; négociant *m* merchant; négociateur, -trice *m/f* negotiator; négociation *f* negotiation; négocier negotiate

neige *f* snow; neiger snow

néon *m* neon

nerf *m* nerve; (*vigueur*) energy; **être à bout de ~s** be at the end of one's tether

nerveux, -euse nervous; (*vigoureux*) full of energy; AUTO responsive; **nervosité** *f* nervousness

n'est-ce pas: **il fait beau, ~?** it's a fine day, isn't it?; **tu la connais, ~?** you know her, don't you?

net, ~te **1** *adj* (*propre*) clean; (*clair*) clear; *différence* distinct; COMM net **2** *adv* (*aussi* **nettement**) *tué* outright; *refuser* flatly; *parler* plainly; **netteté** *f* cleanliness; (*clarté*) clarity

nettoyage *m* cleaning; **~ ethnique** ethnic cleansing; **~ à sec** dry cleaning; **nettoyer** clean; F (*ruiner*) clean out F; **~ à sec** dryclean

neuf[1] nine

neuf[2], neuve *adj* new; **refaire à ~** *maison etc* renovate; *moteur* recondition

neutraliser neutralize; neutralité *f* neutrality; neutre neutral

neuvième ninth

neveu *m* nephew

névralgie *f* MÉD neuralgia

névrosé, ~e *m/f* neurotic

nez *m* nose

ni neither, nor; **je n'ai ~ intérêt ~ désir** I have neither interest nor inclination; **sans sucre ~ lait** without sugar or milk, with neither sugar nor milk; **~ moi non plus** neither *ou* nor do I, me neither

niais stupid; niaiserie *f* stupidity

niche *f dans un mur* niche; *d'un chien* kennel; **nicher** nest; *fig* F live

nicotine *f* nicotine

nid *m* nest; **~ de poule** *fig* pothole

nièce *f* niece

nier: ~ (**avoir fait**) deny (doing)

nigaud **1** *adj* silly **2** *m* idiot, fool

niveau *m* level; ÉDU standard; *outil* spirit level; **~ de vie** standard of living; **niveler** *terrain* level; *fig:* *différences* even out

noble noble; noblesse *f* nobility

noce *f* wedding; **faire la ~** F paint the town red

nocif, -ive harmful, noxious

nocturne **1** *adj* night *atr*; ZO nocturnal **2** *f:* **un match joué en ~** an evening match

Noël *m* Christmas; **joyeux ~!**

Merry Christmas!; *le père ~* Santa Claus, *Br aussi* Father Christmas

nœud *m* knot (*aussi* NAUT); *fig: d'un problème* nub; *~ papillon* bow tie

noir 1 *adj* black; (*sombre*) dark; *il fait ~* it's dark **2** *m* black; (*obscurité*) dark; *travail m au ~* moonlighting

Noir *m* black man

noircir blacken

Noire *f* black woman

noisetier *m* hazel; **noisette** *f* & *adj inv* hazelnut

noix *f* walnut

nom *m* name; GRAM noun; *au ~ de qn* in *ou Br* on behalf of s.o.; *~ de famille* surname, family name; *~ de jeune fille* maiden name

nombre *m* number; *sans ~* countless; **nombreux**, *-euse* many; *famille ~* large

nombril *m* navel

nomination *f* appointment; *à un prix* nomination

nommer name, call; *à une fonction* appoint; *se ~* be called

non no; *j'espère que ~* I hope not; *moi ~ plus* me neither; *c'est normal, ~?* that's normal, isn't it?

non-alcoolisé non-alcoholic

nonchalant nonchalant, casual

nonobstant notwithstanding

non-polluant environ-

mentally friendly, non-polluting

nord 1 *m* north; *au ~ de* (to the) north of **2** *adj* north; *hémisphère* northern

nord-américain, *~e* North--American; **Nord-Américain**, *~e* *m/f* North-American

nord-est *m* north-east

nord-ouest *m* north-west

normal, *~e* **1** *adj* normal **2** *f*: *inférieur/supérieur à la ~e* above/below average; **normalement** normally; **normalisation** *f* normalization; TECH standardization; **normalité** *f* normality

norme *f* norm; TECH standard

Norvège: *la ~* Norway; **norvégien**, *~ne* **1** *adj* Norwegian **2** *m langue* Norwegian; **Norvégien**, *~ne* *m/f* Norwegian

nos → *notre*

nostalgie *f* nostalgia; *avoir la ~ de son pays* be homesick

notaire *m* notary

notamment particularly

note *f* note; *à l'école* grade, *Br* mark; (*facture*) check, *Br* bill; *~ de frais* expense account; *~ de service* memo; **noter** (*écrire*) write down; (*remarquer*) note

notice *f* note; (*mode d'emploi*) instructions *pl*

notifier *v/t*: *~ qch à qn* notify s.o. of sth

notion *f* (*idée*) notion, concept; **~s** basics *pl*

notre, *pl* **nos** our

nôtre: **le/la ~**, **les ~s** ours

nouer tie; *relations* establish

nougat *m* nougat

nouilles *fpl* noodles

nounou *f* F nanny

nounours *m* teddy bear

nourrice *f* child minder

nourrir feed; *fig*: *espoir* nurture

nourrisson *m* infant

nourriture *f* food

nous *sujet* we; *complément d'objet direct* us; *complément d'objet indirect* (to) us; **~ ~ sommes levés tôt** we got up early; **~ ~ aimons** we love each other

nouveau, **nouvelle** (*m* **nouvel** *before a vowel or silent* h; *mpl* **nouveaux**) **1** *adj* new; **de** *ou* **à ~** again; **Nouvel An** *m* New Year('s) **2** *m/f* new person

nouveau-né *m adj* newborn **2** *m* newborn baby

nouveauté *f* novelty

nouvelle *f* (*récit*) short story; **une ~** *dans les médias* a piece of news; **nouvelles** *fpl* news *sg*; **Nouvelle Zélande** *f* New Zealand

novembre *m* November

novice **1** *m/f* novice **2** *adj* inexperienced

noyade *f* drowning

noyau *m* pit, *Br* stone; PHYS nucleus; *fig* (small) group

noyer[1] *v/t* drown; AUTO flood;

se ~ drown; **se suicider** drown o.s.

noyer[2] *m arbre*, *bois* walnut

nu **1** *adj* naked; *arbre*, *bras*, *tête etc* bare **2** *m* ART nude

nuage *m* cloud; **nuageux**, **-euse** cloudy

nuance *f* shade; *fig* slight difference; (*subtilité*) subtlety; **nuancé** subtle; **nuancer** qualify

nucléaire **1** *adj* nuclear **2** *m*: **le ~** nuclear power

nudiste *m/f* & *adj* nudist; **nudité** *f* nudity

nuée *f* *d'insectes* cloud; *de journalistes* horde

nuire: **~ à** hurt, harm

nuit *f* night; **il fait ~** it's dark

nul, **~le 1** *adj* no; (*non valable*) invalid; (*sans valeur*) hopeless; (*inexistant*) nonexistent; **~le part** nowhere **2** *pron* no-one; **nullement** not in the least; **nullité** *f* JUR invalidity; *fig* hopelessness; *personne* loser

numérique numerical; INFORM digital

numéro *m* number; **~ vert** toll-free number, *Br* Freefone number; **numéroter 1** *v/t* number **2** *v/i* TÉL dial

nuque *f* nape of the neck

nurse *f* nanny

nutritif, **-ive** nutritional; *aliment* nutritious; **nutrition** *f* nutrition

nylon *m* nylon

O

obéir obey; **~ à** obey; **obéissance** *f* obedience; **obéissant** obedient

obèse obese; **obésité** *f* obesity

objecter: **~ qch pour ne pas faire qch** give sth as a reason; **~ que** object that; **objectif, -ive 1** *adj* (*forcer*) force; **2** *m* objective; PHOT lens; **objection** *f* objection; **objectivité** *f* objectivity

objet *m* object; *de réflexions, d'une lettre* subject

obligation *f* obligation; COMM bond; **obligatoire** compulsory, obligatory

obligeant obliging; **obliger** oblige; (*forcer*) force; **être obligé de faire qc** be obliged to do sth

oblique oblique

oblitérer *timbre* cancel

obscène obscene

obscur obscure; *nuit, rue* dark; **obscurcir** darken; **s'~** grow dark; **obscurité** *f* obscurity; *de la nuit, d'une rue* darkness

obséder obsess

obsèques *fpl* funeral

observateur, -trice *m/f* observer; **observation** *f* observation; *d'une règle* observance; **observatoire** *m* observatory; **observer** ob-

serve; *changement* notice; **faire ~ qc à qn** point sth out to s.o.

obsession *f* obsession

obstacle *m* obstacle; SP hurdle; *pour cheval* jump; **faire ~ à qc** stand in the way of sth

obstination *f* obstinacy; **obstiné** obstinate; **obstiner**: **s'~ à faire qc** persist in doing sth

obstruction *f* obstruction; *dans tuyau* blockage; **obstruer** obstruct, block

obtenir get, obtain

obturer seal; *dent* fill

obtus MATH, *fig* obtuse

obus *m* MIL shell

occasion *f* opportunity; *marché* bargain; **d'~** second-hand; **à l'~** when the opportunity arises; **occasionner** cause

Occident *m*: **l'~** the West; **occidental, ~e** western; Occidental, **~e** *m/f* Westerner

occulte occult

occupant 1 *adj* occupying **2** *m* occupant; **occupation** *f* occupation; **occupé** busy; *pays, appartement* occupied; *chaise* taken; TÉL busy; **occuper** occupy; *personnel* employ; **s'~ de politique etc** take an interest in; *malade, organisation* look after

occurrence *f*: **en l'~** as it hap-

173

ondée

pens

océan m ocean
octet m INFORM byte
octobre m October
oculaire eye atr
oculiste m/f eye specialist
odeur f smell; **~ corporelle** BO
odieux, -euse hateful, odious
odorant scented
odorat m sense of smell
œil m (pl yeux) eye; **à vue d'~** visibly
œillet m BOT carnation
œuf m egg; **~s brouillés** scrambled eggs; **~ à la coque** soft-boiled egg; **~ sur le plat** fried egg
œuvre 1 f work; **~ d'art** work of art; **mettre en ~** (employer) use; (exécuter) carry out **2** m ART, littérature works pl
offense f (insulte) insult; (péché) sin; **offenser** offend; **s'~ de** take offense ou Br offence at
office m office; REL service; **d'~** automatically; **faire ~ de** act as
officiel, ~le official
officier m officer
officieux, -euse semi-official
officinal plante medicinal
offre f offer; **~ d'emploi** job offer; **offrir** offer; cadeau give; **s'~ qc** treat o.s. to sth
offusquer offend
oie f goose
oignon m onion; BOT bulb

oiseau m bird; **à vol d'~** as the crow flies
oiseux, -euse idle
oisif, -ive idle; **oisiveté** f idleness
olive f olive; **olivier** m olive (tree)
olympique Olympic
ombrage m shade; **ombragé** shady; **ombrageux, -euse** cheval skittish; personne touchy; **ombre** f shade; (silhouette) shadow; fig (anonymat) obscurity; de regret hint
ombrelle f sunshade
omelette f omelet, Br omelette
omettre leave out, omit; **~ de faire** fail ou omit to do; **omission** f omission
omnibus m: **(train m) ~** slow train
on (après que, et, où, qui, si souvent l'on) (nous) we; (tu, vous, indéterminé) you; (quelqu'un) someone; (eux, les gens) they, people; autorités they; **~ m'a dit que...** I was told that ...; **~ ne sait jamais** you never know, one never knows fml
oncle m uncle
onction f REL unction; **onctueux, -euse** smooth; fig smarmy F, unctuous
onde f wave; **sur les ~s** RAD on the air; **grandes ~s** long wave
ondée f downpour

174

on-dit *m* rumor, *Br* rumour
ondoyer *du blés* sway
ondulation *f de terrain* undulation; *de coiffure* wave; **onduler** *d'ondes* undulate; *de cheveux* be wavy
onéreux, -euse expensive
ongle *m* nail; ZO claw
onguent *m* cream, salve
onze eleven; **le ~** the eleventh; **onzième** eleventh
opaque opaque
opéra *m* opera; *bâtiment* opera house
opérable MÉD operable; **opérateur, -trice** *m/f* operator; *en cinéma* cameraman; FIN trader; **opération** *f* operation; *action* working; FIN transaction; **opérer 1** *v/t* MÉD operate on; *(produire)* make; *(exécuter)* implement **2** *v/i* MÉD operate; *(avoir effet)* work; *(procéder)* proceed; **se faire ~** have an operation
opiner: **~ de la tête** nod in agreement
opiniâtre stubborn; **opiniâtreté** *f* stubbornness
opinion *f* opinion
opium *m* opium
opportun *ou* opportune; *moment* right; **opportuniste** *m/f* opportunist; **opportunité** *f* timeliness; *(occasion)* opportunity
opposant, ~e 1 *adj* opposing **2** *m/f* opponent; **les ~s** the opposition; **opposé 1** *adj*

pôles opposite; *opinions* conflicting; **être ~ à qc** be opposed to sth **2** *m* opposite; **à l'~ de qn** unlike s.o.; **opposer** bring into conflict; *argument* put forward; **s'~ à qn/à qc** oppose s.o./sth; **opposition** *f* opposition; *(contraste)* contrast
oppresser oppress, weigh down; **oppression** *f* oppression
opprimer oppress
opter: **~ pour** opt for
opticien, ~ne *m/f* optician
optimisme *m* optimism; **optimiste 1** *adj* optimistic **2** *m/f* optimist
option *f* option
optique 1 *adj nerf* optic; *verre* optical **2** *f science* optics; *fig* viewpoint
opulent wealthy; *poitrine* ample
or¹ *m* gold
or² *conj* now
orage *m* storm; **orageux, -euse** stormy
oraison *f* REL prayer
oral *adj* & *m* oral
orange *f* & *adj inv* orange; **oranger** *m* orange tree
orateur, -trice *m/f* orator
orbital orbital
orbite *f* ANAT eyesocket; ASTR orbit *(aussi fig)*
orchestre *m* orchestra; *de théâtre* orchestra, *Br* stalls *pl*
orchidée *f* orchid
ordinaire 1 *adj* ordinary **2** *m*

essence regular; *d'~* ordinarily

ordinateur *m* computer

ordonnance *f* arrangement, layout; (*ordre*) order (*aussi* JUR); MÉD prescription; **ordonné** tidy; **ordonner** organize; (*commander*) order; MÉD prescribe

ordre *m* order; *~ du jour* agenda; *de premier ~* first-rate; *mettre en ~* tidy

ordures *fpl* (*détritus*) garbage, *Br* rubbish; *fig* filth

oreille *f* ear; *d'un bol* handle; *dur d'~* hard of hearing

oreiller *m* pillow

oreillons *mpl* MÉD mumps *sg*

orfèvre *m* goldsmith

organe *m* organ; (*voix, porte-parole*) voice; *d'un mécanisme* part

organisation *f* organization; **organiser** organize; *s'~ d'une personne* get organized; **organiseur** *m* INFORM personal organizer

organisme *m* organism; ANAT system; (*organisation*) organization, body

orgue *m* organ

orgueil *m* pride; **orgueilleux, -euse** proud

Orient *m*: *l'~* the East; *Asie* the East, the Orient; **oriental, ~e** east, eastern; *d'Asie* eastern, Oriental; **Oriental, ~e** *m/f* Oriental

orientation *f* direction; *d'une maison* exposure; **orienter**

orient, *Br* orientate; (*diriger*) direct; *s'~* get one's bearings; *s'~ vers fig* go in for

orifice *m* opening

originaire original; *être ~ de* come from; **original 1** *adj* original; *péj* eccentric **2** *m ouvrage* original; *personne* eccentric; **origine** *f* origin; *à l'~* originally; **originel, ~le** original

orme *m* BOT elm

ornement *m* ornament; **ornementer** ornament

orner decorate; (*de* with)

orphelin, ~e *m/f* orphan; **orphelinat** *m* orphanage

orteil *m* toe

orthographe *f* spelling

ortie *f* BOT nettle

os *m* bone

osciller PHYS oscillate; *d'un pendule* swing; *~ entre fig* waver between

osé daring; **oser**: *~ faire* dare to do

osier *m* BOT osier; *en ~* wicker

ossements *mpl* bones; **osseux, -euse** ANAT bone *atr*; *visage, mains* bony

ostensible evident

otage *m* hostage

ôter remove; MATH take away

ou or; *~ bien* or (else); *~ ... ~ ...* either ... or

où where; *d'~ vient-il?* where does he come from?; *d'~ l'on peut déduire que ...* from which it can be deduced that

...; **le jour ~** ... the day when ...

ouate f absorbent cotton, Br cotton wool; **ouater** pad, quilt

oubli m forgetting; (*omission*) oversight; **tomber dans l'~** sink into oblivion; **oublier** forget; **~ de faire** forget to do

ouest 1 m west; **à l'~ de** (to the) west of **2** adj west, western

oui yes

ouï-dire: par ~ by hearsay

ouïe f hearing; **~s** zo gills

ouragan m hurricane

ourler hem; **ourlet** m hem

ours m bear; **ourse** f she-bear; **la Grande Ourse** ASTR the Great Bear

oursin m zo sea urchin

outil m tool; **outillage** m tools pl

outrage m insult; **outrager** insult

outrance f excessiveness; **à ~** excessively

outre 1 prép in addition to **2** adv: **en ~** besides; **passer ~** ignore

outré: être ~ de ou **par** be outraged by

outre-Atlantique on the other side of the Atlantic

outre-Manche on the other side of the Channel

outre-mer: d'~ overseas atr

ouvert open; **ouverture** f opening; MUS overture

ouvrable working; **jour** m ~ workday; **ouvrage** m work; **ouvragé** ornate

ouvre-boîtes m can opener, Br aussi tin opener; **ouvre--bouteilles** m bottle opener

ouvrier, -ère 1 adj working-class **2** m/f worker

ouvrir 1 v/t open; *radio, gaz* turn on **2** v/i *d'un magasin* open; **s'~** open; *fig* open up

ovale m & adj oval

ovni m (= **objet volant non identifié**) UFO (= unidentified flying object)

oxygène m oxygen

P

pacifier pacify; **pacifique 1** adj *personne* peace-loving; *coexistence* peaceful **2** m **le Pacifique** the Pacific; **pacifiste** m/f & adj pacifist

pacte m pact; **pactiser: ~ avec** come to terms with

pagaie f paddle

pagaïe, pagaille f F mess

page f page; **~ d'accueil** INFORM home page

paie, paye f pay; **paiement** m payment

païen, ~ne m/f & adj pagan

paillasson m doormat

paille f straw

pain *m* bread; ~ *au chocolat* chocolate croissant; ~ *complet* whole wheat *ou Br* wholemeal bread; ~ *d'épice* gingerbread; *petit* ~ roll

pair **1** *adj nombre* even **2** *m*: *hors* ~ unrivaled, *Br* unrivalled; *fille f au* ~ au pair

paire *f*: *une* ~ *de* a pair of

paisible peaceful; *personne* quiet

paître graze

paix *f* peace; (*calme*) peace and quiet

Pakistan: *le* ~ Pakistan; pakistanais, ~e Pakistani; Pakistanais, ~e *m/f* Pakistani

palais *m* **1** palace; ~ *de justice* law courts *pl* **2** ANAT palate

pale *f* blade

pâle pale; *fig*: *style* colorless, *Br* colourless; *imitation* pale

Palestine: *la* ~ Palestine; palestinien, ~ne Palestinian; Palestinien, ~ne *m/f* Palestinian

palette *f de peinture* palette

pâleur *f* paleness, pallor

palier *m d'un escalier* landing; TECH bearing; (*phase*) stage

pâlir go pale; *de couleurs* fade

palissade *f* fence

pallier alleviate; *manque* make up for

palme *f* BOT palm; *de natation* flipper; **palmier** *m* BOT palm tree

pâlot, ~te pale

palper feel; MÉD palpate

palpitant *fig* exciting, thrilling; **palpitations** *fpl* palpitations; **palpiter** *du cœur* pound

pamplemousse *m* grapefruit

pan *m de vêtement* tail; *de mur* section

panache *m* plume; *avoir du* ~ have panache; **panaché** *m* shandy-gaff, *Br* shandy

pancarte *f* sign; *de manifestation* placard

pané breaded

panier *m* basket

panique *f* breakdown; ~ *en panne* have a breakdown; *tomber en* ~ *sèche* run out of gas *ou Br* petrol; ~ *d'électricité* power outage, *Br* power failure

panne *f* panic; **paniquer** panic

panneau *m* board; TECH panel; ~ *de signalisation* roadsign

panorama *m* panorama

pansement *m* dressing; **panser** *blessure* dress; *cheval* groom

pantalon *m* pants *pl*, *Br* trousers *pl*; *un* ~ a pair of pants

pantelant panting

pantois *inv*: *rester* ~ be speechless

pantoufle *f* slipper

paon *m* peacock

papa *m* dad

papal REL papal; **pape** *m* REL pope

paperasse *f* (*souvent au pl* *~s*) *péj* papers *pl*

papeterie *f magasin* stationery store, *Br* stationer's

papi, papy *m* F grandpa

papier *m* paper; *~* (**d'**)**aluminium** kitchen foil; *~* **hygiénique** toilet tissue; *~s* **d'identité** identification, ID

papillon *m* butterfly; TECH wing nut; F (*contravention*) (parking) ticket

paquebot *m* liner

pâquerette *f* BOT daisy

Pâques *msg ou fpl* Easter; **joyeuses** *~!* happy Easter

paquet *m* packet; *de sucre, café* bag; *de la poste* parcel

par *lieu* through; *passif, moyen* by; *~* **terre** on the ground; *~* **beau temps** in fine weather; *~* **curiosité** out of curiosity; *~* **hasard** by chance; **diviser** *~* **quatre** divide by four; *~* **an** a year; **finir** *~* **faire** finish by doing

parabolique: **antenne** *f* *~* satellite dish

paracétamol *m* paracetamol

parachute *m* parachute; **parachutiste** *m/f* parachutist; MIL para(trooper)

parade *f* parade; *en escrime* parry; *à un argument* counter

paradis *m* paradise

paradoxe *m* paradox

parages *mpl*: ; **dans les** *~* around; **dans les** *~* **de** in the vicinity of

paragraphe *m* paragraph

paraître appear; *d'un livre* come out, be published; *il* **paraît que** it seems that, it would appear that; **laisser** *~* show

parallèle 1 *adj* parallel (*à* to) **2** *f* MATH parallel (line) **3** *m* GÉOGR parallel (*aussi fig*)

paralyser paralyse; **paralysie** *f* paralysis

paramètre *m* parameter

paranoïaque *m/f* & *adj* paranoid

parapharmacie *f* (non-dispensing) pharmacy; *produits toiletries* *pl*

paraplégique *m/f* & *adj* paraplegic

parapluie *m* umbrella

parasite 1 *adj* parasitic **2** *m* parasite; *~s radio* interference

parasol *m* parasol; *de plage* beach parasol

paratonnerre *m* lightning rod, *Br* lightning conductor

paravent *m* windbreak

parc *m* park; *pour enfant* playpen

parcelle *f* *de terrain* parcel

parce que because

par-ci *adv*: *~,* **par-là** *espace* here and there; *temps* now and then

parcimonie *f*: **avec** *~* parcimoniously

parcourir *région* travel through; *distance* cover; *texte* read quickly

partager

parcours *m* route; *course d'automobiles* circuit
par-derrière from behind
par-dessous underneath
pardessus *m* overcoat
par-dessus over
par-devant from the front
pardon *m* forgiveness; **~!** sorry!; **~?** excuse me?; **pardonner: ~ qc à qn** forgive s.o. sth
pare-brise *m* windshield, *Br* windscreen
pare-chocs *m* bumper
pareil, ~le 1 *adj* similar (**à** to); *(tel)* such; **c'est toujours ~** it's always the same **2** *adv*: **habillés ~** similarly dressed, dressed the same way
parent, ~e 1 *adj* related **2** *m/f* relative; **~s** *(mère et père)* parents; **parenté** *f* relationship
parenthèse *f* parenthesis, *Br* (round) bracket; **entre ~s** *fig* by the way
parer *attaque* ward off; *en escrime* parry
paresse *f* laziness; **paresseux, -euse** lazy
parfait 1 *adj* perfect; *avant le substantif* complete **2** *m* GRAM perfect (tense)
parfois sometimes
parfum *m* perfume; *d'une glace* flavour, *Br* flavour
pari *m* bet; **parier** bet
parisien, ~ne Parisian, of/ from Paris; **Parisien, ~ne** *m/f* Parisian
parité *f* ÉCON parity

parking *m* parking lot, *Br* car park; *édifice* parking garage, *Br* car park
parlant *comparaison* striking; *preuves* decisive
Parlement *m* Parliament; **parlementaire 1** *adj* Parliamentary **2** *m/f* Parliamentarian
parler 1 *v/i* speak, talk; **sans ~ de** not to mention **2** *v/t*: **~ affaires** talk business; **~ anglais** speak English
parmi among
parodie *f* parody
paroi *f* partition
paroisse *f* REL parish
parole *f* word; *faculté* speech; **donner la ~ à qn** give s.o. the floor
parquer *bétail* pen; *réfugiés* dump
parquet *m* (parquet) floor; JUR public prosecutor's office
parrain *m* godfather; *dans un club* sponsor
parsemer sprinkle (**de** with)
part *f* share; *(fraction)* part; **faire ~ de qc à qn** inform s.o. of sth; **de la ~ de qn** on *ou Br* on behalf of s.o.; **d'une ~ ... d'autre ~** on the one hand ... on the other hand; **autre ~** elsewhere; **nulle ~** nowhere; **quelque ~** somewhere; **à ~ traiter** *etc* separately; **à ~ cela** apart from that
partage *m* division; **partager**

share; (*couper, diviser*) divide (up)

partenaire *m/f* partner

parterre *m* de fleurs bed; *au théâtre* rear orchestra, Br rear stalls *pl*

parti[1] *m* side; POL party; **prendre ~ pour** side with; **tirer ~ de qc** turn sth to good use; **~ pris** preconceived idea

parti[2] *adj* F: **être ~** (*ivre*) tight

partial biassed

participant, ~e *m/f* participant; participer: **~ à** participate in, take part in; *bénéfices* share; *frais* contribute to; *douleur, succès* share in

particularité *f* special feature; **particulier, -ère 1** *adj* particular, special; *privé* private; **~ à** peculiar to **2** *m* (*privé*) individual; **particulièrement** particularly

partie *f part*; *d'un jeu* game; JUR party; *lutte* struggle; **en ~** partly; **faire ~ de qch** be part of sth

partiel, ~le partial

partir leave (**à, pour** for); SP start; *de la saleté* come out; *d'un film* show; **~ chez qn** come from sth; **à ~ de** (starting) from

partisan, ~e *m/f* supporter; MIL *m* partisan

partition *f* MUS score; POL partition

partout everywhere

parure *f* finery; *de bijoux* set

parvenir arrive; **faire ~ qc à qn** forward sth to s.o.; **~ à faire** manage to do

parvenu, ~e *m/f* upstart

pas[1] *m* step, pace; **faux ~** stumble; *fig* blunder, faux pas

pas[2] *adv* not; **ne ... ~** not; **il ne pleut ~** it's not raining; **il n'a ~ plu** it didn't rain

passable acceptable

passage *m* passage; *fig* (*changement*) changeover; **~ à niveau** grade crossing, Br level crossing; **de ~** passing

passager, -ère 1 *adj* passing **2** *m/f* passenger

passant, ~e *m/f* passerby

passe *f* SP pass

passé 1 *adj* past **2** *prép*: **~ dix heures** after ten o'clock **3** *m* past; **~ composé** GRAM perfect

passe-partout *m* skeleton key

passe-passe *m*: **tour** *m* **de ~** conjuring trick

passeport *m* passport

passer 1 *v/i* pass, go past; *d'un film* show; **~ chez qn** drop by at s.o.'s place; **~ de mode** go out of fashion; **~ en seconde** AUTO shift into second; **~ pour qc** pass as sth; **faire ~** *personne* let past; *plat, journal* pass; **laisser ~** *personne* let past; *lumière* let in; *chance* let slip **2** *v/t*

181 pauvre

frontière cross; (*omettre*) miss (out); *temps* spend; *examen* take; *vêtement* slip on; *film* show; *contrat* enter into; **~ qc à qn** pass s.o. sth, pass sth to s.o. **3: se~** (*se produire*) happen; **se ~ de qc** do without sth

passerelle *f* footbridge; MAR gangway; AVIAT steps *pl*

passe-temps *m* hobby, pastime

passif, -ive **1** *adj* passive **2** *m* GRAM passive; COMM liabilities *pl*

passion *f* passion; passionnant exciting; passionné, ~e **1** *adj* passionate **2** *m/f* enthusiast; passionner excite; **se ~ pour** have a passion for

passivité *f* passiveness, passivity

passoire *f* sieve

pastel *m* pastel

pastèque *f* BOT watermelon

pasteur *m* REL pastor

pasteuriser pasteurize

pastille *f* pastille

patate *f* F potato, spud F

patauger flounder

pâte *f* paste; CUIS: *à pain* dough; *à tarte* pastry; **~s** pasta *sg*

pâté *m* paté; **~ de maisons** block of houses

patère *f* coat peg

paternaliste paternalistic

paternel, ~le paternal

pâteux, -euse doughy; *bouche* dry

pathétique touching; F (*mauvais*) pathetic

pathologique pathological

patience *f* patience; patient, ~e *m/f* & *adj* patient; patienter wait

patin *m*: **faire du ~** go skating; **~ à roulettes** roller skate; patinage *m* skating; patiner skate; AUTO skid; *de roues* spin; patineur, -euse *m/f* skater; patinoire *f* skating rink

pâtisserie *f* cake shop; *gâteaux* cakes; pâtissier, -ère *m/f* pastrycook

patois *m* dialect

patrie *f* homeland

patrimoine *m* heritage

patriote **1** *adj* patriotic **2** *m/f* patriot

patron *m* boss; (*propriétaire*) owner; *d'une auberge* landlord; REL patron saint; *de couture* pattern

patronne *f* boss; (*propriétaire*) owner; *d'une auberge* landlady; REL patron saint

patronner sponsor

patrouille *f* patrol

patte *f* paw; *d'un oiseau* foot; *d'un insecte* leg; F hand, paw péj

paume *f* palm

paumer F lose

paupière *f* eyelid

pause *f* (*silence*) pause; (*interruption*) break; **~ café** coffee break

pauvre **1** *adj* poor **2** *m/f* poor

person; **les ~s** the poor *pl*;
pauvreté *f* poverty
pavé *m* paving; (*chaussée*)
pavement, *Br* road surface;
pierres rondes cobbles *pl*;
un ~ a paving stone; *rond*
a cobblestone; **paver** pave
pavillon *m* (*maisonnette*)
small house; MAR flag
pavot *m* BOT poppy
payable payable
payant *spectateur* paying;
parking which charges; *fig*
profitable
payer 1 *v/t* pay; **~ qc dix euros** pay ten euros for sth **2**
v/i pay **3**: **se ~ qc** treat o.s.
to sth
pays *m* country; **mal m du ~**
homesickness
paysage *m* landscape
paysan, ~ne 1 *m/f* small farmer; HIST peasant **2** *adj mœurs*
country *atr*
Pays-Bas *mpl*: **les ~** the
Netherlands
PC *m* (= **personal computer**)
PC
PDG *m* (= **président-directeur général**) President,
CEO (= Chief Executive
Officer),
péage *m d'une autoroute* toll-
booth; **autoroute à ~** turnpike, toll road
peau *f* skin; *cuir* leather
pêche[1] *f* BOT peach
pêche[2] *f* fishing; *poissons*
catch
péché *m* sin; **pécher** sin

pêcher[1] *m* BOT peach tree
pêcher[2] **1** *v/t* fish for; (*attraper*) catch **2** *v/i* fish; **~ à la ligne** go angling
pêcheur, -eresse *m/f* sinner
pêcheur *m* fisherman; **~ à la
ligne** angler
pédagogie *f* education,
teaching; **pédagogique** educational; *méthode* teaching
pédale *f* pedal; **pédaler** *à vélo*
pedal
pédéraste *m* homosexual
pédestre: *sentier m ~* footpath; *randonnée f ~* hike
pédiatre *m/f* MÉD pediatrician
pédicure *m/f* podiatrist, *Br*
chiropodist
pègre *f* underworld
peigne *m* comb; **peigner**
comb; **se ~** comb one's hair
peignoir *m* robe, *Br* dressing
gown
peindre paint; (*décrire*) depict
peine *f* (*punition*) punishment; (*effort*) trouble; (*difficulté*) difficulty; (*chagrin*)
sorrow; **ce n'est pas la ~**
there's no point, it's not
worth it; **valoir la ~ de faire
qc** be worth doing sth; **à ~**
scarcely, hardly
peiner 1 *v/t* upset **2** *v/i* labor,
Br labour
peintre *m* painter
peinture *f* paint; *action, tableau* painting; *description*
depiction

péjoratif, -ive pejorative
pelage *m* coat
peler peel
pèlerin *m* pilgrim
pelle *f* spade
pellicule *f* film; **~s** dandruff
pelote *f de fil* ball
peloter F grope, feel up
peloton *m* ball; MIL platoon;
SP pack; **pelotonner** wind
into a ball; **se ~ contre qn**
snuggle up to s.o.
pelouse *f* lawn
peluche *f* soft toy; **ours**
m **en ~** teddy bear
pelure *f de fruit* peel
pénaliser penalize; **pénalité** *f*
penalty
penchant *m* (*inclination*) liking, penchant
pencher 1 *v/t pot* tilt; **penché**
écriture sloping; **~ la tête en
avant** bend over **2** *v/i* lean; *d'un plateau* tilt;
d'un bateau list; **se ~ sur
un problème** *fig* examine a
problem
pendant¹ 1 *prép* during; *avec
chiffre* for **2** *conj:* **~ que**
while
pendant² *adj oreilles* pendu-
lous; (*en instance*) pending
penderie *f armoire, Br* wardrobe
pendre hang; **se ~** hang o.s.
pendule 1 *m* pendulum **2** *f*
(*horloge*) clock
pénétrer 1 *v/t* penetrate; *pensées, personne* fathom out **2**
v/i: **~ dans** penetrate; *mai-*

son, bureaux get into
pénible *travail, vie* hard; *nouvelle* painful; *caractère* difficult
pénicilline *f* penicillin
péninsule *f* peninsula
pénis *m* penis
pénitence *f* REL penitence;
(*punition*) punishment; **pénitencier** *m* penitentiary,
Br prison
pénombre *f* semi-darkness
pense-bête *m* reminder
pensée *f* thought; BOT pansy;
penser think; **~ à** (*réfléchir
à*) think about; **faire ~ à
qn à faire qch** remind s.o.
to do sth; **~ faire qch** (*avoir
l'intention*) be thinking of
doing sth; **penseur** *m* think-
er; **pensif, -ive** thoughtful
pension *f* (*allocation*) allowance; *logement* rooming
house, *Br* boarding house; **~
école** boarding school; **~
complète** American plan,
Br full board; **pensionnaire**
m/f d'un hôtel guest; *écolier*
boarder; **pensionnat** *m*
boarding school
pente *f* slope; **en ~** sloping
Pentecôte: **la ~** Pentecost
pénurie *f* shortage
pépin *m de fruit* seed
perçant *regard, froid* piercing
percée *f* breakthrough
percepteur *m* tax collector
perception *f* perception; *des
impôts* collection; *bureau*
tax office

percer 1 v/t make a hole in; *porte* make; *(transpercer)* pierce **2** v/i *du soleil* break through; **perceuse** f drill

percevoir perceive; *impôts* collect

perche f zo perch; *en bois, métal* pole

percher: *(se)* ~ *d'un oiseau* perch; F live; **perchoir** m perch

percolateur m percolator

percussion f MUS percussion

percuter crash into

perdant, ~e **1** adj losing **2** m/f loser

perdre 1 v/t lose; *occasion* miss; *son temps* waste; *se* ~ *disparaître* disappear; *d'une personne* get lost **2** v/i: ~ *au change* lose out

perdrix f partridge

père m father (*aussi* REL)

perfection f perfection; **perfectionnement** m perfecting; **perfectionner** perfect; *se* ~ *en anglais* improve one's English

perfide treacherous

perforer perforate; *cuir* punch

performance f performance; **performant** high-performance

péril m peril; **périlleux, -euse** perilous

périmé out of date

périmètre m MATH perimeter

période f period; *en* ~ *de* in times of; **périodique 1** adj

periodic **2** m periodical

périphérie f *d'une ville* outskirts pl; **périphérique** m beltway, Br ringroad

périr perish; **périssable** *nourriture* perishable

péritel: *prise* f ~ scart

perle f pearl; *(boule percée)* bead; *fig: personne* gem; *de sang* drop; **perler:** *la sueur perlait sur son front* he had beads of sweat on his forehead

permanence f permanence; *être de* ~ be on duty; *en* ~ constantly; **permanent,** ~e **1** adj permanent **2** f *coiffure* perm

perméable permeable

permettre allow, permit; ~ *à qn de faire qch* allow s.o. to do sth; *se* ~ *qc* allow o.s. sth

permis m permit; *passer son* ~ sit one's driving test; ~ *de conduire* driver's license, Br driving licence; ~ *de séjour* residence permit

permission f permission; MIL leave

perpendiculaire perpendicular (*à* to)

perpétrer JUR perpetrate

perpétuel, ~le perpetual; **perpétuer** perpetuate; **perpétuité** f: *à* ~ in perpetuity; JUR *condamné* to life imprisonment

perplexe perplexed, puzzled

perron m steps pl

perroquet *m* parrot

perruque *f* wig

persécuter persecute

persévérance *f* perseverance; **persévérer** persevere (**dans** in)

persienne *f* shutter

persil *m* BOT parsley

persistance *f* persistence; **persister** persist (**à faire** in doing); **~ dans sa décision** stick to one's decision

personnage *m* character; (*dignitaire*) important person

personnalité *f* personality

personne[1] *f* person; **deux ~s** two people; **par ~** per person, each; **les ~s âgées** the old *pl*, old people *pl*

personne[2] *pron* no-one, nobody; **il n'y avait ~** no-one was there, there wasn't anyone there; **je ne vois jamais ~** I never see anyone; **qui que ce soit** anyone, anybody

personnel, **~le 1** *adj* personal; *conversation*, *courrier* private **2** *m* personnel *pl*, staff *pl*

perspective *f* perspective; *fig: pour l'avenir* prospect

perspicace shrewd; **perspicacité** *f* shrewdness

persuader persuade (**de faire** to do); **se ~** convince o.s.

perte *f* loss; *fig* (*destruction*) ruin; **à ~ de vue** as far as the eye can see; **une ~ de temps** a waste of time

pertinent relevant

perturbateur, **-trice** disruptive; **perturber** *personne* upset; *trafic* disrupt

pervers perverse; **pervertir** pervert

pesant heavy; **pesanteur** *f* PHYS gravity

pèse-personne *f* scales *pl*

peser weigh; *fig* weigh up; *mots* weigh

pessimisme *m* pessimism; **pessimiste 1** *adj* pessimistic **2** *m/f* pessimist

pétale *f* petal

pétard *m* firecracker; F (*bruit*) racket

péter F fart F

pétillant sparkling; **pétiller** *du feu* crackle; *d'une boisson*, *d'yeux* sparkle

petit, **~e 1** *adj* small, little; **~ à ~** gradually, little by little; **~ ami** *m* boyfriend; **~e amie** *f* girlfriend **2** *m/f* child; **une chatte et ses ~s** a cat and her young; **attendre des ~s** be pregnant

petite-fille *f* granddaughter

petit-fils *m* grandson

pétition *f* petition

pétrifier turn to stone; *fig* petrify

pétrin *m* *fig* F mess

pétrir knead

pétrole *m* oil, petroleum; **~ brut** crude (oil); **pétrolier**, **-ère 1** *adj* oil *atr* **2** *m* tanker

peu 1 *adv*: **~ gentil** not very nice; **~ après** a little after;

j'ai ~ dormi I didn't sleep much; **~ de pain** not much bread; **~ de choses à faire** not many things to do; **~ de gens** few people; **dans ~ de temps** in a little while; **un ~** a little, a bit; **un tout petit ~** just a very little, just a little bit; **un ~ de chocolat** a little chocolate, a bit of chocolate; **un ~ plus long** a bit *ou* little longer; **de ~ rater le bus** *etc* only just; **à ~ peu près** (*plus ou moins*) more or less; (*presque*) almost

peuple *m* people; **peupler** *région* populate; *maison* live in

peuplier *m* BOT poplar

peur *f* fear (**de** of); **avoir ~** be frightened, be afraid (**de** of); **faire ~ à qn** frighten s.o.; **de ~ que** (+*subj*) in case; **peureux, -euse** fearful, timid

peut-être perhaps, maybe

phare *m* MAR lighthouse; AVIAT beacon; AUTO headlight; **se mettre en (pleins) ~s** switch to full beam

pharmacie *f* pharmacy, Br *aussi* chemist's; *science* pharmacy; **médicaments** pharmaceuticals *pl*; **pharmacien, ~ne** *m/f* pharmacist

phénomène *m* phenomenon

philosophe *m* philosopher; **philosophie** *f* philosophy; **philosophique** philosophical

phobie *f* phobia

photo *f* photo; *l'art* photography; **prendre qn en ~** take a photo of s.o.

photocopie *f* photocopy; **photocopier** photocopy; **photocopieur** *m*, **photocopieuse** *f* photocopier

photographe *m/f* photographer; **photographie** *f* photograph; *l'art* photography; **photographier** photograph

phrase *f* GRAM sentence; MUS phrase; **sans ~s** straight out

physicien, ~ne *m/f* physicist

physique 1 *adj* physical **2** *m* physique **3** *f* physics

piailler *d'un oiseau* chirp; F *d'un enfant* scream

pianiste *m/f* pianist; **piano** *m* piano; **~ à queue** grand piano

pic *m* pick; *d'une montagne* peak; **à ~ tomber** steeply

pichet *m* pitcher, Br jug

pickpocket *m* pickpocket

pick-up *m* pick-up (truck)

pie *f* ZO magpie

pièce *f* piece; *de machine* part; (*chambre*) room; (*document*) document; *de monnaie* coin; *de théâtre* play; **cinq euros (la) ~** five euros each; **mettre en ~s** smash to smithereens; **~ jointe** enclosure

pied *m* foot; *d'un meuble* leg; *d'un champignon* stalk; **à ~** on foot; **~s nus** barefoot; **au ~ de** at the foot of; **mettre**

sur ~ set up

piège *m* trap; piégé: *voiture f* ~*e* car bomb; piéger trap; *voiture* booby-trap

piercing *m* body piercing

pierre *f* stone; ~ *tombale* gravestone; pierreux, -euse *sol* stony

piétiner **1** *v/t* trample; *fig* trample underfoot **2** *v/i fig* (*ne pas avancer*) mark time

piéton, ~ne **1** *m/f* pedestrian **2** *adj*: *zone f* ~*ne* pedestrianized zone, *Br* pedestrian precinct

pieu *m* stake; *F* pit *F*

pieuvre *f* octopus

pieux, -euse *pious*

pigeon *m* pigeon

piger *F* understand, get *F*

pigment *m* pigment

pile¹ *f* (*tas*) pile; ÉL battery; *monnaie* tails

pile² *adv*: *s'arrêter* ~ stop dead; *à deux heures* ~ at two o'clock on the dot

piler *ail* crush; *amandes* grind

pilier *m* pillar (*aussi fig*)

pillage *m* pillage, plunder; piller pillage

pilote **1** *m* pilot; AUTO driver **2** *adj*: *usine f* ~ pilot plant; piloter pilot; AUTO drive

pilule *f* pill

piment *m* pimento; *fig* spice

pimenter spice up

pin *m* BOT pine

pinard *m* F wine

pince *f* pliers *pl*; *d'un crabe* pincer; ~ *à épiler* tweezers

pl; ~ *à linge* clothespin, *Br* clothespeg

pinceau *m* brush

pincer pinch; MUS pluck

ping-pong *m* ping-pong

pinson *m* chaffinch

pintade *f* guinea fowl

pioche *f* pickax, *Br* pickaxe; piocher dig

pioncer *F* sleep, *Br* kip *F*

pipe *f* pipe

pipi *m* F pee *F*

pique *m aux cartes* spades

pique-nique *m* picnic

piquer *d'une abeille, des orties* sting; *d'un moustique, serpent* bite; *d'épine* prick; *fig*: *curiosité* excite; *fig F* (*voler*) pinch F; *se* ~ prick o.s.; *se faire une piqûre* inject o.s.

piquet *m* stake; ~ *de tente* tent peg; ~ *de grève* picket line

piquette *f* cheap wine

piqûre *f d'abeille* sting; *de moustique* bite; MÉD injection

pirate *m* pirate; ~ *informatique* hacker; ~ *de l'air* hijacker; pirater pirate

pire WOISE; *le/la* ~ the worst

piscine *f* (swimming) pool; ~ *couverte/en plein air* indoor/outdoor pool

pisser *F* pee *F*, piss *F*

piste *f* track; AVIAT runway; *ski alpin* piste; *ski de fond* trail; ~ *cyclable* cycle path

pistolet *m* pistol

piston m piston; **pistonner** F pull strings for

pitié f pity; **avoir ~ de qn** take pity on s.o.

pitoyable pitiful

pittoresque picturesque

pivot m pivot

pizza f pizza

PJ (= **pièce(s) jointe(s)**) enclosure(s)

placard m (armoire) cabinet, Br cupboard; (affiche) poster; **placarder** avis stick up

place f de ville square; (lieu) place; (siège) seat; (espace libre) room, space; (emploi) position; **sur ~** on the spot; **à la ~ de** instead of; **~ de place ce avec** change places with

placement m (emploi) placement; FIN investment; **agence f de ~** employment agency; **placer** put, place; (procurer emploi à) find a job for; argent invest; dans une famille etc find a place for; **se ~** take one's place

plafond m ceiling

plage f beach; lieu seaside resort

plagiat m plagiarism

plaider 1 v/i JUR plead **2** v/t: **~ la cause de qn** defend s.o.; fig plead s.o.'s cause

plaidoyer m JUR speech for the defense ou Br defence; fig plea

plaie f cut; fig wound

plaignant, ~e m/f JUR plaintiff

plaindre pity; **se ~** complain

(de about; à to)

plaine f plain

plainte f complaint; (lamentation) moan

plaire: s'il vous plaît, s'il te plaît please; **Paris me plaît** I like Paris; **ça me plairait d'aller ...** I would like to go ...; **se ~ de personnes** be attracted to each other

plaisance f: **port m de ~** marina

plaisanter joke; **plaisanterie** f joke

plaisir m pleasure; **par ~, pour le ~** for pleasure; **faire ~ à** please

plan 1 adj flat, level **2** m (surface) surface; (projet, relevé) plan; **premier ~** foreground; **sur ce ~** in that respect; **sur le ~ économique** in economic terms

planche f plank; **~ à voile** sailboard

plancher m floor

planer hover; fig live in another world

planète f planet

planeur m glider

planifier plan

planning m: **~ familial** family planning

planquer F hide; **se ~** hide

plant m AGR seedling; (plantation) plantation

plante[1] f plant

plante[2] f: **~ du pied** sole of the foot

planter plant; jardin plant up;

poteau hammer in; *tente* put up

plaque *f* plate; (*inscription*) plaque; **~ électrique** hot-plate; **~ tournante** turntable; *fig* hub

plaquer *argent, or* plate; *meuble* veneer; *fig* pin (**contre** to, against); F (*abandonner*) dump F; *au rugby* tackle

plastique *adj & m* plastic

plat 1 *adj* flat; *eau* still **2 ~** dish

plateau *m* tray; *de théâtre* stage; TV, *d'un film* set; GÉOGR plateau; **~ de fromages** cheeseboard

plate-bande *f* flower bed

plate-forme *f* platform; **~ de lancement** launch pad

platine 1 *m* CHIM platinum **2** *f*: **~ laser** *ou* **CD** CD player

platitude *f* dullness; (*lieu commun*) platitude

plâtre *m* plaster; **plâtrer** plaster

plausible plausible

plein 1 *adj* full (**de** of); **en ~ air** in the open (air); **en ~ Paris** in the middle of Paris; **en ~ jour** in broad daylight **2** *adv*: **~ de** F lots of, a whole bunch of F **3** *m*: **faire le ~** AUTO fill up

pleurer 1 *v/i* cry; **~ sur** complain about **2** *v/t* (*regretter*) mourn

pleurnicher F snivel

pleuvoir rain; *il pleut* it's raining

pli *m* fold; *d'une jupe* pleat; *d'un pantalon* crease; (*enveloppe*) envelope; (*lettre*) letter; **plier 1** *v/t* (*rabattre*) fold; (*courber, ployer*) bend **2** *v/i* bend; *fig* (*céder*) give in; **se ~ à** (*se soumettre*) submit to

plomb *m* lead; **sans ~** *essence* unleaded

plombage *m* filling

plomberie *f* plumbing; **plombier** *m* plumber

plongée *f* diving; **plonger 1** *v/i* dive **2** *v/t* plunge; **se ~ dans** bury o.s. in; **plongeur, -euse** *m/f* diver

pluie *f* rain; *fig* shower

plumage *m* plumage; **plume** *f* feather; **plumer** pluck; *fig* fleece

plupart: **la ~ d'entre nous** most of us; **pour la ~** mostly; **la ~ du temps** most of the time

pluriel, ~le *adj & m* plural

plus 1 *adv* more (**que, de** than); **~ grand** bigger; **~ efficace** more efficient; **le ~ grand** the biggest; **le ~ efficace** the most efficient; **~ il vieillit ~ il dort** the older he gets the more he sleeps; **le ~** the most; **tu en veux ~?** do you want some more?; **20 euros de ~** 20 euros more; **nous n'avons ~ d'argent** we have no more money, we don't have any more money; **elle n'y habite ~**

she doesn't live there any more, she no longer lives there; **je ne le reverrai ~ jamais** I won't see him ever again; **moi non ~** me neither **2** *prép* MATH plus

plusieurs several

plutôt rather

pluvieux, -euse rainy

pneu *m* tire, *Br* tyre

pneumonie *f* pneumonia

poche *f* pocket; zo pouch; **livre** *m* **de ~** paperback; **argent de ~** pocket money

pocher œufs poach

pochette *f pour photos etc* folder; *d'un disque,* CD sleeve; (*sac*) bag

poêle 1 *m* stove **2** *f* frypan, *Br* frying pan

poème *m* poem

poésie *f* poetry; (*poème*) poem

poète *m* poet; **poétique** poetic; *atmosphère* romantic

poids *m* weight; *fig* (*charge, fardeau*) burden; (*importance*) weight; **perdre/prendre du ~** lose/gain weight

poignard *m* dagger; **poignarder** stab

poignée *f petit nombre* handful; *d'une valise etc* handle; **~ de main** handshake

poignet *m* wrist

poil *m* hair; **à ~** naked; **poilu** hairy

poinçonner argent hallmark; billet punch

poing *m* fist; **coup** *m* **de ~** punch

point¹ *m* point; *de couture* stitch; **deux ~s** colon; **être sur le ~ de faire** be on the point of doing; **à ~** viande medium; **à ce ~** so much; **du jour** dawn; **~ de vue** point of view

point² *adv litt*: **il ne le fera ~** he will not do it

pointe *f* point; *d'asperge* tip; **en ~** pointed; **de ~** technologie leading-edge; secteur high-tech; **une ~ de** a touch of

pointer 1 *v/t sur liste* check, *Br* tick off **2** *v/i d'un employé* clock in

pointillé *m*: **les ~s** the dotted line

pointilleux, -euse fussy

pointu pointed; *voix* high-pitched

pointure *f* (shoe) size

point-virgule *m* GRAM semi-colon

poire *f* pear

poireau *m* BOT leek

poirier *m* BOT pear (tree)

pois *m* BOT pea; **petits ~** garden peas

poison 1 *m* poison **2** *m/f fig* F nuisance, pest

poisson *m* fish; **Poissons** *mpl* ASTROL Pisces

poissonnerie *f* fish shop, *Br* fishmonger's

poitrine *f* chest; (*seins*) bosom

poivre *m* pepper; **poivrer**

pepper

poivron m bell pepper, Br pepper

polaire polar; **pôle** m pole; fig center, Br centre, focus; **~ Nord** North Pole; **~ Sud** South Pole

poli (courtois) polite; métal, caillou polished

police f police; **~ d'assurance** insurance policy

policier, -ère 1 adj police atr; film, roman detective atr **2** m police officer

polir polish

politesse f politeness

politicien, ~ne m/f politician

politique 1 adj political; **homme** m **~** politician **2** f d'un parti etc policy; (affaires publiques) politics sg

pollen m pollen

polluer pollute; **pollution** f pollution; **~ atmosphérique** air pollution

Pologne: la ~ Poland; **polonais, ~e** adj Polish **2** m langue Polish; **Polonais, ~e** m/f Pole

poltron, ~ne m/f coward

polyclinique f (general) hospital

polycopié m (photocopied) handout

polystyrène m polystyrene

polyvalence f versatility; **polyvalent** multipurpose; personne versatile

pommade f MÉD ointment

pomme f apple; **~ de terre** potato

pommette f ANAT cheekbone

pommier m BOT apple tree

pompe[1] f faste pomp; **~s funèbres** funeral director

pompe[2] f TECH pump; **~ à essence** gas pump, Br petrol pump; **pomper** pump; fig (épuiser) knock out

pompeux, -euse pompous

pompier m firefighter; **~s** fire department, Br fire brigade

pomponner F: **se ~** get dolled up F

poncer sand

ponctualité f punctuality; **ponctuel, ~le** personne punctual; fig: action one-off

ponctuer punctuate

pondération f d'une personne level-headedness; de forces balance; ÉCON weighting; **pondéré** personne level-headed; forces balanced; ÉCON weighted

pondre œufs lay; fig F come up with; roman churn out

poney m pony

pont m bridge; MAR deck; **faire le ~** make a long weekend of it

pontage m: **~ coronarien** (heart) bypass

pop f MUS pop

populaire popular; **populariser** popularize; **popularité** f popularity

population f population

porc m hog, pig; fig pig; viande pork

porcelaine *f* porcelain

porcherie *f* hog *ou* pig farm

pore *m* pore; poreu*x*, -eu*se* porous

pornographique pornographic

port[1] *m* port; **~ de pêche** fishing port

port[2] *m* *d'armes* carrying; *courrier* postage

portable **1** *adj* portable **2** *m* *ordinateur* laptop; *téléphone* cellphone, cell, *Br* mobile

portail *m* ARCH portal; *d'un parc* gate

portant *mur* load-bearing; **à bout ~** at point-blank range; **bien ~** well; **mal ~** not well

portatif, -ive portable

porte *f* door; *d'une ville* gate; **mettre qn à la ~** show s.o. the door

porte-bagages *m* AUTO roof rack; *filet* luggage rack; porte-bonheur *m* lucky charm; porte-clés *m* keyring; porte-documents *m* briefcase

portée *f* ZO litter; *d'une arme* range; (*importance*) significance; **être à la ~ de qn** *fig* be accessible to s.o.

portefeuille *m* portfolio (*aussi* POL, FIN); (*porte-monnaie*) billfold, *Br* wallet

portemanteau *m* coat rack; *sur pied* coatstand

porte-monnaie *m* coin purse, *Br* purse

porte-parole *m* spokesperson

porter **1** *v/t* carry; *un vêtement, des lunettes etc* wear; (*apporter*) take; *yeux, attention* turn (**sur** to); *toast* drink; *fruits, nom* bear; **~ plainte** make a complaint **2** *v/i* *d'une voix* carry; **~ sur** (*appuyer sur*) rest on; (*concerner*) be about **3**: **il se porte bien/mal** he's well/not well; **se ~ candidat** be a candidate, run

porteur *m d'un message* bearer

portier *m* doorman

portière *f de train, voiture* door

portion *f* portion

portrait *m* portrait

portugais, ~e **1** *adj* Portuguese **2** *m langue* Portuguese; Portugais, ~e *m/f* Portuguese; Portugal: **le ~** Portugal

pose *f d'un radiateur* installation; *de moquette* fitting; *de papier peint, rideaux* hanging; (*attitude*) pose; posé poised, composed; poser **1** *v/t* (*mettre*) put (down); *compteur, radiateur* install, *Br* instal; *moquette* fit; *papier peint, rideaux* hang; *problème* pose; *question* ask; **se ~ en** set o.s. up as **2** *v/i* pose

positif, -ive positive

position *f* position

possédé possessed (**de** by); posséder own, possess;

possesseur *m* owner; possession *f* possession, ownership

possibilité *f* possibility; possible **1** *adj* possible; *le plus souvent* ~ as often as possible; *autant que* ~ as far as possible **2** *m*: *faire tout son* ~ do everything one can

poste[1] *m* mail, *Br aussi* post; (*bureau m de*) ~ post office; *mettre à la* ~ mail, *Br aussi* post

poste[2] *m* post; (*profession*) position; RAD, TV set; TÉL extension; ~ *de secours* first-aid post; ~ *de travail* INFORM work station

poster *soldat* post; *lettre* mail, *Br aussi* post

postérieur **1** *adj dans l'espace* back *atr*, rear *atr*; *dans le temps* later; ~ *à qch* after sth **2** *m* F posterior F

postérité *f* posterity

posthume posthumous

postier, -ère *m/f* post office employee

postillonner splutter

postuler apply for

posture *f* position, posture; *fig* position

pot *m* pot; ~ *à eau* water jug; *prendre un* ~ F have a drink; *avoir du* ~ F be lucky

potable fit to drink; *eau* ~ drinking water

potage *m* soup; potager, -ère: *jardin m* ~ kitchen garden

pot-au-feu *m* boiled beef dinner

pot-de-vin *m* F kickback F, bribe

poteau *m* post; ~ *indicateur* signpost

poterie *f* pottery; *objet* piece of pottery

potion *f* potion

potiron *m* BOT pumpkin

pou *m* louse

poubelle *f* trash can, *Br* dustbin

pouce *m* thumb

poudre *f* powder; *chocolat m en* ~ chocolate powder; poudrier *m* powder compact

pouffer: ~ *de rire* burst out laughing

poulailler *m* henhouse; *au théâtre* gallery, *Br* gods *pl*

poulain *m* zo foal

poule *f* hen; poulet *m* chicken

poulpe *m* octopus

pouls *m* pulse

poumon *m* lung

poupée *f* doll (*aussi fig*)

poupon *m* little baby

pour *m* prép for; ~ *20 euros de courses* 20 euros' worth of shopping; *je l'ai dit* ~ *te prévenir* I said that to warn you **2** *conj*: ~ *que* (+ *subj*) so that; *il parle trop vite* ~ *que je le comprenne* he speaks too fast for me to understand **3** *m*: *le* ~ *et le contre* the pros and the cons *pl*

pourboire *m* tip

pourcentage *m* percentage
pourparlers *mpl* talks
pourpre purple
pourquoi why
pourri rotten (*aussi fig*);
pourrir 1 *v/i* rot; *fig: d'une
situation* deteriorate 2 *v/t*
rot; *fig* (*corrompre*) corrupt;
(*gâter*) spoil; pourriture *f* rot
(*aussi fig*)
poursuite *f* chase, pursuing; *fig*
pursuit; **~s** JUR proceedings;
poursuivre pursue, chase;
fig: bonheur pursue; *de pensées* haunt; JUR sue; *malfaiteur* prosecute; (*continuer*)
carry on with
pourtant yet
pourvoir 1 *v/t emploi* fill; **~ de
voiture, maison** equip with 2
v/i: **~ à besoins** provide for;
se ~ de provide o.s.
pourvu: **~ que** (+ *subj*) provided that; *exprimant désir*
hopefully
pousse *f* AGR shoot; poussée
f thrust; MÉD outbreak; *de
fièvre* rise; *fig: de racisme
etc* upsurge; pousser 1 *v/t*
push; *du vent* drive; *cri, soupir* give; *fig: recherches* pursue; **se ~ d'une foule** push
forward; *pour faire de la place* move over 2 *v/i* push; *de
cheveux, plantes* grow;
poussette *f pour enfants*
stroller, *Br* pushchair
poussière *f* dust; *particule*
speck of dust
poussin *m* chick

poutre *f* beam
pouvoir 1 *v/aux* be able to,
can; **je ne peux pas aider**
I can't *ou* cannot help; **je
ne pouvais pas accepter** I
couldn't accept, I wasn't
able to accept; **il se peut
que** (+ *subj*) it's possible
that; **tu aurais pu me prévenir!** you could have *ou* might
have warned me! 2 *m* power;
procuration power of attorney; **les ~s publics** the
authorities
prairie *f* meadow; *plaine* prairie
praline *f* praline
praticable *projet* feasible;
route passable
pratique 1 *adj* practical 2 *f*
practice; *expérience* practical experience; pratique-
ment (*presque*) practically;
dans la pratique in practice;
pratiquer practice, *Br* practise; *sports* play; *technique*
use; TECH *trou, passage*
make
pré *m* meadow
préado *m/f* pre-teen
préalable 1 *adj* (*antérieur*)
prior; (*préliminaire*) preliminary 2 *m* condition; **au ~** beforehand
préavis *m* notice
précaire precarious
précaution *f* caution; *mesure*
precaution; **par ~** as a precaution
précédent 1 *adj* previous 2 *m*

prendre

precedent; **précéder** precede

prêcher preach

précieux, -euse precious

précipice *m* precipice

précipitamment hastily, in a rush; **précipitation** *f* haste; **~s** *temps* precipitation; **précipiter** *(faire tomber)* plunge *(dans* into); *(pousser)* hurl; *(brusquer)* precipitate; *pas* hasten; **se ~** *(se jeter)* throw o.s.; *(se dépêcher)* rush

précis 1 *adj* precise **2** *m* precis, summary; **préciser** specify; **~ que** *(souligner)* make it clear that; **précision** *f* accuracy; *d'un geste* preciseness; *pour plus de* **~s** for further details

précoce early; *enfant* precocious; **précocité** *f* earliness; *d'un enfant* precociousness

préconçu preconceived

précurseur 1 *m* precursor **2** *adj*: *signe m* **~** warning sign

prédateur, -trice 1 *adj* predatory **2** *m/f* predator

prédécesseur *m* predecessor

prédestiner predestine *(à qc* for sth; *à faire* to do)

prédiction *f* prediction

prédilection *f* predilection; *de* **~** favorite, *Br* favourite

prédire predict

prédominer predominate

préfabriqué prefabricated

préface *f* preface

préférable preferable *(à* to);

préféré favorite, *Br* favourite; **préférence** *f* preference; *de* **~** preferably; **préférer** prefer *(à* to); **~ faire qc** prefer to do sth; *je préfère que tu viennes* *(subj)* **demain** I would *ou* I'd prefer you to come tomorrow, I'd rather you came tomorrow

préfet *m* prefect; **~ de police** chief of police

préfixe *m* prefix

préjudice *m* harm; **porter ~ à** harm

préjugé *m* prejudice

prélever *échantillon* take; *montant* deduct *(sur* from)

préliminaire preliminary

préluder *fig*: **~ à** be the prelude to

prématuré premature

préméditer premeditate

premier, -ère 1 *adj* first; *rang* front; *objectif, cause* primary; *nombre* prime; **au ~ étage** on the second floor, *Br* on the first floor; **Premier ministre** Prime Minister; *le* **~ août** August first, *Br* the first of August **2** *m/f: partir le* **~** leave first **3** *m* second floor, *Br* first floor; *en* **~** first **4** *f* THÉÂT first night; AUTO first (gear); *en train* first (class)

prémisse *f* premise

prémonition *f* premonition; **prémonitoire** *rêve* prophetic

prendre 1 *v/t* take; *(enlever)* take away; *froid* catch; *poids* put on; **~ qch à qn** take sth (away) from s.o. **2** v/i (durcir) set; de mode catch on; d'un feu take hold; **~ à droite** turn right **3**: **se ~** (se laisser attraper) get caught; **se ~ d'amitié pour qn** take a liking to s.o.

prénom m first name; **deuxième ~** middle name

préoccuper preoccupy; (inquiéter) worry; **se ~ de** worry about

préparatifs mpl preparations; **préparation** f preparation; **préparer** prepare; (organiser) arrange; **~ qn à qch** prepare s.o. for sth; **~ un examen** prepare for an exam; **se ~** get ready; de dispute, d'orage be brewing

prépondérant predominant

préposé m (facteur) mailman, Br postman; au vestiaire attendant; des douanes official; **préposée** f (factrice) mailwoman, Br postwoman

préretraite f early retirement

près 1 adv close, near; **de ~** closely **2** prép: **~ de qch** near sth, close to sth; **~ de 500** nearly 500

présage m omen

presbyte farsighted, Br longsighted

prescription f rule; MÉD prescription; **prescrire** stipulate; MÉD prescribe

présence f presence; **en ~ de** in the presence of; **présent 1** adj present **2** m present (aussi GRAM); **les ~s** those present; **à ~** at present; **à ~ que** now that; **jusqu'à ~** till now

présentateur, -trice m/f TV presenter; **~ météo** weatherman; **présentation** f presentation; **présenter** present; chaise offer; personne introduce; pour un concours put forward; billet show, present; condoléances, félicitations offer; difficultés, dangers involve; **se ~** introduce o.s.; pour un poste, un emploi apply; aux élections run; de difficultés come up

préservatif m condom

préserver protect (**de** from); bois, patrimoine preserve

présidence f chairmanship; POL presidency; **président**, **~e** m/f d'une réunion chair; POL president; **présidentiel**, **~le** presidential; **présider** réunion chair

présomption f presumption; **présomptueux, -euse** presumptuous

presque almost, nearly

presqu'île f peninsula

pressant besoin pressing, urgent; personne insistent

presse f press; **mise ~ sous ~** going to press

pressé lettre, requête urgent; citron fresh; **je suis ~** I'm in a hurry

197

prime

pressentiment *m* foreboding, presentiment; pressentir: **~** *qch* have a premonition that sth is going to happen; **~** *qn pour un poste* approach s.o., sound s.o. out

presser **1** *v/t bouton* push, press; *fruit* squeeze; (*harceler*) press; *pas* quicken; *affaire* speed up; (*étreindre*) press, squeeze; **se ~** *contre* press (o.s.) against **2** *v/i* be urgent; **se ~** hurry up

pressing *m magasin* dry cleaner

pression *f* pressure; *bouton* snap fastener, *Br aussi* press-stud fastener; (*bière f*) **~** draft beer, *Br* draught beer; **faire ~** *sur* pressure, put pressure on

prestance *f* presence

prestation *f* (*allocation*) allowance; **~s familiales** child benefit

prestige *m* prestige

présumer **1** *v/t*: **~** *que* presume *ou* assume that **2** *v/i*: **~** *de* overrate

prêt¹ *adj* ready (*à* for; *à faire* to do)

prêt² *m* loan; **~** *immobilier* mortgage

prêt-à-porter *m* ready-to-wear clothes *pl*

prétendre **1** *v/t* maintain; **~** *faire qch* claim to do sth **2** *v/i*: **~** *à* lay claim to; **prétendu** so-called

prétentieux, -euse pretentious

prêter **1** *v/t* lend **2** *v/i*: **~** *à* give rise to; **se ~** *à d'une chose* lend itself to; *d'une personne* be a party to

prétexte *m* pretext; **sous ~ de faire** on the pretext of doing

prêtre *m* priest; **prêtresse** *f* woman priest

preuve *f* proof, evidence; MATH proof; **faire ~** *de courage* show courage

prévenance *f* consideration

prévenir (*avertir*) warn (*de* of); (*informer*) inform (*de* of); *besoin, question* anticipate; *crise, maladie* avert

préventif, -ive preventive; prévention *f* prevention; **~ routière** road safety

prévision *f* forecast; **~s météorologiques** weather forecast

prévoir (*pressentir*) foresee; (*planifier*) plan; **comme prévu** as expected; **prévoyance** *f* foresight; **prévoyant** farsighted

prier **1** *v/i* REL pray **2** *v/t* (*supplier*) beg; REL pray to; **~** *qn de faire qc* ask s.o. to do sth; **je vous en prie** don't mention it

prière *f* REL prayer; (*demande*) entreaty; **faire sa ~** say one's prayers

primaire primary; *péj* narrow-minded

prime¹: **de ~ abord** at first sight

prime² f d'assurance premium; de fin d'année bonus; (cadeau) free gift

primer 1 v/i take precedence **2** v/t take precedence over

primeur f: **avoir la ~ de la nouvelle** be the first to hear; objet have first use of; **~s** early fruit and vegetables

primitif, -ive primitive; couleur, sens original

primordial essential

prince m prince; **princesse** princess

principal, ~e 1 adj main, principal **2** m: **le ~** the main thing **3** m/f principal, Br head teacher

principe m principle; **par ~** on principle; **en ~** in principle

printemps m spring

priorité f priority (**sur** over); sur la route right of way

pris place taken; personne busy

prise f hold; d'un pion, une ville etc capture, taking; de poissons catch; ÉL outlet, Br socket; d'un film take; **être aux ~s avec** be struggling with; **~ de conscience** awareness; **~ de courant** outlet, Br socket

prison f prison; **prisonnier, -ère** m/f prisoner

privation f deprivation

privatisation f privatization; **privatiser** privatize

privé 1 adj private **2** m: **en ~** in

private; **priver**: **~ qn de** deprive s.o. of; **se ~ de** go without

privilège m privilege; **privilégier** favor, Br favour

prix m price; (valeur) value; (récompense) prize; **à tout ~** at all costs; **hors de ~** prohibitive; **au ~ de** at the cost of; **~ fort** full price; **~ de revient** cost price

probabilité f probability; **probable** probable

probant convincing

problème m problem

procédé m (méthode) method; TECH process; **~s** (comportement) behavior, Br behaviour

procéder proceed; **~ à qc** carry out sth

procès m JUR trial

processus m process

procès-verbal m minutes pl; (contravention) ticket

prochain, ~e 1 adj next **2** m/f: **son ~** one's neighbor ou Br neighbour

proche 1 adj close (**de** to), near; ami close; événement recent; **~ de** fig close to **2** mpl: **~s** family and friends

proclamer roi, république proclaim; résultats, innocence declare

procréer procreate

procuration f proxy, power of attorney; **procurer** get, procure fml

prodigieux, -euse enormous,

tremendous

prodigue extravagant; **prodiguer** lavish

producteur, -trice 1 adj producing **2** m/f producer; **productif, -ive** productive; **production** f production; **produire** produce; **se~** happen; **produit** m product; **d'un investissement** yield; **~ d'entretien** cleaning product; **~ fini** end product

profane 1 adj art, musique secular **2** m/f fig lay person; **profaner** desecrate, profane

proférer menaces utter

professeur m teacher; **d'université** professor

profession f profession; **professionnel, ~le** m/f & adj professional

profil m profile

profit m COMM profit; (avantage) benefit; **profitable** beneficial; COMM profitable; **profiter: ~ de qc** take advantage of sth; **~ à qn** be to s.o.'s advantage

profond deep; personne, pensées deep, profound; influence profound; **profondément** deeply, profoundly; **profondeur** f depth

programme m program, Br programme; INFORM program; **~ télé** TV program; **programmer** TV schedule; INFORM program; **programmeur, -euse** m/f programmer

progrès m progress; d'un incendie, d'une épidémie spread; **progresser** progress; d'une incendie, d'une épidémie spread; **progressif, -ive** progressive; **progression** f progress

prohiber ban, prohibit; **prohibition** f ban; **la Prohibition** HIST Prohibition

proie f prey (aussi fig); **en ~ à** prey to

projecteur m (spot) spotlight; au cinéma projector

projection f projection

projet m project; personnel plan; (ébauche) draft; **~ de loi** bill; **projeter** (jeter) throw; film screen; travail, voyage plan

proliférer proliferate

prologue m prologue

prolongation f extension; **~s** SP overtime, Br extra time; **prolonger** prolong; mur, route extend; **se ~** continue

promenade f walk; en voiture drive; **promener** take for a walk; **se ~** go for a walk; en voiture go for a drive; **promeneur, -euse** m/f stroller, walker

promesse f promise; **prometteur, -euse** promising; **promettre** promise (**qc à qn** s.o. sth, sth to s.o., **de faire** to do); **se ~ de faire qc** make up one's mind to do sth

promiscuité f overcrowding;

sexuelle promiscuity

promontoire *m* promontory

promoteur, -trice 1 *m/f (instigateur)* instigator **2** *m:* **~ immobilier** property developer; **promotion** *f* promotion; *sociale* advancement; ÉDU class, *Br* year; **en ~** on special offer; **promouvoir** promote

prompt swift

pronom *m* GRAM pronoun

prononcé *fig* marked, pronounced; *accent, traits* strong; **prononcer** *(dire)* say, utter; *(articuler)* pronounce; *discours* give; JUR *sentence* pass, pronounce; **se ~ d'un mot** be pronounced; *(se déterminer)* express an opinion; **se ~ pour/contre qch** come out in favor *ou Br* favour of /against sth; **prononciation** *f* pronunciation; JUR passing

propager *idée, nouvelle* spread; BIOL propagate; **se ~** spread; BIOL reproduce

propension *f* propensity (**à** for)

propice favorable, *Br* favourable; *moment* right

proportion *f* proportion; **toutes ~s gardées** on balance; **proportionnel, ~le** proportional (**à** to)

propos 1 *mpl (paroles)* words **2** *m (intention)* intention; **à ~** at the right moment; **mal à ~, hors de ~** at the wrong moment; **à ~!** by the way; **à ~ de** *(au sujet de)* about

proposer suggest, propose; *(offrir)* offer; **se ~ de faire** propose doing; **se ~** offer one's services; **proposition** *f (suggestion)* proposal, suggestion; *(offre)* offer; GRAM clause

propre 1 *adj* own; *(net)* clean; *(approprié)* suitable; **~ à** *(particulier à)* characteristic of **2** *m:* **mettre au ~** make a clean copy of; **propreté** *f* cleanliness

propriétaire *m/f* owner; *qui loue* landlord; *femme* landlady; **propriété** *f* ownership; *(caractéristique)* property

propulser propel; **propulsion** *f* propulsion

proscrire *(interdire)* ban; *(bannir)* banish

prospectus *m* brochure; FIN prospectus

prospère prosperous; **prospérer** prosper; **prospérité** *f* prosperity

prosterner: se ~ prostrate o.s.

prostituée *f* prostitute; **prostitution** *f* prostitution

protecteur, -trice 1 *adj* protective; *péj: ton* patronizing **2** *m/f* protector; *(mécène)* sponsor, patron; **protection** *f* protection; **protéger** protect (**contre, de** from); *arts, artistes* be a patron of

protéine *f* protein

201 pull(-over)

protestant, ~e REL m/f & adj
Protestant
protestation f (plainte) protest; (déclaration) protestation; protester protest
prothèse f prosthesis
protocole m protocol
prototype m prototype
prouesse f prowess
prouver prove
provenance f origin; en ~ de
avion, train from
provenir: ~ de come from
proverbe m proverb
providence f providence
province f province
proviseur m principal, Br
head (teacher)
provision f supply; ~s (vi-
vres) provisions; (achats)
shopping; d'un chèque funds
pl; chèque m sans ~ bad
check ou Br cheque
provisoire provisional
provocant, provocateur, -tri-
ce provocative; provoquer
provoke; accident cause
proximité f proximity; à ~ de
near, in the vicinity of
prude prudish
prudence f caution, pru-
dence; prudent cautious,
prudent; conducteur careful
prune f BOT plum
pruneau m prune
prunier m plum (tree)
PS m (= Parti socialiste) Socialist Party; (= Post Scrip-
tum) PS (= postscript)
psaume m psalm

pseudonyme m pseudonym
psychanalyser psychoana-
lyze; psychanalyste m/f
psychoanalyst
psychiatre m/f psychiatrist
psychologie f psychology;
psychologique psychologi-
cal; psychologue m/f psy-
chologist
psychopathe m/f psycho-
path
puant stinking; fig arrogant;
puanteur f stink
pub f: une ~ an ad; faire de la
~ do some advertising
publication f publication
publicitaire advertising atr;
publicité f publicity; COMM
advertising; (affiche) ad
publier publish
publipostage m mailshot
puce f ZO flea; INFORM chip
pudeur f modesty; pudique
modest; discret discreet
puer 1 v/i stink; ~ des pieds
have smelly feet 2 v/t stink of
puéril childish
puis then
puiser draw (dans from)
puisque since
puissance f power; d'une armée strength; puissant
powerful; musculature, médicament strong
puits m well; d'une mine
shaft; ~ de pétrole oil well
pull(-over) m sweater, Br

aussi pullover
pulluler swarm
pulsation f beat, beating
pulsion f drive; **~s** fpl **de mort** death wish
pulvériser *solide* pulverize (*aussi fig*); *liquide* spray
punaise f zo bug; (*clou*) thumbtack, *Br* drawing pin
punir punish; **punition** f punishment
pupille 1 m/f JUR ward **2** f ANAT pupil
pur pure; *whisky* straight
purée f puree; **~ (de pommes de terre)** mashed potatoes pl
pureté f purity

purge f purge; **purger** TECH bleed; POL purge; JUR *peine* serve
purification f purification; **purifier** purify
pur-sang m thoroughbred
pus m pus
pute f F slut
puzzle m jigsaw (puzzle)
P.-V. m (= *procès-verbal*) ticket
pyjama m pajamas pl, *Br* pyjamas pl
pyramide f pyramid
Pyrénées fpl Pyrenees
pyromane m pyromaniac; JUR arsonist

Q

quadragénaire m/f & adj forty-year old
quadrillé *papier* squared; **quadriller** *fig: région* put under surveillance
quadruple quadruple
quai m *d'un port* quay; *d'une gare* platform
qualification f qualification; (*appellation*) name; **qualifier** qualify; **~ qn d'idiot** describe s.o. as an idiot; **se ~** SP qualify
qualité f quality; **de ~** atr; **en ~ d'ambassadeur** as ambassador, in his capacity as ambassador
quand when; **~ je serai de retour** when I'm back

quant à as for
quantifier quantify
quantité f quantity; **une ~ de grand nombre** a great many; **abondance** a great deal of
quarantaine f MÉD quarantine; **une ~ de** about forty, forty or so; **avoir la ~** be in one's forties; **quarante** forty
quart m quarter; *de vin* quarter liter, *Br* quarter litre; **~ d'heure** quarter of an hour; **~ de finale** quarter-final
quartier m (*quart*) quarter; *d'orange* segment; *d'une ville* area; **~ général** MIL headquarters pl
quasiment virtually
quatorze fourteen

quatre four; **quatre-vingt(s)** eighty; **quatre-vingt-dix** ninety; **quatrième** fourth

quatuor *m* MUS quartet

que 1 *pron relatif personne* who, that; *chose, animal* which, that; *les étudiants ~ j'ai rencontrés* the students (who *ou* that) I met **2** *pron interrogatif* what; *qu'y a-t-il?* what's the matter?; *qu'est-ce que c'est?* what's that? **3** *adv dans exclamations:* *~ c'est beau!* it's so beautiful!; *~ de fleurs!* what a lot of flowers! **4** *conj* that; *je croyais ~ ...* I thought that ...; *plus grand ~ moi* bigger than me; *aussi petit ~ cela* as small as that; *ne ... ~* only

quel, ~le what, which; *~le femme!* what a woman!

quelconque (*médiocre*) mediocre; *un travail ~* some sort of job

quelque some; *~s* some, a few; *~ ... que* (+ *subj*) whatever, whichever

quelque chose something; *avec interrogatif, conditionnel aussi* anything

quelquefois sometimes

quelques-uns, quelques-unes a few, some

quelqu'un someone, somebody; *avec interrogatif, conditionnel aussi* anyone, anybody

querelle *f* quarrel; **quereller:** *se ~* quarrel; **querelleur, -euse** quarrelsome

question *f* question; **questionnaire** *m* questionnaire; **questioner** question (*sur* about)

quête *f* search; (*collecte*) collection

queue *f* d'un animal tail; d'un fruit stalk; d'une casserole handle; d'un train rear; d'une classe bottom; d'une file line, Br queue; faire la ~ stand in line, Br queue (up); *à la ~, en ~* at the rear

qui *interrogatif* who; *relatif, personne* who, that; *relatif, chose, animal* which, that

quiconque whoever; (*n'importe qui*) anyone, anybody

quincaillerie *f* hardware; *magasin* hardware store

quinquagénaire *m/f & adj* fifty-year old

quintal *m* hundred kilos *pl*

quinte *f*: (*de toux*) coughing fit

quinzaine *f de jours* two weeks *pl*, Br *aussi* fortnight; *une ~ de personnes* about fifteen people *pl*; **quinze** fifteen; *~ jours* two weeks, Br *aussi* fortnight

quitte: *être ~ envers qn* be quits with s.o.

quitter leave; *vêtement* take off; *se ~* part; *ne quittez pas* TÉL hold the line please

quoi what; *après ~, il ...* after which he ...; *à ~ bon?* what's the point?; **il n'y a pas de ~!** don't mention it; **~ que** (+ *subj*) whatever

quoique (+ *subj*) although, though

quotidien, ~ne 1 *adj* daily; **de tous les jours** everyday **2** *m* daily

R

rabâcher keep on repeating

rabais *m* discount, reduction; **rabaisser** *prix* reduce; *mérites* belittle

rabattre 1 *v/t siège* pull down; *couvercle* shut; *col* turn down **2** *v/i fig:* **se ~ sur** fall back on; *d'une voiture* pull back into

râblé stocky

rabot *m* plane

rabougri stunted

rabrouer snub

racaille *f* rabble

raccommoder mend; *chaussettes* darn

raccompagner: je vais vous ~ chez vous à pied I'll take you home

raccord *m* join; *d'un film* splice; **raccorder** join

raccourci *m* shortcut; **en ~** briefly; **raccourcir 1** *v/t* shorten **2** *v/i* get shorter

raccrocher 1 *v/t* put back up; **~ le téléphone** hang up; **se ~ à** cling to **2** *v/i* TÉL hang up

race *f* race; (*ascendance*) descent; **zo** breed

rachat *m d'un otage* ransoming; *d'une société* buyout; **racheter** buy back; *otage*

ransom; *fig: faute* make up for; **se ~** make amends

racine *f* root

racisme *m* racism; **raciste** *m/f* & *adj* racist

racler scrape; **se ~ la gorge** clear one's throat

raconter tell

radar *m* radar

radeau *m* raft

radiateur *m* radiator

radiation *f* radiation; *d'une liste* deletion

radical *adj* & *m* radical

radier strike out

radieux, -euse radiant; *temps* glorious

radin F mean, tight

radio *f* radio; (*radiographie*) X-ray

radioactif, -ive radioactive

radiocassette *f* radio cassette player

radiographie *f procédé* radiography; *photo* X-ray

radioréveil radio alarm

radis *m* BOT radish

radoter ramble

radoucir make milder; **se ~ du temps** get milder

rafale *f de vent* gust; MIL burst

raffermir *chair* firm up; *auto-*

ramification

rité re-assert

raffinage *m* refining; **raffiné** refined; **raffiner** refine; **raffinerie** *f* refinery

raffoler: ~ **de** adore

rafraîchir 1 *v/t* cool down; *mémoire* refresh **2** *v/i du vin* chill; **se** ~ *de la température* get cooler; *d'une personne* have a drink (in order to cool down); **rafraîchissant** refreshing (*aussi fig*); **rafraîchissement** *m de la température* cooling; **~s** (*boissons*) refreshments

rage *f* rage; MÉD rabies *sg*; **rageur, -euse** furious

ragoût *m* CUIS stew

raide *personne, membres* stiff; *pente* steep; *cheveux* straight; (*ivre, drogué*) stoned; **raideur** *f* stiffness; *d'une pente* steepness; **raidir**: **se** ~ *de membres* stiffen up

raie *f* (*rayure*) stripe; *des cheveux* part, *Br* parting; *zo* skate

rail *m* rail; ~ **de sécurité** crash barrier

railler mock; **raillerie** *f* mockery

raisin *m* grape; ~ **sec** raisin

raison *f* reason; **avoir** ~ be right; **avoir** ~ **de** get the better of; **à** ~ **de** at a rate of; **à plus forte** ~ all the more so; **en** ~ **de** (*à cause de*) because of; ~ **sociale** company name; **raisonnable** reasona-

ble; **raisonnement** *m* reasoning; **raisonner 1** *v/i* reason **2** *v/t*: ~ **qn** make s.o. see reason

rajeunir 1 *v/t thème* modernize; ~ **qn** make s.o. look (years) younger **2** *v/i* look younger

rajouter add

rajuster adjust; *coiffure* put straight

ralenti *m* AUTO idle; *dans un film* slow motion; **au** ~ *fig* at a snail's pace; **ralentir** slow down; **ralentissement** *m* slowing down; **ralentisseur** *m de circulation* speed-bump

râler moan; F beef F; **râleur, -euse** F **1** *adj* grumbling **2** *m/f* grumbler

rallier rally; (*s'unir à*) join; **se** ~ **à** rally to

rallonger 1 *v/t* lengthen **2** *v/i* get longer

rallumer *télé, lumière* switch on again; *fig* revive

ramassage *m* collection; *de fruits* picking; **ramasser** collect; *ce qui est par terre* pick up; *fruits* pick; F *coup* get

rame *f* oar; *de métro* train

rameau *m* branch

ramener take back; (*rapporter*) bring back; *l'ordre* restore; **se** ~ **à** (*se réduire à*) come down to

ramer row; **rameur, -euse** *m/f* rower

ramification *f* ramification

ramollir soften; *se ~* soften; *fig* go soft
rampant crawling; BOT creeping; *fig:* inflation rampant
rampe *f* ramp; *d'escalier* bannisters *pl*; *au théâtre* footlights *pl*
ramper crawl; BOT creep
rance rancid
rancœur *f* resentment (*contre* toward)
rançon *f* ransom; *la ~ de fig* the price of
rancune *f* resentment; rancunier, -ère resentful
randonnée *f* walk; *en montagne* hill walk; **randonneur** *m* walker; *en montagne* hillwalker
rang *m* row; (*niveau*) rank; *être au premier ~* be in the forefront
rangée *f* row
ranger put away; *chambre* tidy up; *voiture* park; (*classer*) arrange; *se ~* (*s'écarter*) move aside; AUTO pull over; *fig* (*assagir*) settle down; *se ~ à une opinion* come around to a point of view
ranimer *personne* bring around; *fig: force* revive
rap *m* MUS rap
rapace 1 *adj animal* predatory; *personne* greedy **2** *m* bird of prey
rapatrier repatriate
râpe *f* grater; TECH rasp; **râper** CUIS grate; *bois* file; **râpé** CUIS grated; *manteau*

threadbare
rapide 1 *adj* fast, rapid; *coup d'œil, décision* quick **2** *m* *dans l'eau* rapid; *train* fast train; **rapidité** *f* speed, rapidity
rapiécer patch
rappel *m* reminder; *d'un ambassadeur, produit* recall; THÉÂT curtain call; MÉD booster; **rappeler** call back; *ambassadeur* recall; *~ qc/qn à qn* remind s.o. of sth/s.o.; *se ~ qc* remember sth
rapport *m* écrit, oral report; (*lien*) connection; (*proportion*) proportion; COMM return; MIL briefing; *~s* (*sexuels*) sexual relations; *par ~ à* compared with; *être en ~ avec* be in touch with; **rapporter** return, bring/take back; *d'un chien* fetch; COMM bring in; (*relater*) report; *se ~ à* be connected with; **rapporteur** *m* reporter; *enfant* sneak
rapprochement *m* *fig* reconciliation; POL rapprochement; *analogie* connection; **rapprocher** bring closer (*de* to); *établir un lien* connect; *se ~* come closer
rapt *m* abduction
raquette *f* racket
rare rare; *marchandises* scarce; (*peu dense*) sparse; **raréfier**: *se ~* become rare; *de l'air* become rarefied; **rarement** rarely; **rareté** *f* rarity

ras short; **rempli à ~ bord** full to the brim; **faire table ~e** make a clean sweep

raser shave; *barbe* shave off; (*démolir*) raze to the ground; *murs* hug; F (*ennuyer*) bore

rasoir *m* razor; **~ électrique** electric shaver

rassasier satisfy

rassembler collect, assemble; **se ~** gather

rasseoir replace; **se ~** sit down again

rassis stale; *fig* sedate

rassurer reassure; **rassurez--vous** don't be concerned

rat *m* rat

ratatiner: **se ~** shrivel up

rate *f* ANAT spleen

raté, ~e **1** *adj* unsuccessful; *occasion* missed **2** *m/f personne* failure

râteau *m* rake

rater **1** *v/t* miss; *examen* fail **2** *v/i d'une arme* misfire; *d'un projet* fail

ration *f* ration; *fig* (fair) share

rationaliser rationalize; rationnel, ~le rational; rationner ration

ratisser rake; (*fouiller*) scarch

rattacher *chien* tie up again; *cheveux* put up again; *lacets* do up again; *conduites d'eau* connect; *idées* connect; **se ~ à** be linked to

rattraper recapture; *objet qui tombe* catch; (*rejoindre*) catch up (with); *retard* make up; *imprudence* make up for; **se ~** make up for it; (*se raccrocher*) get caught

rature *f* deletion

rauque hoarse

ravages *mpl* devastation; **les ~ du temps** the ravages of time; *ravager* devastate

ravaler swallow; *façade* clean up

rave *f*: **céléri ~** celeriac

rave *f* rave

ravi delighted (**de** with; **de faire** to do)

ravir (*enchanter*) delight

raviser: **se ~** change one's mind

ravissant delightful

ravisseur, -euse *m/f* abductor

ravitaillement *m* supplying; *en carburant* refueling, *Br* refuelling; *ravitailler* supply; *en carburant* refuel

raviver revive

rayé striped; *papier* lined; *verre, carrosserie* scratched; *rayer* scratch; *mot* score *ou* scratch out

rayon *m* ray; MATH radius; *d'une roue* spoke; (*étagère*) shelf; *de magasin* department; **~ laser** laser beam; *rayonner de chaleur* radiate; *d'un visage* shine; **~ de** *fig* radiate

rayure *f* stripe; *sur un meuble, du verre* scratch

raz *m*: **~ de marée** tidal wave

réacteur *m* reactor; AVIAT jet engine; **réaction** *f* reaction; **avion** *m* **à ~** jet (aircraft); **réactionnaire** *m/f* & *adj* reactionary

réagir react (**à** to; **contre** against)

réalisable feasible; **réalisateur**, **-trice** *m/f* director; **réalisation** *f* *d'un projet* execution, realization; *création*, *œuvre* creation; *d'un film* direction; **réaliser** *projet* carry out; *rêve* fulfill; *Br* fulfil; *vente* make; *film* direct; *bien, capital* realize; *(se rendre compte)* realize; **se ~** *d'un rêve* come true; *d'un projet* be carried out

réalisme *m* realism; **réaliste** **1** *adj* realistic **2** *m/f* realist; **réalité** *f* reality

réanimer resuscitate

rébarbatif, **-ive** off-putting, daunting

rebelle **1** *adj* rebellious **2** *m/f* rebel; **rebeller**: **se ~** rebel; **rébellion** *f* rebellion

rebondir bounce; *(faire un ricochet)* rebound; **faire ~ qch** *fig* get sth going again; **rebondissement** *m fig* unexpected development

rebord *m* edge; *d'une fenêtre* sill

rebours *m*: **compte à ~** countdown

rebrousser: **~ chemin** retrace one's footsteps

rebut *m* dregs *pl*; **mettre au ~** get rid of

rebuter *(décourager)* dishearten; *(choquer)* offend

récapituler recap

récemment recently

recenser *population* take a census of

récent recent

récépissé *m* receipt

récepteur *m* receiver

réception *f* reception; *d'une lettre, de marchandises* receipt; **réceptionniste** *m/f* receptionist, desk clerk

récession *f* ÉCON recession

recette *f* COMM takings *pl*; CUIS, *fig* recipe

recevoir receive; **être reçu à un examen** pass an exam

rechange *m*: **de ~** spare *atr*

rechargeable *pile* rechargeable; **recharger** *camion, arme* reload; *accumulateur* recharge; *briquet* refill

réchaud *m* stove

réchauffement *m* warming; **~ de la planète** global warming; **réchauffer** warm up

recherche *f* search (**de** for); *scientifique* research; **~s de la police** search; **rechercher** look for, search for; *(prendre)* fetch

rechute *f* MÉD relapse

récif *m* reef

récipient *m* container

réciproque reciprocal

récit *m* account; *(histoire)* story; **réciter** recite

réclamation *f* claim; *(protes-*

tation) complaint

réclame *f* advertisement

réclamer *secours, aumône* ask for; *son dû* claim; (*nécessiter*) call for

réclusion *f* imprisonment

récolte *f* harvesting; *de produits* harvest, crop; *fig* crop; récolter harvest

recommander recommend; *lettre* register

recommencer start again

récompense *f* reward; récompenser reward (*de* for)

réconcilier reconcile

reconduire: ~ *qn chez lui* take s.o. home; *à la porte* see s.o. out

réconforter console, comfort

reconnaissance *f* recognition; *d'une faute* acknowledg(e)ment; (*gratitude*) gratitude; MIL reconnaissance; reconnaissant grateful (*de* for); reconnaître recognize; *faute* acknowledge; *se* ~ *de deux personnes* recognize each other; *se* ~ *à* be recognizable by; reconnu known

reconstituer reconstitute; *ville, maison* restore; *événement* reconstruct

reconstruire rebuild

reconvertir: *se* ~ retrain

recopier *notes* copy out

record *m* record; recordman *m* record holder; recordwoman *f* record holder

recourbé bent

recours *m* recourse, resort;

avoir ~ *à* resort to

recouvrer recover; *santé* regain

recouvrir recover; *enfant* cover up again; (*couvrir entièrement*) cover (*de* with); (*cacher, embrasser*) cover

récréation *f* relaxation; ÉDU recess, *Br* recreation

récriminations *fpl* recriminations

recrudescence *f* new outbreak

recrue *f* recruit; recruter recruit

rectangle *m* rectangle; rectangulaire rectangular

rectifier rectify; (*ajuster*) adjust; (*corriger*) correct

recto *m* *d'une feuille* front

reçu *m* receipt

recueil *m* collection; recueillir collect; *personne* take in; *se* ~ meditate

recul *m* *d'un fusil* recoil; *d'une armée* retreat; *de la production* drop; *fig* detachment; reculer 1 *v/t* push back; *décision* postpone 2 *v/i* back away, recoil; MIL retreat; *d'une voiture* back, reverse; ~ *devant fig* back away from; reculons: *à* ~ backward, *Br* backwards

récupérer 1 *v/t* recover, retrieve; *ses forces* regain; *vieux matériel* salvage; *temps* make up 2 *v/i* recover

recyclable recyclable; recyclage *m du personnel* re-

training; TECH recycling; recycler retrain; TECH recycle
rédacteur, -trice *m/f* editor;
(*auteur*) writer; **~ en chef**
editor-in-chief; **rédaction** *f*
editing; (*rédacteurs*) editorial team
redescendre 1 *v/i* come/go
down again; **~ d'une voiture**
get out of a car again **2** *v/t*
bring/take down again;
montagne come down again
redevable *être* **~ de qc à qn**
owe s.o. sth; **redevance** *f*
d'un auteur royalty; TV licence fee
rédiger write
redire repeat, say again; (*rapporter*) repeat; **trouver à ~ à**
find fault with
redoubler 1 *v/t* double **2** *v/i*
ÉDU repeat a class; *d'une
tempête* intensify; **~ d'efforts** redouble one's efforts
redoutable formidable; *hiver*
harsh; **redouter** dread (**de
faire** doing)
redresser *ce qui est courbe*
straighten; *ce qui est tombé*
set upright; **se ~ d'un pays**
recover
réduction *f* reduction; MÉD
setting; **réduire** reduce; *personnel* cut back; **se ~ à**
amount to; **réduit 1** *adj* reduced; *possibilités* limited
2 *m* small room
rééducation *f* MÉD rehabilita-
tion
réel, ~le real

refaire do again; *examen* re-
take; *erreur* repeat; *remettre
en état: maison* do up
réfectoire *m* refectory
référence *f* reference; **~s** (*recommandation*) reference
référendum *m* referendum
référer: en ~ à consult; **se ~ à**
refer to
réfléchir 1 *v/t* reflect **2** *v/i*
think (**à, sur** about)
reflet *m* *de lumière* glint; *dans
miroir* reflection (*aussi fig*)
réflexe *m* reflex
réflexion *f* reflection; (*remarque*) remark
réforme *f* reform; **la Réforme**
REL the Reformation; **réformer** reform; MIL discharge
refouler push back; PSYCH repress
refrain *m* refrain, chorus
réfréner control
réfrigérateur *m* refrigerator
refroidir cool down; *fig* cool;
se ~ du temps get colder;
MÉD catch a chill; **refroidis-
sement** *m* cooling; MÉD chill
refuge *m* refuge, shelter;
pour piétons traffic island;
en montagne (mountain)
hut; **réfugié, ~e** *m/f* refugee;
réfugier: se ~ take shelter
refus *m* refusal; **refuser** refuse; **~ de** *ou* **se ~ à faire** refuse to do
réfuter refute
regagner win back, regain;
endroit get back to
régal *m* treat; **régaler** regale

(*de* with)

regard *m* look; **regardant**
avec argent careful with
one's money; **ne pas être
~ sur** not be too worried
about; **regarder 1** *v/t* look
at; *télé* watch; (*concerner*)
regard, concern; **~ qn faire
qch** watch s.o. doing sth **2**
v/i look; **se ~** look at o.s.;
de plusieurs personnes look
at each other

régate *f* regatta

régime *m* POL government,
régime; MÉD diet; *fiscal system*

région *f* region; **~ sinistrée**
disaster area; **régional** regional

régir govern

régisseur *m* THÉÂT stage
manager; *dans le film* assistant director

réglage *m* adjustment

règle *f* rule; *instrument* ruler;
en ~ générale as a rule; **~s**
(*menstruation*) period

réglé *organisé* settled; *vie*
well-ordered; *papier* ruled

règlement *m* settlement; (*règles*) regulations *pl*; **réglementaire** in accordance with
the rules; *tenue* regulation
atr; **réglementer** control,
regulate

régler *affaire* settle; TECH adjust; COMM pay, settle; *épicier etc* pay, settle up with

règne *m* reign; **régner** reign

régression *f* regression

regret *m* regret (*de* about); **à ~**
with regret, reluctantly; **être
au ~ de faire** regret to do; regrettable regrettable; regretter regret; *personne ab-
sente* miss; **~ d'avoir fait qc**
regret doing sth, regret having done sth; **je ne regrette
rien** I have no regrets; **je regrette mais ...** I'm sorry
(but) ...

régulariser put in order; *situation* regularize; TECH regulate; **régularité** *f* regularity; *d'élections* legality; **régulier**, **-ère** regular; *allure*, *progrès* steady; *écriture* even;
(*réglementaire*) lawful; (*correct*) honest; **régulièrement**
regularly

réhabiliter rehabilitate; *quartier* renovate, redevelop

rehausser raise; *fig* (*accentuer*) emphasize

rein *m* ANAT kidney; **~s** lower
back

reine *f* queen

réitérer reiterate

rejaillir spurt

rejeter reject; (*relancer*)
throw back; (*vomir*) bring
up; *responsabilité*, *faute* lay
(*sur* on)

rejoindre *personne* join,
meet; (*rattraper*) catch up
with; MIL rejoin; *autoroute*
get back onto; **se ~** meet

réjouir make happy, delight;
se ~ de be delighted about;
réjouissance *f* rejoicing

relâche f: **sans ~** without a break, nonstop

relâcher corde, emprise loosen; prisonnier release; **se ~** d'un élève, de la discipline become slack

relais m SP, ÉL relay; **prendre le ~ de** take over from

relancer balle throw back; moteur restart; fig: économie kickstart; personne contact again

relater relate

relatif, -ive relative; **~ à** relating to; relation f relationship; (connaissance) acquaintance; **être en ~ avec qn** be in touch with s.o.; **~s** relations; (connaissances) contacts; relativement relatively; **~ à** compared with; (en ce qui concerne) relating to; relativiser look at in context

relaxer: **se ~** relax

relayer take over from; TV, radio relay; **se ~** take turns

reléguer relegate

relève f relief; **prendre la ~** take over

relevé 1 adj manche turned up; style elevated; CUIS spicy **2** m de compteur reading; **~ de compte** bank statement; relever 1 v/t raise; (remettre debout) pick up; col, chauffage turn up; manches roll up; siège put up; économie improve; (ramasser) collect; défi take up; faute find;

adresse, date copy; (relayer) take over from; **se ~** get up; fig recover **2** v/i: **~ de** (dépendre de) be answerable to; (ressortir de) be the responsibility of

relief m relief; **mettre en ~** fig highlight

relier connect (à to); livre bind

religieux, -euse 1 adj religious **2** m monk **3** f nun; religion f religion

reliure f binding

reluire shine

remanier texte re-work; POL reshuffle

remarquable remarkable

remarque f remark; remarquer notice; (dire) remark; **faire ~ qc à qn** point sth out to s.o.; **se faire ~** d'un acteur etc get o.s. noticed; d'un écolier get into trouble; **se différencier** be conspicuous

rembourrer stuff

remboursement m refund; de dettes repayment; rembourser frais refund, reimburse; dettes, emprunt pay back

remède m remedy; remédier: **~ à** remedy

remerciement m: **~s** thanks; remercier thank (de, pour for); (congédier) dismiss

remettre put back; vêtement put on again; peine remit; décision postpone; (ajouter) add; **~ qc à qn** give sth to s.o.; **se ~ à qc** take sth up again; **se ~ à faire qc** start doing sth again; **se ~ de qc** recover from sth; **s'en ~ à qn** rely on s.o.

remise f (*hangar*) shed; *d'une lettre* delivery; *de peine* remission; COMM discount; *d'une décision* postponement; **~ à neuf** reconditioning; **~ en question** questioning

rémission f MÉD remission

remonte-pente m ski lift

remonter 1 v/i come/go up again; *dans une voiture* get back in; *de prix, température* go up again; *d'un avion, chemin* climb, rise **2** v/t *choses* bring/take back up; *rue, escalier* come/go back up; *montre* wind; TECH reassemble; *col* turn up; *stores* raise

remords mpl remorse

remorque f *véhicule* trailer; *câble* towrope; **remorquer** *voiture* tow

remplaçant, ~e m/f replacement; **remplacement** m replacement; **remplacer** replace (**par** with)

remplir fill (**de** with); *formulaire* fill out; *conditions* fulfill, Br fulfil; *tâche* carry out; **remplissage** m filling

remporter take away; *prix* win

remue-ménage m (*agitation*) commotion

remuer 1 v/t move (*aussi fig*);

sauce stir; *salade* toss; *terre* turn over **2** v/i move; **se ~** move; *fig* F get a move on F

rémunération f pay, remuneration; **rémunérer** pay

renaître REL be born again; *fig* be reborn

renard m fox

renchérir go up; **~ sur** outdo

rencontre f meeting; **aller à la ~ de** go and meet; **rencontrer** meet; *accueil* meet with; *difficulté* encounter; *amour* find; (*heurter*) hit; **se ~** meet

rendement m AGR yield; *d'un employé, d'une machine* output; *d'un placement* return

rendez-vous m appointment; *amoureux* date; *lieu* meeting place; **prendre ~** make an appointment

rendre 1 v/t give back; *salut, invitation* return; (*donner*) give; (*traduire*) render; (*vomir*) bring up; MIL surrender; **~ visite à** visit **2** v/i *de terre, d'un arbre* yield; **se ~ à un endroit** go; MIL surrender; **se ~ malade** make o.s. sick

rêne f rein

renfermer (*contenir*) contain; **se ~ dans le silence** withdraw into silence

renforcer reinforce

renfort m reinforcements pl; **à grand ~ de** with copious amounts of

renier 214

renier *qn* disown

renifler sniff

renne *m* reindeer

renom *m* (*célébrité*) fame, renown; (*réputation*) reputation; **renommée** *f* fame

renoncement *m* renunciation (*à* of); **renoncer**: ~ *à qc* give sth up; ~ *à faire* give up doing

renouer 1 *v/t amitié etc* renew **2** *v/i*: ~ *avec* get back in touch with; *après brouille* get back together with

renouveler renew; *demande, promesse* repeat; **se** ~ (*se reproduire*) happen again; **renouvellement** *m* renewal

rénovation *f* renovation; *fig* (*modernisation*) updating

renseignement *m* piece of information (*sur* about); ~**s** information; MIL intelligence; **prendre des ~s sur** find out about; **renseigner**: ~ *qn sur qc* tell *ou* inform s.o. about sth; **se** ~ find out

rentabilité *f* profitability; **rentable** cost-effective; *entreprise* profitable; **ce n'est pas** ~ there's no money in it

rente *f revenu d'un bien* private income; (*pension*) annuity; *versée à sa femme etc* allowance

rentrée *f* return; ~ *des classes* beginning of the new school year; ~**s** COMM takings

rentrer 1 *v/i* go/come in; *de nouveau* go/come back in; *chez soi* go/come home; *dans un récipient* go in, fit; *de l'argent* come in; ~ *dans* (*heurter*) collide with; *serrure, sac* go into; *responsabilités* be part of **2** *v/t* bring/take in; *voiture* put away; *ventre* pull in

renversement *m d'un régime* overthrow; **renverser** *image* reverse; (*mettre à l'envers*) upturn; (*faire tomber*) knock over; *liquide* spill; *gouvernement* overthrow

renvoi *m de personnel* dismissal; *d'un élève* expulsion; *d'une lettre* return; *dans un texte* cross-reference (*à* to); **renvoyer** (*faire retourner*) send back; *ballon* return; *personnel* dismiss; *élève* expel; *rencontre, décision* postpone

repaire *m* den

répandre spread; (*renverser*) spill; **se** ~ spread; (*être renversé*) spill; **répandu** widespread

réparation *f* repair; (*compensation*) reparation; **en** ~ being repaired; **réparer** repair; *fig* make up for

repartie *f* retort; **avoir de la** ~ have a gift for repartee

repartir set off again; ~ **de zéro** start again from scratch

répartir share out; *chargement* distribute; *en catégories* divide; **répartition** *f* distribution; *en catégories* division

repas *m* meal

repassage *m* ironing; **repasser 1** *v/t* come/go back again **2** *v/t linge* iron; *examen* take again

repentir 1: *se* ~ REL repent; *se* ~ *de* be sorry for **2** *m* penitence

répercussions *fpl* repercussions

repère *m* mark; (*point m de*) ~ landmark; **repérer** (*situer*) pinpoint; (*trouver*) find; (*marquer*) mark

répertoire *m* directory; THÉÂT repertoire

répéter repeat; THÉÂT rehearse; **répétition** *f* repetition; THÉÂT rehearsal

répit *m* respite

replacer put back, replace

repli *m* fold; *d'une rivière* bend; **replier** fold; *jambes* draw up; *journal* fold up; *manches* roll up; **se** ~ **sur soi-même** retreat into one's shell

répliquer retort; *d'un enfant* answer back

répondeur *m*: ~ **automatique** answering machine; **répondre 1** *v/t* answer, reply **2** *v/i* answer; (*réagir*) respond; ~ **à** answer, reply to; (*réagir à*) respond to; *besoin* meet; *attente* come up to; *signalement* match; **réponse** *f* answer; (*réaction*) response

reportage *m* report; **reporter** *m/f* reporter

repos *m* rest; **reposer 1** *v/t* (*remettre*) put back; *question* ask again; (*détendre*) rest; **se** ~ rest **2** *v/i*: ~ **sur** rest on

repoussant repulsive; **repousser 1** *v/t* (*dégoûter*) repel; (*différer*) postpone; *pousser en arrière*, MIL push back; (*rejeter*) reject **2** *v/i* grow again

reprendre 1 *v/t* take back; (*prendre davantage de*) take more; *ville* recapture; (*recommencer*) start again; (*corriger*) correct; *entreprise* take over (*à* from) **2** *v/i* (*recommencer*) start again; **se** ~ (*se corriger*) correct o.s.; (*se maîtriser*) pull o.s. together

représailles *fpl* reprisals

représentant, ~**e** *m/f* representative; **représentation** *f* representation; *au théâtre* performance; **représenter** represent; THÉÂT perform; **se** ~ *qc* imagine sth

répression *f* repression; **mesures** *fpl* **de** ~ crackdown (**contre** on)

réprimander reprimand

réprimer suppress

reprise *f de ville* recapture; *de marchandise* taking back; *de travail, de lutte* resumption; **à plusieurs** ~**s** on several occasions

repriser darn, mend

reproche 216

reproche *m* reproach; reprocher reproach; ~ *qch à qn* reproach s.o. for sth

reproduction *f* reproduction; reproduire reproduce; *se* ~ happen again; BIOL reproduce

républicain, ~e *m/f & adj* republican; république *f* republic

répugnant repugnant; répugner: ~ *à* be repelled by; ~ *à faire* be reluctant to do

répulsion *f* repulsion

réputation *f* reputation

requérir require

requête *f* request

requin *m* shark

requis necessary

réseau *m* network

réservation *f* booking, reservation

réserve *f* reserve; (*entrepôt*) storeroom; *sans* ~ unreservedly; *sous* ~ *de* subject to

réserver reserve; *dans hôtel, restaurant* book, reserve; (*mettre de côté*) put aside; ~ *qc à qn* keep *ou* save sth for s.o.

réservoir *m* tank; *lac etc* reservoir

résidence *f* residence; ~ *universitaire* dormitory, *Br* hall of residence; résider live; ~ *dans fig* lie in

résidu *m* residue; MATH remainder

résigner resign; *se* ~ resign o.s. (*à* to)

resilier *contrat* cancel

résistance *f* resistance; (*endurance*) stamina; *d'un matériau* strength; *la Résistance* HIST the Resistance; résister resist; ~ *à tentation, personne* resist; *sécheresse* withstand

résolu determined (*à faire* to do); résolution *f* (*décision*) resolution; (*fermeté*) determination; *d'un problème* solving

résonner echo, resound

résoudre 1 *v/t problème* solve 2 *v/i:* ~ *de faire, se* ~ *à faire* decide to do

respect *m* respect; respecter respect; ~ *le(s) délai(s)* meet the deadline; *se* ~ have some self-respect; *mutuellement* respect each other; *se faire* ~ command respect; respectif, -ive respective; respectueux, -euse respectful

respiration *f* breathing; *retenir sa* ~ hold one's breath; ~ *artificielle* MÉD artificial respiration; respirer breathe

resplendir glitter

responsabilité *f* responsibility (*de* for); JUR liability; responsable responsible (*de* for)

ressaisir: *se* ~ pull o.s. together

ressemblance *f* resemblance; ressembler: ~ *à* resemble, be like; *se* ~ resemble each other, be like each other

ressemeler resole

ressentiment *m* resentment

ressentir feel; *se ~ de* still feel the effects of

resserrer tighten; *fig: amitié* strengthen

ressort *m* TECH spring; *fig* motive; (*énergie*) energy; (*compétence*) province; JUR jurisdiction

ressortir 1 come/go out again **2** (*se détacher*) stand out; *faire ~* bring out; *~ à* JUR fall within the jurisdiction of

ressource *f* resource

restant 1 *adj* remaining **2** *m* remainder

restaurant *m* restaurant

restauration *f* catering; ART restoration; *~ rapide* fast food; **restaurer** restore

reste *m* rest, remainder; *~s* CUIS leftovers; *du ~, au ~* moreover; **rester** (*subsister*) be left, remain; (*demeurer*) stay, remain; *on en reste là* we'll stop there; *il reste du vin* there's some wine left

restituer (*rendre*) return; (*reconstituer*) restore; **restitution** *f* restitution

restreindre restrict

restriction *f* restriction; *sans ~* unreservedly

résultat *m* result; **résulter** result (**de** from)

résumé *m* summary

rétablir restore; *se ~* recover

retard *m* lateness; *dans travail, paiement* delay; *avoir deux heures de ~* be two hours late; *avoir du ~ sur qn* be behind s.o.; *être en ~* be late; **retarder 1** *v/t* delay, hold up; *montre* put back **2** *v/i a d'une montre* be slow; *~ de cinq minutes* be five minutes slow; *~ sur son temps* *fig* be behind the times

retenir *personne* keep; *argent* withhold; (*rappeler*) remember; *proposition* accept; (*réserver*) reserve; *se ~* restrain o.s.

retentir sound; *du tonnerre* boom; *~ sur* impact on; **retentissant** resounding (*aussi fig*)

retenu (*réservé*) reserved; (*empêché*) delayed

retenue *f sur salaire* deduction; *fig* (*modération*) restraint

réticence *f* (*omission*) omission; (*hésitation*) hesitation

retirer withdraw; *vêtement* take off; *promesse* take back; *profit* derive; *~ qch de* remove sth from; *se ~* withdraw; (*prendre sa retraite*) retire

retombées *fpl* fallout; **retomber** fall again; (*tomber*) land; *de cheveux, d'un rideau* fall; *~ dans qc* sink back into sth

rétorsion POL: **mesure** f **de** ~ retaliatory measure

retoucher texte, vêtement alter; photographie retouch

retour m return; **être de** ~ be back; **bon** ~! have a good trip home!; **retourner 1** v/i return, go back; ~ **sur ses pas** backtrack **2** v/t matelas, tête turn; lettre return; vêtement turn inside out; **se** ~ **au lit** turn over (aussi AUTO); (tourner la tête) turn (around)

retrait m withdrawal; **en** ~ set back

retraite f retirement; (pension) retirement pension; MIL retreat; **prendre sa** ~ retire; **retraité,** ~e m/f pensioner, retired person

retrancher (enlever) remove, cut (**de** from); (déduire) deduct

rétrécir 1 v/t shrink; fig narrow **2** v/i de tissu shrink; **se** ~ narrow

rétrograder 1 v/t demote **2** v/i retreat; AUTO downshift

rétrospectif, -ive 1 adj retrospective **2** f: **rétrospective** retrospective

retrousser manches roll up

retrouver (trouver) find; de nouveau find again; (rejoindre) meet; santé regain; **se** ~ meet; **se** ~ **seul** find o.s. alone

rétroviseur m AUTO rear-view mirror

réunion f meeting; POL reunion; **réunir** bring together; pays reunite; documents collect; **se** ~ meet

réussi successful; **réussir 1** v/i succeed; ~ **à faire** manage to do, succeed in doing **2** v/t vie, projet make a success of; examen be successful in; **réussite** f success; aux cartes solitaire, Br aussi patience

revanche f revenge; **en** ~ on the other hand

rêve m dream

réveil m awakening; (pendule) alarm (clock); **réveiller** wake up; fig revive; **se** ~ wake up

révélation f revelation; **révéler** reveal; **se** ~ **faux** prove to be false

revenant m ghost

revendeur, -euse m/f retailer

revendication f claim, demand; **revendiquer** claim

revendre resell

revenir come back, return (**à** to); ~ **sur** thème go back to; décision go back on; ~ **à qn** d'une part be due to s.o.; ~ **de** évanouissement come around from; étonnement get over; illusion lose

revenu m income; ~**s** revenue

rêver dream (**de, à** about)

réverbère m street lamp

rêverie f daydream

revers m back; d'un pantalon cuff, Br turn-up; fig (échec) reversal

revêtir *vêtement* put on; *forme, caractère* assume; *importance* take on

rêveur, -euse 1 *adj* dreamy **2** *m/f* dreamer

revirement *m*: ~ **d'opinion** sudden change in the public's attitude

réviser *texte* revise; *machine* service; **révision** *f* revision; AUTO service

révocation *f* revocation; *d'un dirigeant etc* dismissal

revoir 1 *v/t* see again; *texte* review; ÉDU review, *Br* revise **2** *m*: **au** ~! goodbye!

révolte *f* revolt; **révolter** revolt; **se** ~ rebel, revolt

révolution *f* revolution; **révolutionner** revolutionize

revolver *m* revolver

révoquer *fonctionnaire* dismiss; *contrat* revoke

revue *f* review; **passer en** ~ *fig* review

rez-de-chaussée *m* first floor, *Br* ground floor

rhubarbe *f* rhubarb

rhum *m* rum

rhumatismes *mpl* rheumatism

rhume *m* cold; ~ **des foins** hay fever

ricaner sneer; *bêtement* snigger

riche rich; *sol* fertile; *décoration* elaborate; **richesse** *f* wealth; *du sol* fertility

rictus *m* grimace

ride *f* wrinkle, line

rideau *m* drape, *Br* curtain

rider *peau* wrinkle; **se** ~ become wrinkled

ridicule 1 *adj* ridiculous **2** *m* ridicule; *(absurdité)* ridiculousness; **ridiculiser** ridicule; **se** ~ make a fool of o.s.

rien 1 *pron* nothing; *quelque chose* anything; **de** ~ *comme réponse* you're welcome; **ne** ... ~ nothing, not anything **2** *m* trifle; **en un** ~ **de temps** in no time

rigide rigid

rigole *f* *(conduit)* channel

rigoler F *(plaisanter)* joke; *(rire)* laugh

rigolo, ~**te** F *(amusant)* funny

rigoureux, -euse rigorous; **rigueur** *f* rigor, *Br* rigour; **à la** ~ if absolutely necessary; **de** ~ compulsory

rincer rinse

riposte *f* riposte, response; *avec armes* return of fire; **riposter** reply, response; *avec armes* return fire

rire *v/i* laugh *(de* about, at); *(s'amuser)* have fun; ~ **aux éclats** roar with laughter; ~ **de qn** laugh at s.o. **2** *m* laugh; ~**s** laughter

risque *m* risk; **à tes** ~**s et périls** at your own risk; **risqué** risky; *plaisanterie* risqué; **risquer** risk; ~ **de faire** risk doing; **se** ~ **dans** venture into

rituel, ~**le** *adj* & *m* ritual

rivage *m* shore

rival, ~e m/f & adj rival; rivaliser compete, vie; rivalité f
rivalry
rive f d'un fleuve bank; d'une
mer, d'un lac shore
riverain, ~e m/f resident
rivet m TECH rivet
rivière f river
riz m BOT rice
robe f dress; d'un juge robe; ~
de chambre robe, Br dressing gown
robinet m faucet, Br tap
robuste robust
roche f rock
rocher m rock; rocheux, -eu-
se rocky
rôder prowl
rogne f: être en ~ F be in a
bad mood
rogner cut, trim
rognon m CUIS kidney
roi m king
rôle m role; (registre) roll; à
tour de ~ turn and turn
about
roman m novel
romancier, -ère m/f novelist
romantique m/f & adj ro-
mantic; romantisme m ro-
manticism
romarin m BOT rosemary
rompre 1 v/i break; ~ avec petit ami break it off with; tradition break with; habitude
break 2 v/t break; négociations, fiançailles break off
ronce f BOT: ~s brambles
rond, ~e 1 adj round; joues,
personne plump; F (ivre)

drunk 2 adv: tourner ~ run
smoothly 3 m figure circle
m 4 f: faire sa ronde do
one's rounds; de soldat, policier be on patrol; à la ronde
around
rondelle f disk, Br disc; de
saucisson slice; TECH washer
rondement (promptement)
briskly; (carrément) frankly
rond-point m traffic circle,
Br roundabout
ronflement m snoring; d'un
moteur purr; ronfler snore;
d'un moteur purr
ronger gnaw at; fig torment;
se ~ les ongles bite one's
nails; rongeur m ZO rodent
ronronner purr
rosbif m CUIS roast beef
rose 1 f BOT rose 2 m couleur
pink 3 adj pink
rosé 1 m rosé 2 adj pinkish
roseau m BOT reed
rosée f dew
rosier m rose bush
rossignol m ZO nightingale
rot m F belch; roter F belch
rôti m roast; rôtir roast; rôtis-
serie f grill-room
rouage m cogwheel; ~s d'une
montre works; fig machinery
roue f wheel; deux ~s m two-
-wheeler; quatre ~s motrices all-wheel drive
roué crafty
rouer: ~ qn de coups beat
s.o. black and blue
rouge 1 adj red 2 adv fig: voir
~ see red 3 m red; ~ à lèvres

lipstick
rouge-gorge *m* robin (red-breast)
rougeole *f* MÉD measles *sg*
rougir go red; *d'une personne aussi* blush (**de** with); *de colère* flush (**de** with)
rouille *f* rust; **rouillé** rusty; **rouiller** rust; **se ~** rust; *fig* go rusty
rouleau *m* roller; *de pellicule etc* roll; CUIS rolling pin
rouler 1 *v/i* roll; *d'une voiture* travel; **~ sur qc** *d'une conversation* be about sth **2** *v/t* roll; **~ qn** F cheat s.o.
roulette *f* **de meubles** caster; *jeu* roulette
roumain, ~e 1 *adj* Romanian **2** *m langue* Romanian; Roumain, ~e *m/f* Romanian; Roumanie: **la ~** Romania
rouspéter F complain
rousseur *f*: **taches** *fpl* **de ~** freckles
route *f* road; (*parcours*) route; *fig* (*chemin*) path; **en ~** on the way; **se mettre en ~** set off; *fig* get under way; **faire~ vers** be heading for
routier, -ère 1 *adj* road *atr* **2** *m* (*conducteur*) truck driver, *Br* long-distance lorry driver; *restaurant* truck stop, *Br aussi* transport café
routine *f* routine; **de~** routine *atr*
roux, rousse *personne* red-haired; *cheveux* red

royal royal; *fig*: *pourboire, accueil* superb, right royal
royaume *m* kingdom; le Royaume-Uni the United Kingdom
R.-U. (= **Royaume-Uni**) UK (= United Kingdom)
ruban *m* ribbon; **~ adhésif** adhesive tape
rubéole *f* MÉD German measles *sg*
rubrique *f* heading
ruche *f* hive
rude *manières* uncouth; (*sévère*) harsh; *travail, lutte* hard
rudimentaire rudimentary; **rudiments** *mpl* rudiments
rue *f* street; **dans la ~** on the street
ruée *f* rush
ruelle *f* alley
rugby *m* rugby
rugir roar; *du vent* howl
rugueux, -euse rough
ruine *f* ruin; **ruiner** ruin
ruisseau *m* stream; (*caniveau*) gutter
ruisseler run
rumeur *f* hum; *de personnes* murmuring; (*nouvelle*) rumor, *Br* rumour
ruminer 1 *v/i* chew the cud, ruminate **2** *v/t fig*: **~ qch** mull sth over
rupture *f* breaking; *fig* split; *de négociations* breakdown; *de relations* breaking off; *de contrat* breach
ruse *f* ruse; **la~** cunning; **rusé** crafty, cunning

russe 1 *adj* Russian **2** *m langue*, *Br* Russian; **Russe** *m/f* Russian; **Russie:** *la ~* Russia
rustique rustic

rustre *péj* **1** *adj* uncouth **2** *m* oaf
rythme *m* rhythm; (*vitesse*) pace; **rythmique** rhythmical

S

sa → son¹
S.A. *f* (= *société anonyme*) Inc, *Br* plc
sable *m* sand; **sabler** sand; *~ le champagne* break open the champagne
sablier *m* CUIS eggtimer
sabot *m* clog; ZO hoof
sabotage *m* sabotage; **saboter** sabotage; F *travail* make a mess of
sac *m* bag; *de pommes de terre* sack; *~ de couchage* sleeping bag; *~ à dos* backpack; *~ à main* purse, *Br* handbag
saccadé *mouvements* jerky; *voix* breathless
saccager (*piller*) sack; (*détruire*) destroy
saccharine *f* saccharine
sachet *m* sachet; *~ de thé* teabag
sacoche *f* bag; *de vélo* saddlebag
sacré sacred; F damn F
sacrement *m* REL sacrament
sacrifice *m* sacrifice; **sacrifier** sacrifice; *se ~* sacrifice o.s.
sacrilège 1 *adj* sacrilegious **2** *m* sacrilege

sadique 1 *adj* sadistic **2** *m/f* sadist
safran *m* saffron
sagace shrewd; **sagacité** *f* shrewdness
sage 1 *adj* wise; *enfant* good **2** *m* sage, wise man; **sage-femme** *f* midwife; **sagesse** *f* wisdom; *d'un enfant* goodness
Sagittaire *m* ASTROL Sagittarius
saignant bleeding; CUIS rare; **saigner 1** *v/i* bleed **2** *v/t fig* bleed dry
saillant *pommettes* prominent; *fig* salient; **saillie** *f* ARCH projection; *fig* quip; **saillir** ARCH project
sain healthy; *gestion* sound; *~ d'esprit* sane
saint, *~e* **1** *adj* holy **2** *m/f* saint; **sainteté** *f* holiness; **Saint-Sylvestre:** *la ~* New Year's Eve
saisie *f* seizure; *~ de données* INFORM data capture; **saisir** seize; *sens, intention* grasp; INFORM capture; **saisissant** striking; *froid* penetrating
saison *f* season; **saisonnier**,

-ère **1** *adj* seasonal **2** *m ouvrier* seasonal worker

salade *f* salad; **saladier** *m* salad bowl

salaire *m d'un ouvrier* wages *pl*; *d'un employé* salary; ~ **net** take-home pay

salarié, ~e **1** *adj travail* paid **2** *m/f ouvrier* wage-earner; *employé* salaried employee

salaud *m* P bastard P

sale *après le substantif* dirty; *devant le substantif* nasty

salé *eau* salt; **cuis** salted; *histoire* daring; *prix* steep; **saler** salt

saleté *f* dirtiness; ~**s** *fig* (*grossièretés*) filthy remarks; F *choses sans valeur, mauvaise nourriture* junk

salière *f* salt cellar

salir: ~ *qch* get sth dirty

salive *f* saliva

salle *f* room; ~ *d'attente* waiting room; ~ *d'eau* shower room; ~ *à manger* dining room

salon *m* living room; *d'un hôtel* lounge; (*foire*) show; ~ *de l'automobile* auto show, *Br* motor show; ~ *de thé* tea room

salope *f* P bitch; **saloperie** *f* F *chose sans valeur* piece of junk; (*bassesse*) dirty trick

salopette *f* dungarees *pl*

salubre healthy

saluer greet; **mil** salute; ~ *qn* (*de la main*) wave to s.o.

salut *m* greeting; **mil** salute;

(*sauvegarde*) safety; **rel** salvation; ~*!* F hi!; (*au revoir*) bye!

salutaire salutary

samedi *m* Saturday

sanction *f* sanction

sanctuaire *m* sanctuary

sandale *f* sandal

sandwich *m* sandwich

sang *m* blood; **sang-froid** *m composure;* **garder son** ~ keep one's cool; **tuer qn de** ~ kill s.o. in cold blood; **sanglant** bloodstained; *combat, mort* bloody

sanglot *m* sob; **sangloter** sob

sanguin blood *atr*; *tempérament* sanguine; **groupe** *m* ~ blood group

sanitaire sanitary

sans without; ~ *manger* without eating; ~ *balcon* without a balcony

sans-abri *m/f:* **les** ~ the homeless *pl*

sans-emploi *m:* **les** ~ the unemployed *pl*

santé *f* health; **à votre** ~*!* cheers!, your very good health!

saper undermine

sapeur-pompier *m* firefighter

saphir *m* sapphire

sapin *m* **bot** fir

sarcasme *m* sarcasm; **sarcastique** sarcastic

sardine *f* sardine

sardonique sardonic

S.A.R.L. *f* (= *société à res-*

ponsabilité limitée) Inc, *Br* Ltd

satellite *m* satellite

satin *m* satin

satirique satirical

satisfaction *f* satisfaction; **satisfaire 1** *v/i*: **~ à 2** *v/t* satisfy; *attente* come up to; **satisfaisant** satisfactory; **satisfait** satisfied (**de** with)

saturer saturate

sauce *f* sauce

saucisse *f* sausage

saucisson *m* (dried) sausage

sauf[1] *prép* except; **~ avis contraire** unless you/I / *etc* hear to the contrary

sauf[2], **sauve** *adj* safe

sauf-conduit *m* safe-conduct

saugrenu ridiculous

saule *m* BOT willow; **~ pleureur** weeping willow

saumon *m* salmon

sauna *m* sauna

saupoudrer sprinkle (**de** with)

saut *m* jump; **faire un ~ chez qn** *fig* drop in briefly on s.o.; **~ à l'élastique** bungee jumping; **~ en longueur** broad jump, *Br* long jump; **~ à la perche** pole vault

sauter 1 *v/i* jump; (*exploser*) blow up; *d'un fusible* blow; *d'un bouton* come off; **~ sur** *personne* pounce on; *occasion, offre* jump at; **cela saute aux yeux** it's obvious **2** *v/t fossé* jump (over); *mot, repas* skip

sauterelle *f* grasshopper

sautiller hop

sauvage 1 *adj* wild; (*insociable*) unsociable; (*primitif, barbare*) savage; *pas autorisé* unauthorized **2** *m/f* savage; (*solitaire*) unsociable person

sauvegarde *f* safeguard; INFORM back-up

sauver save; *personne en danger* save, rescue; *navire* salvage; **se ~** run away; F (*partir*) be off; (*déborder*) boil over

sauvetage *m* rescue; *de navire* salvaging; **sauveteur** *m* rescuer

sauveur *m* savior, *Br* saviour

savant 1 *adj* (*érudit*) learned; (*habile*) skillful, *Br* skilful **2** *m* scientist

saveur *f* taste

savoir 1 *v/i & v/i* know; **sais-tu nager?** can you swim?, do you know how to swim? **2** *m* knowledge

savoir-faire *m* expertise, knowhow

savoir-vivre *m* good manners *pl*

savon *m* soap

savourer savor, *Br* savour; **savoureux, -euse** tasty; *fig: récit* spicy

saxophone *m* saxophone, sax

scandale *m* scandal; **faire ~** cause a scandal; **faire tout un ~** make a scene; **scanda-**

liser scandalize; **se ~ de** be shocked by

scanner 1 v/t scan **2** m scanner

scaphandrier m diver

scarlatine f scarlet fever

sceau m seal; fig (marque, signe) stamp

scellé m official seal; **sceller** seal

scénario m scenario; (script) screenplay; **~ catastrophe** worst-case scenario

scène f scene (aussi fig); (plateau) stage; **mettre en ~** pièce, film direct; présenter stage; **~ de ménage** domestic argument

sceptique 1 adj skeptical, Br sceptical **2** m skeptic, Br sceptic

schéma m diagram; **schématiser** oversimplify

sciatique f sciatica

scie f saw; fig F bore

sciemment knowingly

science f science; (connaissance) knowledge; **scientifique 1** adj scientific **2** m/f scientist

scier saw; branche etc saw off

scinder fig split; **se ~** split up

scintiller sparkle

scission f split

scolaire school atr; succès, échec academic; **scolarité** f education, schooling

scooter m (motor) scooter

score m SP score; POL share of the vote

scorpion m ZO scorpion; ASTROL **Scorpion** Scorpio

scotch® m Scotch tape®, Br sellotape®

scrupule m scruple; **scrupuleux, -euse** scrupulous

scruter scrutinize

scrutin m ballot; **~ majoritaire** majority vote system; **~ proportionnel** proportional representation

sculpter sculpt; pierre carve; **sculpteur** m sculptor; **sculpture** f sculpture

SDF m/f (= **sans domicile fixe**) homeless person

se réfléchi masculin himself; féminin herself; chose, animal itself; pluriel themselves; avec 'one' oneself; réciproque each other; **cela ne ~ fait pas** that isn't done; **ils ~ lèvent à …** they get up at …

séance f session; de cinéma show, performance; **~ tenante** fig immediately

seau m bucket

sec, sèche 1 adj dry; fruits, légumes dried; (maigre) thin; réponse, ton curt **2** m: **tenir au ~** keep in a dry place **3** adv boire neat, straight

sèche-cheveux m hair dryer; **sèche-linge** m clothes dryer; **sécher** dry; d'un lac dry up; **sécheresse** f dryness; manque de pluie drought; de réponse, ton curtness

second, ~e **1** adj second **2** m étage third floor, Br second floor; (adjoint) second in command **3** f second; en train second class; secondaire secondary; seconder personne assist

secouer shake; poussière shake off

secouriste m/f first-aider; secours m help; matériel aid; au ~! help!; sortie f de ~ emergency exit; premiers ~s first aid

secousse f jolt; électrique shock; tellurique tremor

secret, -ète **1** adj secret **2** m secret; (discrétion) secrecy; en ~ in secret

secrétaire 1 m/f secretary **2** m writing desk

secrétariat m secretariat; profession secretarial work

secte f REL sect

secteur m sector; (zone) area, district; ÉL mains pl

section f section; sectionner (couper) sever; région etc divide up

séculaire a hundred years old; très ancien centuries--old

séculier, -ère secular

sécurité f security; (manque de danger) safety; **Sécurité sociale** welfare, Br social security; **être en ~** be safe

sédatif m sedative

sédentaire sedentary; population settled

séduction f seduction; fig (charme) attraction; séduire seduce; fig (charmer) appeal to; d'une personne charm; séduisant appealing; personne attractive

ségrégation f segregation

seigle m AGR rye

seigneur m HIST the lord of the manor; REL: **le Seigneur** the Lord

sein m breast; fig bosom; au ~ de within

seize sixteen; **seizième** sixteenth

séjour m stay; (salle f de) ~ living room; séjourner stay

sel m salt

sélection f selection; sélectionner select

selle f saddle; MÉD stool

selon according to; ~ moi in my opinion; c'est ~ it all depends

semaine f week; à la ~ by the week; en ~ during the week, on weekdays

semblable 1 adj similar; tel such; ~ à like, similar to **2** m (être humain) fellow human being

semblant m semblance; **faire ~ de faire** pretend to do

sembler seem

semelle f sole; pièce intérieure insole

semence f AGR seed

semer sow; fig (répandre) spread; ~ qn F shake s.o. off

semestre m half-year

séminaire *m* seminar; REL seminary

semi-remorque *m* semi, *Br* articulated lorry

semonce *f* reproach

semoule *f* CUIS semolina

Sénat *m* POL Senate; **sénateur** *m* senator

sénile senile

sens *m* sense; (*direction*) direction; **~ interdit** no entry; **~ dessus dessous** upside down; **~ de l'humour** sense of humor *ou Br* humour; (*rue f à*) **~ unique** one-way street

sensation *f* feeling, sensation; *effet de surprise* sensation; **faire ~** cause a sensation; **sensationnel,** ~**le** sensational

sensé sensible

sensibilité *f* sensitivity; **sensible** sensitive; (*notable*) appreciable; **sensiblement** appreciably; **plus ou moins** more or less

sensualité *f* sensuality; **sensuel,** ~**le** sensual

sentence *f* JUR sentence

sentier *m* path

sentiment *m* feeling; **sentimental** *vie* love *atr*; *péj* sentimental

sentinelle *f* MIL guard

sentir 1 *v/t* feel; (*humer*) smell; (*dégager une odeur de*) smell of; **se ~ bien** feel well **2** *v/i*: **~ bon** smell good

séparable separable; **sépa-**

ration *f* separation; (*cloison*) partition; **séparatisme** *m* POL separatism; **séparé** separate; *époux* separated; **séparément** separately; **séparer** separate; **se ~** separate

sept seven

septembre *m* September

septennat *m* term of office (of French President)

septentrional northern

septième seventh

septique septic

séquelles *fpl* MÉD after-effects; *fig* aftermath

séquence *f* sequence

serein calm

sérénité *f* serenity

série *f* series *sg*; *de casseroles, timbres* set; SP (*épreuve*) heat; **hors~** *numéro* special; **fabriquer en ~** mass-produce

sérieux, -euse 1 *adj* serious; *entreprise, employé* professional; (*consciencieux*) conscientious **2** *m* seriousness; **prendre au ~** take seriously

seringue *f* MÉD syringe

serment *m* oath; **prêter ~** take the oath

sermon *m* sermon

séropositif, -ive HIV-positive

serpent *m* snake; **serpenter** wind, meander

serpillière *f* floor cloth

serre *f* greenhouse; **~s** ZO talons

serré tight; *pluie* heavy; *per-*

sonnes closely packed; *café* strong

serrer 1 *v/t* (*tenir*) clasp; *ceinture* tighten; *d'un vêtement* be too tight for **2** *v/i*: **se ~** (*s'entasser*) squeeze up; **se ~ contre qn** press against s.o.

serrure *f* lock; **serrurier** *m* locksmith

serveur *m dans un café* bartender, *Br* barman; *dans un restaurant* waiter; INFORM server

serveuse *f dans un café* bartender, *Br* barmaid; *dans un restaurant* server, waitress

serviable helpful

service *m* service; (*faveur*) favor, *Br* favour; *au tennis* service, serve; *d'une entreprise, d'un hôpital* department; **être de ~** be on duty; **rendre~ à qn** do s.o. a favor; **mettre en ~** put into service; **hors ~** out of order

serviette *f* serviette; *de toilette* towel; *pour documents* briefcase; **~ hygiénique** sanitary napkin

servile servile

servir serve; (*être utile*) be useful; **~ à qn** be of use to s.o.; **~ à qch/à faire qch** be used for sth/for doing sth; **~ de qc** act as sth; **se ~** *à table* help o.s. (**en** to); **se ~ de** (*utiliser*) use

ses → son¹

seuil *m* doorstep; *fig* threshold

seul 1 *adj* alone; (*solitaire*) lonely; *devant le subst* only, sole **2** *adv* alone; **faire qch tout ~** do sth all by o.s. *ou* all on one's own

seulement only; **non ~ ... mais encore** *ou* **mais aussi** not only ... but also

sévère severe; **sévérité** *f* severity

sévices *mpl* abuse

sévir *d'une épidémie* rage; **~ contre qn** come down hard on s.o.; **~ contre qc** clamp down on sth

sexagénaire *m/f & adj* sixty--year old

sexe *m* sex; *organes* genitals *pl*; **sexiste** *m/f & adj* sexist; **sexualité** *f* sexuality; **sexuel, ~le** sexual

shampo(o)ing *m* shampoo

short *m* shorts *pl*

si 1 *conj* (**s'il, s'ils**) if; **~ bien que** with the result that **2** *adv* (*tellement*) so; *après négation* yes; **de ~ bonnes vacances** such a good vacation; **~ riche qu'il soit** (*subj*) however rich he may be; **tu ne veux pas? - mais ~!** you don't want to? - oh yes, I do

sida *m* MÉD Aids

sidéré F thunderstruck

siècle *m* century; *fig* (*époque*) age

siège *m* seat; *d'une entreprise* headquarters *pl*; MIL siege; **~**

social COMM head office; **siéger** sit; ***~ à*** *d'une entreprise* be headquartered in

sien: *le sien, la sienne, les* **siens, les siennes** *d'homme* his; *de femme* hers; *de chose, d'animal* its; *avec 'one'* one's

sieste f siesta, nap

sifflement m whistle; **siffler** whistle; *d'un serpent* hiss; **sifflet** m whistle; ***coup*** m ***de ~*** blow on the whistle

signal m signal; ***~ d'alarme*** alarm (signal); **signalement** m description; **signaler** par un signal signal; (faire remarquer) point out; (dénoncer) report; ***se ~ par*** distinguish o.s. by

signature f signature

signe m sign; ***faire~ à*** gesture ou signal to s; (contacter) get in touch with; ***~ de ponctuation*** punctuation mark; **signer** sign

signet m bookmark

signification f meaning; **signifier** mean; ***~ qch à qn*** (faire savoir) notify s.o. of sth

silence m silence; **silencieux, -euse 1** adj silent **2** m d'une arme muffler, Br silencer

silhouette f outline, silhouette; (figure) figure

sillage m wake (aussi fig)

sillon m dans un champ furrow; d'un disque groove; sil-

lonner (parcourir) criss-cross

similaire similar; **similitude** f similarity

simple 1 adj simple **2** m au tennis singles pl; **simplicité** f simplicity

simplifier simplify

simulateur, -trice 1 m/f: ***c'est un ~*** he's pretending **2** m TECH simulator; **simulation** f simulation; **simuler** simulate

simultané simultaneous

sincère sincere; **sincérité** f sincerity

singe m monkey; **singer** ape; **singerie** f imitation; ***~s*** F antics

singulier, -ère 1 adj odd, strange **2** m GRAM singular

sinistre 1 adj sinister; (triste) gloomy **2** m disaster; **sinistré 1** adj stricken **2** m/f disaster victim

sinon (autrement) or else, otherwise; (sauf) except; (si ce n'est) if not

sinueux, -euse route winding; ligne squiggly; explication complicated

sinus m sinus; **sinusite** f sinusitis

sirène f siren

sirop m syrup

siroter sip

sismique seismic

sitcom m ou f sitcom

site m site; (paysage) area; ***~ Web*** website

sitôt 1 *adv*: ~ **parti, il** ... as soon as he had left he ... **2** *conj*: ~ **que** as soon as

situation *f* situation; (*emplacement, profession*) position; **situé** situated

six six; **sixième** sixth

skateboard *m* skateboard; *activité* skateboarding

sketch *m* sketch

ski *m* ski; *activité* skiing; ~ **alpin** downhill (skiing); ~ **de fond** cross-country (skiing); ~ **nautique** water-skiing; **skier** ski; **skieur, -euse** *m/f* skier

slip *m* **de femme** panties *pl*; *d'homme* briefs; ~ **de bain** swimming trunks *pl*

slogan *m* slogan

slovaque *adj* Slovak(ian); Slovaque *m/f* Slovak(ian)

slovène *adj* Slovene, Slovenian; Slovène *m/f* Slovene, Slovenian

smoking *m* tuxedo, *Br* dinner jacket

SMS *m* text (message)

S.N.C.F. *f* (= *Société nationale des chemins de fer français*) French national railroad company

sobre sober; *style* restrained

sociable sociable

social social; COMM company *atr*; **socialiser** socialize; **socialisme** *m* socialism; **socialiste** *m/f* & *adj* socialist

société *f* society; *firme* company; ~ **anonyme** corpora-

tion, *Br* public limited company, plc

sociologie *f* sociology

socquette *f* anklet, *Br* ankle sock

soda *m* soda, *Br* fizzy drink; *un whisky* ~ a whiskey and soda

sœur *f* sister; REL nun

sofa *m* sofa

soi oneself; *avec* ~ with one; *ça va de* ~ that goes without saying

soi-disant *inv* so-called

soie *f* silk

soif *f* thirst; *avoir* ~ be thirsty

soigné *personne* well-groomed; *travail* careful; **soigner** look after, take care of; *d'un médecin* treat; *se* ~ take care of o.s.; **soigneux, -euse** careful (**de** about)

soi-même oneself

soin *m* care; ~**s** care; MÉD care, treatment; *prendre* ~ *de* look after, take care of; *être sans* ~ be untidy

soir *m* evening; *le* ~ in the evening; **soirée** *f* evening; (*fête*) party

soit[1] *adv* very well, so be it

soit[2] *conj* ~ ..., ~ ... either ..., or ...; (*à savoir*) that is, ie

soixantaine *f* about sixty; **soixante** sixty; **soixante-dix** seventy

soja *m* BOT soy bean, *Br* soya

sol *m* ground; (*plancher*) floor; (*patrie*), GÉOL soil

solaire solar

soldat *m* soldier
solde[1] *f* MIL pay
solde[2] *m* COMM balance; **~s marchandises** sale goods; *vente au rabais* sale; **solder compte** close, balance; *marchandises* sell off
sole *f* ZO sole
soleil *m* sun; **il y a du ~** it's sunny; **coup** *m* **de ~** sunburn
solennel, **~le** solemn
solidaire: **être ~ de qn** suport s.o.; **solidarité** *f* solidarity
solide 1 *adj* solid; *tissu* strong; *argument* sound; *personne* sturdy **2** *m* PHYS solid; **solidité** *f* solidity; *d'un matériau* strength; *d'un argument* soundness
solitaire 1 *adj* solitary **2** *m/f* loner **3** *m diamant* solitaire; **solitude** *f* solitude
sollicitation *f* plea; **solliciter** request; *attention* attract; *curiosité* arouse; **~ un emploi** apply for a job; **sollicitude** *f* solicitude
solstice *m* ASTR solstice
soluble soluble; **café** *m* **~** instant coffee
solution *f* solution
solvable solvent; *digne de crédit* creditworthy
sombre *couleur*, *salle* dark; *temps* overcast; *avenir*, *regard* somber; *Br* sombre
sommaire 1 *adj* brief; *exécution* summary **2** *m* summary
somme[1] *f* sum; *(quantité)* amount; **en ~,** **~ toute** in short
somme[2] *m* nap, snooze
sommeil *m* sleep; **avoir ~** be sleepy; **sommeiller** doze
sommelier *m* wine waiter
sommer: **~ qn de faire qc** order s.o. to do sth
sommet *m* **d'une montagne** summit, top; *d'un arbre*, *d'une tour* top; *fig* pinnacle; POL summit
sommier *m* mattress
somnambule *m/f* sleepwalker
somnifère *m* sleeping tablet
somnolence *f* drowsiness, sleepiness; **somnoler** doze
somptueux, **-euse** sumptuous; **somptuosité** *f* sumptuousness
son[1] *m*, **sa** *f*, **ses** *pl d'homme* his; *de femme* her; *de chose*, *d'animal* its; *avec 'one'* one's
son[2] *m* sound
sondage *m* probe; TECH drilling; **~ (d'opinion)** opinion poll, survey
sonde *f* probe; **sonder** MÉD probe; *personne*, *atmosphère* sound out
songe *m litt* dream; **songer**: **~ à (faire) qc** think about (doing) sth; **songeur**, **-euse** thoughtful
sonner 1 *v/i de cloches*, *sonnette* ring; *d'un réveil* go off; *d'un instrument*, *d'une voix* sound; *d'une horloge* strike; **midi a sonné** it has struck noon; **~ creux/faux**

fig ring hollow/false **2** *v/t cloches* ring; **sonnerie** *f de cloches* ringing; *(sonnette)* bell; **sonnette** *f* bell

sonore *voix* loud; *rire* resounding; *cuivres* sonorous; *onde, film* sound *atr*; **sonorité** *f* sound, tone; *d'une salle* acoustics *pl*

sophistiqué sophisticated

soporifique sleep-inducing, soporific

soprano 1 *f* soprano **2** *m* treble

sorcellerie *f* sorcery, witchcraft

sorcier *m* sorcerer; **sorcière** *f* witch

sordide filthy; *fig* sordid

sort *m* fate; *(condition)* lot; *tirer au ~* draw lots; *jeter un ~ à fig* cast a spell on

sorte *f (manière)* way; *(espèce)* sort, kind; *en quelque ~* in a way; *de (telle) ~ que* and so

sortie *f* exit; *(promenade, excursion)* outing; *d'un livre* publication; *d'un disque* release; *d'une voiture* launch; TECH outlet; MIL sortie; *(sur) imprimante* printout

sortir 1 *v/i* come/go out; *pour se distraire* go out *(avec* with); *d'un livre, un disque* come out; *au loto* come up; *~ de endroit* leave; *accident, entretien* emerge from; *(provenir de)* come from **2** *v/t chose* bring/take out;

chien, personne take out; COMM bring out; F *bêtises* come out with **3**: *s'en ~ d'un malade* pull through

sot, ~te 1 *adj* silly, foolish **2** *m/f* fool; **sottise** *f* foolishness; *action/remarque* foolish thing to do/say

sou *m fig* penny; *être sans le ~* be penniless

souche *f d'un arbre* stump; *d'un carnet* stub

souci *m* worry, care; *sans ~* carefree; **soucier**: *se ~ de* worry about; **soucieux, -euse** anxious, concerned *(de* about)

soucoupe *f* saucer

soudain 1 *adj* sudden **2** *adv* suddenly

souder TECH weld; *fig* bring closer together

soudoyer bribe

souffle *m* breath; *d'une explosion* blast; *à bout de ~* breathless, out of breath; **souffler 1** *v/i du vent* blow; *(haleter)* puff; *(respirer)* breathe; *(reprendre son souffle)* get one's breath back **2** *v/t chandelle* blow out; ÉDU, *au théâtre* prompt; *~ qc à qn* F *(dire)* whisper sth to s.o.; *(enlever)* steal sth from s.o.

souffrance *f* suffering; **souffrant** unwell; **souffrir 1** *v/i* be in pain; *~ de* suffer from **2** *v/t* suffer

soufre *m* CHIM sulfur, *Br* sulphur

souhait *m* wish; **à vos ~s!** bless you!; **souhaitable** desirable; **souhaiter** wish for; **~ que** (+ *subj*) hope that

souiller dirty, soil; *fig: réputation* tarnish

soûl drunk

soulagement *m* relief; **soulager** relieve; **~ qn au travail** help s.o. out

soûler F: **~ qn** get s.o. drunk; **se ~** get drunk

soulèvement *m* uprising; **soulever** raise; *enthousiasme* arouse; *protestations* generate; **se ~** raise o.s.; (*se révolter*) rise up

souligner underline

soumettre *pays, peuple* subdue; *à un examen* subject (*à* to); (*présenter*) submit; **se ~** à submit to; **soumis** *peuple* subject; (*obéissant*) submissive; **soumission** *f* submission; COMM tender

soupçon *m* suspicion; **un ~ de** a hint of; **soupçonner** suspect; **soupçonneux, -euse** suspicious

soupe *f* CUIS (thick) soup

souper 1 *v/i* have dinner *ou* supper **2** *m* dinner, supper

soupir *m* sigh; **soupirer** sigh

souple flexible; **souplesse** *f* flexibility

source *f* spring; *fig* source

sourcil *m* eyebrow

sourd deaf; *voix* low; *douleur, bruit* dull; *colère* re-

pressed; **~-muet** deaf-and--dumb

souriant smiling

souricière *f* mousetrap; *fig* trap

sourire *v/i* & *m* smile

souris *f* mouse

sournois, ~e 1 *adj* underhanded **2** *m/f* underhanded person

sous under; **~ peu** soon; **~ la pluie** in the rain

souscription *f* subscription; **souscrire: ~ à** subscribe to (*aussi fig*); *emprunt* approve

sous-entendre imply; **sous--entendu 1** *adj* implied **2** *m* implication

sous-estimer underestimate

sous-jacent underlying

sous-louer sublet

sous-marin 1 *adj* underwater **2** *m* submarine

sous-sol *m* *d'une maison* basement

sous-titre *m* subtitle

soustraire MATH subtract (*de* from); *fig: au regard de re-move*; *à un danger* protect (*à* from)

sous-traitance *f* sub-contracting

sous-vêtements *mpl* underwear

soutane *f* REL cassock

soute *f* MAR, AVIAT hold

soutenir support; *pression* withstand; *conversation* keep going; *opinion* maintain; **~ que** maintain that;

se ~ support each other; **soutenu** *effort* sustained; *style* elevated

souterrain 1 *adj* underground, subterranean **2** *m* underground passage

soutien *m* support

soutien-gorge *m* brassiere, bra

souvenir 1: *se* ~ *de qn/qch* remember s.o./sth; *se* ~ *que* remember that **2** *m* memory; *objet* souvenir

souvent often; *le plus* ~ most of the time

souverain, ~e *m/f* sovereign

soyeux, -euse silky

spacieux, -euse spacious

spaghetti *mpl* spaghetti *sg*

sparadrap *m* Band-Aid®, *Br* Elastoplast®

spasme *m* MÉD spasm; **spasmodique** spasmodic

spatial spatial; ASTR space *atr*

spécial special; **spécialiser:** *se* ~ specialize; **spécialiste** *m/f* specialist; **spécialité** *f* speciality

spécifier specify

spécifique specific

spécimen *m* specimen

spectacle *m* spectacle; *théâtre, cinéma* show, performance; **spectaculaire** spectacular

spectateur, -trice *m/f* (*témoin*) onlooker; SP spectator; *au théâtre* member of the audience

spectre *m* ghost; PHYS spectrum

spéculer speculate

spéléologie *f* caving

spermatozoïde *m* BIOL sperm

sperme *m* BIOL sperm

sphère *f* MATH sphere (*aussi fig*)

spirale *f* spiral

spirituel, ~le spiritual; (*amusant*) witty

spiritueux *mpl* spirits

splendeur *f* splendor, *Br* splendour, magnificence; **splendide** splendid

sponsor *m* sponsor; **sponsoriser** sponsor

spontané spontaneous

sport 1 *m* sport; *faire du* ~ do sport **2** *adj vêtements* casual *atr*

sportif, -ive 1 *adj résultats, association* sports *atr*; *allure* sporty; (*fair-play*) sporting **2** *m* sportsman **3** *f* sportswoman

square *m* public garden

squash *m* SP squash

squatter *m* squat; **squatteur, -euse** *m/f* squatter

squelette *m* skeleton

stabilisateur, -trice 1 *adj* stabilizing **2** *m* stabilizer; **stabiliser** stabilize; **stabilité** *f* stability; **stable** stable

stade *m* SP stadium; *d'un processus* stage

stage *m* training period; (*cours*) training course; *pour professeur* teaching practice; (*expérience professionnelle*) work placement; **stagiaire** *m/f* trainee

stagnant *eau* stagnant

stalle *f d'un cheval* box; **~s** REL stalls

stand *m de foire* booth, *Br* stand; *de kermesse* stall

standard *m* standard; TÉL switchboard

standardiser standardize

standardiste *m/f* TÉL (switchboard) operator

starter *m* AUTO choke

station *f* station; *de bus* stop; *de vacances* resort; **~ de taxis** cab stand, *Br* taxi rank; **~ thermale** spa

stationnement *m* parking; **stationner** park

station-service *f* gas station, *Br* petrol station

statistique 1 *adj* statistical **2** *f* statistic; *science* statistics *sg*

statue *f* statue

stature *f* stature

statut *m* status; **~s** *d'une société* statutes

stéréo *f* stereo

stéréotype *m* stereotype; **stéréotypé** stereotype

stérile sterile; **stériliser** sterilize; **stérilité** *f* sterility

steward *m* flight attendant, steward

stigmate *m* mark; **~s** REL stigmata

stimuler stimulate

stipulation *f* stipulation; **stipuler** stipulate

stock *m* stock; **stocker** stock; INFORM store

stoïque stoical

stop *m* stop; *écriteau* stop sign; *(feu m)* ~ AUTO brake light; **faire du ~** F hitchhike; **stopper** stop

store *m d'une fenêtre* shade, *Br* blind; *d'un magasin, d'une terrasse* awning

strapontin *m* tip-up seat

stratagème *m* stratagem

stratégie *f* strategy

stress *m* stress; **stressant** stressful; **stressé** stressed-out

strict strict; **le ~ nécessaire** the bare minimum

strident strident

strip-tease *m* strip(tease)

structure *f* structure

studieux, -euse studious

stupéfait stupefied; **stupéfiant 1** *adj* stupefying **2** *m* drug; **stupéfier** stupefy

stupeur *f* stupor

stupide stupid

style *m* style; **styliste** *m de mode, d'industrie* stylist

stylo *m* pen; **~ plume** fountain pen

suave *voix, goût* sweet

subalterne 1 *adj* junior **2** *m/f* junior, subordinate

subir *(endurer)* suffer; *(se soumettre volontairement à)* undergo

subit sudden

subjectif, -ive subjective

subjuguer *fig* captivate

sublime sublime

submerger submerge; **être submergé de** fig be buried in

subordonné, ~e adj & m/f subordinate; subordonner subordinate (à to)

subrepticement surreptitiously

subsidiaire subsidiary

subsistance f subsistence; subsister survive; d'une personne aussi live

substance f substance; substantiel, ~le substantial

substituer: ~ **X à Y** substitute X for Y

subterfuge m subterfuge

subtil subtle; subtilité f subtlety

subvenir: ~ à provide for

subvention f grant, subsidy; subventionner subsidize

subversif, -ive subversive

suc m: ~s gastriques gastric juices

succéder: ~ à follow; personne succeed; se ~ follow each other

succès m success

successeur m successor; succession f succession; JUR (biens dévolus) inheritance

succomber (mourir) die, succumb; ~ à succumb to

succulent succulent

succursale f COMM branch

sucer suck; sucette f bonbon lollipop; de bébé pacifier, Br

dummy

sucre m sugar; sucré sweet; au sucre sugared; péj sugary; sucrer sweeten; avec sucre sugar; sucreries fpl sweet things

sud 1 m south; au ~ de (to the) south of 2 adj south; hemisphère southern

sud-américain, ~e South American; Sud-Américain, ~e m/f South American

sud-est m south-east

sud-ouest m south-west

Suède: la ~ Sweden; suédois, ~e 1 adj Swedish 2 m langue Swedish; Suédois, ~e m/f Swede

suer 1 v/i sweat 2 v/t sweat; fig (dégager) ooze; sueur f sweat

suffire be enough; **il suffit que tu le lui dises** (subj) all you have to do is tell her; **ça suffit!** that's enough!

suffisamment sufficiently, enough; ~ **intelligent** sufficiently intelligent, intelligent enough; ~ **de ...** enough ..., sufficient ...; suffisance f arrogance; suffisant sufficient, enough; (arrogant) arrogant

suffocant suffocating; fig breath-taking; suffocation f suffocation; suffoquer suffocate

suffrage m vote; ~ **universel** universal suffrage

suggérer suggest (**à** to); suggestion *f* suggestion
suicide *m* suicide; suicider:
se ~ commit suicide
suinter *d'un mur* ooze
suisse Swiss; Suisse 1 *m/f*
Swiss 2 la Suisse Switzerland
suite *f* pursuit; (*série*) series
sg; (*continuation*) continuation; *d'un film, un livre* sequel; MUS, *appartement*
suite; *la ~ de l'histoire* the
rest of the story; *~s* (*conséquences*) consequences;
d'un choc, d'une maladie after-effects; *trois fois de ~*
three times in a row; *et ainsi
de ~* and so on; *par ~ de* as a
result of; *tout de ~* immediately
suivant, ~e 1 *adj* next, following 2 *m/f* next person; *au ~!*
next! 3 *prép* (*selon*) according to 4 *conj*: *~ que* depend-
ing on whether
suivi *effort* sustained; *relations* continuous; *argumen-
tation* coherent
suivre 1 *v/t* follow; *cours* take
2 *v/i* follow; *à l'école* keep
up; *faire ~ lettre* please forward; *à ~* to be continued
sujet, ~te 1 *adj*: *~ à* subject to
2 *m* subject; *au ~ de* on the
subject of
sulfureux, -euse sultry
super 1 *adj* F great F, neat F 2
m essence premium
superbe superb

supercherie *f* hoax
superficie *f* fig surface; (*surface, étendue*) (surface) area;
superficiel, ~le superficial
superflu 1 *adj* superfluous 2
m surplus
supérieur, ~e 1 *adj* higher;
étages, mâchoire upper;
(*meilleur, dans une hiérarchie*) superior (*aussi péj*) 2
m/f superior; supériorité *f*
superiority
supermarché *m* supermar-
ket
superposer stack; *couches*
superimpose; *lits mpl su-
perposés* bunk beds
superstitieux, -euse superstitious; superstition *f* superstition
superviser supervise
supplanter supplant
suppléant, ~e 1 *adj* acting 2
m/f stand-in, replacement;
suppléer: *~ à* make up for
supplément *m* supplement;
un ~ de ... additional *ou* extra ...; supplémentaire additional
supplication *f* plea
supplice *m* torture; *fig* agony; supplicier torture
supplier: *~ qn de faire* beg
s.o. to do
support *m* support; supportable bearable; supporter[1]
v/t TECH, ARCH support, hold
up; *conséquences* take; *frais,
douleur, personne* bear; *chaleur, alcool* tolerate; sup-

porter² *m* SP supporter, fan

supposer suppose; (*impliquer*) presuppose; **supposition** *f* supposition

suppression *f* suppression; **supprimer** *institution, impôt* abolish; *emplois* cut; *mot* delete; *concert* cancel

suprême supreme

sur on; *prendre qch ~ l'étagère* take sth off the shelf; *une fenêtre ~ la rue* a window looking onto the street; *tirer ~ qn* shoot at s.o.; *un film ~ ...* a movie on *ou* about ...; *un ~ dix* one out of ten

sûr sure; (*non dangereux*) safe; (*fiable*) reliable; *bien ~* of course; *à coup ~ il sera ...* he's bound to be ...

surcharge *f* overloading; (*poids excédentaire*) excess weight

surchauffer overheat

surclasser outclass

surcroît *m*: *un ~ de travail* extra work; *de ~, par ~* moreover

surdité *f* deafness

surdoué extremely gifted

surélever raise

sûrement surely

surenchère *f dans vente aux enchères* higher bid

surestimer overestimate

sûreté *f* safety; MIL security; *de jugement* soundness

surexciter overexcite

surexposer overexpose

surface *f* surface; *grande ~* COMM supermarket

surfait overrated

surfer surf; *~ sur Internet* surf the Net

surgelé **1** *adj* deep-frozen **2** *mpl*: *~s* frozen food

surgir suddenly appear; *d'un problème* crop up

sur-le-champ at once, straightaway

surlendemain *m* day after tomorrow

surligner highlight

surmener overwork; *se ~* overwork, overdo it F

surmonter dominate; *fig* overcome, surmount

surnaturel, *~le* supernatural

surnom *m* nickname; **surnommer** nickname

surpasser surpass

surpeuplé *pays* overpopulated; *endroit* overcrowded

surplomber overhang

surplus *m* surplus; *au ~* moreover

surprenant surprising; **surprendre** surprise; *voleur* catch (in the act); *se ~ à faire qch* catch o.s. doing sth; **surpris** surprised; **surprise** *f* surprise

sursaut *m* jump, start; **sursauter** jump

sursis *m fig* reprieve, stay of execution; *peine avec ~* JUR suspended sentence

surtaxe *f* surcharge

surtout especially; (*avant*

tout) above all; **~ que** F especially since

surveillance *f* supervision; *par la police etc* surveillance; **surveillant**, **~e** *m/f* supervisor; *de prison* guard; **surveiller** watch; *élèves, employés* supervise; **se ~** *comportement* watch one's step; *poids* watch one's figure

survenir *d'une personne* arrive unexpectedly; *d'un événement* happen; *d'un problème* come up, arise

survêtement *m* sweats *pl*, *Br* tracksuit

survie *f* survival; REL afterlife; **survivant**, **~e 1** *adj* surviving **2** *m/f* survivor; **survivre**: **~ à** survive

susceptible sensitive, touchy; **~ de faire qch** likely to do sth

susciter arouse

suspect (*équivoque*) suspicious; (*d'une qualité douteuse*) suspect; **~ de qc** suspected of sth; **suspecter** suspect

suspendre suspend; (*accrocher*) hang up; **suspendu** suspended

suspens: **en ~** *personne* in suspense; *affaire* outstanding

suspense *m* suspense

suspension *f* suspension

suspicion *f* suspicion

svelte trim, slender

sweat(-shirt) *m* sweatshirt

syllabe *f* syllable

symbole *m* symbol; **symboliser** symbolize

symétrie *f* symmetry

sympathie *f* sympathy; (*amitié, inclination*) liking; **sympathique** nice, friendly; **sympathiser** get on

symphonie *f* symphony

symptôme *m* symptom

synagogue *f* synagogue

synchroniser synchronize

syndical labor *atr*, *Br* (trade) union *atr*

syndicat *m* (labor) union, *Br* (trade) union; **~ d'initiative** tourist information office

syndiqué unionized

synonyme 1 *adj* synonymous (**de** with) **2** *m* synonym

synthèse *f* synthesis; **synthétiseur** *m* MUS synthesizer

systématique systematic; **système** *m* system; **~ antidémarrage** immobilizer; **~ d'exploitation** INFORM operating system

T

ta → **ton²**

tabac *m* tobacco; **bureau** *m* **de~** tobacco store; *Br* tobacconist's

table *f* table; **se mettre à ~** sit down to eat

tableau *m* **à l'école** board; *(peinture)* painting; *fig* picture; *(liste)* list; *(schéma)* table; **~ de bord** AVIAT instrument panel

tablette *f* shelf; **~ de chocolat** chocolate bar

tablier *m* apron

tabouret *m* stool

tache *f* stain

tâche *f* task

tacher stain

tâcher: ~ de faire try to do

tacheté stained

tacite tacit

taciturne taciturn

tact *m* tact; **avoir du ~** be tactful

tactique 1 *adj* tactical **2** *f* tactics *pl*

taie *f*: **~ (d'oreiller)** pillowslip

taille¹ *f* BOT pruning; **de la pierre** cutting

taille² *f* *(hauteur)* height; *(dimension)* size; ANAT waist

taille-crayon(s) *m* pencil sharpener

tailler BOT prune; *vêtement* cut out; *crayon* sharpen; *pierre* cut; **tailleur** *m* *(coutu-* rier) tailor; *vêtement* (woman's) suit

taire: se ~ keep quiet *(sur* about); *s'arrêter de parler* stop talking; **tais-toi!** be quiet!, shut up!

talc *m* talc

talent *m* talent; **talentueux, -euse** talented

talon *m* heel; *d'un chèque* stub; **talonner** *(serrer de près)* follow close behind; *(harceler)* harass

talus *m* bank

tambour *m* MUS, TECH drum; **tambouriner** drum

Tamise: la ~ the Thames

tamiser sieve; *lumière* filter

tampon *m d'ouate* pad; *hygiène féminine* tampon; *(amortisseur)* buffer; *(cachet)* stamp; **tamponnement** *m* AUTO collision; **tamponner** *plaie* clean; *(cacheter)* stamp; AUTO collide with

tandis que while

tangente *f* MATH tangent

tangible tangible

tango *m* tango

tanière *f* lair, den *(aussi fig)*

tanné tanned; *peau* weatherbeaten; **tanner** tan; *fig* F pester

tant 1 *adv* so much; **~ de vin** so much wine; **~ d'erreurs** so many errors; **~ mieux** so much the better; **~ pis** too bad, tough **2** *conj*: **~ que temps** as long as; **en ~ que Français** as a Frenchman; **~ ... que ...** both ... and ...

tante *f* aunt

tantôt this afternoon; **à ~** see you soon; **~ ... ~ ...** now ... now ...

taon *m* horsefly

tapage *m* racket; *fig* fuss; **tapageur, -euse** (*voyant*) flashy, loud; (*bruyant*) noisy

tape *f* pat

taper 1 *v/t personne* hit; *table* bang on; **~ (à l'ordinateur)** F key, type **2** *v/i* hit; *à l'ordinateur* key; **~ sur les nerfs de qn** F get on s.o.'s nerves

tapir: **se ~** crouch

tapis *m* carpet; SP mat; **~ roulant** TECH conveyor belt; *pour personnes* traveling *ou* Br travelling walkway; **~ de souris** mouse mat

tapisser *avec du papier peint* (wall)paper; **tapisserie** *f* tapestry; (*papier peint*) wallpaper

tapoter tap; *personne* pat

taquiner tease; **taquinerie** *f* teasing

tard 1 *adv* late; **plus ~** later (on); **au plus ~** at the latest **2** *m*: **sur le ~** late in life

tarder delay; **~ à faire** take a long time doing; **il me tarde de te revoir** I'm longing to see you again

tardif, -ive late

targuer: **se ~ de qc** *litt* pride o.s. on sth

tarif *m* rate; **~ unique** flat rate

tarir dry up (*aussi fig*); **se ~** dry up

tartan *m* tartan

tarte *f* tart; **tartelette** *f* tartlet

tartine *f* slice of bread; **~ de confiture** slice of bread and jam

tas *m* heap, pile; **un ~ de choses** heaps *pl ou* piles *pl* of things

tasse *f* cup; **une ~ de café** a cup of coffee; **une ~ à café** a coffee cup

tasser (*bourrer*) cram; **se ~** settle

tâter 1 *v/t* feel **2** *v/i* F: **~ de qc** try sth

tatillon, ~ne fussy

tâtons: **avancer à ~** feel one's way forward

tatouage *m action* tattooing; *signe* tattoo

taudis *m* slum

taupe *f* zo mole

taureau *m* bull; ASTROL **Taureau** Taurus

taux *m* rate; **~ d'alcoolémie** blood alcohol level; **~ de change** exchange rate; **~ d'intérêt** interest rate

taxe *f* duty; (*impôt*) tax; **~ sur ou à la valeur ajoutée** sales tax, Br value added tax, VAT; **taxer** tax; **~ qn de qc** *fig* (*accuser*) tax s.o. with sth

taxi *m* taxi, cab

tchèque 1 *adj* Czech **2** *m lan-*

gue Czech; **Tchèque** *m/f*
Czech

te you; *complément d'objet indirect* (to) you; *tu t'es coupé*
you've cut yourself; *si tu ~
lèves à ...* if you get up at ...

technicien, **-ne** *m/f* technicien

technique 1 *adj* technical **2** *f*
technique

technologie *f* technology; **~
*informatique*** computer
technology; **~ de pointe**
high-tech; **technologique**
technological

tee-shirt *m* T-shirt

teindre dye

teint, **~e 1** *adj* dyed **2** *m* complexion; **fond m de ~** foundation (cream) **3** *f* tint; *fig*
tinge; **teinter** tint; *bois* stain;
teinture *f action* dyeing;
produit dye; **~ pharm** tincture

tel, **~le** such; *une ~le surprise*
such a surprise; *de ce genre* a
surprise like that; **~(s) ou
~le(s) que** such as, like

télé *f* F TV, tube F, *Br* telly F

télécharger *inform* download

télécommande *f* remote control

télécommunications *f pl* telecommunications

téléconférence *f* teleconference

téléguidage *m* remote control

téléobjectif *m* telephoto lens

télépathie *f* telepathy

téléphone *m* phone, telephone; **~ *portable*** cellphone, *Br* mobile (phone);
coup m de ~ (phone) call;
~ avec appareil photo intégré camera phone; **téléphoner 1** *v/i* phone, telephone; **~
à qn** call s.o., *Br aussi* phone
s.o. **2** *v/t* phone, telephone;
téléphonique phone *atr*, telephone *atr*; **appel m ~**
phone

téléréalité *f* reality TV

télescope *m* telescope; **télescoper** crash into; **se ~**
crash

télésiège *m* chair lift

téléski *m* ski lift

téléspectateur, **-trice** *m/f*
(TV) viewer

télévision *f* television; **~ *câblée*** cable (TV)

tellement so; *avec verbe* so
much; *pas ~* not really; **~
de chance** so much good
luck; **~ de filles** so many girls

téméraire reckless; **témérité** *f*
recklessness

témoignage *m jur* testimony,
evidence; *(rapport)* account;
fig: d'estime token; **témoigner** *jur* testify, give evidence; **~ de** *(être le témoignage de)* show; **témoin** *m*
witness; **être (le) ~ de qch**
witness sth

tempe *f anat* temple

tempérament *m* temperament; **à ~** in installments
ou Br instalments

tenu

température f temperature;
  avoir de la ~ have a fever,
  Br aussi have a temperature
tempérer moderate
tempête f storm
temple m temple; *protestant*
  church
temporaire temporary
temporel, ~le temporal
temporiser stall, play for
  time
temps m time; *atmosphérique* weather; TECH stroke;
  à ~ in time; *de* ~ *en* ~ from
  time to time; *il est* ~ *de partir* it's time to go; *il est* ~ *que
  tu t'en ailles* (subj) it's time
  you left; *en même* ~ at the
  same time; *par beau* ~ in
  good weather; *quel* ~ *fait-il?* what's the weather like?
tenace tenacious
tenailles fpl pincers
tendance f trend; (disposition) tendency; *avoir* ~ *à faire* have a tendency to do,
  tend to do
tendon m ANAT tendon
tendre[1] 1 v/t filet, ailes
  spread; *piège* set; *bras, main
  hold out; *muscles* tense; *corde* tighten; ~ *qch à qn* hold
  sth out to s.o.; *se* ~ *de rapports* become strained 2
  v/i: ~ *à qc* strive for sth; ~
  à faire qch tend to do sth
tendre[2] adj tender; *couleur*
  soft
tendresse f tenderness
tendu *corde* tight; *fig* tense;

relations strained
ténèbres fpl darkness; **ténébreux**, *-euse* dark
teneur f *d'une lettre* contents
  pl; (concentration) content
tenir 1 v/t hold; (maintenir)
  keep; *registre, promesse*
  keep; *caisse* be in charge
  of; *restaurant* run; *place* take
  up; ~ *à qc/qn* (donner de
  l'importance à) value sth/
  s.o.; *à un objet be attached
  to sth; ~ *à faire qc* really
  want to do sth; *cela ne tient
  qu'à toi* (dépend de) it's entirely up to you 2 v/i hold; ~
  dans fit into 3: *se* ~ *d'un
  spectacle* be held; (être, se
  trouver) stand; *se* ~ *à qch*
  hold on to sth; *s'en* ~ *à* confine o.s. to
tennis m tennis; *terrain* tennis
  court; ~ *pl* sneakers, *Br*
  trainers; SP tennis shoes
ténor m MUS tenor
tension f tension; MÉD blood
  pressure; *faire de la* ~ F have
  high blood pressure
tentacule m tentacle
tentant tempting; **tentation** f
  temptation
tentative f attempt
tente f tent
tenter tempt; (essayer) attempt, try (*de faire* to do)
tenture f wallhanging
tenu: *être* ~ *de faire qc* be
  obliged to do sth; *bien* ~ well
  looked after; *mal* ~ badly
  kept; *enfant* neglected

ténu fine; *espoir* slim

tenue *f de comptes* keeping; *de ménage* running; *(conduite)* behavior, *Br* behaviour; *du corps* posture; *(vêtements)* clothes *pl*; **~ de soirée** evening wear

tergiverser hum and haw

terme *m (fin)* end; *(échéance)* time limit; *(expression)* term; **à court/long ~** in the short/long term; *emprunt, projet* short-/long-term

terminaison *f* GRAM ending; **terminer** finish; **se ~** end; **se ~ par** end with; *d'un mot* end in

terminus *m* terminus

ternir tarnish

terrain *m* ground; GÉOL, MIL terrain; SP field; **un ~** a piece of land; **sur le ~** *essai* field *atr*; *essayer* in the field; **~ d'aviation** airfield; **~ à bâtir** building lot; **~ de jeu** play park; **véhicule m tout ~** 4x4, off-road vehicle

terrasse *f* terrace; **terrasser** *adversaire* fell

terre *f (sol, surface)* ground; *matière* earth, soil; *opposé à mer, propriété* land; *(monde)* earth, world; *pays, région* land, country; ÉL ground, *Br* earth; **à ~** *personne* down to earth; **à ou par~** on the ground; **tomber par ~** fall down; **sur ~** on earth; **sur la ~** on the ground

terre-plein *m*: **~ central** me-

dian strip, *Br* central reservation

terrestre *animaux* land *atr*; REL earthly; TV terrestrial

terreur *f* terror

terrible terrible; F *(extraordinaire)* terrific; **c'est pas ~** it's not that good

terrien *ne* **1** *adj*: **propriétaire m ~** landowner **2** *m/f (habitant de la Terre)* earthling

terrier *m de renard* earth; ZO terrier

territoire *m* territory

terroir *m viticulture* soil; **du ~** *(régional)* local

terroriser terrorize; **terrorisme m** terrorism; **terroriste** *m/f & adj* terrorist

tertre *m* mound

tes → ton²

test *m* test; **~ de résistance** endurance test

testament *m* JUR will; **Ancien/Nouveau Testament** REL Old/New Testament

tester test

testicule *m* testicle

tête *f* head; *(cheveux)* hair; *(visage)* face; SP header; **de ~ calculer** in one's head; **répondre** without looking anything up; **avoir la ~ dure** be stubborn; **se casser la ~** *fig* rack one's brains; **n'en faire qu'à sa ~** do exactly as one likes; **tenir ~ à qn** stand up to s.o.; *péj* defy s.o.; **faire la ~** sulk; **il se paie ta ~** *fig* he's making a fool of you; **en** ~ in the lead

tête-à-queue *m* AUTO spin; tête-à-tête *m* tête-à-tête; **en** ~ in private

têtu obstinate

texte *m* text; ~**s choisis** selected passages

textile *m* textile; **le** ~ **industrie** the textile industry, textiles *pl*

texto *m* text (message); **envoyer un** ~ **à qn** send s.o. a text, text s.o.

texture *f* texture

T.G.V. *m* (= **train à grande vitesse**) high-speed train

thé *m* tea

théâtre *m* theater, *Br* theatre; *fig*: **cadre** scene

théière *f* teapot

thème *m* theme; ÉDU translation (into a foreign language)

théorie *f* theory; théorique theoretical

thérapeute *m/f* therapist; thérapeutique **1** *f* (*thérapie*) therapy **2** *adj* therapeutic; thérapie *f* therapy

thermal thermal

thermomètre *m* thermometer

thermos *f ou m* thermos®

thèse *f* thesis

thon *m* tuna

thym *m* BOT thyme

tic *m* tic, twitch; *fig* habit

ticket *m* ticket; ~ **de caisse** receipt

tiède warm; *péj* tepid, lukewarm (*aussi fig*); **tiédir** cool down; *devenir plus chaud* warm up

tien, ~ne: **le tien, la tienne, les tiens, les tiennes** yours

tiers, tierce **1** *adj* third; **le** ~ **monde** the Third World **2** *m* MATH third; JUR third party

tige *f* BOT stalk; TECH stem

tigre *m* tiger; **tigresse** *f* tigress

tilleul *m* BOT lime (tree); *boisson* lime-blossom tea

timbre *m* stamp; (*sonnette*) bell; (*son*) timbre; (*tampon*) stamp; **timbre-poste** *m* postage stamp

timide timid; *en sociéte* shy

timoré timorous

tintement *m* tinkle; *de clochettes* ringing; **tinter** *de verres* clink; *de clochettes* ring

tir *m* fire; *action*, SP shooting; ~ **à l'arc** archery

tirage *m* à *la loterie* draw; PHOT print; TYP printing; (*exemplaires de journal*) circulation; *d'un livre* print run; COMM *d'un chèque* drawing; F (*difficultés*) trouble; **par un** ~ **au sort** by drawing lots

tirailler pull; **tiraillé entre** *fig* torn between

tire *f* P AUTO car, jeep P; **vol** *m* **à la** ~ pickpocketing

tiré *traits* drawn

tire-bouchon *m* corkscrew

tirelire *f* piggy bank

tirer

tirer 1 v/t pull; *chèque, ligne, conclusions* draw; *coup de fusil* fire; *oiseau, cible* fire at; PHOT, TYP print; *plaisir, satisfaction* derive **2** v/i pull (**sur** on); *avec arme* shoot (**sur** at); **à sa fin** draw to a close **3**: **se ~ de** *situation difficile* get out of; **se ~** F take off

tiret m dash; (*trait d'union*) hyphen

tiroir m drawer

tisane f herbal tea

tisser weave; *d'une araignée* spin; *fig* hatch

tissu m fabric, material; BIOL tissue

titre m title; *d'un journal* headline; FIN security; **à ce ~** therefore; **à juste ~** rightly; **à ~ d'essai** on a trial basis; **au même ~** on the same basis

tituber stagger

titulaire m/f *d'un document, d'une charge* holder

toast m (*pain grillé*) piece of toast; *de bienvenue* toast

toboggan m slide; *rue* flyover

tocsin m alarm bell

toi you

toile f *de lin* linen; (*peinture*) canvas; **~ d'araignée** spiderweb, Br spider's web; **~ cirée** oilcloth; **~ de fond** backcloth; *fig* backdrop

toilette f (*lavage*) washing; (*mise*) outfit; (*vêtements*) clothes pl; **~s** toilet; **aller aux ~s** go to the toilet; **faire sa ~** get washed

toi-même yourself

toiser *fig*: **~ qn** look s.o. up and down

toison f *de laine* fleece; (*cheveux*) mane of hair

toit m roof; **~ ouvrant** AUTO sun roof; **toiture** f roof

tôle f sheet metal; **~ ondulée** corrugated iron

tolérance f *aussi* TECH tolerance; **tolérant** tolerant; **tolérer** tolerate

tomate f tomato

tombe f grave

tombeau m tomb

tombée f: **à la ~ de la nuit** at nightfall

tomber fall; *de cheveux* fall out; *d'une colère* die down; *d'une fièvre, d'un prix, d'une demande* drop, fall; **~ malade** fall sick; **laisser ~** drop (*aussi fig*); **~ sur** MIL attack; (*rencontrer*) bump into; **~ d'accord** reach agreement

tome m volume

ton¹ m tone; MUS key; **il est de bon ~** it's the done thing

ton² m, **ta** f, **tes** pl your

tondeuse f lawnmower; *de coiffeur* clippers pl; AGR shears pl; **tondre** *mouton* shear; *haie* clip; *herbe* mow, cut; *cheveux* shave off

tonifier tone up

tonique 1 m tonic **2** adj *climat* bracing

247

tourbillon

tonitruant thunderous
tonne f (metric) ton
tonneau m barrel; MAR ton
tonner thunder; fig rage
tonnerre m thunder
tonton m F uncle
tonus m d'un muscle tone; (dynamisme) dynamism
toqué F mad (**de** about)
torche f flashlight, Br torch
torchon m dishtowel
tordre twist; linge wring; **se ~** twist; **se ~ le pied** twist one's ankle
tornade f tornado
torpille f torpedo; **torpiller** torpedo (aussi fig)
torrent m torrent; fig: de larmes flood; d'injures torrent
torse m torso
tort m fault; (préjudice) harm; **à ~** wrongly; **à ~ et à travers** wildly; **avoir ~** be wrong (**de faire** to do); **donner ~ à qn** prove s.o. wrong; (désapprouver) blame s.o.; **faire du ~ à** hurt, harm
torticolis m MÉD stiff neck
tortiller twist; **se ~** wriggle
tortue f tortoise; **~ de mer** turtle
tortueux, -euse winding; fig tortuous; esprit, manœuvres devious
torture f torture; **torturer** torture
tôt early; (bientôt) soon; **le plus ~ possible** as soon as possible; **au plus ~** at the soonest ou earliest; **~ ou**

tard sooner or later
total 1 adj total 2 m total; **au ~** in all; fig on the whole; totalement totally; totaliser total; **totalité** f: **la ~ de** all of; **en ~** in full; **totalitaire** POL totalitarian
touchant touching
touche f touch; de clavier key; SP touchline; (remise en jeu) throw-in; pêche bite; **être mis sur la ~** fig F be sidelined
toucher¹ v/t touch; but hit; (émouvoir) touch, move; (concerner) concern; (contacter) contact, get in touch with; argent get; réserves break into; d'une maison adjoin; **~ au but** near one's goal; **se ~** touch; de maisons, terrains adjoin
toucher² m touch
touffu dense, thick
toujours always; (encore) still; **pour ~** for ever
toupet m F nerve
tour¹ f tower; (immeuble) high-rise
tour² m turn; (circonférence) circumference; (circuit) lap; (promenade) stroll, walk; (excursion, voyage) tour; (ruse) trick; TECH lathe; de potier wheel; **à mon ~, c'est mon ~** it's my turn; **en un ~ de main** in no time at all
tourbe f matière peat
tourbillon m de vent whirl-

tourelle

tourelle *f* turret

tourisme *m* tourism; **~ écologique** ecotourism; **touriste**
m/f tourist

tourment *m litt* torture, torment

tourmente *f litt* storm

tourmenter torment; **se ~**
worry, torment o.s.

tournant **1** *adj* revolving **2** *m*
turn; *fig* turning point

tournée *f* round; *d'un artiste*
tour

tourner **1** *v/t* turn; *sauce* stir;
salade toss; *difficulté* get
around; *film* shoot; **bien
tourné(e)** well-put **2** *v/i* turn;
du lait turn; **j'ai la tête qui
tourne** my head is spinning;
faire ~ *clé* turn; *entreprise*
run **3**: **se ~** turn; **se ~ vers**
fig turn to

tournesol *m* BOT sunflower

tournevis *m* screwdriver

tournoyer *d'oiseaux* wheel;
de feuilles swirl

tournure *f* (*expression*) turn
of phrase; *des événements*
turn

tourterelle *f* turtledove

tous → **tout**

Toussaint: **la ~** All Saints'
Day

tousser cough

toussoter have a slight cough

tout *m*, toute *f*, tous *mpl*, toutes *fpl* **1** *adj* all; (*n'importe
lequel*) any; **~ Français** every Frenchman, all French-

men; **tous les deux jours**
every two days; **tous les
ans** every year **2** *pron sg*
tout everything; *pl* **tous,
toutes** all of us/them; **après
~** after all; **facile comme ~** F
as easy as anything; **nous
tous** all of us; **3** *adv* **tout**
very, quite; **c'est ~ comme
un ...** it's just like a ...; **~
nu** completely naked; **c'est
~ près d'ici** it's just nearby;
je suis ~e seule I'm all
alone; **~ à fait** altogether;
oui, ~ à fait yes, absolutely;
~ de suite straight away; **~
pauvres qu'ils sont** (*ou
soient* (*subj*) however poor
they are **4** *m* **tout** the whole
lot, everything; **pas du ~** not
at all

toutefois however

toux *f* cough m

toxique **1** *adj* toxic **2** *m* poison

trac *m* nervousness; *pour un
acteur* stage fright

traçabilité *f* traceability

tracas *m*: **des ~** worries; **tra-
casser**: **~ qn** *d'une chose*
worry s.o.; *d'une personne*
pester s.o.; **se ~** worry

trace *f* (*piste*) track, trail;
(*marque*) mark; *fig* impression; **~s de sang, poison**
traces; **des ~s de pas** foot-
prints; **tracer** *plan* draw

trachée *f* windpipe, trachea

tractation *f péj*: **~s** horsetrad-
ing

tracteur *m* tractor

tradition *f* tradition; **traditionaliste** *m/f* & *adj* traditionalist; **traditionnel**, **~le** traditional

traducteur, **-trice** *m/f* translator; **traduction** *f* translation; **traduire** translate (**en** into); *fig* be indicative of; **se ~ par** result in

trafic *m* traffic; **trafiquant** *m* trafficker; **~ de drogue(s)** drug trafficker; **trafiquer** traffic in; *moteur* tinker with

tragédie *f* tragedy; **tragique 1** *adj* tragic **2** *m* tragedy

trahir betray; **trahison** *f* betrayal; *crime* treason

train *m* train; *fig: de lois, décrets etc* series *sg*; **être en ~ de faire qc** be doing sth; **mettre en ~** set in motion; **au ~ où vont les choses** at the rate things are going; **~ d'atterrissage** undercarriage, landing gear; **~ de vie** lifestyle

traîner 1 *v/t* drag; *d'une voiture* pull, tow **2** *v/i de vêtements, livres* lie around; *d'une discussion* drag on; **~ dans les rues** hang around street corners **3**: **se ~** drag o.s. along

train-train *m* F: **le ~ quotidien** the daily routine

traire milk

trait *m* (*ligne*) line; *du visage* feature; *de caractère* trait; *d'une œuvre, époque* feature, characteristic; **avoir ~**

à be about; **~ d'esprit** witticism; **~ d'union** hyphen

traite *f* COMM draft, bill of exchange; *d'une vache* milking; **d'une seule ~** in one go

traité *m* treaty

traitement *m* treatment; (*salaire*) pay; TECH, INFORM processing; **traiter 1** *v/t* treat; TECH, INFORM process; **~ qn de menteur** call s.o. a liar **2** *v/i* (*négocier*) negotiate; **~ de qc** deal with sth

traître, **~sse 1** *m/f* traitor **2** *adj* treacherous

trajet *m* (*voyage*) journey; (*chemin*) way

trame *f fig: d'une histoire* background; *de la vie* fabric

tramway *m* streetcar, *Br* tram

tranchant *adj* cutting **2** *m d'un couteau* cutting edge

tranche *f* (*morceau*) slice; (*bord*) edge; **~ d'âge** age bracket

tranché *fig* clear-cut; *couleur* definite

tranchée *f* trench

trancher 1 *v/t* cut; *fig* settle **2** *v/i*: **~ sur** stand out against

tranquille quiet; (*sans inquiétude*) easy in one's mind; **laisse-moi ~!** leave me alone!; **tranquillisant** *m* tranquilizer, *Br* tranquillizer; **tranquilliser**: **~ qn** set s.o.'s mind at rest; **tranquillité** *f* quietness, tranquillity; *du sommeil* peacefulness; (*stabilité morale*) peace of

mind
transaction f JUR compromise; COMM transaction
transatlantique 1 adj transatlantic **2** m bateau transatlantic liner; chaise deck chair
transcription f transcription; transcrire transcribe
transférer transfer; **transfert** m transfer; PSYCH transference
transformation f transformation; TECH processing; en rugby conversion; **transformer** transform; TECH process; appartement, en rugby convert
transfuge m defector
transfusion f: ~ (**sanguine**) (blood) transfusion
transgénique genetically modified
transgresser loi break, transgress
transi: ~ (**de froid**) frozen
transiger come to a compromise
transistor m transistor
transit m: **en** ~ in transit
transition f transition
transmettre transmit; message, talen, maladie pass on; tradition, titre hand down; **transmissible**: **sexuellement** ~ sexually transmitted; **transmission** f transmission; d'un message passing on; d'une tradition, d'un titre handing down; RAD, TV

broadcast
transparence f transparency; transparent transparent
transpercer pierce; de l'eau, de la pluie go right through
transpiration f perspiration; transpirer perspire
transplant m transplant; **transplantation** f transplanting; MÉD transplant; transplanter transplant
transport m transport; ~**s publics** mass transit; Br public transport; **transporter** transport, carry
transposer transpose
transversal cross atr
trapèze m trapeze
trappe f (ouverture) trapdoor
trapu stocky
traquer hunt
traumatiser PSYCH traumatize; **traumatisme** m MÉD, PSYCH trauma
travail m work; **être sans** ~ be out of work; **travaux** (construction) construction work; **travailler 1** v/i work **2** v/t work on; d'une pensée trouble; **travailleur, -euse 1** adj hard-working **2** m/f worker
travers 1 adv: **de** ~ crooked; marcher not straight; **en** ~ across **2** prép: **à** ~ qc, **au** ~ **de qc** through sth **3** m shortcoming
traversée f crossing; **traverser** rue, mer cross; forêt, crise go through; (percer) go right through

travesti **1** *adj pour fête* fancy-dress **2** *m (déguisement)* fancy dress; *(homosexuel)* transvestite; *travestir vérité* distort; *se ~* dress up (*en* as a)

trébucher trip (*sur* over)

trèfle *m* BOT clover; *aux cartes* clubs *pl*

treize thirteen; treizième thirteenth

tremblant trembling, quivering; tremblement *m* trembling; *~ de terre* earthquake; trembler tremble, shake (*de* with); *de la terre* shake

trémousser: *se ~* wriggle

trempe *f fig* caliber, *Br* calibre

trempé soaked; *sol* saturated; tremper soak; *pain dans café etc* dunk; *pied dans l'eau* dip; *acier* harden; *~ dans fig* be involved in

tremplin *m* springboard; *pour ski* ski jump; *fig* stepping stone

trentaine *f: une ~ de personnes* about thirty people *pl*; trente thirty; trentième thirtieth

trépied *m* tripod

trépigner stamp (one's feet)

très very; *~ lu/visité* much read/visited

trésor *m* treasure; *Trésor* Treasury; trésorier, -ère *m/f* treasurer

tressaillir jump

tresse *f de cheveux* braid, *Br* plait

trève *f* truce; *~ de ...* that's enough ...; *sans ~* without respite

tri *m* sort; *faire un ~ dans qc* sort sth out

triangle *m* triangle

tribord *m* MAR starboard

tribu *f* tribe

tribulations *fpl* tribulations

tribunal *m* court

tribune *f* platform; *(débat)* discussion; *~s dans stade* bleachers, *Br* stands

tributaire: *être ~ de* be dependent on

tricher cheat; tricheur, -euse *m/f* cheat

tricolore: *drapeau m ~* tricolor *ou Br* tricolour

tricot *m* knitting; *vêtement* sweater; tricoter knit

trier *(choisir)* pick through; *(classer)* sort

trimballer F hump F, lug

trimer F work like a dog F

trimestre *m* quarter; ÉDU trimester, *Br* term

trinquer *(porter un toast)* clink glasses; *~ à fig* F toast, drink to

triomphe *m* triumph; triompher triumph (*de* over)

tripes *fpl* guts; CUIS tripe

triple *m* triple; triplés, -ées *mpl, fpl* triplets

tripoter *(objet)* play around with; *femme* feel up

triste sad; *temps, paysage* dreary; tristesse *f* sadness

trivial vulgar; *litt (banal)* trite

troc *m* barter

trognon *m d'un fruit* core; *d'un chou* stump

trois 1 *adj* three; **le ~ mai** May third, *Br* the third of May **2** *m* three; **troisième** third

trombe *f*: **des ~s d'eau** sheets of water; **en ~** *fig* at top speed

trombone *m* MUS trombone; *pour papiers* paper clip

trompe *f* MUS horn; *d'un éléphant* trunk

tromper deceive; *époux* be unfaithful to; *confiance* abuse; **se ~** be mistaken; **se ~ de numéro** get the wrong number; **tromperie** *f* deception

trompette 1 *f* trumpet **2** *m* trumpet player

trompeur, -euse deceptive; *(traître)* deceitful

tronc *m* BOT, ANAT trunk; *à l'église* collection box

tronçon *m* section

trône *m* throne

trop too; *avec verbe* too much; **~ de lait/gens** too much milk/too many people

tropical tropical; **tropique** *m* tropic

trot *m* trot; **aller au ~** trot; **trotter** *d'un cheval* trot; *d'une personne* run around

trottiner scamper

trottinette *f* scooter

trottoir *m* sidewalk, *Br* pavement

trou *m* hole; **~ de mémoire** lapse of memory

trouble 1 *adj eau, liquide* cloudy; *explication* unclear; *situation* murky **2** *m (désarroi)* trouble; *(émoi)* excitement; MÉD disorder; **~s** POL unrest; **trouble-fête** *m* party-pooper F

troubler *liquide* make cloudy; *silence, sommeil* disturb; *réunion* disrupt; *(inquiéter)* bother; **se ~** get flustered *d'un liquide* go cloudy

trouée *f* gap; **trouer** make a hole in

troupe *f* troop; *de comédiens* troupe

troupeau *m de vaches* herd; *de moutons* flock

trousse *f* kit; **être aux ~s de qn** *fig* be on s.o.'s heels; **~ de toilette** toilet bag

trousseau *m d'une mariée* trousseau; **~ de clés** bunch of keys

trouver find; *plan* come up with; *(rencontrer)* meet; **~ que** think that; **se ~** *(être)* be; **il se trouve que** it turns out that

truc *m* F *(chose)* thing, thingamajig F; *(astuce)* trick

truffe *f* BOT truffle; *d'un chien* nose; **truffé** with truffles; **~** *de fig: citations* peppered with

truie *f* sow

truite *f* trout

truquage *m dans film* special

effect; *d'une photo* faking; **truquer** *élections, cartes* rig

tu you

tuba *m* snorkel; MUS tuba

tube *m* tube; F (*chanson*) hit

tuberculose *f* MÉD tuberculosis, TB

tuer kill; *fig* (*épuiser*) exhaust; (*peiner*) bother; **se ~** (*se suicider*) kill o.s.; (*trouver la mort*) be killed; **tue-tête: à ~** at the top of one's voice; **tueur** *m* killer

tulipe *f* tulip

tumeur *f* MÉD tumor, *Br* tumour

tumulte *m* uproar; *fig* (*activité*) hustle and bustle; **tumultueux, -euse** noisy; *passion* tumultuous, stormy

tunique *f* tunic

Tunisie: la ~ Tunisia; **tunisien, ~ne** Tunisian; **Tunisien, ~ne** *m/f* Tunisian

tunnel *m* tunnel

turbo-réacteur *m* AVIAT turbojet

turbulence *f* turbulence; *d'un élève* unruliness; **turbulent** turbulent; *élève* unruly

turc, turque 1 *adj* Turkish **2** *m langue* Turkish; **Turc, Turque** *m/f* Turk

turf *m* SP horseracing; *terrain* racecourse

Turquie: la ~ Turkey

tutelle *f* JUR guardianship; *d'un état, d'une société* supervision, control; *fig* protection

tuteur, -trice 1 *m/f* JUR guardian **2** *m* BOT stake

tutoyer address as 'tu'

tuyau *m* pipe; *flexible* hose; F (*information*) tip; **~ d'arrosage** garden hose; **tuyauter** F: **~ qn** tip s.o. off

T.V.A. *f* (= *taxe sur ou à la valeur ajoutée*) sales tax, *Br* VAT (= value added tax)

type *m* type; F (*gars*) guy F; **contrat** *m* **~** standard contract

typhon *m* typhoon

typique typical (**de** of)

tyran *m* tyrant; **tyrannie** *f* tyranny; **tyranniser** tyrannize; *petit frère etc* bully

U

U.E. *f* (= *Union européenne*) EU (= European Union)

ulcère *m* MÉD ulcer; **ulcérer** *fig* aggrieve

ultérieur later, subsequent

ultimatum *m* ultimatum

ultime last

ultrason *m* PHYS ultrasound

ultraviolet, ~te *adj* & *m* ultraviolet

un, une 1 *article* a; *devant voyelle* an **2** *pron* one; **à la une** on the front page; **l'un des touristes** one of the tourists; *les uns avaient ...* some (of them) had ...; *elles s'aident les unes les autres* they help each other; *l'un et l'autre* both of them 3 *chiffre* one

unanime unanimous; **unanimité** *f* unanimity; *à l'~* unanimously

uni *pays* united; *surface* smooth; *tissu* solid(-colored), *Br* self-coloured; *famille* close-knit

unification *f* unification; **unifier** unite, unify

uniforme 1 *adj* uniform; *existence* unchanging **2** *m* uniform; **uniformité** *f* uniformity

unilatéral unilateral

union *f* union; (*cohésion*) unity; **Union européenne** European Union

unique (*seul*) single; *fils* only; (*extraordinaire*) unique; **uniquement** only

unir POL unite; *par moyen de communication* link; *couple* marry; *s'~* unite; (*se marier*) marry

unité *f* unit

univers *m* universe; *fig* world; **universel**, *~le* universal

universitaire 1 *adj* university *atr* **2** *m/f* academic; **université** *f* university

uranium *m* CHIM uranium

urbain urban; **urbaniser** ur-banize; **urbanisme** *m* town planning

urgence *f* urgency; *une ~* an emergency; *d'~* emergency *atr*; **urgent** urgent

urine *f* urine; **uriner** urinate

urne *f*: *aller aux ~s* go to the polls

usage *m* use; (*coutume*) custom; *linguistique* usage; *hors d'~* out of use; *à l'~ de qn* for use by s.o.; *d'~* customary; **usager** *m* user

usé worn; *vêtement, personne* worn-out; **user** *du gaz, de l'eau* use, consume; *vêtement* wear out; *yeux* ruin; *s'~* wear out; *personne* wear o.s. out; *~ de qc* use sth

usine *f* plant, factory; **usiner** machine

usité *mot* common

ustensile *m* tool; *~ de cuisine* kitchen utensil

usuel, *~le* usual; *expression* common

usure *f* (*détérioration*) wear; *du sol* erosion

utérus *m* ANAT womb, uterus

utile useful; *en temps ~* in due course

utilisateur, *-trice* *m/f* user; *~ final* end user; **utilisation** *f* use; **utiliser** use

utilitaire utilitarian

utilité *f* usefulness, utility; *ça n'a aucune ~* it's no use whatever

V

vacance f poste opening, Br vacancy; **~s** vacation, Br holiday(s); **vacancier, -ère** m/f vacationer, Br holiday-maker

vacarme m din, racket

vaccin m vaccine; **vaccination** f vaccination; **vacciner** vaccinate

vache 1 f cow **2** adj F mean

vachement F bon, content damn F, Br bloody F; changer, vieillir one helluva lot F

vaciller sur ses jambes sway; d'une flamme flicker; (hésiter) vacillate

vagabond, ~e 1 adj wandering **2** m/f hobo, Br tramp

vagin m vagina

vague¹ f wave (aussi fig); **~ de froid** cold snap

vague² **1** adj vague; regard faraway; **terrain** m **~** waste ground **2** m vagueness; **regarder dans le ~** stare into the middle distance

vaillant brave, valiant

vain vain; mots empty; **en ~** in vain

vaincre conquer; SP defeat; fig: angoisse overcome, conquer; obstacle overcome; **vaincu 1** adj conquered; SP defeated **2** m loser; **vainqueur** m winner, victor

vaisseau m ANAT, litt (bateau) vessel; **~ spatial** spaceship

vaisselle f dishes pl; **laver** ou **faire la ~** do ou wash the dishes

valable valid

valeur f value, worth; d'une personne worth; **~s** COMM securities; **sans ~** worthless; **mettre en ~** emphasize, highlight

valide (sain) fit; passeport, ticket valid; **valider** validate; ticket stamp; **validité** f validity

valise f bag, suitcase

vallée f valley

valoir be worth; (coûter) cost; **~ mieux** be better (**que** than); **faire ~** droits assert; capital make work; (mettre en valeur) emphasize

valoriser enhance the value of; personne enhance the image of

valse f waltz

vandale m/f vandal; **vandaliser** vandalize

vanille f vanilla

vanité f (fatuité) vanity; (inutilité) futility; **vaniteux, -euse** vain

vanne f sluice gate; F dig F

vantard, ~e 1 adj boastful **2** m/f boaster; **vanter** praise; **se ~ de qch** pride o.s. on sth

vapeur f vapor, Br vapour; **~**

(*d'eau*) steam; *cuire à la* ~ steam

vaporeux, **-euse** *paysage* misty; *tissu* filmy

vaporisateur *m* spray; **vaporiser** spray

varappe *f* rock-climbing

variable variable; *temps, humeur* changeable; *variante f* variant; *variation f* (*changement*) change; (*écart*) variation

varice *f* ANAT varicose vein

varicelle *f* MÉD chickenpox

varié varied; **varier** vary; **variété** *f* variety; **~s** *spectacle* vaudeville, *Br* variety show

variole *f* MÉD smallpox

vase[1] *m* vase

vase[2] *m* mud; **vaseux**, **-euse** muddy; F (*nauséeux*) off-color, *Br* off-colour; F *explication* muddled

vasistas *m* fanlight

vaurien, **~ne** *m/f* good-for-nothing

vautour *m* vulture

veau *m* calf; *viande* veal

vedette *f* star; (*bateau*) launch; **mettre en** ~ highlight

végétal 1 *adj* plant *atr*; *huile vegetable* **2** *m* plant; **végétalien**, **~ne** *m/f* & *adj* vegan

végétarien, **~ne** *m/f* & *adj* vegetarian

végétation *f* vegetation; **végéter** vegetate

véhémence *f* vehemence; **véhément** vehement

véhicule *m* vehicle (*aussi fig*)

veille *f* previous day; *absence de sommeil* wakefulness; **à la** ~ **de** on the eve of; **veiller** stay up late; **~ à faire qch** see to it that sth is done; **~ sur qn** watch over s.o.

veinard, **~e** *m/f* F lucky devil F; **veine** *f* vein; F luck

vélo *m* bike; **faire du** ~ go cycling; **vélomoteur** *m* moped

velours *m* velvet; **~ côtelé** corduroy

velouté velvety; (*soupe*) creamy

velu hairy

venaison *f* venison

vendable saleable

vendange *f* grape harvest

vendeur *m* sales clerk, *Br* shop assistant; **vendeuse** *f* sales clerk, *Br* shop assistant; **vendre** sell; *fig* betray; **à** ~ for sale

vendredi *m* Friday; **Vendredi saint** Good Friday

vendu, **~e 1** *adj* sold **2** *m/f péj* traitor

vénéneux, **-euse** poisonous

vénérable venerable; **vénération** *f* veneration; **vénérer** revere

vénérien, **~ne**: **maladie** *f* **~ne** venereal disease

vengeance *f* vengeance; **venger** avenge (*qn de qc* s.o. for sth); **se** ~ **de qn** get one's revenge on s.o.; **se** ~ **de qc sur qn** get one's revenge for sth on s.o.

venimeux, -euse poisonous;
venin *m* venom (*aussi fig*)
venir come; **à ~** to come; **où veut-il en ~?** what's he getting at?; **~ de** come from; **je viens de faire la vaisselle** I have just washed the dishes; **faire ~** *médecin* send for
vent *m* wind; **coup** *m* **de ~** gust of wind; **il y a du ~** it's windy
vente *f* sale; *activité* selling; **~ à crédit** installment plan, *Br* hire purchase
venteux, -euse windy
ventilateur *m* ventilator; *électrique* fan; **ventilation** *f* ventilation; **ventiler** *pièce* air; *montant* break down
ventre *m* stomach; **~ à bière** beer belly
ventriloque *m* ventriloquist
venu, ~e 1 *adj*: **bien/mal ~** appropriate/inappropriate **2** *m/f*: **le premier ~, la première ~e** the first to arrive; (*n'importe qui*) anybody; **venue** *f* arrival
ver *m* worm; **~ de terre** earthworm; **~ à soie** silkworm
verbal verbal; **verbe** *m* verb
verdâtre greenish
verdict *m* verdict
verdir turn green
verdure *f* (*feuillages*) greenery; (*salade*) greens *pl*
verge *f* ANAT penis; (*baguette*) rod
verger *m* orchard

verglas *m* black ice
vergogne *f*: **sans ~** shameless; *avec verbe* shamelessly
véridique truthful
vérification *f* check; **vérifier** check; **se ~** turn out to be true
véritable real; *amour* true
vérité *f* truth; **en ~** actually; **à la ~** to tell the truth
vermeil, ~le bright red, vermillion
vermine *f* vermin
verni varnished; F lucky; **vernir** varnish; *céramique* glaze; **vernis** *m* varnish; *de céramique* glaze; **~ à ongle** nail polish, *Br aussi* nail varnish
verre *m* glass; **prendre un ~** have a drink; **~s de contact** contact lenses
verrerie *f* glassmaking; *fabrique* glassworks *sg*; *objets* glassware
verrière *f* (*vitrail*) stained-glass window; *toit* glass roof
verrou *m* bolt; **verrouillage** *m*: **~ central** AUTO central locking; **verrouiller** bolt; F lock up
verrue *f* wart
vers¹ *m* verse
vers² *prép* toward, *Br* towards; (*environ*) around
versant *m* slope
versatile changeable
Verseau *m* ASTROL Aquarius
versement *m* payment; **verser 1** *v/t* pour (out); *sang,*

version

larmes shed; *argent à un compte* pay in; *intérêts, pension* pay **2** *v/i* (*basculer*) overturn

version *f* version; (*traduction*) translation

verso *m d'une feuille* back

vert 1 *adj* green; *fruit* unripe; *vin* too young; *fig: personne âgée* spry; *propos risqué* **2** *m* green; **les ~s** POL *mpl* the Greens

vertébral vertebral; **colonne** *f* **~e** spine, spinal column; **vertèbre** *f* vertebra

vertical, ~e 1 *adj* vertical **2** *f* vertical (line)

vertige *m* vertigo, dizziness; *fig* giddiness; **un ~** a dizzy spell; **j'ai le ~** I feel dizzy

vertu *f* virtue; (*pouvoir*) property; **en ~ de** in accordance with; **vertueux, -euse** virtuous

verve *f* wit

vésicule *f* ANAT: **~ biliaire** gall bladder

vessie *f* ANAT bladder

veste *f* jacket

vestiaire *m de théâtre* checkroom, *Br* cloakroom; *d'un stade* locker room

vestibule *m* hall

vestiges *mpl* traces

veston *m* jacket, coat

vêtement *m* item of clothing, garment; **~s** clothes; (**industrie** *f* **du**) **~** clothing industry

vétérinaire 1 *adj* veterinary **2** *m/f* veterinarian, vet

vêtu dressed

vétuste *bâtiment* dilapidated, ramshackle

veuf 1 *adj* widowed **2** *m* widower

veuve 1 *adj* widowed **2** *f* widow

vexant humiliating; **vexation** *f* humiliation; **vexer: ~ qn** hurt s.o.'s feelings; **se ~** get upset

viable *projet*, BIOL viable

viaduc *m* viaduct

viager, -ère: rente *f* **viagère** life annuity

viande *f* meat

vibration *f* vibration; **vibrer** vibrate

vice *m* (*défaut*) defect; (*péché*) vice

vice-président *m* COMM, POL vice-president; *Br* COMM vice-chairman

vicié *air* stale

vicieux, -euse lecherous; *cercle* vicious

victime *f* victim

victoire *f* victory; SP win, victory; **victorieux, -euse** victorious

vidange *f* emptying, draining; AUTO oil change

vide 1 *adj* empty **2** *m* (*néant*) emptiness; *physique* vacuum; (*espace non occupé*) (empty) space; **avoir peur du ~** be afraid of heights

vidéo *adj & f* video **~ amateur** home movie; **vidéocassette** *f* video cassette

vide-ordures *m* rubbish chute

vider empty (out); F *personne* throw out; CUIS *volaille* draw; *salle* vacate, leave; **se ~** empty; **videur** *m* F bouncer

vie *f* life; *moyens matériels* living; **à ~** for life; **être en ~** be alive; *coût de la* **~** cost of living; *gagner sa* **~** earn one's living

vieil → *vieux*

vieillard *m* old man; *les* **~s** old people *pl*, the elderly *pl*

vieille → *vieux*

vieillesse *f* old age

vieillir 1 *v/t*: **~ qn** age s.o. **2** *v/i d'une personne* get old, age; *d'un visage* age; *d'une théorie, d'un livre* become dated; *d'un vin* age, mature

viennoiseries *fpl* croissants and similar types of bread

vierge 1 *f* virgin; **Vierge** ASTROL Virgo **2** *adj* virgin; *feuille* blank

Việt-nam: **le ~** Vietnam; **vietnamien, ~ne 1** *adj* Vietnamese **2** *m langue* Vietnamese; **Vietnamien, ~ne** *m/f* Vietnamese

vieux, (*m vieil before a vowel or silent h*), **vieille** (*f*) **1** *adj* old **2** *m/f* old man/old woman; *les* **~** old people *pl*, the aged *pl*

vif, **vive 1** *adj* lively; (*en vie*) alive; *plaisir, satisfaction* great; *critique, douleur*

sharp; *air* bracing; *froid* biting; *couleur* bright **2** *m* **à ~** *plaie* open; *piqué au* **~** cut to the quick; *le* **~** *du sujet* the heart of the matter; *avoir les nerfs à* **~** be on edge

vigilance *f* vigilance; **vigilant** vigilant

vigile *m* (*gardien*) security man, guard

vigne *f* (*arbrisseau*) vine; (*plantation*) vineyard

vigneron, ~ne *m/f* wine grower

vignoble *m plantation* vineyard; *région* wine-growing area

vigoureux, -euse robust, vigorous; **vigueur** *f* vigor, *Br* vigour, robustness; *entrer en* **~** come into force

V.I.H. *m* (= *Virus de l'Immunodéficience Humaine*) HIV (= human immunodeficiency virus)

vilain nasty; *enfant* naughty; (*laid*) ugly

villa *f* villa

village *m* village; **villageois, ~e 1** *adj* village *atr* **2** *m/f* villager

ville *f* town; *grande* city; *aller en* **~** go into town

vin *m* wine; **~** *d'honneur* reception; **~** *de pays* regional wine

vinaigre *m* vinegar

vinaigrette *f* salad dressing

vingt twenty; **vingtaine**: *une*

~ de personnes about twenty people *pl;* vingtième twentieth

viol *m* rape; *d'un lieu saint* violation; **violation** *f d'un traité* violation; *d'une église* desecration

violemment violently; *fig* intensely; **violence** *f* violence; *fig* intensity; **violent** violent; *fig* intense

violer *loi* break, *sexuellement* rape; *(profaner)* desecrate

violet, ~te violet

violette *f* BOT violet

violon *m* violin; *musicien* violinist

violoncelle *m* cello

virage *m de la route* curve, corner; *d'un véhicule* turn; *fig* change of direction; **virement** *m* COMM transfer; **virer 1** *v/i (changer de couleur)* change color *ou Br* colour; *d'un véhicule* corner **2** *v/t argent* transfer; **~ qn** F kick s.o. out

virginité *f* virginity

virgule *f* comma

viril male; *(courageux)* manly; **virilité** *f* manhood; *(vigueur sexuelle)* virility

virtuel, ~le virtual; *(possible)* potential

virulent virulent

virus *m* MÉD, INFORM virus

vis *f* screw; **escalier** *m* à **~** spiral staircase

visa *m* visa

visage *m* face

vis-à-vis 1 *prép:* **~ de** opposite; *(envers)* toward, *Br* towards; *(en comparaison de)* compared with **2 ~** *m* person sitting opposite; *(rencontre)* face-to-face meeting

viser 1 *v/t* aim at; *(s'adresser à)* be aimed at **2** *v/i* aim *(à* at); **~ à faire** aim to do

viseur *m d'une arme* sights *pl;* PHOT viewfinder

visibilité *f* visibility; **visible** visible; *(évident)* clear

vision *f* sight; *(conception, apparition)* vision; **visionnaire** *m/f & adj* visionary

visite *f* visit; *d'une ville* tour; **rendre ~ à qn** visit s.o.; **avoir droit de ~** *d'un parent divorcé* have access; **~ de douane** customs inspection; **~ médicale** medical (examination); **visiter** visit; *(faire le tour de)* tour; *bagages* inspect; **visiteur, -euse** *m/f* visitor

vison *m* mink

visqueux, -euse viscous; *péj* slimy

visser screw

visuel, ~le visual; **champ** *m* **~** field of vision

vital vital; **vitalité** *f* vitality

vitamine *f* vitamin

vite fast, quickly; *(sous peu, bientôt)* soon; **~!** quick!; **vitesse** *f* speed; AUTO gear; **à toute ~** at top speed

viticulture *f* wine-growing

vitrage *m cloison* glass partition; *action* glazing; *ensem-*

ble de vitres windows *pl*

vitrail *m* stained-glass window

vitre *f* window (pane); *de voiture* window; **vitrer** glaze; **vitrier** *m* glazier

vitrine *f* (*étalage*) (store) window; *meuble* display cabinet

vivace hardy; *(doué de vie)* lasting; **vivacité** *f* liveliness, vivacity

vivant 1 *adj* alive; *(plein de vie)* lively; *(vite)* living; *langue* modern **2** *m* living person; *de son* ~ in his lifetime

vivement *(d'un ton vif)* sharply; *(vite)* briskly; *ému, touché* deeply

vivoter just get by

vivre 1 *v/i* live **2** *v/t* experience **3** *mpl:* ~s supplies

vocabulaire *m* vocabulary

vociférer shout

vodka *f* vodka

vœu *m* REL vow; *(souhait)* wish; **tous mes** ~*x!* best wishes!

voici here is *sg*, here are *pl*; **me** ~*!* here I am!; **le livre que** ~ this book

voie *f* way; *de chemin de fer* track; *d'autoroute* lane; **en** ~ **de développement** developing; **être en** ~ **de guérison** be on the mend; **par** ~ **aérienne** by air; **par la** ~ **hiérarchique** through channels; ~ **d'eau** leak; ~ **express** expressway

voilà there is *sg*, there are *pl*; **(et)** ~*!* there you are!; **en** ~ **assez!** that's enough!; ~ **tout** that's all

voile 1 *m* veil **2** *f* MAR sail; SP sailing

voiler¹ *v/t* veil; **se** ~ *d'une femme* wear the veil; *du ciel* cloud over

voiler²: **se** ~ *du bois* warp; *d'une roue* buckle

voir see; **faire** ~ show; **se** ~ see each other; **cela se voit** that's obvious; **je ne peux pas le** ~ I can't stand him

voisin, ~**e 1** *adj* neighboring, *Br* neighbouring; *(similaire)* similar **2** *m/f* neighbor, *Br* neighbour; **voisinage** *m* neighborhood, *Br* neighbourhood; *(proximité)* vicinity

voiture *f* car; *d'un train* car, *Br* carriage; **en** ~ by car; ~ **de fonction** company car

voix *f* voice *(aussi* GRAM*)*; POL vote; **à haute** ~ in a loud voice, aloud; **à** ~ **basse** in a low voice, quietly

vol¹ *m* theft; ~ **à main armée** armed robbery

vol² *m* flight; **à** ~ **d'oiseau** as the crow flies; **au** ~ in flight; ~ **à voile** gliding

volaille *f* poultry; *(poulet etc)* bird

volant *m* AUTO (steering) wheel; SP shuttlecock; *d'un vêtement* flounce

volcan *m* volcano

volée *f d'oiseaux* flock; *en tennis, de coups de feu* volley; **à la ~** in mid-air

voler¹ *v/t* steal; **~ qch à qn** steal sth from s.o.

voler² *v/i* fly

volet *m de fenêtre* shutter; *fig* part; **trier sur le ~** *fig* handpick

voleur, -euse 1 *adj* thieving **2** *m/f* thief; **~ à l'étalage** shoplifter

volontaire 1 *adj* voluntary; *(délibéré)* deliberate; *(décidé)* headstrong **2** *m/f* volunteer

volonté *f* will; *(souhait)* wish; *(fermeté)* willpower; **de l'eau à ~** as much water as you like; **faire preuve de bonne ~** show willing

volontiers willingly, with pleasure

volt *m* ÉL volt; **voltage** *m* ÉL voltage

volte-face *f* about-turn *(aussi fig)*

volubilité *f* volubility

volume *m* volume; **volumineux, -euse** bulky

voluptueux, -euse voluptuous

vomir 1 *v/i* vomit, throw up **2** *v/t* bring up; *fig* spew out; **vomissement** *m* vomiting

vorace voracious

vos → *votre*

vote *m* vote; *action* voting; **voter 1** *v/i* vote **2** *v/t loi* pass

votre, *pl* **vos** your

vôtre: le/la ~, les ~s yours

vouer dedicate *(à* to); **se ~ à** *fig* dedicate o.s. to

vouloir want; **il veut que tu partes** *(subj)* he wants you to leave; **je voudrais** I would like, I'd like; **je veux bien** I'd like to; **veuillez ne pas fumer** please do not smoke; **~ dire** mean; **en ~ à qn** have something against s.o.; **veux-tu te taire!** will you shut up!

voulu requisite; *délibéré* deliberate

vous *sg et pl* you; *complément d'objet indirect, sg et pl* (to) you; *avec verbe pronominal* yourself; *pl* yourselves; **~ ~ êtes coupé** you've cut yourself; **si ~ ~ levez à …** if you get up at …

vous-même, *pl* **vous-mêmes** yourself; *pl* yourselves

voûte *f* ARCH vault; **voûté** *personne* hunched; *dos* bent; ARCH vaulted

vouvoyer adress as 'vous'

voyage *m* trip, journey; *en paquebot* voyage; **~ d'affaires** business trip; **~ de noces** honeymoon; **~ organisé** package holiday; **voyager** travel; **voyageur, -euse** *m/f* traveler, *Br* traveller; *par train, avion* passenger; **~ de commerce** traveling *ou Br* travelling salesman

voyant, ~e 1 *adj couleur* garish **2** *m (signal)* light **3** *m/f* *(devin)* clairvoyant

voyelle *f* GRAM vowel

voyou *m jeune* lout

vrac *m*: **en ~** COMM loose; *fig* jumbled together

vrai 1 *adj (après le subst)* true; *(devant le subst)* real, genuine; *ami* true **2** *m*: **à ~ dire, à dire ~** to tell the truth; **vraiment** really

vraisemblable likely, probable; **vraisemblance** *f* likelihood, probability

vrombir throb

VTT *m* (= *vélo tout terrain*) mountain bike

vu in view of

vue *f* view; *sens, faculté* sight; **à première ~** at first sight; **connaître qn de ~** know s.o. by sight; **avoir la ~ basse** be shortsighted; **point** *m* **de ~** viewpoint, point of view; **en ~ de faire** with a view to doing

vulgaire *(banal)* common; *(grossier)* common, vulgar

vulnérable vulnerable

W

wagon *m* car, *Br* carriage; *de marchandises* car, *Br* wagon; **wagon-lit** *m* sleeping car; **wagon-restaurant** *m* dining car

walkman *m* Walkman®

watt *m* ÉL watt

W.-C. *mpl* WC *sg*

week-end *m* weekend; **ce ~** on the weekend

whisky *m* whiskey, *Br* whisky

X, Y

xénophobe xenophobic; **xénophobie** *f* xenophobia

xérès *m* sherry

y there; **on ~ va!** let's go!; **ça ~ est!** that's it!; **j'~ suis** *(je comprends)* now I get it; **~**

compris including; **j'~ travaille** I'm working on it

yacht *m* yacht; **yachting** *m* yachting

yaourt *m* yoghurt

yeux *pl* → **œil**

Z

zapper channel-hop, *Br aussi* zap

zèbre *m* zebra

zèle *m* zeal; **faire du ~** be overzealous; **zélé** zealous

zéro 1 *m* zero, *Br aussi* nought; SP *Br* nil; *fig* nonentity **2** *adj*: **~ faute** no mistakes; **partir de ~** start from nothing

zeste *m* peel, zest

zézayer lisp

zigouiller F bump off F

zigzag *m* zigzag; **zigzaguer** zigzag

zinc *m* zinc

zona *m* shingles *sg*

zone *f* area, zone; *péj* slums *pl*; **~ euro** euro zone; **~ industrielle** industrial park, *Br* industrial estate; **~ interdite** prohibited area

zoo *m* zoo

zoologie *f* zoology; **zoologiste** *m/f* zoologist

zut! F blast!

English – French
Anglais – Français

A

a [ə] un(e)

abandon [əˈbændən] abandonner

abbreviate [əˈbriːvɪeɪt] abréger; abbreviation abréviation *f*

abduct [əbˈdʌkt] enlever

ability [əˈbɪlətɪ] capacité *f*; *skill* faculté *f*

able [ˈeɪbl] (*skillful*) compétent; *be ~ to do* pouvoir faire

abnormal [æbˈnɔːrml] anormal

aboard [əˈbɔːrd] à bord

abolish [əˈbɑːlɪʃ] abolir; abolition abolition *f*

abort [əˈbɔːrt] suspendre; abortion MED avortement *m*; *have an ~* se faire avorter; abortive avorté

about [əˈbaʊt] 1 *prep* (*concerning*) à propos de; *a book ~* un livre sur; *talk ~* parler de; *what's it ~? of book, movie* de quoi ça parle? 2 *adv* (*roughly*) à peu près; *~ noon* aux alentours de midi; *be ~ to do* (*be going to*) être sur le point de faire

above [əˈbʌv] au-dessus de; *on the floor ~* à l'étage du dessus

abrasive [əˈbreɪsɪv] *personality* abrupt

abreast [əˈbrest]: *three ~* les trois l'un à côté de l'autre; *keep ~ of* se tenir au courant de

abridge [əˈbrɪdʒ] abréger

abroad [əˈbrɔːd] à l'étranger

abrupt [əˈbrʌpt] brusque

abscess [ˈæbsɪs] abcès *m*

absence [ˈæbsəns] absence *f*; absent absent; absentee absent(e) *m(f)*; absenteeism absentéisme *m*; absent-minded distrait

absolute [ˈæbsəluːt] absolu; absolution REL absolution *f*; absolve absoudre

absorb [əbˈsɔːrb] absorber; absorbent absorbant; absorbent cotton coton *m* hydrophile; absorbing absorbant

abstain [əbˈsteɪn] *in vote* s'abstenir; abstention *in vote* abstention *f*

abstract [ˈæbstrækt] abstrait

absurd [əbˈsɜːrd] absurde; absurdity absurdité *f*

abundance [əˈbʌndəns] abondance *f*; abundant abondant

abuse¹ [əˈbjuːs] *n verbal* insultes *fpl*; *physical* violences *fpl physiques*; *sexual* sévices *mpl* sexuels; *of power etc* abus *m*

abuse² [əˈbjuːz] *v/t verbally* insulter; *physically* maltraiter; *sexually* faire subir des sévices sexuels à; *power etc* abuser de

abysmal [əˈbɪzml] *(very bad)* lamentable

academic [ækəˈdemɪk] **1** *n* universitaire *m/f* **2** *adj year*: *at school* scolaire; *at university* universitaire; *interests* intellectuel; *academy* académie *f*

accelerate [əkˈseləreɪt] accélérer; *acceleration* accélération *f*; *accelerator* accélérateur *m*

accent [ˈæksənt] accent *m*; *accentuate* accentuer

accept [əkˈsept] accepter; *acceptable* acceptable; *acceptance* acceptation *f*

access [ˈækses] **1** *n* accès *m* **2** *v/t also* COMPUT accéder à; *accessible* accessible

accessory [əkˈsesərɪ] *for wearing* accessoire *m*; LAW complice *m/f*

accident [ˈæksɪdənt] accident *m*; *by ~* par hasard; *accidental* accidentel; *accidentally* accidentellement

acclimate, acclimatize [əˈklaɪmət, əˈklaɪmətaɪz] s'acclimater

accommodate [əˈkɑːmədeɪt] loger; *needs* s'adapter à; *accommodations* logement *m*

accompaniment [əˈkʌmpənɪmənt] MUS accompagnement *m*; *accompany also* MUS accompagner

accomplice [əˈkʌmplɪs] complice *m/f*

accomplished [əˈkʌmplɪʃt] accompli; *accomplishment of task* accomplissement *m*; *(achievement)* réussite *f*; *(talent)* talent *m*

accord [əˈkɔːrd] accord *m*; *of one's own ~* de son plein gré

accordance [əˈkɔːrdəns]: *in ~ with* conformément à

according [əˈkɔːrdɪŋ]: *~ to* selon; *accordingly (consequently)* par conséquent; *(appropriately)* en conséquence

account [əˈkaʊnt] *financial* compte *m*; *(report)* récit *m*; *give an ~ of* faire le récit de; *on no ~* en aucun cas; *on ~ of* en raison de; *take ... into ~* tenir compte de; *accountable*: *be held ~* être tenu responsable; *accountant* comptable *m/f*; *accounts* comptabilité *f*

accumulate [əˈkjuːmjʊleɪt] **1** *v/t* accumuler **2** *v/i* s'accumuler; *accumulation* accumulation *f*

accuracy [ˈækjʊrəsɪ] justesse *f*; *accurate* juste; *accurately* avec justesse

accusation [ækjuː'zeɪʃn] accusation *f*; accuse: *~ s.o. of doing sth* accuser qn de faire qch; accused LAW accusé(e) *m(f)*; accusing accusateur

accustom [ə'kʌstəm]: *get ~ed to* s'accoutumer à

ace [eɪs] *in cards* as *m*; *tennis shot* ace *m*

ache [eɪk] **1** *n* douleur *f* **2** *v/i*: *my arm ~s* j'ai mal au bras

achieve [ə'tʃiːv] accomplir; achievement (*thing achieved*) accomplissement *m*; *of ambition* réalisation *f*

acid ['æsɪd] acide *m*

acknowledge [ək'nɑːlɪdʒ] reconnaître; *~ receipt of* accuser réception de; acknowledg(e)ment reconnaissance *f*; *of a letter* accusé *m* de réception

acoustics [ə'kuːstɪks] acoustique *f*

acquaint [ə'kweɪnt]: *be ~ed with* connaître; acquaintance *person* connaissance *f*

acquire [ə'kwaɪr] acquérir; acquisition acquisition *f*

acquit [ə'kwɪt] LAW acquitter; acquittal LAW acquittement *m*

acre ['eɪkər] acre *m* (4.047*m²*)

across [ə'krɔːs] **1** *prep* de l'autre côté de; *walk ~ the street* traverser la rue; *~ Europe* all over dans toute l'Europe; *~ from* en face de **2** *adv*: *swim ~* traverser à la na-

---

ge; *10m ~* 10 *m* de large

act [ækt] **1** *v/i* (*take action*) agir; THEA faire du théâtre **2** *n* (*deed*) fait *m*; *of play* acte *m*; *in vaudeville* numéro *m*; (*law*) loi *f*

action ['ækʃn] action *f*; *take ~* prendre des mesures

active ['æktɪv] actif; activist POL activiste *m/f*; activity activité *f*

actor ['æktər] acteur *m*

actress ['æktrɪs] actrice *f*

actual ['æktʃʊəl] véritable; actually ['æktʃʊəli] en fait; *expressing surprise* vraiment

acute [ə'kjuːt] *pain* intense; *sense* très développé

AD [eɪ'diː] (= *anno domini*) apr. J.-C. (= après Jésus Christ)

ad [æd] → *advertisement*

adamant ['ædəmənt]: *be ~ that ...* soutenir catégoriquement que ...

adapt [ə'dæpt] **1** *v/t* adapter **2** *v/i* *of person* s'adapter; adaptability faculté *f* d'adaptation; adaptable adaptable; adaptation *of play etc* adaptation *f*; adapter ELEC adaptateur *m*

add [æd] **1** *v/t* ajouter; MATH additionner **2** *v/i* *of person* faire des additions
◆ add on *15% etc* ajouter
◆ add up **1** *v/t* additionner **2** *v/i* avoir du sens

addict ['ædɪkt] (*drug ~*) drogué(e) *m(f)*; *of TV program etc* accro *m/f*; **addicted to** *drugs* drogué; *to TV program etc* accro F; **addiction to** *drugs* dépendance *f* (**to** de); **addictive**: **be ~** entraîner une dépendance

addition [ə'dɪʃn] MATH addition *f*; *to list* ajout *m*; *to company* recrue *f*; **in ~ to** en plus de; **additional** supplémentaire; **additive** additif *m*; **add-on** accessoire *m*

address [ə'dres] **1** *n* adresse *f* **2** *v/t letter* adresser; *audience* s'adresser à; **addressee** destinataire *m/f*

adequate ['ædɪkwət] (*sufficient*) suffisant; (*satisfactory*) satisfaisant; **adequately** suffisamment

◆ **adhere to** [əd'hɪr] adhérer à

adhesive [əd'hiːsɪv] adhésif *m*

adjacent [ə'dʒeɪsnt] adjacent

adjective ['ædʒɪktɪv] adjectif *m*

adjoining [ə'dʒɔɪnɪŋ] attenant

adjourn [ə'dʒɜːrn] ajourner; **adjournment** ajournement *m*

adjust [ə'dʒʌst] ajuster; **adjustable** ajustable; **adjustment** ajustement *m*

ad lib [æd'lɪb] **1** *adj* improvisé **2** *v/i* improviser

administer [əd'mɪnɪstər] *country* administrer; **administration** administration *f*;

(*administrative work*) tâches *fpl* administratives; **administrative** administratif; **administrator** administrateur(-trice) *m(f)*

admirable ['ædmərəbl] admirable; **admiration** admiration *f*; **admire** admirer; **admirer** admirateur(-trice) *m(f)*; **admiring** admiratif; **admiringly** admirativement

admissible [əd'mɪsəbl] admis; **admission** (*confession*) aveu *m*; **~ free** entrée *f* gratuite; **admit** *to a place*, (*accept*) admettre; (*confess*) avouer; **admittance**: **no ~** entrée *f* interdite

adolescence [ædə'lesns] adolescence *f*; **adolescent 1** *adj* adolescent **2** *n* adolescent(e) *m(f)*

adopt [ə'dɑːpt] adopter; **adoption** adoption *f*

adorable [ə'dɔːrəbl] adorable; **adoration** adoration *f*; **adore** adorer

adrenalin [ə'drenəlɪn] adrénaline *f*

adult ['ædʌlt] **1** *adj* adulte **2** *n* adulte *m/f*; **adultery** adultère *m*

advance [əd'væns] **1** *n money* avance *f*; *in science etc* avancée *f*; MIL progression *f*; **in ~** à l'avance; **payment in ~** paiement *m* anticipé; **make ~s** (*progress*) faire des progrès; *sexually* faire des avances **2** *v/i* MIL, (*make progress*) avancer **3** *v/t theory, sum of money* avancer; *human knowledge, cause* faire avancer; advanced avancé

advantage [əd'vɑ:ntɪdʒ] avantage *m*; *take ~ of opportunity* profiter de; **advantageous** avantageux

adventure [əd'ventʃər] aventure *f*; **adventurous** aventureux

adverb ['ædvɜ:rb] adverbe *m*

adversary ['ædvərsəri] adversaire *m/f*

adverse ['ædvɜ:rs] adverse

advertise ['ædvərtaɪz] *product* faire de la publicité pour; *job* mettre une annonce pour; **advertisement** *for product* publicité *f*, pub *f*; *for job* annonce *f*; **advertiser** annonceur(-euse) *m(f)*; **advertising** publicité *f*

advice [əd'vaɪs] conseils *mpl*; *a bit of ~* un conseil; **advisable** conseillé; **advise** conseiller

advocate ['ædvəkeɪt] recommander

aerial ['erɪəl] *Br* antenne *f*; **aerial photograph** photographie *f* aérienne

aerobics [e'roubɪks] aérobic *m*

aerodynamic [eroudaɪ'næmɪk] aérodynamique

aeroplane ['eroupleɪn] avion *m*

aerosol ['erəsɑ:l] aérosol *m*

aesthetic *etc* → **esthetic** *etc*

affair [ə'fer] *(matter)* affaire *f*; *(love ~)* liaison *f*

affection [ə'fekʃn] affection *f*; **affectionate** affectueux; **affectionately** affectueusement

affirmative [ə'fɜ:rmətɪv] affirmatif

affluence ['æfluəns] richesse *f*; **affluent** riche

afford [ə'fɔ:rd]: *be able to ~ sth financially* pouvoir se permettre d'acheter qch

afloat [ə'flout] *boat* sur l'eau

afraid [ə'freɪd]: *be ~* avoir peur (*of* de); *I'm ~ expressing regret* je crains

afresh [ə'freʃ]: *start ~* recommencer

Africa ['æfrɪkə] Afrique *f*

African ['æfrɪkən] **1** *adj* africain **2** *n* Africain(e) *m(f)*; **African-American 1** *adj* afro--américain(e) **2** *n* Afro-Américain(e) *m(f)*

after ['æftər] **1** *prep* après; *it's ten ~ two* il est deux heures dix **2** *adv (afterward)* après; *the day ~* le lendemain

afternoon [æftər'nu:n] après--midi *m*; *in the ~* l'après-midi; *this ~* cet après-midi; *good ~* bonjour

'**after sales service** service *m* après-vente; **aftershave** lotion *f* après-rasage; **afterward** ensuite

again [ə'geɪn] encore; *I never saw him ~* je ne l'ai jamais revu

against [ə'genst] contre

age [eɪdʒ] âge *m*; **she's five years of ~** elle a cinq ans; **aged**: **~ 16** âgé de 16 ans; **age group** catégorie *f* d'âge; **age limit** limite *f* d'âge

agency ['eɪdʒənsɪ] agence *f*

agenda [ə'dʒendə] ordre *m* du jour

agent ['eɪdʒənt] COM agent *m*

aggravate ['ægrəveɪt] faire empirer; (*annoy*) agacer

aggression [ə'greʃn] agression *f*; **aggressive** agressif; **aggressively** agressivement

aghast [ə'gæst] horrifié

agile ['ædʒəl] agile; **agility** agilité *f*

agitated ['ædʒɪteɪtd] agité; **agitation** agitation *f*; **agitator** agitateur(-trice) *m(f)*

agnostic [æg'nɒstɪk] agnostique *m/f*

ago [ə'goʊ]: **two days ~** il y a deux jours; **long ~** il y a longtemps

agonize ['ægənaɪz] se tourmenter (**over** sur); **agonizing** terrible; **agony** ['ægənɪ] *mental* tourment *m*; *physical* grande douleur *f*

agree [ə'griː] **1** *v/i* être d'accord; *of figures* s'accorder; (*reach agreement*) s'entendre **2** *v/t price* s'entendre sur; **agreeable** (*pleasant*) agréable; **agreement** accord *m*

agricultural [ægrɪ'kʌltʃərəl] agricole; **agriculture** agri-

culture *f*

ahead [ə'hed] devant; **plan/ think ~** prévoir/penser à l'avance

aid [eɪd] **1** *n* aide *f* **2** *v/t* aider

aide [eɪd] aide *m/f*

Aids [eɪdz] sida *m*

ailing ['eɪlɪŋ] *economy* mal en point

ailment ['eɪlmənt] mal *m*

aim [eɪm] **1** *n* (*objective*) but *m* **2** *v/i in shooting* viser; **~ to do sth** essayer de faire qch **3** *v/t*: **be ~ed at** *of remark* viser; *of gun* être pointé sur; **aimless** ['eɪmlɪs] sans but

air [er] **1** *n* air *m*; **by ~** par avion; **in the open ~** en plein air **2** *v/t room* aérer; *views* exprimer; **airbag** airbag *m*; **air-conditioned** climatisé; **air-conditioning** climatisation *f*; **aircraft** avion *m*; **aircraft carrier** porte-avions *m inv*; **air force** armée *f* de l'air; **air hostess** hôtesse *f* de l'air; **airline** compagnie *f* aérienne; **airliner** avion *m* de ligne; **airmail**: **by ~** par avion; **airplane** avion *m*; **airport** aéroport *m*; **air terminal** aérogare *f*; **air-traffic controller** contrôleur(-euse) aérien(ne) *m(f)*

aisle [aɪl] *in airplane* couloir *m*; *in theater* allée *f*

ajar [ə'dʒɑːr]: **be ~** être entrouvert

alarm [ə'lɑːrm] **1** *n* (*fear*) inquiétude *f*; *device* alarme *f*;

alongside

(~ *clock*) réveil *m* **2** *v/t* alarmer; **alarming** alarmant; **alarmingly** de manière alarmante

album ['ælbəm] album *m*

alcohol ['ælkəhɒl] alcool *m*; **alcoholic 1** *adj drink* alcoolisé **2** *n* alcoolique *m/f*

alert [ə'lɜːrt] **1** *adj* vigilant **2** *n signal* alerte *f* **3** *v/t* alerter

alibi ['ælɪbaɪ] alibi *m*

alien ['eɪlɪən] **1** *adj* étranger (**to** à) **2** *n* étranger(-ère) *m(f); from space* extra-terrestre *m/f*; **alienate** s'aliéner

align [ə'laɪn] aligner

alike [ə'laɪk] **1** *adj:* **be** ~ se ressembler **2** *adv:* **old and young** ~ les vieux comme les jeunes

alimony ['ælɪmənɪ] pension alimentaire

alive [ə'laɪv]: **be** ~ être en vie

all [ɔːl] **1** *adj* tout **2** *pron* tout; ~ **of us/them** nous/eux tous; **he ate** ~ **of it** il l'a mangé en entier; **for** ~ **I know** pour autant que je sache; ~ **but him** (*except*) tous sauf lui **3** *adv:* ~ **at once** (*suddenly*) tout d'un coup; (*at the same time*) tous ensemble; ~ **but** (*nearly*) presque; ~ **the better** encore mieux; **they're not at** ~ **alike** ils ne se ressemblent pas du tout; **not at** ~*!* pas du tout!; **two** ~ SP deux à deux

allegation [ælɪ'geɪʃn] allégation *f*; **allege** alléguer; **alleged** supposé; **allegedly:**

he ~ **killed two women** il aurait assassiné deux femmes

allegiance [ə'liːdʒəns] loyauté *f* (**to** à)

allergic [ə'lɜːrdʒɪk] allergique (**to** à)

alleviate [ə'liːvɪeɪt] soulager

alley ['ælɪ] ruelle *f*

alliance [ə'laɪəns] alliance *f*

allocate ['æləkeɪt] assigner; **allocation** [ælə'keɪʃn] *action* assignation *f*; *amount allocated* part *f*

allot [ə'lɒt] assigner

allow [ə'laʊ] (*permit*) permettre; (*calculate for*) compter

♦ **allow for** prendre en compte

allowance [ə'laʊəns] *money* allocation *f*; (*pocket money*) argent *m* de poche

alloy ['ælɔɪ] alliage *m*

'all-purpose universel; *vehicle* tous usages; **all-round** général; *athlete* complet;

♦ **allude to** [ə'luːd] faire allusion à

alluring [ə'lʊrɪŋ] alléchant

all-wheel 'drive quatre roues motrices *fpl*; *vehicle* 4x4 *m*

ally ['ælaɪ] allié(e) *m(f)*

almond ['ɑːmənd] amande *f*

almost ['ɒːlmoʊst] presque

alone [ə'loʊn] seul

along [ə'lɒːŋ] **1** *prep* le long de; *walk* ~ **this path** prenez ce chemin **2** *adv:* **bring** ~ amener; ~ **with** *in addition to* ainsi que

alongside [əlɒːŋ'saɪd] *paral-*

lel to à côté de; *in cooperation with* aux côtés de

aloof [əˈluːf] distant

aloud [əˈlaud] à haute voix

alphabet [ˈælfəbet] alphabet *m*; **alphabetical** alphabétique

already [ɔːlˈredɪ] déjà

alright [ɔːlˈraɪt] (*permitted*) permis; (*acceptable*) convenable; **be ~** (*in working order*) fonctionner; **she's ~** not hurt elle n'est pas blessée; **everything is ~** tout va bien

altar [ˈɔːltər] autel *m*

alter [ˈɔːltər] modifier; *person* changer; **alteration** modification *f*

alternate 1 [ˈɔːltərneɪt] *v/i* alterner **2** [ˈɔːltərnət] *adj:* **on ~ Mondays** un lundi sur deux

alternative [ɔːlˈtɜːrnətɪv] **1** *adj* alternatif **2** *n* alternative *f*; **alternatively** sinon; **or ~** bien

although [ɔːlˈðou] bien que (+*subj*), quoique (+*subj*)

altitude [ˈæltɪtuːd] altitude *f*

altogether [ɔːltəˈgeðər] (*completely*) totalement; (*in all*) en tout

altruism [ˈæltruːɪzm] altruisme *m*; **altruistic** altruiste

aluminum [əˈluːmənəm] aluminium [æljuˈmɪnɪəm] aluminium *m*

always [ˈɔːlweɪz] toujours

a.m. [ˈeɪem] (= **ante meridiem**) du matin

amass [əˈmæs] amasser

amateur [ˈæməʧʊr] sp amateur *m/f*; **amateurish** *attempt* d'amateur; *painter* sans talent

amaze [əˈmeɪz] étonner; **amazed** étonné; **amazement** étonnement *m*; **amazing** étonnant; (*very good*) impressionnant; **amazingly** étonnamment

ambassador [æmˈbæsədər] ambassadeur(-drice) *m(f)*

amber [ˈæmbər]: **at ~** à l'orange

ambience [ˈæmbɪəns] ambiance *f*

ambiguity [æmbɪˈgjuːətɪ] ambiguïté *f*; **ambiguous** ambigu

ambition [æmˈbɪʃn] ambition *f*; **ambitious** ambitieux

ambivalent [æmˈbɪvələnt] ambivalent

amble [ˈæmbl] déambuler

ambulance [ˈæmbjuləns] ambulance *f*

ambush [ˈæmbʊʃ] **1** *n* embuscade *f* **2** *v/t* tendre une embuscade à

amend [əˈmend] modifier; **amendment** modification *f*; **amends**: **make ~** se racheter

amenities [əˈmiːnətɪz] facilités *fpl*

America [əˈmerɪkə] (*United States*) États-Unis *mpl*; *continent* Amérique *f*; **American 1** *adj* américain **2** *n* Américain(e) *m(f)* amicable ['æmɪkəbl] à l'amiable; amicably à l'amiable

ammunition [æmju'nɪʃn] munitions *fpl*

amnesia [æm'niːzɪə] amnésie *f*

amnesty ['æmnəstɪ] amnistie *f*

among(st) [ə'mʌŋ(st)] parmi

amoral [eɪ'mɔːrəl] amoral

amount [ə'maʊnt] quantité *f*; (*sum of money*) somme *f*
♦ **amount to** s'élever à; (*be equivalent to*) revenir à

amphibian [æm'fɪbɪən] amphibien *m*

ample ['æmpl] beaucoup de

amplifier ['æmplɪfaɪr] amplificateur *m*; amplify amplifier

amputate ['æmpjuːteɪt] amputer; amputation amputation *f*

amuse [ə'mjuːz] (*make laugh*) amuser; (*entertain*) distraire; amusement (*merriment*) amusement *m*; (*entertainment*) divertissement *m*; amusement park parc *m* d'attractions; amusing amusant

an [æn] → **a**

anaemia *etc* → **anemia** *etc*

anaesthetic *etc* → **anesthetic** *etc*

analog ['ænəlɒg] analogique; analogy analogie *f*

analysis [ə'næləsɪs] analyse *f*; analyst PSYCH analyste *m/f*; analytical analytique; analyze *also* PSYCH analyser

anarchy ['ænəkɪ] anarchie *f*

ancestor ['ænsestər] ancêtre *m/f*

anchor ['æŋkər] **1** *n* NAUT ancre *f*; TV présentateur(-trice) principal(e) *m(f)* **2** *v/i* NAUT ancrer

ancient ['eɪnʃənt] ancien; *Rome etc* antique

and [ænd] et

anemia [ə'niːmɪə] anémie *f*; anemic anémique

anesthetic [ænəs'θetɪk] anesthésiant *m*

angel ['eɪndʒl] ange *m*

anger ['æŋgər] **1** *n* colère *f* **2** *v/t* mettre en colère

angle ['æŋgl] angle *m*

angry ['æŋgrɪ] *person* en colère; *mood, look* fâché

animal ['ænɪml] animal *m*

animated ['ænɪmeɪtɪd] animé; animated cartoon dessin *m* animé; animation animation *f*

animosity [ænɪ'mɑːsətɪ] animosité *f*

ankle ['æŋkl] cheville *f*

annex ['æneks] **1** *n* annexe *f* **2** *v/t state* annexer

annihilate [ə'naɪəleɪt] anéantir; annihilation anéantissement *m*

anniversary [ænɪ'vɜːrsərɪ] anniversaire *m*

announce [ə'naʊns] annoncer; announcement annonce *f*; announcer [ə'naʊnsər] TV, RAD speaker *m*, speakrine *f*

annoy [əˈnɔɪ] agacer; **annoyance** (*anger*) agacement *m*; (*nuisance*) désagrément *m*; **annoying** agaçant

annual [ˈænʊəl] annuel

annul [əˈnʌl] annuler; **annulment** annulation *f*

anonymous [əˈnɑːnɪməs] anonyme

anorexia [ænəˈreksɪə] anorexie *f*

another [əˈnʌðər] **1** *adj* autre **2** *pron* un(e) autre *m(f)*; **they know one ~** ils se connaissent

answer [ˈænsər] **1** *n* réponse *f*; (*solution*) solution *f* (**to** à) **2** *v/t* répondre à **3** *v/i* répondre; **answerphone** répondeur *m*

ant [ænt] fourmi *f*

antagonism [ænˈtægənɪzm] antagonisme *m*; **antagonistic** hostile; **antagonize** provoquer

Antarctic [æntˈɑːrktɪk]: **the ~** l'Antarctique *m*

antenatal [æntɪˈneɪtl] prénatal

antenna [ænˈtenə] antenne *f*

antibiotic [æntɪbaɪˈɑːtɪk] antibiotique *m*

anticipate [ænˈtɪsɪpeɪt] prévoir; **anticipation** prévision *f*

antics [ˈæntɪks] singeries *fpl*

antidote [ˈæntɪdoʊt] antidote *m*

antifreeze [ˈæntaɪfriːz] antigel *m*

antipathy [ænˈtɪpəθɪ] antipathie *f*

antiquated [ˈæntɪkweɪtɪd] antique

antique [ænˈtiːk] antiquité *f*

antiseptic [æntaɪˈseptɪk] **1** *adj* antiseptique **2** *n* antiseptique *m*

antisocial [æntaɪˈsoʊʃl] asocial, antisocial

antivirus program [æntaɪˈvaɪrəs] COMPUT programme *m* antivirus

anxiety [æŋˈzaɪətɪ] inquiétude *f*; **anxious** inquiet; (*eager*) soucieux

any [ˈenɪ] **1** *adj*: **are there ~ glasses?** est-ce qu'il y a des verres?; **is there ~ bread/improvement?** est-ce qu'il y a du pain/une amélioration?; **there isn't/aren't ~ ...** il n'y a pas de ...; **have you ~ idea at all?** est-ce que vous avez une idée? **2** *pron*: **do you have ~?** est-ce que vous en avez?; **there aren't/isn't ~ left** il n'y en a plus; **~ of them could be guilty** ils pourraient tous être coupables

anybody [ˈenɪbɑːdɪ] quelqu'un; *with negatives* personne; *no matter who* n'importe qui; **there wasn't ~ there** il n'y avait personne

anyhow [ˈenɪhaʊ] (*anyway*) enfin; (*in any way*) de quelque façon que ce soit

anyone [ˈenɪwʌn] → **anybody**

anything ['enιθιŋ] quelque chose; *with negatives* rien; *I didn't hear* ~ je n'ai rien entendu ~ *but ...* tout sauf ...

anyway ['enιweι] → *anyhow*

anywhere ['enιwer] quelque part; *with negatives* nulle part; *I can't find it* ~ je ne le trouve nulle part

apart [ə'pɑːrt] séparé; ~ *from* (*except*) à l'exception de; (*in addition to*) en plus de

apartment [ə'pɑːrtmənt] appartement *m*; **apartment block** immeuble *m*

ape [eıp] singe *m*

aperitif [ə'perιtiːf] apéritif *m*

apologize [ə'pɑːlədʒaız] s'excuser (*to s.o.* auprès de qn); **apology** excuses *fpl*

appalling [ə'pɔːlιŋ] scandaleux

apparatus [æpə'reιtəs] appareils *mpl*

apparent [ə'pærənt] (*obvious*) évident; (*seeming*) apparent; **apparently** apparemment

appeal [ə'piːl] (*charm*) charme *m*; *for funds etc*, LAW appel *m*

◆ **appeal for** *calm etc* appeler à; *funds* demander

◆ **appeal to** (*be attractive to*) plaire à

appealing [ə'piːlιŋ] séduisant

appear [ə'pιr] apparaître; *in court* comparaître; (*seem*) paraître; ~ *to be ...* avoir l'air d'être ...; **appearance**

apparition *f*; *in court* comparution *f*; (*look*) apparence *f*

appendicitis [əpendι'saιtιs] appendicite *f*

appendix [ə'pendιks] MED, *of book etc* appendice *m*

appetite ['æpιtaιt] appétit *m*; **appetizer** *to drink* apéritif *m*; *to eat* amuse-gueule *m*; **appetizing** appétissant

applaud [ə'plɔːd] applaudir; **applause** applaudissements *mpl*

apple ['æpl] pomme *f*

appliance [ə'plaιəns] appareil *m*

applicable [ə'plιkəbl] applicable; **applicant** *for job* candidat(e) *m(f)*; **application** *for job* candidature *f*; *for passport etc* demande *f*; **apply 1** *v/t* appliquer **2** *v/i* of *rule, law* s'appliquer

◆ **apply for** *job* poser sa candidature pour; *passport etc* faire une demande de

◆ **apply to** (*contact*) s'adresser à; *of rules etc* s'appliquer à

appoint [ə'pɔınt] *to position* nommer; **appointment** *to position* nomination *f*; (*meeting*) rendez-vous *m*

appraisal [ə'preιzəl] évaluation *f*

appreciable [ə'priːʃəbl] considérable; **appreciate 1** *v/t* apprécier; (*acknowledge*) reconnaître **2** *v/i* FIN s'apprécier; **appreciative** *grateful* reconnaissant; *understanding* approbateur; *audience* réceptif

apprehensive [æprɪˈhensɪv] appréhensif

approach [əˈprəʊtʃ] **1** *n* approche *f*; (*proposal*) proposition *f* **2** *v/t* (*get near to*) approcher; (*contact*) faire des propositions à; *problem* aborder; **approachable** *person* d'un abord facile

appropriate [əˈprəʊprɪət] approprié

approval [əˈpruːvl] approbation *f*; **approve 1** *v/i* être d'accord **2** *v/t plan* approuver

approximate [əˈprɒksɪmət] approximatif; **approximately** approximativement

apricot [ˈeɪprɪkɒt] abricot *m*

April [ˈeɪprəl] avril *m*

apt [æpt] *remark* pertinent; *aptitude* aptitude *f*

aquarium [əˈkweərɪəm] aquarium *m*

Arab [ˈærəb] **1** *adj* arabe **2** *n* Arabe *m/f*; **Arabic 1** *adj* arabe **2** *n* arabe *m*

arbitrary [ˈɑːrbɪtrərɪ] arbitraire

arbitrate [ˈɑːrbɪtreɪt] arbitrer; **arbitration** arbitrage *m*

arch [ɑːrtʃ] voûte *f*

archaeology *etc* → **archeology** *etc*

archaic [ɑːrˈkeɪɪk] archaïque

archeological [ɑːrkɪəˈlɒdʒ-ɪkl] archéologique; **archeologist** archéologue *m/f*; ar-

cheology archéologie *f*

architect [ˈɑːrkɪtekt] architecte *m/f*; **architectural** architectural; **architecture** architecture *f*

archives [ˈɑːrkaɪvz] archives *fpl*

Arctic [ˈɑːrktɪk]: **the ~** l'Arctique *m*

ardent [ˈɑːrdənt] fervent

arduous [ˈɑːrdjʊəs] ardu

area [ˈeɪrɪə] *of city* quartier *m*; *of country* région *f*; *of research* domaine *m*; *of room* surface *f*; GEOM, *of land* superficie *f*; **area code** TELEC indicatif *m* régional

arena [əˈriːnə] SP arène *f*

Argentina [ɑːrdʒənˈtiːnə] Argentine *f*

Argentinian [ɑːrdʒənˈtɪnɪən] **1** *adj* argentin **2** *n* Argentin(e) *m(f)*

arguably [ˈɑːrgjʊəblɪ]: **it was ~** ... on peut dire que ...; **argue** (*quarrel*) se disputer; (*reason*) argumenter; **argument** (*quarrel*) dispute *f*; (*discussion*) discussion *f*; (*reasoning*) argument *m*

arid [ˈærɪd] *land* aride

arise [əˈraɪz] *of situation* survenir

arithmetic [əˈrɪθmətɪk] arithmétique *f*

arm[1] [ɑːrm] *n* bras *m*

arm[2] [ɑːrm] *v/t* armer

armaments [ˈɑːrməmənts] armes *fpl*

'armchair fauteuil *m*

armed [ɑːrmd] armé; **armed forces** forces *fpl* armées; **armed robbery** vol *m* à main armée

'**armpit** aisselle *f*

arms [ɑːrmz] (*weapons*) armes *fpl*

army ['ɑːrmɪ] armée *f*

around [ə'raund] **1** *prep* (*encircling*) autour de; **it's ~ the corner** c'est juste à côté **2** *adv* (*in the area*) dans les parages; (*encircling*) autour; (*roughly*) à peu près; *with expressions of time* à environ

arouse [ə'rauz] susciter; *sexually* exciter

arrange [ə'reɪndʒ] arranger; *furniture* disposer; *meeting etc* organiser; *time* fixer; *appointment* prendre; **I've ~d to meet her** j'ai prévu de la voir; **arrangement** (*agreement*), *music* arrangement *m*; *of furniture* disposition *f*; *flowers* composition *f*

arrears [ə'rɪərz] arriéré *m*

arrest [ə'rest] **1** *n* arrestation *f*; **be under ~** être en état d'arrestation **2** *v/t* arrêter

arrival [ə'raɪvl] arrivée *f*; **arrive** arriver

♦ **arrive at** arriver à

arrogance ['ærəgəns] arrogance *f*; **arrogant** arrogant

arrow ['ærou] flèche *f*

arson ['ɑːrsn] incendie *m* criminel

art [ɑːrt] art *m*

artery ['ɑːrtərɪ] artère *f*

'**art gallery** galerie *f* d'art

arthritis [ɑːr'θraɪtɪs] arthrite *f*

artichoke ['ɑːrtɪtʃouk] artichaut *m*

article ['ɑːrtɪkl] article *m*

articulate [ɑːr'tɪkjulət] *person* qui s'exprime bien

artificial [ɑːrtɪ'fɪʃl] artificiel

artillery [ɑːr'tɪlərɪ] artillerie *f*

artist ['ɑːrtɪst] artiste *m/f*; **artistic** artistique

'**arts degree** licence *f* de lettres

as [æz] **1** *conj* (*while, when*) alors que; (*because*) comme; (*like*) comme; **~ if** comme si; **~ usual** comme d'habitude **2** *adv*: **~ high ~ ...** aussi haut que ...; **~ much ~ that?** autant que ça?; **~ soon ~ possible** aussi vite que possible **3** *prep*: **work ~ a teacher** travailler comme professeur; **~ for** quant à; **~ from** *or* **of Monday** à partir de lundi

ash [æʃ] cendres *fpl*

ashamed [ə'ʃeɪmd] honteux; **be ~ of** avoir honte de

'**ash can** poubelle *f*

ashore [ə'ʃɔːr] à terre; **go ~** débarquer

ashtray ['æʃtreɪ] cendrier *m*

Asia ['eɪʒə] Asie *f*; **Asian 1** *adj* asiatique **2** *n* Asiatique *m/f*; **Asian-American 1** *adj* américain(e) d'origine asiatique **2** *n* Américain(e) *m(f)* d'origine asiatique

aside [ə'saɪd] de côté; **move ~**

please poussez-vous, s'il vous plaît; ***take s.o.*** ~ prendre qn à part; ~ ***from*** à part

ask [æsk] demander; *question* poser; *(invite)* inviter; ~ ***s.o. for sth*** demander qch à qn

◆ ask after *person* demander des nouvelles de

◆ ask for *sth* demander; *person* demander à parler à

◆ ask out: ***he's asked me out*** il m'a demandé de sortir avec lui

asleep [ə'sli:p]: ***be (fast)*** ~ être (bien) endormi; ***fall*** ~ s'endormir

asparagus [ə'spærəgəs] asperges *fpl*

aspect ['æspekt] aspect *m*

aspirations [æspə'reɪʃnz] aspirations *fpl*

aspirin ['æsprin] aspirine *f*

ass¹ [æs] *(idiot)* idiot(e) *m(f)*

ass² [æs] *(butt)* cul *m*

assassin [ə'sæsin] assassin *m*; assassinate assassiner

assassination assassinat *m*

assault [ə'sɔːlt] 1 *n* agression *f*; MIL attaque *f* (***on*** contre) 2 *v/t* agresser

assemble [ə'sembl] 1 *v/t parts* assembler 2 *v/i of people* se rassembler; assembly POL assemblée *f*; *of parts* assemblage *m*; assembly line chaîne *f* de montage

assent [ə'sent] consentir

assertive [ə'sɜːrtɪv] *person* assuré

assess [ə'ses] *situation* éva-

luer; *value* estimer; assessment *of situation* évaluation *f*; *of value* estimation *f*

asset ['æset] FIN actif *m*; atout *m*

assign [ə'saɪn] assigner; assignment mission *f*; EDU devoir *m*

assimilate [ə'sɪmɪleɪt] assimiler

assist [ə'sɪst] aider; assistance aide *f*; assistant assistant(e) *m(f)*; assistant manager sous-directeur *m*, sous-directrice *f*; *of department* assistant(e) *m(f)* du/de la responsable

associate 1 *v/t* [ə'soʊʃieɪt] associer 2 *n* [ə'soʊʃiət] *(colleague)* collègue *m/f*; association association *f*

assortment [ə'sɔːrtmənt] assortiment *m*

assume [ə'suːm] *(suppose)* supposer; assumption supposition *f*

assurance [ə'ʃʊrəns] *(reassurance, confidence)* assurance *f*; assure *(reassure)* assurer

asthma ['æsmə] asthme *m*

astonish [ə'stɑːnɪʃ] étonner; astonishing étonnant; astonishment étonnement *m*

astound [ə'staʊnd] stupéfier

astride [ə'straɪd] à califourchon sur

astrology [ə'strɑːlədʒɪ] astrologie *f*

astronaut ['æstrənɔːt] astronaute *m/f*

astronomer [əˈstrɒnəmər] astronome *m/f*; astronomical *price etc* astronomique; astronomy astronomie *f*

astute [əˈstuːt] fin

asylum [əˈsaɪləm] *political,* (*mental* ~) asile *m*

at [æt] *with places* à; ~ *Joe's* chez Joe; ~ *10 dollars* au prix de 10 dollars; ~ *the age of 18* à l'âge de 18 ans; ~ *5 o'clock* à 5 heures; *be good/bad* ~ ... être bon/mauvais en ...

atheist [ˈeɪθɪɪst] athée *m/f*

athlete [ˈæθliːt] athlète *m/f*; athletic [æθˈletɪk] d'athlétisme; (*strong, sporting*) sportif; athletics athlétisme *m*

Atlantic [ətˈlæntɪk]: *the* ~ l'Atlantique *m*

atlas [ˈætləs] atlas *m*

ATM [eɪtiːˈem](= *automatic teller machine*) distributeur *m* automatique (de billets)

atmosphere [ˈætməsfɪr] atmosphère *f*

atom [ˈætəm] atome *m*; atomic atomique

◆ atone for [əˈtoʊn] racheter

atrocious [əˈtroʊʃəs] atroce; atrocity atrocité *f*

at-'seat TV télévision que l'on regarde à sa place, par exemple en avion

attach [əˈtætʃ] attacher; attachment *to* e-mail fichier *m* joint

attack [əˈtæk] **1** *n* attaque *f* **2** *v/t* attaquer

attempt [əˈtempt] **1** *n* tentative *f* **2** *v/t* essayer

attend [əˈtend] assister à; *school* aller à

◆ attend to s'occuper de

attendance [əˈtendəns] présence *f*; attendant *in museum etc* gardien(ne) *m(f)*

attention [əˈtenʃn] attention *f*; *pay* ~ faire attention; attentive attentif

attic [ˈætɪk] grenier *m*

attitude [ˈætɪtuːd] attitude *f*

attorney [əˈtɜːrnɪ] avocat *m*

attract [əˈtrækt] attirer; attraction *of job, doing sth* attrait *m*; *romantic* attirance *f*; *touristic* attraction *f*; attractive *person* attirant; *idea, city* attrayant

auction [ˈɔːkʃn] vente *f* aux enchères

audacity [ɔːˈdæsətɪ] audace *f*

audible [ˈɔːdəbl] audible

audience [ˈɔːdɪəns] public *m*

audio [ˈɔːdɪoʊ] audio; audiovisual audiovisuel

audit [ˈɔːdɪt] **1** *n* audit *m* **2** *v/t* contrôler; *course* suivre en auditeur libre

audition [ɔːˈdɪʃn] **1** *n* audition *f* **2** *v/i* passer une audition

auditor [ˈɔːdɪtər] fin auditeur(-trice) *m(f)*

auditorium [ɔːdɪˈtɔːrɪəm] *of theater etc* auditorium *m*

August [ˈɔːgəst] août

aunt [ænt] tante *f*

au pair [oʊˈper] jeune fille *f* au pair

aura ['ɔːrə] aura *f*

auspicious [ɔː'spɪʃəs] favorable

austere [ɔː'stɪər] austère; **austerity** austérité *f*

Australia [ɒ'streɪljə] Australie *f*; **Australian 1** *adj* australien **2** *n* Australien(ne) *m(f)*

Austria [ˈɒːstrɪə] Autriche *f*; **Austrian 1** *adj* autrichien **2** *n* Autrichien(ne) *m(f)*

authentic [ɔː'θentɪk] authentique; **authenticity** authenticité *f*

author ['ɔːtər] auteur *m*

authoritarian [əθɑːrɪˈteːrɪən] autoritaire; **authoritative** *source* qui fait autorité; *person, manner* autoritaire; **authority** [əˈθɑːrəti] autorité *f*; (*permission*) autorisation *f*; **authorization** autorisation *f*; **authorize** autoriser

autistic [ɔː'tɪstɪk] autiste

autobiography [ɒːtəbɑːˈɡrəfi] autobiographie *f*

autocratic [ɒːtəˈkrætɪk] autocratique

autograph ['ɔːtəɡræf] autographe *m*

automate ['ɔːtəmeɪt] automatiser; **automatic 1** *adj* automatique **2** *n* car automatique *f*; gun automatique *m*; **automatically** automatiquement; **automation** automatisation *f*

automobile ['ɔːtəmoubiːl] automobile *f*; **automobile**

industry industrie *f* automobile

autonomous [ɔː'tɑːnəməs] autonome

autopilot ['ɔːtoupaɪlət] pilotage *m* automatique

autopsy ['ɔːtɑːpsi] autopsie *f*

autumn ['ɔːtəm] *Br* automne *m*

auxiliary [ɔːɡ'zɪljəri] auxiliaire

available [əˈveɪləbl] disponible

avalanche ['ævəlænʃ] avalanche *f*

avenue ['ævənuː] avenue *f*; **explore all ~s** explorer toutes les possibilités

average ['ævərɪdʒ] **1** *adj* moyen **2** *n* moyenne *f*; **on ~** en moyenne

◆ **average out at** faire une moyenne de

averse [əˈvɜːrs]: **not be ~ to** ne rien avoir contre; **aversion** aversion *f* (**to** pour)

avid ['ævɪd] avide

avocado [ɑːvəˈkɑːdou] avocat *m*

avoid [ə'vɔɪd] éviter

await [ə'weɪt] attendre

awake [əˈweɪk] éveillé; **it's keeping me ~** ça m'empêche de dormir

award [ə'wɔːrd] **1** *n* (*prize*) prix *m* **2** *v/t* décerner; *damages* attribuer; **awards** ceremony cérémonie *f* de remise des prix; EDU cérémonie *f* de remise des diplômes aware [ə'wer]: **be ~ of sth** avoir conscience de qch; **become ~ of sth** prendre conscience de qch; **awareness** conscience f

away [ə'wer]: **be~** être absent, ne pas être là; **walk~** s'en aller; **look ~** tourner la tête; **it's 2 miles ~** c'est à 2 miles d'ici; **take sth ~ from s.o.** enlever qch à qn; **away game** SP match m à l'extérieur

awesome ['ɒːsəm] F (*terrific*) super *inv*

awful ['ɒːfəl] affreux

awkward ['ɒːkwərd] (*clumsy*) maladroit; (*difficult*) difficile; (*embarrassing*) gênant; **feel ~** se sentir mal à l'aise

ax, Br **axe** [æks] **1** n hache f **2** v/t *project* abandonner; *budget* faire des coupures dans; *job* supprimer

axle ['æksl] essieu m

B

baby ['beɪbɪ] bébé m; **baby-sit** faire du baby-sitting

bachelor ['bætʃələr] célibataire m

back [bæk] **1** n of person, clothes dos m; of chair dossier m; of drawer fond m; of house arrière m; SP arrière m; **in ~ (of the car)** à l'arrière (de la voiture); **at the~ of the book** à la fin du livre; **~ to front** à l'envers **2** adj door de derrière; wheels, legs arrière inv **3** adv: **move~** se reculer; **give sth ~to s.o.** rendre qch à qn; **she'll be ~ tomorrow** elle sera de retour demain **4** v/t (*support*) soutenir; car faire reculer; horse miser sur

◆ **back down** faire marche arrière

◆ **back out** of commitment se

dégager

◆ **back up 1** v/t (*support*) soutenir; file sauvegarder **2** v/i in car reculer

'**backache** mal m de dos; **backbone** colonne f vertébrale; **backdate** antidater; **backdoor** porte f arrière; **backer** bailleur m de fonds; for artist, show producteur (-trice) m(f); **background** of picture arrière-plan m; social milieu m; of crime contexte m; **his work~** son expérience professionnelle; **backhand** in tennis revers m; **backing** (*support*) soutien m; MUS accompagnement m; **backing group** groupe m d'accompagnement; **backlash** répercussion(s) f(pl); **backlog** retard m (**of** dans); **backpack** sac m à dos; **back-**

packer randonneur(-euse) *m(f)*; **back seat** siège *m* arrière; **back streets** petites rues *fpl*; *poor area* quartiers *mpl* pauvres; **backstroke** SP dos *m* crawlé; **backtrack** retourner sur ses pas; **backup** (*support*) renfort *m*; COMPUT copie *f* de sauvegarde; **backyard** arrière-cour *f*

bacon ['beɪkn] bacon *m*

bacteria [bæk'tɪrɪə] bactéries *fpl*

bad [bæd] mauvais; *person* méchant; (*rotten*) avarié; *go ~* s'avarier; *it's not ~* c'est pas mal; *that's really too ~* (*shame*) c'est vraiment dommage

badge [bædʒ] insigne *f*

bad 'language grossièretés *fpl*; **badly** mal; *injured* grièvement; *damaged* sérieusement; *he ~ needs ...* il a grand besoin de ...

badminton ['bædmɪntən] badminton *m*

bad-tempered [bæd'tempərd] de mauvaise humeur

baffle ['bæfl] déconcerter; *be ~d* être perplexe

bag [bæg] sac *m*; (*piece of baggage*) bagage *m*

baggage ['bægɪdʒ] bagages *mpl*; **baggage check** contrôle *m* des bagages

baggy ['bægɪ] flottant; *fashionably* large

bail [beɪl] LAW caution *f*; *be*

out on ~ être en liberté provisoire sous caution

bait [beɪt] appât *m*

bake [beɪk] cuire au four; **baked potato** pomme *f* de terre au four; **baker** boulanger(-ère) *m(f)*; **bakery** boulangerie *f*

balance ['bæləns] **1** *n* équilibre *m*; (*remainder*) reste *m*; *of bank account* solde *m* **2** *v/t* mettre en équilibre **3** *v/i* rester en équilibre; *of accounts* équilibrer; **balanced** (*fair*) objectif; *diet, personality* équilibré; **balance sheet** bilan *m*

balcony ['bælkənɪ] balcon *m*

bald [bɔːld] chauve; **balding** qui commence à devenir chauve

ball [bɔːl] *for soccer etc* ballon *m*; *for tennis, golf* balle *f*

ballad ['bæləd] ballade *f*

ballet [bæ'leɪ] ballet *m*; **ballet dancer** danseur(-euse) *m(f)* de ballet

'ball game match *m* de baseball

ballistic missile [bə'lɪstɪk] missile *m* balistique

balloon [bə'luːn] *child's* ballon *m*; *for flight* montgolfière *f*

ballot ['bælət] **1** *n* vote *m* **2** *v/t members* faire voter; **ballot box** urne *f*

'ballpark terrain *m* de baseball; **ballpark figure** chiffre *m* en gros; **ballpoint (pen)**

stylo *m* bille
balls [bɔːlz] V couilles *fpl*
bamboo [bæm'buː] bambou *m*
ban [bæn] **1** *n* interdiction *f* **2** *v/t* interdire
banal [bə'næl] banal
banana [bə'nænə] banane *f*
band [bænd] MUS orchestre *m*; *pop* groupe *m*; *of material* bande *f*
bandage ['bændɪdʒ] **1** *n* bandage *m* **2** *v/t* faire un bandage à
'Band-Aid® sparadrap *m*
bandit ['bændɪt] bandit *m*
bandy ['bændɪ] *legs* arqué
bang [bæŋ] **1** *n noise* boum *m*; (*blow*) coup *m* **2** *v/t door* claquer; (*hit*) cogner
bangle ['bæŋgl] bracelet *m*
bangs [bæŋz] frange *f*
banisters ['bænɪstərz] rampe *f*
banjo ['bændʒoʊ] banjo *m*
bank¹ [bæŋk] *of river* bord *m*, rive *f*
bank² [bæŋk] FIN banque *f*
◆ **bank on** compter sur
'bank account compte *m* en banque; **banker** banquier (-ière) *m(f)*; **banker's card** carte *f* d'identité bancaire; **banking** banque *f*; **bank loan** emprunt *m* bancaire; **bank manager2** directeur (-trice) *m(f)* de banque; **bank rate** taux *m* bancaire; **bankroll** financer; **bankrupt** en faillite; **go ~** faire faillite;

bankruptcy faillite *f*
banner ['bænər] bannière *f*
banquet ['bæŋkwɪt] banquet *m*
baptism ['bæptɪzm] baptême *m*; **baptize** baptiser
bar¹ [bɑːr] *n of iron, chocolate* barre *f*; *for drinks, counter* bar *m*
bar² [bɑːr] *v/t* exclure
barbaric [bɑːr'bærɪk] barbare
barbarism ['bɑːrbərɪkjuː] **1** *n* barbecue *m* **2** *v/t* cuire au barbecue
barbed 'wire [bɑːrbd] fil *m* barbelé
barber ['bɑːrbər] coiffeur *m*
'bar code code *m* barre
bare [ber] nu; *room, shelves* vide; **barefoot**: **be ~** être pieds nus; **bare-headed** tête nue; **barely** à peine
bargain ['bɑːrgɪn] **1** *n* (*deal*) marché *m*; (*good buy*) bonne affaire *f* **2** *v/i* marchander
barge [bɑːrdʒ] NAUT péniche *f*
◆ **barge into** se heurter contre; (*enter noisily*) faire irruption dans
baritone ['bærɪtoʊn] baryton *m*
bark¹ [bɑːrk] **1** *n of dog* aboiement *m* **2** *v/i* aboyer
bark² [bɑːrk] *of tree* écorce *f*
barn [bɑːrn] grange *f*
barometer [bə'rɑːmɪtər] *also fig* baromètre *m*
barracks ['bærəks] MIL caserne *f*
barrel ['bærəl] tonneau *m*

barren

barren ['bærən] *land* stérile
barrette [bə'ret] barrette *f*
barricade [bærɪ'keɪd] barricade *f*
barrier ['bærɪər] barrière *f*
'bar tender barman *m*, barmaid *f*
barter ['bɑːrtər] **1** *n* troc *m* **2** *v/t* troquer (**for** contre)
base [beɪs] **1** *n* base *f* **2** *v/t* baser (**on** sur); baseball baseball *m*; *ball* ballon *m* de baseball; baseball cap casquette *f* de baseball; baseboard plinthe *f*; basement sous-sol *m*
basic ['beɪsɪk] (*rudimentary*) rudimentaire; (*fundamental*), *salary* de base; basically au fond
basin ['beɪsn] *for washing dishes* bassine *f*; *in bathroom* lavabo *m*
basis ['beɪsɪs] base *f*; *of argument* fondement *m*
bask [bæsk] se dorer
basket ['bæskɪt] panier *m*; basketball *game* basket (-ball) *m*; *ball* ballon *m* de basket
bass [beɪs] basse *f*; *double ~* contrebasse *f*; *~ guitar* basse *f*
bastard ['bæstərd] salaud(e) *m(f)*
bat¹ [bæt] **1** *n for baseball* batte *f*; *for table tennis* raquette *f* **2** *v/i in baseball* batter
bat² [bæt] *animal* chauve-souris *f*

batch [bætʃ] *of students, data* lot *m*; *of bread* fournée *f*
bath [bæθ] (*~tub*) baignoire *f*
bathe [beɪð] (*have a bath*) se baigner
'bathrobe peignoir *m*; bathroom salle *f* de bains; *toilet* toilettes *fpl*; bath towel serviette *f* de bains; bathtub baignoire *f*
batter ['bætər] *for cakes, pancakes etc* pâte *f* lisse; *in baseball* batteur *m*; *battered wife, children* battu
battery ['bætərɪ] pile *f*, MOT batterie *f*
battle ['bætl] **1** *n* bataille *f*; *fig* lutte *f* **2** *v/i against illness etc* se battre, lutter; battleship cuirassé *m*
bawl [bɔːl] (*shout, weep*) brailler
bay [beɪ] (*inlet*) baie *f*
BC [biː'siː] (= *before Christ*) av. J.-C.
be [biː] ◇ être; *~ 15* avoir 15 ans; *it's me* c'est moi; *how much is...?* combien coûte ...?; *there is/are* il y a; *how are you?* comment ça va? ◇ *has the mailman been?* est-ce que le facteur est passé?; *I've never been to Japan* je ne suis jamais allé au Japon ◇ *tags: that's right, isn't it?* c'est juste, n'est-ce pas?; *she's American, isn't she?* elle est américaine, n'est-ce pas?

285   behavior

◇ *passive*: *he was killed* il a
été tué; *it hasn't been decid-
ed* on n'a encore rien décidé
beach [biːtʃ] plage *f*; beach-
wear vêtements *mpl* de plage
beads [biːdz] collier *m* de perles
beak [biːk] bec *m*
beam [biːm] **1** *n in ceiling etc*
poutre *f* **2** *v/i (smile)* rayonner
bean [biːn] haricot *m*; *of coffee* grain *m*
bear¹ [ber] *n animal* ours *m*
bear² [ber] **1** *v/t weight* porter;
costs prendre en charge; *(tolerate)* supporter; bearable
supportable
beard [bɪrd] barbe *f*
beat [biːt] **1** *n of heart* battement *m*; *of music* mesure *f*
2 *v/i of heart* battre; *of rain*
s'abattre **3** *v/t in competition,
(hit)* battre; *(pound)* frapper
◆ beat up tabasser
beaten ['biːtən]: *off the ~
track* à l'écart; beating *physical* raclée *f*; beat-up déglin-
gué
beautiful ['bjuːtəfʊl] beau;
beautifully admirablement;
beauty beauté *f*
beaver ['biːvər] castor *m*
because [bɪ'kɑːz] parce que;
~ of à cause de
become [bɪ'kʌm] devenir;
what's ~? qu'est-elle
devenue?; becoming seyant
bed [bed] *also of sea* lit *m*; *of*

flowers parterre *m*; *go to ~*
aller se coucher; bedding literie *f*; bedridden cloué au
lit; bedroom chambre *f* (à
coucher); bedtime heure *f*
du coucher
bee [biː] abeille *f*
beech [biːtʃ] hêtre *m*
beef [biːf] bœuf *m*; beefbur-
ger steak *m* hâché
beep [biːp] **1** *n* bip *m* **2** *v/i* faire
bip
beer [bɪr] bière *f*
beet [biːt] betterave *f*
beetle ['biːtl] coléoptère *m*,
cafard *m*
before [bɪ'foːr] **1** *prep* avant; *~
signing it* avant de le signer;
~ a vowel devant une voyelle
2 *adv* auparavant; *(already)*
déjà; *the week/day ~* la se-
maine/le jour d'avant **3** *conj*
avant que (*+subj*); *I had a
coffee ~ I left* j'ai pris un café
avant de partir; beforehand
à l'avance
befriend [bɪ'frend] se lier
d'amitié avec
beg [beg] **1** *v/i* mendier **2** *v/t*: *~
s.o. to do sth* prier qn de fai-
re qch; beggar mendiant (e)
m (f)
begin [bɪ'gɪn] **1** *v/i* commencer; beginner débutant(e)
m(f); beginning début *m*
behalf [bɪ'hɑːf]: *in or on ~ of*
de la part de
behave [bɪ'heɪv] se comporter; *~ (yourself)!* sois sage!;
behavior, *Br* behaviour

comportement m

behind [bɪˈhaɪnd] **1** prep derrière; **be ~ ...** (responsible for, support) être derrière ... **2** adv (at the back) à l'arrière; leave, stay derrière; **be ~ in match** être derrière

beige [beɪʒ] beige

being [ˈbiːɪŋ] (creature) être m; (existence) existence f

belated [bɪˈleɪtɪd] tardif

belch [beltʃ] **1** n éructation f, rot m **2** v/i éructer, roter

Belgian [ˈbeldʒən] **1** adj belge **2** n Belge m/f; **Belgium** Belgique f

belief [bɪˈliːf] conviction f; REL also croyance f; in person foi f (**in** en); **believe** croire

◆ **believe in** God, person croire en; sth croire à; cacher la vérité aux gens

believer [bɪˈliːvər] in God croyant(e) m(f); in sth partisan(e) m(f) (**in** de)

bell [bel] on bike, door sonnette f; in church cloche f; in school: electric sonnerie f; **bellhop** groom m

belligerent [bɪˈlɪdʒərənt] belligérant

bellow [ˈbeloʊ] brailler; of bull beugler

belly [ˈbeli] of person ventre m; fat bedaine f; of animal panse f

◆ **belong to** of object appartenir à; club, organization faire partie de

belongings [bɪˈlɒːŋɪŋz] affai-

res fpl

beloved [bɪˈlʌvɪd] bien-aimé

below [bɪˈloʊ] **1** prep au-dessous de **2** adv en bas, au-dessous; in text en bas; **10 degrees ~** moins dix

belt [belt] ceinture f

'benchmark référence f

bend [bend] **1** n tournant m **2** v/t head baisser; arm, knees plier; metal, plastic tordre **3** v/i of road tourner; of person se pencher

◆ **bend down** se pencher

beneath [bɪˈniːθ] **1** prep sous **2** adv (au-)dessous

benefactor [ˈbenɪfæktər] bienfaiteur(-trice) m(f)

beneficial [benɪˈfɪʃl] bénéfique

benefit [ˈbenɪfɪt] **1** n bénéfice m **2** v/t bénéficier à **3** v/i bénéficier (**from** de)

benevolent [bɪˈnevələnt] bienveillant

benign [bɪˈnaɪn] doux; MED bénin

bequeath [bɪˈkwiːð] léguer; **bequest** legs m

beret [ˈbeɪeɪ] béret m

berry [ˈberi] baie f

berth [bɜːrθ] couchette f; for ship mouillage m

beside [bɪˈsaɪd] à côté de; **be ~ o.s.** être hors de soi; **that's ~ the point** c'est hors de propos

besides [bɪˈsaɪdz] **1** adv d'ailleurs **2** prep (apart from) à part

best [best] **1** adj meilleur **2** adv le mieux; *I like her ~* c'est elle que j'aime le plus **3** n: *do one's ~* faire de son mieux; *the ~* le mieux; *the ~* (outstanding thing or person) le (la) meilleur(e) m(f); *all the ~!* meilleurs vœux!; **best before date** date f limite de consommation; **best man** at wedding garçon m d'honneur

bet [bet] **1** n pari m & v/t & v/i parier; *you ~!* évidemment!

betray [bɪ'treɪ] trahir; **betrayal** trahison f

better ['betər] **1** adj meilleur; *get ~* s'améliorer; *he's ~ in health* il va mieux **2** adv mieux; *I'd really ~not* je ne devrais vraiment pas; *I like her ~* je l'aime plus; **better-off** (richer) plus aisé

between [bɪ'twiːn] entre

beware [bɪ'wer]: *~ of* attention à

bewilder [bɪ'wɪldər] confondre; **bewilderment** confusion f

beyond [bɪ'jɑːnd] au-delà de

bias ['baɪəs] parti m pris, préjugé m; **bias(s)ed** partial, subjectif

Bible ['baɪbl] Bible f; **biblical** biblique

bicentennial [baɪsen'teniəl] bicentenaire m

bicker ['bɪkər] se chamailler

bicycle ['baɪsɪkl] bicyclette f

bid [bɪd] **1** n at auction enchè-

re m; (attempt) tentative f; in takeover offre f **2** v/i at auction faire une enchère; **bidder** enchérisseur(-euse) m(f)

biennial [baɪ'enɪəl] biennal

big [bɪg] **1** adj grand; sum of money, mistake gros; *my ~ brother/sister* mon grand frère/ma grande sœur **2** adv: *talk ~* se vanter

bigamist ['bɪgəmɪst] bigame m/f

'bighead crâneur(-euse) m(f)

bigot ['bɪgət] fanatique m/f, sectaire m/f

bike [baɪk] vélo m; (motorbike) moto f; **biker** ['baɪkər] motard(e) m(f)

bikini [bɪ'kiːnɪ] bikini m

bilingual [baɪ'lɪŋgwəl] bilingue

bill [bɪl] facture f; money billet m (de banque); POL projet m de loi; (poster) affiche f; **billboard** panneau m d'affichage; **billfold** portefeuille m

billion ['bɪljən] milliard m

bin [bɪn] for storage boîte f

bind [baɪnd] (connect) unir; (tie) attacher; LAW (oblige) obliger; **binding** agreement obligatoire

binoculars [bɪ'nɑːkjʊlərz] jumelles fpl

biodegradable [baɪoʊdɪ'greɪdəbl] biodégradable

biographer [baɪ'ɑːgrəfər] biographe m/f; **biography** biographie f

biological [baɪoʊ'lɑːdʒɪkl]

biologique; **biology** biologie
f
bird [bɜːrd] oiseau m
biro® ['baɪrou] Br stylo m bille
birth [bɜːrθ] naissance f; (labor) accouchement m; **give
~ to** child donner naissance
à; **date of ~** date f de naissance; **birth certificate** acte m
de naissance; **birth control**
contrôle m des naissances;
birthday anniversaire m
happy ~! bon anniversaire!
biscuit ['bɪskɪt] biscuit m
bisexual ['baɪseksjʊəl] **1** adj
bisexuel **2** n bisexuel(le)
m(f)
bishop ['bɪʃəp] évêque m
bit [bɪt] (piece) morceau m;
(part: of book) passage m;
(part: of garden, road) partie
f; COMPUT bit m; **a ~ of** (a little) un peu de
bitch [bɪtʃ] **1** n dog chienne f;
F: woman garce f **2** v/i F
(complain) rouspéter
bite [baɪt] **1** n of dog, snake
morsure f; of flea, mosquito
piqûre f; of food morceau
m **2** v/t & v/i of dog, snake,
person mordre; of flea, mosquito piquer
bitter ['bɪtər] taste, person
amer
black [blæk] **1** adj noir; tea nature; future sombre **2** n color
noir m; person Noir(e) m(f)
♦ **black out** (faint) s'évanouir
'**blackboard** tableau m noir;

black coffee café m noir;
black economy économie f
souterraine; **black eye** œil
m poché; **blacklist** liste f noire; **blackmail 1** n chantage m
2 v/t faire chanter; **black
market** marché m noir;
blackness noirceur f; **black-
out** ELEC panne f d'électricité; MED évanouissement m
bladder ['blædər] vessie f
blade [bleɪd] of knife lame f;
of propeller ailette f; of grass
brin m
blame [bleɪm] **1** n responsabilité f **2** v/t: **~ s.o. for sth** reprocher qch à qn
bland [blænd] fade
blank [blæŋk] **1** adj paper, tape
vierge; look vide **2** n (empty
space) espace m vide; blank
check, Br blank cheque
chèque m en blanc
blanket ['blæŋkɪt] couverture
f
blast [blæst] **1** n (explosion)
explosion f; (gust) rafale f **2**
v/t tunnel etc percer (à l'aide
d'explosifs); **~!** mince!; **blast-
-off** lancement m
blatant ['bleɪtənt] flagrant;
person éhonté
blaze [bleɪz] **1** n (fire) incendie m **2** v/i of fire flamber
blazer ['bleɪzər] blazer m
bleach [bliːtʃ] **1** n for clothes
eau f de Javel; for hair déco-
lorant m **2** v/t hair décolorer
bleak [bliːk] countryside désolé; weather morne; future

sombre

bleary-eyed ['blɪrɪaɪd] aux yeux troubles

bleat [bliːt] *of sheep* bêler

bleed [bliːd] saigner; **bleeding** saignement *m*

bleep [bliːp] **1** *n* bip *m* **2** *v/i* faire bip

blemish ['blemɪʃ] tache *f*

blend [blend] **1** *n* mélange *m* **2** *v/t* mélanger; **blender** *machine* mixeur *m*

bless [bles] bénir; **~ you!** *in response to sneeze* à vos souhaits!; **blessing** bénédiction *f*

blind [blaɪnd] **1** *adj* aveugle; **~ corner** virage *m* masqué **2** *v/t of sun* aveugler; **blind alley** impasse *f*; **blind date** rendez-vous *m* arrangé; **blindfold 1** *n* bandeau *m* sur les yeux **2** *v/t* bander les yeux à; **blinding** *light* aveuglant; *headache* terrible; **blindly** sans rien voir; *fig* aveuglément; **blind spot** *in road* angle *m* mort

blink [blɪŋk] *of person* cligner des yeux; *of light* clignoter

blizzard ['blɪzərd] tempête *f* de neige

bloc [blɑːk] POL bloc *m*

block [blɑːk] **1** *n* bloc *m*; *buildings* pâté *m* de maisons; *(blockage)* obstruction *f* *m*; **it's three ~s away** c'est à trois rues d'ici **2** *v/t* bloquer; **blockage** obstruction *f*; **blockbuster** *movie* film *m*

à grand succès; *novel* roman *m* à succès; **block letters** capitales *fpl*

blond [blɑːnd] blond; **blonde** *woman* blonde *f*

blood [blʌd] sang *m*; **blood donor** donneur(-euse) *m(f)* de sang; **blood group** groupe *m* sanguin

'**blood poisoning** empoisonnement *m* du sang; **blood pressure** tension *f* (artérielle); **blood sample** prélèvement *m* sanguin; **bloodshed** carnage *m*; **without ~** sans effusion de sang; **bloodshot** injecté de sang; **bloodstained** taché de sang; **blood test** test *m* sanguin; **bloodthirsty** sanguinaire

bloom [bluːm] *also fig* fleurir

blossom ['blɑːsəm] **1** *n* fleur *f* **2** *v/i* fleurir; *fig* s'épanouir

blot [blɑːt] tache *f*

◆ **blot out** effacer

blouse [blauz] chemisier *m*

blow[1] [bloʊ] *n also fig* coup *m*

blow[2] [bloʊ] **1** *v/t* souffler; **~ one's whistle** donner un coup de sifflet **2** *v/i of wind, person* souffler; *of whistle* retentir; *of fuse* sauter; *of tire* éclater

◆ **blow out 1** *v/t candle* souffler **2** *v/i of candle* s'éteindre

◆ **blow over 1** *v/t* renverser **2** *v/i* se renverser; *(pass)* passer

◆ **blow up 1** *v/t with explosives* faire sauter; *balloon* gonfler; *photograph* agrandir **2** v/i of boiler etc sauter, exploser

'**blow-dry** sécher (au sèche--cheveux); **blow-out** of tire éclatement m

blue [bluː] bleu; movie porno; **blueberry** myrtille f; **blue chip** de premier ordre; **blues** MUS blues m; **have the ~** avoir le cafard

bluff [blʌf] **1** n (deception) bluff m **2** v/i bluffer

blunder ['blʌndər] **1** n gaffe f **2** v/i faire une gaffe

blunt [blʌnt] émoussé; person franc; **bluntly** franchement

blur [blɜːr] **1** n masse f confuse **2** v/t brouiller

◆ **blurt out** [blɜːrt] lâcher

blush [blʌʃ] **1** n rougissement m **2** v/i rougir; **blusher** cosmetic rouge m

blustery ['blʌstəri] à bourrasques

BO [biː'ou] (= **body odor**) odeur f corporelle

board [bɔːrd] **1** n of wood planche f; cardboard carton m; for game plateau m de jeu; for notices panneau m; **~ (of directors)** conseil m d'administration; **on ~** à bord **2** v/t plane, ship monter à bord de; train, bus monter dans **3** v/i of passengers embarquer; on train, bus monter (à bord)

◆ **board up** windows condamner

boarder ['bɔːrdər] pension-

naire m/f; EDU interne m/f; **board game** jeu m de société; **boarding card** carte f d'embarquement; **boarding school** internat m, pensionnat m; **board meeting** réunion f du conseil d'administration; **board room** salle f du conseil

boast [boust] se vanter (**about** de)

boat [bout] bateau m; small, for leisure canot m

bodily ['bɑːdɪlɪ] **1** adj corporel **2** adv: **they ~ ejected him** ils l'ont saisi à bras-le-corps et l'ont mis dehors **body** corps m; dead cadavre m; **bodyguard** garde m du corps; **bodywork** MOT carrosserie f

bogus ['bougəs] faux

boil[1] [bɔɪl] n (swelling) furoncle m

boil[2] [bɔɪl] **1** v/t faire bouillir **2** v/i bouillir

◆ **boil down to** se ramener à

boiler ['bɔɪlər] chaudière f **boisterous** ['bɔɪstərəs] bruyant

bold [bould] **1** adj courageux; text en caractères gras **2** n print caractères mpl gras

bolster ['boulstər] confidence soutenir

bolt [boult] **1** n (metal pin) boulon m; on door verrou m **2** adv: **~ upright** tout droit **3** v/t (fix with bolts) boulonner; close verrouiller **4** v/i (run off) décamper; of horse s'emballer

bomb [bɑːm] **1** *n* bombe *f* **2** *v/t*
MIL. bombarder; *of terrorist*
faire sauter; **bombard**
[bɑːm'bɑːrd] *also fig* bombarder; **bomb attack** attaque
f à la bombe; **bomber** *airplane* bombardier *m*; *terrorist* poseur *m(f)* de bombes;
bomb scare alerte *f* à la
bombe; **bombshell: come
as a ~** faire l'effet d'une
bombe

bond [bɑːnd] **1** *n (tie)* lien *m*;
FIN obligation *f* **2** *v/i of glue*
se coller

bone [boʊn] os *m*; *in fish* arête
f

bonnet ['bɑːnɪt] *Br of car* capot *m*

bonus ['boʊnəs] *money* prime *f*; *(something extra)* plus
m

boob [buːb] P *(breast)* nichon
m

booboo ['buːbuː] F bêtise *f*

book [bʊk] **1** *n* livre *m* **2** *v/t
seat* réserver; *ticket* prendre;
of policeman donner un P.V.
à; **bookcase** bibliothèque *f*;
booked up complet; *perso*
complètement pris; **bookie**
F bookmaker *m*; **booking** réservation *f*; **bookkeeper**
comptable *m*

'**bookkeeping** comptabilité *f*;
booklet livret *m*; **bookmaker** bookmaker *m*; **books** *(accounts)* comptes *mpl*; **book-
seller** libraire *m/f*; **book-**

store librairie *f*

boom[1] [buːm] **1** *n* boum *m* **2**
v/i of business aller très fort

boom[2] [buːm] *n noise* boum
m

boost [buːst] **1** *n*: **give sth a ~**
stimuler qc **2** *v/t* stimuler

boot [buːt] botte *f*; *for climbing, football* chaussure *f*

◆ **boot up** COMPUT **1** *v/i* démarrer **2** *v/t* faire démarrer

booth [buːð] *at market* tente *f*
(de marché); *at fair* baraque
f; *at trade fair* stand *m*; *in restaurant* alcôve *f*

booze [buːz] boisson *f* (alcoolique)

border ['bɔːrdər] **1** *n* frontière
f; *(edge)* bordure *f* **2** *v/t country* avoir une frontière avec

◆ **border on** avoir une frontière avec; *(be almost)* friser

bore[1] [bɔːr] *v/t hole* percer

bore[2] [bɔːr] **1** *n person* ra-
seur(-euse) *m(f)* **2** *v/t* ennuyer

bored [bɔːrd] ennuyé; **be ~**
s'ennuyer; **boredom** ennui
m; **boring** ennuyeux, chiant

born [bɔːrn]: **be ~** être né

borrow ['bɑːroʊ] emprunter

bosom ['bʊzm] poitrine *f*

boss [bɑːs] patron(-onne)
m(f)

◆ **boss around** donner des
ordres à

bossy ['bɑːsɪ] autoritaire

botanical [bə'tænɪkl] botanique

botch [bɑːtʃ] bâcler

both [bəυθ] **1** *adj & pron* les deux; **~ of them** tous(-tes) *m(f)* les deux **2** *adv:* **~ ... and ...** à la fois ... et ...

bother ['bɒðər] **1** *n* problèmes *mpl* **2** *v/t* (*disturb*) déranger; (*worry*) ennuyer **3** *v/i* s'inquiéter (**with** de)

bottle ['bɒtl] bouteille *f*; *for medicines* flacon *m*; *for baby* biberon *m*

♦ **bottle up** *feelings* réprimer

'**bottle bank** conteneur *m* à verre; **bottled water** eau *f* en bouteille; **bottleneck** rétrécissement *m*; *in production* goulet *m* d'étranglement; **bottle-opener** ouvre-bouteilles *m inv*

bottom ['bɒtəm] **1** *adj* du bas **2** *n of drawer, pan, garden* fond *m*; (*underside*) dessous *m*; (*lowest part*) bas *m*; *of street* bout *m*; (*buttocks*) derrière *m*

♦ **bottom out** se stabiliser

bottom 'line *financial* résultat *m*; (*real issue*) la question principale

boulder ['bəυldər] rocher *m*

bounce [baυns] **1** *v/t ball* faire rebondir **2** *v/i of ball* rebondir; *on sofa etc* sauter; *of check* être refusé; **bouncer** videur *m*

bound[^1] [baυnd] *adj:* **be ~ to do sth** (*sure to*) aller forcément faire qch

bound[^2] [baυnd] *adj:* **be ~ for** *of ship* être à destination de

bound[^3] [baυnd] *n* (*jump*) bond *m*

boundary ['baυndərɪ] frontière *f*

bouquet [bυ'keɪ] bouquet *m*

bourbon ['bɜːrbən] bourbon *m*

bout [baυt] MED accès *m*; *in boxing* match *m*

bow[^1] [baυ] **1** *n as greeting* révérence *f* **2** *v/i* faire une révérence **3** *v/t head* baisser

bow[^2] [bəυ] (*knot*) nœud *m*; MUS archet *m*; *for archery* arc *m*

bow[^3] [baυ] *of ship* avant *m*

bowels ['baυəlz] intestins *mpl*

bowl[^1] [bəυl] *n* bol *m*; *for soup etc* assiette *f* creuse; *for serving salad etc* saladier *m*; *for washing dishes* cuvette *f*

bowl[^2] [bəυl] *v/i* jouer au bowling

bowling ['bəυlɪŋ] bowling *m*; **bowling alley** bowling *m*

bow 'tie [bəυ] (nœud *m*) papillon *m*

box[^1] [bɒks] *n container* boîte *f*; *on form* case *f*

box[^2] [bɒks] *v/i* boxer

boxer ['bɒksər] boxeur *m*; **boxing** boxe *f*; **boxing glove** gant *m* de boxe; **boxing match** match *m* de boxe

box number boîte *f* postale; **box office** bureau *m* de location

boy [bɔɪ] garçon *m*; (*son*) fils *m*

boycott ['bɔɪkɑːt] **1** *n* boycott

m **2** *v/t* boycotter

'**boyfriend** petit ami *m*; *younger* copain *m*

bra [brɑː] soutien-gorge *m*

bracelet ['breɪslɪt] bracelet *m*

bracket ['brækɪt] *for shelf* support *m* (d'étagère)

brag [bræg] se vanter (*about* de)

braid [breɪd] *in hair* tresse *f*; *trimming* galon *m*

braille [breɪl] braille *m*

brain [breɪn] ANAT cerveau *m*; **brainless** écervelé; **brains** cerveau *m*; **brain surgeon** neurochirurgien(ne) *m(f)*; **brain tumor**, *Br* **brain tumour** tumeur *f* au cerveau; **brainwash** conditionner

brake [breɪk] **1** *n* frein *m* **2** *v/i* freiner

branch [bræntʃ] *of tree, company* branche *f*

brand [brænd] **1** *n* marque *f* **2** *v/t*: **be ~ed a liar** être étiqueté comme voleur; **brand image** image *f* de marque

brandish ['brændɪʃ] brandir

brand 'leader marque *f* dominante; **brand name** nom *m* de marque; **brand-new** flambant neuf

brandy ['brændɪ] brandy *m*

brassière [brəˈzɪr] soutien-gorge *m*

brat [bræt] garnement *m*

brave [breɪv] courageux; **bravery** courage *m*

brawl [brɔːl] **1** *n* bagarre *f* **2** *v/i* se bagarrer

Brazil [brəˈzɪl] Brésil *m*; **Brazilian 1** *adj* brésilien **2** *n* Brésilien(ne) *m(f)*

breach [briːtʃ] (*violation*) violation *f*; *in party* désaccord *m*; **breach of contract** rupture *f* de contrat

bread [bred] pain *m*

breadth [bredθ] largeur *m*; *of knowledge* étendue *f*

'**breadwinner** soutien *m* de famille

break [breɪk] **1** *n* fracture *f*; (*rest*) repos *m*; *in relationship* séparation *f* **2** *v/t* casser; *rules, law, promise* violer; *news* annoncer; *record* battre **3** *v/i* se casser; *of news, storm* éclater

◆ **break down** *v/i of vehicle, machine* tomber en panne; *of talks* échouer; *in tears* s'effondrer; *mentally* faire une dépression **2** *v/t door* défoncer; *figures* détailler

◆ **break even** rentrer dans ses frais

◆ **break in** (*interrupt*) interrompre qn; *of burglar* s'introduire par effraction

◆ **break up 1** *v/t into parts* décomposer; *fight* interrompre **2** *v/i of ice* se briser; *of couple, band* se séparer; *of meeting* se dissoudre

breakable ['breɪkəbl] cassable; **breakage** casse *f*; **breakdown** *of talks* échec *m*; (*nervous* ~) dépression *f* (nerveuse); *of figures* détail

m

breakfast ['brekfəst] petit déjeuner *m*; **have ~** prendre son petit déjeuner; **break-in** cambriolage *m*; **breakthrough** percée *f*; **breakup** *of partnership* échec *m*

breast [brest] *of woman* sein *m*; **breastfeed** allaiter; **breaststroke** brasse *f*

breath [breθ] souffle *m*; **out of ~** à bout de souffle

breathe [bri:ð] respirer
◆ **breathe in** inspirer
◆ **breathe out** expirer

breathing ['bri:ðɪŋ] respiration *f*

breathtaking ['breθteɪkɪŋ] à vous couper le souffle

breed [bri:d] **1** *n* race *f* **2** *v/t animals* élever; *plants, also fig* cultiver **3** *v/i of animals* se reproduire; **breeding** *of animals* élevage *m*; *of person* éducation *f*

breeze [bri:z] brise *f*; **breezy** venteux

brew [bru:] **1** *v/t beer* brasser **2** *v/i* couver; **brewery** brasserie *f*

bribe [braɪb] **1** *n* pot-de-vin *m* **2** *v/t* soudoyer; **bribery** corruption *f*

brick [brɪk] brique *m*

bride [braɪd] *about to be married* (future) mariée *f*; *married* jeune mariée *f*; **bridegroom** *about to be married* (futur) marié *m*; *married* jeune marié *m*; **bridesmaid** demoiselle *f* d'honneur

bridge [brɪdʒ] **1** *n* pont *m*; *of ship* passerelle *f* **2** *v/t gap* combler

bridle ['braɪdl] bride *f*

brief[1] [bri:f] *adj* bref, court

brief[2] [bri:f] **1** *n* (*mission*) instructions *fpl* **2** *v/t:* **~ s.o. on sth** (*give information*) informer qn de qch

briefcase serviette *f*; **briefing session** séance *f* d'information; *instructions* instructions *fpl*; **briefly** brièvement; (*to sum up*) en bref; **briefs** slip *m*

bright [braɪt] *color* vif; *smile* radieux; *future* brillant; (*sunny*) clair; (*intelligent*) intelligent; **brightly** *smile* d'un air radieux; *colored* vivement; **shine ~** resplendir

brilliance ['brɪljəns] *of person* esprit *m* lumineux; *of color* vivacité *f*; *brilliant sunshine etc* resplendissant; (*very good*) génial; (*very intelligent*) brillant

brim [brɪm] *of container, hat* bord *m*

bring [brɪŋ] *object* apporter; *person, peace* amener; *hope, happiness* donner
◆ **bring back** (*return*) ramener; (*re-introduce*) réintroduire; *it brought back memories of ... childhood* ça m'a rappelé ...
◆ **bring down** *also fig: government* faire tomber; *air-*

plane abattre; *price* faire
baisser
◆ **bring on** *illness* donner
◆ **bring out** *(produce)* sortir
◆ **bring up** *child* élever; *subject* soulever; *(vomit)* vomir
brink [brɪŋk] bord *m*
brisk [brɪsk] vif; *(businesslike)*
énergique; *trade* florissant
bristles ['brɪslz] *on chin* poils
mpl raides; *of brush* poils
mpl
Britain ['brɪtn] Grande-Bretagne; **British 1** *adj* britannique **2** *npl*: **the ~** les Britanniques
brittle ['brɪtl] fragile
broad [brɔːd] **1** *adj* large;
smile grand; *(general)* général; **in ~ daylight** en plein jour **2** *n* F gonzesse *f*; **broadcast 1** *n* émission *f* **2** *v/t*
transmettre; **broadcaster**
présentateur(-trice)   *m(f)*
(radio/télé); **broad jump**
saut *m* en longueur; **broadly:**
~ speaking en gros; **broad-minded** large d'esprit
broccoli ['brɑːkəlɪ] brocoli(s)
m(pl)
brochure ['brəʊʃər] brochure
f
broil [brɔɪl] griller; **broiler** *on
stove* grill *m*; *chicken* poulet
m à rôtir
broke [brəʊk] fauché; **broken**
cassé; *home* brisé; **broker**
courtier *m*
bronchitis   [brɑːŋ'kaɪtɪs]
bronchite *f*

bronze [brɑːnz] bronze *m*
brooch [brəʊtʃ] broche *f*
brothel ['brɑːθl] bordel *m*
brother ['brʌðər] frère *m*;
brother-in-law   beau-frère
m; **brotherly** fraternel
brow [braʊ] *(forehead)* front
m; *of hill* sommet *m*
brown [braʊn] **1** *adj* marron
inv; *(tanned)* bronzé **2** *n* marron *m*; **brownie** brownie *m*
brown paper 'bag sac *m* en
papier kraft
browse [braʊz] *in store* flâner; COMPUT surfer; **~
through a book** feuilleter
un livre; **browser** COMPUT navigateur *m*
bruise [bruːz] bleu *m*; *on fruit*
meurtrissure *f*
brunette [bruː'net] brune *f*
brush [brʌʃ] **1** *n* brosse *f*;
(conflict) accrochage *m* **2**
v/t brosser; *(touch lightly)* effleurer
◆ **brush aside** *person* mépriser; *remark, criticism* écarter
◆ **brush up** réviser
brusque [brʊsk] brusque
brutal ['bruːtl] brutal; **brutality** brutalité *f*; **brutally** brutalement; **brute** brute *f*
bubble ['bʌbl] bulle *f*
buck¹ [bʌk] *n* F *(dollar)* dollar
m
buck² [bʌk] *v/i of horse* ruer
bucket ['bʌkɪt] seau *m*
buckle¹ ['bʌkl] **1** *n* boucle *f* **2**
v/t belt boucler
buckle² ['bʌkl] *v/i of metal* dé-

former

bud [bʌd] BOT bourgeon *m*

buddy ['bʌdɪ] copain *m*, copine *f*; *form of address* mec

budge [bʌdʒ] **1** *v/t (move)* déplacer **2** *v/i (move)* bouger

budget ['bʌdʒɪt] budget *m*

buff [bʌf] passionné(e) *m(f)*

buffalo ['bʌfəlou] buffle *m*

buffer ['bʌfər] RAIL, COMPUT, *fig* tampon *m*

buffet ['bufeɪ] *meal* buffet *m*

bug [bʌg] **1** *n (insect)* insecte *m*; *(virus)* virus *m*; COMPUT bogue *f*; *(spying device)* micro *m* **2** *v/t room, telephone* mettre sur écoute; F *(annoy)* énerver

buggy ['bʌgɪ] *for baby* poussette *f*

build [bɪld] **1** *n of person* carrure *f* **2** *v/t* construire

◆ **build up 1** *v/t strength* développer; *relationship* construire **2** *v/i* s'accumuler; *fig* s'intensifier

builder ['bɪldər] constructeur(-trice) *m(f)*; *building* bâtiment *m*; *activity* construction *f*

building site chantier *m*; **building society** *Br* caisse *f* d'épargne-logement; **building trade** (industrie *f* du) bâtiment *m*; **build-up** accumulation *f*; **give s.o./sth a big ~** faire beaucoup de battage autour de qn/qch; **built-in** encastré; *flash* incorporé

bulb [bʌlb] BOT bulbe *m*; *(light*

~) ampoule *f*

bulge [bʌldʒ] **1** *n* gonflement *m*, saillie *f* **2** *v/i* être gonflé, faire saillie

bulky ['bʌlkɪ] encombrant; *sweater* gros

bull [bʊl] *animal* taureau *m*; **bulldozer** ['bʊldouzər] bulldozer *m*

bullet ['bʊlɪt] balle *f*

bulletin ['bʊlɪtɪn] bulletin *m*

bulletin board tableau *m* d'affichage; COMPUT serveur *m* télématique

bullet-proof protégé contre les balles; *vest* pare-balles

bull's-eye mille *m*; **hit the ~** *also fig* mettre dans le mille; **bullshit** merde *f* V, conneries *fpl* V

bully ['bʊlɪ] **1** *n* brute *f* **2** *v/t* brimer; **bullying** brimades *fpl*

bum [bʌm] **1** *n* F *(worthless person)* bon à rien *m*; *(tramp)* clochard *m* **2** *v/t*: **can I ~ a cigarette?** est-ce que je peux vous taper une cigarette?

bump [bʌmp] **1** *n* bosse *f* **2** *v/t* se cogner; **bumper** MOT pare-chocs *mpl*; **bumpy** *road* cahoteux; **we had a ~ flight** nous avons été secoués pendant le vol

bunch [bʌntʃ] *of people* groupe *m*; *of keys* trousseau *m*; *of grapes* grappe *f*; *of flowers* bouquet *m*; **thanks a ~** merci beaucoup

bungle ['bʌŋgl] bousiller

bunk [bʌŋk] couchette f

buoy [bɔɪ] NAUT bouée f;
buoyant *mood* jovial; *econo-my* prospère

burden ['bɜːrdn] **1** *n* fardeau
m **2** *v/t*: ~ *s.o. with sth* accabler qn de qch

bureau ['bjʊrou] bureau m;
bureaucrat bureaucrate
m/f; bureaucratic bureaucratique

burger ['bɜːrgər] steak m haché; *in roll* hamburger m

burglar ['bɜːrglər] cambrioleur(-euse) m(f); burglar
alarm alarme f antivol; burglarize cambrioler; burglary
cambriolage m

burial ['beriəl] enterrement m

burn [bɜːrn] **1** n brûlure f **2** v/t
& v/i brûler
◆ burn down **1** v/t incendier
2 v/i être réduit en cendres

burp [bɜːrp] **1** n rot m **2** v/i roter

burst [bɜːrst] **1** n *in pipe* trou
m **2** adj tire creuvé **3** v/t & v/i
crever; *of pipe* éclater; ~ *into
tears* fondre en larmes; ~ *out
laughing* éclater de rire

bus [bʌs] (auto)bus m; *long
distance* (auto)car m

bush [bʊʃ] *plant* buisson m

bushy ['bʊʃɪ] *beard* touffu

business ['bɪznɪs] commerce
m; (*company*) entreprise f;
(*work*) travail m; (*sector*) secteur m; (*matter*) affaire f; **on
~** en déplacement (profes-sionnel); **mind your own ~!**
occupe-toi de tes affaires!;
business card carte f de visite; business class classe f
affaires; businesslike sérieux; businessman homme
m d'affaires; business
meeting réunion f d'affaires;
business school école f de
commerce; business studies *course* études fpl de commerce; business trip voyage
m d'affaires; businesswoman femme f d'affaires

'bus station gare f routière;
bus stop arrêt m d'autobus

bust¹ [bʌst] n *of woman* poitrine f

bust² [bʌst] F (*broken*) cassé

'bust-up F brouille f; busty à
la poitrine plantureuse

busy ['bɪzɪ] *person*, TELEC occupé; *day, life* bien rempli;
street, shop plein de monde;
busybody curieux(-se) m(f)

but [bʌt] **1** conj mais **2** prep:
all ~ him tous sauf lui; **the
last ~ one** l'avant-dernier;
~ **for you** si tu n'avais pas
été là; **nothing ~ the best**
rien que le meilleur

butcher ['bʊtʃər] boucher
(-ère) m(f)

butt [bʌt] **1** n *of cigarette* mégot m; F (*backside*) cul m **2**
v/t donner un coup de tête à

butter ['bʌtər] beurre m; butterfly *also swimming* papillon m

buttocks ['bʌtəks] fesses fpl

button ['bʌtn] bouton *m*; (*badge*) badge *m*
buy [baɪ] acheter
◆ **buy out** COM racheter la part de
buyer ['baɪr] acheteur(-euse) *m* (*f*)
buzz [bʌz] **1** *n* bourdonnement *m* **2** *v/i of insect* bourdonner; **buzzer** sonnerie *f*
by [baɪ] *to show agent* par; (*near, next to*) près de; (*no*

later than) pour; *mode of transport* en; **~ bus** en bus; **~ day** le jour; **~ my watch** selon ma montre; **~ o.s.** tout seul
bye(-bye) [baɪ] au revoir
'bypass *road* déviation *f*; MED pontage *m* (coronarien); **by--product** sous-produit *m*; **by-stander** spectateur(-trice) *m*(*f*)

C

cab [kæb] taxi *m*; *of truck* cabine *f*; **cab driver** chauffeur *m* de taxi
cabin ['kæbɪn] *of plane, ship* cabine *f*; **cabin attendant** *male* steward *m*; *female* hôtesse *f* (de l'air); **cabin crew** équipage *m*
cabinet ['kæbɪnɪt] *furniture* meuble *m* (de rangement); POL cabinet *m*; **display** ~ vitrine *f*
cable ['keɪbl] câble *m*; **cable car** téléphérique *m*; *on rail* funiculaire *m*; **cable television** (télévision *f* par) câble *m*
'cab stand station *f* de taxis
cactus ['kæktəs] cactus *m*
cadaver [kə'dævər] cadavre *m*
caddie ['kædɪ] *in golf* caddie *m*
Caesarean *Br* → **Cesarean**

café ['kæfeɪ] café *m*; **cafeteria** cafétéria *f*
caffeine ['kæfi:n] caféine *f*
cage [keɪdʒ] cage *f*; **cagey** évasif
cake [keɪk] gâteau *m*
calculate ['kælkjʊleɪt] (*work out*) évaluer; *in arithmetic* calculer; **calculating** calculateur; **calculation** calcul *m*; **calculator** calculatrice *f*
calendar ['kælɪndər] calendrier *m*
calf[1] [kæf] (*young cow*) veau *m*
calf[2] [kæf] *of leg* mollet *m*
caliber, *Br* **calibre** ['kælɪbər] *of gun* calibre *m*
call [kɔ:l] **1** *n* appel *m*; (*phone ~ also*) coup *m* de téléphone **2** *v/t on phone* appeler; **~ed ...** s'appeler ... **3** *v/i on phone* appeler; (*visit*) passer
◆ **call back 1** *v/t* rappeler **2** *v/i*

on phone rappeler; (*make another visit*) repasser
◆ **call for** (*collect*) venir chercher; (*demand*) demander
◆ **call off** annuler
caller ['kɔːlər] *on phone* personne *f* qui appelle; (*visitor*) visiteur *m*
callous ['kæləs] dur
calm [kɑːm] **1** *adj* calme, tranquille **2** *n* calme *m*
◆ **calm down 1** *v/t* calmer **2** *v/i* se calmer
calmly ['kɑːmlɪ] calmement
calorie ['kælərɪ] calorie *f*
camcorder ['kæmkɔːrdər] caméscope *m*
camera ['kæmərə] appareil *m* photo; **tv** caméra *f*; **cameraman** cadreur *m*, caméraman *m*; **camera phone** téléphone *m* avec appareil photo intégré
camouflage ['kæməflɑːʒ] **1** *n* camouflage *m* **2** *v/t* camoufler
camp [kæmp] **1** *n* camp *m* **2** *v/i* camper
campaign [kæm'peɪn] **1** *n* campagne *f* **2** *v/i* faire campagne
camper ['kæmpər] *person* campeur *m*; *vehicle* camping-car *m*; *camping* camping *m*; **campsite** (terrain *m* de) camping *m*
campus ['kæmpəs] campus *m*
can[1] [kæn] *v/aux* pouvoir; ~ **you hear me?** tu m'entends?; ~ **she swim?** sait-elle

nager?; ~ **I help you?** est-ce que je peux t'aider?
can[2] [kæn] *n for food* boîte *f*; *for drinks* canette *f*; *of paint* bidon *m*
Canada ['kænədə] Canada *m*; **Canadian 1** *adj* canadien **2** *n* Canadien *m*
canal [kə'næl] canal *m*
cancel ['kænsl] annuler; **cancellation** annulation *f*
cancer ['kænsər] cancer *m*
candid ['kændɪd] franc
candidacy ['kændɪdəsɪ] candidature *f*; **candidate** candidat *m*
candle ['kændl] bougie *f*; *in church* cierge *m*
candor, *Br* **candour** ['kændər] franchise *f*
candy ['kændɪ] (*sweet*) bonbon *m*; (*sweets*) bonbons *mpl*
cane [keɪn] canne *f*
canister ['kænɪstər] boîte *f* (métallique); *for gas, spray* bombe *f*
canned [kænd] *en conserve*, en boîte; (*recorded*) enregistré
cannot ['kænɑːt] = **can not**
canny ['kænɪ] (*astute*) rusé
canoe [kə'nuː] canoë *m*
'can opener ouvre-boîte *m*
can't [kænt] = **can not**
canteen [kæn'tiːn] *in factory* cantine *f*
canvas ['kænvəs] toile *f*
canyon ['kænjən] canyon *m*
cap [kæp] *hat* bonnet *m*; *with peak* casquette *f*; *of soldier,*

policeman képi *m*

capability [keɪpə'bɪlətɪ] capacité *f*; **capable** capable

capacity [kə'pæsətɪ] capacité *f*

capital ['kæpɪtl] *of country* capitale *f*; *letter* majuscule *f*; *money* capital *m*; **capitalism** capitalisme *m*; **capitalist 1** *adj* capitaliste **2** *n* capitaliste *m/f*; **capital punishment** peine *f* capitale

capsize [kæp'saɪz] chavirer

capsule ['kæpsʊl] *of medicine* gélule *f*; *(space ~)* capsule *f* spatiale

captain ['kæptɪn] capitaine *m*; *of aircraft* commandant *m* de bord

caption ['kæpʃn] légende *f*

captivate ['kæptɪveɪt] captiver, fasciner; **captive** captif; **captivity** captivité *f*; **capture 1** *n of city* prise *f*; *of person, animal* capture *f* **2** *v/t person, animal* capturer; *city, building* prendre; *market share* conquérir

car [kɑːr] voiture *f*, automobile *f*; *of train* wagon *m*, voiture *f*; **by ~** en voiture

carbon monoxide [kɑːrbənmən'ɑːksaɪd] monoxyde *m* de carbone

carburetter, carburetor [kɑːrbʊ'retər] carburateur *m*

carcass ['kɑːrkəs] carcasse *f*

card [kɑːrd] carte *f*; **cardboard box** carton *m*

cardiac ['kɑːrdɪæk] cardiaque

cardinal ['kɑːrdɪnl] REL cardinal *m*

care [ker] **1** *n of baby, pet* garde *f*; *of the elderly, sick* soins *mpl*; *(medical ~)* soins *mpl* médicaux; *(worry)* souci *m*; **care of** → **c/o**; **take ~** *(be cautious)* faire attention; **take ~ of** s'occuper de **2** *v/i* se soucier; **I don't ~!** ça m'est égal!
◆ **care about** s'intéresser à
◆ **care for** *(look after)* s'occuper de

career [kə'rɪr] carrière *f*

careful ['kerfl] *(cautious)* prudent; *(thorough)* méticuleux; *(be) ~!* (fais) attention!; **carefully** *(with caution)* prudemment; *worded etc* soigneusement; **careless** négligent; *work* négligé; **carelessly** négligemment

caress [kə'res] caresser

car ferry (car-)ferry *m*, transbordeur

cargo ['kɑːrgoʊ] cargaison *f*

caricature ['kærɪkətʃər] caricature *f*

carnival ['kɑːrnɪvl] fête *f* foraine; *with processions etc* carnaval *m*

carpenter ['kɑːrpɪntər] charpentier *m*; *for smaller objects* menuisier *m*

carpet ['kɑːrpɪt] tapis *m*; *fitted* moquette *f*

car phone téléphone *m* de voiture; **carpool** faire du co-voiturage; **car rental** location *f* de voitures

carrier ['kærɪər] *company* entreprise *f* de transport; *of disease* porteur(-euse) *m(f)*
carrot ['kærət] carotte *f*
carry ['kærɪ] **1** *v/t* porter; *of ship, bus etc* transporter **2** *v/i of sound* porter
◆ **carry on 1** *v/i* (*continue*) continuer (**with sth** qch) **2** *v/t business* exercer
◆ **carry out** *survey etc* faire; *orders etc* exécuter
cart [kɑːrt] charrette *f*
carton ['kɑːrtn] carton *m*; *of cigarettes* cartouche *f*
cartoon [kɑːr'tuːn] dessin *m* humoristique; *on TV* dessin *m* animé; (*strip ~*) BD *f*, bande *f* dessinée
carve [kɑːrv] *meat* découper; *wood* sculpter
case[1] [keɪs] *for eyeglasses, camera* étui *m*; *for gadget* pochette *f*; *of wine etc* caisse *f*; *Br* (*suitcase*) valise *f*
case[2] [keɪs] (*instance*), MED cas *m*; *for police* affaire *f*; LAW procès *m*; **in ~** . au cas où …; **in any ~** en tout cas
cash [kæʃ] **1** *n* (*money*) argent *m*; (*coins and notes*) (argent *m*) liquide *m* **2** *v/t check* toucher; cash desk caisse *f*; cash flow COM trésorerie *f*; **I've got ~ problems** j'ai des problèmes d'argent; **cashier** *in store etc* caissier(-ère) *m(f)*; cashpoint *Br* distributeur *m* automatique de (billets); cash register caisse *f*

enregistreuse
casino [kə'siːnou] casino *m*
casket ['kæskɪt] (*coffin*) cercueil *m*
casserole ['kæsəroul] *meal* ragoût *m*; *container* cocotte *f*
cassette [kə'set] cassette *f*; cassette player lecteur *m* de cassettes
cast [kæst] **1** *n of play* distribution *f*; (*mold*) moule *m* **2** *v/t doubt* jeter; *metal* couler
cast 'iron fonte *f*
castle ['kæsl] chateau *m*
casual ['kæʒuəl] (*chance*) fait au hasard; (*offhand*) désinvolte; (*not formal*) décontracté; **casually** *dressed* de manière décontractée; *say* de manière désinvolte; **casualty** victime *f*
cat [kæt] chat(te) *m(f)*
catalog, *Br* **catalogue** ['kætəlɑːg] catalogue *m*
catalyst ['kætəlɪst] catalyseur *m*
catastrophe [kə'tæstrəfɪ] catastrophe *f*; **catastrophic** catastrophique
catch [kætʃ] **1** *n* prise *f* (au vol); *of fish* pêche *f*; (*lock: on door*) loquet *m*; (*problem*) entourloupette *f* **2** *v/t ball, prisoner, bus, illness* attraper; (*get on: bus, train*) prendre; (*hear*) entendre; **catching** *also fig* contagieux; **catchy** facile à retenir
categoric [kætə'gɑːrɪk] catégorique; **category** catégorie

f
caterer ['keɪtərər] traiteur *m*
cathedral [kə'θiːdrl] cathédrale *f*
Catholic ['kæθəlɪk] **1** *adj* catholique **2** *n* catholique *m/f*; Catholicism catholicisme *m*
catty ['kætɪ] méchant
cause [kɔːz] **1** *n* cause *f*; (*grounds*) raison *f* **2** *v/t* causer
caution ['kɔːʃn] **1** *n* (*carefulness*) prudence *f* **2** *v/t* (*warn*) avertir; cautious prudent; cautiously prudemment
cave [keɪv] caverne *f*, grotte *f*
cavity ['kævətɪ] cavité *f*
CD [siː'diː] (= *compact disc*) CD *m* (= compact-disc *m*, disque *m* compact)
C'D player lecteur *m* de CD; CD-ROM CD-ROM *m*
cease [siːs] cesser
'cease-fire cessez-le-feu *m*
ceiling ['siːlɪŋ] plafond *m*
celebrate ['selɪbreɪt] **1** *v/i* faire la fête **2** *v/t* fêter; *Christmas, event* célébrer; celebrated célèbre; celebration fête *f*; *of event, wedding* célébration *f*; celebrity célébrité *f*
cell [sel] *for prisoner, of spreadsheet*, BIO cellule *f*
cellar ['selər] cave *f*
cello ['tʃelou] violoncelle *m*
cell phone, cellular phone ['seljuːlər] (téléphone *m*) portable *m*
cement [sɪ'ment] ciment *m*

cemetery ['semətərɪ] cimetière *m*
censor ['sensər] censurer
census ['sensəs] recensement *m*
cent [sent] cent *m*
centenary [sen'tiːnərɪ] centenaire *m*
center ['sentər] **1** *n* centre *m* **2** *v/t* centrer
centigrade ['sentɪgreɪd] centigrade
centimeter, *Br* centimetre ['sentɪmiːtər] centimètre *m*
central ['sentrəl] central
central 'heating chauffage *m* central; centralize centraliser; central locking MOT verrouillage *m* centralisé
centre *Br* → **center**
century ['sentʃərɪ] siècle *m*
CEO [siːiː'ou] (= *Chief Executive Officer*) directeur *m* général
ceramic [sɪ'ræmɪk] en céramique
cereal ['sɪrɪəl] céréale *f*; (*breakfast ~*) céréales *fpl*
ceremonial [serɪ'mounɪəl] **1** *adj* de cérémonie **2** *n* cérémonial *m*; ceremony cérémonie *f*
certain ['sɜːrtn] (*sure*) certain, sûr; (*particular*) certain; certainly certainement; certainty certitude *f*
certificate [sər'tɪfɪkət] certificat *m*
certified public accountant ['sɜːrtɪfaɪd] expert *m* comp-

table; **certify** certifier

Cesarean [sɪˈzeɪrɪən] césarienne f

CFO [siːefˈəʊ] (= *chief financial officer*) directeur m financier

chain [tʃeɪn] **1** n also of stores etc chaîne f **2** v/t: **~ sth. to sth** enchaîner qch à qch

chair [tʃer] **1** n chaise f; (*arm~*) fauteuil m; *at university* chaire f **2** v/t *meeting* présider; **chair lift** télésiège m; **chairman** président m; **chairmanship** présidence f; **chairperson** président(e) m(f)

chalk [tʃɔːk] craie f

challenge [ˈtʃælɪndʒ] **1** n défi m, challenge m **2** v/t (*defy*) défier; (*call into question*) mettre en doute; **~ s.o. to a game** proposer à qn de faire une partie; **challenger** challenger m; **challenging** *job, undertaking* stimulant

Chamber of 'Commerce Chambre f de commerce

champagne [ʃæmˈpeɪn] champagne m

champion [ˈtʃæmpɪən] **1** n SP, *of cause* champion(ne) m(f) **2** v/t *cause* être le (la) champion(ne) m(f) de; **championship** *event* championnat m; *title* titre m de champion(ne)

chance [tʃæns] (*possibility*) chances fpl; (*opportunity*) occasion f; (*luck*) hasard m; **by ~** par hasard; **take a ~**

prendre un risque

change [tʃeɪndʒ] **1** n changement m; (*money*) monnaie f; **for a ~** pour changer un peu **2** v/t changer; *bankbill* faire la monnaie sur **3** v/i changer; (*put on different clothes*) se changer; **changeover** changement m; **changing room** SP vestiaire m; *in shop* cabine f d'essayage

channel [ˈtʃænl] *on TV, radio* chaîne f; (*waterway*) chenal m

chant [tʃænt] **1** n *slogans* scandés; REL chant m **2** v/i of *crowds etc* scander des slogans; REL psalmodier

chaos [ˈkeɪɑːs] chaos m; **chaotic** [keɪˈɑtɪk] chaotique

chapel [ˈtʃæpl] chapelle f

chapter [ˈtʃæptər] chapitre m

character [ˈkærɪktər] caractère m; (*person*) personne f; *in book* personnage m; **characteristic 1** n caractéristique f **2** adj caractéristique; **characterize** caractériser

charge [tʃɑːrdʒ] **1** n (*fee*) frais mpl; LAW accusation f; **free of ~** gratuit; **be in ~** être responsable **2** v/t *sum of money* faire payer; LAW inculper (**with** de); *battery* charger; **can you ~ it?** (*put on account*) pouvez-vous le mettre sur mon compte? **3** v/i (*attack*) charger; **charge account** compte m; **charge card** carte f de paiement

charitable ['ʧærɪtəbl] charitable; **charity** charité f; (*organization*) organisation f caritative

charm [ʧɑːrm] **1** n also on bracelet charme m **2** v/t (delight) charmer; **charming** charmant

charred [ʧɑːrd] carbonisé

chart [ʧɑːrt] diagramme m; (map) carte f

'**charter flight** (vol m) charter m

chase [ʧeɪs] **1** n poursuite f **2** v/t poursuivre

◆ **chase away** v/t chasser

chassis ['ʃæsɪ] of car châssis m

chat [ʧæt] **1** n causette f **2** v/i causer; **chatline** chat m téléphonique; **chat room** chat m

chatter ['ʧætər] **1** n bavardage m **2** v/i (talk) bavarder; **my teeth were ~ing** je claquais des dents

chauffeur ['ʃoʊfər] chauffeur m

chauvinist ['ʃoʊvɪnɪst] (male ~) machiste m

cheap [ʧiːp] bon marché, pas cher; (nasty) méchant; (mean) pingre

cheat [ʧiːt] **1** n person tricheur(-euse) m(f) **2** v/t tromper **3** v/i tricher

check[1] [ʧek] **1** adj shirt à carreaux **2** n carreaux m

check[2] [ʧek] n FIN chèque m; in restaurant etc addition f

check[3] [ʧek] **1** n to verify sth contrôle m, vérification f **2** v/t vérifier; with a ~mark cocher; coat etc mettre au vestiaire **3** v/i vérifier

◆ **check in** v/i at airport se faire enregistrer; at hotel s'inscrire

◆ **check out 1** v/i of hotel régler sa note **2** v/t (look into) enquêter sur; club etc essayer

◆ **check up on** se renseigner sur

'**checkbook** carnet m de chèques; **checked** material à carreaux

checkered ['ʧekərd] pattern à carreaux; career varié

'**check-in** (**counter**) enregistrement m; **checking account** compte m courant; **checklist** liste f (de contrôle); **check mark**: **put a ~ against sth** cocher qch; **check-out** caisse f; **checkpoint** contrôle m; **checkroom** for coats vestiaire m; for baggage consigne f; **checkup** medical examen m médical; dental examen m dentaire

cheek [ʧiːk] on face joue f

cheer [ʧɪr] **1** n hourra m **2** v/t acclamer **3** v/i pousser des hourras

◆ **cheer up 1** v/i reprendre courage; **cheer up!** courage! **2** v/t remonter le moral à

cheerful ['ʧɪrfəl] gai, joyeux; **cheering** acclamations fpl; **cheerleader** meneuse f de ban

cheese [tʃiːz] fromage *m*

chef [ʃef] chef *m* (de cuisine)

chemical ['kemɪkl] **1** *adj* chimique **2** *n* produit *m* chimique; **chemist** *in laboratory* chimiste *m/f*; *Br* pharmacien(ne) *m(f)*; **chemistry** chimie *f*

chemotherapy [kiːmou'θerəpɪ] chimiothérapie *f*

cheque [tʃek] *Br* → **check²**

chess [tʃes] (jeu *m* d'échecs *mpl*; **play ~** jouer aux échecs

chest [tʃest] poitrine *f*; (*box*) coffre *m*, caisse *f*

chew [tʃuː] mâcher; *of rat* ronger; **chewing gum** chewing-gum *m*

chick [tʃɪk] poussin *m*; F *girl* nana

chicken ['tʃɪkɪn] poulet *m*

chief [tʃiːf] **1** *n* chef *m* **2** *adj* principal; **chiefly** principalement

child [tʃaɪld] enfant *m/f*; **childhood** enfance *f*; **childish** puéril; **childlike** enfantin

children ['tʃɪldrən] *pl* → **child**

Chile ['tʃɪlɪ] Chili *m*; **Chilean 1** *adj* chilien **2** *n* Chilien(ne) *m(f)*

◆ **chill out** se relaxer

chilly ['tʃɪlɪ] *also fig* froid

chimney ['tʃɪmnɪ] cheminée *f*

chin [tʃɪn] menton *m*

China ['tʃaɪnə] Chine *f*

china ['tʃaɪnə] **1** *n* porcelaine *f* **2** *adj* en porcelaine

Chinese [tʃaɪ'niːz] **1** *adj* chi-

nois **2** *n language* chinois *m*; *person* Chinois(e) *m(f)*

chip [tʃɪp] **1** *n damage* brèche *f*; *in gambling* jeton *m*; COMPUT puce *f*; **~s** (*potato ~s*) chips *mpl*; *Br* pommes frites *fpl* **2** *v/t damage* ébrécher

chipmunk tamia *m* rayé

chisel ['tʃɪzl] ciseau *m*, burin *m*

chlorine ['klɔːriːn] chlore *m*

chocolate ['tʃɑːkələt] chocolat *m*

choice [tʃɔɪs] **1** *n* choix *m*; **I had no ~** je n'avais pas le choix **2** *adj* (*top quality*) de choix

choir ['kwaɪr] chœur *m*

choke [tʃouk] **1** *v/i* s'étrangler **2** *v/t* (*strangle*) étrangler

cholesterol [kə'lestəroul] cholestérol *m*

choose [tʃuːz] choisir; **choosey** difficile

chop [tʃɑːp] **1** *n of meat* côtelette *f* **2** *v/t* couper

◆ **chop down** *tree* abattre

chore [tʃɔːr] **~s** travaux *mpl* domestiques

choreography [kɔːrɪ'ɑːgrəfɪ] chorégraphie *f*

chorus ['kɔːrəs] *singers* chœur *m*; *of song* refrain *m*

Christ [kraɪst] Christ *m*; **~!** mon Dieu!

christen ['krɪsn] baptiser

Christian ['krɪstʃən] **1** *n* chrétien(ne) *m(f)* **2** *adj* chrétien; **Christianity** christianisme *m*

Christmas ['krɪsməs] Noël *m*;
Merry ~! Joyeux Noël!;
Christmas card carte *f* de
Noël; Christmas Day jour
m de Noël; Christmas Eve
veille *f* de Noël; Christmas
present cadeau *m* de Noël;
Christmas tree arbre *m* de
Noël

chronic ['krɒnɪk] chronique

chubby ['tʃʌbɪ] potelé

chuck [tʃʌk] lancer

chuckle ['tʃʌkl] **1** *n* petit rire
m **2** *v/i* rire tout bas

chunk [tʃʌŋk] gros morceau *m*

church [tʃɜːrtʃ] église *f*;
church service office *m*;
churchyard cimetière *m* (autour d'une église)

chute [ʃuːt] *for garbage* vide-ordures *m*; *for escape* toboggan *m*

cigar [sɪ'gɑːr] cigare *m*

cigarette [sɪgə'ret] cigarette
f; cigarette lighter briquet *m*

cinema ['sɪnɪmə] *Br* cinéma
m

circle ['sɜːrkl] **1** *n* cercle *m* **2**
v/i of plane tournoyer

circuit ['sɜːrkɪt] circuit *m*;
(*lap*) tour *m* (de circuit); circuit board COMPUT plaquette
f; circular ['sɜːrkjʊlər] **1** *n*
circulaire *f* **2** *adj* circulaire;
circulate ['sɜːrkjʊleɪt] **1** *v/i*
circuler **2** *v/t memo* faire circuler; circulation circulation
f; *of newspaper* tirage *m*

circumstances ['sɜːrkəmstænsɪs] circonstances *fpl*;

financial situation *f* financière

circus ['sɜːrkəs] cirque *m*

cistern ['sɪstərn] réservoir *m*;
of WC réservoir *m* de chasse
d'eau

citizen ['sɪtɪzn] citoyen(ne)
m(f); citizenship citoyenneté *f*

city ['sɪtɪ] (grande) ville *f*

city 'center, *Br* 'city 'centre
centre-ville *m*; city hall hôtel
m de ville

civic ['sɪvɪk] municipal; *pride,
responsibilities* civique

civil ['sɪvl] civil; (*polite*) poli;
civil ceremony mariage *m*
civil; civil engineer ingénieur *m* des travaux publics

civilian [sɪ'vɪljən] civil(e)
m(f); civilization civilisation
f; civilize civiliser; civil
rights droits *mpl* civils; civil
servant fonctionnaire *m/f*;
civil service fonction *f* publique, administration *f*; civil
war guerre *f* civile

claim [kleɪm] **1** *n* (*request*) demande *f*; (*assertion*) affirmation *f* **2** *v/t* (*ask for as a right*)
demander, réclamer; (*assert*)
affirmer; *lost property* réclamer; claimant ['kleɪmənt]
demandeur(-euse) *m(f)*

clam [klæm] palourde *f*, clam
m

clammy ['klæmɪ] moite

clamp [klæmp] *fastener* pince
f, crampon *m*

◆ clamp down on sévir con-

clerk

tre
clandestine [klæn'destɪn]
clandestin
clap [klæp] (*applaud*) applaudir
clarification [klærɪfɪ'keɪʃn]
clarification *f*; **clarify** clarifier; **clarity** clarté *f*
clash [klæʃ] **1** *n between people* affrontement *m* **2** *v/i* s'affronter; *of colors* détonner; *of events* tomber en même temps
clasp [klæsp] **1** *n* agrafe *f* **2** *v/t in hand* serrer
class [klæs] **1** *n* (*lesson*) cours *m*; (*group of people, category*) classe *f*; **the ~ of 2002** la promo(tion) 2002 **2** *v/t* classer
classic ['klæsɪk] **1** *adj* classique **2** *n* classique *m*; **classical music** musique classique; **classification** classification *f*; **classified** *information* secret; **classified ad**(vertisement) petite annonce *f*; **classify** classifier; **classroom** salle *f* de classe; **classy** F *restaurant etc* chic *inv*; *person* classe
clause [klɔːz] (*in agreement*) clause *f*; GRAM proposition *f*
claustrophobia [klɔːstrə-'foʊbɪə] claustrophobie *f*
claw [klɔː] *of cat* griffe *f*; *of lobster* pince *f*
clay [kleɪ] argile *f*, glaise *f*
clean [kliːn] **1** *adj* propre **2** *adv* (*completely*) complètement **3** *v/t* nettoyer; **cleaner**

male agent *m* de propreté; *female* femme *f* de ménage; (*dry~*) teinturier(-ère) *m(f)*
cleanse [klenz] *skin* nettoyer; **cleanser** *for skin* démaquillant *m*
clear [klɪr] **1** *adj voice, photo* net; *to understand, sky, water* clair; *conscience* tranquille **2** *v/t roads etc* dégager; *place* (faire) évacuer; *table* débarrasser; *ball* dégager; (*acquit*) innocenter; (*authorize*) autoriser **3** *v/i of sky* se dégager; *of mist* se dissiper; *of face* s'éclairer
◆ **clear out 1** *v/t closet* vider **2** *v/i* ficher le camp
◆ **clear up 1** *v/i in room etc* ranger; *of weather* s'éclaircir; *of illness* disparaître **2** *v/t* (*tidy*) ranger; *problem* résoudre
clearance ['klɪrəns] (*space*) espace *m* (libre); (*authorization*) autorisation *f*; **clearance sale** liquidation *f*; **clearing** clairière *f*; **clearly** *speak, see* clairement; *hear* distinctement; (*evidently*) manifestement
cleavage ['kliːvɪdʒ] décolleté *m*
clench [klentʃ] serrer
clergy ['klɜːrdʒɪ] clergé *m*; **clergyman** ecclésiastique *m*; *Protestant* pasteur *m*
clerk [klɜːrk] *administrative* employé(e) *m(f)* de bureau; *in store* vendeur(-euse) *m(f)*

clever ['klevər] intelligent; *gadget* ingénieux; *(skillful)* habile

click [klɪk] **1** *n* COMPUT clic *m* **2** *v/i* cliqueter

♦ **click on** COMPUT cliquer sur

client ['klaɪənt] client(e) *m(f)*; **clientele** clientèle *f*

climate ['klaɪmət] *also fig* climat *m*

climax ['klaɪmæks] point *m* culminant

climb [klaɪm] **1** *n up mountain* ascension *f f* **2** *v/t* monter sur; *mountain* escalader **3** *v/i* monter; **climber** alpiniste *m/f*

clinch [klɪntʃ] *deal* conclure

cling [klɪŋ] *of clothes* coller

♦ **cling to** s'accrocher à

clingy ['klɪŋɪ] *person* collant

clinic ['klɪnɪk] clinique *f*; **clinical** clinique

clip[1] [klɪp] **1** *n fastener* pince *f*; *for hair* barrette *f* **2** *v/t*: ~ *sth to sth* attacher qch à qch

clip[2] [klɪp] **1** *n (extract)* extrait *m* **2** *v/t hair, grass* couper; *clipping from press* coupure *f* (de presse)

clock [klɑːk] horloge *f*; **clock radio** radio-réveil *m*; **clockwise** dans le sens des aiguilles d'une montre

clone [kloun] **1** *n* clone *m* **2** *v/t* cloner; **cloning** clonage *m*

close[1] [klous] **1** *adj family, friend* proche **2** *adv* près; ~ *at hand*, ~ *by* tout près; ~ *to* près de

close[2] [klouz] *v/t* fermer

closed-circuit 'television télévision *f* en circuit fermé; **close-knit** très uni; **closely** *listen* attentivement; *watch* de près; *cooperate* étroitement

closet ['klɑːzɪt] armoire *f*, placard *m*

close-up ['klousʌp] gros plan *m*

closing date ['klouzɪŋ] date *f* limite

closure ['klouʒər] fermeture *f*

clot [klɑːt] **1** *n of blood* caillot *m* **2** *v/i of blood* coaguler

cloth [klɑːθ] tissu *m*; *for drying* torchon *m*; *for washing* lavette *f*

clothes [klouðz] vêtements *mpl*; **clothing** vêtements *mpl*

cloud [klaud] nuage *m*; **cloudless** sans nuages; **cloudy** nuageux

clout [klaut] *fig (influence)* influence *f*

clove of 'garlic [klouv] gousse *f* d'ail

clown [klaun] *also pej* clown *m*

club [klʌb] club *m*; *weapon* massue *f*

clue [kluː] indice *m*

clumsiness ['klʌmzɪnɪs] maladresse *f*; **clumsy** maladroit

cluster ['klʌstər] groupe *m*

clutch [klʌtʃ] **1** *n* MOT embrayage *m* **2** *v/t* étreindre

♦ **clutch at** s'agripper à

c/o(= *care of*) chez

Co. (= *Company*) Cie (= Compagnie)

coach [kəʊtʃ] **1** *n* (*trainer*) entraîneur(-euse) *m(f)*; *Br* (*bus*) (auto)car *m* **2** *v/t* SP entraîner; **coaching** entraînement *m*

coagulate [kəʊˈægjʊleɪt] *of blood* coaguler

coal [kəʊl] charbon *m*

coalition [kəʊəˈlɪʃn] coalition *f*

'coalmine mine *f* de charbon

coarse [kɔːrs] *fabric* rugueux; *hair* épais; (*vulgar*) grossier; **coarsely** (*vulgarly*), *ground* grossièrement

coast [kəʊst] côte *f*; **coastal** côtier; **coastguard** gendarmerie *f* maritime; *person* gendarme *m* maritime; **coastline** littoral *m*

coat [kəʊt] **1** *n* veston *m*; (*over*∼) pardessus *m*; *of animal* pelage *m*; *of paint etc* couche *f* **2** *v/t* (*cover*) couvrir (**with** de); **coathanger** cintre *m*; **coating** couche *f*

coax [kəʊks] cajoler

cocaine [kəˈkeɪn] cocaïne *f*

cock [kɑːk] *chicken* coq *m*; *any male bird* (oiseau *m*) mâle *m*; **cockpit** *of plane* poste *m* de pilotage; **cockpit** *m*; **cockroach** cafard *m*; **cocktail** cocktail *m*

cocoa [ˈkəʊkəʊ] cacao *m*

coconut [ˈkəʊkənʌt] noix *m* de coco; **coconut palm** cocotier *m*

code [kəʊd] code *m*; **in** ∼ codé

coeducational [kəʊedʊˈkeɪʃnl] mixte

coerce [kəʊˈɜːrs] forcer

coexist [kəʊɪɡˈzɪst] coexister; **coexistence** coexistence *f*

coffee [ˈkɑːfɪ] café *m*; **coffee maker** machine *f* à café; **coffee pot** cafetière *f*; **coffee shop** café *m*

cohabit [kəʊˈhæbɪt] cohabiter

coherent [kəʊˈhɪrənt] cohérent

coil [kɔɪl] *of rope* rouleau *m*; *of snake* anneau *m*

coin [kɔɪn] pièce *f* (de monnaie)

coincide [kəʊɪnˈsaɪd] coïncider; **coincidence** coïncidence *f*

Coke® [kəʊk] coca® *m*

cold [kəʊld] **1** *adj* froid; **I'm** ∼ j'ai froid; **it's** ∼ *of weather* il fait froid **2** *n* froid *m*; MED rhume *m*; **cold-blooded** à sang froid; *murder* commis de sang-froid; **coldly** froidement; **coldness** froideur *f*; **cold sore** bouton *m* de fièvre

collaborate [kəˈlæbəreɪt] collaborer; **collaboration** collaboration *f*; **collaborator** collaborateur(-trice) *m(f)*

collapse [kəˈlæps] s'effondrer; *of building* s'écrouler; **collapsible** pliant

collar [ˈkɑːlər] col *m*; *for dog* collier *m*

colleague ['kɒliːg] collègue *m/f*

collect [kə'lekt] **1** *v/t person, cleaning etc* aller/venir chercher; *as hobby* collectionner; (*gather together*) recueillir **2** *v/i* (*gather together*) s'assembler; **collect call** communication *f* en PCV; **collection** collection *f; in church* collecte *f;* **collective** collectif *f;* **collector** collectionneur(-euse) *m(f)*

college ['kɒlɪdʒ] université *f*

collide [kə'laɪd] se heurter; **collision** collision *f*

colon ['kəʊlən] *punctuation* deux-points *mpl*

colonel ['kɜːnl] colonel *m*

colonial [kə'ləʊnɪəl] colonial; **colonize** coloniser; **colony** colonie *f*

color ['kʌlər] couleur *f;* **color-blind** daltonien; **colored** *person* de couleur; **colorful** *also fig* coloré

colossal [kə'lɒsl] colossal

colour *Br* → **color**

colt [kəʊlt] poulain *m*

column ['kɒləm] *architectural, of text* colonne *f;* **columnist** chroniqueur(-euse) *m(f)*

coma ['kəʊmə] coma *m*

comb [kəʊm] **1** *n* peigne *m* **2** *v/t* peigner; *area* passer au peigne fin

combat ['kɒmbæt] **1** *n* combat *m* **2** *v/t* combattre

combination [kɒmbɪ'neɪʃn]

also of safe combinaison *f;* **combine 1** *v/t* combiner; *ingredients* mélanger **2** *v/i* se combiner

come [kʌm] venir; *of train, bus* arriver

◆ **come across** (*find*) tomber sur

◆ **come along** (*come too*) venir (aussi); (*turn up*) arriver; (*progress*) avancer

◆ **come back** revenir

◆ **come down** descendre; *in price etc* baisser; *of rain, snow* tomber

◆ **come for** (*attack*) attaquer; (*to collect*) venir chercher

◆ **come forward** se présenter

◆ **come from** venir de

◆ **come in** entrer; *of train, in race* arriver; *of tide* monter

◆ **come in for** *criticism* recevoir

◆ **come off** *of handle etc* se détacher

◆ **come out** sortir; *of results* être communiqué; *of sun, product* apparaître; *of stain* partir

◆ **come to 1** *v/t* (*reach*) arriver à; **that comes to $70** ça fait 70 $ **2** *v/i* (*regain consciousness*) revenir à soi

◆ **come up** monter; *of sun* se lever

'**comeback** retour *m,* come-back *m*

comedian [kə'miːdɪən] (*comic*) comique *m/f; pej* pitre *m/f;* **comedy** comédie *f*

comfort ['kʌmfərt] **1** n confort m; (*consolation*) réconfort m **2** v/t réconforter; **comfortable** confortable; *be ~ of person* être à l'aise

comic ['kɑ:mɪk] **1** n *to read* bande f dessinée; (*comedian*) comique m/f **2** adj comique; **comical** comique; **comic book** bande f dessinée, BD f; **comics** bandes fpl dessinées; **comic strip** bande f dessinée

comma ['kɑ:mə] virgule f

command [kə'mænd] **1** n (*order*) ordre m; MIL commandement m **2** v/t commander

commandeer [kɑ:mən'dɪr] réquisitionner

commander [kə'mændər] commandant(e) m(f); **commander-in-chief** commandant(e) m(f) en chef

commemorate [kə'meməreɪt] commémorer

commence [kə'mens] commencer

commendable [kə'mendəbl] louable; **commendation** *for bravery* éloge m

comment ['kɑ:ment] **1** n commentaire m **2** v/t: *~ on* commenter; **commentary** commentaire m; **commentator** commentateur(-trice) m(f)

commerce ['kɑ:mɜ:rs] commerce m; **commercial 1** adj commercial **2** n (*ad*) publicité f; **commercial break** page f de publicité; **commercial-**ize commercialiser

commission [kə'mɪʃn] (*payment, committee*) commission f; (*job*) commande f

commit [kə'mɪt] *crime* commettre; *money* engager; **commitment** *in relationship* engagement m; (*responsibility*) responsabilité f; **committee** comité m

commodity [kə'mɑ:dətɪ] marchandise f

common ['kɑ:mən] courant; *species etc* commun; (*shared*) commun; *have sth in ~ with s.o.* avoir qch en commun; **commonly** communément; **common sense** bon sens m

commotion [kə'mouʃn] agitation f

communal [kəm'ju:nl] en commun

communicate [kə'mju:nɪkeɪt] communiquer; **communication** communication f; **communicative** communicatif

Communion [kə'mju:njən] REL communion f

Communism ['kɑ:mjʊnɪzəm] communisme m; **Communist 1** adj communiste **2** n communiste m/f

community [kə'mju:nətɪ] communauté f

commute [kə'mju:t] v/i faire la navette (pour aller travailler) **2** v/t LAW commuer

compact 1 adj [kəm'pækt] compact **2** n ['kɑ:mpækt]

MOT petite voiture *f*

companion [kəmˈpænjən] compagnon *m*

company [ˈkʌmpəni] COM société *f*; (*companionship*) compagnie *f*; (*guests*) invités *mpl*

comparable [ˈkɑːmpərəbl] comparable; **comparative** comparativement; **compare** comparer; **comparison** comparaison *f*

compartment [kəmˈpɑːrtmənt] compartiment *m*

compass [ˈkʌmpəs] compas *m*

compassion [kəmˈpæʃn] compassion *f*; **compassionate** compatissant

compatibility [kəmpætəˈbɪlɪti] compatibilité *f*; **compatible** compatible

compel [kəmˈpel] obliger

compensate [ˈkɑːmpənseɪt] **1** *v/t* dédommager **2** *v/i*: **~ for** compenser; **compensation** (*money*) dédommagement *m*; (*reward*) compensation *f*; (*comfort*) consolation *f*

compete [kəmˈpiːt] être en compétition; (*take part*) participer (**in** à)

competence [ˈkɑːmpɪtəns] compétence *f*; **competent** *person* compétent, capable; *piece of work* (très) satisfaisant

competition [kɑːmpəˈtɪʃn] (*contest*) concours *m*; SP

compétition *f*; (*competing, competitors*) concurrence *f*; **competitive** compétitif; *price, offer* concurrentiel; **competitiveness** COM compétitivité *f*; *of person* esprit *m* de compétition; **competitor** concurrent *m*

complacent [kəmˈpleɪsənt] complaisant, suffisant

complain [kəmˈpleɪn] se plaindre; **complaint** plainte *f*; IN SHOP réclamation *f*; MED maladie *f*

complementary [kɑːmplɪˈmentəri] complémentaire

complete [kəmˈpliːt] **1** *adj* complet; (*finished*) terminé **2** *v/t task, building etc* terminer, achever; *form* remplir; **completely** complètement; **completion** achèvement *m*

complex [ˈkɑːmpleks] **1** *adj* complexe **2** *n building*, PSYCH complexe *m*; **complexion** *facial* teint *m*; **complexity** complexité *f*

compliance [kəmˈplaɪəns] conformité *f*

complicate [ˈkɑːmplɪkeɪt] compliquer; **complicated** compliqué; **complication** complication *f*

complimentary [kɑːmplɪˈmentəri] élogieux, flatteur; (*free*) gratuit

comply [kəmˈplaɪ] obéir; **~ with ...** se conformer à

component [kəmˈpoʊnənt] composant *m*

compose [kəm'pəʊz] composer; composed (*calm*) calme; composer MUS compositeur *m*; composition composition *f*; composure calme *m*

compound ['kɑːmpaʊnd] CHEM composé *m*

comprehend [kɑːmprɪ'hend] comprendre; comprehension compréhension *f*; comprehensive complet

compress [kəm'pres] comprimer; *information* condenser

comprise [kəm'praɪz] comprendre; (*make up*) constituer; *be ~d of* se composer de

compromise ['kɑːmprəmaɪz] **1** *n* compromis *m* **2** *v/i* trouver un compromis **3** *v/t* compromettre

compulsion [kəm'pʌlʃn] PSYCH compulsion *f*; compulsive *behavior* compulsif; *reading* captivant; compulsory obligatoire

computer [kəm'pjuːtər] ordinateur *m*; computer game jeu *m* informatique; computerize informatiser; computer science informatique *f*; computing informatique *f*

comrade ['kɑːmreɪd] camarade *m/f*; comradeship camaraderie *f*

conceal [kən'siːl] cacher; concealment dissimulation *f*

conceit [kən'siːt] vanité *f*; conceited vaniteux

conceivable [kən'siːvəbl] concevable; conceive *of woman* concevoir

concentrate ['kɑːnsəntreɪt] **1** *v/i* se concentrer **2** *v/t energies* concentrer; concentration concentration *f*

concept ['kɑːnsept] concept *m*; conception *of child* conception *f*

concern [kən'sɜːrn] **1** *n* (*anxiety, care*) inquiétude *f*, souci *m*; (*business*) affaire *f*; (*company*) entreprise *f* **2** *v/t* (*involve*) concerner; (*worry*) préoccuper; concerned (*anxious*) inquiet; (*caring, involved*) concerné; concerning concernant, au sujet de

concert ['kɑːnsərt] concert *m*; concerted concerté

concession [kən'seʃn] concession *f*

concise [kən'saɪs] concis

conclude [kən'kluːd] conclure; *~ sth from sth* déduire qch de qch; conclusion conclusion *f*; conclusive concluant

concrete ['kɑːŋkriːt] **1** *n* béton *m* **2** *adj* concret

concussion [kən'kʌʃn] commotion *f* cérébrale

condemn [kən'dem] condamner; condemnation condamnation *f*

condescend [kɑːndɪ'send]

daigner (**to do** faire); conde-
scending condescendant
condition [kənˈdɪʃn] **1** n
(*state, requirement*) condition f; MED maladie f **2** v/t
PSYCH conditionner; conditioning PSYCH conditionnement m
condo [ˈkɑːndoʊ] *building*
immeuble m (en copropriété); *apartment* appart m
condolences [kənˈdoʊlənsɪz]
condoléances fpl
condom [ˈkɑːndəm] préservatif m
condominium [kɑːndəˈmɪn-
ɪəm] → **condo**
condone [kənˈdoʊn] excuser
conduct [ˈkɑːndʌkt] **1** n (*behavior*) conduite f **2** v/t
[kənˈdʌkt] (*carry out*) mener; ELEC conduire; MUS diriger; conducted tour visite f
guidée; conductor MUS chef
m d'orchestre; on train chef
m de train
cone [koʊn] cône m; *for ice
cream* cornet m; *of pine tree*
pomme f de pin
conference [ˈkɑːnfərəns]
conférence f; *discussion* réunion f; conference room salle f de conférences
confess [kənˈfes] **1** v/t avouer,
confesser **2** v/i *also to police*
avouer; REL se confesser;
confession confession f
confide [kənˈfaɪd] **1** v/t confier **2** v/i: ~ **in s.o.** (*trust*) faire
confiance à qn; confidence

confiance f; (*in self*) assurance f; **confident** (*self-assured*)
sûr de soi; (*convinced*) confiant; **confidential** confidentiel; **confidently** avec assurance
confine [kənˈfaɪn] (*imprison*)
enfermer; (*restrict*) limiter;
confined space restreint
confirm [kənˈfɜːrm] confirmer; confirmation confirmation f
confiscate [ˈkɑːnfɪskeɪt] confisquer
conflict [ˈkɑːnflɪkt] **1** n conflit
m **2** v/i [kənˈflɪkt] être en
conflit; *of dates* coïncider
confront [kənˈfrʌnt] (*face*) affronter; (*tackle*) confronter;
confrontation confrontation
f; (*clash, dispute*) affrontement m
confuse [kənˈfjuːz] (*muddle*)
compliquer; *person* embrouiller; ~ **s.o. with s.o.**
confondre qn avec qn; confused *person* désorienté;
ideas, situation confus; confusing déroutant; confusion confusion f
congestion [kənˈdʒestʃn] *on
roads* encombrement m
congratulate [kənˈɡrætʊleɪt]
féliciter (**on** pour); congratulations félicitations fpl
congregate [ˈkɑːnɡrɪɡeɪt] se
rassembler; congregation
REL assemblée f
Congress [ˈkɑːnɡres] le Congrès; **Congressional** du

Congrès; **Congressman** membre *m* du Congrès; **Congresswoman** membre *m* du Congrès

conjecture [kənˈdʒektʃər] conjecture *f*

con man [ˈkɑːnmæn] escroc *m*, arnaqueur *m*

connect [kəˈnekt] raccorder, relier; TELEC passer; (*link*) associer; *to power supply* brancher; **connected: be well~** avoir des relations; **be ~ with** être lié à; **connection** *in wiring* branchement *m*, connexion *f*; *causal etc* rapport *m*; *when traveling* correspondance *f*; (*personal contact*) relation *f*

connoisseur [kɑːnəˈsɜːr] connaisseur *m*, connaisseuse *f*

conquer [ˈkɑːŋkər] conquérir; *fear etc* vaincre; **conqueror** conquérant *m*; **conquest** conquête *f*

conscience [ˈkɑːnʃəns] conscience *f*; **conscientious** consciencieux; **conscientiousness** conscience *f*

conscious [ˈkɑːnʃəs] conscient; (*deliberate*) délibéré; **consciously** (*knowingly*) consciemment; (*deliberately*) délibérément; **consciousness** conscience *f*; **lose/regain ~** perdre/reprendre connaissance

consecutive [kənˈsekjʊtɪv] consécutif

consensus [kənˈsensəs] consensus *m*

consent [kənˈsent] **1** *n* consentement *m* **2** *v/i* consentir (**to** à)

consequence [ˈkɑːnsɪkwəns] conséquence *f*; **consequently** par conséquent

conservation [kɑːnsərˈveɪʃn] protection *f*; **conservationist** écologiste *m/f*; **conservative** conservateur; *clothes* classique; *estimate* prudent; **conserve 1** *n* (*jam*) confiture *f* **2** *v/t energy* économiser

consider [kənˈsɪdər] considérer; (*show regard for*) prendre en compte; **considerable** considérable; **considerably** considérablement; **considerate** attentionné; **considerately** gentiment; **consideration** (*thought*) réflexion *f*; (*factor*) facteur *m*; (*thoughtfulness, concern*) attention *f*; **take sth into ~** prendre qch en considération

◆ **consist of** [kənˈsɪst] consister en

consistency [kənˈsɪstənsɪ] (*texture*) consistance *f*; (*unchangingness*) constance *f*; (*logic*) cohérence *f*; **consistent** (*unchanging*) constant; *logically etc* cohérent

consolidate [kənˈsɑːlɪdeɪt] consolider

conspicuous [kənˈspɪkjʊəs]

voyant; **look~** se faire remarquer

conspiracy [kən'spɪrəsɪ]
conspiration f; **conspirator**
conspirateur(-trice)   m(f);
conspire conspirer

constant ['kɑːnstənt] constant; **constantly** constamment

constipated ['kɑːnstɪpeɪtɪd]
constipé; **constipation** constipation f

constitute   ['kɑːnstɪtuːt]
constituer;   **constitution**
constitution f; **constitution-
al** POL constitutionnel

constraint [kən'streɪnt] (*restriction*) contrainte f

construct [kən'strʌkt] construire;   **construction** construction f; (*trade*) bâtiment
m; **constructive** constructif

consul ['kɑːnsl] consul m;
consulate consulat m

consult [kən'sʌlt] consulter;
consultancy *company* cabi-
net-conseil m; (*advice*) conseil m; **consultant** consultant m; **consultation** consultation f

consume [kən'suːm] consommer; **consumer** con-
sommateur m; **consump-
tion** consommation f

contact ['kɑːntækt] **1** n contact m **2** v/t contacter; **contact lens** lentille f de contact

contagious [kən'teɪdʒəs]
contagieux

contain [kən'teɪn] contenir;

container récipient m; COM
conteneur m, container m

contaminate [kən'tæmɪneɪt]
contaminer; **contamination**
contamination f

contemporary [kən'tem-
pərerɪ] **1** *adj* contemporain
2 n contemporain m

contempt [kən'tempt] mépris
m; **contemptible** méprisable; **contemptuous** méprisant

contender [kən'tendər] *in
sport* prétendant m; *in compétition* concurrent m; POL
candidat m

content[1] ['kɑːntent] n contenu m

content[2] [kən'tent] **1** *adj* content **2** v/t: **~ o.s. with** se contenter de

contented [kən'tentɪd] satisfait; **contentment** contente-
ment m

contents ['kɑːntents] contenu m

contest[1] ['kɑːntest] n (*compétition*) concours m; *in sport*
compétition f; (*struggle for
power*) lutte f

contest[2] [kən'test] *leadership
etc* disputer; (*oppose*) contester; **~ an election** se présenter à une élection

contestant [kən'testənt] concurrent m

context ['kɑːntekst] contexte
m

continent ['kɑːntɪnənt] continent m; **continental** conti-

nental

continual [kən'tɪnuəl] continuel; **continually** continuellement; **continuation** continuation *f*; *of story* suite *f*; **continue** continuer; **continuous** continu; **continuously** continuellement

contort [kən'tɔːrt] *face* tordre; ~ **one's body** se contorsionner

contraception [kɑːntrə'sepʃn] contraception *f*; **contraceptive** contraceptif *m*

contract[1] ['kɑːntrækt] *n* contrat *m*

contract[2] [kən'trækt] **1** *v/i* (*shrink*) se contracter **2** *v/t illness* contracter

contractor [kən'træktər] entrepreneur *m*

contractual [kən'træktuəl] contractuel

contradict [kɑːntrə'dɪkt] contredire; **contradiction** contradiction *f*; **contradictory** contradictoire

contrary[1] ['kɑːntrərɪ] **1** *adj* contraire; ~ **to …** contrairement à … **2** *n*: **on the** ~ au contraire

contrary[2] [kən'trerɪ] *adj* (*perverse*) contrariant

contrast ['kɑːntræst] **1** *n* contraste *m* **2** *v/t* mettre en contraste **3** *v/i* contraster; **contrasting** contrastant; **views** opposé

contravene [kɑːntrə'viːn] enfreindre

contribute [kən'trɪbjuːt] **1** contribuer (**to** à); *to magazine* collaborer (**to** à) **2** *v/t money, suggestion* donner, apporter; **contribution** contribution *f*; *to political party, church* don *m*; **contributor** *of money* donateur *m*; *to magazine* collaborateur(-trice) *m(f)*

control [kən'troul] **1** *n* contrôle *m*; **be in** ~ **of** contrôler **2** *v/t* contrôler; *company* diriger

controversial [kɑːntrə'vɜːrʃl] controversé; **controversy** controverse *f*

convenience [kən'viːnɪəns] commodité *f*; **at your** ~ à votre convenance; **convenience store** magasin *m* de proximité; **convenient** commode, pratique

convent ['kɑːnvənt] couvent *m*

convention [kən'venʃn] (*tradition*) conventions *fpl*; (*conference*) convention *f*; **conventional** conventionnel; *person* conformiste

conversation [kɑːnvər'seɪʃn] conversation *f*; **conversational** de conversation

conversion [kən'vɜːrʃn] conversion *f*; *of building* aménagement *m*; **convert 1** *n* converti *m* **2** *v/t* convertir; *building* aménager; **convertible** *car* (voiture *f*) décapotable *f*

convey [kən'veɪ] (*transmit*) transmettre; (*carry*) trans-

porter; **conveyor belt** convoyeur *m*, tapis *m* roulant
convict 1 ['kɑːnvɪkt] *n* détenu *m* **2** [kən'vɪkt] *v/t* LAW déclarer coupable; **conviction** LAW condamnation *f*; (*belief*) conviction *f*
convince [kən'vɪns] convaincre
convoy ['kɑːnvɔɪ] convoi *m*
cook [kuk] **1** *n* cuisinier(-ière) *m(f)* **2** *v/t meal* préparer; *food* faire cuire **3** *v/i* faire la cuisine; *of food* cuire; **cookery** cuisine *f*; **cookbook** livre *m* de cuisine; **cookie** cookie *m*; **cooking** cuisine *f*
cool [kuːl] **1** *n:* **keep one's ~** garder son sang-froid **2** *adj* frais; *dress* léger; (*calm*) calme; (*unfriendly*) froid; P (*great*) cool **3** *v/i refroidir; of tempers* se calmer; *of interest* diminuer **4** *v/t :* **~ it** on se calme
◆ **cool down 1** *v/i* refroidir; *of weather* se rafraîchir; *: of tempers* se calmer **2** *v/t food* (faire) refroidir; *fig* calmer
cooperate [kouˈɑːpəreɪt] coopérer; **cooperation** coopération *f*; **cooperative 1** *n* COM coopérative *f* **2** *adj* coopératif
coordinate [kouˈɔːrdɪneɪt] coordonner; **coordination** coordination *f*
cop [kɑːp] F flic *m* F
cope [koup] se débrouiller; **~**

with ... faire face à ...
copier ['kɑːpɪər] *machine* photocopieuse *f*
copper ['kɑːpər] cuivre *m*
copy ['kɑːpɪ] **1** *n* copie *f*; *of book* exemplaire *m* **2** *v/t* copier; (*photocopy*) photocopier
cord [kɔːrd] (*string*) corde *f*; (*cable*) fil *m*, cordon *m*
cordon ['kɔːrdn] cordon *m*
cords [kɔːrdz] *pants* pantalon *m* en velours (côtelé)
core [kɔːr] **1** *n of fruit, problem* cœur *m*; *of party* noyau *m* **2** *adj issue* fondamental
cork [kɔːrk] *in bottle* bouchon *m*; *material* liège *m*; **corkscrew** tire-bouchon *m*
corn [kɔːrn] *grain* maïs *m*
corner ['kɔːrnər] **1** *n* coin *m*; *in road* virage *m*, tournant *m*; *in soccer* corner *m*; **on the ~** *of street* au coin **2** *v/t person* coincer; **~ the market** accaparer le marché **3** *v/i of driver, car* prendre le/les virage(s)
coronary ['kɑːrənerɪ] **1** *adj* coronaire **2** *n* infarctus *m* (du myocarde)
coroner ['kɑːrənər] coroner *m*
corporal ['kɔːrpərəl] caporal *m*; **corporal punishment** châtiment *m* corporel
corporate ['kɔːrpərət] COM d'entreprise; **corporation** (*business*) société *f*, entreprise *f*

counter-attack

corpse [kɔːrps] cadavre *m*, corps *m*
corral [kəˈræl] corral *m*
correct [kəˈrekt] **1** *adj* correct; ***the ~ answer*** la bonne réponse; ***that's ~*** c'est exact **2** *v/t* corriger; **correction** correction *f*; **correctly** correctement
correspond [kɑːrɪˈspɑːnd] correspondre (**to** à); **correspondence** correspondance *f*; **correspondent** correspondant(e) *m(f)*
corridor [ˈkɑːrɪdɔːr] couloir *m*
corroborate [kəˈrɑːbəreɪt] corroborer
corrosion [kəˈrouʒn] corrosion *f*
corrupt [kəˈrʌpt] **1** *adj also* COMPUT corrompu; MORALS, YOUTH dépravé **2** *v/t* corrompre; **corruption** corruption *f*
cosmetic [kɑːzˈmetɪk] cosmétique *f*; *fig* esthétique; **cosmetics** cosmétiques *mpl*; **cosmetic surgery** chirurgie *f* esthétique
cosmopolitan [kɑːzməˈpɑːlɪtən] cosmopolite
cost [kɑːst] **1** *n also fig* coût *m* **2** *v/t* coûter; ***how much does it ~?*** combien ça coûte?
cost-effective rentable; **cost of living** coût *m* de la vie
costume [ˈkɑːstuːm] *for actor* costume *m*
cosy *Br* → **cozy**
cot [kɑːt] (*camp-bed*) lit *m* de camp; *Br for child* lit *m* d'en-

fant
cottage [ˈkɑːtɪdʒ] cottage *m*
cotton [ˈkɑːtn] **1** *n* coton *m* **2** *adj* en coton; **cotton candy** barbe *f* à papa; **cotton wool** *Br* coton *m* hydrophile, ouate *f*
couch [kautʃ] canapé *m*; **couch potato** téléphage *m/f*
cough [kɑːf] **1** *n* toux *f* **2** *v/i* tousser; **cough medicine**, **cough syrup** sirop *m* contre la toux
could [kud]: ***~ I have my key?*** pourrais-je avoir ma clef?; ***~ you help me?*** pourrais-tu m'aider?; ***you ~ be right*** vous avez peut-être raison; ***you ~ have warned me!*** tu aurais pu me prévenir!
council [ˈkaunsl] (*assembly*) conseil *m*, assemblée *f*; **councilor** conseiller *m*
counsel [ˈkaunsl] **1** *n* (*advice*) conseil *m*; (*lawyer*) avocat *m* **2** *v/t* conseiller; **counseling**, *Br* **counselling** aide *f* (*psychologique*); **counselor**, *Br* **counsellor** (*adviser*) conseiller *m*; LAW maître *m*
count [kaunt] **1** *n* compte *m* **2** *v/t & v/i* compter
♦ **count on** compter sur
countdown compte *m* à rebours
counter [ˈkauntər] *in shop, café* comptoir *m*; *in game* pion *m*
counteract neutraliser, contrecarrer; **counter-attack 1**

n contre-attaque *f* **2** *v/i* contre-attaquer; **counterclockwise** dans le sens inverse des aiguilles d'une montre; **counterespionage** contre-espionnage *m*; **counterfeit 1** *v/t* contrefaire **2** *adj* faux; **counterpart** *person* homologue *m/f*; **counterproductive** contre-productif

countless ['kaʊntlɪs] innombrable

country ['kʌntrɪ] pays *m*; *as opposed to town* campagne *f*

county ['kaʊntɪ] comté *m*

coup [kuː] POL coup *m* d'État; *fig* beau coup *m*

couple ['kʌpl] (*two people*) couple *m*; **a ~ of** (*a pair*) deux; (*a few*) quelques

courage ['kʌrɪdʒ] courage *m*; **courageous** courageux

courier ['kʊrɪər] (*messenger*) coursier *m*; *with tourist party* guide *m/f*

course [kɔːrs] *of lessons* cours *m(pl)*; *of meal* plat *m*; *of ship, plane* route *f*; *for sports* piste *f*; *for golf* terrain *m*; **of ~** bien sûr; **of ~ not** bien sûr que non

court [kɔːrt] LAW tribunal *m*, cour *f*; FOR TENNIS court *m*; *for basketball* terrain *m*; **take s.o. to ~** faire un procès à qn; **court case** affaire *f*, procès *m*

courtesy ['kɜːrtəsɪ] courtoisie *f*

'**courthouse** palais *m* de justi-

ce, tribunal *m*; **courtroom** salle *f* d'audience; **courtyard** cour *f*

cousin ['kʌzn] cousin(e) *m(f)*

cover ['kʌvər] **1** *n protective housse f*; *of book, magazine* couverture *f*; (*shelter*) abri *m*; (*insurance*) couverture *f*, assurance *f* **2** *v/t* couvrir

◆ **cover up 1** *v/t* couvrir; *scandal* dissimuler **2** *v/i* cacher la vérité

coverage ['kʌvərɪdʒ] *by media* couverture *f* (médiatique)

covert ['koʊvɜːrt] secret, clandestin

'**cover-up** black-out *m inv*

cow [kaʊ] vache *f*

coward ['kaʊərd] lâche *m/f*; **cowardice** lâcheté *f*

'**cowboy** cow-boy *m*

co-worker ['koʊwɜːrkər] collègue *m/f*

cozy ['koʊzɪ] confortable, douillet

crab [kræb] crabe *m*

crack [kræk] **1** *n* fissure *f*; *in cup, glass* fêlure *f*; (*joke*) vanne *f* **2** *v/t cup, glass* fêler; *nut* casser; (*solve*) résoudre; *code* décrypter **3** *v/i* se fêler; *crack* (*cocaine*) crack *m*; **cracked** *cup* fêlé; **cracker** *to eat* cracker *m*

cradle ['kreɪdl] berceau *m*

craft[1] [kræft] NAUT embarcation *f*

craft[2] (*trade*) métier *m*; *weaving, pottery etc* artisanat *m*;

(*craftsmanship*) art *m*;
craftsman (*artisan*) artisan *m*; **crafty** malin, rusé

crag [kræg] (*rock*) rocher *m* escarpé

cram [kræm] fourrer; *food* enfourner; *people* entasser

cramps [kræmps] crampe *f*

crane [kreɪn] **1** *n* (*machine*) grue *f* **2** *v/t*: ~ **one's neck** tendre le cou

crank [kræŋk] *person* allumé *m*; **cranky** (*bad-tempered*) grognon

crash [kræʃ] **1** *n noise* fracas *m*; *accident* accident *m*; COM faillite *f*; *of stock exchange* krach *m*; COMPUT plantage *m* **2** *v/i* s'écraser; *of car* avoir un accident; *of market* s'effondrer; COMPUT se planter **3** *v/t car* avoir un accident avec; **crash course** cours *m* intensif; **crash diet** régime *m* intensif; **crash helmet** casque *m*; **crash-land** atterrir en catastrophe

crate [kreɪt] caisse *f*

crater ['kreɪtər] cratère *m*

crave [kreɪv] avoir très envie de; **craving** envie *f* (irrépressible)

crawl [krɔːl] **1** *n in swimming* crawl *m* **2** *v/i on belly* ramper; *on hands and knees* marcher à quatre pattes; (*move slowly*) se traîner

crayon ['kreɪɑːn] crayon *m* de couleur

craze [kreɪz] engouement *m*;

the latest ~ la dernière mode; **crazy** fou

creak [kriːk] craquer, grincer; **creaky** qui craque, grinçant

cream [kriːm] **1** *n* crème *f*; *color* crème *m* **2** *adj* crème *inv*

crease [kriːs] **1** *n* pli *m* **2** *v/t accidentally* froisser

create [kriː'eɪt] créer; **creation** création *f*; **creative** créatif; **creator** créateur(-trice) *m(f)*

creature ['kriːtʃər] animal *m*; (*person*) créature *f*

credibility [kredə'bɪlətɪ] crédibilité *f*; **credible** crédible

credit ['kredɪt] crédit *m*; (*honor*) honneur *m*, mérite *m*; **creditable** honorable; **credit card** carte *f* de crédit; **credit limit** limite *f* de crédit; **creditor** créancier *m*; **creditworthy** solvable

creep [kriːp] **1** *n pej* sale type *m* **2** *v/i* se glisser (en silence); (*move slowly*) avancer lentement; **creepy** flippant F

cremate [krɪ'meɪt] incinérer; **cremation** incinération *f*, crémation *f*

crest [krest] crête *f*

crevice ['krevɪs] fissure *f*

crew [kruː] *of ship, airplane* équipage *m*; **crew cut** cheveux *mpl* en brosse

crib [krɪb] *for baby* lit *m* d'enfant

crime [kraɪm] crime *m*; **criminal 1** *n* criminel *m* **2** *adj* cri-

minel; (*shameful*) honteux
crimson ['krɪmzn] cramoisi
cripple ['krɪpl] **1** *n* handicapé(e) *m(f)* **2** *v/t person* estropier; *fig* paralyser
crisis ['kraɪsɪs] crise *f*
crisp [krɪsp] *weather* vivifiant; *lettuce, apple* croquant; *bacon, toast* croustillant; **crisps** *Br* chips *fpl*
criterion [kraɪ'tɪrɪən] critère *m*
critic ['krɪtɪk] critique *m*; **critical** critique; **criticism** critique *f*; **criticize** critiquer
crocodile ['krɑːkədaɪl] crocodile *m*
crony ['krouni] pote *m* , copain *m*
crook [krʊk] escroc *m*; **crooked** de travers; *streets* tortueux; (*dishonest*) malhonnête
crop [krɑːp] **1** *n* culture *f*; (*harvest*) récolte *f* **2** *v/t hair, photo* couper
♦ **crop up** surgir
cross [krɑːs] **1** *adj* (*angry*) fâché **2** *n* croix *f* **3** *v/t* (*go across*) traverser; **~ o.s.** REL se signer **4** *v/i* (*go across*) traverser; *of lines* se croiser
♦ **cross off, cross out** rayer
'crosscheck 1 *n* recoupement *m* **2** *v/t* vérifier par recoupement; **cross-examine** LAW faire subir un contre-interrogatoire à; **cross-eyed** qui louche; **crossing** NAUT traversée *f*; **crossroads** *also*

fig carrefour *m*; **crosswalk** passage *m* (pour) piétons; **crossword** (**puzzle**) mots *mpl* croisés
crotch [krɑːtʃ] entrejambe *m*
crouch [kraʊtʃ] s'accroupir
crowd [kraʊd] foule *f*; *at sports event* public *m*; **crowded** bondé, plein (de monde)
crown [kraʊn] *also on tooth* couronne *f*
crucial ['kruːʃl] crucial
crucifix ['kruːsɪfɪks] crucifix *m*; **crucifixion** *of Christ* crucifixion *f*; **crucify** REL crucifier; *fig* assassiner
crude [kruːd] **1** *adj* (*vulgar*) grossier; (*unsophisticated*) rudimentaire **2** *n*: **~ (oil)** pétrole *m* brut
cruel ['kruːəl] cruel; **cruelty** cruauté *f*
cruise [kruːz] **1** *n* croisière *f* **2** *v/i of people* faire une croisière; *of car* rouler (à une vitesse de croisière); *of plane* voler (à une vitesse de croisière)
crumb [krʌm] miette *f*
crumble ['krʌmbl] *of bread* s'émietter; *of stonework* s'effriter; *fig: of opposition etc* s'effondrer
crumple ['krʌmpl] **1** *v/t* (*crease*) froisser **2** *v/i* (*collapse*) s'écrouler
crush [krʌʃ] **1** *n* (*crowd*) foule *f* **2** *v/t* écraser; (*crease*) froisser

crust [krʌst] *on bread* croûte *f*

crutch [krʌtʃ] *for injured person* béquille *f*

cry [kraɪ] **1** *n* (*call*) cri *m* **2** *v/i* (*weep*) pleurer

◆ **cry out** crier

cryptic [ˈkrɪptɪk] énigmatique

crystal [ˈkrɪstl] cristal *m*

cube [kjuːb] cube *m*; **cubic** cubique; **~ meter** mètre cube

cubicle [ˈkjuːbɪkl] (*changing room*) cabine *f*

cuddle [ˈkʌdl] câliner

cue [kjuː] *for actor etc* signal *m*; *for pool* queue *f*

cuff [kʌf] *of shirt* poignet *m*; *of pants* revers *m*; (*blow*) gifle *f*

culminate [ˈkʌlmɪneɪt]: **~ in** se terminer par; **culmination** apogée *f*

culprit [ˈkʌlprɪt] coupable *m/f*

cult [kʌlt] (*sect*) secte *f*

cultivate [ˈkʌltɪveɪt] *land, person* cultiver; **cultivated** *person* cultivé; **cultivation** *of land* culture *f*

cultural [ˈkʌltʃərəl] culturel; **culture** culture *f*; **cultured** cultivé

cumulative [ˈkjuːmjʊlətɪv] cumulatif

cunning [ˈkʌnɪŋ] **1** *n* ruse *f* **2** *adj* rusé

cup [kʌp] tasse *f*; (*trophy*) coupe *f*

cupboard [ˈkʌbərd] placard *m*

curb [kɜːrb] **1** *n of street* bord *m* du trottoir; *on powers etc* frein *m* **2** *v/t* réfréner

cure [kjʊr] **1** *n* MED remède *m* **2** *v/t* MED guérir; *meat* saurer

curiosity [kjʊriˈɑːsəti] curiosité *f*; **curious** curieux

curl [kɜːrl] **1** *n in hair* boucle *f*; *of smoke* volute *f* **2** *v/t hair* boucler; (*wind*) enrouler **3** *v/i of hair* boucler; *of leaf, paper etc* se gondoler

◆ **curl up** se pelotonner

curly [ˈkɜːrlɪ] *hair* bouclé; *tail* en tire-bouchon

currency [ˈkʌrənsɪ] monnaie *f*; **foreign ~** devise étrangère; **current 1** *n in sea,* ELEC courant *m* **2** *adj* actuel; **current affairs** actualité *f*

curse [kɜːrs] **1** *n* (*spell*) malédiction *f*; (*swearword*) juron *m* **2** *v/t* maudire **3** *v/i* (*swear*) jurer

cursor [ˈkɜːrsər] COMPUT curseur *m*

cursory [ˈkɜːrsərɪ] superficiel

curt [kɜːrt] abrupt

curtain [ˈkɜːrtn] *also* THEA rideau *m*

curve [kɜːrv] **1** *n* courbe *f* **2** *v/i* (*bend*) s'incurver; *of road* faire une courbe

cushion [ˈkʊʃn] **1** *n* coussin *m* **2** *v/t blow, fall* amortir

custody [ˈkʌstədɪ] *of children* garde *f*; **in ~** LAW en détention

custom [ˈkʌstəm] coutume *f*; COM clientèle *f*; **customer** client *m*; **customer service** service *m* clientèle

customs [ˈkʌstəmz] douane

f; **customs officer** douanier *m*

cut [kʌt] **1** *n with knife, scissors* entaille *f*; *(injury)* coupure *f*; *of garment, hair* coupe *f*; *(reduction)* réduction *f* **2** *v/t* couper; *(reduce)* réduire; **get one's hair ~** se faire couper les cheveux

◆ **cut down 1** *v/t tree* abattre **2** *v/i on smoking etc* réduire

◆ **cut off** couper; *(isolate)* isoler

◆ **cut up** *meat etc* découper

cutback réduction *f*

cute [kjuːt] *in appearance* mignon; *(clever)* malin

'cutoff date date *f* limite; **cut-price** à prix *m* réduit; **cut-**-throat *competition* acharné; **cutting 1** *n from newspaper* coupure *f* **2** *adj remark* blessant

cyber ... ['saɪbər] cyber...

cycle ['saɪkl] **1** *n* vélo *m*; *of events* cycle *m* **2** *v/i* aller en vélo; **cycling** cyclisme *m*; **cyclist** cycliste *m/f*

cylinder ['sɪlɪndər] *in engine* cylindre *m*; **cylindrical** cylindrique

cynic ['sɪnɪk] cynique *m/f*; **cynical** cynique; **cynicism** cynisme *m*

Czech [tʃek] **1** *adj* tchèque; **the ~ Republic** la République tchèque **2** *n person* Tchèque *m/f*; *language* tchèque *m*

D

DA [diː'eɪ] (= **district attorney**) procureur *m*

◆ **dabble** in toucher à

dad [dæd] papa *m*

daily ['deɪlɪ] **1** *n paper* quotidien *m* **2** *adj* quotidien

'dairy products produits *mpl* laitiers

dam [dæm] *for water* barrage *m*

damage ['dæmɪdʒ] **1** *n* dommage(s) *m(pl)*; *to reputation* préjudice *m* **2** *v/t* endommager; *fig: reputation* nuire à; **damages** LAW dommages--intérêts *mpl*; **damaging** préjudiciable

damn [dæm] F **1** *interj* zut **2** *adj* sacré **3** *adv* (*very*) vachement F; **damning** *evidence, report* accablant

damp [dæmp] humide

dance [dæns] **1** *n* danse *f*; *social event* bal *m* **2** *v/i* danser; **dancer** danseur(-euse) *m(f)*; **dancing** danse *f*

Dane [deɪn] Danois(e) *m(f)*

danger ['deɪndʒər] danger *m*; **dangerous** dangereux

dangle ['dæŋgl] **1** *v/t* balancer **2** *v/i* pendre

Danish ['deɪnɪʃ] **1** *adj* danois **2** *n language* danois *m*

Danish (**pastry**) feuilleté *m*

(sucré)

dare [der] **1** v/i oser; **~ to do sth** oser faire qch **2** v/t: **s.o. to do sth** défier qn de faire qch; **daring** audacieux

dark [dɑ:rk] **1** n noir m **2** adj room sombre, noir; hair brun; eyes, color, clothes foncé; **dark glasses** lunettes fpl noires; **darkness** obscurité f

darling ['dɑ:rlɪŋ] chéri(e) m(f)

dart [dɑ:rt] **1** n for game fléchette f **2** v/i se précipiter

dash [dæʃ] **1** n punctuation tiret m; **a~ of** un peu de **2** v/i se précipiter **3** v/t hopes anéantir; **dashboard** tableau m de bord

data ['deɪtə] données fpl; **database** base f de données

date[1] [deɪt] fruit datte f

date[2] [deɪt] date f; meeting, person rendez-vous m; **out of ~** clothes démodé; passport périmé; **up to~** information à jour; style à la mode; **dated** démodé

daughter ['dɔ:tər] fille f; **daughter-in-law** belle-fille f

dawn [dɔ:n] also fig aube f

day [deɪ] jour m; stressing duration journée f; **the ~ after** le lendemain; **the ~ after tomorrow** après-demain; **the ~ before** la veille; **the ~ before yesterday** avant-hier; **in those ~s** en ce temps-là, à l'époque; **the other ~** (recently) l'autre jour; day-

break aube f, point m du jour; **daydream 1** n rêverie f **2** v/i rêvasser; **daylight** jour m; **day spa** spa m urbain

dazed [deɪzd] by news hébété; by blow étourdi

dazzle ['dæzl] éblouir

dead [ded] **1** adj mort; battery à plat; **the phone's ~** il n'y a pas de tonalité **2** adv F (very) très; **~ beat, ~ tired** crevé **3** npl: **the ~** les morts mpl; **dead end** street impasse f; **dead heat** arrivée f ex æquo; **deadline** date f limite; heure f limite, délai m; for newspaper heure f de clôture; **meet the ~** respecter le(s) délai(s); **deadlock** in talks impasse f; **deadly** mortel

deaf [def] sourd; **deafening** assourdissant; **deafness** surdité f

deal [di:l] **1** n accord m, marché m; **a great ~ of** beaucoup de **2** v/t cards distribuer

♦ **deal in** COM être dans le commerce de; drugs dealer

♦ **deal with** (handle) s'occuper de; (do business with) traiter avec; (be about) traiter de

dealer ['di:lər] marchand m; (drug ~) dealer m, dealeuse f; large-scale trafiquant m de drogue; **dealing** (drug ~) trafic m de drogue; **dealings** (business) relations fpl

dear [dɪr] cher; **Dear Sir** Monsieur

death [deθ] mort *f*; **death toll** nombre *m* de morts

debatable [dɪ'beɪtəbl] discutable; **debate 1** *n* débat *m* **2** *v/i* débattre **3** *v/t* débattre de

debit ['debɪt] **1** *n* débit *m* **2** *v/t account* débiter; *amount* porter au débit; **debit card** carte *f* bancaire

debris [də'briː] débris *mpl*

debt [det] dette *f*; **be in ~** être endetté; **debtor** débiteur *m*

debug [diː'bʌg] COMPUT déboguer

decade ['dekeɪd] décennie *f*

decadent ['dekədənt] décadent

decaffeinated [dɪ'kæfɪneɪtɪd] décaféiné

decay [dɪ'keɪ] **1** *n* détérioration *f*; *in wood, plant* pourriture *f*; *in teeth* carie *f* **2** *v/i of wood, plant* pourrir; *of civilization* tomber en décadence; *of teeth* se carier

deceased [dɪ'siːst]: *the ~* le défunt/la défunte

deceit [dɪ'siːt] duplicité *f*; **deceitful** fourbe; **deceive** tromper

December [dɪ'sembər] décembre *m*

decency ['diːsənsɪ] décence *f*; **decent** *person* correct, honnête; *salary* correct, décent; *meal, sleep* bon

deception [dɪ'sepʃn] tromperie *f*; **deceptive** trompeur

decide [dɪ'saɪd] décider; de-

cided (*definite*) décidé; *views* arrêté; *improvement* net

decimal ['desɪml] décimale *f*

decipher [dɪ'saɪfər] déchiffrer

decision [dɪ'sɪʒn] décision *f*; **decisive** décidé; (*crucial*) décisif

deck [dek] *of ship* pont *m*; *of cards* jeu *m* (de cartes)

declaration [deklə'reɪʃn] déclaration *f*; **declare** déclarer

decline [dɪ'klaɪn] **1** *n* baisse *f*; *of civilization, health* déclin *m* **2** *v/t invitation* décliner; **~ to comment** refuser de commenter **3** *v/i* (*refuse*) refuser; (*decrease*) baisser; *of health* décliner

decode [diː'koʊd] décoder

décor ['deɪkɔːr] décor *m*

decorate ['dekəreɪt] *room* refaire; *with paint* peindre; *with paper* tapisser; (*adorn*), *soldier* décorer; **decoration** décoration *f*; **decorator** (*interior ~*) décorateur *m* (d'intérieur)

decoy ['diːkɔɪ] appât *m*, leurre *m*

decrease ['diːkriːs] **1** *n* baisse *f*, diminution *f*; *in size* réduction *f* **2** *v/t* & *v/i* diminuer

dedicate ['dedɪkeɪt] *book etc* dédicacer; **dedicated** dévoué; **dedication** *in book* dédicace *f*; *to cause, work* dévouement *m*

deduce [dɪ'duːs] déduire

deduct [dɪ'dʌkt] déduire

(*from* de); **deduction** *from salary* prélèvement *m*; (*conclusion*) déduction *f*

deed [di:d] (*act*) acte *m*; LAW acte *m* (notarié)

deep [di:p] profond; *voice* grave; *color* intense; **deepen 1** *v/t* creuser **2** *v/i* devenir plus profond; *of mystery* s'épaissir; **deep freeze** congélateur *m*

deer [dɪr] cerf *m*; *female* biche *f*

deface [dɪ'feɪs] abîmer

defamation [defə'meɪʃn] diffamation *f*; **defamatory** diffamatoire

defeat [dɪ'fi:t] **1** *n* défaite *f* **2** *v/t* battre

defect ['di:fekt] défaut *m*; **defective** défectueux

defence *Br* → **defense**

defend [dɪ'fend] défendre; *decision* justifier; **defendant** défendeur *m*, défenderesse *f*; *in criminal case* accusé(e) *m(f)*; **defense** défense *f*; **defenseless** sans défense; **Defense Secretary** POL ministre de la Défense; **defensive 1** *n*: **go on(to) the** ~ se mettre sur la défensive **2** *adj* défensif

deference ['defərəns] déférence *f*

defiance [dɪ'faɪəns] défi *m*; **defiant** [dɪ'faɪənt] provocant; *look* de défi

deficiency [dɪ'fɪʃənsɪ] manque *m*; MED carence *f*

deficit ['defɪsɪt] déficit *m*

define [dɪ'faɪn] définir

definite ['defɪnɪt] définitif; *improvement* net; (*certain*) catégorique; **definitely** sans aucun doute; ~ **not** certainement pas!

definition [defɪ'nɪʃn] définition *f*

deformity [dɪ'fɔ:rmətɪ] difformité *f*

defrost [di:'frɒst] *food* décongeler; *fridge* dégivrer

defuse [di:'fju:z] *bomb, situation* désamorcer

defy [dɪ'faɪ] défier; *superiors* braver

degrading [dɪ'greɪdɪŋ] dégradant

degree [dɪ'gri:] degré *m*; *from university* diplôme *m*

dehydrated [di:haɪ'dreɪtɪd] déshydraté

deign [deɪn]: ~ **to** daigner

dejected [dɪ'dʒektɪd] déprimé

delay [dɪ'leɪ] **1** *n* retard *m* **2** *v/t* retarder; **be ~ed** être en retard **3** *v/i* tarder

delegate ['delɪɡət] **1** *n* délégué(e) *m(f)* **2** *v/t* déléguer; **delegation** délégation *f*

delete [dɪ'li:t] effacer; (*cross out*) rayer; **deletion** *act* effacement *m*; *that deleted* rature *f*

deliberate 1 [dɪ'lɪbərət] *adj* délibéré **2** [dɪ'lɪbəreɪt] *v/i* délibérer; (*reflect*) réfléchir; **deliberately** délibérément, exprès

delicate ['delɪkət] délicat

delicatessen [delɪkə'tesn] traiteur *m*, épicerie *f* fine

delicious [dɪ'lɪʃəs] délicieux

delight [dɪ'laɪt] joie *f*, plaisir *m*; **delighted** ravi; **delightful** charmant

deliver [dɪ'lɪvər] livrer; *letters* distribuer; *parcel etc* remettre; *message* transmettre; *baby* mettre au monde; *speech* faire; **delivery** *of goods* livraison *f*; *of mail* distribution *f*; *of baby* accouchement *m*; *of speech* débit *m*; **delivery date** date *f* de livraison

de luxe [dɪ'lʌks] de luxe; *model* haut de gamme *inv*

demand [dɪ'mænd] **1** *n also* COM demande *f*; *of terrorist, unions etc* revendication *f*; **in** ∼ demandé **2** *v/t* exiger; *pay rise etc* réclamer; **demanding** *job* éprouvant; *person* exigeant

demo ['deməʊ] (*protest*) manif *f*; *of video etc* démo *f*

democracy [dɪ'mɑːkrəsɪ] démocratie *f*; **democrat** démocrate *m/f*; **democratic** démocratique

demolish [dɪ'mɑːlɪʃ] *building, argument* démolir; **demolition** démolition *f*

demonstrate ['demənstreɪt] **1** *v/t* (*prove*) démontrer; *machine etc* faire une démonstration de **2** *v/i politically* manifester; **demonstration** démonstration *f*; (*protest*) manifestation *f*; **demonstrator** (*protester*) manifestant(e) *m(f)*

demoralized [dɪ'mɔːrəlaɪzd] démoralisé; **demoralizing** démoralisant

demote [diː'məʊt] rétrograder

den [den] *room* antre *f*

denial [dɪ'naɪəl] *of accusation* démenti *m*, dénégation *f*; *of request* refus *m*

denim ['denɪm] jean *m*

Denmark ['denmɑːrk] le Danemark

denomination [dɪnɑːmɪ'neɪʃn] *of money* coupure *f*; *religious* confession *f*

dense [dens] (*thick*) dense; **density** ['densɪtɪ] densité *f*

dent [dent] **1** *n* bosse *f* **2** *v/t* bosseler

dental ['dentl] dentaire

dented ['dentɪd] bosselé

dentist ['dentɪst] dentiste *m/f*; **dentures** dentier *m*

Denver boot ['denvər] sabot *m* de Denver

deny [dɪ'naɪ] *charge* nier; *right, request* refuser

deodorant [diː'əʊdərənt] déodorant *m*

department [dɪ'pɑːrtmənt] *of company* service *m*; *of university* département *m*; *of government* ministère *m*; *of store* rayon *m*; **Department of State** ministère *m* des Affaires étrangères; **depart-**

ment store grand magasin *m*

departure [dɪ'pɑːrtʃər] départ *m*; *from standard etc* entorse *f* (**from** à); **departure lounge** salle *f* d'embarquement; **departure time** heure *f* de départ

depend [dɪ'pend] dépendre; *that* **~s** cela dépend; **dependence, dependency** dépendance *f*

depict [dɪ'pɪkt] représenter

deplorable [dɪ'plɔːrəbl] déplorable; **deplore** déplorer

deploy [dɪ'plɔɪ] (*use*) faire usage de; (*position*) déployer

deport [dɪ'pɔːrt] expulser; **deportation** expulsion *f*

deposit [dɪ'pɑːzɪt] **1** *n* in bank dépôt *m*; *on purchase* acompte *m*; *security* caution *f*; *of mineral* gisement *m* **2** *v/t money, object* déposer; **deposition** LAW déposition *f*

depot ['depou] *for storage* dépôt *m*, entrepôt *m*

depreciation [dɪpriːʃɪ'eɪʃn] FIN dépréciation *f*

depress [dɪ'pres] *person* déprimer; **depressed** déprimé; **depressing** déprimant; **depression** MED, *meteorological* dépression *f*, *economic* crise *f*, récession *f*

deprivation [deprɪ'veɪʃn] privation(s) *f(pl)*; **deprive**: **~ s.o. of sth** priver qn de qch; **deprived** défavorisé

depth [depθ] profondeur *f*; *of color* intensité *f*; **in ~** en pro-

fondeur

deputy ['depjʊt] adjoint(e) *m(f)*; *of sheriff* shérif *m* adjoint

derail [dɪ'reɪl]: **be ~ed** of train dérailler

derelict ['derəlɪkt] délabré

deride [dɪ'raɪd] se moquer de; **derision** dérision *f*; **derisory** dérisoire

derivative [dɪ'rɪvətɪv] (*not original*) dérivé

derive [dɪ'raɪv] tirer (**from** de); **be ~d from** dériver de

dermatologist [dɜːrmə-'tɑːlədʒɪst] dermatologue *m/f*

derogatory [dɪ'rɑːɡətɔːrɪ] désobligeant; *term* péjoratif

descendant [dɪ'sendənt] descendant(e) *m(f)*; **descent** descente *f*; (*ancestry*) descendance *f*

describe [dɪ'skraɪb] décrire; **description** description *f*; *of criminal* signalement *m*

desegregate [diː'seɡrəɡeɪt] supprimer la ségrégation dans

desert[1] ['dezərt] *n* désert *m*

desert[2] [dɪ'zɜːrt] **1** *v/t* abandonner **2** *v/i* of soldier déserter; **deserted** désert; **deserter** MIL déserteur *m*; **desertion** abandon *m*; MIL désertion *f*

deserve [dɪ'zɜːrv] mériter

design [dɪ'zaɪn] **1** *n* (*subject*) design *m*; (*style*) style *m*; (*drawing, pattern*) dessin *m*

2 v/t (draw) dessiner; building, car concevoir

designate ['dezɪgneɪt] person désigner

designer [dɪ'zaɪnər] designer m/f; of car, ship concepteur(-trice) m(f); of clothes styliste m/f; **designer clothes** vêtements mpl de marque

desirable [dɪ'zaɪrəbl] souhaitable; sexually, change désirable; house beau; **desire** désir m

desk [desk] bureau m; in hotel réception f; **desk clerk** réceptionniste m/f; **desktop publishing** publication f assistée par ordinateur

desolate ['desələt] place désolé

despair [dɪ'sper] **1** n désespoir m; **in ~** désespéré **2** v/i désespérer (**of** de); **desperate** désespéré; **be ~ for sth** avoir très envie de qch; **desperation** désespoir m; **in ~** en désespoir de cause

despicable [dɪs'pɪkəbl] méprisable; **despise** mépriser

despite [dɪ'spaɪt] malgré, en dépit de

dessert [dɪ'zɜːrt] dessert m

destination [destɪ'neɪʃn] destination f

destroy [dɪ'strɔɪ] détruire; **destroyer** NAUT destroyer m; **destruction** destruction f; **destructive** power destructeur; **a ~ child** un enfant qui casse tout

detach [dɪ'tætʃ] détacher; **detached** (objective) neutre; **detachment** (objectivity) neutralité f

detail ['diːteɪl] détail m; **detailed** détaillé

detain [dɪ'teɪn] (hold back) retenir; as prisoner détenir; **detainee** détenu(e) m(f); **political ~** prisonnier m politique

detect [dɪ'tekt] déceler; of device détecter; **detection** of criminal découverte f; of smoke etc détection f; **detective** inspecteur m de police; **detector** détecteur m

détente ['deɪtɑːnt] POL détente f

deter [dɪ'tɜːr] dissuader

detergent [dɪ'tɜːrdʒənt] détergent m

deteriorate [dɪ'tɪrɪəreɪt] se détériorer

determination [dɪtɜːrmɪ'neɪʃn] (resolution) détermination f; **determine** (establish) déterminer; **determined** déterminé, résolu; effort délibéré

detest [dɪ'test] détester; **detestable** détestable

detour ['diːtʊr] détour m; (diversion) déviation f

devaluation [diːvæljʊ'eɪʃn] dévaluation f; **devalue** dévaluer

devastate ['devəsteɪt] dévaster; fig: person anéantir

develop [dɪ'veləp] **1** v/t *film, business* développer; *site* aménager; *technique, vaccine* mettre au point; *illness* attraper **2** v/i (*grow*) se développer; **developing country** pays m en voie de développement; **development** *of film, business* développement m; *of site* aménagement m; (*event*) événement m; *of technique, vaccine* mise f au point

device [dɪ'vaɪs] (*tool*) appareil m

devil ['devl] diable m; **a little ~** un petit monstre

devise [dɪ'vaɪz] concevoir

devote [dɪ'vəʊt] consacrer; **devoted** *son etc* dévoué (**to** à); **devotion** dévouement m

devour [dɪ'vaʊər] dévorer

devout [dɪ'vaʊt] pieux

diabetes [daɪə'biːtiːz] diabète m; **diabetic** diabétique m/f

diagnose ['daɪəgnəʊz] diagnostiquer; **diagnosis** diagnostic m

diagonal [daɪ'ægənl] diagonal; **diagonally** en diagonale

diagram ['daɪəgræm] diagramme m

dial ['daɪl] **1** n cadran m **2** v/i TELEC faire le numéro **3** v/t TELEC *number* composer

dialog, Br dialogue ['daɪəlɒːg] dialogue m

'dial tone tonalité f

diameter [daɪ'æmɪtər] diamètre m

diamond ['daɪmənd] diamant m; *shape* losange m

diaper ['daɪpər] couche f

diaphragm ['daɪəfræm] diaphragme m

diarrhea, Br diarrhoea [daɪə'riːə] diarrhée f

diary ['daɪrɪ] journal m; *for appointments* agenda m

dice [daɪs] dé m; pl dés mpl

dictate [dɪk'teɪt] dicter; **dictator** POL dictateur m; **dictatorship** dictature f

dictionary ['dɪkʃənrɪ] dictionnaire m

die [daɪ] mourir

♦ **die down** *of storm* se calmer; *of excitement* s'apaiser

♦ **die out** disparaître

diet ['daɪət] **1** n (*regular food*) alimentation f; *to lose weight, for health* régime m **2** v/i faire un régime

differ ['dɪfər] différer; (*disagree*) différer; **difference** différence f; **different** différent; **differently** différemment

difficult ['dɪfɪkəlt] difficile; **difficulty** difficulté f

dig [dɪg] creuser

digest [daɪ'dʒest] digérer; *information* assimiler; **digestion** digestion f

digit ['dɪdʒɪt] chiffre m; **digital** numérique; **digital camera** appareil m photo numérique; **digital photo** photo f numérique

dignified ['dɪgnɪfaɪd] digne; **dignity** dignité f

dilapidated [dɪˈlæpɪdeɪtɪd] délabré

dilemma [dɪˈlemə] dilemme *m*

dilute [daɪˈluːt] diluer

dim [dɪm] **1** *adj* *room, prospects* sombre; *light* faible; *outline* vague; *(stupid)* bête **2** *v/i of lights* baisser

dime [daɪm] *(pièce f de)* dix cents *mpl*

dimension [daɪˈmenʃn] dimension *f*

diminish [dɪˈmɪnɪʃ] diminuer

din [dɪn] brouhaha *m*

dine [daɪn] dîner

dinghy [ˈdɪŋɡɪ] *small yacht* dériveur *m*; *rubber boat* canot *m* pneumatique

dining car [ˈdaɪnɪŋ] RAIL wagon-restaurant *m*; dining room salle *f* à manger; *in hotel* salle *f* de restaurant

dinner [ˈdɪnər] dîner *m*; *at midday* déjeuner *f*; *gathering* repas *m*; dinner party dîner *m*, repas *m*

dip [dɪp] **1** *n for food* sauce *f* *(dans laquelle on trempe des aliments)*; *in road* inclinaison *f* **2** *v/i of road* s'incliner

diploma [dɪˈploʊmə] diplôme *m*

diplomacy [dɪˈploʊməsɪ] *also* *(tact)* diplomatie *f*; diplomat diplomate *m/f*; diplomatic diplomatique; *(tactful)* diplomate

direct [daɪˈrekt] **1** *adj* direct **2**

v/t to a place indiquer **(to sth** qch)*; *play* mettre en scène; *movie* réaliser; *attention* diriger

direction [dɪˈrekʃn] direction *f*; *of movie* réalisation *f*; **~s** *(instructions)* indications *fpl*; *for use* mode *m* d'emploi; *for medicine* instructions *fpl*; **ask for ~s** *to a place* demander son chemin; directly *(straight)* directement; *(soon)* dans très peu de temps; *(immediately)* immédiatement; director *of company* directeur(-trice) *m(f)*; *of movie* réalisateur(-trice) *m(f)*; *of play* metteur(-euse) *m(f)* en scène; directory répertoire *m* (d'adresses); TELEC annuaire *m* (des téléphones)

dirt [dɜːrt] saleté *f*; dirty **1** *adj* sale; *(pornographic)* cochon **2** *v/t* salir

disability [dɪsəˈbɪlɪtɪ] infirmité *f*; disabled handicapé

disadvantage [dɪsədˈvæntɪdʒ] désavantage *m*; disadvantaged défavorisé

disagree [dɪsəˈɡriː] *of person* ne pas être d'accord; disagreeable désagréable

disagreement désaccord *m*; *(argument)* dispute *f*

disappear [dɪsəˈpɪr] disparaître; disappearance disparition *f*

disappoint [dɪsəˈpɔɪnt] décevoir; disappointing décevant; disappointment déception f

disapproval [dɪsə'pruːvl] désapprobation f; disapprove désapprouver; ~ of actions désapprouver; s.o. ne pas aimer; disapproving désapprobateur

disarm [dɪs'ɑːrm] désarmer; disarmament désarmement m

disaster [dɪ'zæstər] désastre m; disastrous désastreux

disband [dɪs'bænd] 1 v/t disperser 2 v/i se disperser

disbelief [dɪsbə'liːf] incrédulité f

disc [dɪsk] disque m; CD CD m

discard [dɪs'kɑːrd] old clothes etc se débarrasser de; boyfriend abandonner

disciplinary [dɪsɪ'plɪnərɪ] disciplinaire; discipline discipline f

'disc jockey disc-jockey m

disclaim [dɪs'kleɪm] nier

disclose [dɪs'kloʊz] révéler

disco ['dɪskoʊ] discothèque f; type of dance, music disco m

discomfort [dɪs'kʌmfərt] gêne f; be in ~ être incommodé

disconcert [dɪskən'sɜːrt] déconcerter

disconnect [dɪskə'nekt] hose détacher; electrical appliance débrancher; supply, phones couper

discontent [dɪskən'tent] mécontentement m

discontinue [dɪskən'tɪnuː]

product arrêter; bus service supprimer

discotheque ['dɪskətek] discothèque f

discount ['dɪskaʊnt] remise f

discourage [dɪs'kʌrɪdʒ] décourager

discover [dɪs'kʌvər] découvrir; discovery découverte f

discredit [dɪs'kredɪt] discréditer

discreet [dɪ'skriːt] discret

discrepancy [dɪ'skrepənsɪ] divergence f

discretion [dɪ'skreʃn] discrétion f

discriminate [dɪ'skrɪmɪneɪt]: ~ against pratiquer une discrimination contre; discriminating avisé; discrimination sexual etc discrimination f

discuss [dɪ'skʌs] discuter de; of article traiter de; discussion discussion f

disease [dɪ'ziːz] maladie f

disembark [dɪsəm'bɑːrk] débarquer

disentangle [dɪsən'tæŋgl] démêler

disfigure [dɪs'fɪgər] défigurer

disgrace [dɪs'greɪs] 1 n honte f 2 v/t faire honte à; disgraceful honteux

disguise [dɪs'gaɪz] 1 n déguisement m 2 v/t déguiser; fear, anxiety dissimuler

disgust [dɪs'gʌst] 1 n dégoût m 2 v/t dégoûter; disgusting dégoûtant

dish [dɪʃ] plat *m*; **~es** vaisselle *f*

disheartening [dɪs'hɑːrtnɪŋ] décourageant

dishonest [dɪs'ɑːnɪst] malhonnête; **dishonesty** malhonnêteté *f*

dishonour [dɪs'ɑːnər] déshonneur *m*; **dishonorable** dishonorant

dishonour *etc Br* → **dishonor** *etc*

disillusion [dɪsɪ'luːʒn] désillusionner; **disillusionment** désillusion *f*

disinfect [dɪsɪn'fekt] désinfecter; **disinfectant** désinfectant *m*

disinherit [dɪsɪn'herɪt] déshériter

disintegrate [dɪs'ɪntɪgreɪt] se désintégrer; *of marriage* se désagréger

disjointed [dɪs'dʒɔɪntɪd] décousu

disk [dɪsk] *also* COMPUT disque *m*; *floppy* disquette *f*; **disk drive** COMPUT lecteur *m* de disque/disquette; **diskette** disquette *f*

dislike [dɪs'laɪk] **1** *n* aversion *f* **2** *v/t* ne pas aimer

dislocate ['dɪsləkeɪt] disloquer

disloyalty [dɪs'lɔɪəltɪ] déloyauté *f*

dismal ['dɪzməl] *weather* morne; *prospect* sombre; *person (sad)* triste; *person (negative)* lugubre; *failure* lamentable

dismantle [dɪs'mæntl] *object* démonter; *organization* démanteler

dismay [dɪs'meɪ] consternation *f*

dismiss [dɪs'mɪs] *employee* renvoyer; *suggestion* rejeter; *idea* écarter; **dismissal** *of employee* renvoi *m*

disobedience [dɪsə'biːdɪəns] désobéissance *f*; **disobedient** désobéissant; **disobey** désobéir à

disorganized [dɪs'ɔːrgənaɪzd] désorganisé

disoriented [dɪs'ɔːrɪəntɪd] désorienté

disparaging [dɪ'spærɪdʒɪŋ] désobligeant

disparity [dɪ'spærətɪ] disparité *f*

dispassionate [dɪ'spæʃənət] impartial, objectif

dispatch [dɪ'spætʃ] *(send)* envoyer

disperse [dɪ'spɜːrs] se disperser

display [dɪ'spleɪ] **1** *n of paintings etc* exposition *f*; *of emotion, in store window* étalage *m*; COMPUT affichage *m* **2** *v/t emotion* montrer; *at exhibition, for sale* exposer; COMPUT afficher

displease [dɪs'pliːz] déplaire à; **displeasure** mécontentement *m*

disposable [dɪ'spouzəbl] jetable; **disposal** *of waste* élimination *f*; *(sale)* cession *f*;

put sth at s.o.'s ~ mettre qch à la disposition de qn
♦ **dispose of** [dɪˈspəʊz] (*get rid of*) se débarrasser de
disprove [dɪsˈpruːv] réfuter
dispute [dɪˈspjuːt] **1** *n* contestation *f; between two countries* conflit *m; industrial* ~ conflit *m* social **2** *v/t* contester; (*fight over*) se disputer
disqualification [dɪskwɔːlɪfɪˈkeɪʃn] disqualification *f;* **disqualify** disqualifier
disregard [dɪsrəˈgɑːrd] **1** *n* indifférence *f* (*for* à l'égard de) **2** *v/t* ne tenir aucun compte de
disreputable [dɪsˈrepjʊtəbl] peu recommandable
disrespect [dɪsrəˈspekt] manque *m* de respect, irrespect *m;* **disrespectful** irrespectueux
disrupt [dɪsˈrʌpt] perturber; **disruption** perturbation *f*
dissatisfaction [dɪssætɪsˈfækʃn] mécontentement *m;* **dissatisfied** mécontent
dissident [ˈdɪsɪdənt] dissident(e) *m(f)*
dissolve [dɪˈzɑːlv] **1** *v/t* dissoudre **2** *v/i* se dissoudre
distance [ˈdɪstəns] distance *f; in the* ~ au loin; *distant* éloigné; *fig* (*aloof*) distant
distaste [dɪsˈteɪst] dégoût *m;* **distasteful** désagréable
distinct [dɪsˈtɪŋkt] (*clear*) net; (*different*) distinct; **distinctive** distinctif; **distinctly** dis-

tinctement; (*decidedly*) vraiment
distinguish [dɪsˈtɪŋgwɪʃ] distinguer; ~ *between X and Y* distinguer X de Y; **distinguished** distingué
distort [dɪsˈtɔːrt] déformer
distract [dɪsˈtrækt] *person* distraire; *attention* détourner; **distraught** [dɪsˈtrɔːt] angoissé
distress [dɪsˈtres] **1** *n* douleur *f* **2** *v/t* (*upset*) affliger; **distressing** pénible
distribute [dɪsˈtrɪbjuːt] *also* COM distribuer; **distribution** *also* COM distribution *f; of wealth* répartition *f;* **distributor** COM distributeur *m*
district [ˈdɪstrɪkt] *of town* quartier *m; of country* région *f;* **district attorney** procureur *m*
distrust [dɪsˈtrʌst] méfiance *f*
disturb [dɪsˈtɜːrb] (*interrupt*) déranger; (*upset*) inquiéter; **disturbance** (*interruption*) dérangement *m;* ~*s* (*civil unrest*) troubles *mpl;* **disturbed** perturbé; *mentally* dérangé; **disturbing** perturbant
disused [dɪsˈjuːzd] désaffecté
ditch [dɪtʃ] **1** *n* fossé *m* **2** *v/t* F (*get rid of*) se débarrasser de; *boyfriend, plan* laisser tomber
dive [daɪv] **1** *n* plongeon *m; underwater* plongée *f; of*

plane (vol *m*) piqué *m*; F *bar etc* bouge *m* **2** *v/i* plonger; *underwater* faire de la plongée sous-marine; *of plane* descendre en piqué; **diver** plongeur(-euse) *m(f)*

diverge [daɪˈvɜːrdʒ] diverger

diversification [daɪvɜːrsɪfɪˈkeɪʃn] COM diversification *f*; **diversify** COM se diversifier

diversion [daɪˈvɜːrʃn] *for traffic* déviation *f*; *to distract attention* diversion *f*; **divert** *traffic* dévier; *attention* détourner

divide [dɪˈvaɪd] (*share*) partager; MATH, *country, family* diviser

dividend [ˈdɪvɪdend] FIN dividende *m*

diving [ˈdaɪvɪŋ] *from board* plongeon *m*; *underwater* plongée *f* (sous-marine); **diving board** plongeoir *m*

division [dɪˈvɪʒn] division *f*

divorce [dɪˈvɔːrs] **1** *n* divorce *m* **2** *v/t* divorcer de **3** *v/i* divorcer; **divorced** divorcé; **divorcee** divorcé(e) *m(f)*

divulge [daɪˈvʌldʒ] divulguer

DIY [diːaɪˈwaɪ] (= *do-it-yourself*) bricolage *m*

dizziness [ˈdɪzɪnɪs] vertige *m*; **dizzy**: *feel* ~ avoir un vertige des vertiges

DJ [ˈdiːdʒeɪ] (= *disc jockey*) D.J. *m/f* (= disc-jockey)

DNA [diːenˈeɪ] (= *deoxyribonucleic acid*) AND *m* (= acide *m* désoxyribonucléïque)

do [duː] **1** *v/t* faire; ~ *one's hair* se coiffer **2** *v/i* (*be suitable, enough*) aller; *that will* ~*!* ça va!; ~ *well* in health, of business aller bien; (*be successful*) réussir; *well done!* (*congratulations!*) bien!; *how* ~ *you* ~*?* enchanté
◆ **do away with** supprimer
◆ **do up** *building* rénover; *street* refaire; (*fasten*), *coat etc* fermer; *laces* faire
◆ **do with**: *I could do with* ... j'aurais bien besoin de ...
◆ **do without** **1** *v/i* s'en passer **2** *v/t* se passer de

docile [ˈdoʊsaɪl] docile

dock[1] [dɑːk] **1** *n* NAUT bassin *m* **2** *v/i* of ship entrer au bassin; *of spaceship* s'arrimer

dock[2] [dɑːk] *n* LAW banc *m* des accusés

doctor [ˈdɑːktər] MED docteur *m*, médecin *m*; *form of address* docteur; **doctorate** doctorat *m*

doctrine [ˈdɑːktrɪn] doctrine *f*

document [ˈdɑːkjʊmənt] document *m*; **documentary** documentaire *m*; **documentation** documentation *f*

dodge [dɑːdʒ] *blow, person* éviter; *question* éluder

dog [dɔːg] **1** *n* chien *m* **2** *v/t* of bad luck poursuivre

dogma [ˈdɔːgmə] dogme *m*; **dogmatic** dogmatique

dog tag MIL plaque *f* d'identification; **dog-tired** F crevé

do-it-yourself [duːɪtjərˈself]

bricolage *m*

doldrums ['douldrəmz]: *be in the*~ *of economy* être dans le marasme; *of person* avoir le cafard

doll [dɑːl] *also* F *woman* poupée *f*

dollar ['dɑːlər] dollar *m*

dolphin ['dɑːlfɪn] dauphin *m*

dome [doum] *of building* dôme *m*

domestic [də'mestɪk] *chores* domestique; *news* national; *policy* intérieur; **domestic flight** vol *m* intérieur

dominant ['dɑːmɪnənt] dominant; **dominate** dominer; **domination** domination *f*; **domineering** dominateur

donate [dou'neɪt] faire don de; **donation** don *m*

donkey ['dɑːŋkɪ] âne *m*

donor ['dounər] *of money* donateur(-trice) *m(f)*; MED donneur(-euse) *m(f)*

donut ['dounʌt] beignet *m*

doom [duːm] *(fate)* destin *m*; *(ruin)* ruine *f*; **doomed** *project* voué à l'échec

door [dɔːr] porte *f*; *of car* portière *f*; **doorbell** sonnette *f*; **doorman** portier *m*; **doorway** embrasure *f* de porte

dope [doup] **1** *n (drugs)* drogue *f*; *(idiot)* idiot(e) *m(f)*

dormant ['dɔːrmənt]: ~ *volcano* volcan *m* en repos

dormitory ['dɔːrmɪtɔːrɪ] résidence *f* universitaire; *Br* dortoir *m*

dose [dous] dose *f*

dot [dɑːt] point *m*

double ['dʌbl] **1** *n* double *m*; *of film star* doublure *f* **2** *adj* double **3** *adv* deux fois (plus); ~ *the size* deux fois plus grand **4** *v/t & v/i* doubler; **double bed** grand lit *m*; **doublecheck** revérifier; **double-click** double-cliquer; **doublecross** trahir; **doublepark** stationner en double file; **double room** chambre *f* pour deux personnes; **doubles** *in tennis* double *m*

doubt [daut] **1** *n* doute *m*; *be in* ~ être incertain; *no* ~ *(probably)* sans doute **2** *v/t* douter de; **doubtful** *look* douteux; *be* ~ *of person* avoir des doutes; **doubtless** sans aucun doute

dough [dou] pâte *f*; *download* compu **1** *v/t* télécharger **2** *n* fichier *m* téléchargé;

dove [dʌv] colombe *f*

down [daun] **1** *adv (downward)* en bas, vers le bas; ~ *there* là-bas; *$200* ~ *(as deposit)* 200 dollars d'acompte; ~ *south* dans le sud; *be* ~ *of price, numbers* être en baisse; *(not working)* être en panne; F *(depressed)* être déprimé **2** *prep (along)* le long de; *run* ~ *the stairs* descendre les escaliers en courant; *it's just* ~ *the street* c'est à deux pas; **down-and-out** clochard(e) *m(f)*; **download**

downmarket *Br* bas de gamme; **down payment** paiement *m* au comptant; **downplay** minimiser; **downpour** averse *f*; **downscale** bas de gamme; **downside** (*disadvantage*) inconvénient *m*; **downsize** *car etc* réduire la taille *de*; *company* réduire les effectifs *de*; **downstairs 1** *adj* neighbors *etc* d'en bas **2** *adv* en bas; **down-town 1** *adj* du centre-ville **2** *adv* en ville

doze [dəʊz] sommeiller

dozen ['dʌzn] douzaine *f*

draft [dræft] **1** *n of air* courant *m* d'air; *of document* brouillon *m*; MIL conscription *f*; ∼ **beer** bière *f* à la pression **2** *v/t document* faire le brouillon *de*; MIL appeler; **draft dodger** réfractaire *m*; **draftsman** dessinateur(-trice) *m(f)*

drag [dræg] **1** *v/t* traîner, tirer; (*search*) draguer **2** *v/i of time* se traîner; *of show, movie* traîner en longueur

drain [dreɪn] **1** *n* tuyau *m* d'écoulement; *under street* égout *m* **2** *v/t oil* vidanger; *vegetables* égoutter; *land* drainer; *glass, tank* vider; (*exhaust: person*) épuiser; **drainage** (*drains*) système *m* d'écoulement des eaux usées; *of water from soil* drainage *m*; **drainpipe** tuyau *m* d'écoulement

drama ['drɑːmə] drame *m*; **dramatic** dramatique; *scenery* spectaculaire; **dramatist** dramaturge *m/f*; **dramatize** *story* adapter (**for** pour); *fig* dramatiser

drapes [dreɪps] rideaux *mpl*

drastic ['dræstɪk] radical; *measures also* drastique

draught [drɑːft] *Br* → **draft**

draw [drɔː] **1** *n in competition* match *m* nul; *in lottery* tirage *m* (au sort); (*attraction*) attraction *f* **2** *v/t picture* dessiner; (*pull*), *in lottery, gun* tirer; (*attract*) attirer; (*lead*) emmener; *from bank account* retirer **3** *v/i of artist* dessiner; *in competition* faire match nul

◆ **draw back 1** *v/i* (*recoil*) reculer **2** *v/t* (*pull back*) retirer; *drapes* ouvrir

◆ **draw out** *wallet, from bank* retirer

◆ **draw up 1** *v/t document* rédiger; *chair* approcher **2** *v/i of vehicle* s'arrêter

drawback désavantage *m*, inconvénient *m*

drawer [drɔːr] *of desk* tiroir *m*

drawing ['drɔːɪŋ] dessin *m*

drawl [drɔːl] voix *f* traînante

dread [dred]: ∼ **doing** redouter de faire; **dreadful** épouvantable

dream [driːm] **1** *n* rêve *m* **2** *v/i* rêver (**about, of** de)

◆ **dream up** inventer

dreary ['drɪrɪ] morne

dress [dres] **1** *n for woman* robe *f*; (*clothing*) tenue *f* **2** *v/t person* habiller; *wound* panser; **get ~ed** s'habiller **3** *v/i* s'habiller
◆ **dress up** s'habiller chic; (*wear a disguise*) se déguiser (**as** en)
'**dress circle** premier balcon *m*; **dresser** (*dressing table*) coiffeuse *f*; *in kitchen* buffet *m*; **dressing** *for salad* assaisonnement *m*; *for wound* pansement *m*; **dress rehearsal** (répétition *f*) générale *f*

dribble ['drɪbl] *of person* baver; *of water* dégouliner; SP dribbler

dried [draɪd] *fruit etc* sec

drier ['draɪr] → **dryer**

drift [drɪft] *of snow* s'amonceler; *of ship* être à la dérive; (*go off course*) dériver; *of person* aller à la dérive; **drifter** personne qui vit au jour le jour

drill [drɪl] **1** *n tool* perceuse *f*; *exercise*, MIL exercice *m* **2** *v/t hole* percer **3** *v/i for oil* forer; MIL faire l'exercice

drily ['draɪlɪ] *say* d'un ton pince-sans-rire

drink [drɪŋk] **1** *n* boisson *f*; **can I have a ~ of water** est-ce que je peux avoir de l'eau? **2** *v/t & v/i* boire; **I don't ~** je ne bois pas; **drinkable** buvable; *water* potable
drinker ['drɪŋkər] buveur(-eu-

se) *m(f)*; **drinking water** eau *f* potable

drip [drɪp] **1** *n liquid* goutte *f*; MED goutte-à-goutte *m*, perfusion *f* **2** *v/i* goutter

drive [draɪv] **1** *n outing* promenade *f* (en voiture); (*energy*) dynamisme *m*; COMPUT unité *f*, lecteur *m*; (*campaign*) campagne *f* **2** *v/t vehicle* conduire; (*be owner of*) avoir; (*take in car*) amener; TECH actionner **3** *v/i* conduire; **~ to work** aller au travail en voiture; **drive-in** *movie theater* drive-in *m*

drivel ['drɪvl] bêtises *fpl*

driver ['draɪvər] conducteur (-trice) *m(f)*; *of truck* camionneur(-euse) *m(f)*; COMPUT pilote *m*; **driver's license** permis *m* de conduire
'**driveway** allée *f*; **drive-thru** drive-in *m inv*

drizzle ['drɪzl] **1** *n* bruine *f* **2** *v/i* bruiner

drop [drɑːp] **1** *n* goutte *f*; *in price, temperature* chute *f* **2** *v/t object* faire tomber; *bomb* lancer; *person from car* déposer; *person from team* écarter; (*stop seeing*), *charges, subject* laisser tomber; (*give up*) arrêter **3** *v/i* tomber
◆ **drop in** (*visit*) passer
◆ **drop off 1** *v/t person, goods* déposer **2** *v/i* (*fall asleep*) s'endormir; (*decline*) diminuer
◆ **drop out** (*withdraw*) se re-

tirer (**of** de); *of school* abandonner (**of sth** qch)

drought [draʊt] sécheresse *f*

drown [draʊn] se noyer

drug [drʌg] **1** *n* MED médicament *m*; *illegal* drogue *f* **2** *v/t* droguer; **drug addict** toxicomane *m/f*; **drug dealer** dealer *m*, dealeuse *f*; *large-scale* trafiquant(e) *m(f)* de drogue; **druggist** pharmacien(ne) *m(f)*; **drugstore** drugstore *m*; **drug trafficking** trafic *m* de drogue

drum [drʌm] MUS tambour *m*; *container* tonneau *m*; **~s** batterie *f*; **drumstick** MUS baguette *f* de tambour

drunk [drʌŋk] **1** *n* ivrogne *m/f*; *habitually* alcoolique *m/f* **2** *adj* ivre, soûl; **get ~** se soûler; **drunk driving** conduite *f* en état d'ivresse

dry [draɪ] **1** *adj* sec **2** *v/t* clothes faire sécher; *dishes, eyes* essuyer **3** *v/i* sécher; **dryclean** nettoyer à sec; **dry cleaner** pressing *m*; **dryer** *machine* sèche-linge *m*

dual [ˈduːəl] double

dub [dʌb] *movie* doubler

dubious [ˈduːbɪəs] douteux; **I'm still ~ about ...** j'ai encore des doutes quant à ...

duck [dʌk] **1** *n* canard *m*; *female* cane *f* **2** *v/i* se baisser

dud [dʌd] F (*false bill*) faux *m*

due [duː] (*owed*) dû; **the rent is ~ tomorrow** il faut payer le loyer demain

dull [dʌl] *weather* sombre; *sound, pain* sourd; (*boring*) ennuyeux

duly [ˈduːlɪ] (*as expected*) comme prévu; (*properly*) dûment, comme il se doit

dumb [dʌm] (*mute*) muet; F (*stupid*) bête

dump [dʌmp] **1** *n for garbage* décharge *f*; (*unpleasant place*) trou *m*; *house, hotel* taudis *m* **2** *v/t* (*deposit*) déposer; (*throw away*) jeter; (*leave*) laisser; *waste* déverser

dune [duːn] dune *f*

duplex (*apartment*) [ˈduːpleks] duplex *m*

duplicate [ˈduːplɪkət] double *m*

durable [ˈdʊrəbl] *material* résistant

during [ˈdʊrɪŋ] pendant

dusk [dʌsk] crépuscule *m*

dust [dʌst] **1** *n* poussière *f* **2** *v/t* épousseter; **duster** chiffon *m* (à poussière); **dustpan** pelle *f* à poussière; **dusty** poussiéreux

duty [ˈduːtɪ] devoir *m*; (*task*) fonction *f*; *on goods* droit(s) *m(pl)*; **be on ~** être de service; **dutyfree** hors taxe

DVD [diːviːˈdiː] (= *digital versatile disk*) DVD *m*; **DVD-ROM** DVD-ROM *m*

dwarf [dwɔːrf] **1** *n* nain(e) *m(f)* **2** *v/t* rapetisser

dwindle [ˈdwɪndl] diminuer

dye [daɪ] **1** *n* teinture *f* **2** *v/t*

teindre
dying ['daɪɪŋ] *person* mourant; *industry* moribond; *tradition* qui se perd
dynamic [daɪ'næmɪk] dynamique; **dynamism** dynamis-

dynasty ['daɪnəstɪ] dynastie *f*
dyslexic [dɪs'leksɪk] **1** *adj* dyslexique **2** *n* dyslexique *m/f*

me *m*

E

each [iːtʃ] **1** *adj* chaque **2** *adv* chacun; **they're $1.50 ~** ils coûtent $1.50 chacun, ils sont 1,50 $ pièce **3** *pron* chacun(e) *m(f)*; **~ of them** chacun(e) d'entre eux(elles) *m(f)*; **we know ~ other** nous nous connaissons
eager ['iːgər] désireux; *look* avide; **be ~ to do sth** désirer vivement faire qch; **eagerly** avec empressement; *wait* impatiemment; **eagerness** empressement *m*
eagle ['iːgl] aigle *m*; **eagle-eyed: be ~** avoir des yeux d'aigle
ear¹ [ɪr] oreille *f*
ear² [ɪr] *of corn* épi *m*
'earache mal *m* d'oreilles
early ['ɜːrlɪ] **1** *adv* (*not late*) tôt; (*ahead of time*) en avance **2** *adj stages, Romans* premier; *arrival* en avance; *retirement* anticipé; *music* ancien; (*in the near future*) prochain; (*in*) **~ October** début octobre; **have an ~ supper** dîner tôt *or* de bonne heure; **early bird: be an ~** (*early ris-*

er) être matinal
earmark ['ɪrmɑːrk] réserver
earn [ɜːrn] gagner; *interest* rapporter
earnest ['ɜːrnɪst] sérieux
earnings ['ɜːrnɪŋz] salaire *m*; *of company* profits *mpl*
'earphones écouteurs *mpl*;
earring boucle *f* d'oreille
earth [ɜːrθ] terre *f*; *earthenware* poterie *f*; *earthly terrestre*; **it's no ~ use doing that** F ça ne sert strictement à rien de faire cela; **earthquake** tremblement *m* de terre; **earth-shattering** stupéfiant
ease [iːz] **1** *n* facilité *f*; **feel at ~** se sentir à l'aise **2** *v/t pain, mind* soulager; *suffering, shortage* diminuer **3** *v/i of pain* diminuer
easel ['iːzl] chevalet *m*
easily ['iːzəlɪ] facilement; (*by far*) de loin
east [iːst] **1** *n* est *m* **2** *adj* est *inv*; *wind* d'est **3** *adv travel* vers l'est
Easter ['iːstər] Pâques *fpl*; **Easter Day** (jour *m* de) Pâ-

ques m; **Easter egg** œuf m de Pâques

easterly ['iːstərlɪ] *wind* de l'est; *direction* vers l'est

Easter Monday lundi m de Pâques

eastern ['iːstərn] de l'est; (*oriental*) oriental; **easterner** habitant(e) m(f) de l'Est des États-Unis

Easter Sunday (jour m de) Pâques m

eastward ['iːstwərd] vers l'est

easy ['iːzɪ] facile; (*relaxed*) tranquille; **easy chair** fauteuil m; **easy-going** accommodant

eat [iːt] manger

◆ **eat out** manger au restaurant

eatable ['iːtəbl] mangeable

eavesdrop ['iːvzdrɑːp] écouter de façon indiscrète (**on s.o.** qn)

ebb [eb] *of tide* descendre

e-book ['iːbʊk] livre m électronique; **e-business** commerce m électronique

eccentric [ɪk'sentrɪk] **1** *adj* excentrique **2** *n* original(e) m(f); **eccentricity** excentricité f

echo ['ekoʊ] **1** *n* écho m **2** *v/i* faire écho **3** *v/t words* répéter; *views* se faire l'écho de

eclipse [ɪ'klɪps] **1** *n* éclipse f **2** *v/t fig* éclipser

ecological [iːkə'lɑːdʒɪkl] écologique; **ecologically** écologiquement; **ecologically**

friendly écologique; **ecologist** écologiste m/f; **ecology** écologie f

economic [iːkə'nɑːmɪk] économique; **economical** (*cheap*) économique; (*thrifty*) économe; **economics** économie f; *financial aspects* aspects mpl économiques; **economist** économiste m/f; **economize** économiser

◆ **economize on** économiser

economy [ɪ'kɑːnəmɪ] économie f; **economy class** classe f économique

ecosystem ['iːkoʊsɪstm] écosystème m; **ecotourism** tourisme m écologique

ecstasy ['ekstəsɪ] extase f; **ecstatic** extatique

eczema ['eksmə] eczéma m

edge [edʒ] **1** *n* bord m; *of knife* tranchant m; **on ~** énervé **2** *v/i (move slowly)* se faufiler; **edgewise**: *I couldn't get a word in ~* je n'ai pas pu en placer une F; **edgy** énervé

edible ['edɪbl] comestible

edit ['edɪt] *text* mettre au point; *book* préparer pour la publication; *newspaper* diriger; *TV program* réaliser; *film* monter; **edition** édition f; **editor** *of text, book* rédacteur(-trice) m(f); *of newspaper* rédacteur(-trice) m(f) en chef; *of TV program* réalisateur(-trice) m(f); *of film* monteur(-euse) m(f); **edito-**

electrify

rial **1** adj de la rédaction **2** n éditorial m

educate ['edʒəkeɪt] instruire (**about** sur); **she was ~d in France** elle a fait sa scolarité en France; **educated** instruit; **education** éducation f; as subject pédagogie f; **educational** scolaire; (informative) instructif

eerie ['ɪrɪ] inquiétant

effect [ɪ'fekt] effet m; **effective** (efficient) efficace; (striking) frappant

effeminate [ɪ'femɪnət] efféminé

efficiency [ɪ'fɪʃənsɪ] efficacité f; in motel chambre f avec coin-cuisine; **efficient** efficace; **efficiently** efficacement

effort ['efət] effort m; **effortless** aisé, facile

e.g. [iː'dʒiː] ex; spoken par example

egg [eg] œuf m; **eggcup** coquetier m; **egghead** F intello m/f F; **eggplant** aubergine f

ego ['iːgəʊ] PSYCH ego m; **egocentric** égocentrique; **egoism** égoïsme m; **egoist** égoïste m/f

eiderdown ['aɪdərdaʊn] (quilt) édredon m

eight [eɪt] huit; **eighteen** dix-huit; **eighteenth** dix-huitième; **eighth** huitième; **eightieth** quatre-vingtième; **eighty** quatre-vingts; **~-two/four** etc quatre-vingt-deux/-quatre etc

either ['iːðər] **1** adj l'un ou l'autre; (both) chaque **2** pron l'un(e) ou l'autre **3** adv: **I won't go ~** je n'irai pas non plus **4** conj: **~ ... or** soit ...; with negative ni ... ni ...

eject [ɪ'dʒekt] **1** v/t éjecter **2** v/i from plane s'éjecter

♦ eke out [iːk] suppléer à l'insuffisance de; **eke out a living** vivoter

el [el] métro m aérien

elaborate [ɪ'læbərət] **1** adj compliqué **2** v/i [ɪ'læbəreɪt] donner des détails (**on** sur)

elapse [ɪ'læps] (se) passer

elastic [ɪ'læstɪk] **1** adj élastique **2** n élastique m; **elasticated** élastique

elated [ɪ'leɪtɪd] transporté (de joie); **elation** exultation f

elbow ['elbəʊ] coude m

elder ['eldər] **1** adj aîné **2** n aîné(e) m(f); **elderly 1** adj âgé **2** npl: the ~ les personnes fpl âgées; **eldest 1** adj aîné **2** n: **the ~** l'aîné(e) m(f)

elect [ɪ'lekt] élire; **elected** élu; **election** élection f; **election campaign** campagne f électorale; **election day** jour m des élections; **electorate** électorat m

electric [ɪ'lektrɪk] also fig électrique; **electrical** électrique; **electric chair** chaise f électrique; **electrician** électricien(ne) m(f); **electricity** électricité f; **electrify** électrifier; fig électriser

electrocute [ɪ'lektrəkju:t]
électrocuter

electron [ɪ'lektra:n] électron
m; **electronic** électronique;
electronics électronique *f*

elegance ['elɪgəns] élégance
f; **elegant** élégant

element ['elɪmənt] élément
m; **elementary** élémentaire;
elementary schoo école *f*
primaire

elephant ['elɪfənt] éléphant
m

elevate ['elɪveɪt] élever; **elevated railroad** métro *m* aérien; **elevation** (*altitude*) altitude *f*; **elevator** ascenseur *m*

eleven [ɪ'levn] onze; **eleventh**
onzième

eligible ['elɪdʒəbl]: **be ~ to do
sth** avoir le droit de faire qch

eliminate [ɪ'lɪmɪneɪt] élimi-
ner; **elimination** élimination
f

elite [eɪ'li:t] **1** *n* élite *f* **2** *adj*
d'élite

eloquence ['eləkwəns] éloquence *f*; **eloquent** éloquent

else [els]: **anything ~?** autre
chose?; **nothing ~** rien d'autre; **no one ~** personne d'autre; **everyone ~ is going** tous
les autres y vont; **someone ~**
quelqu'un d'autre; **something ~** autre chose; **let's
go somewhere ~** allons autre part; **or ~** sinon; **elsewhere** ailleurs

elude [ɪ'lu:d] (*escape from*)
échapper à; (*avoid*) éviter;

elusive insaisissable

emaciated [ɪ'meɪsɪeɪtɪd]
émacié

e-mail ['i:meɪl] **1** *n* e-mail *m*,
courrier *m* électronique **2**
v/t person envoyer un e-mail
à; **e-mail address** adresse *f*
e-mail, adresse *f* électronique

emancipation [ɪmænsɪ-
'peɪʃn] émancipation *f*

embalm [ɪm'ba:m] embau-
mer

embankment
[ɪm'bæŋkmənt] *of river* berge *f*; RAIL remblai *m*

embargo [em'ba:rgoʊ] em-
bargo *m*

embark [ɪm'ba:rk] (s')embar-
quer

embarrass [ɪm'bærəs] gêner,
embarrasser; **embarrassed**
gêné, embarrassé; **embarrassing** gênant, embarrassant; **embarrassment** gêne
f, embarras *m*

embassy ['embəsɪ] ambassade *f*

embezzle [ɪm'bezl] détourner; **embezzlement** détournement *m* de fonds

emblem ['embləm] emblème
m

embodiment [ɪm'ba:dɪmənt]
personnification *f*; **embody**
personnifier

embrace [ɪm'breɪs] **1** *n* étreinte *f* **2** *v/t* (*hug*) serrer dans ses
bras, étreindre; (*take in*) embrasser **3** *v/i of two people* se

serrer dans les bras, s'étreindre

embroider [ɪmˈbrɔɪdər] broder; *fig* enjoliver

embryo [ˈembrɪou] embryon *m*; **embryonic** *fig* embryonnaire

emerald [ˈemərəld] émeraude *f*

emerge [ɪˈmɜːrdʒ] sortir; *from mist, of truth* émerger

emergency [ɪˈmɜːrdʒənsɪ] urgence *f*; **emergency exit** sortie *f* de secours; **emergency landing** atterrissage *m* forcé; **emergency services** services *mpl* d'urgence

emigrate [ˈemɪɡreɪt] émigrer; **emigration** émigration *f*

Eminence [ˈemɪnəns] REL: **His ~** son Éminence; **eminent** éminent

emission [ɪˈmɪʃn] *of gases* émission *f*; **emit** émettre

emotion [ɪˈmouʃn] émotion *f*; **emotional** *problems* émotionnel, affectif; *(full of emotion)* ému; *reunion* émouvant

emphasis [ˈemfəsɪs] accent *m*; **emphasize** *syllable* accentuer; *fig* souligner; **emphatic** catégorique

empire [ˈempaɪr] *also fig* empire *m*

employ [ɪmˈplɔɪ] employer; **employee** employé(e) *m(f)*; **employer** employeur(-euse) *m(f)*; **employment** *(jobs)* emplois *mpl*; *(work)* emploi *m*

emptiness [ˈemptɪnɪs] vide *m*; **empty 1** *adj* vide; *promises* vain **2** *v/t* vider **3** *v/i of room, street* se vider

emulate [ˈemjuleɪt] imiter

enable [ɪˈneɪbl] permettre

enchanting [ɪnˈtʃæntɪŋ] ravissant

encircle [ɪnˈsɜːrkl] encercler

enclose [ɪnˈklouz] *in letter* joindre; *area* entourer; **enclosure** *with letter* pièce *f* jointe

encore [ˈɑːŋkɔːr] bis *m*

encounter [ɪnˈkauntər] **1** *n* rencontre *f* **2** *v/t person* rencontrer; *problem, resistance* affronter

encourage [ɪnˈkʌrɪdʒ] encourager; **encouragement** encouragement *m*; **encouraging** encourageant

encyclopedia [ɪnsaɪkləˈpiːdɪə] encyclopédie *f*

end [end] **1** *n (conclusion, purpose)* fin *f*; *(extremity)* bout *m*; **in the ~** à la fin **2** *v/t* terminer, finir **3** *v/i* se terminer, finir

◆ **end up** finir

endanger [ɪnˈdeɪndʒər] mettre en danger; **endangered species** espèce *f* en voie de disparition

endeavor, *Br* **endeavour** [ɪnˈdevər] **1** *n* effort *m* **2** *v/t* essayer (**to do sth** de faire qch)

endemic [ɪnˈdemɪk] endémique

ending ['endɪŋ] fin *f*; GRAM terminaison *f*; **endless** sans fin

endorse [ɪnˈdɔːrs] *candidacy* appuyer; *product* associer son image à; **endorsement** *of candidacy* appui *m*; *of product* association *f* de son image à

end 'product produit *m* fini

endurance [ɪnˈdʊrəns] *of person* endurance *f*; *of car* résistance *f*; **endure 1** *v/t* endurer **2** *v/i* (*last*) durer; **enduring** durable

enemy ['enəmɪ] ennemi(e) *m(f)*

energetic [enərdʒetɪk] *also fig* énergique; **energy** énergie *f*; **energy supply** alimentation *f* en énergie

enforce [ɪnˈfɔːrs] mettre en vigueur

engage [ɪnˈɡeɪdʒ] **1** *v/t* (*hire*) engager **2** *v/i of machine part* s'engrener; **engaged** *to be married* fiancé; *Br* TELEC occupé; *get* ~ se fiancer; **engagement** *to be married* fiançailles *fpl*; MIL engagement *m*; **engagement ring** bague *f* de fiançailles

engine ['endʒɪn] moteur *m*; **engineer** ingénieur *m/f*; NAUT, RAIL mécanicien(ne) *m(f)*; **engineering** ingénierie *f*

England ['ɪŋɡlənd] Angleterre *f*; **English 1** *adj* anglais **2** *n language* anglais *m*; **the**

~ les Anglais *mpl*; **English-man** Anglais *m*; **Englishwoman** Anglaise *f*

engrave [ɪnˈɡreɪv] graver; **engraving** gravure *f*

engrossed [ɪnˈɡroʊst]: ~ *in* absorbé dans

engulf [ɪnˈɡʌlf] engloutir

enhance [ɪnˈhæns] *flavor* rehausser; *reputation* accroître; *performance* améliorer; *enjoyment* augmenter

enigma [ɪˈnɪɡmə] énigme *f*

enjoy [ɪnˈdʒɔɪ] aimer; ~ *o.s.* s'amuser; ~*!* *said to s.o. eating* bon appétit!; **enjoyable** agréable; **enjoyment** plaisir *m*

enlarge [ɪnˈlɑːrdʒ] agrandir; **enlargement** agrandissement *m*

enlighten [ɪnˈlaɪtn] éclairer

enlist [ɪnˈlɪst] MIL enrôler

enmity ['enmətɪ] inimitié *f*

enormous [ɪˈnɔːrməs] énorme

enough [ɪˈnʌf] **1** *adj* assez de **2** *pron* assez; *will $50 be* ~*?* est-ce que $50 suffiront?; *that's* ~ ça suffit **3** *adv* assez; *big* ~ assez grand

enquire *etc* [ɪnˈkwaɪr] → *inquire etc*

enroll, *Br* **enrol** [ɪnˈroʊl] s'inscrire

en suite (bathroom) ['ɑːnswiːt] salle *f* de bains attenante

ensure [ɪnˈʃʊər] assurer; ~ *that ...* s'assurer que ...

entail [ɪnˈteɪl] entraîner

entangle [ɪnˈtæŋgl] *in rope* empêtrer

enter [ˈentər] **1** *v/t room, house* entrer dans; *competition* entrer en; COMPUT entrer **2** *v/i* entrer; *in competition* s'inscrire **3** *n* COMPUT touche *f* entrée

enterprise [ˈentərpraɪz] *(initiative)* (esprit *m* d')initiative *f*; *(venture)* entreprise *f*; **enterprising** entreprenant

entertain [entərˈteɪn] *(amuse)* amuser; *(consider: idea)* envisager; **entertainer** artiste *m/f* de variété; **entertaining** amusant, divertissant; **entertainment** divertissement *m*

enthusiasm [ɪnˈθuːzɪæzəm] enthousiasme *m*; **enthusiast** enthousiaste *m/f*; **enthusiastic** enthousiaste; **enthusiastically** avec enthousiasme

entire [ɪnˈtaɪr] entier; **entirely** entièrement

entitle [ɪnˈtaɪtl]: ~ *s.o.* **to sth** donner à qn droit à qch; **be ~d to** avoir droit à

entrance [ˈentrəns] entrée *f*

entranced [ɪnˈtrænst] enchanté

'entrance exam(ination) examen *m* d'entrée

entrant [ˈentrənt] inscrit(e) *m(f)*

entrepreneur [ɑːntrəprəˈnɜːr] entrepreneur(-euse) *m(f)*; **entrepre-**

neurial *skills* d'entrepreneur

entrust [ɪnˈtrʌst] confier

entry [ˈentri] entrée *f*; *for competition:* entrée *f*; *person* participant(e) *m(f)*; **entryphone** interphone *m*

envelop [ɪnˈveləp] envelopper

envelope [ˈenvəloʊp] enveloppe *f*

enviable [ˈenviəbl] enviable; **envious** envieux; **be ~ of s.o.** envier qn

environment [ɪnˈvaɪrənmənt] environnement *m*; **environmental** écologique; **environmentalist** écologiste *m/f*; **environmentally friendly** écologique; **environs** environs *mpl*

envisage [ɪnˈvɪzɪdʒ] envisager

envoy [ˈenvɔɪ] envoyé(e) *m(f)*

envy [ˈenvi] **1** *n* envie *f* **2** *v/t:* ~ *s.o.* **sth** envier qch à qn

epic [ˈepɪk] **1** *n* épopée *f*; *movie* film *m* à grand spectacle **2** *adj journey* épique

epicenter *Br* **epicentre** [ˈepɪsentər] épicentre *m*

epidemic [epɪˈdemɪk] *also fig* épidémie *f*

episode [ˈepɪsoʊd] épisode *m*

epitaph [ˈepɪtæf] épitaphe *f*

equal [ˈiːkwl] **1** *adj* égal; **be ~ to task** être à la hauteur de **2** *n* égal *m* **3** *v/t* égaler; **equality** égalité *f*; **equalize 1** *v/t* égaliser **2** *v/i* Br SP égaliser; **equalizer** Br SP but *m* égalisateur; **equally** *divide* de manière égale; *qualified, intelligent* tout aussi; **equal rights** égalité *f* des droits

equation [ɪ'kweɪʒn] MATH équation *f*

equator [ɪ'kweɪtər] équateur *m*

equip [ɪ'kwɪp] équiper; **equipment** équipement *m*

equity ['ekwətɪ] FIN capitaux *mpl* propres

equivalent [ɪ'kwɪvələnt] **1** *adj* équivalent **2** *n* équivalent *m*

era ['ɪrə] ère *f*

eradicate [ɪ'rædɪkeɪt] éradiquer

erase [ɪ'reɪz] effacer

erect [ɪ'rekt] **1** *adj* droit **2** *v/t* ériger, élever; **erection** *of building, penis* érection *f*

ergonomic [ɜːrgoʊ'nɑːmɪk] ergonomique

erode [ɪ'roʊd] éroder; *fig: power* miner; *rights* supprimer progressivement; **erosion** érosion *f*; *fig: of rights* suppression *f* progressive

errand ['erənd] commission *f*

erratic [ɪ'rætɪk] *performance, course* irrégulier; *driving* capricieux; *behavior* changeant

error ['erər] erreur *f*

erupt [ɪ'rʌpt] *of volcano* entrer en éruption; *of violence* éclater; *of person* exploser F; **eruption** *of volcano* éruption *f*; *of violence* explosion *f*

escalate ['eskəleɪt] s'intensifier; **escalation** intensifica-

tion *f*; **escalator** escalier *m* mécanique, escalator *m*

escape [ɪ'skeɪp] **1** *n of prisoner* évasion *f*; *of animal, gas* fuite *f* **2** *v/i* s'échapper

escort ['eskɔːrt] **1** *n* cavalier (-ière) *m(f)*; *(guard)* escorte *f* **2** *v/t* [ɪ'skɔːrt] *socially* accompagner; *(act as guard to)* escorter

especially [ɪ'speʃlɪ] particulièrement

espionage ['espɪənɑːʒ] espionnage *m*

espresso (coffee) [es'presoʊ] expresso *m*

essay ['eseɪ] *at school* rédaction *f*; *at university* dissertation *f*; *by writer* essai *m*

essential [ɪ'senʃl] essentiel

establish [ɪ'stæblɪʃ] *company* fonder; *(create, determine)* établir; **establishment** *firm, shop etc* établissement *m*

estate [ɪ'steɪt] *land* propriété *f*; *of dead person* biens *mpl*

esthetic [ɪs'θetɪk] esthétique

estimate ['estɪmət] **1** *n* estimation *f*; *from builder etc* devis *m* **2** *v/t* estimer

estuary ['estʃəwerɪ] estuaire *m*

etc [et'setrə] (= **et cetera**) etc.

eternal [ɪ'tɜːrnl] éternel; **eternity** éternité *f*

ethical ['eθɪkl] *problem* éthique; *(morally right)* moral; **ethics** éthique *f*

ethnic ['eθnɪk] ethnique

EU [iː'juː] (= **European Un-**

ion) U.E. *f* (= Union *f* euro-péenne)

euphemism ['ju:fəmɪzm] eu-phémisme *m*

euro ['juərou] FIN euro *m*

Europe ['juərəp] Europe *f*; Eu-ropean **1** *adj* européen **2** *n* Européen(ne) *m(f)*

euthanasia [juθə'neɪzɪə] eu-thanasie *f*

evacuate [ɪ'vækjueɪt] (*clear people from*) faire évacuer; (*leave*) évacuer

evade [ɪ'veɪd] éviter; *question* éluder

evaluate [ɪ'væljueɪt] évaluer; **evaluation** évaluation *f*

evaporate [ɪ'væpəreɪt] *also fig* s'évaporer; **evaporation** évaporation *f*

evasion [ɪ'veɪʒn] fuite *f*; eva-sive évasif

eve [i:v] veille *f*

even ['i:vn] **1** *adj breathing* régulier; *distribution* égal; (*level*) plat; *surface* plan; *number* pair; **get ~ with ...** prendre sa revanche sur ... **2** *adv* même; **~ bigger** encore plus grand; **not ~** pas même; **~ so** quand même; **~ if** même si **3** *v/t:* **~ the score** égaliser

evening ['i:vnɪŋ] soir *m*, **in the ~** le soir; **this ~** ce soir; **good ~** bonsoir; **evening class** cours *m* du soir; **eve-ning dress** *for woman* robe *f* du soir; *for man* tenue *f* de soirée

evenly ['i:vnlɪ] (*regularly*) de

manière égale; *breathe* régu-lièrement

event [ɪ'vent] événement *m*; SP épreuve *f*; **eventful** mou-vementé

eventually [ɪ'ventʃuəlɪ] fina-lement

ever ['evər] jamais; **have you ~ been to Japan?** est-ce que tu es déjà allé au Japon?; **for ~** pour toujours; **~ since** depuis lors; **~ since we ...** depuis le jour où nous ...; **ever-lasting** éternel

every ['evrɪ]: **~ day** tous les jours, chaque jour; **~ one of ...** chacun de ...; **every-body → everyone**; **every-day** de tous les jours; **every-one** tout le monde; **~ who ...** tous ceux qui ...; **everything** tout; **everywhere** partout; (*wherever*) partout où

evict [ɪ'vɪkt] expulser

evidence ['evɪdəns] preuve(s) *f(pl)*; LAW témoignage *m*; **give ~** témoigner; **evident** évident; **evidently** (*clearly*) à l'évidence; (*apparently*) de toute évidence

evil ['i:vl] **1** *adj* mauvais **2** *n* mal *m*

evolution [i:və'lu:ʃn] évolu-tion *f*; **evolve** évoluer

ex [eks] F *wife, husband* ex *m/f* F

exact [ɪg'zækt] exact; **exact-ing** exigeant; **exactly** exacte-ment

exaggerate   [ɪg'zædʒəreɪt]

exagérer; **exaggeration** exagération *f*

exam [ɪgˈzæm] examen *m*; **examination** examen *m*; **examine** examiner

example [ɪgˈzɑːmpl] exemple *m*; **for ~** par exemple

excavate [ˈekskəveɪt] (*dig*) excaver; *of archeologie* fouiller; **excavation** excavation *f*; *archeological* fouille(s) *f(pl)*

exceed [ɪkˈsiːd] dépasser; *authority* outrepasser; **exceedingly** extrêmement

excel [ɪkˈsel] **1** *v/i* exceller (**at** en) **2** *v/t*: **~ o.s.** se surpasser; **excellence** excellence *f*; **excellent** excellent

except [ɪkˈsept] sauf; **~ for** à l'exception de; **exception** exception *f*; **exceptional** exceptionnel

excerpt [ˈeksɜːrpt] extrait *m*

excess [ɪkˈses] **1** *n* excès **m 2** *adj*: **~ water** excédent *m* d'eau; **excessive** excessif

exchange [ɪksˈtʃeɪndʒ] **1** *n* échange **m 2** *v/t* échanger; **exchange rate** FIN cours *m* du change

excite [ɪkˈsaɪt] (*make enthusiastic*) enthousiasmer; **excited** excité; **get~** s'exciter; **excitement** excitation *f*; **exciting** passionnant

exclaim [ɪkˈskleɪm] s'exclamer; **exclamation** exclamation *f*; **exclamation point** point *m* d'exclamation

exclude [ɪkˈskluːd] exclure; **excluding** sauf; **exclusive** *hotel* huppé; *rights, interview* exclusif

excuse [ɪkˈskjuːs] **1** *n* excuse *f* **2** *v/t* [ɪkˈskjuːz] excuser; (*forgive*) pardonner; **~ me** excusez-moi

ex-directory *Br* : **be ~** être sur liste rouge

execute [ˈeksɪkjuːt] *criminal, plan* exécuter; **execution** *of criminal, plan* exécution *f*; **executive** cadre *m*

exempt [ɪgˈzempt] exempt

exercise [ˈeksərsaɪz] **1** *n* exercice **m 2** *v/t muscle* exercer; *dog* promener; (*caution, restraint* user de **3** *v/i* prendre de l'exercice

exhale [eksˈheɪl] exhaler

exhaust [ɪgˈzɔːst] **1** *n fumes* gaz *m* d'échappement; *pipe* tuyau *m* d'échappement **2** *v/t* (*tire, use up*) épuiser; **exhausted** (*tired*) épuisé; **exhausting** épuisant; **exhaustion** épuisement *m*; **exhaustive** exhaustif

exhibit [ɪgˈzɪbɪt] **1** *n in exhibition* objet *m* exposé **2** *v/t of artist* exposer; (*give evidence of*) montrer; **exhibition** exposition *f*; *of bad behavior* étalage *m*; *of skill* démonstration *f*

exhilarating [ɪgˈzɪləreɪtɪŋ] *weather* vivifiant; *sensation* grisant

exile [ˈeksaɪl] **1** *n* exil *m*; *per-*

son exilé(e) *m(f)* **2** *v/t* exiler

exist [ɪg'zɪst] exister; **~ on** subsister avec; **existence** existence *f*; **be in ~** exister; **existing** existant

exit ['eksɪt] **1** *n* sortie *f* **2** *v/i* COMPUT sortir

exonerate [ɪg'zɑːnəreɪt] *(clear)* disculper

exotic [ɪg'zɑːtɪk] exotique

expand [ɪk'spænd] **1** *v/t* étendre **2** *v/i* of *population* s'accroître; of *business, city* se développer; of *metal, gas* se dilater; **expanse** étendue *f*; **expansion** of *population* accroissement *m*; of *business, city* développement *m*; of *metal, gas* dilatation *f*

expect [ɪk'spekt] **1** *v/t also baby* attendre; *(suppose)* penser; *(demand)* exiger **2** *v/i*: **be ~ing** attendre un bébé; **I ~ so** je pense que oui; **expectant mother** future maman *f*; **expectation** attente *f*, espérance *f*

expedition [ekspɪ'dɪʃn] expédition *f*

expel [ɪk'spel] expulser

expendable [ɪk'spendəbl] *person* pas indispensable

expenditure [ɪk'spendɪtʃər] dépenses *fpl* (**on** de)

expense [ɪk'spens] dépense *f*; **expenses** frais *mpl*; **expensive** cher

experience [ɪk'spɪrɪəns] **1** *n* expérience *f* **2** *v/t pain, pleasure* éprouver; *difficulty* connaître; **experienced** expérimenté

experiment [ɪk'sperɪmənt] **1** *n* expérience *f* **2** *v/i* faire des expériences; **experimental** expérimental

expert ['ekspɜːrt] **1** *adj* expert **2** *n* expert(e) *m(f)*; **expertise** savoir-faire *m*

expiration date ['ekspɪ'reɪʃn] date *f* d'expiration; **expire** expirer; **expiry** expiration *f*; **expiry date** *Br* date *f* d'expiration

explain [ɪk'spleɪn] expliquer; **explanation** explication *f*; **explanatory** explicatif

explicit [ɪk'splɪsɪt] *instructions* explicite

explode [ɪk'sploud] **1** *v/i* of *bomb*, *fig* exploser **2** *v/t bomb* faire exploser

exploit[1] ['eksplɔɪt] *n* exploit *m*

exploit[2] [ɪk'splɔɪt] *v/t person, resources* exploiter

exploitation [eksplɔɪ'teɪʃn] of *person* exploitation *f*

exploration [eksplə'reɪʃn] exploration *f*; **explore** *country, possibility* explorer; **explorer** explorateur(-trice) *m(f)*

explosion [ɪk'splouʒn] *also in population* explosion *f*; **explosive** explosif *m*

export ['ekspɔːrt] **1** *n* exportation *f* **2** *v/t also* COMPUT exporter; **exporter** exportateur(-trice) *m(f)*

expose [ɪk'spouz] *(uncover)*

mettre à nu; *scandal* dévoiler; *person* démasquer; **~ X to Y** exposer X à Y; **exposure** exposition *f*; **~** mpl du froid; *of dishonest behavior* dénonciation *f*; PHOT pose *f*; *in media* couverture *f*

express [ɪk'spres] **1** *adj* (*fast*) express; (*explicit*) explicite **2** *n train* express *m* **3** *v/t* exprimer; **expression** expression *f*; **expressive** expressif; **expressly** (*explicitly*) expressément; (*deliberately*) exprès; **expressway** voie *f* express

expulsion [ɪk'spʌlʃn] expulsion *f*

extend [ɪk'stend] **1** *v/t house, garden* agrandir; *search* étendre (**to** à); *runway, contract, visa* prolonger **2** *v/i of garden etc* s'étendre; **extension** *to house* agrandissement *m*; *of contract, visa* prolongation *f*; TELEC poste *m*; **extensive** *search, knowledge* vaste, étendu; *damage* considérable; (*extent* étendue *f*, ampleur *f*; **to a certain ~** jusqu'à un certain point

exterior [ɪk'stɪrɪər] **1** *adj* extérieur **2** *n of building* extérieur *m*; *of person* dehors *mpl*

exterminate [ɪk'stɜːrmɪneɪt] exterminer

external [ɪk'stɜːrnl] extérieur

extinct [ɪk'stɪŋkt] *species* disparu; **extinction** *of species* extinction *f*; **extinguish** *fire,*

cigarette éteindre; **extinguisher** extincteur *m*

extortion [ɪk'stɔːrʃn] extortion *f*

extra ['ekstrə] **1** *n* extra *m* **2** *adj* (*spare*) en plus; (*additional*) en plus; **be ~** (*cost more*) être en supplément **3** *adv* ultra-

extract[1] ['ekstrækt] *n* extrait *m*

extract[2] [ɪk'strækt] extraire; *tooth also* arracher; *information* arracher; **extraction** extraction *f*

extradite ['ekstrədaɪt] extrader; **extradition** extradition *f*

extramarital [ekstrə'mærɪtl] extraconjugal

extraordinary [ɪkstrəˈɔːrdɪnerɪ] extraordinaire

extra 'time *Br* sp prolongation(s) *f(pl)*

extravagance [ɪk'strævəgəns] dépenses fpl extravagantes; *single act* dépense *f* extravagante; **extravagant** *person* dépensier; *price* exorbitant; *claim* excessif

extreme [ɪk'striːm] **1** *n* extrême *m* **2** *adj* extrême; **extremely** extrêmement; **extremist** extrémiste *m/f*

extrovert ['ekstrəvɜːrt] **1** *n* extraverti(e) *m(f)* **2** *adj* extraverti

exuberant [ɪg'zuːbərənt] exubérant

eye [aɪ] **1** *n* œil *m* **2** *v/t* regarder; **eye-catching** accrocheur; **eyeglasses** lunettes *fpl*; **eyeliner** eye-liner *m*;

eyeshadow ombre *f* à paupières; **eyesight** vue *f*; **eyewitness** témoin *m* oculaire

F

fabric ['fæbrɪk] tissu *m*
fabulous ['fæbjʊləs] fabuleux
façade [fə'saːd] façade *f*
face [feɪs] **1** *n* visage *m*, figure *f* **2** *v/t person, sea* faire face à
♦ **face up to** *bully* affronter; *responsibilities* faire face à
'**facecloth** gant *m* de toilette; **facelift** lifting *m*
facial ['feɪʃl] soin *m* du visage
facilitate [fə'sɪlɪteɪt] faciliter; **facilities** *of school, town etc* installations *fpl*; *(equipment)* équipements *mpl*
fact [fækt] fait *m*; **in ~, as a matter of ~** en fait
faction ['fækʃn] faction *f*
factor ['fæktər] facteur *m*
faculty ['fækltɪ] faculté *f*
fad [fæd] lubie *f*
fade [feɪd] *of colors* passer; **faded** *color* passé
fag [fæg] *pej* F *(homosexual)* pédé *m* F
fail [feɪl] *v/i* échouer **2** *v/t exam* être refusé à; **failing** défaut *m*, faiblesse *f*; **failure** échec *m*
faint [feɪnt] **1** *adj* faible, léger **2** *v/i* s'évanouir; **faintly** légèrement
fair¹ [fer] *(fun~)*, COM foire *f*

fair² [fer] *hair* blond; *complexion* blanc
fairly ['ferlɪ] *treat* équitablement; *(quite)* assez; **fairness** *of treatment* équité *f*
faith [feɪθ] *also* REL foi *f*; **faithful** fidèle; **faithfully** fidèlement
fake [feɪk] **1** *n (article m)* faux *m* **2** *adj* faux; *suicide attempt* simulé **3** *v/t (forge)* falsifier; *(feign)* feindre; *suicide, kidnap* simuler
fall¹ [fɔːl] *n season* automne *m*
fall² [fɔːl] **1** *v/i* tomber; *of prices* baisser **2** *n* chute *f*; *in price, temperature* baisse *f*
♦ **fall behind** prendre du retard
♦ **fall for** *person* tomber amoureux de; *(be deceived by)* se laisser prendre à
♦ **fall through** *of plans* tomber à l'eau
fallible ['fæləbl] faillible
false [fɔːls] faux; **false start** *in race* faux départ *m*; **false teeth** fausses dents *fpl*; **falsify** falsifier
fame [feɪm] célébrité *f*
familiar [fə'mɪljər] familier; **be ~ with sth** bien connaître

qch; **familiarity** *with subject etc* (bonne) connaissance *f* (**with** de); **familiarize:** ~ *o.s.* **with** se familiariser avec

family ['fæməlɪ] famille *f*; **family doctor** médecin *m* de famille; **family planning clinic** centre *m* de planning familial; **family tree** arbre *m* généalogique

famine ['fæmɪn] famine *f*

famous ['feɪməs] célèbre

fan[1] [fæn] *n in sport* fana *m/f* F; *of singer, band* fan *m/f*

fan[2] [fæn] **1** *n electric* ventilateur *m*; *handheld* éventail *m* **2** *v/t:* ~ *o.s.* s'éventer

fanatical [fə'nætɪkl] fanatique; **fanaticism** fanatisme *m*

fanatize ['fæntəsaɪz] fantasmer (**about** sur); **fantastic** fantastique; **fantasy** *hopeful* rêve *m*; *unrealistic, sexual* fantasme *m*

fanzine ['fænziːn] fanzine *m*

far [fɑːr] loin; (*much*) bien; ~ **away** très loin; **as** ~ **as the corner** jusqu'au coin

farce [fɑːrs] farce *f*

fare [fer] *for ticket* prix *m* du billet; *for taxi* prix *m*

Far 'East Extrême-Orient *m*

farewell [fer'wel] adieu *m*

farfetched [fɑːr'fetʃ] tiré par les cheveux

farm [fɑːrm] ferme *f*; **farmer** fermier(-ière) *m(f)*; **farming** agriculture *f*; **farmworker** ouvrier(-ière) *m(f)* agricole; **farmyard** cour *f* de ferme

far-'off lointain, éloigné; **far-sighted** prévoyant; *visually* hypermétrope; **farther** plus loin; **farthest** le plus loin

fascinate ['fæsɪneɪt] fasciner; **fascinating** fascinant; **fascination** fascination *f*

fascism ['fæʃɪzm] fascisme *m*; **fascist 1** *n* fasciste *m/f* **2** *adj* fasciste

fashion ['fæʃn] mode *f*; (*manner*) manière *f*, façon *f*; **in** ~ à la mode; **out of** ~ démodé; **fashionable** à la mode; **fashionably** à la mode; **fashion-conscious** au courant de la mode; **fashion designer** créateur(-trice) *m(f)* de mode; **fashion show** défilé *m* de mode

fast[1] [fæst] **1** *adj* rapide; **be** ~ *of clock* avancer **2** *adv* vite; **be** ~ **asleep** dormir à poings fermés

fast[2] [fæst] *n (not eating)* jeûne *m*

fasten ['fæsn] **1** *v/t* attacher; *lid, window* fermer **2** *v/i of dress etc* s'attacher; **fastener** ['fæsnər] *for dress* agrafe *f*; *for lid* fermeture *f*

fast 'food fast-food *m*; **fast lane** voie *f* rapide; **fast train** train *m* rapide

fat [fæt] **1** *adj* gros **2** *n on meat* gras *m*; *for baking* graisse *f*

fatal ['feɪtl] *also error* fatal; *fatality accident* *m* mortel; *fatally* fatalement; ~ **injured** mortellement blessé

fermentation

fate [feɪt] destin *m*

'fat free sans matières grasses;
yoghurt etc 0%

father ['fɑːðər] père *m*; fatherhood paternité *f*; father-in-law beau-père *m*; fatherly paternel

fatigue [fəˈtiːg] fatigue *f*

fatten ['fætn] *animal* engraisser; fatty 1 *adj* adipeux 2 *n* F *person* gros(se) *m(f)*

faucet ['fɔːsɪt] robinet *m*

fault [fɔːlt] *(defect)* défaut *m*; **it's your/my ~** c'est de ta/ma faute; faultless impeccable; faulty défectueux

favor ['feɪvər] 1 *n* faveur *f*; **do s.o. a ~** rendre (un) service à qn 2 *v/t (prefer)* préférer; favorable favorable; favorite 1 *n person* préféré(e) *m(f)*; *food* plat *m* préféré; *in race* 2 *adj* préféré; favoritism favoritisme *m*

favour *Br* → **favor**

fax [fæks] 1 *n* fax *m* 2 *v/t* faxer

fear [fɪr] 1 *n* peur *f* 2 *v/t* avoir peur de; fearless sans peur; fearlessly sans peur

feasibility study [fiːzəˈbɪlətɪ] étude *f* de faisabilité; feasible faisable

feast [fiːst] festin *m*

feat [fiːt] exploit *m*

feather ['feðər] plume *f*

feature ['fiːtʃər] *on face* trait *m*; *of city, building, style* caractéristique *f*; *article in paper* chronique *f*; feature film long métrage *m*

February ['februərɪ] février *m*

federal ['fedərəl] fédéral; federation fédération *f*

fed 'up F: **be ~ with** en avoir ras-le-bol de F

fee [fiː] *of lawyer, doctor etc* honoraires *mpl*; *for membership* frais *mpl*

feeble ['fiːbl] faible

feed [fiːd] nourrir; feedback réactions *fpl*

feel [fiːl] 1 *v/t (touch)* toucher; *(sense)* sentir; *pain, pleasure* ressentir; *(think)* penser 2 *v/i*: **it ~s like silk** on dirait de la soie; **do you ~ like a drink?** est-ce que tu as envie de boire quelque chose?

◆ feel up to se sentir capable de

feeler ['fiːlər] *of insect* antenne *f*; feeling sentiment *m*; *(sensation)* sensation *f*

fellow 'citizen concitoyen(ne) *m(f)*

felony ['felənɪ] crime *m*

felt [felt] feutre *m*; felt tip stylo *m* feutre

female ['fiːmeɪl] 1 *adj* femelle; *relating to people* féminin 2 *n* femelle *f*; *person* femme *f*

feminine ['femɪnɪn] 1 *adj* féminin 2 *n* GRAM féminin *m*; feminism féminisme *m*; feminist 1 *n* féministe *m/f* 2 *adj* féministe

fence [fens] barrière *f*, clôture *f*

fender ['fendər] MOT aile *f*

fermentation [fɜːrmenˈteɪʃn]

fermentation *f*

ferocious [fəˈrouʃəs] féroce

ferry [ˈferɪ] ferry *m*

fertile [ˈfɜːrtl] fertile; **fertility** fertilité *f*; **fertilize** féconder; **fertilizer** *for soil* engrais *m*

fervent [ˈfɜːrvənt] fervent

fester [ˈfestər] *of wound* suppurer

festival [ˈfestɪvl] festival *m*; **festive** de fête; **festivities** festivités *fpl*

fetal [ˈfiːtl] fœtal

fetch [fetʃ] *(go and ~)* aller chercher (**from** à); *(come and ~)* venir chercher (**from** à); *price* atteindre

fetus [ˈfiːtəs] fœtus *m*

feud [fjuːd] querelle *f*

fever [ˈfiːvər] fièvre *f*; **feverish** *also fig* fiévreux

few [fjuː] **1** *adj (not many)* peu de; **a ~** quelques; **quite a ~**, **a good ~** *(a lot)* beaucoup de **2** *pron (not many)* peu; **a ~** quelques-un(e)s *m(f)*; **quite a ~**, **a good ~** beaucoup; **fewer** moins de

fiancé [fɪˈɑːnseɪ] fiancé *m*; **fiancée** fiancée *f*

fiber [ˈfaɪbər] fibre *f*; **fiberglass** *n* fibre *f* de verre; **fiber optics** fibres *fpl* optiques

fibre *Br* → **fiber**

fickle [ˈfɪkl] inconstant

fiction [ˈfɪkʃn] romans *mpl*; *(made-up story)* fiction *f*; **fictional** de roman; **fictitious** fictif

fiddle [ˈfɪdl] **1** *n (violin)* violon

m **2** *v/i*: **~ around with** tripoter **3** *v/t accounts, results* truquer

fidgety [ˈfɪdʒɪtɪ] remuant

field [fiːld] champ *m*; *for sport* terrain *m*; *(competitors in race)* concurrent(e)s *m(f)pl*; **fielder** *in baseball* joueur *m* de champ

fierce [fɪrs] *animal* féroce; *wind, storm* violent; **fiercely** avec férocité

fiery [ˈfaɪrɪ] ardent, fougueux

fifteen [fɪfˈtiːn] quinze; **fifteenth** quinzième; **fifth** cinquième; **fiftieth** cinquantième; **fifty** cinquante; **fifty-fifty** moitié-moitié

fight [faɪt] **1** *n* combat *m*; *(argument)* dispute *f*; *for survival etc* lutte *f* **2** *v/t enemy, person* combattre; *in boxing* se battre contre; *injustice* lutter contre **3** *v/i* se battre; *(argue)* se disputer; **fighter** combattant(e) *m(f)*; *airplane* avion *m* de chasse; *(boxer)* boxeur *m*; **fighting** *physical* combat *m*; *verbal* dispute *f*

figure [ˈfɪgjər] **1** *n (digit)* chiffre *m*; *of person* ligne *f*; *(form, shape)* figure *f* **2** *v/t* F *(think)* penser:

◆ **figure on** F *(plan)* compter

◆ **figure out** *(understand)* comprendre; *calculation* calculer

file[1] [faɪl] **1** *n of documents* dossier *m*; COMPUT fichier *m* **2** *v/t documents* classer

file[2] [faɪl] *for wood etc* lime *f*

'**file cabinet** classeur *m*

fill [fɪl] remplir; *tooth* plomber; *prescription* préparer

◆ **fill in** *form* remplir; *hole* boucher

◆ **fill out 1** *v/t form* remplir **2** *v/i* (*get fatter*) grossir

fillet ['fɪlɪt] filet *m*

filling ['fɪlɪŋ] **1** *n in sandwich* garniture *f*; *in tooth* plombage *m* **2** *adj food* nourrissant; **filling station** station-service *f*

film [fɪlm] **1** *n* pellicule *f*; (*movie*) film *m* **2** *v/t* filmer; **film-maker** réalisateur(-trice) *m(f)* de films; **film star** star *f* de cinéma

filter ['fɪltər] **1** *n* filtre *m* **2** *v/t* filtrer

filth [fɪlθ] saleté; filthy sale; *language etc* obscène

final ['faɪnl] **1** *adj* dernier; *decision* définitif, irrévocable **2** *n* SP finale *f*; **finale** apothéose *f*; **finalist** finaliste *m/f*; **finalize** finaliser, mettre au point; **finally** finalement, enfin

finance ['faɪnæns] **1** *n* finance *f*; (*funds*) financement *m* **2** *v/t* financer; **financial** financier; **financially** financièrement; **financier** financier (-ière) *m(f)*

find [faɪnd] trouver

◆ **find out** découvrir; (*enquire about*) se renseigner sur

findings ['faɪndɪŋz] *of report*

constatations *fpl*

fine[1] [faɪn] *day* beau; (*good*) bon, excellent; *distinction* subtil; *line* fin; **how's that?** **– that's ~** que dites-vous de ça? – c'est bien

fine[2] [faɪn] **1** *n* amende *f* **2** *v/t* condamner à une amende de $5.000

finger ['fɪŋgər] **1** *n* doigt *m* **2** *v/t* toucher; **fingerprint** empreinte *f* digitale

finicky ['fɪnɪkɪ] *person* tatillon; *design* alambiqué

finish ['fɪnɪʃ] **1** *v/t* finir, terminer **2** *v/i* finir **3** *n of product* finition *f*; *of race* arrivée *f*

◆ **finish with** *boyfriend etc* en finir avec

fire ['faɪr] **1** *n* feu *m*; (*blaze*) incendie *m*; (*electric, gas*) radiateur *m*; **be on ~** être en feu; **set ~ to sth** mettre le feu à qch **2** *v/i* (*shoot*) tirer **3** *v/t* F (*dismiss*) virer F; **fire alarm** signal *m* d'incendie; **firearm** arme *f* à feu; **firecracker** pétard *m*; **fire department** sapeurs-pompiers *mpl*; **fire engine** *esp Br* voiture *f* de pompiers; **fire escape** *ladder* échelle *f* de secours; *stairs* escalier *m* de secours; **fire extinguisher** extincteur *m* (d'incendie); **fire fighter** pompier *m*; **fireplace** cheminée *f*; **fire station** caserne *f* de pompiers; **fire truck** voiture *f* de pompiers; **firework** pièce *f* d'artifice; **~s**

firm

(display) feu *m* d'artifice

firm¹ [fɜːrm] *adj* ferme

firm² [fɜːrm] *n* COM firme *f*

first [fɜːrst] **1** *adj* premier **2** *n* premier(-ière) *m(f)* **3** *adv* arrive, finish le/la premier(-ière) *m(f)*; (*beforehand*) d'abord; **at ~** au début; **first aid** premiers secours *mpl*; **first class 1** *adj* ticket de première classe; (*very good*) de première qualité **2** *adv* travel en première classe; **first floor** rez-de-chaussée *m*; *Br* premier étage *m*; **First Lady** première dame *f*; **firstly** premièrement; **first name** prénom *m*; **first night** première *f*; **first-rate** de premier ordre

fiscal ['fɪskl] fiscal; **fiscal year** année *f* fiscale

fish [fɪʃ] **1** *n* poisson *m* **2** *v/i* pêcher; **fisherman** pêcheur *m*; **fishing** pêche *f*; **fishing boat** bateau *m* de pêche; **fish stick** bâtonnet *m* de poisson; **fishy** F (*suspicious*) louche

fist [fɪst] poing *m*

fit¹ [fɪt] *n* MED crise *f*, attaque *f*

fit² [fɪt] *adj* physically en forme; *morally* digne

fit³ [fɪt] **1** *v/t of clothes* aller à; (*install, attach*) poser; **it doesn't ~ me any more** je ne rentre plus dedans **2** *v/i of clothes* aller

fitness ['fɪtnɪs] *physical* (bonne) forme *f*; **fitting** approprié; **fittings** installations *fpl*

five [faɪv] cinq

fix [fɪks] **1** *n* (*solution*) solution *f* **2** *v/t* (*attach*) attacher; (*repair*) réparer; *meeting etc* arranger; *lunch* préparer; *dishonestly: match etc* truquer; **fixed** fixe; **fixings** garniture *f*

flab [flæb] *on body* graisse *f*; **flabby** *muscles etc* mou

flag¹ [flæg] *n* drapeau *m*; NAUT pavillon *m*

flag² [flæg] *v/i* (*tire*) faiblir

'flagpole mât *m* (de drapeau)

flagrant ['fleɪgrənt] flagrant

flair [fler] (*talent*) flair *m*; **have a natural ~ for** avoir un don pour

flake [fleɪk] *of snow* flocon *m*; *of plaster* écaille *f*

flamboyant [flæm'bɔɪənt] extravagant; **flamboyantly** avec extravagance

flame [fleɪm] flamme *f*

flammable ['flæməbl] inflammable

flank [flæŋk] **1** *n* flanc *m* **2** *v/t*: **be ~ed by** être flanqué de

flap [flæp] **1** *n of envelope, pocket* rabat *m* **2** *v/t wings* battre **3** *v/i of flag etc* battre

♦ flare up [fler] *of violence, rash* éclater; *of fire* s'enflammer; (*get very angry*) s'emporter

flash [flæʃ] **1** *n of light* éclair *m*; PHOT flash *m*; **in a ~** F en un rien de temps; **~ of lightning** éclair *m* **2** *v/i of light* clignoter; **flashback** *in movie* flash-back *m*; **flashlight** lam-

flow

pe *f* de poche; PHOT flash *m*;
flashy *pej* voyant

flask [flæsk] (*hip* ~) fiole *f*

flat¹ [flæt] **1** *adj* plat; *beer*
éventé; *battery, tire* à plat;
bémol **2** *adv* MUS trop bas **3**
n pneu *m* crevé

flat² [flæt] *n Br* (*apartment*)
appartement *m*

flatly ['flætlɪ] *deny* catégoriquement; **flat rate** tarif *m*
unique; **flatten** *land, road*
aplanir; *by bombing, demolition* raser

flatter ['flætər] flatter; **flatterer** flatteur(-euse) *m(f)*; **flattering** *comments* flatteur;
color, clothes avantageux;
flattery flatterie *f*

flavor ['fleɪvər] **1** *n* goût *m*; *of
ice cream* parfum *m* **2** *v/t
food* assaisonner; **flavoring**
arôme *m*

flavour *Br* → **flavor**

flaw [flɔː] défaut *m*; **flawless**
parfait

flee [fliː] s'enfuir

fleet [fliːt] NAUT flotte *f*; *of vehicles* parc *m*

fleeting ['fliːtɪŋ] *visit etc* très
court

flesh [fleʃ] *also of fruit* chair *f*

flex [fleks] *muscles* fléchir,
flexibility flexibilité *f*; **flexible** flexible; **flextime** horaire
m à la carte

flicker ['flɪkər] vaciller

flier [flaɪr] (*circular*) prospectus *m*

flight [flaɪt] *in airplane* vol *m*;

(*fleeing*) fuite *f*; ~ (*of stairs*)
escalier *m*; **flight attendant**
male steward *m*; *female* hôtesse *f* de l'air; **flight path**
trajectoire *f* de vol; **flight recorder** enregistreur *m* de vol;
flight time *departure* heure *f*
de vol; *duration* durée *f* de
vol; **flighty** frivole

flimsy ['flɪmzɪ] *furniture* fragile; *dress, material* léger; *excuse* faible

flinch [flɪntʃ] tressaillir

flipper ['flɪpər] nageoire *f*

flirt [flɜːrt] **1** *v/i* flirter **2** *n* flir-
teur(-euse) *m(f)*; **flirtatious**
flirteur

float [fləʊt] *also* FIN flotter

flock [flɑːk] **1** *n of sheep* troupeau *m* **2** *v/i* venir en masse

flood [flʌd] **1** *n* inondation *f* **2**
v/t of river inonder; **flooding**
inondation(s) *f(pl)*

¹floodlight projecteur *m*;
flood waters inondations *fpl*

floor [flɔːr] *sol m*; *wooden*
plancher *m*; (*story*) étage *m*

flop [flɑːp] **1** *v/i* s'écrouler;
(*fail*) faire un bide **F 2** *n F
(failure)* bide *m* **F**; **floppy**
(*disk*) disquette *f*

florist ['flɔːrɪst] fleuriste *m/f*

flour ['flaʊr] farine *f*

flourish ['flʌrɪʃ] *of plants*
fleurir; *fig* prospérer; **flourishing** *business* fleurissant,
prospère

flow [fləʊ] **1** *v/i of river* couler;
of electric current passer; *of
traffic* circuler; *of work* se

dérouler **2** *n of river* cours *m*;
of information circulation *f*;
flowchart organigramme *m*

flower ['flaʊr] **1** *n* fleur *f* **2** *v/i* fleurir

flu [fluː] grippe *f*

fluctuate ['flʌktʃʊeɪt] fluctuer; **fluctuation** fluctuation *f*

fluency ['fluːənsɪ] *in a language* maîtrise *f* (**in** de); **fluent** *person* qui s'exprime avec aisance; *he speaks ~ Spanish* il parle couramment l'espagnol; **fluently** couramment; *in own language* avec aisance

fluid ['fluːɪd] fluide *m*

flunk [flʌŋk] F *subject* rater

flush [flʌʃ] **1** *v/t*: *~ the toilet* tirer la chasse d'eau **2** *v/i* (*go red*) rougir

flutter ['flʌtər] *of bird* voleter; *of wings* battre; *of flag* s'agiter; *of heart* palpiter

fly[1] [flaɪ] *n* (*insect*) mouche *f*

fly[2] [flaɪ] *n on pants* braguette *f*

fly[3] [flaɪ] **1** *v/i* voler; *in airplane* prendre l'avion; *of flag* flotter **2** *v/t airplane* piloter, voler; *airline* voyager par; (*transport by air*) envoyer par avion

◆ **fly past** *of time* filer

flying ['flaɪɪŋ]: *I hate ~* je déteste prendre l'avion

foam [fəʊm] *on sea* écume *f*; *on drink* mousse *f*; **foam rubber** caoutchouc *m* mous-

se

focus ['fəʊkəs] *of attention* centre *m*; PHOT mise *f* au point

◆ **focus on** se concentrer sur; PHOT mettre au point sur

fodder ['fɑːdər] fourrage *m*

fog [fɑːg] brouillard *m*; **foggy** brumeux

foil[1] [fɔɪl] *n silver* feuille *f* d'aluminium

foil[2] [fɔɪl] *v/t* (*thwart*) faire échouer

fold [fəʊld] **1** *v/t paper etc* plier; *~ one's arms* croiser les bras **2** *v/i of business* fermer (ses portes) **3** *n in cloth etc* pli *m*

◆ **fold up 1** *v/t* plier **2** *v/i of chair, table* se (re)plier

folder ['fəʊldər] *for documents* chemise *f*; COMPUT dossier *m*; **folding** pliant

foliage ['fəʊlɪdʒ] feuillage *m*

folk [fəʊk] (*people*) gens *mpl*; **folk music** folk *m*; **folk singer** chanteur(-euse) *m(f)* folk

follow ['fɑːləʊ] **1** *v/t also* (*understand*) suivre **2** *v/i logically* s'ensuivre

◆ **follow up** *inquiry* donner suite à

follower ['fɑːləʊər] *of politician etc* partisan(e) *m(f)*; *of football team* supporteur (-trice) *m(f)*; **following 1** *adj* suivant **2** *n people* partisans *mpl*

fond [fɑːnd] (*loving*) aimant;

memory agréable; **be ~ of** beaucoup aimer

fondle ['fɑ:ndl] caresser

fondness ['fɑ:ndnɪs] *for s.o.* tendresse *f*; *for sth* penchant *m*

font [fɑ:nt] *for printing* police *f*; *in church* fonts *mpl* baptismaux

food [fu:d] nourriture *f*; **French ~** la cuisine française; **food poisoning** intoxication *f* alimentaire

fool [fu:l] **1** *n* idiot(e) *m(f)* **2** *v/t* berner; **foolhardy** téméraire; **foolish** idiot, bête; **foolproof** à toute épreuve

foot [fʊt] *also measurement* pied *m*; *of animal* patte *f*; **put one's ~ in it** F mettre les pieds dans le plat F; **footage** séquences *fpl*; **football** football *m* américain; (*soccer*) football *m* F; (*ball*) ballon *m* de football; **football player** joueur(-euse) *m(f)* de football américain; *soccer* joueur(-euse) *m(f)* de football; **foothills** contreforts *mpl*; **footnote** note *f* (de bas de page); **footpath** sentier *m*; **footprint** trace *f* de pas; **footstep** pas *m*

for [fər], [fɔ:r] pour; **a train ~ ...** un train à destination de ...; **what is this ~?** pour quoi est-ce que c'est fait?; **what ~?** pourquoi?; **~ three days** pendant trois jours; **it lasted ~ three days** ça a duré trois

jours; **I've been waiting ~ an hour** j'attends depuis une heure

forbid [fər'bɪd] interdire; **forbidden** interdit; **forbidding** menaçant

force [fɔ:rs] **1** *n* force *f*; **come into ~** *of law* etcr entrer en vigueur **2** *v/t door, lock* forcer; **~ s.o. to do sth** forcer qn à faire qch; **forced** forcé; **forced landing** atterrissage *m* forcé; **forceful** *argument, speaker* puissant; *character* énergique

forceps ['fɔ:rseps] MED forceps *m*

forcibly ['fɔ:rsəblɪ] *restrain* par force

foreboding [fər'boʊdɪŋ] pressentiment *m*; **forecast 1** *n* of *results* pronostic *m*; *of weather* prévisions *fpl* **2** *v/t result* pronostiquer; *future, weather* prévoir; **forefathers** ancêtres *mpl*; **forefinger** index *m*; **foreground** premier plan *m*; **forehead** front *m*

foreign ['fɒrən] étranger; **foreign affairs** affaires *fpl* étrangères; **foreign body** corps *m* étranger; **foreign currency** devises *fpl* étrangères; **foreigner** étranger (-ère) *m(f)*; **foreign exchange** devises *fpl* étrangères

'foreman chef *m* d'équipe; **foremost 1** *adv* (*uppermost*) le plus important **2** *adj* (*lead-

ing) premier

forensic 'medicine [fəˈrensɪk] médecine *f* légale; **forensic scientist** expert *m* légiste

'forerunner *person* prédécesseur *m*; *thing* ancêtre *m/f*; **foresee** prévoir; **foresight** prévoyance *f*

forest [ˈfʊrɪst] forêt *f*; **forestry** sylviculture *f*

fore'tell prédire

forever [fəˈrevər] toujours

'foreword avant-propos *m*

forfeit [ˈfɔːrfət] *(lose)* perdre; *(give up)* renoncer à

forge [fɔːrdʒ] contrefaire; **forgery** *bank bill* faux billet *m*; *document* faux *m*; *signature* contrefaçon *f*

forget [fərˈget] oublier; **forgetful: you're so ~** tu as vraiment mauvaise mémoire

forgive [fərˈgɪv] **1** *v/t:* **~ s.o. sth** pardonner qch à qn **2** *v/i* pardonner; **forgiveness** pardon *m*

fork [fɔːrk] fourchette *f*; *for gardening* fourche *f*; *in road* embranchement *m*

form [fɔːrm] **1** *n (shape)* forme *f*; *document* formulaire *m* **2** *v/t* former; *friendship* développer; *opinion* se faire **3** *v/i (take shape, develop)* se former; **formal** *language* soutenu; *dress* de soirée; *manner, reception* cérémonieux; *recognition etc* officiel; **formality** *of language*

caractère *m* soutenu; *of occasion* cérémonie *f*; **it's just a ~** c'est juste une formalité; **formally** *speak* cérémonieusement; *recognized* officiellement

format [ˈfɔːrmæt] **1** *v/t* formater **2** *n* format *m*

formation [fɔːrˈmeɪʃn] formation *f*

former [ˈfɔːrmər] ancien; **the ~** le premier, la première; **formerly** autrefois

formidable [ˈfɔːrmɪdəbl] redoutable

formula [ˈfɔːrmjʊlə] MATH, CHEM formule *f*; *fig* recette *f*

fort [fɔːrt] MIL fort *m*

forthcoming [ˈfɔːrθkʌmɪŋ] *(future)* futur; *personality* ouvert

'forthright franc

fortieth [ˈfɔːrtɪɪθ] quarantième

fortnight [ˈfɔːrtnaɪt] *Br* quinze jours *mpl*, quinzaine *f*

fortress [ˈfɔːrtrɪs] MIL forteresse *f*

fortunate [ˈfɔːrtʃnət] *decision* heureux; **be ~** avoir de la chance; **fortunately** heureusement; **fortune** *(fate)* destin *m*; *(luck)* chance *f*; *(lot of money)* fortune *f*

forty [ˈfɔːrtɪ] quarante

forward [ˈfɔːrwərd] **1** *adv* en avant **2** *adj pej: person* effronté **3** *n* SP avant **m 4** *v/t letter* faire suivre; **forward-looking** moderne

freezer

fossil ['fɒsl] fossile *m*

foster ['fɒstər] *child* servir de famille d'accueil à; *attitude, belief* encourager

foul [faʊl] **1** *n* sp faute *f* **2** *adj smell* infect; *weather* sale **3** *v/t* sp commettre une faute contre

found [faʊnd] *school etc* fonder; **foundation** *of theory etc* fondement *m*; *(organization)* fondation *f*; **foundations** *of building* fondations *fpl*; **founder** fondateur(-trice) *m(f)*

fountain ['faʊntɪn] fontaine *f*; *with vertical spout* jet *m* d'eau

four [fɔːr] quatre; **four-star** quatre étoiles; **fourteen** quatorze; **fourteenth** quatorzième; **fourth** quatrième; **four-wheel drive** MOT quatre-quatre *m*

fox [fɑːks] **1** *n* renard *m* **2** *v/t (puzzle)* mystifier

foyer ['fɔɪər] hall *m* d'entrée

fraction ['frækʃn] fraction *f*; **fractionally** très légèrement

fracture ['fræktʃər] **1** *n* fracture *f* **2** *v/t* fracturer

fragile ['frædʒəl] fragile

fragment ['frægmənt] fragment *m*

fragrance ['freɪɡrəns] parfum *m*; **fragrant** parfumé

frail [freɪl] frêle, fragile

frame [freɪm] **1** *n* of picture, bicycle cadre *m*; of window châssis *m*; of eyeglasses monture *f* **2** *v/t picture* encadrer; F *person* monter un coup contre; **framework** structure *f*; **within the ~ of** dans le cadre de

France [fræns] France *f*

franchise ['fræntʃaɪz] *for business* franchise *f*

frank [fræŋk] franc; **frankly** franchement; **frankness** franchise *f*

frantic ['fræntɪk] frénétique

fraternal [frə'tɜːrnl] fraternel

fraud [frɔːd] fraude *f*; *person* imposteur *m*; **fraudulent** frauduleux

frayed [freɪd] *cuffs* usé

freak [friːk] **1** *n (unusual event)* phénomène *m* étrange; *(two-headed animal etc)* monstre *m*; F *(strange person)* taré(e) *m(f)*F **2** *adj storm etc* anormalement violent

free [friː] **1** *adj* libre; *no cost* gratuit **2** *v/t prisoners* libérer; **freedom** liberté *f*; **free enterprise** libre entreprise *f*; **free kick** *in soccer* coup *m* franc; **freelance** indépendant, free-lance *inv*; **freely** *admit* volontiers; **free speech** libre parole *f*; **freeway** autoroute *f*

freeze [friːz] **1** *v/t* congeler; *bank account* bloquer; **~ a video** faire un arrêt sur image **2** *v/i of water* geler; **freeze-dried** lyophilisé; **freezer** congélateur *m*;

freezing **1** *adj* glacial **2** *n:* **10 below** ~ 10 degrés au-dessous de zéro

freight [freɪt] fret *m*; freighter ship cargo *m*; airplane avion-cargo *m*

French [frenʃ] **1** *adj* français **2** *n* language français *m*; **the** ~ les Français *mpl*; French fries frites *fpl*; Frenchman Français *m*; Frenchwoman Française *f*

frenzied [ˈfrenzɪd] attack, activity forcené; mob déchaîné; frenzy frénésie *f*

frequency [ˈfriːkwənsɪ] also of radio fréquence *f*

frequent[1] *adj* fréquent

frequent[2] [frɪˈkwent] *v/t* bar etc fréquenter

frequently [ˈfriːkwəntlɪ] fréquemment

fresh [freʃ] frais; start nouveau; sheets propre; (impertinent) insolent; fresh air air *m*

◆ freshen up **1** *v/i* se rafraîchir **2** *v/t* paintwork rafraîchir

freshly [ˈfreʃlɪ] fraîchement; freshman étudiant(e) *m(f)* de première année; freshwater d'eau douce

fret [fret] s'inquiéter

friction [ˈfrɪkʃn] friction *f*

Friday [ˈfraɪdeɪ] vendredi *m*

fridge [frɪdʒ] frigo *m* F

friend [frend] ami(e) *m(f)*; friendliness amabilité *f*; friendly amical; hotel, city sympathique; argument entre amis; friendship amitié *f*

fries [fraɪz] frites *fpl*

fright [fraɪt] peur *f*; frighten faire peur à; **be** ~**ed** avoir peur (**of** de); frightening effrayant

frill [frɪl] on dress etc, (extra) falbala *m*

fringe [frɪndʒ] frange *f*; of city périphérie *f*; of society marge *f*; fringe benefits avantages *mpl* sociaux

frisk [frɪsk] fouiller

◆ fritter away [ˈfrɪtər] time, fortune gaspiller

frivolity [frɪˈvɑːlətɪ] frivolité *f*; frivolous frivole

frizzy [ˈfrɪzɪ] hair crépu

frog [frɑːg] grenouille *f*; frogman homme-grenouille *m*

from [frɑːm] de; ~ **9 to 5** (o'clock) de 9 heures à 5 heures; ~ **the 18th century** à partir du XVIIIe siècle; ~ **today on** à partir d'aujourd'hui; ~ **here to there** d'ici à là(-bas); **I am** ~ **New Jersey** je viens du New Jersey; **tired** ~ **the journey** fatigué par le voyage; **it's** ~ **overeating** c'est d'avoir trop mangé

front [frʌnt] **1** *n* of building façade *f*, devant *m*; of book devant *m*; (cover organization) façade *f*; MIL, of weather front *m*; **in** ~ devant; **in** ~ in a race en tête; **in** ~ **of** devant **2** *adj* wheel, seat avant **3** *v/t* TV program présenter; front door porte *f* d'entrée

frontier [ˈfrʌntɪr] also fig

frontière f

'**front line** MIL front m; **front page** of newspaper une f; **front-wheel drive** traction f avant

frost [frɑ:st] gel m; **frostbite** gelure f; **frosting** on cake glaçage m; **frosty** also fig glacial

froth [frɑ:θ] écume f, mousse f

frown [fraun] froncer les sourcils

frozen [ˈfrouzn] gelé; food surgelé

fruit [fru:t] fruit m; collective fruits mpl; **fruitful** discussions etc fructueux; **fruit juice** jus m de fruit; **fruit salad** salade f de fruits

frustrate [ˈfrʌstreɪt] person frustrer; plans contrarier; **frustrating** frustrant; **frustration** frustration f

fry [fraɪ] (faire) frire; **frypan** poêle f (à frire)

fuck [fʌk] V baiser V; **~ puterin!** V

fuel [ˈfjuːəl] **1** n carburant m **2** v/t fig entretenir

fugitive [ˈfjuːdʒətɪv] fugitif (-ive) m(f)

fulfill, Br **fulfil** [fulˈfɪl] dreams réaliser; task accomplir; contract remplir; **fulfillment**, Br **fulfilment** of contract etc exécution f; moral, spiritual accomplissement m

full [ful] plein (**of** de); hotel, account complet; **pay in ~** tout payer; **full moon** pleine

lune f; **full stop** Br point m; **full-time** à plein temps; **fully** complètement; describe en détail

fumble [ˈfʌmbl] catch mal attraper

fumes [fjuːmz] s fumée f

fun [fʌn] **1** n amusement m; **it was great ~** on s'est bien amusé; **have ~!** amuse-toi bien! **2** adj F marrant F

function [ˈfʌŋkʃn] **1** n fonction f; (reception etc) réception f **2** v/i fonctionner; **~ as** faire fonction de; **functional** fonctionnel

fund [fʌnd] **1** n fonds m **2** v/t project etc financer

fundamental [fʌndəˈmentl] fondamental; **fundamentalist** fondamentaliste m/f; **fundamentally** fondamentalement

funding [ˈfʌndɪŋ] (money) financement m

funeral [ˈfjuːnərəl] enterrement m; **funeral home** établissement m de pompes funèbres

fungus [ˈfʌŋgəs] champignon m; mold moisissure f

funnies [ˈfʌnɪz] F pages fpl drôles; **funnily** (oddly) bizarrement; (comically) comiquement; **~ enough** chose curieuse; **funny** (comical) drôle; (odd) bizarre, curieux

fur [fɜːr] fourrure f

furious [ˈfjʊrɪəs] furieux

furnace [ˈfɜːrnɪs] four(neau)

m
furnish ['fɜːrnɪʃ] *room* meubler; (*supply*) fournir; **furniture** meubles *mpl*; *a piece of ~* un meuble
further ['fɜːrðər] **1** *adj* supplémentaire; (*more distant*) plus éloigné **2** *adv* walk, drive plus loin **3** *v/t cause etc* faire avancer, promouvoir; **furthermore** de plus, en outre
furtive ['fɜːrtɪv] furtif
fury ['fjʊrɪ] fureur *f*
fuse [fjuːz] **1** *n* ELEC fusible *m*, plomb *m* F **2** *v/i* ELEC: *the*

lights have ~d les plombs ont sauté **3** *v/t* ELEC faire sauter; **fusebox** boîte *f* à fusibles
fusion ['fjuːʒn] fusion *f*
fuss [fʌs] agitation *f*; **fussy** *person* difficile; *design etc* trop compliqué
futile ['fjuːtl] futile; **futility** futilité *f*
future ['fjuːtʃər] **1** *n* avenir *f*; GRAM futur *m* **2** *adj* futur; **futuristic** *design* futuriste
fuzzy ['fʌzɪ] *hair* crépu; (*out of focus*) flou

G

gadget ['gædʒɪt] gadget *m*
gag [gæg] **1** *n* bâillon *m*; (*joke*) gag *m* **2** *v/t also fig* bâillonner
gain [geɪn] acquérir; *victory* remporter; *advantage, sympathy* gagner
gala ['gælə] gala *m*
galaxy ['gæləksɪ] galaxie *f*
gale [geɪl] tempête *f*
gallery ['gælərɪ] *for art, in theater* galerie *f*
gallon ['gælən] gallon *m* (*0,785l, en GB 0,546l*)
gallop ['gæləp] galoper
gamble ['gæmbl] jouer; **gambler** joueur(-euse) *m(f)*; **gambling** jeu *m*
game [geɪm] *also in tennis* jeu *m*; *have a ~ of tennis* faire une partie de tennis

gang [gæŋ] gang *m*; *of friends* bande *f*; **gangster** gangster *m*; **gangway** passerelle *f*
gap [gæp] trou *m*; *in time* intervalle *m*; *between personalities* fossé *m*
gape [geɪp] rester bouche bée; *gaping hole* béant
garage [gəˈrɑːʒ] garage *m*
garbage ['gɑːrbɪdʒ] ordures *fpl*; (*fig : nonsense*) bêtises *fpl*; **garbage can** poubelle *f*; **garbage truck** benne *f* à ordures
garbled ['gɑːrbld] *message* confus
garden ['gɑːrdn] jardin *m*; **gardening** jardinage *m*
garish ['gerɪʃ] criard
garlic ['gɑːrlɪk] ail *m*
garment ['gɑːrmənt] vête-

ment *m*

garnish ['gɑːrnɪʃ] garnir (**with** de)

gas [gæs] gaz *m*; (*gasoline*) essence *f*

gash [gæʃ] entaille *f*

gasket ['gæskɪt] joint *m* d'étanchéité

gasoline ['gæsəliːn] essence *f*

gasp [gæsp] **1** *n* in surprise hoquet *m*; with exhaustion halètement *m* **2** *v/i* with exhaustion haleter; **with surprise** pousser une exclamation de surprise

'**gas pedal** accélérateur *m*; **gas pump** pompe *f* (à essence); **gas station** station-service *f*

gate [geɪt] also at airport porte *f*; **gateway** entrée *f*; also fig porte *f*

gather ['gæðər] **1** *v/t* facts recueillir; ~ **speed** prendre de la vitesse **2** *v/i* of crowd s'assembler; **gathering** (*group of people*) assemblée *f*

gaudy ['gɔːdɪ] voyant

gauge [geɪdʒ] **1** *n* jauge *f* **2** *v/t* pressure jauger; opinion mesurer

gaunt [gɔːnt] émacié

gawky ['gɔːkɪ] gauche

gawp [gɔːp] F rester bouche bée (**at** devant)

gay [geɪ] gay

gaze [geɪz] **1** *n* regard *m* (fixe) **2** *v/i* regarder fixement

gear [gɪr] (*equipment*) équipement *m*; in vehicles vitesse *f*;

gearbox MOT boîte *f* de vitesses; **gear shift** MOT levier *m* de vitesse

gel [dʒel] for hair, shower gel *m*

gem [dʒem] pierre *f* précieuse; fig perle *f*

gender ['dʒendər] genre *m*

gene [dʒiːn] gène *m*

general ['dʒenrəl] **1** *n* MIL général *m(f)* **2** adj général; **generalization** généralisation *f*; **generalize** généraliser; generally généralement; ~ **speaking** de manière générale

generate ['dʒenəreɪt] produire; **generation** génération *f*; **generator** générateur *m*

generosity [dʒenə'rɑːsətɪ] générosité *f*; **generous** généreux

genetic [dʒɪ'netɪk] génétique; **genetically** génétiquement; **genetically engineered** transgénique; **genetically modified** génétiquement modifié; **genetic engineering** génie *m* génétique; **genetic fingerprint** empreinte *f* génétique; **genetics** génétique *f*

genial ['dʒiːnjəl] agréable

genitals ['dʒenɪtlz] organes *mpl* génitaux

genius ['dʒiːnjəs] génie *m*

genocide ['dʒenəsaɪd] génocide *m*

gentle ['dʒentl] doux; breeze léger; **gentleman** monsieur *m;* **he's a real ~** c'est un vrai gentleman; **gentleness** douceur *f;* **gently** doucement; *blow* légèrement

genuine ['dʒenuɪn] authentique; **genuinely** vraiment, sincèrement

geographical [dʒɪə'græfɪkl] géographique; **geography** géographie *f*

geological [dʒɪə'lɒːdʒɪkl] géologique; **geologist** géologue *m/f;* **geology** géologie *f*

geometric, geometrical [dʒɪə'metrɪk(l)] géométrique; **geometry** géométrie *f*

geriatric [dʒerɪ'ætrɪk] **1** *adj* gériatrique **2** *n* patient(e) *m(f)* gériatrique

germ [dʒɜːrm] *also of idea etc* germe *m*

German ['dʒɜːrmən] **1** *adj* allemand **2** *n person* Allemand(e) *m(f); language* allemand *m;* **German shepherd** berger *m* allemand; **Germany** Allemagne *f*

gesture ['dʒestʃər] *also fig* geste *m*

get [get] *(obtain)* obtenir; *(buy)* acheter; *(fetch)* aller chercher; *(receive: letter)* recevoir; *(receive: knowledge, respect etc)* acquérir; *(catch: bus, train etc)* prendre; *(understand)* comprendre; *(become)* devenir; **when we ~ home** quand nous arrivons chez nous; **~ old/tired** vieil-

lir/se fatiguer; **~ sth done** *(by s.o. else)* faire faire qch; **~ s.o. to do sth** faire faire qch à qn; **~ one's hair cut** se faire couper les cheveux; **~ sth ready** préparer qch; **have got** avoir; **have got to** devoir; **I have got to study** je dois étudier, il faut que j'étudie (subj); **~ to know** commencer à bien connaître

◆ **get at** *(criticize)* s'en prendre à; *(imply, mean)* vouloir dire

◆ **get by** *(pass)* passer; *financially* s'en sortir

◆ **get down 1** *v/i from ladder etc* descendre; *(duck)* se baisser **2** *v/t (depress)* déprimer

◆ **get in 1** *v/i (of train, plane)* arriver; *(come home)* rentrer; *to car* entrer **2** *v/t to suitcase etc* rentrer

◆ **get into** *house* entrar dans; *car* monter dans

◆ **get off 1** *v/i from bus etc* descendre; *(finish work)* finir; *(not be punished)* s'en tirer **2** *v/t (remove)* enlever

◆ **get on 1** *v/i to bike, bus* monter; *(be friendly)* s'entendre; *(advance: of time)* se faire tard; *(become old)* prendre de l'âge; *(progress: of book)* avancer **2** *v/t:* **get on the bus** monter dans le bus

◆ **get out 1** *v/i of car, prison*

etc sortir; ***get out!*** va-t-en! **2**
v/t nail, stain enlever; *gun,
pen* sortir
◆ **get through** *on telephone*
obtenir la communication
◆ **get up 1** *v/i* se lever **2** *v/t*
(*climb: hill*) monter
'**getaway car** voiture utilisée
pour s'enfuir; **get-together**
réunion *f*
ghastly ['gɑːstlɪ] horrible
ghetto ['getou] ghetto *m*
ghost [goust] fantôme *m*,
spectre *m*; **ghostly** spectral
ghoul [guːl] personne *f* morbide
giant ['dʒaɪənt] **1** *n* géant(e)
m(f) **2** *adj* géant
gibberish ['dʒɪbərɪʃ] F charabia *m*
gibe [dʒaɪb] moquerie *f*
giddiness ['gɪdɪnɪs] vertige
m; **giddy: feel ~** avoir le vertige
gift [gɪft] cadeau *m*; *talent* don
m; **gift card** carte *f* cadeau;
gifted doué; **giftwrap**: **~** *sth*
faire un paquet-cadeau
gig [gɪg] F concert *m*
gigabyte ['gɪgəbaɪt] COMPUT
gigaoctet *m*
gigantic [dʒaɪ'gæntɪk] gigantesque
giggle ['gɪgl] **1** *v/i* glousser **2** *n*
gloussement *m*
gimmick ['gɪmɪk] truc F
gin [dʒɪn] gin *m*; **~ and tonic**
gin *m* tonic
gipsy ['dʒɪpsɪ] gitan(e) *m(f)*
girder ['gɜːrdər] poutre *f*

girl [gɜːrl] (jeune) fille *f*; **girlfriend** *of boy* petite amie *f*;
younger also copine *f*; *of girl*
amie *f*, *younger also* copine
f; **girlish** de jeune fille
gist [dʒɪst] essence *f*
give [gɪv] donner; *present* offrir; (*supply: electricity etc*)
fournir; *talk, lecture* faire;
cry, groan pousser
◆ **give away** *as present* donner; (*betray*) trahir
◆ **give back** rendre
◆ **give in 1** *v/i* (*surrender*) se
rendre **2** *v/t* (*hand in*) remettre
◆ **give onto** (*open onto*) donner sur
◆ **give out 1** *v/t leaflets etc*
distribuer **2** *v/i of supplies,
strength* s'épuiser
◆ **give up 1** *v/t smoking etc*
arrêter de **2** *v/i* (*stop making
effort*) abandonner
◆ **give way** *of bridge etc*
s'écrouler
give-and-'take concessions
fpl mutuelles
gizmo ['gɪzmou] F truc *m*
glad [glæd] heureux; **gladly**
volontiers, avec plaisir
glamor ['glæmər] éclat *m*, fascination *f*; **glamorize** donner
un aspect séduisant à; **glam-
orous** séduisant, fascinant;
job prestigieux; **glamour** *Br*
→ **glamor**
glance [glæns] **1** *n* regard *m* **2**
v/i jeter un regard, lancer un
coup d'œil

gland [glænd] glande *f*

glare [gler] **1** *n* of sun, lights éclat *m* (éblouissant) **2** *v/i* of sun, lights briller d'un éclat éblouissant

♦ **glare at** lancer un regard furieux à

glaring ['glerɪŋ] *mistake* flagrant

glass [glæs] *material, for drink* verre *m*; **glasses** lunettes *fpl*

glazed [gleɪzd] *expression* vitreux

gleam [gli:m] **1** *n* lueur *f* **2** *v/i* luire

glee [gli:] joie *f*; **gleeful** joyeux

glib [glɪb] désinvolte; **glibly** avec désinvolture

glide [glaɪd] glisser; *of bird, plane* planer; **glider** planeur *m*; **gliding** *sport* vol *m* à voile

glimpse [glɪmps] **1** *n*: **catch a ~ of ...** entrevoir **2** *v/t* entrevoir

glint [glɪnt] **1** *n* lueur *f* **2** *v/i of light, eyes* luire

glisten ['glɪsn] *of light* luire; *of water* miroiter; *of silk* chatoyer

glitter ['glɪtər] *of light, jewels* briller, scintiller

gloat [glout] jubiler

♦ **gloat over** se réjouir de

global ['gloubl] *(worldwide)* mondial; *(without exceptions)* global; **globalization** mondialisation *f*; **global warming** réchauffement *m*

de la planète; **globe** globe *m*

gloom [glu:m] *(darkness)* obscurité *f*; *mood* tristesse *f*; **gloomy** sombre

glorious ['glɔːrɪəs] *weather* magnifique; *victory* glorieux; **glory** gloire *f*

gloss [glɑːs] *(shine)* brillant *m*; *(general explanation)* glose *f*; **glossary** glossaire *m*; **glossy 1** *adj paper* glacé **2** *n magazine* magazine *m* de luxe

glove [glʌv] gant *m*; **glove compartment** boîte *f* à gants

glow [glou] **1** *n of light* lueur *f*; *of fire* rougeoiement *m*; *in cheeks* couleurs *fpl* **2** *v/i of light* luire; *of fire* rougeoyer; *of cheeks* être rouge; **glowing** *description* élogieux

glucose ['glu:kous] glucose *m*

glue [glu:] **1** *n* colle *f* **2** *v/t* coller

glum [glʌm] morose

glut [glʌt] surplus *m*

glutton ['glʌtən] glouton(ne) *m(f)*

gnaw [nɔː] *bone* ronger

go [gou] aller; *(leave)* partir; *(work, function)* marcher, fonctionner; *(come out: of stain etc)* s'en aller; *(cease: of pain etc)* partir, disparaître; *(match: of colors etc)* aller ensemble; **hamburger to ~** hamburger à emporter

♦ **go away** *of person* s'en aller, partir; *of rain* cesser; *of*

goose bumps

pain, *clouds* partir
◆ **go back** (*return*) retourner; (*date back*) remonter (**to** à)
◆ **go by** *of car*, *time* passer
◆ **go down** descendre; *of sun* se coucher
◆ **go in** *to room*, *house* entrer; *of sun* se cacher; (*fit: of part etc*) s'insérer
◆ **go off** (*leave*) partir; *of bomb* exploser; *of gun* partir; *of alarm* se déclencher
◆ **go on** (*continue*) continuer; (*happen*) se passer
◆ **go out** *of person* sortir; *of light*, *fire* s'éteindre
◆ **go over** (*check*) revoir
◆ **go through** *hard times* traverser; *illness* subir; (*check*) revoir; (*read through*) lire en entier
◆ **go under** (*sink*) couler; *of company* faire faillite
◆ **go up** (*climb*) monter; *of prices* augmenter
◆ **go without 1** *v/t food etc* se passer de **2** *v/i* s'en passer
'**go-ahead 1** *n* feu vert *m* **2** *adj* (*enterprising, dynamic*) entreprenant, dynamique
goal [gəʊl] *in sport*, (*objective*) but *m*; **goalkeeper** gardien *m* de but; **goal kick** remise *f* en jeu; **goalpost** poteau *m* de but
goat [gəʊt] chèvre *m*
gobble ['ɡɑːbl] dévorer
gobbledygook ['ɡɑːbldɪɡuːk] F charabia *m* F
'**go-between** intermédiaire

m/f
god [ɡɑːd] dieu *m*; **thank God!** Dieu merci!
'**godchild** filleul(e) *m(f)*; **godfather** *also in mafia* parrain *m*; **godmother** marraine *m*
gofer ['ɡoʊfər] F coursier(-ière) *m(f)*
goggles ['ɡɑːɡl] lunettes *fpl*
goings-on [ɡəʊɪŋz'ɑːn] activités *fpl*
gold [ɡoʊld] **1** *n* or *m* **2** *adj* en or; **ingot** d'or; **golden** *sky* doré; *hair also* d'or; **golden wedding** noces *fpl* d'or; **gold medal** médaille *f* d'or; **gold mine** *fig* mine *f* d'or
golf [ɡɑːlf] golf *m*; **golf ball** balle *f* de golf; **golf club** *organization*, *stick* club *m* de golf; **golf course** terrain *m* de golf; **golfer** golfeur(-euse) *m(f)*
good [ɡʊd] bon; *weather* beau; *child* sage; **goodbye** au revoir; **good-for-nothing** *n* bon(ne) *m(f)* à rien; **Good Friday** Vendredi *m* saint; **good-humored**, *Br* **good-humoured** jovial; **good-looking** beau; **good-natured** bon, au naturel; **goodness** *moral* bonté *f*; *of fruit etc* bonnes choses *fpl*; **goods** com marchandises *fpl*; **goodwill** bonne volonté *f*
goof [ɡuːf] F gaffer F
goose [ɡuːs] oie *f*; **goose bumps** chair *f* de poule

gorgeous ['gɔːrdʒəs] magnifique, superbe

gospel ['gɑːspl] évangile *m*

gossip ['gɑːsɪp] **1** *n* potins *mpl*; *malicious* commérages *mpl*; *person* commère *f* **2** *v/i* bavarder; *maliciously* faire des commérages; **gossip column** échos *mpl*

gourmet ['gʊrmeɪ] gourmet *m*

govern ['gʌvərn] gouverner; **government** gouvernement *m*; **governor** gouverneur *m*

gown [gaʊn] robe *f*; *wedding dress* robe *f* de mariée; *of academic, judge* toge *f*; *of surgeon* blouse *f*

grab [græb] saisir; *food* avaler

grace [greɪs] *of dancer etc* grâce *f*; *before meals* bénédicité *m*; **graceful** gracieux; **gracious** *person* bienveillant; *style* élégant

grade [greɪd] **1** *n* (*quality*) qualité *f*; EDU classe *f*; (*mark*) note *f* **2** *v/t* classer; **school work** noter; **grade crossing** passage *m* à niveau; **grade school** école *f* primaire

gradient ['greɪdɪənt] pente *f*

gradual ['grædʒuəl] graduel; **gradually** peu à peu, progressivement

graduate 1 ['grædʒuət] *n* diplômé(e) *m(f)* **2** ['grædʒueɪt] *v/i* obtenir son diplôme (*from* de); **graduation** obtention *f* du diplôme

graffiti [grə'fiːtiː] graffitis *mpl*; *single* graffiti *m*

graft [græft] **1** *n* BOT, MED greffe *f*; F (*corruption*) corruption *f* **2** *v/t* BOT, MED greffer

grain [greɪn] blé *m*; *of rice etc*, *in wood* grain *m*

gram [græm] gramme *m*

grammar ['græmər] grammaire *f*; **grammatical** grammatical

grand [grænd] **1** *adj* grandiose; F (*very good*) génial F **2** *n* F (*$1000*) mille dollars *mpl*; **grandchild** petit-fils *m*, petite-fille *f*; **granddaughter** petite-fille *f*; **grandeur** grandeur *f*; **grandfather** grand-père *m*; **grand jury** grand jury *m*; **grandmother** grand-mère *f*; **grandparents** grands-parents *mpl*; **grand piano** piano *m* à queue; **grandson** petit-fils *m*

granite ['grænɪt] granit *m*

grant [grænt] **1** *n money* subvention *f* **2** *v/t wish, visa* accorder

granule ['grænuːl] grain *m*

grape [greɪp] (*grain m de*) raisin *m*; *some* ~s du raisin; **grapefruit juice** jus *m* de pamplemousse

graph [græf] graphique *m*, courbe *f*; **graphic 1** *adj* (*vivid*) très réaliste **2** *n* COMPUT graphique *m*

◆ **grapple with** ['græpl] *attacker* en venir aux prises avec; *problem etc* s'attaquer à

grasp [grɑːsp] **1** *n physical* prise *f*; *mental* compréhension *f* **2** *v/t physically* saisir; *(understand)* comprendre

grass [grɑːs] herbe *f*; **grasshopper** sauterelle *f*; **grass roots** *people* base *f*; **grassy** ['grɑːsɪ] herbeux, herbu

grate[1] [greɪt] *n metal* grille *f*

grate[2] [greɪt] **1** *v/t in cooking* râper **2** *v/i*: ~ **on the ear** faire mal aux oreilles

grateful ['greɪtfʊl] reconnaissant; **gratefully** avec reconnaissance

gratify ['grætɪfaɪ] satisfaire

grating ['greɪtɪŋ] **1** *n* grille *f* **2** *adj sound, voice* grinçant

gratitude ['grætɪtuːd] gratitude *f*, reconnaissance *f*

grave[1] [greɪv] *n* tombe *f*

grave[2] [greɪv] *adj* grave

gravel ['grævl] gravier *m*

'gravestone pierre *f* tombale; **graveyard** cimetière *m*

gravity ['grævətɪ] PHYS, *of situation* gravité *f*

gray [greɪ] gris; **gray-haired** aux cheveux gris

graze[1] [greɪz] *v/i of cow etc* paître

graze[2] [greɪz] **1** *v/t arm etc* écorcher **2** *n* écorchure *f*

grease [griːs] *for cooking* graisse *f*; *for car* lubrifiant *m*; *greasy pas*; *(covered in grease)* graisseux

great [greɪt] grand; *mistake, sum* gros; F *(very good)* su-

per F; **Great Britain** Grande-Bretagne *f*; **greatly** beaucoup; *not ~ different* pas très différent; **greatness** grandeur *f*

Greece [griːs] Grèce *f*

greed [griːd] *for money* avidité *f*; *for food also* gourmandise *f*; **greedily** avec avidité; **greedy** *for money* avide; *for food also* gourmand

Greek [griːk] **1** *n* Grec(que) *m(f)*; *language* grec *m* **2** *adj* grec

green [griːn] vert; **green beans** haricots *mpl* verts; **green belt** ceinture *f* verte; **green card** *(work permit)* permis *m* de travail; **greenhouse effect** effet *m* de serre; **greens** légumes *mpl* verts

greet [griːt] saluer; *(welcome)* accueillir; **greeting** salut *m*

grenade [grɪ'neɪd] grenade *f*

grey [greɪ] *Br* → **gray**

grid [grɪd] grille *f*; **gridiron** SP terrain *m* de football; **gridlock** *in traffic* embouteillage *m*

grief [griːf] chagrin *m*, douleur *f*; **grief-stricken** affligé; **grievance** grief *m*; **grieve** être affligé; ~ *for s.o.* pleurer qn

grill [grɪl] **1** *n on window* grille *f* **2** *v/t (interrogate)* mettre sur la sellette

grille [grɪl] grille *f*

grim [grɪm] sinistre, sombre

grimace

grimace ['grɪməs] grimace f

grime [graɪm] crasse f; grimy crasseux

grin [grɪn] 1 n (large) sourire m 2 v/i sourire

grind [graɪnd] coffee moudre; meat hacher

grip [grɪp] saisir, serrer; gripping prenant, captivant

gristle ['grɪsl] cartilage m

grit [grɪt] 1 n for roads gravillon m 2 v/t: ~ one's teeth grincer des dents; gritty F réaliste

groan [groʊn] 1 n gémissement m 2 v/i gémir

groceries ['groʊsərɪz] provisions fpl; grocery store épicerie f l'épicerie

groggy ['grɑːgɪ] F groggy F

groin [grɔɪn] ANAT aine f

groom [gruːm] 1 n for bride marié m; for horse palefrenier(-ère) m(f) 2 v/t horse panser; (train, prepare) préparer

groove [gruːv] rainure f; on record sillon m

grope [groʊp] 1 v/i in the dark tâtonner 2 v/t sexually peloter F

gross [groʊs] (coarse, vulgar) grossier; exaggeration gros; FIN brut

ground [graʊnd] 1 n sol m, terre f; for football etc, fig terrain; (reason) motif m; ELEC terre f 2 v/t ELEC mettre une prise de terre à; grounding in subject bases fpl;

groundless sans fondement; ground meat viande f hachée; groundwork travail m préparatoire

group [gruːp] 1 n groupe m 2 v/t grouper

groupie ['gruːpɪ] F groupie f F

grouse [graʊs] 1 n F rouspéter F 2 v/i F plainte f

grovel ['grɑːvl] fig ramper (to devant)

grow [groʊ] 1 v/i grandir; of plants, hair pousser; of number augmenter; of business se développer; (become) devenir 2 v/t flowers faire pousser

♦ grow up of person devenir adulte; of city se développer

growl [graʊl] 1 n grognement m 2 v/i grogner

'grown-up 1 n adulte m/f 2 adj adulte

growth [groʊθ] of person, company croissance f; (increase) augmentation f; MED tumeur f

grudge [grʌdʒ] rancune f; grudging accordé à contrecœur; person plein de ressentiment; grudgingly à contrecœur

grueling, Br gruelling ['gruːəlɪŋ] épuisant

gruff [grʌf] bourru, revêche

grumble ['grʌmbl] ronchonner; grumbler grognon(ne) m(f)

grunt [grʌnt] 1 n grognement m 2 v/i grogner

guarantee [gærən'tiː] **1** n garantie f **2** v/t garantir; **guarantor** garant(e) m(f)

guard [gɑːrd] **1** n gardien(ne) m(f); MIL garde f **2** v/t garder; **guard dog** chien m de garde; **guarded** reply prudent; **guardian** LAW tuteur(-trice) m(f)

guerrilla [gə'rɪlə] guérillero m; **guerrilla warfare** guérilla f

guess [ges] **1** n conjecture f **2** v/t answer deviner **2** v/i deviner; **I ~ so** je crois; **guesswork** conjecture(s) f(pl)

guest [gest] invité(e) m(f); in hotel hôte m/f; **guestroom** chambre f d'amis

guidance ['gaɪdəns] conseils mpl; **guide 1** n person guide m/f; book guide m **2** v/t guider; **guidebook** guide m; **guided missile** missile m téléguidé; **guided tour** visite f guidée; **guidelines** directives fpl

guilt [gɪlt] culpabilité f; **guilty** also LAW coupable

guinea pig ['gɪnɪpɪg] also fig cobaye m

guitar [gɪ'tɑːr] guitare f; **guitarist** guitariste m/f

gulf [gʌlf] golfe m; fig gouffre m

gull [gʌl] mouette f; bigger goéland m

gullet ['gʌlɪt] ANAT gosier m

gullible ['gʌlɪbl] crédule

gulp [gʌlp] **1** n of drink gorgée

f **2** v/i in surprise dire en s'étranglant
◆ **gulp down** drink avaler à grosses gorgées; food avaler à grosses bouchées

gum¹ [gʌm] in mouth gencive f

gum² [gʌm] (glue) colle f; (chewing gum) chewing-gum m

gun [gʌn] arme f à feu; pistol pistolet m; revolver revolver m; rifle fusil m; cannon canon m
◆ **gun down** abattre

'gunfire coups mpl de feu; **gunman** homme m armé; **gunshot** coup m de feu; **gunshot wound** blessure f par balle

gurgle ['gɜːrgl] of baby gazouiller; of drain gargouiller

guru ['guːruː] fig gourou m

gush [gʌʃ] of liquid jaillir

gust [gʌst] rafale f, coup m de vent

gusto ['gʌstoʊ]: **with ~** avec enthousiasme

gusty ['gʌstɪ] weather très venteux

gut [gʌt] **1** n intestin m; F (stomach) bide m F **2** v/t (destroy) ravager; **guts** F (courage) cran m F; **gutsy** (brave) qui a du cran F

gutter ['gʌtər] on sidewalk caniveau m; on roof gouttière f

guy [gaɪ] F type m F

guzzle ['gʌzl] food engloutir; drink avaler

gym [dʒɪm] *sports club* club *m* de gym; *in school* gymnase *m; activity* gym(nastique) *f*; **gymnast** gymnaste *m/f*; **gymnastics** gymnastique *f*

gynecology, *Br* gynaecology [gaɪnɪ'kɒlədʒɪ] gynécologie

gypsy ['dʒɪpsɪ] gitan(e) *m(f)*

H

habit ['hæbɪt] habitude *f*

habitable ['hæbɪtəbl] habitable; habitat habitat *m*

habitual [hə'bɪtʃʊəl] habituel; *smoker, drinker* invétéré

hacker ['hækər] COMPUT pirate *m* informatique

hackneyed ['hæknɪd] rebattu

haemorrhage *Br* → hemorrhage

haggard ['hægərd] hagard, égaré

haggle ['hægl] chipoter

hail [heɪl] grêle *f*

hair [her] cheveux *mpl; single* cheveu *m; on body* poils *mpl; single* poil *m*; **hairbrush** brosse *f* à cheveux; **haircut** coupe *f* de cheveux; **have a ~** se faire couper les cheveux

'hairdo coiffure *f*; **hairdresser** coiffeur(-euse) *m(f)*; **hairdryer** sèche-cheveux *m*; **hairpin** épingle *f* à cheveux; **hairpin curve** virage *m* en épingle à cheveux; **hair-raising** horrifique; **hair remover** crème *f* épilatoire; **hairsplitting** ergotage *m*; **hairstyle** coiffure *f*; **hairstylist** coiffeur(-euse) *m(f)*; **hairy** *arm,*

animal poilu; F *(frightening)* effrayant

half [hæf] **1** *n* moitié *f*; **~ past ten** dix heures et demie; **~ an hour** une demi-heure **2** *adj* demi; **at ~ price** à moitié prix **3** *adv* à moitié; **half-hearted** tiède; **half time** SP mi-temps *f*; **halfway 1** *adj*: **reach the ~ point** être à la moitié **2** *adv in space, distance* à mi-chemin

hall [hɔːl] *(large room)* salle *f*; *(hallway in house)* vestibule *m*

Hallowe'en [hæloʊ'wiːn] halloween *f*

halo ['heɪloʊ] auréole *f*

halt [hɔːlt] **1** *v/i* faire halte, s'arrêter **2** *v/t* arrêter

halve [hæv] couper en deux; *input, costs* réduire de moitié

ham [hæm] jambon *m*; **hamburger** hamburger *m*

hammer ['hæmər] **1** *n* marteau *m* **2** *v/i* marteler; **~ at the door** frapper à la porte à coups redoublés

hammock ['hæmək] hamac *m*

hamper¹ ['hæmpər] *n for food* pannier *m*

hamper² ['hæmpər] *v/t (ob-*

struct) entraver, gêner

hand [hænd] **1** n main f; of clock aiguille f; (worker) ouvrier(-ère) m(f); **at ~, to ~** thing sous la main; **at ~** person à disposition; **on the one ~ ..., on the other ~** d'une part ..., d'autre part; **on your right ~** sur votre droite; **give s.o. a ~** donner un coup de main à qn

◆ **hand down** transmettre

◆ **hand out** distribuer

◆ **hand over** donner; to authorities livrer

'**handbag** Br sac m à main; **hand baggage** bagages mpl à main; **handcuff** menotter; **handcuffs** menottes fpl

handicap ['hændɪkæp] handicap m; **handicapped** handicapé; **handiwork** object ouvrage m

handkerchief ['hæŋkərtʃɪf] mouchoir m

handle ['hændl] **1** n of door, suitcase poignée f; of knife, pan manche m **2** v/t goods manier, manipuler; case, deal s'occuper de; **handlebars** guidon m

'**hand luggage** bagages m à main; **handmade** fait (à la) main; **hands-free** mains libres; **handshake** poignée f de main

handsome ['hænsəm] beau

'**handwriting** écriture f; **handwritten** écrit à la main;

handy device pratique

hang ['hæŋ] **1** v/t person pendre **2** v/t of dress, hair tomber

◆ **hang on** (wait) attendre

◆ **hang up** TELEC raccrocher

hangar ['hæŋər] hangar m

hanger ['hæŋər] for clothes cintre m

'**hang glider** person libériste m/f; device deltaplane m; **hang gliding** deltaplane m; **hangover** gueule f de bois

hankie, hanky ['hæŋkɪ] F mouchoir m

haphazard [hæp'hæzərd] au hasard

happen ['hæpn] se passer, arriver

happily ['hæpɪlɪ] gaiement; spend volontiers; (luckily) heureusement; **happiness** bonheur m; **happy** heureux; **happy-go-lucky** insouciant

harass [hə'ræs] harceler; **harassed** surmené; **harassment** harcèlement m

harbor, Br **harbour** ['hɑːrbər] **1** n port m **2** v/t criminal héberger; grudge entretenir

hard [hɑːrd] **1** adj dur; facts brut; evidence concret **2** adv work dur; rain, pull, push fort; **try ~** faire tout son possible; **hardback** livre m cartonné; **hard-boiled** egg dur; **hard copy** copie f sur papier; **hard core** pornography (pornographie f) hard m; **hard currency** monnaie f forte; **hard disk** disque m

harden

378

dur; **harden 1** *v/t* durcir **2** *v/i
of glue, attitude* se durcir;
hard hat casque *m*; (*construction worker*) ouvrier *m*
du bâtiment; **hardheaded**
réaliste; **hardhearted** au
cœur dur; **hard line** ligne *f*
dure; **hardliner** dur(e) *m(f)*
hardly ['hɑːrdlɪ] à peine; *see
s.o. etc* presque pas
hardness ['hɑːrdnɪs] dureté *f*;
(*difficulty*) difficulté *f*; **hard-
ship** privation *f*; **hardware** COMPUT hardware *m*, matériel *m*; **hardware store** quincaillerie *f*; **hard-working** travailleur; **hardy** robuste
harm [hɑːrm] **1** *n* mal *m* **2** *v/t*
faire du mal à; *non-physical-
ly* nuire à; **harmful** *substance*
nocif; *influence* nuisible;
harmless inoffensif
harmonious [hɑːr'moʊnɪəs]
harmonieux; **harmonize**
s'harmoniser; **harmony** harmonie *f*
harsh [hɑːrʃ] *words* dur; *color*
criard; *light* cru; **harshly** durement
harvest ['hɑːrvɪst] moisson *f*
hash browns [hæʃ] pommes
de terre *fpl* sautées; **hash
mark** caractère *m* #, dièse *f*
haste [heɪst] hâte *f*; **hastily** à
la hâte; **hasty** hâtif, précipité
hat [hæt] chapeau *m*
hatch [hætʃ] *for serving* guichet *m*; *on ship* écoutille *f*
◆ **hatch out** éclore
hatchet ['hætʃɪt] hachette *f*;

bury the ~ enterrer la hache
de guerre
hate [heɪt] **1** *n* haine *f* **2** *v/t* détester, haïr; **hatred** haine *f*
haul [hɔːl] **1** *n of fish* coup *m*
de filet **2** *v/t* (*pull*) tirer, traîner; **haulage** transports *mpl*
(routiers)
haunch [hɔːntʃ] *of person*
hanche *f*; *of animal* arrière-
-train *m*
haunt [hɔːnt] hanter; *this
place is ~ed* cet endroit est hanté
have [hæv] **1** *v/t* (*own*) avoir;
breakfast, lunch prendre; **~
(got) to** devoir; *you don't ~
to do it* tu n'es pas obligé
de le faire; *do I ~ to pay?*
est-ce qu'il faut payer?; *I'll
~ it sent to you* je vous le ferai envoyer; *I had my hair
cut* je me suis fait couper
les cheveux 2 *v/aux* (*past
tense*): **~ you seen her?**
l'as-tu vue?; *they ~ arrived*
ils sont arrivés
◆ **have on** (*wear*) porter
haven ['heɪvn] *fig* havre *m*
hawk [hɔːk] *also fig* faucon *m*
hay [heɪ] foin *m*; **hay fever**
rhume *m* des foins
hazard ['hæzərd] danger *m*;
hazard lights *mpl* feux *mpl*
de détresse; **hazardous** dangereux
haze [heɪz] brume *f*; **hazy**
view brumeux; *image* flou;
memories vague
he [hiː] il; *there ~ is* le voilà
head [hed] **1** *n* tête *f*; (*boss,*

leader) chef *m/f*; *Br* : *of school* directeur(-trice) *m(f)*; *on beer* mousse *f* **2** *v/t* (*lead*) être à la tête de; *ball* jouer de la tête
◆ **head for** se diriger vers
'headache mal *m* de tête; **headband** bandeau *m*; **header** *in soccer* (coup *m* de) tête *f*; *in document* en-tête *m*; **headhunter** COM chasseur *m* de têtes; **heading** *in list* titre *m*; **headlamp** phare *m*; **headline** *in newspaper* (gros) titre *m*; **head office** *of company* bureau *m* central; **head-on 1** *adv crash* de front **2** *adj* frontal; **headphones** écouteurs *mpl*; **headquarters** quartier *m* général; **headrest** appui-tête *m*; **headroom** *under bridge* hauteur *f* limite; *in car* hauteur *f* au plafond; **headscarf** foulard *m*; **headstrong** entêté; **head waiter** maître *m* d'hôtel; **heady** *wine etc* capiteux

heal [hiːl] guérir
health [helθ] santé *f*; **health food store** magasin *m* d'aliments diététiques; **health insurance** assurance *f* maladie; **healthy** *person* en bonne santé; *food, lifestyle, economy* sain

heap [hiːp] tas *m*
hear [hɪr] entendre
◆ **hear from** (*have news from*) avoir des nouvelles de

hearing ['hɪrɪŋ] ouïe *f*; LAW audience *f*; **hearing aid** appareil *m* acoustique, audiophone *m*

hearse [hɜːrs] corbillard *m*
heart [hɑːrt] *also fig* cœur *m*; **know sth by ~** connaître qch par cœur; **heart attack** crise *f* cardiaque; **heartbreaking** navrant; **heartbroken**: *be* ~ avoir le cœur brisé; **heartburn** brûlures *fpl* d'estomac
hearth [hɑːrθ] foyer *m*, âtre *f*
heartless ['hɑːrtlɪs] insensible, cruel; **hearty** *appetite* gros; *meal* copieux; *person* jovial

heat [hiːt] chaleur *f*
◆ **heat up** réchauffer
heated ['hiːtɪd] *pool* chauffé; *discussion* passionné; **heater** radiateur *m*; *in car* chauffage *m*; **heating** chauffage *m*; **heatproof**, **heat-resistant** résistant à la chaleur; **heatwave** vague *f* de chaleur

heave [hiːv] (*lift*) soulever
heaven ['hevn] ciel *m*; **heavenly** F divin
heavy ['hevi] *also food, loss* lourd; *cold* grand; *rain, accent* fort; *traffic, smoker, bleeding* gros; **heavy-duty** très résistant; **heavyweight** SP poids lourd

hectic ['hektɪk] agité
hedge [hedʒ] haie *f*
heel [hiːl] talon *m*; **heel bar** talon-minute *m*

hefty ['hefti] gros; *person also*

costaud

height [haɪt] *of person* taille *f*; *of building* hauteur *f*; *of airplane* altitude *f*; **heighten** *tension* accroître

heir [er] héritier *m*; **heiress** héritière *f*

helicopter ['helɪkɑːptər] hélicoptère *m*

hell [hel] enfer *m*; **what the ~ are you doing?** F mais enfin qu'est-ce que tu fais?; **go to ~!** F va te faire foutre! P

hello [hə'loʊ] bonjour; TELEC allô

helmet ['helmɪt] casque *m*

help [help] **1** *n* aide *f* **2** *v/t* aider; **~ o.s.** *to food* se servir; **I can't ~ it** je ne peux pas m'en empêcher; **helper** aide *m/f*, assistant(e) *m(f)*; **helpful** *advice* utile; *person* serviable; **helping** *of food* portion *f*; **helpless** (*unable to cope*) sans défense; (*powerless*) impuissant; **helplessness** impuissance *f*

hem [hem] *of dress etc* ourlet *m*

hemisphere ['hemɪsfɪr] hémisphère *m*

'**hemline** ourlet *m*

hemorrhage ['hemərɪdʒ] **1** *n* hémorragie *f* **2** *v/i* faire une hémorragie

hen [hen] poule *f*; **hen party** soirée *f* entre femmes

hepatitis [hepə'taɪtɪs] hépatite *f*

her [hɜːr] **1** *adj* son, sa; *pl* ses **2**

pron object la; *before vowel* l'; *indirect object* lui, à elle; *with prep* elle; **I know ~** je la connais; **I gave ~ a dollar** je lui ai donné un dollar; **this is for ~** c'est pour elle; **who? – ~** qui? – elle

herb [ɜːrb] herbe *f*; **herb(al) tea** tisane *f*

herd [hɜːrd] troupeau *m*

here [hɪr] ici; **in ~, over ~** ici; **~'s to you!** *as toast* à votre santé!; **~ you are** *giving sth* voilà

hereditary [hə'redɪterɪ] héréditaire; **heredity** hérédité *f*; **heritage** héritage *m*

hero ['hɪroʊ] héros *m*; **heroic** héroïque; **heroically** héroïquement

heroin ['heroʊɪn] héroïne *f*

heroine ['heroʊɪn] héroïne *f*

heroism ['heroʊɪzm] héroïsme *f*

herpes ['hɜːrpiːz] herpès *m*

hers [hɜːrz] le sien, la sienne; *pl* les siens, les siennes; **it's ~** c'est à elle

herself [hɜːr'self] elle-même; *reflexive* se; *after prep* elle; **she hurt ~** elle s'est blessée

hesitant ['hezɪtənt] hésitant; **hesitantly** avec hésitation; **hesitate** hésiter; **hesitation** hésitation *f*

heterosexual [hetəroʊ'sekʃʊəl] hétérosexuel

hi [haɪ] salut

hibernate ['haɪbərneɪt] hiberner

hiccup ['hɪkʌp] hoquet *m*; (*minor problem*) hic *m* F

hidden ['hɪdn] caché

hide[1] [haɪd] **1** *v/t* cacher **2** *v/i* se cacher

hide[2] [haɪd] *n of animal* peau *f*; *as product* cuir *m*

hide-and-'seek cache-cache *m*; **hideaway** cachette *f*

hideous ['hɪdɪəs] affreux, horrible

hiding ['haɪdɪŋ] (*beating*) rossée *f*; **hiding place** cachette *f*

hierarchy ['haɪrɑːrkɪ] hiérarchie *f*

high [haɪ] **1** *adj* haut; *salary, price, rent, temperature* élevé; *wind* fort; *speed* grand; *on drugs* défoncé F **2** *n* MOT quatrième *f*; cinquième *f*; *in statistics* pointe *f*; **on a** ~ en forme; **highbrow** intellectuel; **highchair** chaise *f* haute; **high-class** de première classe; **high-frequency** de haute fréquence; **high-grade** *ore* à haute teneur; ~ **gasoline** supercarburant *m*; **high-handed** arbitraire; **high-heeled** à talons hauts; **high jump** saut *m* en hauteur; **high-level** à haut niveau; **highlight 1** *n* (*main event*) point *m* marquant; *in hair* reflets *mpl*, mèches *fpl* **2** *v/t with pen* surligner; COMPUT mettre en relief; **highlighter** *pen* surligneur *m*; **highly** *desirable, likely* fort, très; **think** ~ **of s.o.** pen-

ser beaucoup de bien de qn; **high performance** *drill, battery* haute performance; **high-pitched** aigu; **high point** *of career* point *m* culminant; **high-powered** *engine* très puissant; *intellectual* très compétent; **high pressure** *weather* anticyclone *m*; **high-pressure** TECH à haute pression; *salesman* de choc; *job, lifestyle* dynamique; **high school** collège *m*, lycée *m*; **high-strung** nerveux, très sensible; **high tech 1** *n* technologie *f* de pointe, high-tech **m 2** *adj* de pointe, high-tech; **highway** grande route *f*

hijack ['haɪdʒæk] **1** *v/t* détourner **2** *n* détournement *m*; **hijacker** *of plane* pirate *m* de l'air; *of bus* pirate *m* de la route

hike[1] [haɪk] **1** *n* randonnée *f* à pied **2** *v/i* marcher à pied

hike[2] [haɪk] *n in prices* hausse *f*

hiker ['haɪkər] randonneur (-euse) *m(f)*; **hiking** randonnée *f* (pédestre)

hilarious [hɪ'lerɪəs] hilarant, désopilant

hill [hɪl] **1** *n* colline *f*; (*slope*) côte *f*; **hilltop** sommet *m* de la colline; **hilly** montagneux; *road* vallonné

hilt [hɪlt] poignée *f*

him [hɪm] *object* le; *before vowel* l'; *indirect object*, with *prep* lui; **I know ~** je le connais; **I gave ~ a dollar** je lui ai donné un dollar; **this is for~** c'est pour lui; **who? – him** qui? – lui; **himself** lui-même; *reflexive* se; *after prep* lui; **he hurt ~** il s'est blessé

hinder ['hɪndər] gêner, entraver; **~ s.o. from doing sth** empêcher qn de faire qch; **hindrance** obstacle *m*

hinge [hɪndʒ] charnière *f*

hint [hɪnt] (*clue*) indice *m*; (*piece of advice*) conseil *m*; (*suggestion*) allusion *f*; *of red, sadness etc* soupçon *m*

hip [hɪp] hanche *f*; **hip pocket** poche *f* revolver

hire ['haɪr] louer

his [hɪz] **1** *adj* son, sa; *pl* ses **2** *pron* le sien, la sienne; *pl* les siens, les siennes; **it's~** c'est à lui

Hispanic [hɪ'spænɪk] **1** *n* Hispano-Américain(e) *m(f)* **2** *adj* hispano-américain

hiss [hɪs] siffler

historian [hɪ'stɔːrɪən] historien(ne) *m(f)*; **historic** historique; **historical** historique; **history** histoire *f*

hit [hɪt] **1** *v/t* frapper; (*collide with*) heurter; **he was ~ by a bullet** il a été touché par une balle **2** *n* (*blow*) coup *m*; MUS, (*success*) succès *m*; *on website* visiteur *m*

hitch [hɪtʃ] **1** *n* (*problem*) anicroche *f*, accroc *m* **2** *v/t* atta-

cher; **hitchhike** faire du stop; **hitchhiker** auto-stoppeur (-euse) *m(f)*

hi-'tech 1 *n* technologie *f* de pointe, high-tech *m* **2** *adj* de pointe, high-tech

'hitman tueur *m* à gages; **hit-or-miss** aléatoire

HIV [eɪtʃaɪ'viː] (= *human immunodeficiency virus*) V.I.H. *m* (= Virus de l'Immunodéficience Humaine); **people with ~** les séropositifs

hive [haɪv] *for bees* ruche *f*

HIV-'positive séropositif

hoard [hɔːrd] **1** *n* réserves *fpl* **2** *v/t money* amasser; *in times of shortage* faire des réserves de

hoarse [hɔːrs] rauque

hoax [hoʊks] canular *m*

hobble ['haːbl] boitiller

hobby ['haːbɪ] hobby *m*

hobo ['hoʊboʊ] F vagabond *m*

hockey ['haːkɪ] (*ice hockey*) hockey *m* (sur glace)

hog [haːg] (*pig*) cochon *m*

hoist [hɔɪst] **1** *n* palan *m* **2** *v/t* hisser

hold [hoʊld] **1** *v/t in hand* tenir; (*support, keep in place*) soutenir; (*passport, license, prisoner*) détenir; (*contain*) contenir; *job, post* occuper; **~ the line** TELEC ne quittez pas! **2** *n in ship* cale *f*; *in plane* soute *f*; **take ~ of sth** saisir qch

◆ **hold back** *crowds* contenir; *facts* retenir

◆ **hold out 1** *v/t hand* tendre; *prospect* offrir **2** *v/i of supplies* durer; *(survive)* tenir *(bon)*

◆ **hold up** *hand* lever; *bank etc* attaquer; *(make late)* retenir

holder ['houldər] *(container)* boîtier *m*; *of passport, ticket, record* détenteur(-trice) *m(f)*; **holding company** holding *m*; **holdup** *(robbery)* hold-up *m*; *(delay)* retard *m*

hole [houl] trou *m*

holiday ['hɑːlədeɪ] jour *m* de congé; *Br: period* vacances *fpl*

hollow ['hɑːloʊ] creux; *promise* faux

holocaust ['hɑːləkɔːst] holocauste *m*

hologram ['hɑːləgræm] hologramme *m*

holster ['houlstər] holster *m*

holy ['houlɪ] saint; **Holy Spirit** Saint-Esprit *m*

home [houm] **1** *n* maison *f*; *(native country, town)* patrie *f*; *for old people* maison *f* de retraite; *at ~* chez moi/lui *etc*; *(in own country)* dans mon/ son *etc* pays; SP à domicile; **make o.s. at ~** faire comme chez soi **2** *adv* à la maison, chez soi; *(in own country)* dans son pays; *(in own town)* dans sa ville; **go ~** rentrer; **home address** adresse *f* personnelle; **home banking** services *mpl* télématiques (ban-

caires); **homecoming** retour *m* (à la maison); **home computer** ordinateur *m* familial; **home game** match *m* à domicile; **homeless 1** *adj* sans abri **2** *npl*: **the ~** les sans-abri *mpl*, les S.D.F. *mpl* (sans domicile fixe); **homeloving** casanier; **homely** *(homelike)* simple, comme à la maison; *(not good-looking)* sans beauté; **homemade** fait (à la) maison; **home page** COMPUT page *f* d'accueil; **homesick**: **be ~** avoir le mal du pays; **home town** ville *f* natale; **homeward** *to own house* vers la maison; *to own country* vers son pays; **homework** EDU devoirs *mpl*

homicide ['hɑːmɪsaɪd] homicide *m*; *department* homicides *mpl*

homophobia [houmə'foubɪə] homophobie *f*

homosexual [houmə'sekʃuəl] **1** *adj* homosexuel **2** *n* homosexuel(le) *m(f)*

honest ['ɑːnɪst] honnête; **honestly** honnêtement; *~!* vraiment!; **honesty** honnêteté *f*

honey ['hʌnɪ] miel *m*; F *(darling)* chéri(e) *m(f)*; **honeymoon** lune *f* de miel

honk [hɑːŋk] *horn* klaxonner

honor ['ɑːnər] **1** *n* honneur *f* **2** *v/t* honorer; **honorable** honorable; **honour** *Br* → **honor**

hood [hʊd] *over head* capuche *f*; *over cooker* hotte *f*; MOT capot *m*; F (*gangster*) truand *m*

hook [hʊk] *to hang clothes on* patère *f*; *for fishing* hameçon *m*; **off the ~** TELEC décroché; hooked accro F; **be ~ on sth** être accro de qch; **hooker** F putain *f* P; *in rugby* talonneur *m*

hoot [huːt] **1** *v/t horn* donner un coup de **2** *v/i of car* klaxonner; *of owl* huer

hop [hɒp] sauter, sautiller

hope [həʊp] **1** *n* espoir *m* **2** *v/i* espérer; **I ~ so** je l'espère, j'espère que oui **3** *v/t*: **~ that** espérer que; **hopeful** plein d'espoir; (*promising*) prometteur; **hopefully** *say, wait* avec espoir; (*I/we hope*) avec un peu de chance; **hopeless** *position* sans espoir, désespéré; (*useless: person*) nul

horizon [həˈraɪzn] horizon *m*; **horizontal** horizontal

hormone [ˈhɔːrməʊn] hormone *f*

horn [hɔːrn] *of animal* corne *f*; MOT klaxon *m*

hornet [ˈhɔːrnɪt] frelon *m*

horny [ˈhɔːrnɪ] F *sexually* excité

horrible [ˈhɒːrɪbl] horrible, affreux; **horrify** horrifier; **horrifying** horrifiant; **horror** horreur *f*

horse [hɔːrs] cheval *m*; **horse race** course *f* de chevaux;

horseshoe fer *m* à cheval

horticulture horticulture *f*

hose [həʊz] tuyau *m*

hospitable [ˈhɒːspɪtəbl] hospitalier

hospital [ˈhɒːspɪtl] hôpital *m*; **hospitality** hospitalité *f*

host [həʊst] *at party* hôte *m/f*; *of TV program* présentateur(-trice) *m(f)*

hostage [ˈhɒːstɪdʒ] otage *m*; **hostage taker** preneur(-euse) *m(f)* d'otages

hostel [ˈhɒːstl] *for students* foyer *m*; (*youth ~*) auberge *f* de jeunesse

hostess [ˈhəʊstɪs] hôtesse *f*

hostile [ˈhɒːstl] hostile; **hostility** hostilité *f*; **hostilities** hostilités

hot [hɒt] chaud; (*spicy*) épicé, fort; **I'm ~** j'ai chaud; **it's ~** *weather* il fait chaud; **hot dog** hot-dog *m*

hotel [həʊˈtel] hôtel *m*

hour [aʊr] heure *f*

house [haʊs] maison *f*; **at your ~** chez vous; **housebreaking** cambriolage *m*; **household** ménage *m*; **household name** nom *m* connu de tous; **housekeeper** femme *f* de ménage; **House of Representatives** Chambre *f* des Représentants; **housewarming** (*party*) pendaison *f* de crémaillère; **housewife** femme *f* au foyer; **housework** travaux *mpl* domestiques; **housing**

logement *m*; TECH boîtier *m*

hovel ['hɒvl] taudis *m*

hover ['hɒvər] planer

how [haʊ] comment; **~ are you?** comment allez-vous?; **~ about a drink?** et si on allait prendre un pot?; **~ much?** combien?; **~ much is it?** *cost* combien ça coûte?; **~ many?** combien?; **~ often?** tous les combien?; **~ sad!** comme c'est triste!; however cependant; **~ big they are** qu'ils soient grands ou non

howl [haʊl] hurler

hub [hʌb] *of wheel* moyeu *m*; **hubcap** enjoliveur *m*

♦ **huddle together** ['hʌdl] se blottir les uns contre les autres

hug [hʌg] serrer dans ses bras

huge [hju:dʒ] énorme

hull [hʌl] coque *f*

hum [hʌm] fredonner

human ['hju:mən] **1** *n* être *m* humain **2** *adj* humain; **human being** être *m* humain

humane [hju:'meɪn] humain, plein d'humanité

humanitarian [hju:mænɪ'terɪən] humanitaire

humanity [hju:'mænətɪ] humanité *f*; **human race** race *f* humaine; **human resources** ressources *fpl* humaines

humble ['hʌmbl] modeste

humdrum ['hʌmdrʌm] monotone, banal

humid ['hju:mɪd] humide; **humidifier** humidificateur *m*; **humidity** humidité *f*

humiliate [hju:'mɪlɪeɪt] humilier; **humiliating** humiliant; **humiliation** humiliation *f*; **humility** humilité *f*

humor ['hju:mər] humour *m*; (*mood*) humeur *f*; **sense of ~** sens *m* de l'humour; **humorous** drôle; **humour** *Br* → **humor**

hunch [hʌntʃ] (*idea*) intuition *f*, pressentiment *m*

hundred ['hʌndrəd] cent *m*; **hundredth** centième

hunger ['hʌŋgər] faim *f*

hung-over: **be ~** avoir la gueule de bois F

hungry ['hʌŋgrɪ] affamé; **I'm ~** j'ai faim

hunk [hʌŋk] gros morceau *m*; F *man* beau mec F

hunt [hʌnt] **1** *n* chasse *f* (**for** à); *for new leader, missing child etc* recherche *f* (**for** de) **2** *v/t* chasser; **hunter** chasseur (-euse) *m(f)*; **hunting** chasse *f*

hurdle ['hɜ:rdl] SP haie *f*; *fig* obstacle *m*

hurl [hɜ:rl] lancer, jeter

hurray [hʊ'reɪ] hourra

hurricane ['hʌrɪkən] ouragan *m*

hurried ['hʌrɪd] précipité; **hurry 1** *n* hâte *f*; **be in a ~** être pressé **2** *v/i* se dépêcher

♦ **hurry up 1** *v/i* se dépêcher; **hurry up!** dépêchez-vous! **2** *v/t* presser

hurt [hɜːrt] **1** *v/i* faire mal **2** *v/t* faire mal à; *emotionally* blesser

husband ['hʌzbənd] mari *m*
hush [hʌʃ] silence *m*
◆ **hush up** *scandal etc* étouffer
husky ['hʌskɪ] *voice* rauque
hut [hʌt] cabane *f*, hutte *f*
hybrid ['haɪbrɪd] hybride *m*
hydrant ['haɪdrənt] prise *f* d'eau; *(fire ~)* bouche *f* d'incendie
hydraulic [haɪ'drɔːlɪk] hydraulique
hydroelectric [haɪdrouɪ'lektrɪk] hydroélectrique
hydrogen ['haɪdrədʒən] hydrogène *m*
hygiene ['haɪdʒiːn] hygiène *f*; **hygienic** hygiénique

hymn [hɪm] hymne *m*
hype [haɪp] battage *m* publicitaire
hyperactive [haɪpər'æktɪv] hyperactif; **hypersensitive** hypersensible; **hypertext** COMPUT hypertexte *m*
hypnosis [hɪp'nousɪs] hypnose *f*; **hypnotize** hypnotiser
hypocrisy [hɪ'pɑːkrəsɪ] hypocrisie *f*; **hypocrite** hypocrite *m/f*; **hypocritical** hypocrite
hypothesis [haɪ'pɑːθəsɪs] hypothèse *f*; **hypothetical** hypothétique
hysterectomy [hɪstə'rektəmɪ] hystérectomie *f*
hysteria [hɪ'stɪrɪə] hystérie *f*; **hysterical** hystérique; F *(very funny)* à mourir de rire F; **hysterics** crise *f* de nerfs; *laughter* fou rire *m*

I

I [aɪ] je; *before vowel* j'; **here ~ am** me voici
ice [aɪs] glace *f*; *on road* verglas *m*; **icebox** glacière *f*; **ice cream** glace *f*; **ice cube** glaçon *m*; **iced** *drink* glacé; **ice hockey** hockey *m* sur glace; **ice rink** patinoire *f*; **ice skate** patin *m* (à glace); **ice skating** patinage *m* (sur glace)
icon ['aɪkɑːn] symbole *m*; COMPUT icône *f*
icy ['aɪsɪ] gelé; *welcome* gla-

cial
ID [aɪ'diː] (= *identity*) identité *f*
idea [aɪ'diːə] idée *f*; **ideal** idéal; **idealistic** idéaliste
identical [aɪ'dentɪkl] identique; **identification** identification *f*; *(papers etc)* papiers *mpl* d'identité; **identify** identifier; **identity** identité *f*; **~ card** carte *f* d'identité
ideological [aɪdɪə'lɑːdʒɪkl] idéologique; **ideology** idéologie *f*

idiomatic [ɪdɪəˈmætɪk] (*natural*) idiomatique

idiot [ˈɪdɪət] idiot(e) *m(f)*; **idiotic** idiot, bête

idle [ˈaɪdl] **1** *adj* (*not working*) inoccupé; (*lazy*) paresseux; *threat* oiseux; *machinery* non utilisé **2** *v/i of engine* tourner au ralenti

idol [ˈaɪdl] idole *f*; **idolize** idolâtrer

if [ɪf] si

ignite [ɪgˈnaɪt] mettre le feu à; **ignition** *in car* allumage *m*; ~ **key** clef *f* de contact

ignorance [ˈɪgnərəns] ignorance *f*; **ignorant** ignorant; (*rude*) grossier; **ignore** ignorer

ill [ɪl] malade; *fall* ~, *be taken* ~ tomber malade

illegal [ɪˈliːgl] illégal

illegible [ɪˈledʒəbl] illisible

illegitimate [ɪlɪˈdʒɪtɪmət] *child* illégitime

illicit [ɪˈlɪsɪt] illicite

illiterate [ɪˈlɪtərət] illettré

illness [ˈɪlnɪs] maladie *f*

illogical [ɪˈlɑːdʒɪkl] illogique

ill'treat maltraiter

illuminating [ɪˈluːmɪneɪtɪŋ] *remarks etc* éclairant

illusion [ɪˈluːʒn] illusion *f*

illustrate [ˈɪləstreɪt] illustrer; **illustration** illustration *f*; **illustrator** illustrateur(-trice) *m(f)*

image [ˈɪmɪdʒ] image *f*

imaginary [ɪˈmædʒɪnərɪ] imaginaire; **imagination** imagi-

nation *f*; **imaginative** imaginatif; **imagine** imaginer; **you're imagining things** tu te fais des idées

IMF [aɪemˈef] (= *International Monetary Fund*) F.M.I. *m* (= Fonds *m* Monétaire International)

imitate [ˈɪmɪteɪt] imiter; **imitation** imitation *f*

immaculate [ɪˈmækjʊlət] impeccable

immature [ɪməˈtjʊr] immature

immediate [ɪˈmiːdɪət] immédiat; **immediately** immédiatement

immense [ɪˈmens] immense

immerse [ɪˈmɜːrs] immerger, plonger

immigrant [ˈɪmɪgrənt] immigrant(e) *m(f)*; **immigrate** immigrer; **immigration** immigration *f*

imminent [ˈɪmɪnənt] imminent

immobilize [ɪˈmoʊbɪlaɪz] immobiliser

immoderate [ɪˈmɑːdərət] immodéré

immoral [ɪˈmɔːrəl] immoral; **immorality** immoralité *f*

immortal [ɪˈmɔːrtl] immortel; **immortality** immortalité *f*

immune [ɪˈmjuːn] *to illness* immunisé (*to* contre); *from ruling* exempt (*from* de); **immune system** MED système *m* immunitaire; **immunity** immunité *f*; *from ruling* exemption *f* impact ['ɪmpækt] impact *m*

impair [ɪm'per] affaiblir

impartial [ɪm'pɑːrʃl] impartial

impassable [ɪm'pæsəbl] *road* impraticable

impassioned [ɪm'pæʃnd] *speech, plea* passionné

impatience [ɪm'peɪʃəns] impatience *f*; impatient impatient

impatiently impatiemment

impeccable [ɪm'pekəbl] impeccable

impede [ɪm'piːd] gêner, empêcher; impediment *obstacle* obstacle *m*; speech ~ défaut *m* d'élocution

impending [ɪm'pendɪŋ] imminent

imperative [ɪm'perətɪv] **1** *adj* impératif **2** *n* GRAM impératif *m*

imperfect [ɪm'pɜːrfekt] **1** *adj* imparfait **2** *n* GRAM imparfait *m*

impersonal [ɪm'pɜːrsənl] impersonnel; impersonate *as a joke* imiter; *illegally* se faire passer pour

impertinence [ɪm'pɜːrtɪnəns] impertinence *f*; impertinent impertinent

impervious [ɪm'pɜːrvɪəs]: ~ to insensible à

impetuous [ɪm'petʃʊəs] impétueux

impetus ['ɪmpɪtəs] *of campaign etc* force *f*, élan *m*

implement ['ɪmplɪmənt] **1** *n*

instrument *m*, outil *m* **2** *v/t* ['ɪmplɪment] appliquer

implicate ['ɪmplɪkeɪt] impliquer; implication implication *f*

implore [ɪm'plɔːr] implorer

imply [ɪm'plaɪ] impliquer; *(suggest)* suggérer

impolite [ɪmpə'laɪt] impoli

import ['ɪmpɔːrt] **1** *n* importation *f* **2** *v/t* importer

importance [ɪm'pɔːrtəns] importance *f*; important important

importer [ɪm'pɔːrtər] importateur(-trice) *m(f)*

impose [ɪm'pouz] *tax* imposer; imposing imposant

impossibility [ɪmpɑːsɪ'bɪlɪtɪ] impossibilité *f*; impossible impossible

impotence ['ɪmpətəns] impuissance *f*; impotent impuissant

impractical [ɪm'præktɪkəl] dénué de sens pratique

impress [ɪm'pres] impressionner; impression impression *f*; *(impersonation)* imitation *f*; impressive impressionnant

imprint ['ɪmprɪnt] *of credit card* empreinte *f*

imprison [ɪm'prɪzn] emprisonner; imprisonment emprisonnement *m*

improbable [ɪm'prɑːbəbəl] improbable

improve [ɪm'pruːv] **1** *v/t* améliorer **2** *v/i* s'améliorer; improvement amélioration f

improvize ['ɪmprəvaɪz] improviser

impudent ['ɪmpjʊdənt] impudent

impulse ['ɪmpʌls] impulsion f; **impulsive** impulsif

in [ɪn] **1** prep dans; with time en; ~ **Rouen** à Rouen; ~ **1999** en 1999; ~ **the morning** le matin; ~ **the summer** l'été; ~ **August** en août, au mois d'août; ~ **two hours** from now dans deux heures; over period of en deux heures; ~ **English** en anglais; ~ **yellow** en jaune; ~ **crossing the road** en traversant la route **2** adv (at home, in the building etc) là; (arrived: train) arrivé; (in its position) dedans; ~ **here** ici **3** adj (fashionable, popular) à la mode

inability [ɪnə'bɪlɪtɪ] incapacité f

inaccurate [ɪn'ækjʊrət] inexact

inadequate [ɪn'ædɪkwət] insuffisant, inadéquat

inadvisable [ɪnəd'vaɪzəbl] peu recommandé

inanimate [ɪn'ænɪmət] inanimé

inappropriate [ɪnə'prəʊprɪət] peu approprié

inaudible [ɪn'ɔːdəbl] inaudible

inaugural [ɪ'nɔːgjʊrəl] speech inaugural; **inaugurate** inaugurer

inborn ['ɪnbɔːrn] inné

inc. (= **incorporated**) S.A. f (= Société f Anonyme)

incalculable [ɪn'kælkjʊləbl] damage incalculable

incapable [ɪn'keɪpəbl] incapable

incentive [ɪn'sentɪv] encouragement m, stimulation f

incessant [ɪn'sesnt] incessant; **incessantly** sans arrêt

incest ['ɪnsest] inceste m

inch [ɪntʃ] pouce m

incident ['ɪnsɪdənt] incident m; **incidental** fortuit; ~ **expenses** frais mpl accessoires; **incidentally** soit dit en passant

incision [ɪn'sɪʒn] incision f; **incisive** incisif

incite [ɪn'saɪt] inciter

inclination [ɪnklɪ'neɪʃn] (liking) penchant m; (tendency) tendance f

inclose, inclosure → **enclose, enclosure**

include [ɪn'kluːd] inclure, comprendre; **including** y compris; ~ **service** service compris; **inclusive 1** adj price tout compris **2** prep: ~ **of** en incluant **3** adv tout compris; from **Monday to Thursday** ~ du lundi au jeudi inclus

incoherent [ɪnkoʊ'hɪrənt] incohérent

income ['ɪnkəm] revenu m; **income tax** impôt m sur le revenu

incomparable [ɪn'kɑːmpə-rəbl] incomparable
incompatibility [ɪnkəmpætɪ-'bɪlɪtɪ] incompatibilité f; incompatible incompatible
incompetence [ɪn'kɑːmpɪ-təns] incompétence f; incompetent incompétent
incomplete [ɪnkəm'pliːt] incomplet
incomprehensible [ɪnkɑːmprɪ'hensɪbl] incompréhensible
inconceivable [ɪnkən'siːvəbl] inconcevable
inconsiderate [ɪnkən'sɪdərət] action inconsidéré; **be ~ of** person manquer d'égards
inconsistent [ɪnkən'sɪstənt] incohérent; person inconstant
inconspicuous [ɪnkən'spɪkjuəs] discret
inconvenience [ɪnkən'viːnɪəns] inconvénient m; inconvenient time inopportun; place, arrangement peu commode
incorporate [ɪn'kɔːrpəreɪt] incorporer
incorrect [ɪnkə'rekt] incorrect
increase 1 [ɪn'kriːs] v/t & v/i augmenter **2** ['ɪnkriːs] n augmentation f; increasing croissant; increasingly de plus en plus
incredible [ɪn'kredɪbl] incroyable

incur [ɪn'kɜːr] costs encourir; debts contracter; s.o.'s anger s'attirer
incurable [ɪn'kjʊrəbl] also fig incurable
indecent [ɪn'diːsnt] indécent
indecisive [ɪndɪ'saɪsɪv] argument peu concluant; person indécis; indecisiveness indécision f
indeed [ɪn'diːd] (in fact) vraiment; (yes, agreeing) en effet; **very much ~** beaucoup
indefinable [ɪndɪ'faɪnəbl] indéfinissable
indefinite [ɪn'defɪnɪt] indéfini; indefinitely indéfiniment
indelicate [ɪn'delɪkət] indélicat
independence [ɪndɪ'pendəns] indépendance f; Independence Day fête f de l'Indépendance; independent indépendant
indescribable [ɪndɪ'skraɪbəbl] indescriptible; (very bad) inqualifiable
index ['ɪndeks] for book index m
India ['ɪndɪə] Inde f; Indian **1** adj indien **2** n also American Indien(ne) m(f)
indicate ['ɪndɪkeɪt] **1** v/t indiquer **2** v/i when driving mettre ses clignotants; indication indication f, signe m
indict [ɪn'daɪt] accuser
indifference [ɪn'dɪfrəns] indifférence f; indifferent indifférent; (mediocre) médio-

cre
indigestion [ɪndɪ'dʒestʃn] indigestion *f*
indignant [ɪn'dɪgnənt] indigné; **indignation** indignation *f*
indirect [ɪndɪ'rekt] indirect; **indirectly** indirectement
indiscreet [ɪndɪ'skriːt] indiscret
indiscriminate [ɪndɪ'skrɪmɪnət] aveugle; *accusations* à tort et à travers
indispensable [ɪndɪ'spensəbl] indispensable
indisposed [ɪndɪ'spəʊzd] (*not well*) indisposé
indisputable [ɪndɪ'spjuːtəbl] incontestable
indistinct [ɪndɪ'stɪŋkt] indistinct
indistinguishable [ɪndɪ'stɪŋgwɪʃəbl] indifférenciable
individual [ɪndɪ'vɪdʒʊəl] **1** *n* individu *m* **2** *adj* (*separate*) particulier; (*personal*) individuel; **individually** individuellement
indoctrinate [ɪn'dɑːktrɪneɪt] endoctriner
Indonesia [ɪndə'niːʒə] Indonésie *f*; **Indonesian 1** *adj* indonésien **2** *n person* Indonésien(ne) *m(f)*
indoor ['ɪndɔːr] *activities, games* d'intérieur; *sport* en salle; *arena* couvert; **indoors** à l'intérieur; (*at home*) à la maison
indorse → **endorse**

indulgent [ɪn'dʌldʒənt] (*not strict enough*) indulgent
industrial [ɪn'dʌstrɪəl] industriel; **industrial dispute** conflit *m* social; **industrialist** industriel(le) *m(f)*; **industrious** travailleur; **industry** industrie *f*
ineffective [ɪnɪ'fektɪv] inefficace
inefficient [ɪnɪ'fɪʃənt] inefficace
inept [ɪ'nept] inepte
inequality [ɪnɪ'kwɑːlɪti] inégalité *f*
inescapable [ɪnɪ'skeɪpəbl] inévitable
inevitable [ɪn'evɪtəbl] inévitable; **inevitably** inévitablement
inexcusable [ɪnɪk'skjuːzəbl] inexcusable
inexhaustible [ɪnɪg'zɔːstəbl] inépuisable
inexpensive [ɪnɪk'spensɪv] bon marché, pas cher
inexperienced [ɪnɪk'spɪrɪənst] inexpérimenté
inexplicable [ɪnɪk'splɪkəbl] inexplicable
infallible [ɪn'fælɪbl] infaillible
infamous ['ɪnfəməs] infâme
infancy ['ɪnfənsɪ] *of person* petite enfance *f*; *of state, institution* débuts *mpl*; **infant** petit(e) enfant *m(f)*; **infantile** *pej* infantile
infantry ['ɪnfəntrɪ] infanterie *f*
infect [ɪn'fekt] contaminer;

become ~ed of wound s'infecter; **infection** contamination f; (disease), of wound infection f; **infectious** disease infectieux; laughter contagieux

infer [ɪnˈfɜːr]: ~ X from Y déduire X de Y

inferior [ɪnˈfɪriər] inférieur; **inferiority** infériorité f; **inferiority complex** complexe m d'infériorité

infertile [ɪnˈfɜːrtl] stérile; **infertility** stérilité f

infidelity [ɪnfɪˈdelɪtɪ] infidélité f

infinite [ˈɪnfɪnət] infini; **infinitive** infinitif m

infinity [ɪnˈfɪnətɪ] infinité f; MATH infini m

inflammable [ɪnˈflæməbl] inflammable; **inflammation** MED inflammation f

inflatable [ɪnˈfleɪtəbl] dinghy gonflable; **inflate** tire, dinghy gonfler; **inflation** inflation f; **inflationary** inflationniste

inflexible [ɪnˈfleksɪbl] attitude, person inflexible

inflict [ɪnˈflɪkt] infliger (on à)

influence [ˈɪnfluəns] **1** n influence f **2** v/t influencer; **influential** influent

inform [ɪnˈfɔːrm] **1** v/t informer **2** v/i: ~ on dénoncer

informal [ɪnˈfɔːrml] meeting, agreement non-officiel; form of address familier; conversation, dress simple; **informality** of meeting, agreement

caractère m non officiel; of form of address familiarité f; of conversation, dress simplicité f

informant [ɪnˈfɔːrmənt] informateur(-trice) m(f); **information** renseignements mpl; **information technology** informatique f; **informative** instructif; **informer** dénonciateur(-trice) m(f)

infra-red [ɪnfrəˈred] infrarouge

infrastructure [ˈɪnfrəstrʌktʃər] infrastructure f

infrequent [ɪnˈfriːkwənt] rare

infuriate [ɪnˈfjʊrɪeɪt] rendre furieux; **infuriating** exaspérant

ingenious [ɪnˈdʒiːnɪəs] ingénieux

ingot [ˈɪŋɡət] lingot m

ingratitude [ɪnˈɡrætɪtuːd] ingratitude f

ingredient [ɪnˈɡriːdɪənt] for cooking ingrédient m; for success recette f

inhabit [ɪnˈhæbɪt] habiter; **inhabitant** habitant(e) m(f)

inhale [ɪnˈheɪl] **1** v/t inhaler **2** v/i when smoking avaler la fumée

inherit [ɪnˈherɪt] hériter; **inheritance** héritage m

inhibited [ɪnˈhɪbɪtɪd] inhibé; **inhibition** inhibition f

inhospitable [ɪnhɑːˈspɪtəbl] inhospitalier

inhuman [ɪnˈhjuːmən] inhumain

initial [ɪ'nɪʃl] **1** adj initial **2** n initiale f **3** v/t (write initials on) parapher; **initially** au début; **initiate** procedure lancer; person initier; **initiation** lancement m; of person initiation f; **initiative** initiative f

inject [ɪn'dʒekt] injecter; **injection** injection f

injure ['ɪndʒər] blesser; **injury** blessure f

injustice [ɪn'dʒʌstɪs] injustice f

ink [ɪŋk] encre f

inland ['ɪnlənd] intérieur

in-laws ['ɪnlɔːz] belle-famille f

inmate ['ɪnmeɪt] of prison détenu(e) m(f); of mental hospital interné(e) m(f)

inn [ɪn] auberge f

innate [ɪ'neɪt] inné

inner ['ɪnər] courtyard intérieur; thoughts intime; ear interne

innocence ['ɪnəsəns] innocence f; **innocent** innocent

innocuous [ɪ'nɑːkjʊəs] inoffensif

innovation [ɪnə'veɪʃn] innovation f; **innovative** innovant; **innovator** innovateur(-trice) m(f)

inoculate [ɪ'nɑːkjʊleɪt] inoculer; **inoculation** inoculation f

inoffensive [ɪnə'fensɪv] inoffensif

'in-patient patient(e) hospitalisé(e) m(f)

input ['ɪnpʊt] **1** n into project etc apport m, contribution f; COMPUT entrée f **2** v/t into project apporter; COMPUT entrer

inquest ['ɪnkwest] enquête f (into sur)

inquire [ɪn'kwaɪr] se renseigner; **inquiry** demande f de renseignements; **government** ~ enquête f officielle

inquisitive [ɪn'kwɪzətɪv] curieux

insane [ɪn'seɪn] fou

insanitary [ɪn'sænɪterɪ] insalubre

insanity [ɪn'sænɪtɪ] folie f

inscription [ɪn'skrɪpʃn] inscription f

insect ['ɪnsekt] insecte m; **insecticide** insecticide m

insecure [ɪnsɪ'kjʊr]: be ~ not safe ne pas se sentir en sécurité; not sure of self manquer d'assurance; **insecurity** psychological manque m d'assurance

insensitive [ɪn'sensɪtɪv] insensible (to à)

insert 1 ['ɪnsɜːrt] n in magazine etc encart m **2** [ɪn'sɜːrt] v/t insérer

inside [ɪn'saɪd] **1** n intérieur m; ~ out à l'envers **2** prep à l'intérieur de; ~ of 2 hours en moins de 2 heures **3** adv à l'intérieur **4** adj: ~ information informations fpl internes; ~ lane SP couloir m intérieur

inside pocket poche *f* intérieure; **insider** initié(e) *m(f)*; **insider trading** FIN délit *m* d'initié; **insides** (*stomach*) ventre *m*

insignificant [ɪnsɪgˈnɪfɪkənt] insignifiant

insincere [ɪnsɪnˈsɪr] peu sincère; **insincerity** manque *f* de sincérité

insinuate [ɪnˈsɪnjʊeɪt] insinuer

insist [ɪnˈsɪst] insister (**on** sur); **insistent** insistant

insolent [ˈɪnsələnt] insolent

insolvent [ɪnˈsɑːlvənt] insolvable

insomnia [ɪnˈsɑːmnɪə] insomnie *f*

inspect [ɪnˈspekt] *work, tickets, baggage* contrôler; *factory, school* inspecter; **inspection** of *work, tickets, baggage* contrôle *m*; of *factory, school* inspection *f*; **inspector** *in factory* inspecteur(-trice) *m(f)*

inspiration [ɪnspəˈreɪʃn] inspiration *f*; **inspire** inspirer

instability [ɪnstəˈbɪlɪtɪ] instabilité *f*

install [ɪnˈstɔːl] installer; **installation** installation *f*; **installment**, *Br* **instalment** of *story etc* épisode *m*; (*payment*) versement *m*; **installment plan** vente *f* à crédit

instance [ˈɪnstəns] (*example*) exemple *m*; **for** ~ par exemple

instant [ˈɪnstənt] **1** *adj* instantané **2** *n* instant *m*; **instantaneous** instantané; **instant coffee** café *m* soluble; **instantly** immédiatement

instead [ɪnˈsted] à la place; ~ **of me** à ma place; ~ **of going home** au lieu de rentrer à la maison

instinct [ˈɪnstɪŋkt] instinct *m*; **instinctive** instinctif

institute [ˈɪnstɪtuːt] **1** *n* institut *m*; (*special home*) établissement *m* **2** *v/t new law, inquiry* instituer; **institution** institution *f*

instruct [ɪnˈstrʌkt] (*order*) ordonner; (*teach*) instruire; **instruction** instruction *f*; ~**s for use** mode *m* d'emploi; **instructive** instructif; **instructor** moniteur(-trice) *m(f)*

instrument [ˈɪnstrəmənt] instrument *m*

insubordinate [ɪnsəˈbɔːrdɪneɪt] insubordonné

insufficient [ɪnsəˈfɪʃnt] insuffisant

insulate [ˈɪnsəleɪt] ELEC, *against cold* isoler; **insulation** isolation *f*; *material* isolement *m*

insulin [ˈɪnsəlɪn] insuline *f*

insult [ˈɪnsʌlt] *n* insulte *f* **2** [ɪnˈsʌlt] *v/t* insulter

insurance [ɪnˈʃʊrəns] assurance *f*; **insurance company** compagnie *f* d'assurance; **insurance policy** police *f* d'assurance; **insurance premium** prime *f* d'assurance; **insure** assurer

insurmountable [ɪnsər'maʊntəbl] insurmontable

intact [ɪn'tækt] (*not damaged*) intact

integrate ['ɪntɪgreɪt] intégrer; **integrity** (*honesty*) intégrité *f*

intellect ['ɪntəlekt] intellect *m*; **intellectual 1** *adj* intellectuel **2** *n* intellectuel(le) *m(f)*

intelligence [ɪn'telɪdʒəns] intelligence *f*; (*information*) renseignements *mpl*; **intelligent** intelligent

intelligible [ɪn'telɪdʒəbl] intelligible

intend [ɪn'tend] *v/i*: **~ to do sth** avoir l'intention de

intense [ɪn'tens] intense; *personality* passionné; **intensify 1** *v/t* intensifier **2** *v/i* of pain, fighting s'intensifier; **intensity** intensité *f*; **intensive** intensif; **intensive care** MED service *m* de soins intensifs

intention [ɪn'tenʃn] intention *f*; **intentional** intentionnel; **intentionally** délibérément

interaction [ɪntər'ækʃn] interaction *f*; **interactive** interactif

intercept [ɪntər'sept] intercepter

interchange ['ɪntərtʃeɪndʒ] *of highways* échangeur *m*; **interchangeable** interchangeable

intercom ['ɪntərkɑːm] interphone *m*

intercourse ['ɪntərkɔːrs] *sexual* rapports *mpl*

interdependent [ɪntərdɪ'pendənt] interdépendant

interest ['ɪntrəst] **1** *n* intérêt *m*; *financial* intérêt(s) *m(pl)* **2** *v/t* intéresser; **interested** intéressé; **interesting** intéressant; **interest rate** taux *m* d'intérêt

interface ['ɪntərfeɪs] **1** *n* interface *f* **2** *v/i* avoir une interface (**with** avec)

interfere [ɪntər'fɪr] se mêler (**with** de); **interference** ingérence *f*; *on radio* interférence *f*

interior [ɪn'tɪrɪər] **1** *adj* intérieur **2** *n* intérieur *m*; **interior design** design *m* d'intérieurs; **interior designer** designer *m/f* d'intérieurs

interlude ['ɪntərluːd] intermède *m*

intermediary [ɪntər'miːdɪeri] intermédiaire *m/f*; **intermediate** *level* intermédiaire; *course* (de niveau) moyen

intermission [ɪntər'mɪʃn] *in theater* entracte *m*

internal [ɪn'tɜːrnl] interne; *trade* intérieur; **internally** *in organization* en interne; ***not to be taken*** à usage externe; **Internal Revenue (Service)** direction *f* générale des) impôts *mpl*

international [ɪntər'næʃnl]

international; **internationally** internationalement
Internet ['ɪntərnet] Internet *m*; **on the ~** sur Internet
interpret [ɪn'tɜːrprɪt] interpréter; **interpretation** interprétation *f*; **interpreter** interprète *m/f*
interrogate [ɪn'terəgeɪt] interroger; **interrogation** interrogatoire *m*; **interrogator** interrogateur(-trice) *m(f)*
interrupt [ɪntə'rʌpt] interrompre; **interruption** interruption *f*
intersect [ɪntər'sekt] **1** *v/t* couper, croiser **2** *v/i* s'entrecouper, s'entrecroiser; **intersection** *of roads* carrefour *m*
interstate ['ɪntərsteɪt] autoroute *f*
interval ['ɪntərvl] intervalle *m*; *in theater* entracte *m*
intervene [ɪntər'viːn] intervenir; **intervention** intervention *f*
interview ['ɪntərvjuː] **1** *n* interview *f*; *for job* entretien *m* **2** *v/t* interviewer; *for job* faire passer un entretien à; **interviewer** interviewer(-euse) *m(f)*; *for job* personne *f* responsable d'un entretien
intimate ['ɪntɪmət] intime
intimidate [ɪn'tɪmɪdeɪt] intimider; **intimidation** intimidation *f*
into ['ɪntu] dans; ***translate ~ English*** traduire en anglais;

be ~ sth F (*like*) aimer qch; *politics etc* être engagé dans qch
intolerable [ɪn'tɑːlərəbl] intolérable; **intolerant** intolérant
intoxicated [ɪn'tɑːksɪkeɪtɪd] ivre
intravenous [ɪntrə'viːnəs] intraveineux
intricate ['ɪntrɪkət] compliqué, complexe
intrigue 1 ['ɪntriːg] *n* intrigue *f* **2** [ɪn'triːg] *v/t* intriguer; **intriguing** intrigant
introduce [ɪntrə'duːs] *new technique etc* introduire; **~ s.o. to s.o.** présenter qn à qn; **introduction** *to person* présentations *fpl*; *in book, of new techniques* introduction *f*
intrude [ɪn'truːd] déranger; **intruder** intrus(e) *m(f)*; **intrusion** intrusion *f*
intuition [ɪntuː'ɪʃn] intuition *f*
invade [ɪn'veɪd] envahir
invalid¹ [ɪn'vælɪd] *adj* non valable
invalid² ['ɪnvəlɪd] *n* MED invalide *m/f*
invalidate [ɪn'vælɪdeɪt] *claim, theory* invalider
invaluable [ɪn'væljʊbl] inestimable
invariably [ɪn'verɪəblɪ] (*always*) invariablement
invasion [ɪn'veɪʒn] invasion *f*
invent [ɪn'vent] inventer; **invention** invention *f*; **inventive** inventif; **inventor** inven-

teur(-trice) *m(f)*
inventory [ˈɪnvəntouri] inventaire *m*
invert [ɪnˈvɜːrt] inverser
invest [ɪnˈvest] investir
investigate [ɪnˈvestɪɡeɪt] *crime* enquêter sur; *scientific phenomenon* étudier; **investigation** *of crime* enquête *f*; *in science* étude *f*
investment [ɪnˈvestmənt] investissement *m*; **investor** investisseur *m*
invincible [ɪnˈvɪnsəbl] invincible
invisible [ɪnˈvɪzɪbl] invisible
invitation [ɪnvɪˈteɪʃn] invitation *f*; **invite** inviter
invoice [ˈɪnvɔɪs] **1** *n* facture *f* **2** *v/t customer* facturer
involuntary [ɪnˈvɑːləntərɪ] involontaire
involve [ɪnˈvɑːlv] *work* nécessiter; *expense* entraîner; *(concern)* concerner; **what does it ~?** qu'est-ce que cela implique?; **involved** *(complex)* compliqué; **involvement** *in project, crime etc* participation *f*; *in politics* engagement *m*
invulnerable [ɪnˈvʌlnərəbl] invulnérable
inward [ˈɪnwərd] **1** *adj* intérieur **2** *adv* vers l'intérieur; **inwardly** intérieurement
IQ [aɪˈkjuː] (= ***intelligence quotient***) Q.I. *m* (= Quotient *m* intellectuel)
Iran [ɪˈrɑːn] Iran *m*; **Iranian 1**

adj iranien **2** *n* Iranien(ne) *m(f)*
Iraq [ɪˈræːk] Iraq *m*; **Iraqi 1** *adj* irakien **2** *n* Irakien(ne) *m(f)*
Ireland [ˈaɪrlənd] Irlande *f*; **Irish 1** *adj* irlandais **2** *npl*: **the ~** les Irlandais
iron [ˈaɪərn] **1** *n* fer *m*; *for clothes* fer *m* à repasser **2** *v/t shirts etc* repasser
ironic(al) [aɪˈrɑːnɪk(l)] ironique
'ironing board planche *f* à repasser
irony [ˈaɪrənɪ] ironie *f*
irrational [ɪˈræʃənl] irrationnel
irreconcilable [ɪrekənˈsaɪləbl] *people* irréconciliable; *positions* inconciliable
irregular [ɪˈreɡjʊlər] irrégulier
irrelevant [ɪˈreləvənt] hors de propos
irreplaceable [ɪrɪˈpleɪsəbl] irremplaçable
irrepressible [ɪrɪˈpresəbl] *sense of humor* à toute épreuve; *person* qui ne se laisse pas abattre
irresistible [ɪrɪˈzɪstəbl] irrésistible
irresponsible [ɪrɪˈspɑːnsəbl] irresponsable
irreverent [ɪˈrevərənt] irrévérencieux
irrevocable [ɪˈrevəkəbl] irrévocable
irrigate [ˈɪrɪɡeɪt] irriguer; **irrigation** irrigation *f*

irritable ['ırıtəbl] irritable; **irritate** irriter; **irritating** irritant; **irritation** irritation f

Islam ['ızlɑːm] *religion* islam m; *peoples, civilization* Islam m; **Islamic** islamique

island ['aılənd] île f

isolate ['aısəleɪt] isoler; **isolated** isolé; **isolation** isolement m

ISP [aıes'piː] (= *Internet service provider*) fournisseur m Internet

Israel ['ızreıl] Israël m; **Israeli** **1** *adj* israélien **2** *n person* Israélien(ne) m(f)

issue ['ıʃuː] **1** *n* (*matter*) question f, problème m; *of magazine* numéro m **2** *v/t supplies* distribuer; *coins, warning* émettre; *passport* délivrer

IT [aı'tiː] (= *information technology*) informatique f

it [ıt] *as subject* il, elle; *as object* le, la; ~'*s through there* c'est par là; *give* ~ *to him*

donne-le lui; *on top of* ~ dessus; *let's talk about* ~ parlons-en; ~'*s raining* il pleut; ~'*s me/him* c'est moi/lui; *that's* ~! (*that's right*) c'est ça!; (*finished*) c'est fini!

Italian [ı'tæljən] **1** *adj* italien **2** *n person* Italien(ne) m(f); *language* italien m

italics [ı'tælıks] italique m

Italy ['ıtəlı] Italie f

itch [ıtʃ] **1** *n* démangeaison f **2** *v/i*: *it* ~*es* ça me démange

item ['aıtəm] *article* m; *on agenda* point m; ~ *of news* nouvelle f; **itemize** *invoice* détailler

itinerary [aı'tınərerı] itinéraire m

its [ıts] son, sa; *pl* ses

it's [ıts] → *it is, it has*

itself [ıt'self] *reflexive* se; *stressed* lui-même; elle-même; *by* ~ (*automatically*) tout(e) seul(e)

J

jab [dʒæb]:~ *a stick into s.o.* donner un coup de bâton à qn

jack [dʒæk] MOT cric m; *in cards* valet m

jacket ['dʒækıt] veste f; *of book* couverture f

'jackpot jackpot m

jagged ['dʒægıd] découpé

jail [dʒeıl] prison f

jam¹ [dʒæm] *n for bread* confiture f

jam² [dʒæm] **1** *n* MOT embouteillage m; F (*difficulty*) pétrin m F **2** *v/t* (*ram*) fourrer; (*cause to stick*) bloquer; *broadcast* brouiller **3** *v/i* (*stick*) se bloquer

janitor ['dʒænıtər] concierge m/f

January ['dʒænjʊeri] janvier *m*

Japan [dʒə'pæn] Japon *m*; **Japanese 1** *adj* japonais **2** *n* Japonais(e) *m(f)*; *language* japonais *m*; **the ~** les Japonais *mpl*

jar [dʒɑːr] *container* pot *m*

jargon ['dʒɑːrɡən] jargon *m*

jaw [dʒɔː] mâchoire *f*

jaywalker ['dʒeɪwɔːkər] piéton(ne) *m(f)* imprudent(e)

jazz [dʒæz] jazz *m*

jealous ['dʒeləs] jaloux; jealousy jalousie *f*

jeans [dʒiːnz] jean *m*

jeep [dʒiːp] jeep *f*

jeer [dʒɪr] **1** *n* raillerie *f*; *of crowd* huée *f* **2** *v/i of crowd* huer

Jello® ['dʒeloʊ] gelée *f*

jelly ['dʒeli] *jam* confiture *f*; jellyfish méduse *f*

jeopardize ['dʒepərdaɪz] mettre en danger

jerk¹ [dʒɜːrk] **1** *n* saccade *f* **2** *v/t* tirer d'un coup sec

jerk² [dʒɜːrk] *n* F couillon *m* F

jerky ['dʒɜːrkɪ] *movement* saccadé

Jesus ['dʒiːzəs] Jésus

jet [dʒet] *(airplane)* avion *m* à réaction, jet *m*; *of water* jet *m*; *(nozzle)* bec *m*; jetlag (troubles *mpl* dus au) décalage *m* horaire

jettison ['dʒetɪsn] jeter par-dessus bord; *fig* abandonner

jetty ['dʒetɪ] jetée *f*

Jew [dʒuː] Juif(-ive) *m(f)*

jewel ['dʒuːəl] bijou *m*; *fig* : *person* perle *f*; jeweler, *Br* jeweller bijoutier(-ère) *m(f)*; jewelry, *Br* jewellery bijoux *mpl*

Jewish ['dʒuːɪʃ] juif

jigsaw (puzzle) ['dʒɪɡsɒ] puzzle *m*

jilt [dʒɪlt] laisser tomber

jingle ['dʒɪŋɡl] **1** *n song* jingle *m* **2** *v/i of keys, coins* cliqueter

jinx [dʒɪŋks] *person* porte-malheur *m/f*; **there's a ~ on this project** ce projet porte malheur

jittery ['dʒɪtərɪ] F nerveux

job [dʒɑːb] travail *m*; jobless sans travail

jockey ['dʒɑːkɪ] jockey *m*

jog [dʒɑːɡ] *as exercise* faire du footing *or* jogging; jogger *person* joggeur(-euse) *m(f)*; jogging jogging *m*

john [dʒɑːn] F *(toilet)* petit coin *m* F

join [dʒɔɪn] **1** *n* joint *m* **2** *v/i of roads, rivers* se rejoindre; *(become a member)* devenir membre **3** *v/t (connect)* relier; *person, of road* rejoindre; *club* devenir membre de ♦ join in participer

joint [dʒɔɪnt] ANAT articulation *f*; *in woodwork* joint *m*; *of meat* rôti *m*; joint account compte *m* joint; joint venture entreprise *f* commune

joke [dʒoʊk] **1** *n* plaisanterie *f*,

blague *f* F; (*practical* ~) tour *m* **2** *v/i* plaisanter; joker farceur(-euse) *m(f)*, blagueur(-euse) *m(f)* F; *in cards* joker *m*; *jokingly* en plaisantant

jostle ['dʒɒsl] bousculer

journal ['dʒɜːrnl] (*magazine*) revue *f*; (*diary*) journal *m*; journalism journalisme *m*; journalist journaliste *m/f*

journey ['dʒɜːrnɪ] voyage *m*; *across town etc* trajet *m*

joy [dʒɔɪ] joie *f*

jubilant ['dʒuːbɪlənt] débordant de joie; jubilation jubilation *f*

judge [dʒʌdʒ] **1** *n* juge *m/f* **2** *v/t* juger; *measurement, age* estimer **3** *v/i* juger; judg(e)ment jugement *m*; (*opinion*) avis *m*; Judg(e)ment Day le Jugement dernier

judicial [dʒuː'dɪʃl] judiciaire

juggle ['dʒʌgl] *also fig* jongler avec

juice [dʒuːs] jus *m*; juicy juteux; *gossip* croustillant

July [dʒʊ'laɪ] juillet *m*

jumbo (jet) ['dʒæmbəʊ] jumbo-jet *m*; jumbo-sized F géant

jump [dʒʌmp] **1** *n* saut *m*; (*increase*) bond *m* **2** *v/i* sauter; *in surprise* sursauter; (*increase*) faire un bond **3** *v/t* *fence etc* sauter; F (*attack*) attaquer; ~ *the lights* griller un feu (rouge)

♦ jump at *opportunity* sauter sur

jumper ['dʒʌmpər] *dress* robe-chasuble *f*; jumpy nerveux

June [dʒuːn] juin *m*

jungle ['dʒʌŋgl] jungle *f*

junior ['dʒuːnjər] **1** *adj* subalterne; (*younger*) plus jeune **2** *n in rank* subalterne *m/f*; *she is ten years my* ~ elle est ma cadette de dix ans; junior high collège *m*

junk [dʒʌŋk] camelote *f* F; junk food cochonneries *fpl*; junkie F drogué(e) *m(f)*; junk mail prospectus *mpl*

jurisdiction [dʒʊrɪs'dɪkʃn] LAW juridiction *f*

juror ['dʒʊrər] juré(e) *m(f)*; jury jury *m*

just [dʒʌst] **1** *adj* cause juste **2** *adv* (*barely, only*) juste; ~ *as intelligent* tout aussi intelligent; *I've* ~ *seen her* je viens de la voir; ~ *about* (*almost*) presque; *I was* ~ *about to leave when* ... j'étais sur le point de partir quand ...; ~ *now* (*a few moments ago*) tout à l'heure; (*at this moment*) en ce moment

justice ['dʒʌstɪs] justice *f*

justifiable [dʒʌstɪ'faɪəbl] justifiable; justifiably à juste titre; justification justification *f*; justify *also text* justifier

justly ['dʒʌstlɪ] (*fairly*) de manière juste; (*rightly*) à juste titre

♦ jut out [dʒʌt] être en saillie

juvenile ['dʒuːvənɪl] *crime* juvénile; *court* pour enfants; *pej* puéril; juvenile delin-

quent mineur(e) délin-quant(e) *m(f)*

K

k [keɪ] (= *kilobyte*) Ko *m* (= ki-lo-octet *m*); (= *thousand*) mille

keel [kiːl] NAUT quille *f*

keen [kiːn] (*intense*) vif

keep [kiːp] **1** *v/t* garder; (*detain*) retenir; *in specific place* mettre; *family* entretenir; *dog etc* avoir; *bees, cattle* éle-ver; *promise* tenir; **~ sth from s.o.** cacher qch à qn; **~ s.o. from doing sth** empê-cher qn de faire qch; **~ try-ing!** essaie encore!; **don't ~ interrupting!** arrête de m'in-terrompre tout le temps! **2** *v/i* (*remain*) rester; *of food, milk* se conserver

◆ **keep back** (*hold in check*) retenir; *information* cacher

◆ **keep down** *costs etc* rédui-re; *food* garder

◆ **keep to** *path* rester sur; *rules* s'en tenir à

◆ **keep up 1** *v/i when walk-ing, running etc* suivre; **keep up with** aller au même rythme que **2** *v/t pace, pay-ments* continuer; *bridge, pants* soutenir

'keepsake souvenir *m*

kennel ['kenl] niche *f*; ken-nels chenil *m*

kerosene ['kerəsiːn] AVIA ké-

rosène *m*; *for lamps* pétrole *m* (lampant)

ketchup ['ketʃʌp] ketchup *m*

kettle ['ketl] bouilloire *f*

key [kiː] **1** *n* clef *f*, clé *f*; COMPUT, MUS touche *f* **2** *adj* (*vital*) clef *inv*, clé *inv* **3** *v/t* & *v/i* COMPUT taper

◆ **key in** *data* taper

'keyboard COMPUT, MUS cla-vier *m*; **keyboarder** COMPUT claviste *m/f*; **keycard** carte-clef *f*; **keyed-up** tendu; **key-ring** porte-clefs *m*

kick [kɪk] **1** *n* coup *m* de pied **2** *v/t* donner un coup de pied dans **3** *v/i* *of horse* ruer

◆ **kick around** *ball* taper dans; F (*discuss*) débattre

◆ **kick off** donner le coup d'envoi; F (*start*) démarrer

◆ **kick out** mettre à la porte; **be kicked out of the compa-ny** être mis à la porte de la société

'kickback F (*bribe*) dessous--de-table *m* F

'kickoff SP coup *m* d'envoi

kid [kɪd] **1** *n* F (*child*) gamin(e) *m(f)* **2** *v/t* F taquiner **3** *v/i* F plaisanter

kidnap ['kɪdnæp] kidnapper; **kidnap(p)er** kidnappeur (-euse) *m(f)*; **kidnap(p)ing** kidnapping m

kidney ['kɪdnɪ] ANAT rein m; in cooking rognon m

kill [kɪl] also time tuer; killer (murderer) tueur(-euse) m(f); killing meurtre m

kiln [kɪln] four m

kilo ['ki:ləu] kilo m; kilobyte kilo-octet m; kilogram kilogramme m; kilometer, Br kilometre kilomètre m

kind¹ [kaɪnd] adj gentil

kind² [kaɪnd] n (sort) sorte f, genre m; (make, brand) marque f; ~ of sad/strange F plutôt triste/bizarre

kind-hearted [kaɪnd'hɑ:rtɪd] bienveillant, bon; kindly gentil, bon; kindness bonté f, gentillesse f

king [kɪŋ] roi m; kingdom royaume m

kinky ['kɪŋkɪ] F bizarre

kiosk ['ki:ɑ:sk] kiosque m

kiss [kɪs] 1 n baiser m 2 v/t embrasser 3 v/i s'embrasser

kit [kɪt] (equipment) trousse f; for assembly kit m

kitchen ['kɪtʃɪn] cuisine f

kitten ['kɪtn] chaton(ne) m(f)

kitty ['kɪtɪ] money cagnotte f

klutz [klʌts] F (clumsy person) empoté(e) m(f) F

knack [næk]: have the ~ of doing avoir le chic pour faire; there's a ~ to it il y a un truc F

knee [ni:] genou m; kneecap rotule f

kneel [ni:l] s'agenouiller

'knee-length à la hauteur du genou

knife [naɪf] couteau m

knit [nɪt] tricoter; knitwear tricot m

knob [nɑ:b] on door bouton m; of butter noix f

knock [nɑ:k] 1 n on door, (blow) coup m 2 v/t (hit) frapper; knee etc se cogner; F (criticize) débiner F 3 v/i on door frapper

♦ knock down renverser; wall, building abattre; F (reduce the price of) solder

♦ knock out assommer; boxer mettre knock-out; power lines etc détruire; (eliminate) éliminer

♦ knock over renverser

'knockout in boxing knock-out m

knot [nɑ:t] 1 n nœud m 2 v/t nouer

know [nou] 1 v/t savoir; person, place, language connaître; (recognize) reconnaître 2 v/i savoir; ~ about sth être au courant de qch; knowhow F savoir-faire m; knowing smile entendu; knowingly (wittingly) sciemment; smile etc d'un air entendu; know-it-all F je-sais-tout m/f; knowledge savoir m; of a subject connaissance(s) f(pl); to the best of my ~ autant que je sache

knuckle ['nʌkl] articulation f du doigt

Koran [kə'ræn] Coran *m*
Korea [kə'riːə] Corée *f*; **Korean 1** *adj* coréen **2** *n* Coréen(ne) *m(f)*; *language* co-

réen *m*
kosher ['kouʃər] REL casher *inv*; F réglo *inv* F
kudos ['kjuːdɑːs] prestige *m*

L

lab [læb] labo *m*
label ['leɪbl] **1** *n* étiquette *f* **2** *v/t also fig* étiqueter
labor ['leɪbər] *also in pregnancy* travail *m*
laboratory ['læbrətɔːrɪ] laboratoire *m*
labored ['leɪbərd] *style, speech* laborieux; **laborer** travailleur *m* manuel; **laborious** laborieux; **labor union** syndicat *m*
labour *Br* → **labor**
lace [leɪs] dentelle *f*; *for shoe* lacet *m*
lack [læk] **1** *n* manque *m* **2** *v/t* manquer de **3** *v/i*: **be ~ing** manquer
lacquer ['lækər] laque *f*
ladder ['lædər] échelle *f*
laden ['leɪdn] chargé (**with** de)
ladies room ['leɪdiːz] toilettes *fpl* (*pour dames*)
lady ['leɪdɪ] dame *f*; **ladybug** coccinelle *f*; **ladylike** distingué
lager ['lɑːgər] *Br* bière *f* blonde
laidback [leɪd'bæk] relax F
lake [leɪk] lac *m*
lamb [læm] agneau *m*
lame [leɪm] boîteux; *excuse*

mauvais,
laminated ['læmɪneɪtɪd] *flooring, paper* stratifié; *wood* contreplaqué; *with plastic* plastifié; **~ glass** verre *m* feuilleté
lamp [læmp] lampe *f*; **lamppost** réverbère *m*; **lampshade** abat-jour *m inv*
land [lænd] **1** *n* terre *f*; (*country*) pays *m*; **by ~** par (voie de) terre **2** *v/t airplane* faire atterrir; *job* décrocher F **3** *v/i of airplane* atterrir; *of ball* tomber; **landing** *of airplane* atterrissage *m*; (*top of staircase*) palier *m*; **landing strip** piste *f* d'atterrissage; **landlady** propriétaire *f*; *of rented room* logeuse *f*; *Br of bar* patronne *f*; **landlord** propriétaire *m*; *of rented room* logeur *m*; *Br of bar* patron *m*; **landmark** point *m* de repère; **be a ~ in** *fig* faire date dans; **land owner** propriétaire *m* foncier; **landscape 1** *n* paysage *m* **2** *adv print* en format paysage; **landslide** glissement *m* de terrain; **landslide victory** victoire *f* écrasante

lane [leɪn] *in country* petite route *f* (de campagne); *(alley)* ruelle *f*; MOT voie *f*

language ['læŋgwɪdʒ] langue *f*; *(style, code etc)* langage *m*; **language lab** laboratoire *m* de langues

lap[1] [læp] *of track* tour *m*

lap[2] [læp] *of water* clapotis *m*

lap[3] [læp] *of person* genoux *mpl*

lapel [lə'pel] revers *m*

lapse [læps] **1** *n (mistake)* erreur *f*; *in behavior* écart *m* (de conduite); *of time* intervalle *m* **2** *v/i* expirer

laptop ['læptɑːp] COMPUT portable *m*

larceny ['lɑːrsənɪ] vol *m*

larder ['lɑːrdər] garde-manger *m inv*

large [lɑːrdʒ] grand; *sum of money, head* gros; **largely** *(mainly)* en grande partie

laryngitis [lærɪn'dʒaɪtɪs] laryngite *f*

laser ['leɪzər] laser *m*; **laser printer** imprimante *f* laser

lash[1] [læʃ] *v/t with whip* fouetter

lash[2] [læʃ] *n (eyelash)* cil *m*

last[1] [læst] **1** *adj* dernier; **~ night** hier soir **2** *adv* arrive, leave en dernier; **at ~** enfin

last[2] [læst] *v/i* durer; **lasting** durable; **lastly** pour finir

late [leɪt] **1** *adj (behind time)* en retard; *in day* tard; **it's getting ~** il se fait tard **2** *adv* arrive, leave tard; **lately**

récemment; **later** plus tard; **latest** dernier

Latin A'merica Amérique *f* latine; **Latin American 1** *n* Latino-Américain *m* **2** *adj* latino-américain

latitude ['lætɪtuːd] *also (freedom)* latitude *f*

latter ['lætər] dernier

laugh [læf] **1** *n* rire *m* **2** *v/i* rire ♦ **laugh at** rire de; *(mock)* se moquer de

laughter ['læftər] rires *mpl*

launch [lɔːntʃ] **1** *n boat* vedette *f*; *of rocket, product* lancement *m*; *of ship* mise *f* à l'eau **2** *v/t rocket, product* lancer; *ship* mettre à l'eau

launder ['lɔːndər] *clothes, money* blanchir; **laundromat** laverie *f* automatique; **laundry** *place* blanchisserie *f*; *clothes* lessive *f*

lavatory ['lævətɑːrɪ] W.-C. *mpl*

lavish ['lævɪʃ] somptueux

law [lɔː] loi *f*; *subject* droit *m*; **be against the ~** être contraire à la loi; **law-abiding** respectueux des lois; **law court** tribunal *m*; **lawful** légal; *wife, child* légitime; **lawless** anarchique

lawn [lɔːn] pelouse *f*; **lawn mower** tondeuse *f* (à gazon)

'lawsuit procès *m*; **lawyer** avocat *m*

lax [læks] laxiste; *security* relâché

laxative ['læksətɪv] laxatif *m*

leaving party

lay [leɪ] (put down) poser; eggs pondre; V sexually s'envoyer V

♦ lay off workers licencier; temporarily mettre au chômage technique

♦ lay out objects disposer; page faire la mise en page de

layer ['leɪr] couche f

'layman REL laïc m; fig profane m

'lay-out agencement m; of page mise f en page

lazy ['leɪzɪ] person paresseux; day tranquille

lb (= pound) livre f

lead¹ [liːd] 1 v/t mener; company être à la tête de 2 v/i in race, competition mener; (provide leadership) diriger

lead² [liːd] for dog laisse f

lead³ [led] substance plomb m; leaded gas au plomb

leader ['liːdər] of state dirigeant m; in race leader m; of group chef m; leadership of party etc direction f

lead-free ['ledfriː] gas sans plomb

leading ['liːdɪŋ] runner en tête (de la course); company, product premier; leading-edge company, technology de pointe

leaf [liːf] feuille f

♦ leaf through feuilleter

leaflet ['liːflət] dépliant m

league [liːg] ligue f

leak [liːk] 1 n also of information fuite f 2 v/i of pipe fuir;

of boat fuire eau 3 v/t information divulguer

lean¹ [liːn] 1 v/i (be at an angle) pencher; ~ against sth s'appuyer contre qch 2 v/t appuyer

lean² [liːn] adj meat maigre

leap [liːp] 1 n saut m 2 v/i sauter; leap year année f bissextile

learn [lɜːrn] apprendre; learner apprenant(e) m(f); learning (knowledge) savoir m; act apprentissage m

lease [liːs] 1 n for apartment bail m; for equipment location f 2 v/t louer

♦ lease out louer

leash [liːʃ] for dog laisse f

least [liːst] 1 adj (slightest) (le ou la) moindre; smallest quantity of le moins de 2 adv (le) moins 3 n le moins; at ~ au moins

leather ['leðər] 1 n cuir m 2 adj de cuir

leave [liːv] 1 n (vacation) congé m 2 v/t quitter; food, scar, memory laisser; (forget, leave behind) oublier; ~ sth alone ne pas toucher à qch; ~ s.o. alone laisser qn tranquille; be left rester 2 v/i of person, plane etc partir

♦ leave behind intentionally laisser; (forget) oublier

♦ leave out omettre; (not put away) ne pas ranger

leaving party ['liːvɪŋ] soirée f d'adieu

lecture ['lektʃər] **1** n conférence f; at university cours m **2** v/i at university donner des cours; **lecturer** conférencier m; at university maître m de conférences

ledge [ledʒ] of window rebord m; on rock face saillie f; **ledger** COM registre m de comptes

left [left] **1** adj gauche **2** also POL gauche f; **on/to the ~** à gauche **3** adv turn, look à gauche; **left-hand** gauche; **left-handed** gaucher; **left luggage (office)** Br consigne f; **left-overs** food restes mpl; **left-wing** POL de gauche

leg [leg] jambe f; of animal patte f; of table etc pied m

legacy ['legəsɪ] héritage m, legs m

legal ['liːgl] (allowed) légal; relating to the law juridique; **legal adviser** conseiller (-ère) m(f) juridique; **legality** légalité f; **legalize** légaliser

legend ['ledʒənd] légende f; **legendary** légendaire

legible ['ledʒəbl] lisible

legislate ['ledʒɪsleɪt] légiférer; **legislation** (laws) législation f; **legislative** législatif; **legislature** POL corps m législatif

legitimate [lɪ'dʒɪtɪmət] légitime

'leg room place f pour les jambes

leisure ['liːʒər] loisir m; (free time) temps m libre; **leisurely** tranquille

lemon ['lemən] citron m; **lemonade** citronnade f; carbonated limonade f

lend [lend] prêter

length [leŋθ] longueur f; (piece: of material) pièce f; of piping, road tronçon m; **at ~** describe, explain en détail; (eventually) finalement; **lengthen** sleeve etc allonger; contract prolonger; **lengthy** long

lenient ['liːnɪənt] indulgent

lens [lenz] of microscope etc lentille f; of eyeglasses verre m; of camera objectif m; of eye cristallin m

Lent [lent] REL Carême m

leotard ['liːəʊtɑːrd] justaucorps m

lesbian ['lezbɪən] **1** n lesbienne f **2** adj lesbien

less [les] **1** adv moins; ~ **than $200** moins de 200 dollars **2** adj never, salt moins de; **lessen 1** v/t réduire **2** v/i diminuer

lesson ['lesn] leçon f; at school cours m

let [let] (allow) laisser; Br house louer; ~**'s stay here** restons ici; ~ **go of sth** lâcher qch

♦ **let down** hair détacher; blinds baisser; (disappoint) décevoir

♦ **let in** to house laisser entrer

◆ **let out** *from room, building*
laisser sortir; *jacket etc*
agrandir; *groan,yell* laisser
échapper; *Br (rent)* louer
◆ **let up** *(stop)* s'arrêter
lethal ['li:θl] mortel
lethargic [lɪ'θɑːrdʒɪk] léthar-
gique; **lethargy** léthargie *f*
letter ['letər] *of alphabet, in
mail* lettre *f*; **letterbox** *Br*
boîte *f* aux lettres; **letterhead**
(heading) en-tête *m*; *(headed
paper)* papier *m* à en-tête
lettuce ['letɪs] laitue *f*
leukemia [luː'kiːmɪə] leucémie *f*
level ['levl] **1** *adj surface* plat;
in competition à égalité **2** *n
niveau m; on scale, in hierarchy* échelon *m*; **on the ~**
F *(honest)* réglo F; **level-
-headed** pondéré
lever ['liːvər] levier *m*; **lever-
age** effet *m* de levier; *(influence)* poids *m*
levy ['levɪ] *taxes* lever
liability [laɪə'bɪlətɪ] *(responsibility)* responsabilité *f*; *(like-
liness)* disposition *f* **(to** à); li-
able responsable **(for** de); **be
~ to** *(likely)* être susceptible
de
◆ **liaise with** [lɪ'eɪz] assurer
la liaison avec
liaison [lɪ'eɪzɑːn] *(contacts)*
communication(s) *f*
liar [laɪr] menteur(-euse) *m(f)*
libel ['laɪbl] **1** *n* diffamation *f* **2**
v/t diffamer
liberal ['lɪbərəl] large d'esprit;

portion etc généreux; POL libéral
liberate ['lɪbəreɪt] libérer; **lib-
erated** libéré; **liberation** libération *f*; **liberty** liberté *f*
librarian [laɪ'brerɪən] biblio-
thécaire *m/f*; **library** bibliothèque *f*
Libya ['lɪbɪə] Libye *f*; **Libyan
1** *adj* libyen **2** *n* Libyen(ne)
m(f)
lice [laɪs] *pl* → **louse**
licence ['laɪsns] *Br* → **license
1** *n*
license ['laɪsns] **1** *n* permis *m*
2 *v/t company* accorder une
licence à **(to do** pour faire);
be ~d *equipment* être autorisé; **license number** numéro
m d'immatriculation; **license plate** *of car* plaque *f*
d'immatriculation
lick [lɪk] lécher
lid [lɪd] couvercle *m*
lie¹ [laɪ] **1** *n (untruth)* mensonge *m* **2** *v/i* mentir
lie² [laɪ] *v/i of person (lie
down)* s'allonger; *(be lying
down)* être allongé; *of object*
être; *(be situated)* être, se
trouver
◆ **lie down** se coucher
lieutenant [luː'tenənt] lieutenant *m*
life [laɪf] vie *f*; **life expectancy**
espérance *f* de vie; **lifeguard**
maître nageur *m*; **life imprisonment** emprisonnement *m*
à vie; **life insurance** assurance vie *f*; **life jacket** gilet *m* de

sauvetage; lifeless *body* inanimé; *personality* mou; *town* mort; lifelike réaliste; lifelong de toute une vie; life-sized grandeur nature; life support (équipement *m* de) maintien *m* artificiel; life-threatening *illness* extrêmement grave; lifetime vie *f*; **in my ~** de mon vivant

lift¹ [lɪft] **1** *n* lumière *f*; **do you have a ~?** vous avez du feu? **2** *v/t fire, cigarette* allumer; *(illuminate)* éclairer **3** *adj (not dark)* clair

light² [laɪt] *adj (not heavy)* léger

◆ **light up 1** *v/t* éclairer **2** *v/i (start to smoke)* s'allumer une cigarette

'light bulb ampoule *f*
lighten¹ ['laɪtn] *color* éclaircir
lighten² ['laɪtn] *load* alléger
lighter ['laɪtər] *for cigarettes* briquet *m*; **light-headed** étourdi; **lighting** éclairage *m*
lightness *of room, color* clarté *f*; *in weight* légèreté *f*; **lightning** éclair *m*, foudre *f*; **lightweight** *in boxing* poids *m* léger; **light year** année-lumière *f*
like¹ [laɪk] **1** *prep* comme; **be**

~ s.o./sth ressembler à qn/ qch; **what is she ~?** comment est-elle? **it's not ~ him** not his character ça ne lui ressemble pas **2** *conj* F *(as)* comme; **~ I said** comme je l'ai dit
like² [laɪk] *v/t* aimer; **I ~ it** ça me plaît (bien); **I ~ Susie** j'aime bien Susie; *romantically* Susie me plaît (bien); **I would ~ …** je voudrais, j'aimerais …; **I would ~ to leave** je voudrais *or* j'aimerais partir; **would you ~ …?** voulez-vous…?; **would you ~ to …?** as-tu envie de …?; **~ to do sth** aimer faire qch; **if you ~** si vous voulez; likeable agréable, plaisant; likelihood probabilité *f*; likely probable; likeness ressemblance *f*; likewise de même, aussi; liking *for person* affection *f*; *for sth* penchant *m*
limb [lɪm] membre *m*
lime¹ [laɪm] *fruit* citron *m* vert; *tree* limettier *m*
lime² [laɪm] *substance* chaux *f*
limit ['lɪmɪt] **1** *n* limite *f* **2** *v/t* limiter; limitation limitation *f*; limited company *Br* société *f* à responsabilité limitée
limousine ['lɪməziːn] limousine *f*
limp¹ [lɪmp] *adj* mou
limp² [lɪmp] **1** *n* claudication *f*; **he has a ~** il boite **2** *v/i* boiter
line¹ [laɪn] *n* ligne *f*; RAIL voie

f; *of people* file f; *of trees* rangée f; *of poem* vers m; **stand in ~** faire la queue

line² [laɪn] v/t *with material* recouvrir, garnir; *clothes* doubler

linear ['lɪnɪər] linéaire

linen ['lɪnɪn] *material* lin m; *(sheets etc)* linge m

liner ['laɪnər] *ship* paquebot m de grande ligne

linesman ['laɪnzmən] SP juge m *de touche*; *tennis* juge m de ligne

linger ['lɪŋgər] *of person* s'attarder; *of pain* persister

lingerie ['lænʒəriː] lingerie f

linguist ['lɪŋgwɪst] linguiste m; linguistique linguistique

lining ['laɪnɪŋ] *of clothes* doublure f; *of brakes, pipes* garniture f

link [lɪŋk] **1** n lien m; *in chain* maillon m **2** v/t lier, relier

lion ['laɪən] lion m

lip [lɪp] lèvre f

liposuction ['lɪpoʊsʌkʃən] liposuccion f

'lipread lire sur les lèvres; **lipstick** rouge m à lèvres

liqueur [lɪ'kjʊr] liqueur f

liquid ['lɪkwɪd] **1** n liquide m **2** adj liquide; **liquidate** liquider; **liquidation** liquidation f; **go into ~** entrer en liquidation; **liquidity** FIN liquidité f; **liquidize** passer au mixeur; **liquidizer** mixeur m

liquor ['lɪkər] alcool m; **liquor store** magasin m de vins et

spiritueux

lisp [lɪsp] **1** n zézaiement m **2** v/i zézayer

list [lɪst] **1** n liste f **2** v/t faire la liste de; *(enumerate)* énumérer

listen ['lɪsn] écouter
♦ **listen to** écouter

listener ['lɪsnər] *to radio* auditeur(-trice) m(f)

listless ['lɪstlɪs] amorphe

liter ['liːtər] litre m

literal ['lɪtərəl] littéral; **literally** littéralement

literary ['lɪtərerɪ] littéraire; **literature** littérature f; *about a product* documentation f

litre ['liːtər] *Br* → **liter**

litter ['lɪtər] détritus mpl, ordures fpl; *of animal* portée f

little ['lɪtl] **1** adj petit **2** n peu m; **a ~ wine** un peu de vin **3** adv peu; **a ~ bigger** un peu plus gros

live¹ [lɪv] v/i vivre

live² [laɪv] adj *broadcast* en direct; *bomb* non désamorcé
♦ **live up to** être à la hauteur de

livelihood ['laɪvlɪhʊd] gagne-pain m inv; **liveliness** vivacité f; **lively** *person, city* plein de vie; *party* animé; *music* entraînant

liver ['lɪvər] foie m

livestock ['laɪvstaːk] bétail m

livid ['lɪvɪd] *(angry)* furieux

living ['lɪvɪŋ] **1** adj vivant **2** n vie f; **living room** salle f de séjour

lizard ['lɪzərd] lézard *m*

load [loud] **1** *n* charge *f* **2** *v/t* charger

loaf [louf]: *a ~ of bread* un pain

◆ **loaf around** F traîner

loafer ['loufər] *shoe* mocassin *m*

loan [loun] **1** *n* prêt *m* **2** *v/t*: *~ s.o. sth* prêter qch à qn

loathe [louð] détester; **loathing** dégoût *m*

lobby ['lɑːbɪ] *in hotel* hall *m*; *in theater* vestibule *m*; POL lobby *m*

lobe [loub] *of ear* lobe *m*

lobster ['lɑːbstər] homard *m*

local ['loukl] **1** *adj* local **2** *n* habitant *m* de la région/du quartier; **local call** TELEC appel *m* local; **local elections** élections *fpl* locales; **local government** autorités *f* locales; **locality** endroit *m*; **localize** localiser; **locally** *live, work* dans le quartier, dans la région; **local time** heure *f* locale

locate [lou'keɪt] *new factory etc* établir; (*identify position of*) localiser; *be ~d* se trouver; **location** (*siting*) emplacement *m*; (*identifying position of*) localisation *f*; *on ~ movie* en extérieur

lock[1] [lɑːk] *n of hair* mèche *f*

lock[2] [lɑːk] **1** *n on door* serrure *f* **2** *v/t door* fermer à clef

◆ **lock up** *in prison* mettre sous les verrous

locker ['lɑːkər] casier *m*; **locker room** vestiaire *m*

locust ['loukəst] locuste *f*, sauterelle *f*

lodge [lɑːdʒ] **1** *v/t complaint* déposer **2** *v/i of bullet* se loger

lofty ['lɑːftɪ] *heights* haut; *ideals* élevé

log [lɑːg] bûche *f*; (*written record*) journal *m* de bord

◆ **log in** se connecter (*to* à)

◆ **log off** se déconnecter

◆ **log on** se connecter (*to* à)

◆ **log out** se déconnecter

log 'cabin cabane *f* en rondins

logic ['lɑːdʒɪk] logique *f*; **logical** logique; **logically** logiquement

logistics [lə'dʒɪstɪks] logistique *f*

logo ['lougou] logo *m*, sigle *m*

loiter ['lɔɪtər] traîner

lollipop ['lɑːlɪpɑːp] sucette *f*

London ['lʌndən] Londres

loneliness ['lounlɪnɪs] *of person* solitude *f*; *of place* isolement *m*; **lonely** *person* seul, solitaire; *place* isolé; **loner** solitaire *m/f*

long[1] [lɑːŋ] **1** *adj* long; *it's a ~ way* c'est loin **2** *adv* longtemps; *how ~ will it take?* combien de temps cela va-t-il prendre?; *he no ~er works here* il ne travaille plus ici; *so ~ as* (*provided*) pourvu que; *so ~!* à bientôt!

long[2] [lɑːŋ] *v/i*: *~ for sth* avoir très envie de qch; *be ~ing to*

do sth avoir très envie de faire qch

long-'distance *phonecall* longue distance; *race* de fond; *flight* long-courrier; **longevity** longévité *f*; **longing** désir *m*, envie *f*; **longitude** longitude *f*; **long jump** saut *m* en longueur; **long-range** *missile* à longue portée; *forecast* à long terme; **long-sleeved** à manches longues; **long-standing** de longue date; **long-term** à long terme; *unemployment* de longue durée

loo [luː] *Br* F toilettes *fpl*

look [lʊk] **1** *n* (*appearance*) air *m*; (*glance*) coup *m* d'œil, regard *m*; **~s** (*beauty*) beauté *f* **2** *v/i* regarder; (*search*) chercher, regarder; (*seem*) avoir l'air

◆ **look after** s'occuper de

◆ **look ahead** *fig* regarder en avant

◆ **look around** jeter un coup d'œil

◆ **look at** regarder; (*examine*) examiner; (*consider*) envisager

◆ **look back** regarder derrière soi

◆ **look down on** mépriser

◆ **look for** chercher

◆ **look into** (*investigate*) examiner

◆ **look onto** *garden etc* donner sur

◆ **look out** *of window etc* regarder dehors; (*pay attention*) faire attention

◆ **look over** *house, translation* examiner

◆ **look through** *magazine, notes* parcourir, feuilleter

◆ **look up 1** *v/i from paper etc* lever les yeux; (*improve*) s'améliorer **2** *v/t word, phone number* chercher; (*visit*) passer voir

◆ **look up to** (*respect*) respecter

'**lookout** *person* sentinelle *f*; **be on the ~ for** être à l'affût de

loop [luːp] boucle *f*; **loophole** *in law etc* lacune *f*

loose [luːs] *knot* lâche; *connection, screw* desserré; *clothes* ample; *morals* relâché; *wording* vague; **~ change** petite monnaie *f*; **loosely** *worded* de manière approximative; **loosen** desserrer

loot [luːt] **1** *n* butin *m* **2** *v/i* se livrer au pillage; **looter** pilleur(-euse) *m(f)*

lop-sided [lɑːpˈsaɪdɪd] déséquilibré, disproportionné

Lord [lɔːrd] (*god*) Seigneur *m*

lorry [ˈlɑːrɪ] *Br* camion *m*

lose [luːz] **1** *v/t* perdre **2** *v/i* SP perdre; *of clock* retarder; **loser** perdant(e) *m(f)*

loss [lɑːs] perte *f*

lost [lɑːst] perdu; **lost-and-found**, *Br* **lost property (office)** (bureau *m* des) objets *mpl* trouvés

lot [lɑːt]: *a* ~ *(of)*, *~s (of)* beaucoup (de)

lotion ['ləʊʃn] lotion *f*

lottery ['lɑːtərɪ] loterie *f*

loud [laʊd] *music, voice* fort; *noise* grand; *color* criard; **loudspeaker** haut-parleur *m*

louse [laʊs] pou *m*; **lousy** F minable F , mauvais

lout [laʊt] rustre *m*

lovable ['lʌvəbl] sympathique, adorable; **love 1** *n* amour *m*; *in tennis* zéro *m*; **fall in** ~ tomber amoureux **(with** de); **make** ~ faire l'amour **(to** avec) **2** *v/t* aimer; *wine, music* adorer; **love affair** aventure *f*; **lovely** beau; *house, wife* ravissant; *character* charmant; *meal* délicieux; **lover** *man* amant *m*; *woman* maîtresse *f*; *person in love* amoureux(-euse) *m(f)*; **loving** affectueux; **lovingly** avec amour

low [ləʊ] **1** *adj* bas; *quality* mauvais **2** *n in weather* dépression *f*; *in statistics* niveau *m* bas; **lowbrow** peu intellectuel; **low-calorie** hypocalorique; **low-cut** *dress* décolleté; **lower** baisser; *to the ground* faire descendre; **low-fat** allégé; **lowkey** discret, mesuré

loyal ['lɔɪəl] fidèle, loyal; **loyally** fidèlement; **loyalty** loyauté *f*

lozenge ['lɑːzɪndʒ] *shape* losange *m*; *tablet* pastille *f*

Ltd (= *limited*) *company* à responsabilité limitée

lubricant ['luːbrɪkənt] lubrifiant *m*; **lubricate** lubrifier; **lubrication** lubrification *f*

lucid ['luːsɪd] *(clear)* clair; *(sane)* lucide

luck [lʌk] chance *f*; **good** ~! bonne chance!; **luckily** heureusement; **lucky** *person* chanceux; *number* porte-bonheur *inv*; *coincidence* heureux; **you were** ~ tu as eu de la chance

lucrative ['luːkrətɪv] lucratif

ludicrous ['luːdɪkrəs] ridicule

lug [lʌɡ] F traîner

luggage ['lʌɡɪdʒ] bagages *mpl*

lukewarm ['luːkwɔːrm] *also fig* tiède

lull [lʌl] *in storm, fighting* accalmie *f*; *in conversation* pause *f*

lumber ['lʌmbər] *(timber)* bois *m* de construction

luminous ['luːmɪnəs] lumineux

lump [lʌmp] *of sugar* morceau *m*; *(swelling)* grosseur *f*; **lump sum** forfait *m*; **lumpy** *liquid, sauce* grumeleux; *mattress* défoncé

lunacy ['luːnəsɪ] folie *f*

lunar ['luːnər] lunaire

lunatic ['luːnətɪk] fou *m*, folle *f*

lunch [lʌntʃ] déjeuner *m*; **have** ~ déjeuner; **lunch box** panier-repas *m*; **lunch**

break pause-déjeuner f;
lunchtime heure f du déjeuner, midi m

lung [lʌŋ] poumon m

lurch [lɜːrtʃ] of person tituber;
of ship tanguer

lure [lʊr] **1** n appât m **2** v/t attirer

lurid ['lʊrɪd] color cru; details
choquant

lurk [lɜːrk] of person se cacher

lush [lʌʃ] vegetation luxuriant

lust [lʌst] désir m

luxurious [lʌgˈʒʊrɪəs]
luxueux; **luxuriously** lu-
xueusement; **luxury 1** n luxe
m **2** adj de luxe

lynch [lɪntʃ] lyncher

lyrics ['lɪrɪks] paroles fpl

M

ma'am [mæm] madame

machine [məˈʃiːn] machine f;
machine gun mitrailleuse f;
machinery machines fpl

machismo [məˈkɪzmoʊ] machisme m

macho ['mætʃoʊ] macho inv;
~ **type** macho m

macro ['mækroʊ] COMPUT macro f

mad [mæd] (insane) fou; F (angry) furieux; **madden** (infuriate) exaspérer; **maddening**
exaspérant; **madhouse** fig
maison f de fous; **madman**
fou m; **madness** folie f

Madonna [məˈdɒːnə] Madon-
ne f

Mafia ['mɑːfɪə]: **the ~** la Mafia

magazine [mægəˈziːn]
printed magazine m

Magi ['meɪdʒaɪ] REL: **the ~** les
Rois mpl mages

magic ['mædʒɪk] **1** adj magique **2** n magie f; **magical** magique; **magician** performer

prestidigitateur(-trice) m(f)

magnanimous
[mægˈnænɪməs] magnanime

magnet ['mægnɪt] aimant m;
magnetic also fig magnétique; **magnetism** also fig ma-
gnétisme m

magnificence [mægˈnɪfɪ-
səns] magnificence f; **magnificent** magnifique

magnify ['mægnɪfaɪ] grossir;
difficulties exagérer; **magnifying glass** loupe f

magnitude ['mægnɪtuːd] ampleur f

maid [meɪd] servant domestique f; in hotel femme f de
chambre

maiden name ['meɪdn] nom
m de jeune fille

mail [meɪl] **1** n courrier m,
poste f **2** v/t letter poster;
mailbox boîte f aux lettres;
mailing list fichier m
d'adresses; **mailman** facteur
m; **mailshot** mailing m, pu-

blipostage *m*

maim [meɪm] estropier, mutiler

main [meɪn] principal; **main course** plat *m* principal; **mainframe** ordinateur *m* central; **mainly** principalement; **main road** route *f* principale; **main street** rue *f* principale

maintain [meɪnˈteɪn] *peace, law, and order* maintenir; *speed* soutenir; *relationship, machine, building* entretenir; *innocence, guilt* affirmer; **maintenance of** *machine, building* entretien *m*; *Br money* pension *f* alimentaire; *of law and order* maintien *m*

majestic [məˈdʒestɪk] majestueux

major [ˈmeɪdʒər] **1** *adj* (*significant*) important, majeur **2** *n* MIL commandant *m*
◆ **major in** se spécialiser en

majority [məˈdʒɑːrətɪ] *also* POL majorité *f*

make [meɪk] **1** *n* (*brand*) marque *f* **2** *v/t* faire; (*manufacture*) fabriquer; (*earn*) gagner; *decision* prendre; **3 and 3 → 6** 3 et 3 font 6; ~ *it* (*catch bus, train*) arriver à temps; (*come*) venir; (*succeed*) réussir; (*survive*) s'en sortir; **what time do you ~ it?** quelle heure est-tu?; ~ *believe* prétendre; ~ *do with* se contenter de, faire avec;

what do you ~ of it? qu'en dis-tu?; ~ *s.o. of sth* (*force to*) forcer qn à faire qch; (*cause to*) faire faire qch à qn; ~ *s.o. happy/angry* rendre qn heureux/furieux
◆ **make out** *list, check* faire; (*see*) distinguer; (*imply*) prétendre
◆ **make up 1** *v/i of woman, actor* se maquiller; *after quarrel* se réconcilier **2** *v/t story* inventer; *face* maquiller; (*constitute*) constituer
◆ **make up for** compenser

'make-believe: *it's just* ~ c'est juste pour faire semblant

maker [ˈmeɪkər] (*manufacturer*) fabricant *m*; **makeshift** de fortune; **make-up** (*cosmetics*) maquillage *m*

maladjusted [mæləˈdʒʌstɪd] inadapté

male [meɪl] **1** *adj* masculin; *animal* mâle **2** *n* (*man*) homme *m*; *animal, bird* mâle *m*; **male chauvinism** machisme *m*; **male chauvinist pig** macho *m*

malevolent [məˈlevələnt] malveillant

malfunction [mælˈfʌŋkʃn] **1** *n* mauvais fonctionnement *m*, défaillance *f* **2** *v/i* mal fonctionner

malice [ˈmælɪs] méchanceté *f*, malveillance *f*; **malicious** méchant, malveillant

malignant [məˈlɪgnənt] *tumor* malin

mall [mɔːl] (*shopping* ~) centre *m* commercial
malnutrition [mælnuːˈtrɪʃn] malnutrition *f*
maltreat [mælˈtriːt] maltraiter; **maltreatment** mauvais traitement *m*
mammal [ˈmæml] mammifère *m*
man [mæn] **1** *n* (*pl* **men** [men]) homme *m*; (*humanity*) l'homme *m*; *in checkers* pion *m* **2** *v/t telephones* être de permanence à; *front desk* être de service à
manage [ˈmænɪdʒ] **1** *v/t business* diriger; *money* gérer; *bags* porter; ~ **to** ... réussir à ... **2** *v/i* (*cope*) se débrouiller; **manageable** gérable; *vehicle* maniable; *task* faisable; **management** (*managing*) gestion *f*, direction *f*; (*managers*) direction *f*; **management consultant** conseiller(-ère) *m(f)* en gestion; **manager** directeur(-trice) *m(f)*; *of store, restaurant, hotel* gérant(e) *m(f)*; *of department* responsable *m/f*; *of singer, band, team* manageur(-euse) *m(f)*; **managerial** de directeur, de gestionnaire; **managing director** directeur(-trice) *m(f)* général(e)
mandate [ˈmændeɪt] mandat *m*; **mandatory** obligatoire
maneuver [məˈnuːvər] **1** *n* manœuvre *f* **2** *v/t* manœuvrer

mangle [ˈmæŋgl] (*crush*) broyer
manhandle [ˈmænhændl] *person* malmener; *object* déplacer manuellement
manhood [ˈmænhʊd] (*maturity*) âge *m* d'homme; (*virility*) virilité *f*; **manhunt** chasse *f* à l'homme
mania [ˈmeɪnɪə] (*craze*) manie *f*; **maniac** F fou *m*, folle *f*
manicure [ˈmænɪkjʊr] manucure *f*
manifest [ˈmænɪfest] **1** *adj* manifeste **2** *v/t* manifester
manipulate [məˈnɪpjəleɪt] manipuler; **manipulation** manipulation *f*; **manipulative** manipulateur
mankind humanité *f*; **manly** viril; **man-made** synthétique
manner [ˈmænər] *of doing sth* manière *f*, façon *f*; (*attitude*) comportement *m*; **manners** manières *fpl*
manoeuvre [məˈnuːvər] *Br* → **maneuver**
'manpower main-d'œuvre *f*
manual [ˈmænjuəl] **1** *adj* manuel **2** *n* manuel *m*; **manually** manuellement
manufacture [mænjuˈfæktʃər] **1** *n* fabrication *f* **2** *v/t equipment* fabriquer; **manufacturer** fabricant *m*; **manufacturing** *in-dustry* industrie *f*
manure [məˈnʊr] fumier *m*
manuscript [ˈmænjʊskrɪpt] manuscrit *m*

many ['menɪ] **1** *adj* beaucoup de; **~ times** bien des fois; **too ~ problems** trop de problèmes; **as ~ as possible** autant que possible **2** *pron* beaucoup; **a great ~, a good ~** un bon nombre; **how ~ do you need?** combien en veux-tu?

map [mæp] carte *f*; *of town* plan *m*

maple ['meɪpl] érable *m*

mar [mɑːr] gâcher

marathon ['mærəθɑːn] *race* marathon *m*

marble ['mɑːrbl] *material* marbre *m*

March [mɑːrʃ] mars *m*

march [mɑːrʃ] **1** *n also (demonstration)* marche *f* **2** *v/i* marcher au pas; *in protest* défiler; marcher manifestant(e) *m(f)*

Mardi Gras ['mɑːrdɪgrɑː] mardi *m* gras

margin ['mɑːrdʒɪn] *of page,* COM marge *f*; **marginal** *(slight)* léger; **marginally** *(slightly)* légèrement

marihuana, marijuana [mærɪ'hwɑːnə] marijuana *f*

marina [mə'riːnə] port *m* de plaisance

marine [mə'riːn] **1** *adj* marin **2** *n* MIL marine *f*

marital ['mærɪtl] conjugal; **marital status** situation *f* de famille

maritime ['mærɪtaɪm] maritime

mark [mɑːrk] **1** *n* marque *f*; *(stain)* tache *f*; *(sign, token)* signe *m*; *(trace)* trace *f*; *Br* EDU note *f* **2** *v/t* marquer; *(stain)* tacher; *Br* EDU noter **3** *v/i of fabric* se tacher; **marked** *(definite)* marqué; **marker** *(highlighter)* marqueur *m*

market ['mɑːrkɪt] **1** *n* marché *m* **2** *v/t* commercialiser; **marketable** commercialisable; **market economy** économie *f* de marché; **marketing** marketing *m*; **market leader** *product* produit *m* vedette; *company* leader *m* du marché; **market place** *in town* place *f* du marché; *for commodities* marché *m*; **market research** étude *f* de marché; **market share** part *f* du marché

mark-up ['mɑːrkʌp] majoration *f*

marriage ['mærɪdʒ] mariage *m*; **marriage certificate** acte *m* de mariage; **married** marié; **be ~ to** être marié à; **married life** vie *f* conjugale; **marry** épouser, se marier avec; *of priest* marier; **get married** se marier

marsh [mɑːrʃ] *Br* marais *m*

marshal ['mɑːrʃl] *in police* chef *m* de la police; *in security service* membre *m* du service d'ordre

martial 'law loi *f* martiale

martyr ['mɑːrtər] *also fig* martyr(e) *m(f)*

marvel ['mɑːrvl] merveille *f*;
marvelous, *Br* **marvellous**
merveilleux

Marxism ['mɑːrksɪzm]
marxisme *m*; **Marxist 1** *adj*
marxiste **2** *n* marxiste *m/f*

mascara [mæ'skærə] mascara
m

mascot ['mæskət] mascotte *f*

masculine ['mæskjʊlɪn] *also*
GRAM masculin; **masculinity**
masculinité *f*

mash [mæʃ] réduire en purée

mask [mæsk] **1** *n* masque *m* **2**
v/t masquer

masochism ['mæsəkɪzm]
masochisme *m*; **masochist**
masochiste *m/f*

mass¹ [mæs] **1** *n* (*great
amount*) masse *f*; **~es of** F
des tas de F **2** *v/i* se masser

mass² [mæs] *n* REL messe *f*

massacre ['mæsəkər] **1** *n also
fig* F massacre *m* **2** *v/t also fig*
F massacrer

massage ['mæsɑːʒ] **1** *n* massage
m **2** *v/t* masser; *figures*
manipuler

massive ['mæsɪv] énorme;
heart attack grave

mass 'media médias *mpl*;
mass-produce fabriquer en
série; **mass production** fabrication *f* en série

mast [mæst] *of ship* mât *m*;
for radio signal pylône *m*

master ['mæstər] **1** *n of dog*
maître *m*; *of ship* capitaine
m **2** *v/t* maîtriser; **master**

bedroom chambre *f* principale; **master key** passe-partout *m inv*; **masterly** magistral; **mastermind 1** *n* cerveau
m **2** *v/t* organiser; **masterpiece** chef-d'œuvre *m*; **master's** (**degree**) maîtrise *f*;
mastery maîtrise *f*

mat [mæt] *for floor* tapis *m*;
for table napperon *m*

match¹ [mætʃ] *n for cigarette*
allumette *f*

match² [mætʃ] **1** *n* (*competition*) match *m*, partie *f* **2** *v/t*
(*be the same as*) être assorti
à; (*equal*) égaler **3** *v/i of colors, patterns* aller ensemble;
matching assorti; **match
stick** allumette *f*

mate [meɪt] **1** *n of animal* mâle *m*, femelle *f*; NAUT second
m **2** *v/i* s'accoupler

material [mə'tɪriəl] **1** *n* (*fabric*) tissu *m*; (*substance*) matériau *m*, matière *f* **2** *adj* matériel; **materialism** matéria-
lisme *m*; **materialist** matérialiste *m/f*; **materialistic**
matérialiste; **materialize**
(*appear*) apparaître; (*happen*) se concrétiser

maternal [mə'tɜːrnl] maternel; **maternity** maternité *f*;
maternity leave congé *m*
de maternité

math [mæθ] maths *fpl*; **mathematical** mathématique; **
mathematician** mathémati-
cien(ne) *m(f)*; **maths** *Br* →
math

matinée ['mætɪneɪ] matinée f
matriarch ['meɪtrɪɑːrk] femme f chef de famille
matrimony ['mætrəmoʊnɪ] mariage m
matt [mæt] mat
matter ['mætər] **1** n (affair) affaire f, question f; PHYS matière f; **what's the ~?** qu'est-ce qu'il y a? **2** v/i importer; **it doesn't ~** cela ne fait rien; matter-of-fact impassible
mattress ['mætrɪs] matelas m
mature [mə'tjʊr] **1** adj mûr **2** v/i of person mûrir; of insurance policy arriver à échéance; **maturity** maturité f
maximize ['mæksɪmaɪz] maximiser; **maximum 1** adj maximal, maximum **2** n maximum m
May [meɪ] mai m
may [meɪ] ◇ possibility: **it ~ rain** il va peut-être pleuvoir; **it ~ not happen** cela n'arrivera peut-être pas
◇ permission: pouvoir; **~ I help?** puis-je aider?
maybe ['meɪbiː] peut-être
mayo, mayonnaise ['meɪoʊ, meɪə'neɪz] mayonnaise f
mayor ['meɪər] maire m
maze [meɪz] labyrinthe m
MB (= **megabyte**) Mo (= mégaocte)
MBA [embiː'eɪ] (= **master of business administration**) MBA m
MD [em'diː] (= **Doctor of Med-**

icine) docteur m en médecine; (= **managing director**) DG m (= directeur m général)
me [miː] me; before vowel m'; after prep moi; **he knows ~** il me connaît; **she gave ~ a dollar** elle m'a donné un dollar; **it's for ~** c'est pour moi; **it's ~** c'est moi
meadow ['medoʊ] pré m
meager, Br meagre ['miːgər] maigre
meal [miːl] repas m; **enjoy your ~!** bon appétit!
mean¹ [miːn] adj with money avare; (nasty) mesquin
mean² [miːn] v/t (signify) signifier, vouloir dire; **be ~t for** être destiné à; of remark être adressé à; **meaning** of word sens m; **meaningful** (comprehensible) compréhensible; (constructive) significatif; glance éloquent; **meaningless** sentence etc dénué de sens; gesture insignifiant
means [miːnz] financial moyens mpl; (way) moyen m; **by all ~** (certainly) bien sûr; **by ~ of** au moyen de
meantime ['miːntaɪm] entre-temps
measles ['miːzlz] rougeole f
measure ['meʒər] **1** n (step) mesure f **2** v/t & v/i mesurer
◆ measure up to être à la hauteur de
measurement ['meʒərmənt] action mesure f; (dimension)

dimension *f*; **measuring tape** mètre *m* ruban

meat [miːt] viande *f*; **meatball** boulette *f* de viande

mechanic [mɪˈkænɪk] mécanicien(ne) *m(f)*; **mechanical device** mécanique; *gesture etc also* machinal; **mechanical engineer** ingénieur *m* mécanicien; **mechanically** mécaniquement; *do sth mechanically* machinalement; **mechanism** mécanisme *m*; **mechanize** mécaniser

medal [ˈmedl] médaille *f*; **medalist**, *Br* **medallist** médaillé *m*

meddle [ˈmedl] se mêler (*in* de)

media [ˈmiːdɪə]: *the ~* les médias *mpl*; **media coverage** couverture *f* médiatique

median strip [miːdɪənˈstrɪp] terre-plein *m* central

'media studies études *fpl* de communication

mediate [ˈmiːdɪeɪt] arbitrer; **mediation** médiation *f*; **mediator** médiateur(-trice) *m(f)*

medical [ˈmedɪkl] **1** *adj* médical **2** *n* visite *f* médicale; **medicated** pharmaceutique, traitant; **medication** médicaments *mpl*; **medicinal** médicinal

medicine *science* médecine *f*; (*medication*) médicament *m*

medieval [medɪˈiːvl] médiéval

mediocre [miːdɪˈoʊkər] médiocre; **mediocrity** *of work etc* médiocrité *f*; *person* médiocre *m/f*

meditate [ˈmedɪteɪt] méditer; **meditation** méditation *f*

Mediterranean [medɪtəˈreɪnɪən] **1** *adj* méditerranéen **2** *n*: *the ~* la Méditerranée

medium [ˈmiːdɪəm] **1** *adj* (*average*) moyen; *steak* à point **2** *n* *in size* taille *f* moyenne; (*vehicle*) moyen *m*; (*spiritualist*) médium *m*

medley [ˈmedlɪ] (*assortment*) mélange *m*

meet [miːt] **1** *v/t* rencontrer; (*be introduced to*) faire la connaissance de; (*collect*) (aller/venir) chercher; *in competition* affronter; *of eyes* croiser; (*satisfy*) satisfaire **2** *v/i* se rencontrer; *by appointment* se retrouver; *of committee etc* se réunir **3** *n* SP rencontre *f*; **meeting** *by accident* rencontre *f*; *in business, of committee* réunion *f*; *he's in a ~* il est en réunion

megabyte [ˈmegəbaɪt] COMPUT méga-octet *m*

mellow [ˈmeloʊ] **1** *adj* doux **2** *v/i of person* s'adoucir

melodious [mɪˈloʊdɪəs] mélodieux

melodramatic [melədrəˈmætɪk] mélodramatique

melody [ˈmelədɪ] mélodie *f*

melon [ˈmelən] melon *m*

melt [melt] **1** *v/i* fondre **2** *v/t*

faire fondre; **melting pot** *fig* creuset *m*

member ['membər] membre *m*; **Member of Congress** membre *m* du Congrès; **membership** adhésion *f*; *number of members* membres *mpl*

membrane ['membreɪn] membrane *f*

memento [me'mentoʊ] souvenir *m*

memo ['memoʊ] note *f* (de service)

memoirs ['memwɑːrz] mémoires *fpl*

memorable ['memərəbl] mémorable

memorial [mɪ'mɔːrɪəl] **1** *adj* commémoratif **2** *n* mémorial *m*; **Memorial Day** *jour commémoration des soldats américains morts à la guerre*

memorize ['meməraɪz] apprendre par cœur; **memory** mémoire *f*; *sth remembered* souvenir *m*

men [men] *pl → **man**

menace ['menɪs] **1** *n* menace *f*; *person* danger *m* **2** *v/t* menacer; **menacing** menaçant

mend [mend] réparer; *clothes* raccommoder

menial ['miːnɪəl] subalterne

menopause ['menoʊpɔːz] ménopause *f*

'men's room toilettes *fpl* pour hommes

menstruate ['menstrʊeɪt] avoir ses règles

mental ['mentl] mental; *ability, powers* intellectuel; *health, suffering* moral; F *(crazy)* malade F; **mental hospital** hôpital *m* psychiatrique; **mental illness** maladie *f* mentale; **mentality** mentalité *f*; **mentally** *(inwardly)* intérieurement; *calculate etc* mentalement

mention ['menʃn] **1** *n* mention *f* **2** *v/t* mentionner; **don't ~ it** *(you're welcome)* il n'y a pas de quoi!

mentor ['mentɔːr] mentor *m*

menu ['menjuː] *also* COMPUT menu *m*

mercenary ['mɜːrsɪnerɪ] **1** *adj* intéressé **2** *n* MIL mercenaire *m*

merchandise ['mɜːrtʃəndaɪz] marchandises *fpl*

merchant ['mɜːrtʃənt] négociant *m*, commerçant *m*

merciful ['mɜːrsɪfl] clément; *God* miséricordieux; **mercifully** *(thankfully)* heureusement; **merciless** impitoyable; **mercy** clémence *f*, pitié *f*

mere [mɪr] simple; **merely** simplement, seulement

merge [mɜːrdʒ] *of two lines etc* se rejoindre; *of companies* fusionner; **merger** COM fusion *f*

merit ['merɪt] **1** *n* mérite *m* **2** *v/t* mériter

mesh [meʃ] *of net* maille(s) *f(pl)*; *of grid* grillage *m* mess [mes] (*untidiness*) désordre *m*, pagaille *f*; (*trouble*) gâchis *m*

message ['mesɪdʒ] *also of movie etc* message *m*

messenger ['mesɪndʒər] (*courier*) messager *m*

messy ['mesɪ] *room* en désordre; *person* désordonné; *job* salissant; *divorce* pénible

metabolism [mə'tæbəlɪzm] métabolisme *m*

metal ['metl] **1** *adj* en métal **2** *n* métal *m*; metallic métallique; *paint* métallisé

metaphor ['metəfər] métaphore *f*

meteor ['miːtɪɔːr] météore *m*; meteoric *fig* fulgurant; meteorite météorite *m* or *f*

meteorological [miːtɪərə'lɑːdʒɪkl] météorologique; meteorologist météorologiste *m/f*; meteorology météorologie *f*

meter¹ ['miːtər] *for gas, electricity* compteur *m*; (*parking* ~) parcmètre *m*

meter² ['miːtər] *unit of length* mètre *m*

method ['meθəd] méthode *f*; methodical méthodique

meticulous [mə'tɪkjuləs] méticuleux

metre ['miːtə(r)] *Br* → **meter²**

metropolis [mə'trɑːpəlɪs] métropole *f*; metropolitan citadin; *area* urbain

mew [mjuː] → **miaow**

Mexican ['meksɪkən] **1** *adj*

mexicain **2** *n* Mexicain(e) *m(f)*; Mexico Mexique *m*

miaow [mɪaʊ] **1** *n* miaou *m* **2** *v/i* miauler

mice [maɪs] *pl* → **mouse**

'microchip puce *f*; microclimate microclimat *m*; microcosm microcosme *m*; microorganism micro-organisme *m*; microphone microphone *m*; microprocessor microprocesseur *m*; microscope microscope *m*; microscopic microscopique; microwave oven micro-ondes *m inv*

midday [mɪd'deɪ] midi *m*

middle ['mɪdl] **1** *adj* du milieu **2** *n* milieu *m*; **be in the ~ of doing sth** être en train de faire qch; middle-aged entre deux âges; middle-class bourgeois; middle class(es) classe(s) moyenne(s) *f(pl)*; Middle East Moyen-Orient *m*; middleman intermédiaire *m*; middle name deuxième prénom *m*; middleweight *boxer* poids moyen *m*

midfielder [mɪd'fiːldər] *in soccer* milieu *m* de terrain

midget ['mɪdʒɪt] miniature

'midnight minuit *m*; midsummer milieu *m* de l'été; midweek en milieu de semaine; Midwest Middle West *m*; midwife sage-femme *f*; midwinter milieu *m* de l'hiver

might¹ [maɪt] *v/aux*: **I ~ be late** je serai peut-être en retard; **you ~ have told me!**

vous auriez pu m'avertir!

might² [maɪt] *n (power)* puissance *f*

mighty ['maɪtɪ] **1** *adj* puissant **2** *adv* F *(extremely)* vachement F, très

migraine ['miːɡreɪn] migraine *f*

migrant worker ['maɪɡrənt] travailleur *m* itinérant; **migrate** migrer; **migration** migration *f*

mike [maɪk] F micro *m*

mild [maɪld] doux; *taste* léger; **mildly** doucement; *spicy* légèrement; **mildness** douceur *f*; *of taste* légèreté *f*

mile [maɪl] mile *m*; **milestone** *fig* événement *m* marquant, jalon *m*

militant ['mɪlɪtənt] **1** *adj* militant **2** *n* militant(e) *m(f)*

military ['mɪlɪterɪ] **1** *adj* militaire **2** *n:* **the ~** l'armée *f*

militia [mɪ'lɪʃə] milice *f*

milk [mɪlk] **1** *n* lait *m* **2** *v/t* traire; **milk chocolate** chocolat *m* au lait; **milkshake** milk-shake *m*

mill [mɪl] *for grain* moulin *m*; *for textiles* usine *f*

millennium [mɪ'lenɪəm] millénaire *m*

milligram ['mɪlɪɡræm] milligramme *m*

millimeter, *Br* **millimetre** ['mɪlɪmiːtər] millimètre *m*

million ['mɪljən] million *m*

millionaire [mɪljə'ner] millionnaire *m/f*

mime [maɪm] mimer

mimic ['mɪmɪk] **1** *n* imitateur(-trice) *m(f)* **2** *v/t* imiter

mince [mɪns] hacher

mind [maɪnd] **1** *n* esprit *m*; **bear** *or* **keep sth in ~** ne pas oublier qch; **change one's ~** changer d'avis; **make up one's ~** se décider; **have sth on one's ~** être préoccupé par qch; **keep one's ~ on sth** se concentrer sur qch **2** *v/t (look after)* surveiller; *(heed)* faire attention à; **I don't ~ what he thinks** il peut penser ce qu'il veut, cela m'est égal; **do you ~ if I smoke?** cela ne vous dérange pas si je fume?; **~ the step!** attention à la marche! **3** *v/i:* **~!** *(be careful)* fais attention!; **never ~!** peu importe!; **I don't ~** cela m'est égal; **mind-boggling** ahurissant; **mindless** *violence* gratuit

mine¹ [maɪn] *pron* le mien, la mienne *f*; *pl* les miens, les miennes; **it's ~** c'est à moi

mine² [maɪn] *n for coal etc* mine *f*

mine³ [maɪn] **1** *n explosive* mine *f* **2** *v/t* miner; **minefield** MIL champ *m* de mines; *fig* poudrière *f*; **miner** mineur *m*

mineral ['mɪnərəl] minéral *m*; **mineral water** eau *f* minérale

'minesweeper NAUT dragueur *m* de mines

mingle ['mɪŋɡl] *of sounds* se

mélanger; *at party* se mêler
(aux gens)
mini ['mɪnɪ] *skirt* minijupe *f*
miniature ['mɪnɪtʃər] miniature
minimal ['mɪnɪməl] minime;
minimalism minimalisme
m; **minimize** réduire au minimum; (*downplay*) minimiser; **minimum 1** *adj* minimal,
minimum **2** *n* minimum *m*
mining ['maɪnɪŋ] exploitation
f minière
miniskirt minijupe *f*
minister ['mɪnɪstər] POL, REL
ministre *m*; **ministerial** ministériel
mink [mɪŋk] vison *m*
minor ['maɪnər] **1** *adj* mineur;
pain léger **2** *n* LAW mineur(e)
m(f); **minority** minorité *f*
mint [mɪnt] *herb* menthe *f*;
chocolate chocolat *m* à la
menthe; *hard candy* bonbon
m à la menthe
minus ['maɪnəs] **1** *n* (∼ *sign*)
moins *m* **2** *prep* moins
minuscule ['mɪnəskjuːl] minuscule
minute[1] ['mɪnɪt] *n of time* minute *f*
minute[2] [maɪ'njuːt] *adj* (*tiny*)
minuscule; (*detailed*) minutieux
minute hand ['mɪnɪt] grande
aiguille *f*
minutely [maɪ'njuːtlɪ] (*in detail*) minutieusement; (*very slightly*) très légèrement
minutes ['mɪnɪts] *of meeting*

procès-verbal *m*
miracle ['mɪrəkl] miracle *m*;
miraculous miraculeux; **miraculously** par miracle
mirror ['mɪrər] **1** *n* miroir *m*;
MOT rétroviseur *m* **2** *v/t* refléter
misanthropist [mɪ'zænθrəpɪst] misanthrope *m/f*
misbehave [mɪsbə'heɪv] se
conduire mal
misbehavior, *Br* **misbehaviour** mauvaise conduite *f*
miscalculate [mɪs'kælkjuleɪt] mal calculer; **miscalculation** erreur *f* de calcul; *fig*
mauvais calcul *m*
miscarriage [mɪs'kærɪdʒ]
MED fausse couche *f*
miscellaneous [mɪsə'leɪnɪəs]
divers; *collection* varié
mischief ['mɪstʃɪf] (*naughtiness*) bêtises *fpl*; **mischievous** (*naughty*) espiègle;
(*malicious*) malveillant
misconception [mɪskən'sepʃn] idée *f* fausse
misconduct [mɪs'kɑːndʌkt]
mauvaise conduite *f*
misconstrue [mɪskən'struː]
mal interpréter
misdemeanor, *Br* **misdemeanour** [mɪsdə'miːnər] délit *m*
miser ['maɪzər] avare *m/f*
miserable ['mɪzrəbl] (*unhappy*) malheureux; *weather, performance* épouvantable
miserly ['maɪzərlɪ] avare; *sum*
dérisoire

misery ['mɪzərɪ] (*unhappiness*) tristesse *f*; (*wretchedness*) misère *f*

misfire [mɪs'faɪr] *of scheme* rater; *of joke* tomber à plat

misfit ['mɪsfɪt] *in society* marginal(e) *m(f)*

misfortune [mɪs'fɔːrtʃən] malheur *m*, malchance *f*

misguided [mɪs'gaɪdɪd] malavisé, imprudent

mishandle [mɪs'hændl] *situation* mal gérer

misinform [mɪsɪn'fɔːrm] mal informer

misinterpret [mɪsɪn'tɜːrprɪt] mal interpréter; **misinterpretation** mauvaise interprétation *f*

misjudge [mɪs'dʒʌdʒ] mal juger

mislay [mɪs'leɪ] égarer

mislead [mɪs'liːd] induire en erreur, tromper; **misleading** trompeur

mismanage [mɪs'mænɪdʒ] mal gérer; **mismanagement** mauvaise gestion *f*

misprint ['mɪsprɪnt] faute *f* typographique

mispronounce [mɪsprə'naʊns] mal prononcer; **mispronunciation** mauvaise prononciation *f*

misread [mɪs'riːd] *word, figures* mal lire; *situation* mal interpréter

misrepresent [mɪsreprɪ'zent] présenter sous un faux jour

miss¹ [mɪs]: **Miss Smith** mademoiselle Smith; **~!** mademoiselle!

miss² [mɪs] **1** *n* sp coup *m* manqué *or* raté; **2** *v/t* manquer, rater; *bus, train etc*, (*not notice*) rater; **I ~ you** tu me manques **3** *v/i* rater son coup

misshapen [mɪs'ʃeɪpən] déformé; *person, limb* difforme

missile ['mɪsaɪl] *mil* missile *m*; *stone etc* projectile *m*

missing ['mɪsɪŋ]: **be ~** *have disappeared* avoir disparu; *member of school party, one of a set etc* ne pas être là

mission ['mɪʃn] mission *f*

misspell [mɪs'spel] mal orthographier

mist [mɪst] brume *f*

mistake [mɪ'steɪk] **1** *n* erreur *f*, faute *f*; **make a ~** faire une erreur, se tromper **2** *v/t* se tromper de; **~ s.o./sth for s.o./sth** prendre qn/qch pour qn/qch d'autre; **mistaken** erroné, faux; **be ~** faire erreur, se tromper

mister ['mɪstər] → **Mr**

mistress ['mɪstrɪs] maîtresse *f*

mistrust [mɪs'trʌst] **1** *n* méfiance *f* **2** *v/t* se méfier de

misunderstand [mɪsʌndər'stænd] mal comprendre; **misunderstanding** malentendu *m*

misuse **1** [mɪs'juːs] *n* mauvais usage *m* **2** [mɪs'juːz] *v/t* faire mauvais usage de; *word* employer à tort

mitigating circumstances
['mɪtɪgeɪtɪŋ] circonstances
fpl atténuantes

mitt [mɪt] in baseball gant m;
mitten moufle f

mix [mɪks] 1 n mélange m; in
cooking: ready to use préparation f 2 v/t mélanger; cement malaxer 3 v/i socially
être sociable

♦ mix up confondre; get out
of order mélanger; be mixed
up in être mêlé à; mixed
economy, school, races mixte; reactions mitigé; mixer
for food mixeur m; drink
boisson non-alcoolisée que
l'on mélange avec certains
alcools; mixture mélange
m; medicine mixture f; mix-
-up confusion f

moan [moʊn] 1 n of pain gémissement m 2 v/i in pain gémir

mob [mɑːb] 1 n foule f 2 v/t assaillir

mobile ['moʊbəl] 1 adj mobile; be ~ have car être motorisé 2 n for decoration mobile
m; Br phone portable m; mobile home mobile home m;
mobile phone Br téléphone
m portable; mobility mobilité f

mobster ['mɑːbstər] gangster
m

mock [mɑːk] 1 adj faux, feint
2 v/t se moquer de; mockery
(derision) moquerie f; (trav-
esty) parodie f

mode [moʊd] mode m
model ['mɑːdl] 1 adj employee, husband modèle; boat,
plane modèle réduit inv 2 n
(miniature) maquette f; (pattern) modèle m; (fashion ~)
mannequin m 3 v/i for de-
signer être mannequin; for
artist, photographer poser
modem ['moʊdem] modem m
moderate 1 ['mɑːdərət] adj
also POL modéré 2
['mɑːdəreɪt] n POL modéré
m 3 ['mɑːdəreɪt] v/t modérer; moderately modéré-
ment; moderation (restraint)
modération f
modern ['mɑːdərn] moderne;
modernization modernisa-
tion f; modernize 1 v/t moderniser 2 v/i se moderniser
modest ['mɑːdɪst] modeste;
wage, amount modique;
modesty of apartment sim-
plicité f; of wage modicité
f; (lack of conceit) modestie f
modification [mɑːdɪfɪ'keɪʃn]
modification f; modify modifier
module ['mɑːdʒuːl] module
m
moist [mɔɪst] humide;
moisten humidifier; mois-
ture humidité f; moisturizer
for skin produit m hydratant
molasses [mə'læsɪz] mélasse
f
mold¹ [moʊld] n on food moisi m, moisissure(s) f(pl)
mold² [moʊld] 1 n moule m 2

v/t clay modeler; *character* façonner

moldy ['mǝʊldɪ] *food* moisi

molecule ['mɑ:lɪkju:l] molécule *f*

molest [mǝ'lest] *child, woman* agresser (sexuellement)

mollycoddle ['mɑ:lɪkɑ:dl] F dorloter

molten ['mǝʊltǝn] en fusion

mom [mɑ:m] F maman *f*

moment ['mǝʊmǝnt] instant *m*, moment *m*; **at the ~** en ce moment; **momentarily** *(for a moment)* momentanément; *(in a moment)* dans un instant; **momentary** momentané; **momentous** capital

momentum [mǝ'mentǝm] élan *m*

monarch ['mɑ:nǝrk] monarque *m*

monastery ['mɑ:nǝstrɪ] monastère *m*; **monastic** monastique

Monday ['mʌndɪ] lundi *m*

monetary ['mɑ:nǝterɪ] monétaire

money ['mʌnɪ] argent *m*; **money belt** sac *m* banane; **money market** marché *m* monétaire; **money order** mandat *m* postal

mongrel ['mʌŋgrǝl] bâtard *m*

monitor ['mɑ:nɪtǝr] **1** *n* COMPUT moniteur *m* **2** *v/t* surveiller, contrôler

monk [mʌŋk] moine *m*

monkey ['mʌŋkɪ] singe *m*; F child polisson *m*; **monkey wrench** clef *f* anglaise

monolog, *Br* **monologue** ['mɑ:nǝlɑ:g] monologue *m*

monopolize [mǝ'nɑ:pǝlaɪz] exercer un monopole sur; *fig* monopoliser; **monopoly** monopole *m*

monotonous [mǝ'nɑ:tǝnǝs] monotone; **monotony** monotonie *f*

monster ['mɑ:nstǝr] monstre *m*; **monstrosity** horreur *f*

month [mʌnθ] mois *m*; **monthly 1** *adj* mensuel **2** *adv* mensuellement **3** *n* magazine mensuel *m*

monument ['mɑ:njumǝnt] monument *m*

mood [mu:d] *(frame of mind)* humeur *f*; *(bad ~)* mauvaise humeur *f*; *of meeting, country* état *m* d'esprit; **moody** *changing moods* lunatique; *(bad-tempered)* maussade

moon [mu:n] lune *f*; **moonlight** clair *m* de lune; **moonlit** éclairé par la lune

moor [mʊr] *boat* amarrer

moose [mu:s] orignal *m*

mop [mɑ:p] **1** *n for floor* balai *m* lave-sol; *for dishes* éponge *f* à manche **2** *v/t floor* laver; *eyes, face* éponger, essuyer

◆ **mop up** éponger; MIL balayer

moral ['mɔ:rǝl] **1** *adj* moral **2** *n of story* morale *f*; **~s** moralité *f*

morale [mǝ'ræl] moral *m*

morality [məˈrælətɪ] moralité f

morbid [ˈmɔːrbɪd] morbide

more [mɔːr] 1 adj plus de; **some ~ tea?** encore un peu de thé?; **there's no ~ coffee** il n'y a plus de café; **~ and ~ students** de plus en plus d'étudiants 2 adv plus; **~ important** plus important; **~ and ~** de plus en plus; **~ or less** plus ou moins; **once ~** une fois de plus;**I don't live there any ~** je n'habite plus là-bas 3 pron plus; **do you want some ~?** est-ce que tu en veux encore or davantage?; **a little ~** un peu plus; **moreover** de plus

morgue [mɔːrg] morgue f

morning [ˈmɔːrnɪŋ] matin m; **in the ~** le matin; (tomorrow) demain matin; **tomorrow ~** demain matin; **good ~** bonjour

moron [ˈmɔːrɑːn] F crétin m

morphine [ˈmɔːrfiːn] morphine f

mortal [ˈmɔːrtl] 1 adj mortel 2 n mortel m; **mortality** condition f mortelle; (death rate) mortalité f

mortar [ˈmɔːrtər] MIL, cement mortier m

mortgage [ˈmɔːrgɪdʒ] 1 n prêt m immobilier; on own property hypothèque f 2 v/t hypothéquer

mosaic [mouˈzeɪk] mosaïque f

Moscow [ˈmɑːskau] Moscou

Moslem [ˈmʊzlɪm] 1 adj musulman 2 . n Musulman(e) m(f)

mosque [mɒsk] mosquée f

mosquito [məːsˈkiːtou] moustique m

moss [mɑːs] mousse f

most [moust] 1 adj la plupart de 2 adv (very) extrêmement, très; play, swim, eat etc le plus; **the ~ beautiful** le plus beau; **~ of all** surtout 3 pron: **~ of** la plupart de; **at (the) ~** au maximum; **make the ~ of** profiter au maximum de; **mostly** surtout

motel [mouˈtel] motel m

moth [mɑːθ] papillon m de nuit

mother [ˈmʌðər] 1 n mère f 2 v/t materner; **motherhood** maternité f; **Mothering Sunday** → **Mother's Day**; **mother-in-law** belle-mère f; **motherly** maternel; **Mother's Day** la fête des Mères; **mother tongue** langue f maternelle

motif [mouˈtiːf] motif m

motion [ˈmouʃn] 1 n (movement) mouvement m; (proposal) motion f; **motionless** immobile

motivate [ˈmoutɪveɪt] motiver; **motivation** motivation f; **motive** for crime mobile m

motor [ˈmoutər] moteur m; **motorbike** moto f; **motorcycle** moto f; **motorcyclist** motocycliste *m/f*; **motor home** camping-car *m*; **motor mechanic** mécanicien(ne) *m(f)*; **motor racing** course *f* automobile; **motor vehicle** véhicule *m* à moteur

motto ['mɔtou] devise *f*

mould *etc Br →* **mold** *etc*

mound [maund] *(hillock)* monticule *m*; *(pile)* tas *m*

mount [maunt] **1** *n (mountain)* mont *m*; *(horse)* monture *f* **2** *v/t steps, photo* monter; *horse, bicycle* monter sur; *campaign* organiser **3** *v/i* monter

◆ **mount up** s'accumuler

mountain ['mauntɪn] montagne *f*; **mountaineer** alpiniste *m/f*; **mountaineering** alpinisme *m*; **mountainous** montagneux

mourn [mɔːrn] pleurer; **mourner** parent/ami *m* du défunt; **mournful** triste, mélancolique

mouse [maus] *(pl* **mice** [maɪs]*) also* COMPUT souris *f*; **mouse mat** tapis *m* de souris

moustache *Br →* **mustache**

mouth [mauθ] bouche *f*; *of animal* gueule *f*; *of river* embouchure *f*; **mouthful** *of food* bouchée *f*; *of drink* gorgée *f*; **mouthpiece** *of instrument* embouchure *f*; *(spokesperson)* porte-parole *m inv*; **mouthwash** bain *m* de bouche; **mouthwatering** allé

chant

move [muːv] **1** *n* mouvement *m*; *in chess etc* coup *m*; *(step, action)* action *f*; *(change of house)* déménagement *m* **2** *v/t object* déplacer; *limbs* bouger; *(transfer)* transférer; *emotionally* émouvoir; **~ house** déménager **3** *v/i* bouger; *(transfer)* être transféré

◆ **move around** bouger, remuer; *from place to place* bouger, déménager

◆ **move in** emménager

movement ['muːvmənt] *also organization,* MUS mouvement *m*; **movers** déménageurs *mpl*

movie ['muːvɪ] film *m*; **go to a/the ~s** aller au cinéma; **moviegoer** amateur *m* de cinéma, cinéphile *m/f*; **movie theater** cinéma *m*

moving ['muːvɪŋ] *parts* mobile; *emotionally* émouvant

mow [mou] *grass* tondre; **mower** tondeuse *f* (à gazon)

mph [empiː'eɪtʃ] (= **miles per hour**) miles à l'heure

Mr ['mɪstər] Monsieur, M.

Mrs ['mɪsɪz] Madame, Mme

Ms [mɪz] Madame, Mme

much [mʌtʃ] **1** *adj* beaucoup de; **so ~ money** tant d'argent; **as ~ ... as ...** autant (de)... que... **2** *adv* beaucoup; **very ~** beaucoup; **too ~** trop **3** *pron* beaucoup; **nothing ~** pas grand-chose; **as ~ as ...** autant que...

429

mustard

mud [mʌd] boue f
muddle ['mʌdl] 1 n (mess) désordre m; (confusion) confusion f 2 v/t embrouiller
muddy ['mʌdɪ] boueux
muffin ['mʌfɪn] muffin m
muffle ['mʌfl] étouffer; muffler мот silencieux m
mug¹ [mʌg] n for coffee chope f; F (face) gueule f F
mug² v/t (attack) agresser
mugger ['mʌgər] agresseur m; mugging agression f; muggy lourd, moite
mule [mjuːl] animal mulet m, mule f; slipper mule f
multicultural [mʌltɪ'kʌltʃərəl] multiculturel; multilateral POL multilatéral; multimedia 1 adj multimédia 2 n multimédia m; multinational 1 adj multinational 2 n COM multinationale f
multiple ['mʌltɪpl] multiple; multiple sclerosis sclérose f en plaques
multiplex ['mʌltɪpleks] (cinéma m) multiplex m
multiplication [mʌltɪplɪ'keɪʃn] multiplication f; multiply 1 v/t multiplier 2 v/i se multiplier
multitasking [mʌltɪ'tæskɪŋ] multitâche m; for persons multiplicité f des tâches
mumble ['mʌmbl] 1 n marmonnement m 2 v/t & v/i marmonner
munch [mʌntʃ] mâcher
municipal [mjuː'nɪsɪpl] municipal

mural ['mjʊrəl] peinture f murale
murder ['mɜːrdər] 1 n meurtre m 2 v/t person assassiner; song massacrer; murderer meurtrier(-ière) m(f)
murky ['mɜːrkɪ] also fig trouble
murmur ['mɜːrmər] 1 n murmure m 2 v/t murmurer
muscle ['mʌsl] muscle m; muscular pain musculaire; person musclé
museum [mjuː'zɪəm] musée m
mushroom ['mʌʃrʊm] 1 n champignon m 2 v/i fig proliférer
music ['mjuːzɪk] musique f; in written form partition f; musical 1 adj musical; person musicien 2 n comédie f musicale; musician musicien(ne) m(f)
mussel ['mʌsl] moule f
must [mʌst] 1 v/aux ◇ necessity devoir; I ~ be on time je dois être à l'heure, il faut que je sois (subj) à l'heure; I ~n't be late je ne dois pas être en retard, il ne faut pas que je sois en retard
◇ probability devoir; it ~ be about 6 o'clock il doit être environ six heures
mustache [mə'stæʃ] moustache f
mustard ['mʌstərd] moutarde f

musty ['mʌstɪ] *room* qui sent
le renfermé; *smell* de renfermé
mutilate ['mjuːtɪleɪt] mutiler
mutiny ['mjuːtɪnɪ] **1** *n* mutine-
rie *f* **2** *v/i* se mutiner
mutter ['mʌtər] marmonner
mutual ['mjuːtʃʊəl] (*reciprocal*) mutuel; (*common*) commun
muzzle ['mʌzl] **1** *n of animal*
museau *m*; *for dog* muselière
f **2** *v/t*: ~ *the press* bâillonner

la presse
my [maɪ] mon *m*, ma *f*; *pl* mes;
myself moi-même; *reflexive*
me; *before vowel* m'; *after
prep* moi; **I hurt** ~ je me suis
blessé
mysterious   [mɪ'stɪrɪəs]
mystérieux;   **mysteriously**
mystérieusement; **mystery**
mystère *m*; **mystify** rendre
perplexe; *of tricks* mystifier
myth [mɪθ] *also fig* mythe *m*;
mythical mythique

N

nag [næg] **1** *v/i of person* faire
des remarques continuelles **2**
v/t harceler; **nagging** *pain*
obsédant; **I have this** ~
doubt that ... je n'arrive
pas à m'empêcher de penser
que ...
nail [neɪl] *for wood* clou *m*; *on
finger, toe* ongle *m*; **nail polish** vernis *m* à ongles; **nail
polish remover** dissolvant *m*
naive [naɪ'iːv] naïf
naked ['neɪkɪd] nu
name [neɪm] **1** *n* nom *m*;
what's your ~? comment
vous appelez-vous? **2** *v/t* appeler; **namely** à savoir;
namesake homonyme *m/f*
nanny ['nænɪ] nurse *f*
nap [næp] sieste *f*
napkin ['næpkɪn] (*table* ~) serviette *f* (de table); (*sanitary*~)
serviette *f* hygiénique

narcotic [nɑːr'kɑːtɪk] stupéfiant *m*
narrate ['næreɪt] raconter;
narrative 1 *adj poem, style*
narratif **2** *n* (*story*) récit *m*;
narrator narrateur(-trice)
m(f)
narrow ['nærou] étroit; *victory* serré; **narrowly** *win* de justesse; *escape* de peu; **narrow-minded** étroit d'esprit
nasty ['næstɪ] *person, thing to
say* méchant; *smell* nauséa-
bond; *weather, cut, wound,
disease* mauvais
nation ['neɪʃn] nation *f*; **national 1** *adj* national **2** *n* national *m*, ressortissant *m*; **national anthem** hymne *m* national; **national debt** dette *f*
publique; **nationalism** na-
tionalisme *m*; **nationality** nationalité *f*; **nationalize** in-

dustry etc nationaliser
native ['neɪtɪv] 1 adj natal 2 n
natif(-ive) m(f); (tribesman)
indigène m; Native Ameri-
can 1 adj amérindien 2 n
Amérindien(ne) m(f)
NATO [(= **North At-
lantic Treaty Organization**)
OTAN f (= Organisation
du traité de l'Atlantique
Nord)
natural ['nætʃrəl] naturel; nat-
uralist naturaliste m/f; natu-
ralize: **become ~d** se faire
naturaliser; **naturally** (of
course) bien entendu; be-
have, speak naturellement,
avec naturel; (by nature) de
nature; **nature** nature f; nature reserve réserve f natu-
relle
naughty ['nɔːtɪ] vilain; photograph , word etc coquin
nausea ['nɔːzɪə] nausée f;
nauseate fig écœurer; nau-
seating écœurant; nause-
ous: **feel ~** avoir la nausée
nautical ['nɔːtɪkl] nautique,
marin
naval ['neɪvl] naval, maritime;
history de la marine
navel ['neɪvl] nombril m
navigate ['nævɪgeɪt] also
COMPUT naviguer; in car diriger; **navigation** navigation f;
in car indications fpl; navi-
gator navigateur m
navy ['neɪvɪ] marine f; navy
blue 1 adj bleu marine inv
2 n bleu m marine

near [nɪr] 1 adv près; **come
~er** approche-toi 2 prep près
de 3 adj proche; **in the ~ future** dans un proche avenir;
nearby tout près; **nearly**
presque; **I ~ lost it** j'ai failli
le perdre; **near-sighted**
myope
neat [niːt] room, desk bien
rangé; person ordonné; in appearance soigné; whiskey etc
sec; solution ingénieux; F
(terrific) super inv F
necessarily ['nesəserəlɪ] né-
cessairement, forcément;
necessary nécessaire; **it is
~ to ...** il faut ...; necessity
nécessité f
neck [nek] cou m; of clothing
col m; **necklace** collier m;
neckline of dress encolure
f; **necktie** cravate f
née [neɪ] née
need [niːd] 1 n besoin m; **if ~
be** si besoin est; **in ~** dans le
besoin 2 v/t avoir besoin de;
you don't ~ to wait vous
n'êtes pas obligés d'attendre;
I ~ to talk to you il faut que je
te parle
needle ['niːdl] aiguille f; nee-
dlework travaux mpl d'ai-
guille
needy ['niːdɪ] nécessiteux
negative ['negətɪv] négatif
neglect [nɪ'glekt] 1 n négligence f; state abandon m 2
v/t négliger; neglected négligé
negligence ['neglɪdʒəns] né-

gligence *f*; **negligent** négligent; **negligible** *quantity* négligeable

negotiable [nɪˈgəʊʃəbl] négociable; **negotiate 1** *v/i* négocier **2** *v/t deal* négocier; *obstacles* franchir; *bend in road* négocier, prendre; **negotiation** négociation *f*; **negotiator** négociateur(-trice) *m(f)*

neighbor [ˈneɪbər] voisin(e) *m(f)*; **neighborhood** *in town* quartier *m*; **neighboring** *house, state* voisin; **neighborly** aimable

neighbour *etc Br* → **neighbor** *etc*

neither [ˈniːðər] **1** *adj:* ~ **player** aucun(e) des deux joueurs **2** *pron* ni l'un ni l'autre **3** *adv:* ~ **...** **nor ...** ni ... ni ... **4** *conj:* ~ **do/can I** moi non plus

neon light [ˈniːɑːn] néon *m*

nephew [ˈnefjuː] neveu *m*

nerve [nɜːrv] nerf *m*; (*courage*) courage *m*; (*impudence*) culot *m* F; **nerve-racking** angoissant, éprouvant; **nervous** nerveux; **nervous breakdown** dépression *f* nerveuse; **nervousness** nervosité *f*; **nervy** (*fresh*) effronté, culotté F

nest [nest] nid *m*

net[1] [net] *n for fishing, tennis etc* filet *m*; *Internet* Net *m*

net[2] [net] *adj price etc* net

nettle [ˈnetl] ortie *f*

'network *also* COMPUT réseau *m*

neurologist [nʊˈrɑːlədʒɪst] neurologue *m/f*

neurosis [nʊˈrəʊsɪs] névrose *f*; **neurotic** névrosé, obsédé

neuter [ˈnuːtər] *animal* castrer; **neutral 1** *adj* neutre **2** *n gear* point *m* mort; **neutrality** neutralité *f*; **neutralize** neutraliser

never [ˈnevər] jamais; *I've* ~ *been to New York* je ne suis jamais allé à New York; **nevertheless** néanmoins

new [nuː] *(not used)* neuf; **newborn** nouveau-né; **newcomer** nouveau venu *m*, nouvelle venue *f*; **newly** (*recently*) récemment, nouvellement; **newly-weds** jeunes mariés *mpl*

news [nuːz] nouvelle *f(pl)*; *on TV, radio* informations *fpl*; **newscast** TV journal *m* télévisé; **newscaster** TV présentateur(-trice) *m(f)*; **news flash** flash *m* d'information; **newspaper** journal *m*; **newsreader** TV *etc* présentateur(-trice) *m(f)*; **news report** reportage *m*; **newsstand** kiosque *m* à journaux; **newsvendor** vendeur(-euse) *m(f)* de journaux

'New Year nouvel an *m*; *Happy* ~*!* Bonne année!; **New Year's Day** jour *m* de l'An; **New Year's Eve** la Saint-Sylvestre

next [nekst] **1** *adj* prochain; *the* ~ *month* le mois suivant

2 *adv* (*after*) ensuite, après; ~ **to** là côté de; **next-door 1** *adj* neighbor d'à côté **2** *adv* live à côté; **next of kin** parent *m* le plus proche

nibble ['nɪbl] *cheese* grignoter; *ear* mordiller

nice [naɪs] agréable; *person also* sympathique; *house, hair* beau; *that's very ~ of you* c'est très gentil de votre part; **nicely** *written, presented* bien; (*pleasantly*) agréablement

niche [niːʃ] *in market* créneau *m*; (*special position*) place *f*

nick [nɪk] (*cut*) coupure *f*

nickel ['nɪkl] MIN nickel *m*; *coin* pièce *f* de cinq cents

'nickname surnom *m*

niece [niːs] nièce *f*

night [naɪt] nuit *f*; (*evening*) soir *m*; **11 o'clock at ~** onze heures du soir; **during the ~** pendant la nuit; **good ~** going to bed bonsoir; leaving office, friends' house etc bonsoir; **nightcap** *drink* boisson *f* du soir; **nightclub** boîte *f* de nuit; **nightdress** chemise *f* de nuit; **night flight** vol *m* de nuit; **nightlife** vie *f* nocturne; **nightly 1** *adj* de toutes les nuits; *in evening* de tous les soirs **2** *adv* toutes les nuits; *in evening* tous les soirs; **nightmare** *also fig* cauchemar *m*; **night porter** gardien *m* de nuit; **night school** cours *mpl* du soir; **night shift**

équipe *f* de nuit; **nightshirt** chemise *f* de nuit (d'homme); **nightspot** boîte *f* de nuit); **nighttime**: *at ~, in the ~* la nuit

nimble ['nɪmbl] agile; *mind* vif

nine [naɪn] neuf; **nineteen** dix-neuf; **nineteenth** dix-neuvième; **ninetieth** quatre-vingt-dixième; **ninety** quatre-vingt-dix; **ninth** neuvième

nip [nɪp] (*pinch*) pincement *m*; (*bite*) morsure *f*

nipple ['nɪpl] mamelon *m*

nitrogen ['naɪtrədʒn] azote *m*

no [noʊ] **1** *adv* non **2** *adj* aucun, pas de; *there's ~ coffee left* il ne reste plus de café; *I have ~ money* je n'ai pas d'argent; *~ smoking* défense de fumer

noble ['noʊbl] noble

nobody ['noʊbədɪ] personne; *~ knows* personne ne le sait; *there was ~ at home* il n'y avait personne

no-brainer [noʊ'breɪnər] jeu *m* d'enfant; *the math test was a ~* le devoir de maths était super facile

nod [nɑːd] **1** *n* signe *m* de tête **2** *v/i* faire un signe de tête

noise [nɔɪz] bruit *m*; **noisy** bruyant; *be ~ of person* faire du bruit

nominal ['nɑːmɪnl] nominal; (*token*) symbolique

nominate ['nɑːmɪneɪt] (*ap-*

point) nommer; **nomination** (*appointment*) nomination *f*; (*person proposed*) candidat *m*; **nominee** candidat *m*

nonalco'holic non alcoolisé

noncommissioned 'officer [ˈnɑːnkəmɪʃnd] sous-officier *m*

noncommittal [nɑːnkəˈmɪtl] évasif

nondescript [ˈnɑːndɪskrɪpt] quelconque; *color* indéfinissable

none [nʌn] aucun(e); *there is/ are ~ left* il n'en reste plus

nonentity [nɑːnˈentɪtɪ] être *m* insignifiant

none'xistent inexistant

non'fiction ouvrages *mpl* non littéraires

noninter'ference non-ingérence *f*

noninter'vention non intervention *f*

no-'nonsense *approach* pragmatique

non'payment non-paiement *m*

nonpol'luting non polluant

non'resident non-résident *m*; *in hotel* client *m* de passage

nonre'turnable non remboursable

nonsense [ˈnɑːnsəns] absurdité(s) *f(pl)*; *don't talk ~* ne raconte pas n'importe quoi

non'smoker non-fumeur (-euse) *m(f)*

non'standard non standard *inv*; *use of word* impropre

non'stop 1 *adj flight, train* direct; *chatter* incessant **2** *adv fly, travel* sans escale; *chatter, argue* sans arrêt

non'union non syndiqué

non'violence non-violence *f*; **nonviolent** non-violent

noodles [ˈnuːdlz] nouilles *fpl*

noon [nuːn] midi *m*

no-one → **nobody**

noose [nuːs] nœud *m* coulant

nor [nɔːr] ni; *~ do I* moi non plus

norm [nɔːrm] norme *f*; **normal** normal; **normality** normalité *f*; **normally** normalement

north [nɔːrθ] **1** *n* nord *m* **2** *adj* nord *inv*; *wind* du nord **3** *adv travel* vers le nord; **North America** Amérique *f* du Nord; **North American 1** *adj* nord-américain **2** *n* Nord-Américain(e) *m(f)*; **northeast** nord-est *m*; **northerly** *wind* du nord; *direction* vers le nord; **northern** du nord; **northerner** habitant *m* du Nord; **North Korea** Corée *f* du Nord; **North Korean 1** *adj* nord-coréen **2** *n* Nord-Coréen(ne) *m(f)*; **North Pole** pôle *m* Nord; **northward** *travel* vers le nord; **northwest** nord-ouest *m*

nose [nouz] nez *m*
♦ **nose around** F fouiner

nostalgia [nɑːˈstældʒə] nostalgie *f*; **nostalgic** nostalgique

nostril ['nɑ:strəl] narine f

nosy ['nouzi] F curieux

not [nɑ:t] pas; ~ **now** pas maintenant; ~ **there** pas là; ~ **a lot** pas beaucoup *with verbs* ne ... pas; *it's ~ allowed* ce n'est pas permis; *he didn't help* il n'a pas aidé

notable ['noutəbl] notable

notch [nɑ:tʃ] entaille f

note [nout] MUS, *written* note f; (*short letter*) mot m; **notebook** carnet m; COMPUT ordinateur m bloc-notes; **noted** célèbre; **notepad** bloc-notes m; **notepaper** papier m à lettres

nothing ['nʌθɪŋ] rien; *she said* ~ elle n'a rien dit; ~ *but* rien que; ~ *much* pas grand-chose; *for* ~ (*for free*) gratuitement; (*for no reason*) pour un rien

notice ['noutɪs] **1** n *on bulletin board, in street* affiche f; (*advance warning*) préavis m; *in newspaper* avis m; *to leave job* démission f; *to leave house* préavis m; *at short* ~ dans un délai très court; *until further* ~ jusqu'à nouvel ordre; *hand in one's* ~ *to employer* donner sa démission; *take no* ~ *of* ne pas faire attention à **2** v/t remarquer; **noticeable** visible

notify ['noutɪfaɪ]: ~ *s.o. of sth* signaler qch à qn

notion ['nouʃn] idée f

notorious [nou'tɔ:rɪəs] notoire

noun [naun] substantif m, nom m

nourishing ['nʌrɪʃɪŋ] nourrissant; **nourishment** nourriture f

novel ['nɑ:vl] roman m; **novelist** romancier(-ière) m(f); **novelty** nouveauté f

November [nou'vembər] novembre m

novice ['nɑ:vɪs] (*beginner*) novice m, débutant m

now [nau] maintenant; ~ *and again*, ~ *and then* de temps à autre; *by* ~ maintenant; **nowadays** aujourd'hui, de nos jours

nowhere ['nouwer] nulle part; *it's* ~ *near finished* c'est loin d'être fini

nuclear ['nu:klɪər] nucléaire; **nuclear energy** énergie f nucléaire; **nuclear power** énergie f nucléaire; POL puissance f nucléaire; **nuclear power station** centrale f nucléaire; **nuclear reactor** réacteur m nucléaire; **nude** [nu:d] **1** adj nu **2** n *painting* nu m; *in the* ~ tout nu

nudge [nʌdʒ] *person* donner un coup de coude à; *parked car* pousser (un peu)

nudist ['nu:dɪst] nudiste m/f

nuisance ['nu:sns] peste f, plaie f F; *event, task* ennui m; *make a* ~ *of o.s.* être embêtant F

null and 'void [nʌl] nul et non avenu

numb [nʌm] engourdi; *emotionally* insensible

number ['nʌmbər] **1** *n* nombre *m*; *symbol* chiffre *m*; *of hotel room, phone* ∼ *etc* numéro *m* **2** *v/t* (*put a* ∼ *on*) numéroter

numeral ['nu:mərəl] chiffre *m*

numerous ['nu:mərəs] nombreux

nun [nʌn] religieuse *f*

nurse [nɜːrs] infirmier(-ière) *m(f)*; **nursery** maternelle *f*; *for plants* pépinière *f*; **nurs-**

ery rhyme comptine *f*; **nursery school** école *f* maternelle; **nursing profession** *f* d'infirmier; **nursing home** *for old people* maison *f* de retraite

nut [nʌt] (*walnut*) noix *f*; (*Brazil*) noix *f* du Brésil; (*hazelnut*) noisette *f*; (*peanut*) cacahuète *f*; *for bolt* écrou *m*; **nutcrackers** casse-noisettes *m inv*

nutrient ['nu:trɪənt] élément *m* nutritif; **nutrition** nutrition *f*; **nutritious** nutritif

nuts [nʌts] F (*crazy*) fou

O

oar [ɔːr] aviron *m*, rame *f*

oasis [ou'eɪsɪs] *also fig* oasis *f*

oath [ouθ] LAW serment *m*; (*swearword*) juron *m*

oats [outs] *npl* avoine *f*

obedience [ou'biːdɪəns] obéissance *f*; **obedient** obéissant; **obediently** docilement

obese [ou'biːs] obèse; **obesity** obésité *f*

obey [ou'beɪ] obéir à

obituary [ou'bɪtʃuerɪ] nécrologie *f*

object[1] ['aːbdʒɪkt] *n* (*thing*) objet *m*; (*aim*) objectif *m*; GRAM complément *m* d'objet

object[2] [əb'dʒekt] *v/i* protester; *if nobody* ∼*s* si personne n'y voit d'objection

objection [əb'dʒekʃn] objection *f*; **objectionable** (*unpleasant*) désagréable; **objective 1** *adj* objectif **2** *n* objectif *m*; **objectively** objectivement; **objectivity** objectivité *f*

obligation [aːblɪ'geɪʃn] obligation *f*; **obligatory** obligatoire; **obliging** serviable, obligeant

oblique [ə'bliːk] **1** *adj* *reference* indirect; *line* oblique **2** *n in punctuation* barre *f* oblique

obliterate [ə'blɪtəreɪt] *city* détruire; *memory* effacer

oblivion [ə'blɪvɪən] oubli *m*

oblong ['aːblaːŋ] **1** *adj* oblong **2** *n* rectangle *m*

obscene [əb'siːn] obscène; *salary, poverty* scandaleux; **obscenity** obscénité f

obscure [əb'skjʊr] obscur; *village* inconnu; **obscurity** obscurité f

observant [əb'zɜːrvnt] observateur; **observation** observation f; **observer** observer; **observer** observateur(-trice) m(f)

obsess [ɑːb'ses]: **be ~ed with** être obsédé par; **obsession** obsession f (**with** de)

obsolete ['ɑːbsəliːt] obsolète

obstacle ['ɑːbstəkl] *also fig* obstacle m

obstetrician [ɑːbstə'trɪʃn] obstétricien(ne) m(f); **obstetrics** obstétrique f

obstinacy ['ɑːbstɪnəsɪ] entêtement m, obstination f; **obstinate** obstiné

obstruct [əb'strʌkt] *road* bloquer, obstruer; *investigation* entraver; *police* gêner; **obstruction** *on road etc* obstacle m; **obstructive** *behavior* qui met des bâtons dans les roues; *tactics* obstructionniste

obtain [əb'teɪn] obtenir; **obtainable** *products* disponible

obtuse [əb'tuːs] *fig* obtus

obvious ['ɑːbvɪəs] évident, manifeste; **obviously** manifestement; **~!** évidemment!

occasion [ə'keɪʒn] occasion f; **occasional** occasionnel; **occasionally** de temps en temps, occasionnellement

occupant ['ɑːkjʊpənt] occupant(e) m(f); **occupation** (*job*) métier m; (*of country*) occupation f; **occupy** occuper

occur [ə'kɜːr] avoir lieu, se produire; **occurrence** (*event*) fait m

ocean ['oʊʃn] océan m

o'clock [ə'klɑːk]: **at five ~** à cinq heures

October [ɑːk'toʊbər] octobre m

odd [ɑːd] (*strange*) bizarre; (*not even*) impair; **oddball** F original m; **odds and ends** petites choses fpl, bricoles fpl; **odds-on**: **the ~ favorite** le grand favori

odometer [oʊ'dɑːmətər] odomètre m

odor, Br **odour** ['oʊdər] odeur f

of [ɑːv] de; **the name ~ the street/hotel** le nom de la rue/de l'hôtel; **the color ~ the paper** la couleur du papier; **five minutes ~ ten** dix heures moins cinq; **die ~ cancer** mourir d'un cancer; **love ~ money** l'amour de l'argent

off [ɑːf] **1** *prep*: **~ the main road** *away from* en retrait de la route principale; *near* près de la route principale; **$20 ~ the price** 20 dollars de réduction **2** *adv*: **be ~** *of light, TV, machine* être éteint; *of brake* être des-

serré; *of lid* ne pas être mis;
not at work ne pas être là;
canceled être annulé; **we're
~ tomorrow** leaving nous
partons demain; **take a day
~** prendre un jour de congé;
it's 3 miles ~ c'est à 3 miles;
it's a long way ~ c'est loin 3
adj: **the ~ switch** le bouton
d'arrêt

offence *Br →* **offense**

offend [əˈfend] (*insult*) offenser; **offender** LAW délin-
quant(e) *m(f)*; **offense** LAW
minor infraction *f*; *serious*
délit *m*; **take ~ at sth** s'offenser de qch; **offensive 1** *adj
behavior, remark* offensant;
smell repoussant **2** *n* MIL offensive *f*

offer [ˈɑːfər] **1** *n* offre *f* **2** *v/t*
offrir

offhand *attitude* désinvolte

office [ˈɑːfɪs] bureau *m*; (*position*) fonction *f*; **officer** MIL
officier *m*; *in police* agent
m de police; **official 1** *adj* officiel **2** *n* *civil servant etc*
fonctionnaire *m/f*; **officially**
officiellement; (*strictly
speaking*) en théorie; **offi-
cious** trop zélé

off-line *work* hors connexion;
go ~ se déconnecter

off-peak *rates* en période
creuse

off-season basse saison *f*

offset *losses* compenser

offshore offshore

offside SP hors jeu

offspring progéniture *f*

off-the-record officieux

often [ˈɑːfn] souvent; **how ~
do you go there?** vous y allez tous les combien?

oil [ɔɪl] **1** *n* huile *f*; *petroleum*
pétrole *m* **2** *v/t* lubrifier, huiler; **oil change** vidange *f*; **oil
company** compagnie *f* pé-
trolière; **oilfield** champ *m*
pétrolifère; **oil painting**
peinture *f* à l'huile; **oil refinery** raffinerie *f* de pétrole; **oil
rig** *at sea* plate-forme *f* de forage; *on land* tour *f* de forage; **oil slick** marée *f* noire;
oil tanker *ship* pétrolier *m*;
oil well puits *m* de pétrole;
oily graisseux

ointment [ˈɔɪntmənt] pommade *f*

ok [oʊˈkeɪ]: **can I? - ~** je peux?
– d'accord; **is it ~ with you if
...?** ça te dérange si ...?;
does that look ~? est-ce
que ça va?; **that's ~ by me**
ça me va; **are you ~?** (*well,
not hurt*) ça va?

old [oʊld] vieux; (*previous*)
ancien; **how ~ is he?** quel
âge a-t-il?; **old age** vieillesse
f; **old-fashioned** démodé

olive [ˈɑːlɪv] olive *f*; **olive oil**
huile *f* d'olive

Olympic Games [əˈlɪmpɪk]
Jeux *mpl* Olympiques

omelet, *Br* **omelette** [ˈɑːmlət]
omelette *f*

ominous [ˈɑːmɪnəs] inquiétant

omission [oʊ'mɪʃn] omission
f; omit [oʊ'mɪt] omettre

on [ɑːn] **1** *prep* sur; ~ *the table*
sur la table; ~ *the bus* dans le
bus; ~ *the third floor* au
deuxième étage; ~ *TV* à la télé; ~ *Sunday* dimanche; ~
Sundays le dimanche; ~ *the 1st of ...* le premier...;
this is ~ *me* (*I'm paying*)
c'est moi qui paie; *have
you any money* ~ *you?* as-tu
de l'argent avoir toi?; ~ *his arrival* à son arrivée; ~ *his departure* au moment de son
départ; ~ *hearing this* en entendant ceci **2** *adv*: *be* ~ *of
light, TV, computer etc* être
allumé; *of brake* être serré;
of lid être mis; *of program*:
being broadcast passer; *of
meeting etc*: *be scheduled to
happen* avoir lieu; *what's* ~
tonight? *on TV etc* qu'est-ce qu'il y a ce soir?; (*what's
planned?*) qu'est-ce qu'on
fait ce soir?; *you're* ~ (*I accept*) c'est d'accord; ~ *you
go* (*go ahead*) vas-y; *talk* ~
continuer à parler; *and so*
~ et ainsi de suite; *and* ~
talk etc pendant des heures
3 *adj*: *the* ~ *switch* le bouton
marche

once [wʌns] **1** *adv* (*one time*)
une fois; (*formerly*) autrefois; ~ *again*, ~ *more* encore
une fois; *at* ~ (*immediately*)
tout de suite **2** *conj* une fois
que; ~ *you have finished*

une fois que tu auras terminé
one [wʌn] **1** *n number* un **2**
adj un(e); ~ *day* un jour **3**
pron: ~ *is bigger than the
other* l'un(e) est plus
grand(e) que l'autre; *which
~?* lequel/laquelle?; ~ *by ~,
enter, deal with* un(e) à la fois;
*the little *~*s* les petits *mpl*; *I
for* ~ pour ma part; *what
can* ~ *say?* qu'est-ce qu'on
peut dire?; *one-parent family* famille *f* monoparentale;
oneself: *hurt* ~ se faire
mal; *for* ~ pour soi *or* soi-même; *do sth by* ~ faire qch
tout seul; *one-way street*
rue *f* à sens unique; *one*-way ticket* aller *m* simple
onion ['ʌnjən] oignon *m*
'on-line en ligne; *go* ~ *to* se
connecter à; *on-line banking* (*services mpl de*) banque
f en ligne; *on-line dating*
rencontres *fpl* en ligne; *on*-line shopping* shopping *m*
en ligne
onlooker ['ɑːnlʊkər] spectateur(-trice) *m(f)*
only ['oʊnlɪ] **1** *adv* seulement;
he's ~ *six* il n'a que six ans **2**
adj unique
'on-the-job 'training formation *f* sur le tas
opaque [oʊ'peɪk] *glass* opaque
open ['oʊpən] **1** *adj* ouvert; *in
the* ~ *air* en plein air **2** *v/t* ouvrir **3** *v/i* *of shop, flower* s'ou-

vrir; **open-air** meeting, concert en plein air; **pool** découvert; **open day** journée f portes ouvertes; **open-ended** contract etc flexible; **opening** in wall etc ouverture f; of film, novel etc début m; (job) poste m (vacant); **openly** (honestly, frankly) ouvertement; **open-minded** à l'esprit ouvert, ouvert; **open ticket** billet m open

opera ['ɑːpərə] opéra m; **opera house** opéra m; **opera singer** chanteur(-euse) m(f) d'opéra

operate ['ɑːpəreɪt] **1** v/i of company opérer; of airline, bus service circuler; of machine fonctionner; MED opérer **2** v/t machine faire marcher

◆ **operate on** MED opérer

'operating room MED salle f d'opération; **operating system** COMPUT système m d'exploitation; **operation** MED opération f (chirurgicale); of machine fonctionnement m; **have an ~** se faire opérer; **operator** of machine opérateur(-trice) m(f); (tour ~) tour-opérateur m, voyagiste m; TELEC standardiste m/f

opinion [ə'pɪnjən] opinion f; **opinion poll** sondage m d'opinion

opponent [ə'pəʊnənt] adversaire m/f

opportunist [ɑːpər'tuːnɪst] opportuniste m/f; **opportunity** occasion f

oppose [ə'pəʊz] s'opposer à; **be ~d to** être opposé à

opposite ['ɑːpəzɪt] **1** adj opposé; meaning contraire **2** adv en face; **the house ~** la maison d'en face **3** prep en face de; **opposite 'number** homologue m/f

opposition [ɑːpə'zɪʃn] opposition f

oppress [ə'pres] people opprimer; **oppressive** rule oppressif; weather oppressant

optician [ɑːp'tɪʃn] opticien (-ne) m(f)

optimism ['ɑːptɪmɪzəm] optimisme m; **optimist** optimiste m/f; **optimistic** optimiste; **optimistically** avec optimisme

optimum ['ɑːptɪməm] optimal

option ['ɑːpʃn] option f; **optional** facultatif

or [ɔːr] ou; **~ else!** sinon …

oral ['ɔːrəl] exam oral; hygiene dentaire

orange ['ɔːrɪndʒ] **1** adj color orange inv **2** n fruit orange f; color orange m; **orange juice** jus m d'orange

orator ['ɔːrətər] orateur(-trice) m(f)

orbit ['ɔːrbɪt] **1** n of earth orbite f **2** v/t the earth décrire une orbite autour de

orchard ['ɔːrtʃərd] verger m

orchestra [ˈɔːrkəstrə] orchestre *m*

orchid [ˈɔːrkɪd] orchidée *f*

ordain [ɔːrˈdeɪn] ordonner

ordeal [ɔːrˈdiːl] épreuve *f*

order [ˈɔːrdər] **1** *n* ordre *m*; *for goods, in restaurant* commande *f*; **an ~ of fries** une portion de frites; **in ~ to** pour; **out of ~** (*not functioning*) hors service; **out of ~** (*not in sequence*) pas dans l'ordre **2** *v/t* (*put in sequence, proper layout*) ranger; *goods, meal* commander; **~ s.o. to do sth** ordonner à qn de faire qch **3** *v/i in restaurant* commander; **orderly 1** *adj lifestyle* bien réglé **2** *n in hospital* aide-soignant *m*

ordinarily [ɔːrdɪˈnerɪlɪ] (*as a rule*) d'habitude; **ordinary** ordinaire

ore [ɔːr] minerai *m*

organ [ˈɔːrɡən] ANAT organe *m*; MUS orgue *m*; **organic** *food, fertilizer* biologique; **organically** *grown* biologiquement; **organism** organisme *m*

organization [ɔːrɡənaɪˈzeɪʃn] organisation *f*; **organize** organiser; **organizer** *person* organisateur(-trice) *m(f)*

Orient [ˈɔːriənt] Orient *m*; **Oriental** oriental

origin [ˈɑːrɪdʒɪn] origine *f*; **original 1** *adj* (*not copied*) original; (*first*) d'origine, initial **2** *n painting etc* original

m; **originality** originalité *f*; **originally** à l'origine; (*at first*) au départ; **originate 1** *v/t idea* être à l'origine de **2** *v/i of idea, belief* émaner (**from** de) *of family* être originaire (**from** de)

ornamental [ɔːrnəˈmentl] décoratif

ornate [ɔːrˈneɪt] *architecture* chargé; *prose style* fleuri

orphan [ˈɔːrfn] orphelin(e) *m(f)*

orthodox [ˈɔːrθədɑːks] orthodoxe

orthopedic [ɔːrθəˈpiːdɪk] orthopédique

ostensibly [ɑːˈstensəblɪ] en apparence

ostentatious [ɑːstenˈteɪʃəs] prétentieux; *tape-à-l'œil inv*

ostracize [ˈɑːstrəsaɪz] frapper d'ostracisme

other [ˈʌðər] **1** *adj* autre; **the ~ day** (*recently*) l'autre jour; **every ~ day** un jour sur deux; **~ people** d'autres **2** *n*: **the ~** l'autre *m/f*

otherwise [ˈʌðərwaɪz] **1** *conj* sinon **2** *adv* (*differently*) autrement

ought [ɔːt]: **I/you ~ to know** je/tu devrais le savoir; **you ~ to have done it** tu aurais dû le faire

ounce [aʊns] once *f*

our [ˈaʊər] notre; *pl* nos; **ours** le nôtre, la nôtre; *pl* les nôtres; **it's ~** c'est à nous; **ourselves** nous-mêmes; *reflex-*

ive nous; *after prep* nous; **we
enjoyed** nous nous sommes
amusé(e)s

oust [aust] *from office* évincer

out [aut]: **be ~** *of light, fire* être
éteint; *of flower* être en
fleur; *of sun* briller; (*not at
home, not in building*) être
sorti; *of calculations* être
faux; (*be published*) être sorti; *of secret* être connu; (*no
longer in competition*) être
éliminé; (*no longer in fashion*) être passé de mode; **~
here in Dallas** ici à Dallas;
(**get**) **~!** dehors!; (**get**) **~ of
my room!** sors de ma cham-
bre!; **that's ~!** (*~ of the question*) hors de question!; **he's
~ to win** (*fully intends to*) il
est bien décidé à gagner;
outbreak *of war* déclenche-
ment *m*; *of violence* éruption
f

'**outcast** exclu(e) *m(f)*
'**outcome** résultat *m*
'**outcry** tollé *m*
out'dated démodé
out'do surpasser
out'door *activities* de plein
air; *life* au grand air; *toilet*
extérieur; **outdoors** dehors
outer ['autər] *wall etc* extérieur
'**outfit** (*clothes*) tenue *f*, ensemble *m*; (*company, organization*) boîte *f* F
out'last durer plus longtemps
que
'**outlet** *of pipe* sortie *f*; for

sales point *m* de vente; ELEC
prise *f* de courant
'**outline 1** *n* silhouette *f*; *of
plan, novel* esquisse *f* **2** *v/t
plans* ébaucher
out'live survivre à
'**outlook** (*prospects*) perspective *f*
out'number être plus nombreux que
out of ◇ *motion* de, hors de;
run ~ the house sortir de
la maison en courant
◇ *position:* **20 miles ~ De-
troit** à 32 kilomètres de Détroit
◇ *cause* par; **~ jealousy** par
jalousie
◇ *without:* **we're ~ gas** nous
n'avons plus d'essence
◇ *from a group* sur; **5 ~ 10** 5
sur 10
out-of-'date dépasse; (*expired*) périmé
'**output 1** *n of factory* production *f*, rendement *m*; COMPUT
sortie *f* **2** *v/t* (*produce*) produire
'**outrage 1** *n feeling* indignation *f*; *act* outrage *m* **2** *v/t* faire outrage à; **outrageous**
acts révoltant; *prices* scandaleux
'**outright 1** *adj winner* incontesté **2** *adv kill* sur le coup;
refuse catégoriquement
'**outset** début *m*
out'shine éclipser
'**outside 1** *adj* extérieur **2** *adv*
dehors, à l'extérieur **3** *prep* à

l'extérieur de; *(apart from)* en dehors de **4** n of building, case etc extérieur m

'out**size** *clothing* grande taille

out'**smart** → **outwit**

'out**source** externaliser

out'**standing** exceptionnel, remarquable; FIN impayé

out**stretched** ['aʊtstretʃt] hands tendu

'out**ward** ['aʊtwərd] *appearance* extérieur; **~ journey** voyage *m* aller; **outwardly** en apparence

'out**weigh** l'emporter sur

out'**wit** se montrer plus malin que

oval ['oʊvl] ovale

oven ['ʌvn] four m

over ['oʊvər] **1** prep (above) au-dessus de; *(across)* de l'autre côté de; *(more than)* plus de; *(during)* pendant; **she walked ~ the street** elle traversa la rue; **travel all ~ Brazil** voyager à travers le Brésil; **we're ~ the worst** le pire est passé; **~ and above** en plus de; **2** adv: **be ~** *(finished)* être fini; *(left)* rester; **there were just 6 ~** il n'en restait que 6; **~ In Japan** au Japon; **~ here** ici; **~ there** là-bas; **it hurts all ~** ça fait mal partout; **painted white all ~** peint tout en blanc; **it's all ~** c'est fini; **~ and again** maintes et maintes fois; **do sth ~** *(again)* refaire

qch; **overall** *measure* en tout; *(in general)* dans l'ensemble; **overalls** bleu *m* de travail

over'**awe** impressionner, intimider

over'**balance** *of person* perdre l'équilibre

over'**bearing** dominateur

'over**cast** *sky* couvert

over'**charge** faire payer trop cher à

'over**coat** pardessus m

over'**come** *difficulties* surmonter

over'**crowded** *city* surpeuplé; *train* bondé

over'**do** *(exaggerate)* exagérer; *in cooking* trop cuire; over'**done** *meat* trop cuit

'over**dose** overdose *f*

'over**draft** découvert *m*; **have an ~** être à découvert; over'**draw** *account* mettre à découvert

over**dressed** trop habillé

over'**estimate** surestimer

overex'**pose** surexposer

'over**flow**[1] *n pipe* trop-plein *m inv*

over'**flow**[2] *v/i of water* déborder

over'**haul** *engine etc* remettre à neuf; *plans* remanier

'over**head 1** *adj* au-dessus *m* **2** *n* FIN frais *mpl* généraux

over'**hear** entendre (par hasard)

over'**heated** *room* surchauffé; *engine* qui chauffe

over**joyed** [oʊvər'dʒɔɪd] ravi,

enchanté

'**overland 1** *adj transport* par terre **2** *adv travel* par voie de terre

over'lap *of tiles, periods etc* se chevaucher; *of theories* se recouper

over'load surcharger

over'look *of tall building etc* surplomber, dominer; *of window* donner sur; (*not see*) laisser passer

overly ['ouvǝrlɪ] trop

'**overnight** *travel* la nuit; *fig: change etc* du jour au lendemain

'**overpass** pont *m*

over'power *physically* maîtriser

overpriced [ouvǝr'praɪst] trop cher

overrated [ouvǝ'reɪtɪd] surfait

over'ride *decision etc* annuler; *technically* forcer; **overriding** *concern* principal

over'rule *decision* annuler

over'seas à l'étranger

over'see superviser

over'shadow *fig* éclipser

'**oversight** omission *f*

over'sleep se réveiller en retard

over'state exagérer; **overstatement** exagération *f*

over'take *also Br* MOT dépasser

over'throw[1] *v/t government* renverser

'**overthrow**[2] *n of government* renversement *m*

'**overtime 1** *n* SP temps *m* supplémentaire **2** *adv:* **work ~** faire des heures supplémentaires

over'turn 1 *v/t also government* renverser **2** *v/i of vehicle* se retourner

'**overview** vue *f* d'ensemble

overwhelming [ouvǝr'welmɪŋ] *feeling* irrépressible; *relief* énorme; *majority* écrasant

over'work 1 *n* surmenage *m* **2** *v/i* se surmener

owe [ou] devoir (**s.o.** à qn); **owing to** à cause de

owl [aul] hibou *m*, chouette *f*

own[1] [oun] *v/t* posséder

own[2] [oun] *pron: an apartment of my ~* un appartement à moi; **on my/his ~** tout seul

◆ **own up** avouer

owner ['ounǝr] propriétaire *m/f*; **ownership** possession *f*, propriété *f*

oxygen ['ɑːksɪdʒǝn] oxygène *m*

oyster ['ɔɪstǝr] huître *f*

ozone ['ouzoun] ozone *m*; **ozone layer** couche *f* d'ozone

P

PA [piː'eɪ] (= **personal assistant**) secrétaire m/f

pace [peɪs] (*step*) pas m; (*speed*) allure f; **pacemaker** MED stimulateur m cardiaque, pacemaker m; SP lièvre m

Pacific [pə'sɪfɪk]: **the ~ (Ocean)** le Pacifique, l'océan m Pacifique

pacifier ['pæsɪfaɪər] *for baby* sucette f; **pacifism** pacifisme m; **pacifist** pacifiste m/f; **pacify** calmer, apaiser

pack [pæk] **1** n (*back~*) sac m à dos; *of cereal, cigarettes etc* paquet m; *of cards* jeu m **2** v/t *item of clothing etc* mettre dans ses bagages; *goods* emballer; ~ **one's bag** faire sa valise **3** v/i faire ses bagages; **package 1** n (*parcel*) paquet m; *of offers etc* forfait m **2** v/t *in packs* conditionner; *idea, project* présenter; **packaging** *of product* conditionnement m; *material* emballage m; *of idea* présentation f; **packet** paquet m

pact [pækt] pacte m

pad¹ [pæd] **1** n *protective* tampon m de protection; *over wound* tampon m; *for writing* bloc m **2** v/t *with material* rembourrer; *speech, report* délayer

pad² [pæd] v/i (*move quietly*) marcher à pas feutrés

padding ['pædɪŋ] *material* rembourrage m; *in speech etc* remplissage m

paddle ['pædl] **1** n *for canoe* pagaie f **2** v/i *in canoe* pagayer

paddock ['pædək] paddock m

padlock ['pædlɑːk] cadenas m

page¹ [peɪdʒ] n *of book etc* page f

page² [peɪdʒ] (*call*) (faire) appeler

pager ['peɪdʒər] pager m, radiomessageur m; *for doctor* bip m

paid em'ployment travail m rémunéré

pain [peɪn] douleur f; **be in ~** souffrir; **painful** *arm, leg etc* douloureux; (*distressing*) pénible; (*laborious*) difficile; **painfully** (*extremely, acutely*) terriblement; **painkiller** analgésique m; **painstaking** minutieux

paint [peɪnt] **1** n peinture f **2** v/t peindre; **paintbrush** pinceau m; **painter** peintre m; **painting** *activity* peinture f; **picture** tableau m; **paintwork** peinture f

pair [per] paire f; *of people, animals* couple m; **a ~ of pants** un pantalon

pajamas [pə'dʒɑːməz] pyjama *m*

Pakistan [pækɪ'stɑːn] Pakistan *m*; Pakistani **1** *adj* pakistanais **2** *n* Pakistanais(e) *m(f)*

pal [pæl] F (*friend*) copain *m*, copine *f*

palace ['pælɪs] palais *m*

palate ['pælət] ANAT, *fig* palais *m*

palatial [pə'leɪʃl] somptueux

pale [peɪl] pâle; **go ~** pâlir

Palestine ['pæləstaɪn] Palestine *f*; Palestinian **1** *adj* palestinien **2** *n* Palestinien(ne) *m(f)*

pallet ['pælɪt] palette *f*

pallor ['pælər] pâleur *f*

palm [pɑːm] *of hand* paume *f*

palm tree palmier *m*

paltry ['pɔːltrɪ] dérisoire

pamper ['pæmpər] gâter

pamphlet ['pæmflɪt] *for information* brochure *f*; *political* tract *m*

pan [pæn] casserole *f*; *for frying* poêle *f*

pancake ['pænkeɪk] crêpe *f*

pandemonium [pændɪ'moʊnɪəm] désordre *m*

pane [peɪn] **a ~ of glass** un carreau

panel ['pænl] panneau *m*; *people* comité *m*; *on TV program* invités *mpl*

paneling, *Br* panelling lambris *m*

panic ['pænɪk] **1** *n* panique *f* **2** *v/i* paniquer; **panic-stricken**

affolé, pris de panique

panorama [pænə'rɑːmə] panorama *m*; panoramic panoramique

pant [pænt] *of person* haleter

panties ['pæntɪz] culotte *f*

pantihose → **pantyhose**

pants [pænts] pantalon *m*

pantyhose ['pæntɪhoʊz] collant *m*

papal ['peɪpəl] papal

paparazzi [pæpə'rætsiː] paparazzi *m/f*

paper ['peɪpər] **1** *n* papier *m*; (*news~*) journal *m*; (*wall~*) papier *m* peint; *academic article m*, exposé *m*; (*examination ~*) épreuve *f*; **~s** (*documents*) documents *mpl*; (*identity ~s*) papiers *mpl* **2** *adj* (*made of ~*) en papier **3** *v/t room* tapisser; **paperback** livre *m* de poche; **paper clip** trombone *m*; **paperwork** tâches *fpl* administratives

parachute ['pærəʃuːt] **1** *n* parachute *m* **2** *v/i* sauter en parachute **3** *v/t troops, supplies* parachuter

parade [pə'reɪd] **1** *n* (*procession*) défilé *m* **2** *v/i of soldiers* défiler; *showing off* parader

paradise ['pærədaɪs] REL, *fig* paradis *m*

paradox ['pærədɑːks] paradoxe *m*; **paradoxical** paradoxal; **paradoxically** paradoxalement

paragraph ['pærəgræf] paragraphe *m*

parallel ['pærəlel] **1** *n* parallèle *f*; GEOG, *fig* parallèle *m* **2** *adj also fig* parallèle **3** *v/t* (*match*) égaler

paralysis [pə'ræləsɪs] *also fig* paralysie *f*; **paralyze** paralyser

paramedic [pærə'medɪk] auxiliaire *m/f* médical(e)

parameter [pə'ræmɪtər] paramètre *m*

paramilitary [pærə'mɪlɪterɪ] **1** *adj* paramilitaire **2** *n* membre *m* d'une organisation paramilitaire

paranoia [pærə'nɔɪə] paranoïa *f*; **paranoid** paranoïaque

paraphrase ['pærəfreɪz] paraphraser

parasite ['pærəsaɪt] *also fig* parasite *m*

parasol ['pærəsɔːl] parasol *m*

paratrooper ['pærətruːpər] parachutiste *m*, para *m* (F

parcel ['pɑːrsl] colis *m*, paquet *m*

pardon ['pɑːrdn] **1** *n* LAW grâce *f*; **I beg your ~?** (*what did you say?*) comment?; (*I'm sorry*) je vous demande pardon **2** *v/t* pardonner; LAW gracier; **~ me?** pardon?

parent ['perənt] père *m*; mère *f*; **my ~s** mes parents; **parental** parental; **parent company** société *f* mère

parent-'teacher association association *f* de parents

d'élèves

parish ['pærɪʃ] paroisse *f*

park[1] ['pɑːrk] *n* parc *m*

park[2] ['pɑːrk] MOT **1** *v/t* garer **2** *v/i* stationner, se garer; **parking** MOT stationnement *m*; **parking brake** frein *m* à main; **parking garage** parking *m* couvert; **parking lot** parking *m*; **parking meter** parcmètre *m*; **parking ticket** contravention *f*

parliament ['pɑːrləmənt] parlement *m*

parole [pə'roʊl] **1** *n* libération *f* conditionnelle **2** *v/t* mettre en liberté conditionnelle

parrot ['pærət] perroquet *m*

part [pɑːrt] **1** *n* partie *f*; *of machine* pièce *f*; *in movie* rôle *m*; *in hair* raie *f*; **take ~ in** participer à, prendre part à **2** *adv* (*partly*) en partie **3** *v/i* *of two people* se quitter, se séparer; **partial** (*incomplete*) partiel; **partially** partiellement

participant [pɑːr'tɪsɪpənt] participant(e) *m(f)*; **participate** participer (*in* à); **participation** participation *f*

particular [pər'tɪkjələr] particulier; (*fussy*) à cheval (*about* sur), exigeant; **particularly** particulièrement

partition [pɑːr'tɪʃn] (*screen*) cloison *f*; *of country* partage *m*, division *f*

partly ['pɑːrtlɪ] en partie

partner ['pɑːrtnər] partenaire

m; COM associé *m*; *in relationship* compagnon(ne) *m(f)*;
partnership COM, *in relationship* association *f*; *in particular activity* partenariat *m*
'**part-time** à temps partiel
party ['pɑːrtɪ] **1** *n* (*celebration*)
fête *f*; *for adults in the evening also* soirée *f*; POL parti
m; (*group of people*) groupe
m **2** *v/i* F faire la fête
pass [pæs] **1** *n* *for entry* laissez-passer *m inv*; SP passe *f*;
in mountains col *m* **2** *v/t*
(*go past*) passer devant; *another car* doubler, dépasser;
(*competitor*) dépasser; (*go beyond*) approuver; (*approve*) approuver;
~ *an exam* réussir (à) un examen **3** *v/i* *of time* passer; *in
exam* être reçu; SP faire une
passe; (*go away*) passer
♦ **pass away** (*euph*: *die*)
s'éteindre
♦ **pass on 1** *v/t* *information,
book* passer **2** *v/i* (*euph*:
die) s'éteindre
♦ **pass out** (*faint*) s'évanouir
♦ **pass up** *opportunity* laisser
passer
passable ['pæsəbl] *road* praticable; (*acceptable*) passable
passage ['pæsɪdʒ] (*corridor*)
couloir *m*; *from book, of
time* passage *m*
passenger ['pæsɪndʒər] pas-
sager(-ère) *m(f)*
passer-by [pæsər'baɪ] pas-
sant(e) *m(f)*
passion ['pæʃn] passion *f*;

passionate *lover* passionné;
(*fervent*) fervent, véhément
passive ['pæsɪv] **1** *adj* passif **2**
n GRAM passif *m*; **passive
smoking** tabagisme *m* passif
passport passeport *m*; **passport control** contrôle *m* des
passeport; **password** mot
m de passe
past [pæst] **1** *adj* (*former*)
passé; *the* ~ *few days* ces
derniers jours **2** *n* passé *m*;
in the ~ autrefois **3** *prep*
après; *it's* ~ *7 o'clock* il est
plus de 7 heures; *it's half* ~
two il est deux heures et
demie **4** *adv*: *run* ~ passer
en courant
pasta ['pæstə] pâtes *fpl*
paste [peɪst] **1** *n* (*adhesive*)
colle *f* **2** *v/t* (*stick*) coller
pastime ['pæstaɪm] passe-
-temps *m inv*
past par'ticiple GRAM participe *m* passé
pastry ['peɪstrɪ] *for pie* pâte *f*;
small cake pâtisserie *f*
'**past tense** GRAM passé *m*
pasty ['peɪstɪ] *complexion*
blafard
pat [pæt] **1** *n* petite tape *f* **2** *v/t*
tapoter
patch [pætʃ] **1** *n* *on clothing*
pièce *f*; (*period of time*) période *f*; (*area*) tache *f*; *go
through a bad* ~ traverser
une mauvaise passe **2** *v/t*
clothing rapiécer
♦ **patch up** (*repair*) rafistoler
F; *quarrel* régler

449

peacefully

patchy ['pætʃɪ] inégal
patent ['peɪtnt] **1** adj (obvious) manifeste **2** n for invention brevet m **3** v/t invention breveter
paternal [pə'tɜːrnl] paternel; **paternalism** paternalisme m; **paternalistic** paternaliste; **paternity** paternité f
path [pæθ] chemin m; surfaced allée f; fig voie f
pathetic [pə'θetɪk] touchant; F (very bad) pathétique
pathological [pæθə'lɑːdʒɪkl] pathologique
patience ['peɪʃns] patience f; **patient 1** adj patient **2** n patient m; **patiently** patiemment
patio ['pætɪoʊ] Br patio m
patriot ['peɪtrɪət] patriote m/f; **patriotic** person patriote; song patriotique; **patriotism** patriotisme m
patrol [pə'troʊl] **1** n patrouille f **2** v/t streets, border patrouiller dans/à; **patrol car** voiture f de police; **patrolman** agent m de police; **patrol wagon** fourgon m cellulaire
patron ['peɪtrən] of store, movie theater client(e) m(f); of artist, charity etc protecteur(-trice) m(f); **patronize** person traiter avec condescendance; **patronizing** condescendant; **patron saint** patron(ne) m(f)
pattern ['pætərn] on fabric motif m; for sewing patron

m; (model) modèle m; in events scénario m
paunch [pɔːntʃ] ventre m
pause [pɔːz] **1** n pause f **2** v/i faire une pause **3** v/t tape mettre en mode pause
pave [peɪv] paver; **pavement** (roadway) chaussée f; Br (sidewalk) trottoir m
paw [pɔː] **1** n patte f **2** v/t F tripoter
pawn [pɔːn] in chess, fig pion m
pay [peɪ] **1** n paye f, salaire m **2** v/t payer; **~ attention** faire attention **3** v/i payer; (be profitable) être rentable; **~ for** purchase payer
♦ **pay back** rembourser; (get revenge on) faire payer à
♦ **pay off 1** v/t debt rembourser; corrupt official acheter **2** v/i (be profitable) être rentable
♦ **pay up** payer
payable ['peɪəbl] payable; **pay check**, Br **pay cheque** chèque m de paie; **payday** jour m de paie; **payee** bénéficiaire m/f; **payment** paiement m; **pay phone** téléphone m public
PC [piː'siː] (= **personal computer**) P.C. m; (= **politically correct**) politiquement correct
pea [piː] petit pois m
peace [piːs] paix f; peaceful paisible, tranquille; demonstration pacifique; peace-

fully paisiblement

peach [piːtʃ] pêche *f*

peak [piːk] **1** *n of mountain* pic *m; fig* apogée *f* **2** *v/i* culminer; **peak hours** *of electricity consumption* heures *fpl* pleines; *of traffic* heures *fpl* de pointe

peanut [ˈpiːnʌt] cacahuète *f;* ***get paid ~s*** F être payé trois fois rien; **peanut butter** beurre *m* de cacahuètes

pear [per] poire *f*

pearl [pɜːrl] perle *f*

pecan [ˈpiːkən] pécan *m*

peck [pek] **1** *n* (*bite*) coup *m* de bec; (*kiss*) bise *f* (rapide) **2** *v/t* (*bite*) donner un coup de bec à; (*kiss*) embrasser rapidement

peculiar [pɪˈkjuːljər] (*strange*) bizarre; **peculiarity** bizarrerie *f;* (*special feature*) particularité *f*

pedal [ˈpedl] **1** *n of bike* pédale *f* **2** *v/i* pédaler; ***he ~ed off home*** il est rentré chez lui à vélo

peddle [ˈpedl] *drugs* faire du trafic de

pedestrian [pɪˈdestriən] piéton(ne) *m(f)*

pediatric [piːdɪˈætrɪk] pédiatrique; **pediatrician** pédiatre *m/f;* **pediatrics** pédiatrie *f*

pedicure [ˈpedɪkjur] soins *mpl* des pieds

pedigree [ˈpedɪɡriː] **1** *adj* avec pedigree **2** *n of dog, racehorse* pedigree *m; of person*

arbre *m* généalogique

pee [piː] F faire pipi F

peek [piːk] **1** *n* coup *m* d'œil (*furtif*) **2** *v/i* jeter un coup d'œil, regarder furtivement

peel [piːl] **1** *n* peau *f* **2** *v/t fruit, vegetables* éplucher, peler **3** *v/i of nose, shoulders* peler; *of paint* s'écailler

peep [piːp] → **peek**

'peephole judas *m*

peer[1] [pɪr] *n* (*equal*) pair *m; of same age group* personne *f* du même âge

peer[2] [pɪr] *v/i* regarder

peg [peɡ] *for hat, coat* patère *f; for tent* piquet *m;* ***off the ~*** de confection

pejorative [pɪˈdʒɑːrətɪv] péjoratif

pellet [ˈpelɪt] boulette *f; for gun* plomb *m*

pen[1] [pen] stylo *m*

pen[2] [pen] (*enclosure*) enclos *m*

pen[3] [pen] → **penitentiary**

penalize [ˈpiːnəlaɪz] pénaliser

penalty [ˈpenltɪ] sanction *f;* JUR peine *f; fine* amende *f;* SP pénalisation *f;* *soccer* penalty *m;* **penalty area** *soccer* surface *f* de réparation; **penalty clause** JUR clause *f* pénale; **penalty kick** *soccer* penalty *m*

pencil [ˈpensl] crayon *m* (de bois); **pencil sharpener** taille-crayon *m* inv

pendant [ˈpendənt] *necklace* pendentif *m*

penetrate ['penitreit] pénétrer; **penetration** pénétration *f*

penguin ['pengwin] manchot *m*

penicillin [peni'sılın] pénicilline *f*

peninsula [pə'nınsʊlə] presqu'île *f*

penitence ['penitəns] pénitence *f*, repentir *m*; **penitentiary** pénitencier *m*

'pen name nom *m* de plume

pennant ['penənt] fanion *m*

penniless ['penilis] sans le sou

'pen pal correspondant(e) *m(f)*

pension ['penʃn] retraite *f*, pension *f*

♦ **pension off** mettre à la retraite

pensive ['pensiv] pensif

Pentagon ['pentəgɑːn]: **the ~** le Pentagone

pentathlon [pen'tæθlən] pentathlon *m*

penthouse ['penthaʊs] penthouse *m*, appartement *m* luxueux (édifié sur le toit d'un immeuble)

pent-up ['pentʌp] refoulé

penultimate [pe'nʌltımət] avant-dernier

people ['piːpl] gens *mpl*; *(race, tribe)* peuple *m*; **10 ~** 10 personnes; **the ~** le peuple; **~ say** ... on dit...

pepper ['pepər] *spice* poivre *m*; *vegetable* poivron *m*; **pep-**

permint *candy* bonbon *m* à la menthe; *flavoring* menthe *f* poivrée

per [pɜːr] par; **~ annum** par an

perceive [pər'siːv] percevoir

percent [pər'sent] pour cent; **percentage** pourcentage *m*

perceptible [pər'septəbl] perceptible; **perceptibly** sensiblement; **perception** perception *f*; *(insight)* perspicacité *f*; **perceptive** perspicace

percolate ['pɜːrkəleit] *of coffee* passer; **percolator** cafetière *f* à pression

perfect **1** ['pɜːrfıkt] *adj* parfait **2** ['pɜːrfıkt] *n* GRAM passé *m* composé **3** [pər'fekt] *v/t* perfectionner; **perfection** perfection *f*; **perfectionist** perfectionniste *m/f*; **perfectly** parfaitement; *(totally)* tout à fait

perforated ['pɜːrfəreitid] perforé; **~ line** pointillé *m*

perform [pər'fɔːrm] **1** *v/t (carry out)* exécuter; *of actor etc* jouer **2** *v/i of actor, musician, dancer* jouer; *of machine* fonctionner; **performance** *by actor, musician etc* interprétation *f*; *(event)* représentation *f*; *of employee, company etc* résultats *mpl*; *of machine* performances *fpl*, rendement *m*; **performer** interprète *m/f*

perfume ['pɜːrfjuːm] parfum *m*

perfunctory [pər'fʌŋktəri]

sommaire

perhaps [pər'hæps] peut-être

peril ['perəl] péril *m*

perimeter [pə'rɪmɪtər] périmètre *m*

period ['pɪrɪəd] période *f*; (*menstruation*) règles *fpl*; *punctuation mark* point *m*; **periodic** périodique; **periodical** périodique *m*

peripheral [pə'rɪfərəl] **1** *adj* (*not crucial*) secondaire **2** *n* COMPUT périphérique *m*; **periphery** périphérie *f*

perish ['perɪʃ] *of rubber* se détériorer; *of person* périr; **perishable** *food* périssable

perjure ['pɜːrdʒər]: ~ **o.s.** faire un faux témoignage; **perjury** faux témoignage *m*

perm [pɜːrm] **1** *n* permanente *f* **2** *v/t*: **have one's hair~ed** se faire faire une permanente

permanent ['pɜːrmənənt] permanent; *address* fixe; **permanently** en permanence

permeate ['pɜːrmɪeɪt] *also fig* imprégner

permissible [pər'mɪsəbl] permis; **permission** permission *f*; **permissive** permissif; **permit 1** *n* permis *m* **2** *v/t* permettre (*s.o. to do* à qn de faire)

perpendicular [pɜːrpən'dɪkjələr] perpendiculaire

perpetual [pər'petʃuəl] perpétuel; **perpetually** perpétuellement

perplex [pər'pleks] laisser perplexe; **perplexity** perplexité *f*

persecute ['pɜːrsɪkjuːt] persécuter; **persecution** persécution *f*; **persecutor** persécuteur(-trice) *m(f)*

perseverance [pɜːrsɪ'vɪrəns] persévérance *f*; **persevere** persévérer

persist [pər'sɪst] persister; **persistent** *person* tenace, têtu; *questions* incessant; *rain, unemployment etc* persistant; **persistently** (*continually*) continuellement

person ['pɜːrsn] personne *f*; **personal** personnel; **personal computer** ordinateur *m* individuel; **personality** personnalité *f*; **personally** personnellement; *come, intervene* en personne; **personal organizer** organiseur *m*, agenda *m* électronique; *in book form* agenda *m*; **personal stereo** baladeur *m*; **personify** *of person* personnifier

personnel [pɜːrsə'nel] (*employees*) personnel *m*; *department* service *m* du personnel

perspective [pər'spektɪv] *in art* perspective *f*; **get sth into** ~ relativiser qch

perspiration [pɜːrspɪ'reɪʃn] transpiration *f*; **perspire** transpirer

persuade [pər'sweɪd] *person*

persuader; **persuasion** persuasion *f*; **persuasive** *person* persuasif; *argument* convaincant

perturb [pər'tɜːrb] perturber; **perturbing** perturbant

pervasive [pər'veɪsɪv] *influence, ideas* envahissant

perversion [pər'vɜːrʃn] *sexual* perversion *f*; **pervert** *sexual* pervers(e) *m*(*f*)

pessimism ['pesɪmɪzm] pessimisme *m*; **pessimist** pessimiste *m*/*f*; **pessimistic** pessimiste

pest [pest] *parasite m*; F *person* peste *f*

pester ['pestər] harceler

pesticide ['pestɪsaɪd] pesticide *m*

pet [pet] **1** *n animal* animal *m* domestique; (*favorite*) chouchou *m* F **2** *adj* préféré, favori **3** *v/t animal* caresser **4** *v/i of couple* se peloter F

petite [pə'tiːt] menu

petition [pə'tɪʃn] pétition *f*

petrify ['petrɪfaɪ] pétrifier

petrochemical [petrou'kemɪkl] pétrochimique

petrol ['petrl] *Br* essence *f*

petroleum [pɪ'trouliəm] pétrole *m*

petting ['petɪŋ] pelotage *m* F

petty ['petɪ] *person, behavior* mesquin; *details* insignifiant

pew [pjuː] banc *m* d'église

pharmaceutical [fɑːrmə'suːtɪkl] pharmaceutique; **pharmaceuticals** produits *mpl* pharmaceutiques

pharmacist ['fɑːrməsɪst] pharmacien(ne) *m*(*f*); **pharmacy** *store* pharmacie *f*

phase [feɪz] phase *f*

phenomenal [fə'nɑːmɪnl] phénoménal; **phenomenon** phénomène *m*

philanthropic [fɪlən'θrɑːpɪk] *person* philanthrope; *action* philanthropique; **philanthropist** philanthrope *m*/*f*; **philanthropy** philanthropie *f*

Philippines ['fɪlɪpiːnz]: **the ~** les Philippines *fpl*

philosopher [fɪ'lɑːsəfər] philosophe *m*/*f*; **philosophical** philosophique; *attitude etc* philosophe; **philosophy** philosophie *f*

phobia ['foubɪə] phobie *f* (*about* de)

phone [foun] **1** *n* téléphone *m* **2** *v/t* téléphoner à **3** *v/i* téléphoner; **phone book** annuaire *m*; **phone booth** cabine *f* téléphonique; **phonecall** coup *m* de fil *or* de téléphone; **phone card** télécarte *f*; **phone number** numéro *m* de téléphone

phon(e)y ['founɪ] F faux

photo ['foutou] photo *f*; **photocopier** photocopieuse *f*; **photocopy 1** *n* photocopie *f* **2** *v/t* photocopier; **photogenic** photogénique; **photograph 1** *n* photographie *f* **2** *v/t* photographier; **photog-**

rapher photographe *m/f*;
photography photographie
f

phrase [freɪz] **1** *n* expression
f; *in grammar* syntagme *m*
2 *v/t* formuler

physical ['fɪzɪkl] **1** *adj* physique **2** *n* MED visite *f* médicale; **physically** physiquement

physician [fɪ'zɪʃn] médecin
m

physicist ['fɪzɪsɪst] physicien(ne) *m(f)*; **physics** physique *f*

physiotherapist [fɪzɪoʊ'θerə-
pɪst] kinésithérapeute *m/f*;
physiotherapy kinésithérapie *f*

physique [fɪ'ziːk] physique *m*

pianist ['pɪənɪst] pianiste *m/f*;
piano piano *m*

pick [pɪk] (*choose*) choisir;
flowers, fruit cueillir

♦ **pick up 1** *v/t* prendre;
phone décrocher; *from
ground* ramasser; (*collect*)
passer prendre; *information*
recueillir; *in car* prendre; *in
sexual sense* lever F; *language, skill* apprendre; *illness* attraper; (*buy*) acheter
2 *v/i of business, economy* reprendre; *of weather* s'améliorer

picket ['pɪkɪt] **1** *n of strikers*
piquet *m* de grève **2** *v/t:* **~ a
factory** faire le piquet de
grève devant une usine

'**pickpocket** voleur *m* à la tire,

pickpocket *m*

pick-up (truck) ['pɪkʌp] pick-
-up *m*, camionnette *f*

picky ['pɪkɪ] F difficile

picnic ['pɪknɪk] **1** *n* pique-nique *m* **2** *v/i* pique-niquer

picture ['pɪktʃər] **1** *n* (*photo*)
photo *f*; (*painting*) tableau
m; (*illustration*) image *f*;
(*movie*) film *m* **2** *v/t* imaginer

picturesque [pɪktʃə'resk] pittoresque

pie [paɪ] tarte *f*; *with top* tourte *f*

piece [piːs] morceau *m*; (*component*) pièce *f*; *in board
game* pion *m*; **a ~ of advice**
un conseil; **take to ~s** démonter

♦ **piece together** *broken
plate* recoller; *evidence* regrouper

piecemeal ['piːsmiːl] petit à
petit

pier [pɪr] *Br at seaside* jetée *f*

pierce [pɪrs] (*penetrate*) transpercer; *ears* percer; **piercing**
noise, eyes perçant; *wind* pénétrant

pig [pɪg] cochon *m*, porc *m*;
(*unpleasant person*) porc *m*;

pigeon ['pɪdʒɪn] pigeon *m*; **pigeonhole** casier *m*

pigheaded ['pɪghedɪd] obstiné; **pigpen** *also fig* porcherie
f

pile [paɪl] *of books, plates etc*
pile *f*; *of sand etc* tas *m*; **a ~ of
work** F un tas de boulot F

♦ **pile up 1** *v/i of work, bills*

s'accumuler **2** v/t empiler

'pile-up MOT carambolage m

pilfering ['pɪlfərɪŋ] chapardage m F

pill [pɪl] pilule f

pillar ['pɪlər] pilier m

pillow ['pɪləʊ] oreiller m; **pillowcase** taie f d'oreiller

pilot ['paɪlət] **1** n in AVIA, NAUT pilote m **2** v/t airplane piloter

pimp [pɪmp] maquereau m, proxénète m

pimple ['pɪmpl] bouton m

PIN [pɪn] (= **personal identification number**) code m confidentiel

pin [pɪn] **1** n for sewing épingle f; in bowling quille f; (badge) badge m; fiche f **2** v/t (hold down) clouer; (attach) épingler

◆ **pin up** notice accrocher

pincers ['pɪnsərz] of crab pinces fpl; tool tenailles fpl

pinch [pɪntʃ] **1** n pincement m; of salt etc pincée f **2** v/t pincer **3** v/i of shoes serrer

pine [paɪn] tree, wood pin m; **pineapple** ananas m

pink [pɪŋk] rose

pinnacle ['pɪnəkl] fig apogée f

'pinpoint indiquer précisément; find identifier, **pins and needles** fourmillements mpl; **pin-up (girl)** pin-up f inv

pioneer [paɪə'nɪr] **1** n fig pionnier(-ière) m(f) **2** v/t lancer; **pioneering** work innovateur

pious ['paɪəs] pieux

pip [pɪp] Br of fruit pépin m

pipe [paɪp] **1** n tuyau m; for smoking pipe f **2** v/t transporter par tuyau; **pipeline** for oil oléoduc m; for gas gazoduc m

pirate ['paɪrət] **1** n pirate m **2** v/t software pirater

pissed [pɪst] P (annoyed) en rogne F; Br P (drunk) bourré

pistol ['pɪstl] pistolet m

piston ['pɪstən] piston m

pit [pɪt] (hole) fosse f; (coalmine) mine f

pitch¹ [pɪtʃ] n ton m

pitch² [pɪtʃ] **1** v/i in baseball lancer **2** v/t tent planter; ball lancer

pitcher¹ ['pɪtʃər] in baseball lanceur m

pitcher² ['pɪtʃər] container pichet m

pitfall ['pɪtfɔːl] piège m

pitiful ['pɪtɪfl] pitoyable; **pitiless** impitoyable

pittance ['pɪtns] somme f dérisoire

pity ['pɪtɪ] **1** n pitié f; **what a~!** quel dommage! **2** v/t person avoir pitié de

pizza ['piːtsə] pizza f

placard ['plækɑːrd] pancarte f

place [pleɪs] **1** n endroit m; in race, competition place f; (seat) place f; **at my/his ~** chez moi/lui; **in~of** à la place de; **take ~** avoir lieu **2** v/t (put) mettre, poser; order passer

placid

456

placid ['plæsɪd] placide
plagiarism ['pleɪdʒərɪzm]
plagiat *m*; **plagiarize** plagier
plain[1] [pleɪn] *n* plaine *f*
plain[2] [pleɪn] **1** *adj* (*clear, obvious*) clair, évident; (*not or- nate*) simple; (*not patterned*)
uni; (*not pretty*) ordinaire;
(*blunt*) franc **2** *adv* tout simplement; **plainly** (*clearly*)
manifestement; (*bluntly*)
franchement; (*simply*) simplement; **plain-spoken** direct
plaintive ['pleɪntɪv] plaintif
plan [plæn] **1** *n* plan *m*, projet
m; (*drawing*) plan *m* **2** *v/t*
(*prepare*) organiser, planifier; (*design*) concevoir **3** *v/i*
faire des projets
plane[1] [pleɪn] AVIA avion *m*
plane[2] [pleɪn] *tool* rabot *m*
planet ['plænɪt] planète *f*
plank [plæŋk] *of wood* planche *f*; *fig: of policy* point *m*
planning ['plænɪŋ] organisation *f*, planification *f*
plant[1] [plænt] **1** *n* BOT plante *f*
2 *v/t* planter
plant[2] [plænt] (*factory*) usine
f; (*equipment*) installation *f*,
matériel *m*
plantation [plæn'teɪʃn] plantation *f*
plaque [plæk] *on wall* plaque
f; *on teeth* plaque *f* dentaire
plaster ['plæstər] **1** *n* plâtre *m*
2 *v/t* wall, ceiling plâtrer
plastic ['plæstɪk] **1** *adj* en
plastique **2** *n* plastique *m*;

plastic money cartes *fpl* de
crédit; **plastic surgeon** spécialiste *m* en chirurgie esthétique; **plastic surgery** chirurgie *f* esthétique
plate [pleɪt] *for food* assiette *f*;
(*sheet of metal*) plaque *f*
plateau ['plætoʊ] plateau *m*
platform ['plætfɔːrm] (*stage*)
estrade *f*; *of railroad station*
quai *m*; *fig: political* plate-
-forme *f*
platinum ['plætɪnəm] **1** *adj* en
platine **2** *n* platine *m*
platonic [plə'tɑːnɪk] platoni-
que
platoon [plə'tuːn] *of soldiers*
section *f*
plausible ['plɔːzəbl] plausible
play [pleɪ] **1** *n* jeu *m*; *in theater,
on TV* pièce *f* **2** *v/t* jouer **3** *v/t
musical instrument* jouer de;
piece of music jouer; *game*
jouer à; *opponent* jouer contre; (*perform: Macbeth etc*)
jouer
◆ **play around** F (*be unfaithful*) coucher à droite et à gauche
◆ **play down** minimiser
player ['pleɪr] SP joueur(-euse)
m(f); (*musician*) musicien
(-ne) *m(f)*; (*actor*) acteur
(-trice) *m(f)*; **playful** enjoué;
playground aire *f* de jeu;
playing card carte *f* à jouer;
playwright dramaturge *m/f*
plaza ['plɑːzə] *for shopping*
centre *m* commercial
plc [piːelˈsiː] *Br* (= *public lim-*

ited company) S.A. *f* (= société anonyme)

plea [pliː] appel
plead [pliːd]: **~ guilty/not guilty** plaider coupable/non coupable; **~ with** supplier
pleasant ['pleznt] agréable
please [pliːz] **1** *adv* s'il vous plaît, s'il te plaît; **~ do** je vous en prie **2** *v/t* plaire à; **~ yourself** comme tu veux; **pleased** content, heureux; **~ to meet you** enchanté; **pleasing** agréable; **pleasure** plaisir *m*; **with ~** avec plaisir
pleat [pliːt] *in skirt* pli *m*
pledge [pledʒ] **1** *n* (*promise*) promesse *f*; *as guarantee* gage *m*; **Pledge of Allegiance** serment *m* d'allégeance **2** *v/t* (*promise*) promettre; *money* mettre en gage
plentiful ['plentifl] abondant; **be ~** abonder; **plenty** (*abundance*) abondance *f*; **~ of** beaucoup de
pliable ['plaɪəbl] flexible
pliers ['plaɪərz] pinces *fpl*
plight [plaɪt] détresse *f*
plod [plɒːd] (*walk*) marcher d'un pas lourd
plot[1] [plɒːt] *of land* parcelle *f*
plot[2] [plɒːt] **1** *n* (*conspiracy*) complot *m*; *of novel* intrigue *f* **2** *v/t & v/i* comploter
plotter ['plɒːtər] conspirateur(-trice) *m(f)*; COMPUT traceur *m*
plow, *Br* **plough** [plaʊ] **1** *n* charrue *f* **2** *v/t & v/i* labourer

◆ **plow back** *profits* réinvestir
pluck [plʌk] *chicken* plumer; **~ one's eyebrows** s'épiler les sourcils
plug [plʌg] **1** *n* for sink, bath bouchon *m*; *electrical* prise *f*; (*spark ~*) bougie *f* **2** *v/t hole* boucher; *new book etc* faire de la pub pour F
◆ **plug in** brancher
plumage ['pluːmɪdʒ] plumage *m*
plumber ['plʌmər] plombier *m*; **plumbing** plomberie *f*
plummet ['plʌmɪt] *of airplane* plonger, piquer; *of share prices* dégringoler
plump [plʌmp] *person, chicken* dodu; *hands, feet* potelé; *face, cheek* rond
plunge [plʌndʒ] **1** *n* plongeon *m*; *in prices* chute *f* **2** *v/i* tomber; *of prices* chuter **3** *v/t* plonger; *knife* enfoncer; **plunging** *neckline* plongeant
plural ['plʊrəl] pluriel *m*
plus [plʌs] **1** *prep* plus **2** *adj* plus de **3** *n sign* signe *m* plus; (*advantage*) plus *m* **4** *conj* (*moreover, in addition*) en plus
plush [plʌʃ] luxueux
plywood ['plaɪwʊd] contreplaqué *m*
PM [piːˈem] *Br* (= **Prime Minister**) Premier ministre
p.m. [piːˈem] (= **post meridiem**) *afternoon* de l'après-midi; *evening* du soir

pneumonia [nuː'məʊnɪə] pneumonie f

poach¹ [pəʊtʃ] cook pocher

poach² [pəʊtʃ] salmon etc braconner

poached egg [pəʊtʃt'eg] œuf m poché

P.O. Box [piː'əʊbɑːks] boîte f postale, B. P. f

pocket ['pɑːkɪt] **1** n poche f **2** adj (miniature) de poche **3** v/t empocher; **pocketbook** purse pochette f; (billfold) portefeuille m; book livre m de poche; **pocket calculator** calculatrice f de poche

podium ['pəʊdɪəm] estrade f; for winner podium m

poem ['pəʊɪm] poème m; poet poète m, poétesse f; poetic poétique; poetry poésie f

poignant ['pɔɪnjənt] poignant

point [pɔɪnt] **1** n of pencil, knife pointe f; in competition, exam point m; (purpose) objet m; (moment) moment m; in argument, discussion point m; in decimals virgule f; that's beside the ~ là n'est pas la question; be on the ~ of doing sth être sur le point de faire qch; get to the ~ en venir au fait; the ~ is ... le fait est (que)...; there's no ~ in waiting ça ne sert à rien d'attendre **2** v/i montrer (du doigt)

◆ **point out** sights montrer; advantages etc faire remarquer

◆ **point to** with finger montrer du doig; fig (indicate) indiquer

pointed ['pɔɪntɪd] remark acerbe, mordant; **pointer** for teacher baguette f; (hint) conseil m; (sign, indication) indice m; **pointless** inutile; **point of view** point m de vue

poise [pɔɪz] assurance f, aplomb m; **poised** person posé

poison ['pɔɪzn] **1** n poison m **2** v/t empoisonner; **poisonous** snake, spider venimeux; plant vénéneux

poke [pəʊk] **1** n coup m **2** v/t (prod) pousser; (stick) enfoncer

◆ **poke around** F fouiner F

poker ['pəʊkər] card game poker m

polar ['pəʊlər] polaire

pole¹ [pəʊl] of wood, metal perche f

pole² [pəʊl] of earth pôle m

police [pə'liːs] police f; **police car** voiture f de police; **policeman** gendarme m; criminal policier m; **police state** État m policier; **police station** gendarmerie f; for criminal matters commissariat m; **policewoman** femme f gendarme; criminal femme f policier

policy¹ ['pɑːləsɪ] politique f

policy² ['pɑːləsɪ] (insurance ~) police f (d'assurance)

polio ['pəʊlɪəʊ] polio f

polish ['pɒlɪʃ] **1** *n for furniture* cire *f*; *for shoes* cirage *m*; *for metal* produit *m* lustrant; (*nail ~*) vernis *m* (à ongles) **2** *v/t* faire briller, lustrer; *shoes* cirer; *speech* parfaire; **polished** *performance* impeccable

polite [pə'laɪt] poli; **politely** poliment; **politeness** politesse *f*

political [pə'lɪtɪkl] politique; **politically correct** politiquement correct; **politician** politicien *m*, homme *m*/femme *f* politique; **politics** politique *f*

poll [pəʊl] **1** *n* (*survey*) sondage *m*; **go to the ~s** (*vote*) aller aux urnes **2** *v/t people* faire un sondage auprès de; *votes* obtenir

pollen ['pɒlən] pollen *m*

pollster ['pəʊlstər] sondeur *m*

pollutant [pə'luːtənt] polluant *m*; **pollute** polluer; **pollution** pollution *f*

'polo shirt polo *m*

polyester [pɒliː'estər] polyester *m*

polystyrene [pɒlɪ'staɪriːn] polystyrène *m*

polyunsaturated [pɒliːʌn-'sætʃəreɪtɪd] polyinsaturé

pond [pɒnd] étang *m*; *artificial* bassin *m*

pontiff ['pɒntɪf] pontife *m*

pony ['pəʊnɪ] poney *m*; **ponytail** queue *f* de cheval

pool¹ [puːl] (*swimming ~*) piscine *f*; *of water, blood* flaque *f*

pool² [puːl] *game* billard *m* américain

pool³ [puːl] **1** *n* (*common fund*) caisse *f* commune **2** *v/t resources* mettre en commun

'pool hall salle *f* de billard; **pool table** table *f* de billard

poop [puːp] F caca *m* F

pooped [puːpt] F crevé F

poor [pʊr] **1** *adj* pauvre; *quality etc* médiocre, mauvais **2** *npl*: **the ~** les pauvres *mpl*; **poorly 1** *adj* (*unwell*) malade **2** *adv* mal

pop¹ [pɒp] MUS pop *f*

pop² [pɒp] F (*father*) papa *m*

'popcorn pop-corn *m*

pope [pəʊp] pape *m*

Popsicle® ['pɒpsɪkl] glace *f* à l'eau

popular ['pɒpjələr] populaire; **popularity** popularité *f*

populate ['pɒpjəleɪt] peupler; **population** population *f*

porch [pɔːrtʃ] porche *m*

pork [pɔːrk] porc *m*

porn [pɔːrn] F porno F; **pornographic** pornographique; **pornography** pornographie *f*

port¹ [pɔːrt] *n* port *m*

port² [pɔːrt] *adj* (*left-hand*) de bâbord

portable ['pɔːrtəbl] **1** *adj* portable, portatif **2** *n* COMPUT portable *m*; *TV* téléviseur

m portable *or* portatif
porter ['pɔːrtər] (*doorman*)
portier m
portion ['pɔːrʃn] partie f, part
f; *of food* portion f
portrait ['pɔːrtreɪt] **1** n portrait m **2** *adv print* en mode
portrait, à la française; **por-
tray** *of artist* représenter; *of
actor* interpréter; *of author*
décrire
Portugal ['pɔːrtʃəgl] le Portugal; **Portuguese 1** *adj* portugais **2** n *person* Portugais(e)
m(f); *language* portugais m
pose [pəʊz] **1** n attitude f **2** v/i
for artist poser; **~ as** se faire
passer pour **3** v/t *problem* poser; *threat* constituer
position [pə'zɪʃn] **1** n position
f **2** v/t placer
positive ['pɑːzətɪv] positif;
be ~ (*sure*) être sûr; **posi-
tively** vraiment
possess [pə'zes] posséder;
possession possession f;
possessive possessif
possibility [pɑːsə'bɪlətɪ] possibilité f; **possible** possible;
possibly (*perhaps*) peut-être
post¹ [pəʊst] **1** n *of wood,
metal* poteau m **2** v/t *notice*
afficher; *profits* enregistrer
post² [pəʊst] **1** n (*place of duty*) poste m **2** v/t *soldier, employee* affecter; *guards* poster
post³ [pəʊst] Br **1** n (*mail*)
courrier m **2** v/t *letter* poster
postage ['pəʊstɪdʒ] affran-

chissement m; **postage
stamp** *fml* timbre m; **postal**
postal; **postcard** carte f postale; **postdate** postdater
poster ['pəʊstər] poster m, affiche f
postgraduate['pəʊstgrædʒʊ-
ət] étudiant(e) m(f) de troisième cycle
posthumous ['pɑːstʃəməs]
posthume
posting ['pəʊstɪŋ] (*assignment*) affectation f
'postmark cachet m de la poste
post-mortem [pəʊst'mɔːr-
təm] autopsie f
'post office poste f
postpone [pəʊst'pəʊn] remettre (à plus tard), reporter; **postponement** report m
pot¹ [pɑːt] *for cooking* casserole f; *for coffee* cafetière f;
for tea théière f; *for plant*
pot m
pot² [pɑːt] F (*marijuana*) herbe f
potato [pə'teɪtəʊ] pomme f
de terre; **potato chips**, Br
potato crisps chips fpl
potent ['pəʊtənt] puissant
potential [pə'tenʃl] **1** *adj* potentiel **2** n potentiel m; **po-
tentially** potentiellement
'pothole *in road* nid-de-poule
m
potter ['pɑːtər] potier(-ière)
m(f); **pottery** poterie f; *items*
poteries fpl
pouch [paʊtʃ] *bag* petit sac m

poultry ['pəʊltrɪ] volaille f

pound¹ [paʊnd] *weight* livre f (0,453kg)

pound² [paʊnd] *n for strays, cars* fourrière f

pound³ [paʊnd] *v/i of heart* battre (la chamade)

pour [pɔːr] **1** *v/t liquid* verser **2** *v/i:* **it's ~ing (with rain)** il pleut à verse

♦ **pour out** *liquid* verser; *troubles* déballer F

poverty ['pɒvərtɪ] pauvreté f

powder ['paʊdər] **1** *n* poudre f **2** *v/t:* **~ one's face** se poudrer le visage

power ['paʊər] **1** *n (strength)* puissance f, force f; *(authority)* pouvoir m; *(energy)* énergie f; *(electricity)* courant m; **power drill** perceuse f; **power failure** panne f d'électricité; **powerful** puissant; **powerless** impuissant; **power line** ligne f électrique; **power outage** coupure f de courant; **power station** centrale f électrique; **power steering** direction f assistée

PR [piːˈɑːr] (= **public relations**) relations *fpl* publiques

practical ['præktɪkl] pratique; **practically** d'une manière pratique; *(almost)* pratiquement

practice ['præktɪs] **1** *n* pratique f; *training also* entraînement m; *(rehearsal)* répétition f; *(custom)* coutume f **2** *v/i* s'entraîner **3** *v/t* travail-

ler; *law, medicine* exercer

practise *Br* → **practice** *v/i & v/t*

prairie ['prerɪ] prairie f

praise [preɪz] **1** *n* louange f, éloge *m* **2** *v/t* louer; **praiseworthy** méritoire, louable

pray [preɪ] prier; **prayer** prière f

preach [priːtʃ] prêcher; **preacher** pasteur m

precaution [prɪˈkɔːʃn] précaution f; **precautionary** *measure* préventif, de précaution

precede [prɪˈsiːd] précéder; **precedent** précédent m; **preceding** précédent

precious ['preʃəs] précieux

precise [prɪˈsaɪs] précis; **precisely** précisément; **precision** précision f

preconceived ['priːkənsiːvd] *idea* préconçu

precondition [priːkənˈdɪʃn] condition f requise

predator ['predətər] prédateur m; **predatory** prédateur

predecessor ['priːdɪsesər] prédécesseur m

predicament [prɪˈdɪkəmənt] situation f délicate

predict [prɪˈdɪkt] prédire, prévoir; **prediction** prédiction f

predominant [prɪˈdɑːmɪnənt] prédominant; **predominantly** principalement

prefabricated [priːˈfæbrɪkeɪtɪd] préfabriqué

preface ['prefɪs] préface f

prefer [prɪ'fɜːr] préférer; **preferable** préférable; **preferably** de préférence; **preference** préférence f; **preferential** préférentiel

pregnancy ['pregnənsɪ] grossesse f; **pregnant** enceinte; *animal* pleine

prehistoric [priːhɪs'tɒrɪk] *also fig* préhistorique

prejudice ['predʒʊdɪs] **1** n (*bias*) préjugé m **2** v/t person influencer; *chances* compromettre; **prejudiced** partial

preliminary [prɪ'lɪmɪnərɪ] préliminaire

premarital [priː'mærɪtl] *sex* avant le mariage

premature [premə'tʊr] prématuré

premier ['premɪr] POL Premier ministre m

première ['premɪer] première f

premises ['premɪsɪz] locaux mpl

premium ['priːmɪəm] *in insurance* prime f

prenatal [priː'neɪtl] prénatal

preoccupied [prɪ'ɑːkjʊpaɪd] préoccupé

preparation [prepə'reɪʃn] préparation f; **~s** préparatifs mpl; **prepare** [prɪ'per] **1** v/t préparer; **be ~d to do sth** *willing, ready* être prêt à faire qch **2** v/i se préparer

preposition [prepə'zɪʃn] préposition f

prerequisite [priː'rekwɪzɪt]

condition f préalable

prescribe [prɪ'skraɪb] *of doctor* prescrire; **prescription** MED ordonnance f

presence ['prezns] présence f; **in the ~ of** en présence de

present¹ ['preznt] **1** adj (*current*) actuel; **be ~** être présent **2** n: **the ~** *also* GRAM le présent

present² ['preznt] n (*gift*) cadeau m

present³ [prɪ'zent] v/t *award, bouquet* remettre; *program* présenter

presentation [prezn'teɪʃn] présentation f; **present-day** actuel; **presenter** présentateur(-trice) m(f); **presently** (*at the moment*) à présent; (*soon*) bientôt

preservative [prɪ'zɜːrvətɪv] conservateur m; **preserve 1** n (*domain*) domaine m **2** v/t *standards, peace etc* maintenir; *wood etc* préserver; *food* conserver

preside [prɪ'zaɪd] *at meeting* présider; **presidency** présidence f; **president** POL président(e) m(f); *of company* président-directeur m général, PDG m; **presidential** présidentiel

press [pres] **1** n: **the ~** la presse **2** v/t *button* appuyer sur; *hand* serrer; *grapes, olives* presser; *clothes* repasser; **pressing** pressant; **pressure 1** n pression f **2** v/t faire pres-

printout

sion sur

prestige [pre'sti:ʒ] prestige *m*; **prestigious** prestigieux

presumably [prɪ'zu:məblɪ] sans doute; **presume** présumer; **presumption** *of innocence, guilt* présomption *f*

presuppose [pri:sə'pəʊz] présupposer

pre-tax ['pri:tæks] avant impôts

pretence *Br* → **pretense**

pretend [prɪ'tend] **1** *v/t* prétendre **2** *v/i* faire semblant; **pretense** semblant *m*; **under the ~ of cooperation** sous prétexte de coopération; **pretentious** prétentieux

pretext ['pri:tekst] prétexte *m*

pretty ['prɪtɪ] **1** *adj* joli **2** *adv* (*quite*) assez

prevail [prɪ'veɪl] (*triumph*) prévaloir, l'emporter; **prevailing** *wind* dominant; *opinion* prédominant; (*current*) actuel

prevent [prɪ'vent] empêcher; *disease* prévenir; **~ s.o. (from) doing sth** empêcher qn de faire qch; **prevention** prévention *f*; **preventive** préventif

preview ['pri:vju:] **1** *n* avant--première *f* **2** *v/t* voir en avant-première

previous ['pri:vɪəs] (*earlier*) antérieur; (*the one before*) précédent; **previously** auparavant, avant

prey [preɪ] proie *f*

price [praɪs] **1** *n* prix *m* **2** *v/t* com fixer le prix de; **priceless** sans prix

prick[1] [prɪk] **1** *n* pain piqûre *f* **2** *v/t* (*jab*) piquer

prick[2] [prɪk] ∨ (*penis*) bite *f*∨; *person* con *m* F

prickle ['prɪkl] *on plant* épine *f*, piquant *m*; **prickly** *beard, plant* piquant; (*irritable*) irritable

pride [praɪd] fierté *f*; (*self-respect*) amour-propre *m*, orgueil *m*

priest [pri:st] prêtre *m*

primarily [praɪ'merɪlɪ] principalement; **primary 1** *adj* principal **2** *n* POL (*élection f*) primaire *f*

prime 'minister Premier ministre *m*

primitive ['prɪmɪtɪv] primitif; *conditions* rudimentaire

prince [prɪns] prince *m*; **princess** princesse *f*

principal ['prɪnsəpl] **1** *adj* principal **2** *n of school* directeur(-trice) *m(f)*; **principally** principalement

principle ['prɪnsəpl] principe *m*; **on ~** par principe; **in ~** en principe

print [prɪnt] **1** *n* *in book etc* texte *m*; (*photograph*) épreuve *f*; **out of ~** épuisé **2** *v/t* imprimer; (*use block capitals*) écrire en majuscules; **printer** ['prɪntər] *person* imprimeur *m*; *machine* imprimante *f*; **printout** impression *f*

prior ['praɪr] **1** adj préalable, antérieur **2** prep: ~ **to** avant
prioritize (put in order of priority) donner un ordre de priorité à; (give priority to) donner la priorité à; **priority** priorité f
prison ['prɪzn] prison f; **prisoner** prisonnier(-ière) m(f); **take s.o.** ~ faire qn prisonnier; **prisoner of war** prisonnier(-ière) m(f) de guerre
privacy ['prɪvəsɪ] intimité f;
private **1** adj privé; letter personnel; secretary particulier **2** n MIL simple soldat m; privately talk to s.o. en privé; (inwardly) intérieurement; ~ **owned** privé
privilege ['prɪvəlɪdʒ] privilège m; **privileged** privilégié
prize [praɪz] **1** n prix m **2** v/t priser, faire (grand) cas de; **prizewinner** gagnant m; **prizewinning** gagnant
probability [prɑːbəˈbɪlətɪ] probabilité f; **probable** probable; **probably** probablement
probation [prəˈbeɪʃn] in job période f d'essai; LAW probation f
probe [proʊb] **1** n (investigation) enquête f; (scientific sonde f **2** v/t sonder; (investigate) enquêter sur
problem ['prɑːbləm] problème m; **no** ~ pas de problème; it doesn't worry me c'est pas grave

procedure [prəˈsiːdʒər] procédure f; **proceed** (go: of people) se rendre; of work etc avancer, se dérouler; **proceedings** (events) événements mpl; **proceeds** bénéfices mpl
process ['prɑːses] **1** n processus m **2** v/t food, raw materials transformer; data, application traiter; **procession** procession f; **processor** processeur m
prod [prɑːd] **1** n (petit) coup m **2** v/t donner un (petit) coup à, pousser
prodigy ['prɑːdɪdʒɪ]: prodige m; (**child**) ~ enfant m/f prodige
produce¹ ['prɑːduːs] n produits mpl (agricoles)
produce² [prəˈduːs] v/t produire; (bring about) provoquer; (bring out) sortir
producer [prəˈduːsər] producteur m; of play, movie, TVprogram producteur m; **product** produit m; **production** production f; **productive** productif; **productivity** productivité f
profess [prəˈfes] prétendre; **profession** profession f; **professional 1** adj professionnel **2** n (doctor, lawyer etc) personne f qui exerce une profession libérale; not amateur professionnel(le) m(f); **professionally** play sport professionnellement;

(*well, skillfully*) de manière professionnelle
professor [prə'fesər] professeur *m*
proficient [prə'fɪʃnt] excellent, compétent
profile ['prəʊfaɪl] profil *m*
profit ['prɑːfɪt] **1** *n* bénéfice *m*, profit *m* **2** *v/i*: **~ from** profiter de; **profitability** rentabilité *f*; **profitable** rentable
profound [prə'faʊnd] profond
prognosis [prɑːg'nəʊsɪs] MED pronostic *m*
program ['prəʊgræm] **1** *n* programme *m*; *on radio, TV* émission *f* **2** *v/t* programmer; **programme** *Br* → **program**; **programmer** programmeur(-euse) *m(f)*
progress 1 ['prɑːgres] *n* progrès *m(pl)* **2** [prə'gres] *v/i* (*in time*) avancer; (*move on*) passer à; (*make ~*) faire des progrès, progresser; **progressive** (*enlightened*) progressiste; (*which progresses*) progressif; **progressively** progressivement
prohibit [prə'hɪbɪt] défendre, interdire; **prohibitive** *prices* prohibitif
project[1] ['prɑːdʒekt] *n* projet *m*; EDU étude *f*; (*housing area*) cité *f* (H.L.M.)
project[2] [prə'dʒekt] **1** *v/t figures, sales* prévoir; *movie* projeter **2** *v/i* (*stick out*) faire saillie

projection [prə'dʒekʃn] (*forecast*) projection *f*, prévision *f*; **projector** *for slides* projecteur *m*
prolog, *Br* **prologue** ['prəʊlɑːg] prologue *m*
prolong [prə'lɒːŋ] prolonger
prominent ['prɑːmɪnənt] *nose, chin* proéminent; *visually* voyant; (*significant*) important
promiscuity [prɑːmɪ'skjuːətɪ] promiscuité *f*; **promiscuous** dévergondé
promise ['prɑːmɪs] **1** *n* promesse *f* **2** *v/t & v/i* promettre; **promising** prometteur
promote [prə'məʊt] *employee, idea* promouvoir; COM *also* faire la promotion de; **promoter** *of sports event* organisateur *m*; **promotion** promotion *f*
prompt [prɑːmpt] **1** *adj* (*on time*) ponctuel; (*speedy*) prompt **2** *v/t* (*cause*) provoquer; *actor* souffler à; **promptly** (*on time*) ponctuellement; (*immediately*) immédiatement
prone [prəʊn]: **be ~ to** être sujet à
pronoun ['prəʊnaʊn] pronom *m*
pronounce [prə'naʊns] prononcer
pronto ['prɑːntəʊ] F illico (*presto*) F
pronunciation [prənʌnsɪ-'eɪʃn] prononciation *f*

proof [pru:f] preuve *f*; *of book* épreuve *f*

prop [prɑːp] THEA accessoire *m*

◆ **prop up** soutenir

propaganda [prɑːpə'gændə] propagande *f*

propel [prə'pel] propulser; **propeller** hélice *f*

proper ['prɑːpər] (*real*) vrai; (*correct*) bon, correct; (*fitting*) convenable; **properly** (*correctly*) correctement; (*fittingly also*) convenablement; **property** propriété *f*

proportion [prə'pɔːrʃn] proportion *f*; **proportional** proportionnel

proposal [prə'pouzl] proposition *f*; *of marriage* demande *f* en mariage; **propose 1** *v/t* (*suggest*) proposer; **~ to do sth** (*plan*) se proposer de faire qch **2** *v/i* (*make offer of marriage*) faire sa demande en mariage (**to** à); **proposition 1** *n* proposition *f* **2** *v/t woman* faire des avances à

proprietor [prə'praiətər] propriétaire *m*

prosecute ['prɑːsɪkjuːt] LAW poursuivre (en justice); **prosecution** LAW poursuites *fpl* (judiciaires); *lawyers* accusation *f*

prospect ['prɑːspekt] (*chance, likelihood*) chance(s) *f(pl)*; (*thought of something in the future*) perspective *f*; **~s** perspectives *fpl*

(d'avenir); **prospective** potentiel

prosper ['prɑːspər] prospérer; **prosperity** prospérité *f*; **prosperous** prospère

prostitute ['prɑːstɪtuːt] prostituée *f*; **male ~** prostitué *m*; **prostitution** prostitution *f*

protect [prə'tekt] protéger; **protection** protection *f*; **protective** protecteur; **protector** protecteur(-trice) *m(f)*

protein ['prouti:n] protéine *f*

protest ['proutest] **1** ['proutest] *n* protestation *f*; (*demonstration*) manifestation *f* **2** [prə'test] *v/t* (*object to*) protester contre **3** [prə'test] *v/i* protester; (*demonstrate*) manifester

Protestant ['prɑːtɪstənt] **1** *adj* protestant **2** *n* protestant(e) *m(f)*

protester [prə'testər] manifestant(e) *m(f)*

prototype ['proutətaɪp] prototype *m*

protrude [prə'truːd] *of eyes, ear* être saillant; *from pocket etc* sortir; **protruding** saillant; *ears* décollé; *chin* avancé; *teeth* en avant

proud [praud] fier; **proudly** fièrement, avec fierté

prove [pruːv] prouver

proverb ['prɑːvɜːrb] proverbe *m*

provide [prə'vaɪd] fournir; **~d that** (*on condition that*) pourvu que (+*subj*), à condition que (+*subj*)

province ['prɒvɪns] province *f*; **provincial** *also pej* provincial; *city* de province

provision [prə'vɪʒn] (*supply*) fourniture *f*; *of services* prestation *f*; *in a law, contract* disposition *f*; **provisional** provisoire

provocation [prɒvə'keɪʃn] provocation *f*; **provocative** provocant; **provoke** provoquer

prowl [praʊl] *of tiger etc* chasser; *of burglar* rôder; **prowler** rôdeur(-euse) *m(f)*

proximity [prɒk'sɪmətɪ] proximité *f*

proxy ['prɒksɪ] (*authority*) procuration *f*; *person* mandataire *m/f*

prudence ['pruːdns] prudence *f*; **prudent** prudent

pry [praɪ] être indiscret

PS ['piːes] (= *postscript*) P.-S. *m*

pseudonym ['suːdənɪm] pseudonyme *m*

psychiatric [saɪkɪ'ætrɪk] psychiatrique; **psychiatrist** psychiatre *m/f*; **psychiatry** psychiaɪrie *f*

psychoanalysis [saɪkəʊən'æləsɪs] psychanalyse *f*; **psychoanalyst** psychanalyste *m/f*; **psychoanalyze** psychanalyser

psychological [saɪkə'lɒdʒ- ɪkl] psychologique; **psychol-**

ogist psychologue *m/f*

psychology psychologie *f*

psychopath ['saɪkəʊpæθ] psychopathe *m/f*

psychosomatic [saɪkəʊ- sə'mætɪk] psychosomatique

pub [pʌb] *Br* pub *m*

public ['pʌblɪk] **1** *adj* public **2** *n*: **the ~** le public

publication [pʌblɪ'keɪʃn] publication *f*

public 'holiday jour *m* férié

publicity [pʌb'lɪsətɪ] publicité *f*; **publicize** (*make known*) faire connaître, rendre public; COM faire de la publicité pour

publicly ['pʌblɪklɪ] en public, publiquement

'public school école *f* publique; *Br* école privée (du secondaire)

publish ['pʌblɪʃ] publier; **publisher** éditeur(-trice) *m(f)*; maison *f* d'édition; **publishing** édition *f*; **publishing company** maison *f* d'édition

puff [pʌf] **1** *n* of wind bourrasque *f*; *of smoke* bouffée *f* **2** *v/i* (*pant*) souffler, haleter; **puffy** *eyes, face* bouffi

pull [pʊl] **1** *n on rope* coup *m*; F (*appeal*) attrait *m*; F (*influence*) influence *f* **2** *v/t* tirer; *tooth* arracher; *muscle* se déchirer **3** *v/i* tirer

◆ **pull ahead** *in race, competition* prendre la tête

◆ **pull down** (*lower*) baisser; (*demolish*) démolir

◆ **pull in** *of bus, train* arriver

◆ **pull up 1** *v/t* (*raise*) remonter; *plant* arracher **2** *v/i of car etc* s'arrêter

pulley ['pʊlɪ] poulie *f*

pulsate [pʌl'seɪt] *of heart, blood* battre; *of rhythm* vibrer

pulse [pʌls] pouls *m*

pulverize ['pʌlvəraɪz] pulvériser

pump [pʌmp] **1** *n* pompe *f* **2** *v/t* pomper

pumpkin ['pʌmpkɪn] potiron *m*

pun [pʌn] jeu *m* de mots

punch [pʌntʃ] **1** *n blow coup m* de poing; *implement* perforeuse *f* **2** *v/t with fist* donner un coup de poing à; *hole* percer; *ticket* composter

punctual ['pʌŋktʃʊəl] ponctuel; **punctuality** ponctualité *f*

punctuation [pʌŋktʃʊ'eɪʃn] ponctuation *f*

puncture ['pʌŋktʃər] **1** *n* piqûre *f* **2** *v/t* percer, perforer

punish ['pʌnɪʃ] punir; **punishing** *pace, schedule* éprouvant, épuisant; **punishment** punition *f*

puny ['pju:nɪ] *person* chétif

pup [pʌp] chiot *m*

pupil¹ ['pju:pl] *of eye* pupille *f*

pupil² ['pju:pl] (*student*) élève *m/f*

puppet ['pʌpɪt] *also fig* marionnette *f*

purchase¹ ['pɜːrtʃəs] **1** *n* achat *m* **2** *v/t* acheter

purchase² ['pɜːrtʃəs] *n* (*grip*) prise *f*

purchaser ['pɜːrtʃəsər] acheteur(-euse) *m(f)*

pure [pjʊr] pur; *white* immaculé; **purely** purement

purge [pɜːrdʒ] **1** *n* POL purge *f* **2** *v/t* POL épurer

purify ['pjʊrɪfaɪ] *water* épurer

puritan ['pjʊrɪtən] puritain(e) *m(f)*

purity ['pjʊrɪtɪ] pureté *f*

purpose ['pɜːrpəs] (*aim, object*) but *m*; **on ~** exprès; **purposely** exprès

purr [pɜːr] *of cat* ronronner

purse [pɜːrs] (*pocketbook*) sac *m* à main; *Br for money* porte-monnaie *m inv*

pursue [pər'su:] poursuivre; **pursuer** poursuivant(e) *m(f)*; **pursuit** poursuite *f*; (*activity*) activité *f*

push [pʊʃ] **1** *n* (*shove*) poussée *f* **2** *v/t* (*shove, pressure*) pousser; *button* appuyer sur; F *drugs* revendre, trafiquer **3** *v/i* pousser; **pusher** F *of drugs* dealer(-euse) *m(f)*; **push-up**: *do ~s* faire des pompes; **pushy** F qui se met en avant

puss, pussy (*cat*) [pʊs, 'pʊsɪ (kæt)] F minou *m*

put [pʊt] mettre; *question* poser; **~ the cost at** estimer le prix à

◆ **put across** *idea etc* faire comprendre

◆ **put aside** *money, work* mettre de côté

◆ **put away** *in closet etc* ranger; *in institution* enfermer; *in prison* emprisonner; F *(consume)* s'enfiler F; *animal* faire piquer

◆ **put back** *(replace)* remettre

◆ **put down** poser; *deposit* verser; *rebellion* réprimer; *(belittle)* rabaisser

◆ **put forward** *idea etc* soumettre, suggérer

◆ **put in for** *(apply for)* demander

◆ **put off** *light, TV* éteindre; *(postpone)* repousser; *(deter)* dissuader; *(repel)* dégoûter

◆ **put on** *light, TV* allumer; *music, jacket etc* mettre; *(perform)* monter; *accent etc* prendre

◆ **put out** *hand* tendre; *fire, light* éteindre

◆ **put together** *(assemble)* monter; *(organize)* organiser

◆ **put up** *hand* lever; *person* héberger; *(erect)* ériger; *prices* augmenter; *poster* accrocher; *money* fournir

◆ **put up with** supporter, tolérer

putty ['pʌtɪ] mastic *m*

puzzle ['pʌzl] **1** *n (mystery)* énigme *f*, mystère *m*; *game* jeu *m*, casse-tête *m*; *(jigsaw* ∼*)* puzzle *m* **2** *v/t* laisser perplexe; **puzzling** curieux

PVC [pi:vi:'si:] (= **polyvinyl chloride**) P.V.C. *m* (= polychlorure de vinyle)

pyjamas *Br* → **pajamas**

pylon ['paɪlən] pylône *m*

quadrangle ['kwɑːdræŋgl] *figure* quadrilatère *m*; *courtyard* cour *f*

quadruped ['kwɑːdruped] quadrupède *m*

quail [kweɪl] flancher

quaint [kweɪnt] *cottage* pittoresque; *(eccentric: ideas etc)* curieux

quake [kweɪk] **1** *n (earthquake)* tremblement *m* de terre **2** *v/i* of earth, with fear trembler

qualification [kwɑːlɪfɪ'keɪʃn] *from university etc* diplôme *m*; **qualified** *doctor, engineer etc* qualifié; *(restricted)* restreint; **qualify 1** *v/t of degree, course etc* qualifier; *remark etc* nuancer **2** *v/t (get degree etc)* obtenir son diplôme; *in competition* se qualifier

quality ['kwɑːlətɪ] qualité *f*; **quality control** contrôle *m* de qualité

quandary ['kwɑːndərɪ] dilemme *m*

quantify ['kwɑːntɪfaɪ] quantifier

quantity ['kwɑːntətɪ] quantité *f*

quarantine ['kwɑːrəntiːn] quarantaine *f*

quarrel ['kwɑːrəl] **1** *n* dispute *f*, querelle *f* **2** *v/i* se disputer

quarry¹ ['kwɑːrɪ] *in hunt* gibier *m*

quarry² ['kwɑːrɪ] *for mining* carrière *f*

quart [kwɔːrt] quart *m* de gallon *(0,946 litre)*

quarter ['kwɔːrtər] quart *m*; *25 cents* vingt-cinq cents *mpl*; *part of town* quartier *m*; **a ~ of an hour** un quart d'heure; **a ~ of 5** cinq heures moins le quart; **a ~ after 5** cinq heures et quart; **quarterfinal** quart *m* de finale; **quarterfinalist** quart de finaliste *m*, quart-finaliste *m*; **quarterly 1** *adj* trimestriel **2** *adv* trimestriellement; **quarters** MIL quartiers *mpl*; **quartet** MUS quatuor *m*

quartz [kwɑːrts] quartz *m*

quash [kwɑːʃ] *rebellion* réprimer, écraser; *court decision* casser, annuler

quaver ['kweɪvər] **1** *n in voice* tremblement *m* **2** *v/i of voice* trembler

queasy ['kwiːzɪ] nauséeux; **feel ~** avoir la nausée

queen [kwiːn] reine *f*

queer [kwɪr] *(peculiar)* bizar-

re

quell [kwel] réprimer

quench [kwentʃ] *thirst* étancher, assouvir; *flames* éteindre

query ['kwɪrɪ] **1** *n* question *f* **2** *v/t (express doubt about)* mettre en doute; *(check)* vérifier

quest [kwest] quête *f*

question ['kwestʃn] **1** *n* question *f* **2** *v/t person* questionner, interroger; *(doubt)* mettre en question; **questionable** contestable; **questioning 1** *adj look* interrogateur **2** *n* interrogatoire *m*; **question mark** point *m* d'interrogation; **questionnaire** questionnaire *m*

queue [kjuː] *Br* **1** *n* queue *f* **2** *v/i* faire la queue

quibble ['kwɪbl] chipoter, chercher la petite bête

quick [kwɪk] rapide; **be ~!** fais vite!; **quickly** vite, rapidement; **quickwitted** à l'esprit vif

quiet ['kwaɪət] *street, life* tranquille; *music* doux; *engine* silencieux; *voice* bas; **~!** silence!; **quietly** doucement, sans bruit; *(unassumingly, peacefully)* tranquillement; **quietness** calme *m*, tranquillité *f*

quilt [kwɪlt] *on bed* couette *f*

quinine [kwɪniːn] quinine *f*

quip [kwɪp] **1** *n* trait *m* d'esprit **2** *v/i* plaisanter

quirk [kwɜːrk] manie *f*, lubie

f; **quirky** bizarre, excentrique

quit [kwɪt] **1** *v/t job* quitter **2** *v/i (leave job)* démissionner; COMPUT quitter

quite [kwaɪt] *(fairly)* assez; *(completely)* tout à fait; **~ a lot** pas mal, beaucoup

quiver ['kwɪvər] trembler

quiz [kwɪz] **1** *n on TV* jeu *m* télévisé; *on radio* jeu *m* ra-

diophonique; *at school* interrogation *f* **2** *v/t* interroger

quota ['kwoʊtə] quota *m*

quotation [kwoʊ'teɪʃn] *from author* citation *f*; *price* devis *m*; **quotation marks** guillemets *mpl*; **quote 1** *n from author* citation *f*; *price* devis *m*; *(quotation mark)* guillemet *m*; **in ~s** entre guillemets **2** *v/t text* citer; *price* proposer

R

rabbit ['ræbɪt] lapin *m*

rabble ['ræbl] cohue *f*, foule *f*;
  rabble-rouser agitateur(-trice) *m(f)*

rabies ['reɪbiːz] rage *f*

raccoon [rə'kuːn] raton *m* laveur

race[1] [reɪs] *n of people* race *f*

race[2] [reɪs] **1** *n* SP course *f* **2** *v/i (run fast)* courir à toute vitesse **3** *v/t: I'll ~ you* le premier arrivé a gagné

'**racecourse** champ *m* de courses, hippodrome *m*;
  racehorse cheval *m* de course; **race riot** émeute *f* raciale;
  racetrack *for cars* circuit *m*, piste *f*, *for horses* hippodrome *m*

racial ['reɪʃl] racial

racing ['reɪsɪŋ] course *f*

racism ['reɪsɪzm] racisme *m*;
  racist 1 *adj* raciste **2** *n* raciste *m/f*

rack [ræk] **1** *n for bags on train*

porte-bagages *m inv*; *for CDs* range-CD *m inv* **2** *v/t:*
  ~ one's brains se creuser la tête

racket[1] ['rækɪt] SP raquette *f*

racket[2] ['rækɪt] *(noise)* vacarme *m*; *criminal activity* escroquerie *f*

radar ['reɪdɑːr] radar *m*

radiance ['reɪdɪəns] éclat *m*;
  radiant *smile* radieux; **radiate** *of heat, light* irradier, rayonner; **radiation** *nuclear* radiation *f*; **radiator** radiateur *m*

radical ['rædɪkl] **1** *adj* radical **2** *n* POL radical(e) *m(f)*; **radicalism** POL radicalisme *m*; **radically** radicalement

radio ['reɪdioʊ] radio *f*; **radioactive** radioactif; **radioactivity** radioactivité *f*; **radio alarm** radio-réveil *m*; **radiographer** radiologue *m/f*; **radiography** radiographie *f*;

radio station station *f* de radio

radius ['reɪdɪəs] rayon *m*

raft [rɑːft] radeau *m*

rafter ['rɑːftər] chevron *m*

rag [ræg] *for cleaning etc* chiffon *m*

rage [reɪdʒ] **1** *n* colère *f*, rage *f* **2** *v/i of storm* faire rage

ragged ['rægɪd] *edge* irrégulier; *appearance* négligé; *clothes* en loques

raid [reɪd] **1** *n by troops*, FIN raid *m*; *by police* descente *f*; *by robbers* hold-up *m* **2** *v/t of troops* attaquer; *of police* faire une descente dans; *of robbers* attaquer; **raider** (*robber*) voleur *m*

rail [reɪl] *on track* rail *m*; (*hand~*) rampe *f*; *for towel* porte-serviettes *m inv*; **by ~** en train; **railings** *around park etc* grille *f*; **railroad** chemin *m* de fer; *track* voie *f* ferrée; **railroad station** gare *f*; **railway** *Br* chemin *m* de fer; *track* voie *f* ferrée

rain [reɪn] **1** *n* pluie *f* **2** *v/i* pleuvoir; **it's ~ing** il pleut; **rainbow** arc-en-ciel *m*; **raincheck**: **can I take a ~ on that?** F peut-on remettre cela à plus tard?; **raincoat** imperméable *m*; **raindrop** goutte *f* de pluie; **rainfall** précipitations *fpl*; **rain forest** forêt *f* tropicale (humide); **rainproof** *fabric* imperméa-

ble; **rainstorm** pluie *f* torrentielle; **rainy** pluvieux

raise [reɪz] **1** *n in salary* augmentation *f* (de salaire) **2** *v/t shelf etc* surélever; *offer* augmenter; *children* élever; *question* soulever; *money* rassembler

rake [reɪk] *for garden* râteau *m*

rally ['rælɪ] (*meeting, reunion*) rassemblement *m*; MOT rallye *m*; *in tennis* échange *m*

RAM [ræm] COMPUT (= **random access memory**) RAM *f*, mémoire *f* vive

ram [ræm] **1** *n* bélier *m* **2** *v/t ship, car* heurter, percuter

ramble ['ræmbl] **1** *n walk* randonnée *f* **2** *v/i walk* faire de la randonnée; *when speaking* discourir; (*talk incoherently*) divaguer; **rambling 1** *adj speech* décousu **2** *n walking* randonnée *f*; *in speech* digression *f*

ramp [ræmp] rampe *f* (d'accès), passerelle *f*; *for raising vehicle* pont *m* élévateur

rampant ['ræmpənt] *inflation* galopant

rampart ['ræmpɑːrt] rempart *m*

ramshackle ['ræmʃækl] délabré

ranch [ræntʃ] ranch *m*; **rancher** propriétaire *m/f* de ranch; **ranchhand** employé *m* de ranch

rancid ['rænsɪd] rance

rancor, *Br* rancour ['ræŋkər]
rancœur *f*

R & D [ɑːrən'diː] (= *research
and development*) R&D *f*
(= recherche et développement)

random ['rændəm] **1** *adj* aléatoire, au hasard; **~ sample**
échantillon *m* pris au hasard
2 *n*: **at ~** au hasard

range [reɪndʒ] **1** *n of products*
gamme *f*; *of gun* portée *f*; *of
airplane* autonomie *f*; *of
voice, instrument* registre *m*;
of mountains chaîne *f*; **at
close ~** de très près **2** *v/i*: **~
from X to Y** aller de X à Y;
ranger garde *m* forestier

rank [ræŋk] **1** *n* MIL grade *m*;
in society rang *m* **2** *v/t* classer
◆ **rank among** compter par-
mi

ransack ['rænsæk] *searching*
fouiller; *plundering* saccager

ransom ['rænsəm] *money*
rançon *f*

rap [ræp] **1** *n at door etc* petit
coup *m* sec; MUS rap *m* **2** *v/t
table etc* taper sur

rape¹ [reɪp] **1** *n* viol *m* **2** *v/t*
violer

rape² [reɪp] *n* BOT colza *m*

rapid ['ræpɪd] rapide; **rapidity**
rapidité *f*; **rapidly** rapidement; **rapids** rapides *mpl*

rapist ['reɪpɪst] violeur *m*

rare [rer] rare; *steak* saignant,
bleu; **rarely** rarement; **rarity**
rareté *f*

rash¹ [ræʃ] *n* MED éruption *f*

(cutanée)

rash² [ræʃ] *adj action*, imprudent, impétueux; **rashly** sans
réfléchir

rat [ræt] rat *m*

rate [reɪt] *taux m*; *(price)* tarif
m; *(speed)* rythme *m*; **at this
~** *(at this speed)* à ce rythme;
(carrying on like this) si ça
continue comme ça; **at any
~** en tout cas

rather ['ræðər] *(fairly, quite)*
plutôt; **I would ~ stay here**
je préférerais rester ici

ratification [rætɪfɪ'keɪʃn] *of
treaty* ratification *f*; **ratify** ra-
tifier

ratings ['reɪtɪŋz] indice *m*
d'écoute

ratio ['reɪʃɪoʊ] rapport *m*, proportion *f*

ration ['ræʃn] **1** *n* ration *f* **2** *v/t
supplies* rationner

rational ['ræʃənl] rationnel;
rationality rationalité *f*; **ra-
tionalization** rationalisation
f; **rationalize 1** *v/t* rationaliser **2** *v/i* (se) chercher des excuses; **rationally** rationnelle-
ment

rattle ['rætl] **1** *n of bottles,
chains* cliquetis *m*; *in engine*
bruit *m* de ferraille; *toy* ho-
chet *m* **2** *v/t chains etc* entrechoquer **3** *v/i* faire du bruit;
of engine faire un bruit de
ferraille; *of crates* s'entrechoquer; *of chains* cliqueter; **rat-
tlesnake** serpent *m* à sonnette

raucous ['rɔːkəs] bruyant

rave [reɪv] **1** n party rave f, rave-party f **2** v/i délirer; ~ **about sth** (be very enthusiastic) s'emballer pour qch

ravenous ['rævənəs] affamé

ravine [rə'viːn] ravin m

raw [rɔː] meat, vegetable cru; sugar, iron brut; **raw materials** matières fpl premières

ray [reɪ] rayon m

razor ['reɪzər] rasoir m; **razor blade** lame f de rasoir

re [riː] COM en référence à

reach [riːtʃ] **1** n: **within ~** à portée; **out of ~** hors de portée **2** v/t atteindre; destination arriver à; decision parvenir à

react [rɪ'ækt] réagir; **reaction** réaction f; **reactionary 1** adj POL réactionnaire **2** n POL réactionnaire m/f; **reactor** nuclear réacteur m

read [riːd] lire

◆ **read out** aloud lire à haute voix

readable ['riːdəbl] lisible; **reader** person lecteur(-trice) m(f)

readily ['redɪlɪ] admit, agree volontiers, de bon cœur

reading ['riːdɪŋ] activity lecture f; from meter etc relevé m

readjust [riːə'dʒʌst] **1** v/t régler (de nouveau) **2** v/i to conditions se réadapter (**to** à)

ready ['redɪ] (prepared, willing) prêt; **get sth ~** préparer qch; **ready cash** (argent m)

liquide m; **ready-made** stew etc cuisiné; solution tout trouvé; **ready-to-wear** de confection; **~ clothing** prêt-à-porter m

real [riːl] not imaginary réel; not fake vrai; **real estate** immobilier m, biens mpl immobiliers; **real estate agent** agent m immobilier; **realism** réalisme m; **realist** réaliste m/f; **realistic** réaliste; **realistically** de façon réaliste; **reality** réalité f; **realize** se rendre compte de; FIN réaliser; **really** vraiment; **real time** COMPUT temps m réel; **real-time** COMPUT en temps réel

realtor ['riːltər] agent m immobilier; **realty** immobilier m

reappear [riːə'pɪr] réapparaître

reappearance réapparition f

rear [rɪr] **1** adj arrière inv, de derrière **2** n arrière m

rearm [riː'ɑːrm] réarmer

rearrange [riːə'reɪndʒ] flowers réarranger; furniture déplacer; schedule, meetings réorganiser

rear-view 'mirror rétroviseur m, rétro m F

reason ['riːzn] **1** n (cause), faculty raison f; **reasonable** raisonnable; **reasonably** act, behave raisonnablement; (quite) relativement; **reasoning** raisonnement m

reassure [riːə'ʃur] rassurer;

reassuring rassurant

rebate ['ri:beɪt] *(refund)* remboursement *m*

rebel 1 ['rebl] *n* rebelle *m/f* 2 [rɪ'bel] *v/i* se rebeller; **rebellion** rébellion *f*; **rebellious** rebelle; **rebelliousness** esprit *m* de rébellion

rebound [rɪ'baʊnd] *of ball etc* rebondir

rebuild [ri:'bɪld] reconstruire

recall [rɪ'kɔ:l] *goods, ambassador* rappeler; *(remember)* se rappeler

recap ['ri:kæp] récapituler

recapture [ri:'kæptʃər] reprendre

recede [rɪ'si:d] *of flood waters* baisser

receipt [rɪ'si:t] *for purchase* reçu *m (for* de), ticket *m* de caisse; **~s** FIN recette(s) *f(pl)*; **receive** recevoir; **receiver** TELEC combiné *m*; *for radio* (poste) récepteur *m*; **receivership**: *be in ~* être en liquidation judiciaire

recent ['ri:snt] récent; **recently** récemment

reception [rɪ'sepʃn] réception *f*; *(welcome)* accueil *m*; **reception desk** réception *f*; **receptionist** réceptionniste *m/f*; **receptive**: *be ~ to sth* être réceptif à qch

recess ['ri:ses] *in wall etc* renfoncement *m*, recoin *m*; EDU récréation *f*; *of legislature* vacances *fpl* judiciaires; **recession** *economic* récession *f*

recharge [ri:'tʃɑ:rdʒ] *battery* recharger

recipe ['resəpɪ] recette *f*

recipient [rɪ'sɪpɪənt] *of parcel etc* destinataire *m/f*; *of payment* bénéficiaire *m/f*

reciprocal [rɪ'sɪprəkl] réciproque

recite [rɪ'saɪt] *poem* réciter; *details, facts* énumérer

reckless ['reklɪs] imprudent; **recklessly** imprudemment

reckon ['rekən] *(think, consider)* penser

◆ **reckon on** compter sur

reclaim [rɪ'kleɪm] *land from sea* gagner sur la mer; *lost property* récupérer

recline [rɪ'klaɪn] s'allonger; **recliner** *chair* chaise *f* longue, relax *m*

recluse [rɪ'klu:s] reclus *m*

recognition [rekəg'nɪʃn] reconnaissance *f*; **recognizable** reconnaissable; **recognize** reconnaître

recoil [rɪ'kɔɪl] reculer

recollect [rekə'lekt] se souvenir de; **recollection** souvenir *m*

recommend [rekə'mend] recommander; **recommendation** recommandation *f*

recompense ['rekəmpens] compensation *f*, dédommagement *m*

reconcile ['rekənsaɪl] réconcilier; *differences* concilier; *facts* faire concorder; **reconciliation** réconciliation *f*; *of* *differences, facts* conciliation f

recondition [riːkən'dɪʃn] refaire, remettre à neuf

reconnaissance [rɪ'kɒn-ɪsəns] MIL reconnaissance f

reconsider [riːkən'sɪdər] **1** v/t reconsidérer **2** v/i reconsidérer la question

reconstruct [riːkən'strʌkt] reconstruire; *crime* reconstituer

record¹ ['rekərd] n MUS disque m; SP etc record m; *written document etc* rapport m; *in database* article m, enregistrement m; **~s** (*archives*) archives fpl, dossiers mpl; **have a criminal ~** avoir un casier judiciaire

record² [rɪ'kɔːrd] v/t *electronically* enregistrer; *in writing* consigner

'record-breaking qui bat tous les records; **record holder** recordman m, recordwoman f

recording [rɪ'kɔːrdɪŋ] enregistrement m

recount [rɪ'kaʊnt] (*tell*) raconter

re-count ['riːkaʊnt] **1** n *of votes* recompte m **2** v/t recompter

recoup [rɪ'kuːp] *financial losses* récupérer

recover [rɪ'kʌvər] **1** v/t retrouver **2** v/i *from illness* se remettre; *of business* reprendre; **recovery** *of sth lost* ré-

cupération f; *from illness* rétablissement m

recreation [rekrɪ'eɪʃn] récréation f; **recreational** *done for pleasure* de loisirs

recruit [rɪ'kruːt] **1** n recrue f **2** v/t recruter; **recruitment** recrutement m

rectangle ['rektæŋgl] rectangle m; **rectangular** rectangulaire

rectify ['rektɪfaɪ] rectifier

recuperate [rɪ'kuːpəreɪt] récupérer

recur [rɪ'kɜːr] *of error, event* se reproduire; *of symptoms* réapparaître; **recurrent** récurrent

recycle [riːˈsaɪkl] recycler; **recycling** recyclage m

red [red] **1** adj rouge **2** n: **in the ~** FIN dans le rouge; **Red Cross** Croix Rouge f

redecorate [riːˈdekəreɪt] refaire

redeem [rɪ'diːm] *debt* rembourser; *sinners* racheter

redevelop [riːdɪ'veləp] *part of town* réaménager

'redhead roux m, rousse f; **red light** *for traffic* feu m rouge; **red light district** quartier m chaud; **red meat** viande f rouge; **redneck** F plouc m F; **red tape** F paperasserie f

reduce [rɪ'duːs] réduire; **reduction** réduction f

reek [riːk] empester (**of sth** qch)

reel [riːl] *of film, thread* bobine f

re-e'lect réélire; re-election
réélection f

re-'entry of spacecraft rentrée
f

ref [ref] F arbitre m
♦ refer to faire allusion à; dictionary etc se reporter à

referee [refə'riː] sɒ arbitre m;
for job: personne qui fournit
des références; reference (allusion) allusion f; for job référence f; (~ number) (numéro m de) référence f; reference book ouvrage m de
référence; reference num-
ber numéro m de référence

referendum [refə'rendəm] référendum m

refill ['riːfɪl] remplir

refine [rɪ'faɪn] oil, sugar raffiner; technique affiner; re-
finement to process, ma-
chine perfectionnement m;
refinery raffinerie f

reflect [rɪ'flekt] 1 v/t refléter 2
v/i (think) réfléchir; reflection also fig reflet m; (consideration) réflexion f

reflex ['riːfleks] in body réflexe m

reform [rɪ'fɔːrm] 1 n réforme f
2 v/t réformer; reformer ré-
formateur(-trice) m(f)

refresh [rɪ'freʃ] rafraîchir; of
sleep, rest reposer; of meal
redonner des forces à; refreshing drink rafraîchissant; experience agréable;
refreshments rafraîchisse-

ments mpl

refrigerate [rɪ'frɪdʒəreɪt] ré-
frigérer; refrigerator réfrigérateur m

refuel [riː'fjuːəl] 1 v/t airplane
ravitailler 2 v/i of airplane se
ravitailler (en carburant)

refuge ['refjuːdʒ] refuge m;
take~ from storm etc se réfugier; refugee réfugié(e) m(f)

refund 1 ['riːfʌnd] n remboursement m 2 [rɪ'fʌnd] v/t rembourser

refusal [rɪ'fjuːzl] refus m; refuse refuser; ~ to do sth refuser de faire qch

regain [rɪ'ɡeɪn] control, territory, the lead reprendre;
composure retrouver

regard [rɪ'ɡɑːrd] 1 n: with~ to
en ce qui concerne; (kind) ~s
cordialement; with no~ for
sans égard pour 2 v/t: ~ as
considérer comme; regard-
ing en ce qui concerne; regardless quand même; ~
of sans se soucier de

regime [reɪ'ʒiːm] (government) régime m

regiment ['redʒɪmənt] régi-
ment m

region ['riːdʒən] région f; regional régional

register ['redʒɪstər] 1 n registre m 2 v/t birth, death déclarer; vehicle immatriculer;
letter recommander; emo-
tion exprimer 3 v/i for a
course s'inscrire; with police
se déclarer (with à); regis-

tered letter lettre f recommandée; **registration** *of birth, death* déclaration f; *of vehicle* immatriculation f; *for a course* inscription f
regret [rɪ'gret] **1** v/t regretter **2** n regret m; **regretful** plein de regrets; **regrettable** regrettable
regular ['regjʊlər] **1** adj régulier; *(normal)* normal **2** n *at bar* habitué(e) m(f); **regularity** régularité f; **regularly** régulièrement
regulate ['regjʊleɪt] régler; *expenditure* contrôler; **regulation** *(rule)* règlement m
rehabilitate [riːhə'bɪlɪteɪt] *ex-criminal* réinsérer; *disabled person* rééduquer
rehearsal [rɪ'hɜːrsl] répétition f; **rehearse** répéter
reign [reɪn] **1** n règne m **2** v/i régner
reimburse [riːɪm'bɜːrs] rembourser
reinforce [riːɪn'fɔːrs] renforcer; *argument* étayer; **reinforced concrete** béton m armé; **reinforcements** MIL renforts mpl
reinstate [riːɪn'steɪt] *person in office* réintégrer, rétablir dans ses fonctions; *paragraph etc* réintroduire
reject [rɪ'dʒekt] rejeter; **rejection** rejet m
relapse ['riːlæps] MED rechute f
related [rɪ'leɪtɪd] *by family*

apparenté; *events, ideas etc* associé; **relation** *in family* parent(e) m(f); *(connection)* rapport m, relation f; **relationship** relation f; *sexual* liaison f; **relative** **1** adj relatif **2** n parent(e) m(f); **relatively** relativement
relax [rɪ'læks] **1** v/i se détendre; **~!** du calme! **2** v/t *muscle* relâcher; **relaxation** détente f, relaxation f; **relaxed** détendu, décontracté; **relaxing** reposant, relaxant
relay 1 v/t [riː'leɪ] *message* transmettre; *radio, TV signals* relayer, retransmettre **2** n ['riːleɪ]: **~** *(race)* (course f de) relais m
release [rɪ'liːs] **1** n *from prison* libération f; *of CD, movie etc* sortie f; *CD, record* nouveauté f **2** v/t *prisoner* libérer; *CD, record, movie* sortir; *parking brake* desserrer; *information* communiquer
relegate ['relɪgeɪt] reléguer
relent [rɪ'lent] se calmer; *of person* s'adoucir; **relentless** *(determined)* acharné; *rain etc* incessant
relevance ['reləvəns] pertinence f; **relevant** pertinent
reliability [rɪlaɪə'bɪlətɪ] fiabilité f; **reliable** fiable; **reliance** [rɪ'laɪəns] confiance f **(on** en); *on equipment* dépendance f **(on** vis-à-vis de)
relic ['relɪk] relique f
relief [rɪ'liːf] soulagement m;

relieve *pain* soulager; *(take over from)* relayer, relever

religion [rɪˈlɪdʒən] religion *f*; **religious** religieux; *person* croyant

relinquish [rɪˈlɪŋkwɪʃ] abandonner

relish [ˈrelɪʃ] **1** *n sauce* relish *f*; *(enjoyment)* délectation *f* **2** *v/t idea, prospect* se réjouir de

relive [riːˈlɪv] *event* revivre

relocate [riːloˈkeɪt] *of business* se réimplanter; *of employee* être muté

reluctance [rɪˈlʌktəns] réticence *f*; **reluctant** réticent; **be ~ to do sth** hésiter à faire qch

◆ **rely on** [rɪˈlaɪ] compter sur; **rely on s.o. to do sth** compter sur qn pour faire qch

remain [rɪˈmeɪn] rester; **~ silent** garder le silence; **remainder** *also* MATH reste *m*; **remaining** restant; **the ~ refugees** le reste des réfugiés; **remains** *of body* restes *mpl*

remake [ˈriːmeɪk] *of movie* remake *m*, nouvelle version *f*

remark [rɪˈmɑːrk] **1** *n* remarque *f* **2** *v/t (comment)* faire remarquer; **remarkable** remarquable; **remarkably** remarquablement

remarry [riːˈmærɪ] se remarier

remedy [ˈremədɪ] MED, *fig* remède *m*

remember [rɪˈmembər] **1** *v/t* se souvenir de, se rappeler

2 *v/i* se souvenir

remind [rɪˈmaɪnd]: **~ s.o. to do sth** rappeler à qn de faire qch; **~ X of Y** rappeler Y à X; **~ s.o. of sth** *(bring to their attention)* rappeler qch à qn; **reminder** rappel *m*

reminisce [remɪˈnɪs] évoquer le passé

remission [rɪˈmɪʃn] MED rémission *f*; **go into ~** *of patient* être en sursis

remnant [ˈremnənt] vestige *m*, reste *m*

remorse [rɪˈmɔːrs] remords *m*; **remorseless** impitoyable; *demands* incessant

remote [rɪˈmoʊt] *village* isolé; *possibility* vague; *ancestor* lointain; **remote control** télécommande *f*; **remotely** *related, connected* vaguement

removable [rɪˈmuːvəbl] amovible; **removal** enlèvement *m*; *of demonstrators* expulsion *f*; *of doubt* dissipation *f*; **remove** enlever; *demonstrators* expulser; *doubt* dissiper

rename [riːˈneɪm] rebaptiser; *file* renommer

rendez-vous [ˈrɑːndeɪvuː] rendez vous *m*

renew [rɪˈnuː] *contract* renouveler; *discussion* reprendre; **renewal** *of contract etc* renouvellement *m*; *of discussion* reprise *f*

renounce [rɪˈnaʊns] renoncer à

renovate ['renəveɪt] rénover;
renovation rénovation *f*

rent [rent] **1** *n* loyer *m*; **for ~** à
louer **2** *v/t* louer; **rental** *for
apartment* loyer *m*; *for TV,
car* location *f*; **rental car** voiture *f* de location; **rent-free**
sans payer de loyer

reopen [riː'oʊpn] **1** *v/t* rouvrir; *negotiations* reprendre
2 *v/i of store etc* rouvrir

reorganization [riːɔːrgənaɪ
'zeɪʃn] réorganisation *f*; **reorganize** réorganiser

repaint [riː'peɪnt] repeindre

repair [rɪ'per] **1** *v/t* réparer **2** *n*
réparation *f*; **repairman** réparateur *m*

repatriate [riː'pætrɪeɪt] rapatrier; **repatriation** rapatriement *m*

repay [riː'peɪ] rembourser;
repayment remboursement
m

repeal [rɪ'piːl] *law* abroger

repeat [rɪ'piːt] **1** *v/t* répéter **2** *n*
TV program etc rediffusion
f; **repeatedly** à plusieurs reprises

repel [rɪ'pel] repousser; (*disgust*) dégoûter; **repellent 1**
adj repoussant, répugnant **2**
n (*insect ~*) répulsif *m*

repercussions [riːpər'kʌʃnz]
répercussions *fpl*

repertoire ['repərtwɑːr] répertoire *m*

repetition [repɪ'tɪʃn] répétition *f*; **repetitive** répétitif

replace [rɪ'pleɪs] (*put back*)

remettre; (*take the place
of*) remplacer; **replacement;
replacement person** remplaçant *m*; *product* produit *m* de remplacement; **replacement part** pièce *f* de rechange

replay ['riːpleɪ] **1** *n recording*
relecture *f*, replay *m*; *match*
nouvelle rencontre *f*, replay
m **2** *v/t match* rejouer

replenish [rɪ'plenɪʃ] *container* remplir (de nouveau); **supplies** refaire

replica ['replɪkə] réplique *f*

reply [rɪ'plaɪ] **1** *n* réponse *f* **2**
v/t & v/i répondre

report [rɪ'pɔːrt] **1** *n* (*account*)
rapport *m*, compte-rendu
m; *in newspaper* bulletin *m*
2 *v/t facts* rapporter; *to
authorities* déclarer **3** *v/i*
(*present o.s.*) se présenter;
reporter reporter *m/f*

repossess [riːpə'zes] COM reprendre possession de

represent [reprɪ'zent] représenter; **representative 1**
adj (*typical*) représentatif **2**
n représentant(e) *m(f)*

repress [rɪ'pres] réprimer; **repression** [rɪ'preʃn] répression *f*;
repressive POL répressif

reprieve [rɪ'priːv] **1** *n* LAW sursis *m*; *fig also* répit *m* **2** *v/t
prisoner* accorder un sursis à

reprimand ['reprɪmænd] réprimander

reprint ['riːprɪnt] **1** *n* réimpression *f* **2** *v/t* réimprimer

reprisal [rɪ'praɪzl] représailles

fpl

reproach [rɪ'prəʊtʃ] **1** *n* reproche *m* **2** *v/t*: **~ s.o. for sth** reprocher qch à qn; **reproachful** réprobateur

reproduce [riːprə'djuːs] **1** *v/t* reproduire **2** *v/i* BIO se reproduire; **reproduction** reproduction *f*

reproductive reproducteur

reptile ['reptaɪl] reptile *m*

republic [rɪ'pʌblɪk] république *f*; **Republican 1** *adj* républicain **2** *n* Républicain(e) *m(f)*

repulsive [rɪ'pʌlsɪv] repoussant

reputable ['repjʊtəbl] de bonne réputation; **reputation** réputation *f*

request [rɪ'kwest] **1** *n* demande *f*; **on ~** sur demande **2** *v/t* demander

require [rɪ'kwaɪr] *(need)* avoir besoin de; **required** *(necessary)* requis; **requirement** *(need)* besoin *m*, exigence *f*; *(condition)* condition *f* (requise)

requisition [rekwɪ'zɪʃn] réquisitionner

re-route [riː'ruːt] *airplane etc* dérouter

rerun ['riːrʌn] **1** *n of TV program* rediffusion *f* **2** *v/t tape* repasser

reschedule [riː'skedjuːl] changer l'heure/la date de

rescue ['reskjuː] **1** *n* sauvetage *m* **2** *v/t* sauver, secourir

research [rɪ'sɜːtʃ] recherche *f*; **research and development** recherche *f* et développement; **researcher** chercheur(-euse) *m(f)*

resemblance [rɪ'zembləns] ressemblance *f*; **resemble** ressembler à

resent [rɪ'zent] ne pas aimer; *person also* en vouloir à; **resentful** plein de ressentiment; **resentment** ressentiment *m* (**of** par rapport à)

reservation [rezər'veɪʃn] réservation *f*; *mental, (special area)* réserve *f*; **reserve 1** *n (store, aloofness)* réserve *f*; SP remplaçant(e) *m(f)* **2** *v/t seat, judgment* réserver; **reserved** *table, manner* réservé

reservoir ['rezərvwɑːr] *for water* réservoir *m*

residence ['rezɪdəns] *fml: house etc* résidence *f*; *(stay)* séjour *m*; **resident** résident(e) *m(f)*; *on street* riverain(e) *m(f)*; *in hotel* client(e) *m(f)*; **residential** résidentiel

residue ['rezɪdjuː] résidu *m*

resign [rɪ'zaɪn] **1** *v/t position* démissionner de; **~ o.s. to** se résigner à **2** *v/i from job* démissionner; **resignation** *from job* démission *f*; *mental* résignation *f*

resilient [rɪ'zɪliənt] *personality* fort; *material* résistant

resist [rɪ'zɪst] *v/t* résister à; *new measures* s'opposer à **2** *v/i* résister; **resistance** résis-

tance *f*; **resistant** *material*
résistant

resolution [rezə'luːʃn] résolution *f*

resort [rɪ'zɔːrt] *place* lieu *m* de vacances; *at seaside* station *f* balnéaire; *for health cures* station *f* thermale; *as a last* ~ en dernier ressort
♦ **resort to** avoir recours à, recourir à

♦ **resound with** [rɪ'zaʊnd] résonner de

resounding [rɪ'zaʊndɪŋ] *success, victory* retentissant

resource [rɪ'sɔːrs] ressource *f*; **resourceful** ingénieux

respect [rɪ'spekt] **1** *n* respect *m*; *in this/that* ~ à cet égard; *in many* ~*s* à bien des égards **2** *v/t* respecter; **respectability** respectabilité *f*; **respectable** respectable, respectueux; **respectful** respectueux; **respective** respectif; **respectively** respectivement

respiration [respɪ'reɪʃn] respiration *f*; **respirator** MED respirateur *m*

respond [rɪ'spɑːnd] répondre; (*react also*) réagir; **response** réponse *f*; (*reaction also*) réaction *f*,

responsibility [rɪspɑːnsɪ'bɪl-ətɪ] responsabilité *f*; **responsible** responsable (*for* de); *a* ~ *job* un poste à responsabilités

rest[1] [rest] **1** *n* repos *m*; *during walk, work* pause *f* **2** *v/i*

se reposer **3** *v/t* (*lean, balance*) poser

rest[2] [rest]: *the* ~ *objects* le reste; *people* les autres

restaurant ['restərɑːnt] restaurant *m*

restful ['restfl] reposant; **rest home** maison *f* de retraite; **restless** agité; **restlessly** nerveusement

restoration [restə'reɪʃn] *of building* restauration *f*; **re-store** *building etc* restaurer; (*bring back*) restituer; *confidence* redonner

restrain [rɪ'streɪn] retenir; **re-straint** (*moderation*) retenue *f*

restrict [rɪ'strɪkt] restreindre; *I'll* ~ *myself to ...* je me limiterai à ...; **restriction** restriction *f*

'rest room toilettes *fpl*

result [rɪ'zʌlt] résultat *m*; *as a* ~ *of this* par conséquent

resume [rɪ'zuːm] reprendre

résumé ['rezumeɪ] *of career* curriculum vitæ *m inv*, C.V. *m inv*

resumption [rɪ'zʌmpʃn] reprise *f*

resurface [riː'sɜːrfɪs] **1** *v/t roads* refaire (le revêtement de) **2** *v/i* (*reappear*) refaire surface

Resurrection [rezə'rekʃn] REL Résurrection *f*

retail ['riːteɪl] **1** *adv*: *sell sth* ~ vendre qch au détail **2** *v/i*: ~ *at* se vendre à; **retailer** détail-

revision

lant(e) *m(f)*

retain [rɪ'teɪn] conserver; **retainer** FIN provision *f*

retaliate [rɪ'tælɪeɪt] riposter, se venger; **retaliation** riposte *f*

rethink [riː'θɪŋk] repenser

reticence ['retɪsns] réserve *f*; **reticent** réservé

retire [rɪ'taɪr] *from work* prendre sa retraite; **retired** à la retraite; **retirement** retraite *f*; **retiring** réservé

retort [rɪ'tɔːrt] **1** *n* réplique *f* **2** *v/t* répliquer

retract [rɪ'trækt] *claws, undercarriage* rentrer; *statement* retirer

're-train se recycler

retreat [rɪ'triːt] **1** *v/i also* MIL battre en retraite **2** *n* MIL, *place* retraite *f*

retrieve [rɪ'triːv] récupérer

retroactive [retroʊ'æktɪv] *law etc* rétroactif; **retroactively** rétroactivement, par rétroaction

retrograde ['retrəgreɪd] rétrograde

retrospective [retrə'spektɪv] rétrospective *f*

return [rɪ'tɜːrn] **1** *n* of book, movie critique *f*; of troops revue *f*; of situation etc bilan *m* **2** *v/t* book, movie faire la critique de; troops passer en revue; situation etc faire le bilan de; EDU réviser; **reviewer** of book, movie critique *m*

(*come back*) revenir

reunification [riːjuːnɪfɪ'keɪʃn] réunification *f*

reunion [riː'juːnjən] réunion *f*; **reunite** réunir; *country* réunifier

reusable [riː'juːzəbl] réutilisable; **reuse** réutiliser

◆ **rev up** [rev] *engine* emballer

revaluation [riːvæljuː'eɪʃn] réévaluation *f*

reveal [rɪ'viːl] révéler; (*make visible*) dévoiler; **revealing** *remark* révélateur; *dress* suggestif; **revelation** révélation *f*

revenge [rɪ'vendʒ] vengeance *f*; **take one's ~** se venger

revenue ['revənuː] revenu *m*

reverberate [rɪ'vɜːrbəreɪt] *of sound* retentir, résonner

revere [rɪ'vɪr] révérer; **reverence** déférence *f*, respect *m*; **reverent** respectueux

reverse [rɪ'vɜːrs] **1** *adj sequence* inverse **2** *n* (*opposite*) contraire *m*; (*back*) verso *m*; MOT *gear* marche *f* arrière **3** *v/i* MOT faire marche arrière

review [rɪ'vjuː] **1** *n* of book, movie critique *f*; of troops revue *f*; of situation etc bilan *m* **2** *v/t* book, movie faire la critique de; troops passer en revue; situation etc faire le bilan de; EDU réviser; **reviewer** of book, movie critique *m*

revise [rɪ'vaɪz] *opinion* revenir sur; *text* réviser; **revision**

of text révision *f*

revival [rɪ'vaɪvl] *of custom, old style* renouveau *m; of patient* rétablissement *m;* re-vive **1** *v/t custom, old style* faire renaître; *patient* ranimer **2** *v/i of business* reprendre

revoke [rɪ'vouk] *law* abroger; *license* retirer

revolt [rɪ'voult] **1** *n* révolte *f* *v/i* se révolter; **revolting** répugnant; **revolution** révolution *f;* **revolutionary 1** *adj* révolutionnaire **2** *n* révolutionnaire *m/f;* **revolutionize** révolutionner

revolve [rɪ'vɑːlv] tourner (**around** autour de); **revolver** revolver *m*

revulsion [rɪ'vʌlʃn] répugnance *f*

reward [rɪ'wɔːrd] **1** *n financial* récompense *f; (benefit derived)* gratification *f* **2** *v/t financially* récompenser; **rewarding** *experience* gratifiant, valorisant; **re-wind** [riː'waɪnd] *film, tape* rembobiner

rewrite [riː'raɪt] réécrire

rhetoric ['retərɪk] rhétorique *f*

rhyme [raɪm] **1** *n* rime *f* **2** *v/i* rimer (**with** avec)

rhythm ['rɪðm] rythme *m*

rib [rɪb] ANAT côte *f*

ribbon ['rɪbn] ruban *m*

rice [raɪs] riz *m*

rich [rɪtʃ] **1** *adj person, food* ri-che **2** *npl:* **the ~** les riches *mpl* (**off** sur)

ricochet ['rɪkəʃeɪ] ricocher (**off** sur)

rid [rɪd]: **get ~ of** se débarrasser de

ride [raɪd] **1** *n on horse* promenade *f* (à cheval); *excursion in vehicle* tour *m; (journey)* trajet *m;* **do you want a ~ in-to town?** est-ce que tu veux que je t'emmène en ville? **2** *v/t horse* monter; *bike* se déplacer en; **can I ~ your bike?** est-ce que je peux monter sur ton vélo? **3** *v/i on horse* monter à cheval; *on bike* rouler (à vélo); **rider** *on horse* cavalier(-ière) *m(f); on bike* cycliste *m/f*

ridge [rɪdʒ] *(raised strip)* arête *f* (saillante); *of mountain* crête *f; of roof* arête *f*

ridicule ['rɪdɪkjuːl] **1** *n* ridicule *m* **2** *v/t* ridiculiser; **ridiculous** ridicule; **ridiculously** ridiculement

riding ['raɪdɪŋ] *on horseback* équitation *f*

rifle ['raɪfl] fusil *m,* carabine *f*

rift [rɪft] *in earth* fissure *f; in party etc* scission *f*

rig [rɪg] **1** *n (oil ~)* tour *f* de forage; *at sea* plateforme *f* de forage; *(truck)* semi-remorque *m* **2** *v/t elections* truquer

right [raɪt] **1** *adj* bon; *(not left)* droit; **be ~** *of answer* être juste; *of person* avoir raison; *of clock* être à l'heure; **it's not ~ to ...** ce n'est pas bien de ...;

put things ~ arranger les choses; ***that's ~!*** c'est ça!; ***that's all ~*** *(doesn't matter)* ce n'est pas grave; *when s.o. says thank you* je vous en prie; ***it's all ~*** *(is acceptable)* ça me va; ***I'm all ~*** *not hurt* je vais bien; ***have enough ~*** ça ira pour moi **2** *adv (directly)* directement, juste; *(correctly)* correctement, bien; *(not left)* à droite; ***~ now*** *(immediately)* tout de suite; *(at the moment)* en ce moment; ***it's ~ here*** c'est juste là **3** *n civil, legal* droit *m*; *(not left)*, POL droite *f*; ***be in the ~*** avoir raison; **right-angle** angle *m* droit; **rightful** *owner etc* légitime; **right-handed** *person* droitier; **right-hand man** bras *m* droit; **right of way** *in traffic* priorité *f*; *across land* droit *m* de passage; **right wing** POL droite *f*; SP ailier *m* droit; **right-wing** POL de droite

rigid ['rɪdʒɪd] *also fig* rigide
rigor ['rɪgər] *of discipline* rigueur *f*; *of rigorous* rigoureux; **rigorously** *check* rigoureusement
rigour *Br* → **rigor**
rile [raɪl] F agacer
rim [rɪm] *of wheel* jante *f*; *of cup* bord *m*; *of eyeglasses* monture *f*
ring¹ [rɪŋ] *n (circle)* cercle *m*; *on finger* anneau *m*; *in box-*

ing ring *m*; *at circus* piste *f*
ring² [rɪŋ] **1** *n of bell* sonnerie *f*; *of voice* son *m* **2** *v/t bell* (faire) sonner; *Br* TELEC téléphoner à **3** *v/i of bell* sonner, retentir
'**ringleader** meneur(-euse) *m(f)*; **ring-pull** anneau *m* (d'ouverture)
rink [rɪŋk] patinoire *f*
rinse [rɪns] **1** *n for hair color* rinçage *m* **2** *v/t* rincer
riot ['raɪət] **1** *n* émeute *f* **2** *v/i* participer à une émeute; ***start to ~*** créer une émeute; **rioter** émeutier(-ière) *m(f)*; **riot police** police *f* anti-émeute
rip [rɪp] **1** *n in cloth etc* accroc *m* **2** *v/t cloth etc* déchirer
◆ **rip-off** F *customers* arnaquer F
ripe [raɪp] *fruit* mûr; **ripen** *of fruit* mûrir; **ripeness** *of fruit* maturité *f*
'**rip-off** F arnaque *f* F
ripple ['rɪpl] *on water* ride *f*
rise [raɪz] **1** *v/i from chair, bed, of sun* se lever; *of rocket, price, temperature* monter **2** *n in price, temperature* hausse *f*; *in water level* élévation *f*; *Br: in salary* augmentation *f*
risk [rɪsk] **1** *n* risque *m*; ***take a ~*** prendre un risque **2** *v/t* risquer; **risky** risqué
ritual ['rɪtʊəl] **1** *adj* rituel **2** *n* rituel *m*
rival ['raɪvl] **1** *n* rival(e) *m(f)* **2**

v/t (*match*) égaler; (*compete with*) rivaliser avec; **rivalry** rivalité *f*

river ['rɪvər] rivière *f*; *bigger* fleuve *m*; **riverbank** rive *f*; **riverbed** lit *m* de la rivière/ du fleuve; **riverside 1** *adj* en bord de rivière **2** *n* berge *f*, bord *m* de l'eau

riveting ['rɪvɪtɪŋ] fascinant

road [roʊd] route *f*; *in city* rue *f*; **roadblock** barrage *m* routier; **road-holding** *of vehicle* tenue *f* de route; **road map** carte *f* routière; **road safety** sécurité *f* routière; **roadsign** panneau *m* (de signalisation); **roadway** chaussée *f*; **roadworthy** en état de marche

roam [roʊm] errer

roar [rɔːr] **1** *n* rugissement *m*; *of traffic* grondement *m*; *of engine* vrombissement *m* **2** *v/i* rugir; *of traffic* gronder; *of engine* vrombir

roast [roʊst] **1** *n of beef etc* rôti *m* **2** *v/t* rôtir **3** *v/i of food* rôtir; **roast beef** rosbif *m*

rob [rɑːb] *person* voler, dévaliser; *bank* cambrioler, dévaliser; **robber** voleur(-euse) *m(f)*; **robbery** vol *m*

robe [roʊb] *of judge, priest* robe *f*; (*bath~*) peignoir *m*; (*dressing gown*) robe *f* de chambre

robot ['roʊbɑːt] robot *m*

robust [roʊ'bʌst] robuste

rock [rɑːk] **1** *n* rocher *m*; MUS

rock *m* **2** *v/t baby* bercer; *cradle* balancer; (*surprise*) secouer **3** *v/i on chair, of boat* se balancer; **rock-bottom** *price* le plus bas possible; **rock climber** varappeur(-euse) *m(f)*; **rock climbing** varappe *f*

rocket ['rɑːkɪt] **1** *n* fusée *f* **2** *v/i of prices etc* monter en flèche

rocking chair ['rɑːkɪŋ] rocking-chair *m*; **rock 'n' roll** rock-and-roll *m inv*; **rocky** *beach* rocheux

rod [rɑːd] baguette *f*; *for fishing* canne *f* à pêche

rodent ['roʊdnt] rongeur *m*

rogue [roʊg] vaurien *m*

role [roʊl] rôle *m*; **role model** modèle *m*

roll [roʊl] **1** *n* (*bread* ~) petit pain *m*; *of film* pellicule *f*; (*list, register*) liste *f* **2** *v/i of ball, boat* rouler

♦ **roll over 1** *v/i* se retourner **2** *v/t person, object* tourner; (*renew*) renouveler; (*extend*) prolonger

'roll call appel *m*; **roller** *for hair* rouleau *m*; **roller blade**® roller *m* (en ligne); **roller coaster** montagnes *fpl* russes; **roller skate** patin *m* à roulettes

ROM [rɑːm] COMPUT (= *read only memory*) ROM *f*, mémoire *f* morte

Roman 'Catholic 1 *adj* REL catholique **2** *n* catholique *m/f*

romance ['roʊmæns] (*affair*)

idylle *f*; *novel, movie* histoire *f* d'amour; **romantic** romantique

roof [ruːf] toit *m*; **roof-rack** MOT galerie *f*

rookie ['rʊkɪ] F bleu *m* F

room [ruːm] pièce *f*, salle *f*; (*bed*~) chambre *f*; (*space*) place *f*; (*space*) réceptionniste *m/f*; **roommate** *in apartment* colocataire *m/f*; *in room* camarade *m/f* de chambre; **room service** service *m* en chambre; **room temperature** température *f* ambiante; **roomy** spacieux; *clothes* ample

root [ruːt] racine *f*

rope [roʊp] corde *f*

rosary ['roʊzərɪ] REL rosaire *m*, chapelet *m*

rose [roʊz] BOT rose *f*

roster ['rɑːstər] tableau *m* de service

rostrum ['rɑːstrəm] estrade *f*

rosy ['roʊzɪ] *also fig* rose

rot [rɑːt] **1** *n* pourriture *f* **2** *v/i* pourrir

rotate [roʊ'teɪt] **1** *v/i* tourner **2** *v/t* (*turn*) (faire) tourner; *crops* alterner; **rotation** rotation *f*

rotten ['rɑːtn] *also* F *weather, luck* pourri

rough [rʌf] **1** *adj* *surface* rugueux; *hands, skin* rêche; *voice* rude; (*violent*) brutal; *crossing, seas* agité; (*approximate*) approximatif; ~ **draft** brouillon *m* **2** *n in golf* rough

m; **roughage** *in food* fibres *fpl*; **roughly** (*approximately*) environ; (*harshly*) brutalement

roulette [ruː'let] roulette *f*

round [raʊnd] **1** *adj* rond **2** *n of mailman, doctor, drinks* tournée *f*; *of competition* manche *f*, tour *m*; *in boxing* round *m* **3** *v/t corner* tourner **4** *adv & prep* → **around**

◆ **round up** *figure* arrondir; *suspects* ramasser

roundabout ['raʊndəbaʊt] **1** *adj* détourné, indirect **2** *n Br: on road* rond-point *m*; **round-the-world** autour du monde; **round trip** aller-retour *m*; **round-up** *of cattle* rassemblement *m*; *of suspects* rafles *f*; *of news* résumé *m*

rouse [raʊz] *from sleep* réveiller; *emotions* soulever; **rousing** exaltant

route [raʊt] itinéraire *m*

routine [ruː'tiːn] **1** *adj* de routine; *behavior* routinier **2** *n* routine *f*

row[1] [roʊ] *n* (*line*) rangée *f*; *of troops* rang *m*; **5 days in a** ~ 5 jours de suite

row[2] [roʊ] *v/i in boat* ramer

rowboat ['roʊboʊt] bateau *m* à rames

rowdy ['raʊdɪ] tapageur, bruyant

royal ['rɔɪəl] royal; **royalty** (*membres mpl* de) la famille royale; *on book, recording*

droits *mpl* d'auteur
rub [rʌb] frotter
rubber ['rʌbər] **1** *n material*
caoutchouc *m* **2** *adj* en caoutchouc; **rubber band** élastique *m*
rubble ['rʌbl] *from building*
gravats *mpl*, décombres *mpl*
ruby ['ruːbɪ] *jewel* rubis *m*
rudder ['rʌdər] gouvernail *m*
ruddy ['rʌdɪ] *complexion* coloré
rude [ruːd] impoli; *language,*
gesture grossier; **rudely** (*impolitely*) impoliment; **rude-**
ness impolitesse *f*
rudimentary [ruːdɪ'mentərɪ]
rudimentaire; **rudiments** rudiments *mpl*
rueful ['ruːfl] contrit, résigné;
ruefully avec regret; *smile*
d'un air contrit
ruffian ['rʌfɪən] voyou *m*, brute *f*
ruffle ['rʌfl] **1** *n on dress* ruche
f **2** *v/t hair* ébouriffer; *person*
énerver
rug [rʌg] tapis *m*; *blanket* couverture *f*
rugby ['rʌgbɪ] rugby *m*
rugged ['rʌgɪd] *scenery, cliffs*
escarpé; *face* aux traits rudes; *resistance* acharné
ruin ['ruːɪn] **1** *n* ruine *f* **2** *v/t*
ruiner; *party, plans* gâcher
rule [ruːl] **1** *n* règle *f*; *of mon-*
arch règne *m*; **as a** ~ en règle
générale **2** *v/t country* gouverner **3** *v/i of monarch* régner; **ruler** *for measuring* rè-

gle *f*; *of state* dirigeant(e)
m(f); **ruling 1** *n* décision *f*
2 *adj party* dirigeant, au pouvoir
rum [rʌm] *drink* rhum *m*
rumble ['rʌmbl] *of stomach*
gargouiller; *of thunder* gronder
rumor, *Br* **rumour** ['ruːmər] **1**
n bruit *m*, rumeur *f* **2** *v/t: it is*
~ed that ... le bruit court que
...
rump [rʌmp] *of animal* croupe
f
rumple ['rʌmpl] *clothes, paper*
froisser
'rumpsteak rumsteck *m*
run [rʌn] **1** *n on foot* course *f*;
in pantyhose échelle *f*; **go for**
a ~ *for exercise* aller courir;
in the short/long ~ à court/
long terme **2** *v/i* courir; *of*
river, paint, makeup couler;
of trains, buses passer, circuler; *of play* être à l'affiche; *of*
engine, machine marcher,
tourner; *of software* fonctionner; *in election* se présenter; ~ **for President** être
candidat à la présidence **3**
v/t race courir; *business, ho-*
tel etc diriger; *software* exécuter, faire tourner; *car* entretenir

◆ **run away** s'enfuir; *from*
home for a while faire une fugue; *for good* s'enfuir de
chez soi

◆ **run down 1** *v/t* (*knock*
down) renverser; (*criticize*)

critiquer; **stocks** diminuer **2** *v/i of battery* se décharger

◆ **run off 1** *v/i* s'enfuir **2** *v/t* (*print off*) tirer

◆ **run out** *of contract* expirer; *of time* s'écouler; *of supplies* s'épuiser

◆ **run out of** ne plus avoir de

◆ **run over 1** *v/t* (*knock down*) renverser **2** *v/i of water etc* déborder

◆ **run up** *debts* accumuler

'**runaway** fugueur(-euse) *m(f)*; **run-down** *person* épuisé; *area* délabré

rung [rʌŋ] *of ladder* barreau *m*

runner ['rʌnər] *athlete* coureur(-euse) *m(f)*; **runner beans** haricots *mpl* d'Espagne; **runner-up** second(e) *m(f)*; **running 1** *n* SP course *f*; *of business* gestion *f* **2** *adj*: *for two days* ~ pendant deux jours de suite; **running water** eau *f* courante; **runny** *substance* liquide; *nose* qui coule; **run-up** SP élan *m*; *in the* ~ *to* pendant la période

qui précède; **runway** AVIA piste *f*

rupture ['rʌptʃər] **1** *n also fig* rupture *f* **2** *v/i of pipe* éclater

rural ['rʊrəl] rural

ruse [ruːz] ruse *f*

rush [rʌʃ] **1** *n* ruée *f*; *do sth in a* ~ faire qch à la hâte; *be in a* ~ être pressé **2** *v/t person* presser; *meal* avaler (à toute vitesse) **3** *v/i* se presser; **rush hour** heures *fpl* de pointe

Russia ['rʌʃə] Russie *f*; **Russian** ['rʌʃən] **1** *adj* russe **2** *n* Russe *m/f*; *language* russe *m*

rust [rʌst] **1** *n* rouille *f* **2** *v/i* se rouiller; **rust-proof** antirouille *inv*; **rusty** *also fig* rouillé

rut [rʌt] *in road* ornière *f*; *be in a* ~ *fig* être tombé dans la routine

ruthless ['ruːθlɪs] impitoyable, sans pitié; **ruthlessly** impitoyablement; **ruthlessness** dureté *f* (impitoyable)

rye [raɪ] seigle *m*; **rye bread** pain *m* de seigle

S

sabotage ['sæbətɑːʒ] **1** *n* sabotage *m* **2** *v/t* saboter; **saboteur** saboteur(-euse) *m(f)*

sachet ['sæʃeɪ] sachet *m*

sack [sæk] **1** *n bag* sac *m* **2** *v/t* F virer F

sacred ['seɪkrɪd] sacré

sacrifice ['sækrɪfaɪs] **1** *n* sacrifice *m* **2** *v/t also fig* sacrifier

sacrilege ['sækrɪlɪdʒ] REL, *fig* sacrilège *m*

sad [sæd] triste

saddle ['sædl] **1** *n* selle *f* **2** *v/t*

horse seller

sadism ['seɪdɪzm] sadisme *m*;
sadist sadique *m/f*; **sadistic**
sadique

sadly ['sædlɪ] tristement; (*regrettably*) malheureusement;
sadness tristesse *f*

safe [seɪf] **1** *adj* (*not dangerous*) pas dangereux; *driver*
prudent; (*not in danger*) en
sécurité **2** *n* coffre-fort *m*;
safeguard 1 *n*: **as a ~
against** par mesure de protection contre **2** *v/t* protéger;
safely *arrive, drive* sans
risque; *of investment, prediction*
sûreté *f*; **safety** sécurité
f; *of investment, prediction*
sûreté *f*; **safety pin** épingle
f de nourrice

sag [sæg] *of ceiling* s'affaisser; *of rope* se détendre;
fig: of output fléchir

saga ['sɑːgə] saga *f*

sage [seɪdʒ] *herb* sauge *f*

sail [seɪl] **1** *n of boat* voile *f*;
trip voyage *m* (en mer) **2**
v/i faire de la voile; (*depart*)
partir; **sailboard 1** *n* planche
f à voile **2** *v/i* faire de la planche à voile; **sailboarding**
planche *f* à voile; **sailboat**
bateau *m* à voiles; **sailing**
SP voile *f*; **sailor** marin *m*

saint [seɪnt] saint(e) *m(f)*

sake [seɪk]: **for my ~** pour moi

salad ['sæləd] salade *f*

salary ['sælərɪ] salaire *m*

sale [seɪl] vente *f*; *reduced
prices* soldes *mpl*; **for ~** *sign*
à vendre; **be on ~** être en

vente; *at reduced prices* être
en solde; **sales department**
vente *f*; **sales clerk** *in store*
vendeur(-euse) *m(f)*; **sales
figures** chiffre *m* d'affaires;
salesman vendeur *m*; (*rep*)
représentant *m*; **saleswoman** vendeuse *f*

salient ['seɪlɪənt] marquant

saliva [sə'laɪvə] salive *f*

salmon ['sæmən] saumon *m*

saloon [sə'luːn] (*bar*) bar *m
Br* MOT berline *f*

salt [sɔːlt] sel *m*; **salty** salé

salute [sə'luːt] **1** *n* MIL salut *m*
2 *v/t* MIL saluer **3** *v/i* MIL faire
un salut

salvage ['sælvɪdʒ] *from
wreck* sauver

salvation [sæl'veɪʃn] *also fig*
salut *m*

same [seɪm] **1** *adj* même **2**
pron: **the ~** le/la même; *pl*
the ~ les mêmes; **Happy
New Year – the ~ to you**
Bonne année – à vous aussi;
all the ~ (*even so*) quand même **3** *adv*: **look/sound the ~**
se ressembler, être pareil

sample ['sæmpl] *of work,
cloth* échantillon *m*; *of blood*
prélèvement *m*

sanction ['sæŋkʃn] **1** *n* (*approval*) approbation *f*; (*penalty*) sanction *f* **2** *v/t* (*approve*)
approuver

sand [sænd] **1** *n* sable *m* **2** *v/t
with sandpaper* poncer au
papier de verre

sandal ['sændl] sandale *f*

'**sandbag** sac *m* de sable; **sand dune** dune *f*; **sander** *tool* ponceuse *f*; **sandpaper 1** *n* papier *m* de verre **2** *v/t* poncer au papier de verre

sandwich ['sænwɪtʃ] sandwich *m*

sandy ['sændɪ] *beach* de sable; *soil* sablonneux; *feet, towel* plein de sable; *hair* blond roux

sane [seɪn] sain (d'esprit)

sanitarium [sænɪ'teriəm] sanatorium *m*

sanitary ['sænɪterɪ] sanitaire; (*clean*) hygiénique; **sanitary napkin** serviette *f* hygiénique; **sanitation installations** *fpl* sanitaires; (*removal of waste*) système *m* sanitaire

sanity ['sænɪtɪ] santé *f* mentale

Santa Claus ['sæntəklɔːz] le Père Noël

sap [sæp] **1** *n in tree* sève *f* **2** *v/t s.o.'s energy* saper

sapphire ['sæfaɪr] saphir *m*

sarcasm ['sɑːrkæzm] sarcasme *m*; **sarcastic** sarcastique; **sarcastically** sarcastiquement

sardine [sɑːr'diːn] sardine *f*

sardonic [sɑːr'dɔːnɪk] sardonique

satellite ['sætəlaɪt] satellite *m*; **satellite dish** antenne *f* parabolique; **satellite TV** télévision *f* par satellite

satin ['sætɪn] satin *m*

satire ['sætaɪr] satire *f*; **satiri-** cal satirique; **satirize** satiriser

satisfaction [sætɪs'fækʃn] satisfaction *f*; **satisfactory** satisfaisant; (*just good enough*) convenable; **satisfy** satisfaire; *conditions* remplir

Saturday ['sætərdeɪ] samedi *m*

sauce [sɔːs] sauce *f*; **saucepan** casserole *f*; **saucer** soucoupe *f*

Saudi Arabia [saudɪə'reɪbɪə] Arabie *f* saoudite; **Saudi Arabian 1** *adj* saoudien **2** *n* Saoudien(ne) *m(f)*

sausage ['sɔːsɪdʒ] saucisse *f*; *dried* saucisson *m*

savage ['sævɪdʒ] **1** *adj* féroce **2** *n* sauvage *m/f*; **savagery** férocité *f*

save [seɪv] **1** *v/t* (*rescue*), SP sauver; (*economize, put aside*) économiser; (*collect*) faire collection de; COMPUT sauvegarder **2** *v/i* (*put money aside*) faire des économies; SP arrêter le ballon **3** *n* SP arrêt *m*; **saver** *person* épargneur (-euse) *m(f)*; **savings** économies *fpl*; **savings account** compte *m* d'épargne; **savings and loan** caisse *f* d'épargne-logement; **savings bank** caisse *f* d'épargne

savior, *Br* **saviour** ['seɪvjər] REL sauveur *m*

savor ['seɪvər] savourer; **savory** *not sweet* salé

savour *etc Br* → **savor** *etc*

saw [sɔː] **1** *n tool* scie *f* **2** *v/t*
scier; sawdust sciure *f*

saxophone ['sæksəfoʊn]
saxophone *m*

say [seɪ] dire; *that is to ~*
c'est-à-dire; saying dicton *m*

scab [skæb] *on wound* croûte
f

scaffolding ['skæfəldɪŋ]
échafaudage *m*

scald [skɔːld] ébouillanter

scale¹ [skeɪl] *n on fish* écaille
f

scale² [skeɪl] **1** *n of project,
map etc, on thermometer*
échelle *f*; MUS gamme *f* **2**
v/t cliffs etc escalader

scales [skeɪlz] *for weighing*
balance *f*

scallop ['skæləp] *shellfish* coquille *f* Saint-Jacques

scalp [skælp] cuir *m* chevelu

scalpel ['skælpl] scalpel *m*

scam [skæm] F arnaque *m* F

scampi ['skæmpɪ] scampi *m*

scan [skæn] **1** *n* MED scanner
m; *during pregnancy* écho-
graphie *f* **2** *v/t horizon, page*
parcourir du regard; MED faire un scanner de; COMPUT
scanner

◆ scan in COMPUT scanner

scandal ['skændl] scandale
m; scandalize scandaliser;
scandalous scandaleux

scanner ['skænər] MED,
COMPUT scanner *m*

scanty ['skæntɪ] *dress* réduit
au minimum

scapegoat ['skeɪpgoʊt] bouc

m émissaire

scar [skɑːr] **1** *n* cicatrice *f* **2** *v/t*
marquer d'une cicatrice

scarce [skers] rare; scarcely
['skersli] à peine; *~ anything*
presque rien; scarcity manque *m*

scare [sker] **1** *v/t* faire peur à;
be ~d of avoir peur de **2** *n*
(*panic, alarm*) rumeurs *fpl*
alarmantes; scaremonger
alarmiste *m/f*

scarf [skɑːrf] *around neck*
écharpe *f*; *over head* foulard
m

scarlet ['skɑːrlət] écarlate

scary ['skeri] effrayant

scathing ['skeɪðɪŋ] cinglant

scatter ['skætər] **1** *v/t leaflets,
seed* éparpiller **2** *v/i of people*
se disperser; *scattered
showers* intermittent; *vil-
lages* éparpillé

scavenge ['skævɪndʒ]: *~ for
sth* fouiller pour trouver
qch; scavenger charognard
m; *person* fouilleur(euse)
m(f)

scenario [sɪˈnɑːrɪoʊ] scénario
m

scene [siːn] scène *f*; *of accident, crime etc* lieu *m*; *make
a ~* faire une scène; *behind
the ~s* dans les coulisses;
scenery paysage *m*; THEA dé-
cor(s) *m(pl)*

scent [sent] odeur *f*; Br (*perfume*) parfum *m*

sceptic *etc* Br → skeptic *etc*

schedule ['skedjuːl] **1** *n of*

events calendrier *m*; *for trains* horaire *m*; *of lessons, work* programme *m*; **be on ~ of work, workers** être dans les temps; *of train* être à l'heure; **be behind ~** être en retard **2** *v/t* (*put on ~*) prévoir; **scheduled flight** vol *m* régulier

scheme [skiːm] **1** *n* plan *m* **2** *v/i* (*plot*) comploter; **scheming** intrigant

schizophrenia [skɪtsəˈfriːnɪə] schizophrénie *f*; **schizophrenic 1** *adj* schizophrène **2** *n* schizophrène *m/f*

scholar [ˈskɑːlər] érudit(e) *m(f)*; **scholarly** savant, érudit; **scholarship** (*learning*) érudition *f*; *financial award* bourse *f*

school [skuːl] école *f*; (*university*) université *f*; **school bag** cartable *m*; **schoolchildren** écoliers *mpl*

science [ˈsaɪəns] science *f*; **scientific** scientifique; **scientist** scientifique *m/f*

scissors [ˈsɪzərz] ciseaux *mpl*

scoff[1] [skɑːf] *food* engloutir

scoff[2] [skɑːf] (*mock*) se moquer

scold [skoʊld] réprimander

scoop [skuːp] **1** *n for ice-cream* cuiller *f* à glace; *of ice cream* boule *f*; *story* scoop *m*

scooter [ˈskuːtər] *with motor* scooter *m*; *child's* trottinette *f*

scope [skoʊp] ampleur *f*;

(*freedom, opportunity*) possibilités *fpl*

scorch [skɔːrtʃ] brûler; **scorching** très chaud

score [skɔːr] **1** *n* SP score *m*; (*written music*) partition *f*; *of movie etc* musique *f* **2** *v/t goal, point* marquer; (*cut: line*) rayer **3** *v/i* SP marquer; (*keep the ~*) marquer les points; **scoreboard** tableau *m* des scores; **scorer** marqueur(-euse) *m(f)*

scorn [skɔːrn] **1** *n* mépris *m* **2** *v/t idea* mépriser; **scornful** méprisant; **scornfully** avec mépris

Scot [skɑːt] Écossais(e) *m(f)*; **Scotch** *whiskey* scotch *m*; **Scotch tape**® scotch *m*; **Scotland** Écosse *f*; **Scottish** écossais

scoundrel [ˈskaʊndrəl] gredin *m*

scour [ˈskaʊər] (*search*) fouiller

scowl [skaʊl] **1** *n* air *m* renfrogné **2** *v/i* se renfrogner

scramble [ˈskræmbl] **1** *n* (*rush*) course *f* folle **2** *v/t message* brouiller **3** *v/i*: **he ~d to his feet** il se releva d'un bond; **scrambled eggs** œufs *mpl* brouillés

scrap [skræp] **1** *n metal* ferraille *f*; (*fight*) bagarre *f*; *of food, paper* bout *m* **2** *v/t idea, plan* abandonner

scrape [skreɪp] **1** *n on paint, skin* éraflure *f* **2** *v/t paint-*

work, arm etc érafler

'**scrap metal** ferraille *f*

scrappy ['skræpɪ] *work, essay* décousu

scratch [skrætʃ] **1** *n mark* égratignure *f*; **start from ~** partir de zéro; **not up to ~** pas à la hauteur **2** *v/t* (*mark: skin, paint*) égratigner; *of cat* griffer; *because of itch* se gratter **3** *v/i of cat* griffer

scrawl [skrɔːl] **1** *n* gribouillis *m* **2** *v/t* gribouiller

scrawny ['skrɔːnɪ] décharné

scream [skriːm] **1** *n* cri *m* **2** *v/i* pousser un cri

screech [skriːtʃ] **1** *n of tires* crissement *m*; (*scream*) cri *m* strident **2** *v/i of tires* crisser; (*scream*) pousser un cri strident

screen [skriːn] **1** *n in room, hospital* paravent *m*; *in movie theater, of TV, computer* écran *m* **2** *v/t* (*protect, hide*) cacher; *movie* projeter; *for security reasons* passer au crible; **screenplay** scénario *m*; **screen saver** COMPUT économiseur m d'écran; **screen test** *for movie* bout *m* d'essai

screw [skruː] **1** *n* vis *m* **2** *v/t attach* visser (**to** à); F (*cheat*) rouler F; V (*have sex with*) baiser V; **screwdriver** tournevis *m*; **screwed up** F *psychologically* paumé F; **screwy** F déjanté F

scribble ['skrɪbl] **1** *n* griffonnage *m* **2** *v/t* (*write quickly*)

griffonner **3** *v/i* gribouiller

script [skrɪpt] *for movie* scénario *m*; *for play* texte *m*; *form of writing* script *m*; Scripture: **the (Holy) ~s** les Saintes Écritures *fpl*; **scriptwriter** scénariste *m/f*

◆ **scroll down** [skrəʊl] COMPUT faire défiler vers le bas

◆ **scroll up** COMPUT faire défiler vers le haut

scrounge [skraʊndʒ] se faire offrir; **scrounger** profiteur(-euse) *m(f)*

scrub [skrʌb] *floor* laver à la brosse

scruples ['skruːplz] scrupules *mpl*; **scrupulous** *morally, (thorough)* scrupuleux; **scrupulously** (*meticulously*) scrupuleusement

scrutinize ['skruːtɪnaɪz] (*examine closely*) scruter; **scrutiny** examen *m* minutieux

scuba diving ['skuːbə] plongée *f* sous-marine autonome

scuffle ['skʌfl] bagarre *f*

sculptor ['skʌlptər] sculpteur(-trice) *m(f)*; **sculpture** sculpture *f*

scum [skʌm] *on liquid* écume *f*; *pej: people* bande *f* d'ordures F

sea [siː] mer *f*; **seabird** oiseau *m* de mer; **seafood** fruits *mpl* de mer; **seagull** mouette *f*

seal[1] [siːl] *n animal* phoque *m*

seal[2] [siːl] **1** *n on document*

sceau m; TECH étanchéité f **2** v/t container sceller

'**sea level**: *above/below* ~ au-dessus/au-dessous du niveau de la mer

seam [si:m] *on garment* couture f; *of ore* veine f

'**seaman** marin m; **seaport** port m maritime

search [sɜːrʃ] **1** n recherche f (*for* de) **2** v/t chercher dans
♦ **search for** chercher

searching ['sɜːrʃɪŋ] *look, question* pénétrant; **searchlight** projecteur m

'**seashore** plage f; **seasick**: *get* ~ avoir le mal de mer; **seaside**: *at the* ~ au bord de la mer

season ['siːzn] saison f; *seasonal vegetables, employment* saisonnier; *seasoned wood* sec; *traveler, campaigner* expérimenté; **seasoning** assaisonnement m; **season ticket** carte f d'abonnement

seat [siːt] *place* f; *chair* siège m; *of pants* fond m; *please take a* ~ veuillez vous asseoir; **seat belt** ceinture f de sécurité

'**seaweed** algues fpl

secluded [sɪ'kluːdɪd] retiré

second ['sekənd] **1** n *of time* seconde f **2** adj deuxième **3** adv *come in* deuxième **4** v/t *motion* appuyer; **secondary** secondaire; **second floor** premier étage m, Br deuxiè-

me étage m; **second-hand** d'occasion; **secondly** deuxièmement; **second-rate** de second ordre

secrecy ['siːkrəsɪ] secret m; **secret 1** n secret m **2** adj secret

secretarial [sekrə'terɪəl] *job* de secrétariat; **secretary** secrétaire m/f; POL ministre m/f; **Secretary of State** secrétaire m/f d'État

secretive ['siːkrətɪv] secret; **secretly** en secret

sect [sekt] secte f

section ['sekʃn] section f

sector ['sektər] secteur m

secular ['sekjʊlər] séculier

secure [sɪ'kjʊr] **1** adj *shelf etc* bien fixé; *job, contract* sûr **2** v/t *shelf etc* fixer; *s.o.'s help, finances* se procurer; **securities market** FIN marché m des valeurs; **security** sécurité f; *for investment* garantie f; **security alert** alerte f de sécurité; **security forces** forces fpl de sécurité; **security guard** garde m de sécurité; **security risk** *menace potentielle à la sécurité de l'État ou d'une organisation*

sedan [sɪ'dæn] MOT berline f

sedate [sɪ'deɪt] donner un calmant à; **sedative** calmant m

sedentary ['sedəntərɪ] *job* sédentaire

sediment ['sedɪmənt] sédiment m

seduce [sɪ'djuːs] séduire; seduction séduction f; seduc-
tive dress, offer séduisant

see [siː] with eyes, (understand) voir; ~ you! F à plus! F
◆ see off at airport etc raccompagner; (chase away)
chasser

seed [siːd] single graine f; collective graines fpl; of fruit pépin m; in tennis tête f de série; seedy miteux

seeing 'eye dog chien m
d'aveugle; seeing (that)
étant donné que

seek [siːk] chercher

seem [siːm] sembler; seem-
ingly apparemment

seesaw ['siːsɔː] bascule f

'see-through transparent

segment ['segmənt] segment
m; of orange morceau m

segregate ['segrɪgeɪt] séparer; segregation ségréga-
tion f; of sexes séparation f

seismology [saɪz'mɒlədʒɪ]
sismologie f

seize [siːz] arm, opportunity,
of police etc saisir; power
s'emparer de; seizure MED
crise f; of drugs etc saisie f

seldom ['seldəm] rarement

select [sɪ'lekt] 1 v/t sélectionner 2 adj group of people
choisi; hotel etc chic inv; selection sélection f; selective
sélectif

self [self] moi m; self-assur-
ance confiance f en soi;
self-assured sûr de soi;

self-centered, Br self-cen-
tred égocentrique; self-confidence confiance en soi;
self-confident sûr de soi;
self-conscious intimidé;
about sth gêné (about par);
self-consciousness timidité f; about sth gêne f (about
par rapport à); self-control
contrôle m de soi; self-defense, Br self-defence autodéfense f; LAW légitime défense f; self-employed indépendant; self-evident évident; self-expression ex-
pression f; self-government
autonomie f; self-interest
intérêt m (personnel); selfish égoïste; selfless désinte-
ressé; self-made man self-
-made man m; self-pity api-
toiement m sur soi-même;
self-portrait autoportrait m;
self-reliant autonome; self-
-respect respect m de soi;
self-satisfied pej suffisant;
self-service libre-service;
self-service restaurant self
m; self-taught autodidacte

sell [sel] 1 v/t vendre 2 v/i of
products se vendre; sell-by
date date f limite de vente;
seller vendeur(-euse) m(f);
selling COM vente f; selling
point COM point m fort

Sellotape® ['seləteɪp] Br
scotch m

semester [sɪ'mestər] semestre m

semi ['semɪ] truck semi-remorque f; **semicircle** demi-cercle m; **semiconductor** ELEC semi-conducteur m; **semifinal** demi-finale f; **semifinalist** demi-finaliste m/f

seminar ['semɪnɑːr] séminaire m

semi'skilled worker spécialisé

senate ['senət] Sénat m; **senator** sénateur(-trice) m(f)

send [send] envoyer (**to** a)
◆ **send back** renvoyer
◆ **send for** doctor faire venir; help envoyer chercher

sender ['sendər] of letter expéditeur(-trice) m(f)

senile ['siːnaɪl] sénile; **senility** sénilité f

senior ['siːnjər] (older) plus âgé; in rank supérieur; **senior citizen** personne f âgée; **seniority** in job ancienneté f

sensation [sen'seɪʃn] sensation f; **sensational** sensationnel

sense [sens] **1** n sens m; (common ~) bon sens m; (feeling) sentiment m; **come to one's ~s** revenir à la raison; **it doesn't make ~** cela n'a pas de sens **2** v/t sentir; **senseless** (pointless) stupide

sensible ['sensəbl] sensé; clothes, shoes pratique; **sensibly** raisonnablement

sensitive ['sensɪtɪv] sensible; **sensitivity** sensibilité f

sensor ['sensər] détecteur m

sensual ['senʃʊəl] sensuel; **sensuality** sensualité f

sensuous ['senʃʊəs] voluptueux

sentence ['sentəns] **1** n GRAM phrase f; LAW peine f **2** v/t LAW condamner

sentiment ['sentɪmənt] (sentimentality) sentimentalité f; (opinion) sentiment m; **sentimental** sentimental; **sentimentality** sentimentalité f

sentry ['sentrɪ] sentinelle f

separate 1 ['sepərət] adj séparé **2** ['sepəreɪt] v/t séparer (**from** de) **3** v/i of couple se séparer; **separated** couple séparé; **separately** séparément; **separation** séparation f

September [sep'tembər] septembre m

septic ['septɪk] septique

sequel ['siːkwəl] suite f

sequence ['siːkwəns] ordre m

serene [sɪ'riːn] serein

sergeant ['sɑːrdʒənt] sergent m

serial ['sɪrɪəl] feuilleton m; **serialize** novel on TV adapter en feuilleton; **serial number** of product numéro m de série

series ['sɪriːz] série f

serious ['sɪrɪəs] person, company sérieux; illness, situation, damage grave; **seriously** injured gravement; understaffed sérieusement; **take s.o.** ~ prendre qn au sérieux; **seriousness** of person, situation, illness etc gravité f

sermon ['sɜːmən] sermon m

servant ['sɜːvənt] domestique m/f

serve [sɜːv] **1** n in tennis service m **2** v/t & v/i serve m; server in tennis serveur(-euse) m(f); COMPUT serveur m; **service** n also in tennis service m; for vehicle, machine entretien m; **~s** services mpl **2** v/t vehicle, machine entretenir; **service charge** service m; **serviceman** MIL militaire m; **service station** station-service f; **serving** of food portion f

session ['seʃn] session f, meeting, talk discussion f

set [set] **1** n (collection) série f; (group of people) groupe m; MATH ensemble m; THEA (scenery) décor m; for movie plateau m; in tennis set m **2** v/t (place) poser; movie, novel etc situer; date, time, limit fixer; alarm mettre; broken limb remettre en place; jewel sertir; **~ the table** mettre la table **3** v/i of sun se coucher; of glue durcir **4** adj ideas arrêté; (ready) prêt

◆ **set off 1** v/i on journey partir **2** v/t alarm etc déclencher

◆ **set out 1** v/i on journey partir **2** v/t ideas, goods exposer

◆ **set up 1** v/t company,

equipment, machine monter; market stall installer; meeting arranger; F (frame) faire un coup à **2** v/i in business s'établir

'**setback** revers m

settee [se'tiː] Br (couch, sofa) canapé m

setting ['setɪŋ] of novel, play, house cadre m

settle ['setl] **1** v/i of bird se poser; of dust se déposer; of building se tasser; to live s'installer **2** v/t dispute, issue, debts régler; nerves, stomach calmer; **that ~s it!** ça règle la question!

◆ **settle down** (stop being noisy) se calmer; (stop wild living) se ranger; in an area s'installer

◆ **settle for** (accept) accepter

settled ['setld] weather stable; **settlement** of claim, debt, dispute, (payment) règlement m; of building tassement m; **settler** in new country colon m

'**set-up** (structure) organisation f; (relationship) relation f; F (frame-up) coup monté

seven ['sevn] sept; **seventeen** dix-sept; **seventeenth** dix-septième; **seventh** septième; **seventieth** soixante-dixième; **seventy** soixante-dix

sever ['sevər] sectionner; relations rompre

several ['sevrl] plusieurs

severe [sɪ'vɪr] *illness* grave; *penalty* lourd; *winter, weather* rigoureux; *teacher* sévère; **severely** *punish, speak* sévèrement; *injured* grièvement; *disrupted* fortement; **severity** *of illness* gravité *f*; *of penalty* lourdeur *f*; *of winter* rigueur *f*; *of teacher* sévérité *f*

sew [soʊ] coudre

sewage ['suːɪdʒ] eaux *fpl* d'égouts; **sewer** égout *m*

sewing ['soʊɪŋ] *skill* couture *f*; *(that being sewn)* ouvrage *m*

sex [seks] sexe *m*; **have ~ with** coucher avec; **sexist 1** *adj* sexiste **2** *n* sexiste *m/f*; **sexual** sexuel; **sexuality** sexualité *f*; **sexually** sexuellement; **sexy** sexy *inv*

shabbily ['ʃæbɪlɪ] *dressed* pauvrement; *treat* mesquinement; **shabby** *coat etc* usé; *treatment* mesquin

shack [ʃæk] cabane *f*

shade [ʃeɪd] **1** *n for lamp* abat-jour *m*; *of color* nuance *f*; *on window* store *m*; **in the ~** à l'ombre **2** *v/t from sun* protéger du soleil; *from light* protéger de la lumière

shadow ['ʃædoʊ] ombre *f*

shady ['ʃeɪdɪ] *spot* ombragé; *character* louche

shaft [ʃæft] *of axle* arbre *m*; *of mine* puits *m*

shake [ʃeɪk] **1** *n*: **give sth a good ~** bien agiter qch **2** *v/t* *bottle* agiter; *emotionally* bouleverser; **~ one's head** *in refusal* dire non de la tête; **~ hands with s.o.** serrer la main à qn *v/i of hands, voice, building* trembler; **shaken** *emotionally* bouleversé; **shake-up** remaniement *m*; **shaky** *table etc* branlant; *after illness, shock* faible; *voice, hand* tremblant; *grasp of sth, grammar etc* incertain

shall [ʃæl] ◇ *future:* **I ~ do my best** je ferai de mon mieux ◇ *suggesting:* **~ we go now?** si nous y allions maintenant?

shallow ['ʃæloʊ] *water* peu profond; *person* superficiel

shame [ʃeɪm] **1** *n* honte *f*; **what a ~!** quel dommage! **2** *v/t* faire honte à; **shameful** honteux; **shameless** effronté

shampoo [ʃæm'puː] shampo(o)ing *m*

shape [ʃeɪp] **1** *n* forme *f* **2** *v/t clay, character* façonner; *the future* influencer; **shapeless** *dress etc* informe; **shapely** *figure* bien fait

share [ʃer] **1** *n* part *f*; FIN action *f* **2** *v/t & v/i* partager; **shareholder** actionnaire *m/f*

shark [ʃɑːrk] requin *m*

sharp [ʃɑːrp] **1** *adj knife* tranchant; *mind, pain* vif; *taste* piquant **2** *adv* MUS trop haut; **at 3 o'clock** à 3 heures pile; **sharpen** *knife, skills* aiguiser

shatter ['ʃætər] **1** v/t glass, illusions briser **2** v/i of glass se briser; **shattered** ['ʃætərd] F (exhausted) crevé F; F (very upset) bouleversé; **shattering** news bouleversant

shave [ʃeɪv] **1** v/t raser **2** v/i se raser **3** n: **have a ~** se raser; **shaven** head rasé; **shaver** rasoir m électrique

shawl [ʃɔːl] châle m

she [ʃiː] elle; **there ~ is** la voilà

sheath [ʃiːθ] for knife étui m; contraceptive préservatif m

shed¹ [ʃed] v/t blood, tears verser; leaves perdre

shed² [ʃed] n abri m

sheep [ʃiːp] mouton m; **sheepdog** chien m de berger; **sheepish** penaud

sheer [ʃɪr] pur; cliffs abrupt

sheet [ʃiːt] drap m; of paper, metal, glass feuille f

shelf [ʃelf] étagère f; **shelves** set of shelves étagère(s) f(pl)

shell [ʃel] **1** n of mussel, egg coquille f; of tortoise carapace f; MIL obus m **2** v/t peas écosser; MIL bombarder; **shellfire** bombardements mpl; **shellfish** fruits mpl de mer

shelter ['ʃeltər] **1** n abri m **2** v/i s'abriter (**from** de) **3** v/t (protect) protéger; **sheltered** place protégée; **lead a ~ life** mener une vie protégée

shelve [ʃelv] fig mettre en suspens

shepherd ['ʃepərd] berger (-ère) m(f)

sheriff ['ʃerɪf] shérif m

shield [ʃiːld] **1** n MIL bouclier m; sports trophy plaque f; badge: of policeman plaque f **2** v/t (protect) protéger

shift [ʃɪft] **1** n (change) changement m; (move, switchover) passage m (**to** à); at work poste m; people équipe f **2** v/t (move) déplacer; production, employee transférer; stains etc faire partir **3** v/i (move) se déplacer; in attitude virer; **shifty** pej: person louche; eyes fuyant

shin [ʃɪn] tibia m

shine [ʃaɪn] **1** v/i briller; fig: of student etc être brillant (**at**, **in** en) **2** n on shoes etc brillant m; **shiny** brillant

ship [ʃɪp] **1** n bateau m, navire m **2** v/t (send) expédier **3** v/t of new product être lancé (sur le marché); **shipment** envoi m; **shipowner** armateur m; **shipping** (sea traffic) navigation f; (sending) expédition f; **shipwreck** naufrage m; **shipyard** chantier m naval

shirt [ʃɜːrt] chemise f

shit [ʃɪt] **1** n P merde f P **2** v/i P chier P **3** int P merde P; **shitty** F dégueulasse F

shiver ['ʃɪvər] trembler

shock [ʃɑːk] **1** n choc m; ELEC décharge f; **be in ~** MED être en état de choc **2** v/t choquer;

shock absorber MOT amortisseur m; **shocking** choquant; F (*very bad*) épouvantable

shoddy ['ʃɑːdɪ] *goods* de mauvaise qualité; *behavior* mesquin

shoe [ʃuː] chaussure f, soulier m; **shoelace** lacet m; **shoemaker** cordonnier(-ière) m(f); **shoe mender** cordonnier(-ière) m(f); **shoestore** magasin m de chaussures

shoot [ʃuːt] **1** n bot pousse f **2** v/t tirer sur; *and kill* tuer d'un coup de feu; *movie* tourner **3** v/i tirer

◆ shoot down *airplane* abattre; *fig: suggestion* descendre

◆ shoot up *of prices* monter en flèche; *of children, new buildings etc* pousser

shooting star ['ʃuːtɪŋ] étoile f filante

shop [ʃɑːp] **1** n magasin m **2** v/i faire ses courses; **go ~ping** faire les courses; **shopkeeper** commerçant m,-ante f; **shoplifter** voleur(-euse) m(f) à l'étalage; **shoplifting** vol m à l'étalage

shopping *items* courses fpl; **go ~** faire les courses; **shopping bag** sac m à provisions; **shopping list** liste f de commissions; **shopping mall** centre m commercial

shore [ʃɔːr] rivage m; **on ~** *not at sea* à terre

short [ʃɔːrt] **1** adj court; in

height petit; **be ~ of** manquer de **2** adv: **cut ~** abréger; **go ~ of** se priver de; **in ~** bref; **shortage** manque m; **shortcoming** défaut m; **shortcut** raccourci m; **shorten** raccourcir; **shortfall** déficit m; **short-lived** de courte durée; **shortly** (*soon*) bientôt; **~ before/after that** peu avant/après; **shortness of visit** brièveté f; *in height* petite taille f; **shorts** short m; *underwear* caleçon m; **short-sighted** myope; *fig* peu perspicace; **short-sleeved** à manches courtes; **short-tempered** *by nature* d'un caractère emporté; *at a particular time* de mauvaise humeur; **short-term** à court terme

shot [ʃɑːt] *from gun* coup m de feu; (*photograph*) photo f; (*injection*) piqûre f; **shotgun** fusil m de chasse

should [ʃʊd]: **what ~ I do?** que dois-je faire?; **you ~n't do that** tu ne devrais pas faire ça; **you ~ have heard him** tu aurais dû l'entendre

shoulder ['ʃoʊldər] épaule f

shout [ʃaʊt] **1** n cri m **2** v/t & v/i crier; **shouting** cris mpl

shove [ʃʌv] **1** n: **give s.o. a ~** pousser qn **2** v/t & v/i pousser

shovel ['ʃʌvl] pelle f

show [ʃoʊ] **1** n THEA, TV spectacle m; (*display*) démonstration f **2** v/t montrer; *at exhibition* présenter; *movie* projeter **3** v/i (be visible) se voir; of movie passer

◆ **show in** faire entrer

◆ **show off 1** v/t skills faire étalage de **2** v/i pej crâner

◆ **show up 1** v/t shortcomings etc faire ressortir **2** v/i (arrive, turn up) se pointer F; (be visible) se voir

'**show business** monde m du spectacle; **showcase** also fig vitrine f; **showdown** confrontation f

shower ['ʃaʊər] **1** n of rain averse f; to wash douche f; party: petite fête avant un mariage ou un accouchement à laquelle tout le monde apporte un cadeau; **take a ~** prendre une douche **2** v/i prendre une douche

'**show-off** pej prétentieux (-euse) m(f); **showroom** salle f d'exposition; **showy** voyant

shred [ʃred] **1** n of paper etc lambeau m; of meat etc morceau m **2** v/t documents déchiqueter; in cooking râper; **shredder** for documents déchiqueteuse f

shrewd [ʃruːd] perspicace; **shrewdness** perspicacité f

shriek [ʃriːk] **1** n cri m aigu **2** v/i pousser un cri aigu

shrill [ʃrɪl] perçant

shrimp [ʃrɪmp] crevette f

shrine [ʃraɪn] lieu m saint

shrink[1] [ʃrɪŋk] v/i of material rétrécir; of support diminuer

shrink[2] [ʃrɪŋk] n F (psychiatrist) psy m F

shrivel ['ʃrɪvl] se flétrir

shrub [ʃrʌb] arbuste m; **shrubbery** massif m d'arbustes

shrug [ʃrʌg]: **~ (one's shoulders)** hausser les épaules

shudder ['ʃʌdər] **1** n of fear, disgust frisson m; of earth vibration f **2** v/i with fear, disgust frissonner; of earth vibrer

shuffle ['ʃʌfl] v/t cards battre

shun [ʃʌn] fuir

shut [ʃʌt] **1** v/t fermer **2** v/i of door, box se fermer; of store fermer

◆ **shut down 1** v/t business fermer; computer éteindre **2** v/i of business fermer ses portes; of computer s'éteindre

◆ **shut up** F (be quiet) se taire; **shut up!** tais-toi!

shutter ['ʃʌtər] on window volet m; PHOT obturateur m

shuttle bus ['ʃʌtl] at airport navette f

shy [ʃaɪ] timide; **shyness** timidité f

sick [sɪk] malade; sense of humor noir; Br (vomit) vomir; **sicken 1** v/t (disgust) écœurer; (make ill) rendre malade **2** v/i: **be ~ing for** couver; **sickening** écœurant; **sick leave** congé m de maladie; **sickness** maladie *f*; (*vomiting*) vomissements *mpl*

side [saɪd] côté *m*; SP équipe *f*; **take ~s** (*favor one ~*) prendre parti; **~ by ~** côte à côte; **side effect** effet *m* secondaire; **sidestep** éviter; *fig also* contourner; **side street** rue *f* transversale; **sidewalk** trottoir *m*; **sideways** de côté

siege [siːdʒ] siège *m*

sieve [sɪv] *for flour* tamis *m*

sift [sɪft] tamiser; *data* passer en revue

sigh [saɪ] **1** *n* soupir *m* **2** *v/i* soupirer

sight [saɪt] **1** *n* spectacle *m*; (*power of seeing*) vue *f*; **~s** *of city* monuments *mpl*; **know by ~** connaître de vue; **sightseeing: go ~** faire du tourisme; **sightseer** touriste *m/f*

sign [saɪn] **1** *n* signe *m*; (*road~*) panneau *m*; *outside shop* enseigne *f* **2** *v/t & v/i* signer

signal ['sɪɡnl] **1** *n* signal *m* **2** *v/i of driver* mettre son clignotant

signatory ['sɪɡnətɔːrɪ] signataire *m/f*

signature ['sɪɡnətʃər] signature *f*

significance [sɪɡ'nɪfɪkəns] importance *f*; **significant** *event, sum of money, improvement etc* important; **significantly** *larger, more expensive* nettement

signify ['sɪɡnɪfaɪ] signifier

sign language langage *m* des signes; **signpost** poteau *m* indicateur

silence ['saɪləns] **1** *n* silence *m* **2** *v/t* faire taire; **silent** silencieux

silhouette [sɪluː'et] silhouette *f*

silicon ['sɪlɪkən] silicium *m*

silk [sɪlk] **1** *adj shirt etc* en soie **2** *n* soie *f*; **silky** soyeux

silliness ['sɪlɪnɪs] stupidité *f*; **silly** bête

silo ['saɪloʊ] silo *m*

silver ['sɪlvər] **1** *adj ring* en argent; *hair* argenté **2** *n* argent *m*; **silverware** argenterie *f*

similar ['sɪmɪlər] semblable (**to** à); **similarity** ressemblance *f*; **similarly** de la même façon

simple ['sɪmpl] simple; **simple-minded** *pej* simple, simplet; **simplicity** simplicité *f*; **simplify** simplifier; **simplistic** simpliste; **simply** (*absolutely*) absolument; (*in a simple way*) simplement

simultaneous [saɪməl'teɪnɪəs] simultané; **simultaneously** simultanément

sin [sɪn] **1** *n* péché *m* **2** *v/i* pécher

since [sɪns] **1** *prep & adv* depuis; **I've been here ~ last week** je suis là depuis la semaine dernière **2** *conj in expressions of time* depuis que; (*seeing that*) puisque

sincere [sɪn'sɪr] sincère; **sincerely** sincèrement; ***Sincerely yours*** Je vous prie d'agréer, Madame/Monsieur, l'expression de mes sentiments les meilleurs; **sincerity** sincérité *f*

sinful ['sɪnfʊl] *deeds* honteux; **~ person** pécheur *m*, pécheresse *f*

sing [sɪŋ] chanter

singe [sɪndʒ] brûler légèrement

singer ['sɪŋər] chanteur(-euse) *m(f)*

single ['sɪŋgl] **1** *adj* (*sole*) seul; (*not double*) simple; *bed* à une place; (*not married*) célibataire **2** *n* MUS single *m*; (*~ room*) chambre *f* à un lit; *person* personne *f* seule; **~s** *in tennis* simple *m*; **single-handed** tout seul; **single-minded** résolu; **single parent** mère/père qui élève ses enfants tout seul; **single parent family** famille *f* monoparentale; **single room** chambre *f* à un lit

singular ['sɪŋgjʊlər] GRAM **1** *adj* au singulier **2** *n* singulier *m*

sinister ['sɪnɪstər] sinistre

sink [sɪŋk] **1** *n* évier *m* **2** *v/i* of *ship, object* couler; *of sun* descendre; *of interest rates etc* baisser **3** *v/t ship* couler; *money* investir

sinner ['sɪnər] pécheur *m*, pécheresse *f*

sip [sɪp] **1** *n* petite gorgée *f* **2** *v/t* boire à petites gorgées

sir [sɜːr] monsieur *m*

siren ['saɪrən] sirène *f*

sirloin ['sɜːrlɔɪn] aloyau *m*

sister ['sɪstər] sœur *f*; **sister-in-law** belle-sœur *f*

sit [sɪt] (*~ down*) s'asseoir; *she was sitting* elle était assise

♦ **sit down** s'asseoir

sitcom ['sɪtkɑːm] sitcom *m*

site [saɪt] **1** *n* emplacement *m*; *of battle* site *m* **2** *v/t new offices etc* situer

sitting ['sɪtɪŋ] *of committee, court, for artist* séance *f*; *for meals* service *m*; **sitting room** salon *m*

situated ['sɪtʃueɪtɪd] situé; **situation** situation *f*; *of building etc* emplacement *m*

six [sɪks] six; **sixteen** seize; **sixteenth** seizième; **sixth** sixième; **sixtieth** soixantième; **sixty** soixante

size [saɪz] *of room, jacket* taille *f*; *of project* envergure *f*; *of loan* montant *m*; *of shoes* pointure *f*; *of meal, house* assez grand; *order, amount* assez important

skate [skeɪt] **1** *n* patin *m* **2** *v/i* patiner; **skateboard** skateboard *m*; **skateboarding** skateboard *m*; **skater** patineur(-euse) *m(f)*; **skating** patinage *m*; **skating rink** patinoire *f*

skeleton ['skelɪtn] squelette

m

skeptic ['skeptık] sceptique *m/f*; **skeptical** sceptique; **skepticism** scepticisme *m*

sketch [sketʃ] **1** *n* croquis *m*; THEA sketch *m* **2** *v/t* esquisser; **sketchy** *knowledge etc* sommaire

ski [skiː] **1** *n* ski *m* **2** *v/i* faire du ski

skid [skɪd] **1** *n* dérapage *m* **2** *v/i* déraper

skier ['skiːər] skieur(-euse) *m(f)*; **skiing** ski *m*

skilful *etc* Br → **skillful**

skill [skɪl] **1** *n* technique *f*; **~s** compétences *fpl*; **skilled** habile; **skillful** habile; **skillfully** habilement

skim [skɪm] *surface* effleurer

skimpy ['skɪmpɪ] *account etc* sommaire; *dress* étriqué

skin [skɪn] **1** *n* peau *f* **2** *v/t* *animal* écorcher; *tomato* peler; **skin diving** plongée *f* sous-marine autonome; **skinny** maigre; **skin-tight** moulant

skip [skɪp] **1** *n* (*little jump*) saut *m* **2** *v/i* sautiller **3** *v/t* (*omit*) sauter; **skipper** capitaine *m/f*

skirt [skɜːrt] jupe *f*

skull [skʌl] crâne *m*

skunk [skʌŋk] mouffette *f*

sky [skaɪ] ciel *m*; **skylight** lucarne *f*; **skyline** silhouette *f*; **skyscraper** gratte-ciel *m inv*

slab [slæb] *of stone, butter* plaque *f*; *of cake* grosse tranche *f*

slack [slæk] *rope* mal tendu; *work* négligé; *period* creux; **slacken** *rope* détendre; *pace* ralentir; **slacks** pantalon *m*

slam [slæm] claquer

slander ['slændər] **1** *n* calomnie *f* **2** *v/t* calomnier; **slanderous** calomnieux

slang [slæŋ] *also of a specific group* argot *m*

slant [slænt] **1** *v/i* pencher **2** *n* inclinaison *f*; *given to a story* perspective *f*; **slanting** *roof* en pente; *eyes* bridé

slap [slæp] **1** *n* (*blow*) claque *f* **2** *v/t* donner une claque à

slash [slæʃ] **1** *n cut* entaille *f*; *in punctuation* barre *f* oblique **2** *v/t* *painting, skin* entailler; *prices* réduire radicalement

slaughter ['slɔːtər] **1** *n* *of animals* abattage *m*; *of people, troops* massacre *m* **2** *v/t* *animals* abattre; *people, troops* massacrer; **slaughterhouse** abattoir *m*

slave [sleɪv] esclave *m/f*

slay [sleɪ] tuer; **slaying** (*murder*) meurtre *m*

sleaze [sliːz] POL corruption *f*; **sleazy** *bar, character* louche

sleep [sliːp] **1** *n* sommeil *m*; **go to** ~ s'endormir **2** *v/i* dormir

♦ **sleep with** (*have sex with*) coucher avec

'**sleeping bag** sac *m* de couchage; **sleeping car** RAIL wagon-lit *m*; **sleeping pill** somnifère *m*; **sleepwalker** somnambule *m/f*; **sleepwalking** somnambulisme *m*; **sleepy** *person* qui a envie de dormir; *yawn, town* endormi; **I'm ~** j'ai sommeil

sleet [sliːt] neige *f* fondue

sleeve [sliːv] *of jacket etc* manche *f*; **sleeveless** sans manches

slender ['slendər] mince; *chance, margin* faible

slice [slaɪs] **1** *n of bread, pie* tranche *f*; *fig: of profits* part *f* **2** *v/t loaf etc* couper en tranches

slick [slɪk] **1** *adj performance* habile; *pej (cunning)* rusé **2** *n of oil* marée *f* noire

slide [slaɪd] **1** *n for kids* toboggan *m*; PHOT diapositive *f* **2** *v/i* glisser; *of exchange rate etc* baisser **3** *v/t item of furniture* faire glisser

slight [slaɪt] *person, figure* frêle; *(small)* léger; **no, not in the ~est** non, pas le moins du monde; **slightly** légèrement

slim [slɪm] *person* mince; *chance* faible

slime [slaɪm] *(mud)* vase *f*; *of slug etc* bave *f*; **slimy** *liquid etc* vaseux

sling [slɪŋ] **1** *n for arm* écharpe *f* **2** *v/t* F *(throw)* lancer

slip [slɪp] **1** *n (mistake)* erreur *f* **2** *v/i* glisser; *in quality, quantity* baisser

◆ **slip up** *(make a mistake)*

faire une gaffe

slipped 'disc [slɪpt] hernie *f* discale

slipper ['slɪpər] chausson *m*

slippery ['slɪpərɪ] glissant

'slip-up *(mistake)* gaffe *f*

slit [slɪt] **1** *n (tear)* déchirure *f*; *(hole), in skirt* fente *f* **2** *v/t* ouvrir, fendre

sliver ['slɪvər] petit morceau *m*; *of wood, glass* éclat *m*

slob [slɑːb] *pej* rustaud(e) *m(f)*

slog [slɑːg] *long walk* trajet *m* pénible; *hard work* corvée *f*

slogan ['slougən] slogan *m*

slop [slɑːp] *(spill)* renverser

slope [sloup] **1** *n* inclinaison *f*; *of mountain* côté *m* **2** *v/i* être incliné

sloppy ['slɑːpɪ] F *work, in dress* négligé; *(too sentimental)* gnangnan F

slot [slɑːt] *tente f*; *in schedule* créneau *m*; **slot machine** *for vending* distributeur *m* (automatique); *for gambling* machine *f* à sous

slovenly ['slʌvnlɪ] négligé

slow [slou] lent; **be ~** *of clock* retarder

◆ **slow down 1** *v/t* ralentir **2** *v/i* ralentir; *in life* faire moins de choses

'slowdown *in production* ralentissement *m*; **slowly** lentement; **slowness** lenteur *f*

sluggish ['slʌgɪʃ] lent; *river* à cours lent

slum [slʌm] *area* quartier *m*

pauvre; *house* taudis *m*

slump [slʌmp] **1** *n in trade* effondrement *m* **2** *v/i of economy* s'effondrer; *of person* s'affaisser

slur [slɜːr] **1** *n on character* tache *f* **2** *v/t words* mal articuler

slush [slʌʃ] neige *f* fondue; *pej (sentimental stuff)* sensiblerie *f*; **slush fund** caisse *f* noire

slut [slʌt] *pej* pute *f* F

sly [slaɪ] *(furtive)* sournois; *(crafty)* rusé

small [smɔːl] petit

smart[1] [smɑːrt] **1** *adj* élégant; *(intelligent)* intelligent; *pace* vif

smart[2] [smɑːrt] *v/i (hurt)* brûler

'smart card carte *f* à puce; **smartly** *dressed* avec élégance

smash [smæʃ] **1** *n noise* fracas *m*; *(car crash)* accident *m*; *in tennis* smash *m* **2** *v/t break* fracasser; *(hit hard)* frapper **3** *v/i break* se fracasser

smattering ['smætərɪŋ]: **have a ~ of Chinese** savoir un peu de chinois

smear [smɪr] **1** *n of ink etc* tache *f*; *Br MED* frottis *m*; *on character* diffamation *f* **2** *v/t character* entacher

smell [smel] **1** *n* odeur *f*; **sense of ~** sens *m* de l'odorat **2** *v/t* sentir **3** *v/i unpleasantly* sentir mauvais; *(sniff)* renifler; **smelly** qui sent mauvais

smile [smaɪl] **1** *n* sourire *m* **2** *v/i* sourire

smirk [smɜːrk] petit sourire *m* narquois

smoke [smoʊk] **1** *n* fumée *f* **2** *v/t also food* fumer **3** *v/i of person* fumer; **smoker** fumeur(-euse) *m(f)*; **smoke-free** non-fumeur *inv*; **smoking: no ~** défense de fumer; **smoky** enfumé

smolder ['smoʊldər] *of fire* couver

smooth [smuːð] **1** *adj surface, skin, sea* lisse; *ride, flight, crossing* bon; *pej: person* mielleux **2** *v/t hair* lisser; **smoothly** *without any problems* sans problème

smother ['smʌðər] *person, flames* étouffer

smoulder *Br* → **smolder**

smudge [smʌdʒ] **1** *n* tache *f* **2** *v/t paint* faire des traces sur; *ink, mascara* étaler

smug [smʌɡ] suffisant

smuggle ['smʌɡl] passer en contrebande; **smuggler** contrebandier(-ière) *m(f)*; **smuggling** contrebande *f*

smutty ['smʌtɪ] *joke* grossier

snack [snæk] en-cas *m*

snag [snæɡ] *(problem)* hic *m* F

snake [sneɪk] serpent *m*

snap [snæp] **1** *n sound* bruit *m* sec; *PHOT* instantané *m* **2** *v/t break* casser **3** *v/i break* se casser net **4** *adj decision, judgement* rapide; subit;

snappy *person, mood* cassant; *decision* prompt; **be a ~ dresser** s'habiller chic; *snapshot photo f*

snarl [snɑːrl] **1** *n of dog* grondement **2** *v/i of dog* gronder en montrant les dents

snatch [snætʃ] (*grab*) saisir; F (*steal*) voler; F (*kidnap*) enlever

snazzy ['snæzɪ] F *necktie etc* qui tape F

sneakers ['sniːkərz] tennis *mpl*

sneaky ['sniːkɪ] F (*underhanded*) sournois

sneer [snɪr] **1** *n* ricanement *m* **2** *v/i* ricaner

sneeze [sniːz] **1** *n* éternuement *m* **2** *v/i* éternuer

snicker ['snɪkər] pouffer de rire

sniff [snɪf] renifler

sniper ['snaɪpər] tireur *m* embusqué

snitch [snɪtʃ] **1** *n* (*telltale*) mouchard(e) *m(f)* **2** *v/i* (*tell tales*) vendre la mèche

snivel ['snɪvl] pleurnicher

snob [snɑːb] snob *m/f*; **snobbery** snobisme *m*; **snobbish** snob *inv*

♦ **snoop around** [snuːp] fourrer le nez partout

snooty ['snuːtɪ] arrogant

snooze [snuːz] **1** *n* petit somme *m* **2** *v/i* roupiller F

snore [snɔːr] ronfler; **snoring** ronflement *m*

snorkel ['snɔːrkl] tuba *m*

snort [snɔːrt] *of bull, horse* s'ébrouer; *of person* grogner

snow [snoʊ] **1** *n* neige *f* **2** *v/i* neiger; **snowball** boule *f* de neige; **snowdrift** amoncellement *m* de neige; **snowman** bonhomme *m* de neige; **snowplow** chasse-neige *m inv*; **snowstorm** tempête *f* de neige; **snowy** *weather* neigeux; *roads, hills* enneigé

snub [snʌb] **1** *n* rebuffade *f* **2** *v/t* snober; **snub-nosed** au nez retroussé

snug [snʌg] bien au chaud; (*tight-fitting*) bien ajusté

so [soʊ] **1** *adv* si, tellement; **~ kind** tellement gentil; **not ~ much for me** pas autant pour moi; **~ much easier** tellement plus facile; **drink ~ much** tellement boire; **~ many people** tellement de gens; **I miss you ~** tu me manques tellement; **~ am/do I** moi aussi; **~ is/does she** elle aussi; **and ~ on** et ainsi de suite **2** *pron*: **I hope ~** je l'espère bien; **I think ~** je pense que oui; **50 or ~** une cinquantaine, à peu près cinquante **3** *conj* (*for that reason*) donc; (*in order that*) pour que (+*subj*); **~ (that) I could come too** pour que je puisse moi aussi venir; **~ what?** F et alors?

soak [soʊk] (*steep*) faire tremper; *of water* tremper; **soaked** trempé

soap [soup] *for washing* savon *m*; **soap** *(opera)* feuilleton *m*; **soapy** savonneux

soar [sɔːr] *of rocket, prices etc* monter en flèche

sob [sɑːb] **1** *n* sanglot *m* **2** *v/i* sangloter

sober ['soubər] en état de sobriété; *(serious)* sérieux

so-'called *(referred to as)* comme on le/la/les appelle; *(incorrectly referred to as)* soi-disant *inv*

soccer ['sɑːkər] football *m*

sociable ['souʃəbl] sociable

social ['souʃl] social; *(recreational)* mondain; **social democrat** social-démocrate *m/f*; **socialism** socialisme *m*; **socialist 1** *adj* socialiste **2** *n* socialiste *m/f*; **socialize** fréquenter des gens; **social worker** assistant sociale *m*, assistante sociale *f*

society [sə'saɪətɪ] société *f*

sociologist [sousɪ'ɑːlədʒɪst] sociologue *m/f*; **sociology** sociologie *f*

sock¹ [sɑːk] *n for wearing* chaussette *f*

sock² [sɑːk] *v/t (punch)* donner un coup de poing à

socket ['sɑːkɪt] ELEC *for light bulb* douille *f*; *Br (wall ~)* prise *f* de courant; *of eye* orbite *f*

soda ['soudə] *(~ water)* eau *f* gazeuse; *(soft drink)* soda *m*; *(ice-cream ~)* soda *m* à la crème glacée

sofa ['soufə] canapé *m*

soft [sɑːft] doux; *(lenient)* gentil; **soften** *position* assouplir; *impact, blow* adoucir; **softly** doucement; **software** logiciel *m*

soggy ['sɑːgɪ] *soil* détrempé; *pastry* pâteux

soil [sɔɪl] **1** *n (earth)* terre *f* **2** *v/t* salir

solar energy ['soulər] énergie *f* solaire

soldier ['souldʒər] soldat *m*

sole¹ [soul] *n of foot* plante *f*; *of shoe* semelle *f*

sole² [soul] *adj* seul; *responsibility* exclusif

solely ['soulɪ] exclusivement

solemn ['sɑːləm] solennel; **solemnity** solennité *f*; **solemnly** solennellement

solicit [sə'lɪsɪt] *of prostitute* racoler

solid ['sɑːlɪd] *(hard)* dur; *(without holes)* compact; *gold, silver etc, support* massif; **solidarity** solidarité *f*; **solidify** se solidifier; **solidly** *built* solidement; *in favor of* massivement

solitaire [sɑːlɪ'ter] *card game* réussite *f*

solitary ['sɑːlɪterɪ] *life, activity* solitaire; *(single)* isolé; **solitude** solitude *f*

solo ['soulou] **1** *adj* en solo **2** *n* MUS solo *m*; **soloist** soliste *m/f*

soluble ['sɑːljubl] *substance, problem* soluble; **solution**

also mixture solution *f*

solve [sɑːlv] résoudre; **solvent** *financially* solvable

somber, *Br* sombre ['sɒmbər] sombre

some [sʌm] **1** *adj:* **~ cream/chocolate/cookies** de la crème/du chocolat/des biscuits; **~ people say that ...** certains disent que ... **2** *pron:* **~ of the money** une partie de l'argent; **~ of the group** certaines personnes du groupe, certains du groupe; **would you like ~?** est-ce que vous en voulez?; **give me ~** donnez-m'en **3** *adv* (*a bit*) un peu; **somebody** quelqu'un; **someday** un jour; **somehow** (*by one means or another*) d'une manière ou d'une autre; (*for some unknown reason*) sans savoir pourquoi; **someone** → **somebody**; **someplace** → **somewhere**

somersault ['sʌmərsɒlt] **1** *n* roulade *f*; *by vehicle* tonneau *m* **2** *v/i of vehicle* faire un tonneau

'**something** quelque chose; **sometime** un de ces jours; **~ last year** dans le courant de l'année dernière; **sometimes** parfois; **somewhat** quelque peu; **somewhere 1** *adv* quelque part **2** *pron:* **let's go ~ quiet** allons dans un endroit calme; **~ to park** un endroit où se garer

son [sʌn] fils *m*

song [sɑːŋ] chanson *f*

'**son-in-law** beau-fils *m*; **son of a bitch** V fils *m* de pute V

soon [suːn] (*in a short while*) bientôt; (*quickly*) vite; (*early*) tôt; **how~?** dans combien de temps?; **as ~ as** dès que; **as ~ as possible** le plus tôt possible; **~er or later** tôt ou tard; **the ~er the better** le plus tôt sera le mieux

soothe [suːð] calmer

sophisticated [səˈfɪstɪkeɪtɪd] sophistiqué; **sophistication** [səˈfɪstɪkeɪʃn] sophistication *f*

sophomore ['sɑːfəmɔːr] étudiant(e) *m(f)* de deuxième année

soprano [səˈprɑːnou] soprano *m/f*

sordid ['sɔːrdɪd] sordide

sore [sɔːr] **1** *adj* F (*angry*) fâché; (*painful*): **is it ~?** ça vous fait mal? **2** *n* plaie *f*

sorrow ['sɑːrou] chagrin *m*

sorry ['sɑːrɪ] *day* triste; *sight* misérable; (**I'm**) **~!** (*apologizing*) pardon!; **be ~** être désolé

sort [sɔːrt] **1** *n* sorte *f*; **~ of ...** F plutôt **2** *v/t also* COMPUT trier

SOS [esouˈes] S.O.S. *m*; *fig: plea for help* appel *m* à l'aide

so-'so F comme ci comme ça F

soul [soul] *also fig* âme *f*

sound¹ [saund] **1** *adj* (*sensible*) judicieux; *construction* solide; (*healthy*) en bonne santé; *sleep* profond **2** *adv:* **be ~**

asleep être profondément endormi

sound² [saʊnd] **1** *n* son *m*; (*noise*) bruit *m* **2** *v/i*: *that ~s interesting* ça a l'air intéressant

soundly ['saʊndlɪ] *sleep* profondément; *beaten* à plates coutures; *soundproof* insonorisé; *soundtrack* bande *f* sonore

soup [su:p] soupe *f*

sour ['saʊər] *apple, milk* aigre; *comment* désobligeant

source [sɔ:rs] *of river, information etc* source *f*

south [saʊθ] **1** *n* sud *m*; *the South of France* le Midi **2** *adj* sud *inv*; *wind* du sud **3** *adv travel* vers le sud; **South Africa** Afrique *f* du sud; **South African 1** *adj* sud-africain **2** *n* Sud-Africain *m*, Sud-Africaine *f*; **South America** Amérique *f* du sud; **South American 1** *adj* sud-américain **2** *n* Sud-Américain(e) *m(f)*; **southeast 1** *n* sud-est *m* **2** *adj* sud-est *inv* **3** *adv travel* vers le sud-est; **southeastern** sud-est *inv*; **southerly** *wind* du sud; *direction* vers le sud; **southern** du Sud; **southerner** habitant(e) *m(f)* du Sud; **southernmost** le plus au sud; **South Pole** pôle *m* Sud; **southward** vers le sud; **southwest 1** *n* sud-ouest *m* **2** *adj* sud-ouest *inv* **3** *adv* vers

le sud-ouest; **southwestern** sud-ouest *inv*

souvenir [su:vəˈnɪr] souvenir *m*

sovereign ['sɑːvrɪn] *state* souverain

sow¹ [saʊ] *n* (*female pig*) truie *f*

sow² [soʊ] *v/t seeds* semer

space [speɪs] espace *m*; (*room*) place *f*; **space shuttle** navette *f* spatiale; **space station** station *f* spatiale; **spacious** spacieux

spade [speɪd] *for digging* bêche *f*; **~s** *in card game* pique *m*

spaghetti [spəˈgetɪ] spaghetti *mpl*

Spain [speɪn] Espagne *f*

spam (mail) [spæm] spam *m*

span [spæn] (*cover*) recouvrir; *of bridge* traverser

Spaniard ['spænjərd] Espagnol *m*, Espagnole *f*; **Spanish 1** *adj* espagnol **2** *n language* espagnol *m*; *the ~* les Espagnols

spanner ['spænər] *Br* clef *f*

spare [sper] **1** *v/t time* accorder; (*lend: money*) prêter; (*do without*) se passer de; *can you ~ the time?* est-ce que vous pouvez trouver un moment? **2** *adj* (*extra*) *cash* en trop; *pair of glasses, clothes* de rechange **3** *n* pièce *f* de rechange; **spare part** pièce *f* de rechange; **spare ribs** côtelette *f* de porc dans l'échine; **spare room** chambre *f* d'ami; **spare time** temps *m* libre; **spare wheel** roue *f* de secours; **sparing:** *be ~ with* économiser; **sparingly** en petite quantité

spark [spɑːrk] étincelle *f*

sparkle ['spɑːrkl] étinceler; **sparkling wine** vin *m* mousseux

'spark plug bougie *f*

sparse [spɑːrs] *vegetation* épars

spartan ['spɑːrtn] *room* spartiate

spasmodic [spæz'mɑːdɪk] intermittent; *conversation* saccadé

spate [speɪt] *fig* série *f*, avalanche *f*

spatial ['speɪʃl] spatial

speak [spiːk] **1** *v/i* parler (**to,** **with** à); *~ing* TELEC lui-même, elle-même *f*; *v/t foreign language* parler; **speaker** *at conference* intervenant(e) *m(f)*; *(orator)* orateur(-trice) *m(f)*; *of sound system* haut-parleur *m*; *French/Spanish* ~ francophone *m/f* / hispanophone *m/f*

special ['speʃl] spécial; *effort,* *day etc* exceptionnel; **specialist** spécialiste *m/f*; **specialize** se spécialiser (*in* en, dans); **specially** → **especially**; **specialty** spécialité *f*

species ['spiːʃiːz] espèce *f*

specific [spə'sɪfɪk] spécifique; **specifically** spécifique-

ment; **specifications** *of machine etc* spécifications *fpl*; **specify** préciser

specimen ['spesɪmən] *of work* spécimen *m*; *of blood,* *urine* prélèvement *m*

spectacular [spek'tækjʊlər] spectaculaire

spectator [spek'teɪtər] spectateur(-trice) *m(f)*

spectrum ['spektrəm] *fig* éventail *m*

speculate ['spekjʊleɪt] *also* FIN spéculer; **speculation** spéculations *fpl*; FIN spéculation *f*; **speculator** [spek'spekjʊ-lateur(-trice) *m(f)*

speech [spiːtʃ] discours *m*; *(ability to speak)* parole *f*; *(way of speaking)* élocution *f*; **speechless** *with shock,* *surprise* sans voix

speed [spiːd] **1** *n* vitesse *f* **2** *v/i* *(go quickly)* se précipiter; *of vehicle* foncer; *drive too quickly* faire de la vitesse; **speedboat** vedette *f*; *with outboard motor* hors-bord *m inv*; **speed bump** dos d'âne *m*, ralentisseur *m*; **speed-dial button** bouton *m* de numérotation abrégée; **speedily** rapidement; **speeding** *when driving* excès *m* de vitesse; **speed limit** limitation *f* de vitesse; **speedometer** compteur *m* de vitesse; **speedy** rapide

spell[1] [spel] **1** *v/t word* écrire, épeler; *how do you ~ it?*

513

split

comment ça s'écrit? **2** v/i: **he
can/can't ~** il a une bonne/
mauvaise orthographe
spell² n of time période f
spelling ['spelɪŋ] orthographe
f
spend [spend] money dépenser; time passer; **spendthrift**
pej dépensier(-ière) m(f)
sperm [spɜːrm] spermatozoïde m; (semen) sperme m
sphere [sfɪr] also fig sphère f
spice [spaɪs] (seasoning) épice f; **spicy** food épicé
spider ['spaɪdər] araignée f;
spiderweb toile f d'araignée
spike [spaɪk] pointe f; on
plant, animal piquant m
spill [spɪl] **1** v/t renverser **2** v/i
se répandre **3** n of oil déver-
sement m accidentel
spin¹ [spɪn] **1** n (turn) tour m **2**
v/t faire tourner **3** v/i of wheel
tourner
spin² v/t wool etc filer; web
tisser
spinach ['spɪnɪdʒ] épinards
mpl
spinal ['spaɪnl] de vertèbres;
spinal column colonne f
vertébrale; **spinal cord**
moelle f épinière; **spine** colonne f vertébrale; of book
dos m; on plant, hedgehog
épine f; **spineless** (cowardly) lâche
'**spin-off** retombée f
spiny ['spaɪnɪ] épineux
spiral ['spaɪrəl] **1** n spirale f **2**
v/i rise quickly monter en

spirale
spire [spaɪr] of church flèche
f
spirit ['spɪrɪt] esprit m; (courage) courage m; (spirited (energetic) énergique; **spirits**
(alcohol) spiritueux mpl;
(morale) moral m; **be in
good/poor ~** avoir/ne pas
avoir le moral; **spiritual** spirituel
spit [spɪt] of person cracher
spite [spaɪt] malveillance f; **in
~ of** en dépit de; **spiteful**
malveillant; **spitefully** avec
malveillance
splash [splæʃ] **1** n noise plouf
m; small amount of liquid
goutte f; of color tache f **2**
v/t person éclabousser; water,
mud asperger **3** v/i of person
patauger; **~ against sth** of
waves s'écraser contre qch;
splashdown amerrissage m
splendid ['splendɪd] magnifique; **splendor**, Br **splendour** splendeur f
splint [splɪnt] MED attelle f
splinter ['splɪntər] **1** n of
wood, glass éclat m; in finger
écharde f **2** v/i se briser
split [splɪt] **1** n damage fente
f; (disagreement) division f;
(of profits etc) partage m;
(share) part f **2** v/t wood fendre; log fendre en deux;
(cause disagreement in, divide) diviser **3** v/i of wood
etc se fendre; (disagree) se diviser

◆ **split up** *of couple* se séparer

spoil [spɔɪl] *child* gâter; *surprise, party* gâcher; **spoilsport** F rabat-joie *m/f*; **spoilt** *child* gâté

spoke [spəʊk] *of wheel* rayon *m*

spokesperson ['spəʊkspɜːrsən] porte-parole *m/f*

sponge [spʌndʒ] éponge *f*; **sponger** F parasite *m/f*

sponsor ['spɒnsər] **1** *n for club membership* parrain *m*, marraine *f*; RAD, TV, SP sponsor *m/f* **2** *v/t for club membership* parrainer; RAD, TV, SP sponsoriser; **sponsorship** RAD, TV, SP sponsorisation *f*

spontaneous [spɑːn'teɪnɪəs] spontané; **spontaneously** spontanément

spool [spuːl] bobine *f*

spoon [spuːn] cuillère *f*; **spoonful** cuillerée *f*

sporadic [spə'rædɪk] intermittent

sport [spɔːrt] *n* sport *m*; *sporting event;* sportif; *(fair, generous)* chic *inv*; **sports car** voiture *f* de sport; **sportsman** sportif *m*; **sportswoman** sportive *f*; **sporty** *person* sportif

spot[1] [spɑːt] *n on skin* bouton *m*; *in pattern* pois *m*

spot[2] *n (place)* endroit *m*

spot[3] *v/t (notice, identify)* repérer

'**spot check** contrôle *m* au hasard; **spotless** impeccable; **spotlight** *beam* feu *m* de projecteur; *device* projecteur *m*; **spotty** *with pimples* boutonneux

spouse [spaʊs] *fml* époux *m*, épouse *f*

spout [spaʊt] **1** *n* bec *m* **2** *v/i of liquid* jaillir **3** *v/t* F débiter

sprain [spreɪn] **1** *n* foulure *f*; *serious* entorse *f* **2** *v/t ankle, wrist* se fouler; *seriously* se faire une entorse à

sprawl [sprɔːl] *s'affaler; of city* s'étendre; **sprawling** tentaculaire

spray [spreɪ] **1** *n of sea water* embruns *mpl*; *from fountain* gouttes *fpl* d'eau; *for hair* laque *f*; *container* atomiseur *m* **2** *v/t perfume, lacquer* vaporiser; *paint, weed-killer etc* pulvériser; ~ **graffiti on sth** peindre des graffitis à la bombe sur qch; **spraygun** pulvérisateur *m*

spread [spred] **1** *n of disease, religion etc* propagation *f*; F *(big meal)* festin *m* **2** *v/t (lay), butter* étaler; *news, rumor, disease* répandre; *arms, legs* étendre **3** *v/i* se répandre; **spreadsheet** COMPUT feuille *f* de calcul; *program* tableur *m*

sprightly ['spraɪtlɪ] alerte

spring[1] [sprɪŋ] *n season* printemps *m*

spring² [sprɪŋ] n device ressort m

spring³ [sprɪŋ] **1** n (jump)
bond m; (stream) source f **2**
v/i bondir

'springboard tremplin m;
springtime printemps m

sprinkle ['sprɪŋkl] saupoudrer; sprinkler for garden ar-
roseur m; in ceiling extincteur m

sprint [sprɪnt] **1** n sprint m **2**
v/i SP sprinter; fig piquer
un sprint F; sprinter SP sprin-
teur(-euse) m(f)

spy [spaɪ] **1** n espion(ne) m(f)
2 v/i faire de l'espionnage **3**
v/t (see) apercevoir

♦ spy on espionner

squabble ['skwɒbl] **1** n querelle f **2** v/i se quereller

squalid ['skwɒlɪd] sordide;
squalor misère f

squander ['skwɒndər] gas-
piller

square [skwer] **1** adj in shape
carré; **~ mile** mile carré **2** n
shape, MATH carré m; in town
place f; in board game case f

squash¹ [skwɑːʃ] n vegetable
courge f

squash² [skwɑːʃ] n game
squash m

squash³ [skwɑːʃ] v/t (crush)
écraser

squat [skwɒt] **1** adj in shape
ramassé **2** v/i sit s'accroupir;
illegally squatter

squeak [skwiːk] **1** n of mouse
couinement m; of hinge grin-

cement m **2** v/i of mouse
couiner; of brakes grincer

squeal [skwiːl] **1** n cri m aigu;
of brakes grincement m **2** v/i
pousser des cris aigus; of
brakes grincer

squeamish ['skwiːmɪʃ] trop
sensible

squeeze [skwiːz] hand serrer;
shoulder, (remove juice
from) presser; fruit, parcel
palper

squid [skwɪd] calmar m

squirm [skwɜːrm] se tortiller

St (= **saint**) St(e) (= saint(e));
(= **street**) rue

stab [stæb] poignarder

stability [stəˈbɪlətɪ] stabilité f;
stabilize **1** v/t stabiliser **2** v/i
se stabiliser; stable **1** adj stable **2** n for horses écurie f

stack [stæk] **1** n (pile) pile f **2**
v/t empiler

stadium ['steɪdɪəm] stade m

staff [stæf] (employees) personnel m; (teachers) personnel m enseignant

stage¹ [steɪdʒ] n in project etc
étape f

stage² [steɪdʒ] **1** n THEA scène
f **2** v/t play mettre en scène;
demonstration organiser

stagger ['stægər] **1** v/i tituber
2 v/t (amaze) ébahir; coffee
breaks etc échelonner; stag-
gering stupéfiant

stagnant ['stægnənt] water,
economy stagnant; stagnate
fig stagner

'stag party enterrement m de

vie de garçon

stain [steɪn] **1** n (dirty mark) tache f; for wood teinture f **2** v/t (dirty) tacher; wood teindre; **stained-glass window** vitrail m; **stainless steel** acier m inoxydable

stair [ster] marche f; **the ~s** l'escalier m; **staircase** escalier m

stake [steɪk] **1** n of wood pieu m; when gambling enjeu m; (investment) investissements mpl; **be at ~** être en jeu **2** v/t tree soutenir avec un pieu; money jouer; person financer

stale [steɪl] bread rassis; air empesté; fig: news plus très frais

stalk[1] [stɔːk] n of fruit, plant tige f

stalk[2] [stɔːk] v/t animal, person traquer

stall[1] [stɔːl] n at market étalage m; for cow, horse stalle f

stall[2] [stɔːl] **1** v/i of vehicle, engine caler; (play for time) chercher à gagner du temps **2** v/t engine caler; person faire attendre

stalls [stɔːlz] THEA orchestre m

stalwart ['stɔːlwərt] supporter fidèle

stamina ['stæmɪnə] endurance f

stammer ['stæmər] **1** n bégaiement m **2** v/i bégayer

stamp[1] [stæmp] **1** n for letter

timbre m; device, mark tampon m **2** v/t letter timbrer; passport tamponner

stamp[2] [stæmp] v/t: **~ one's foot** taper du pied

stance [stæns] position f

stand [stænd] **1** n at exhibition stand m; (witness ~) barre f des témoins; (support, base) support m; **take the ~** LAW venir à la barre **2** v/i (be situated) se trouver; as opposed to sit rester debout; (rise) se lever **3** v/t (tolerate) supporter; (put) mettre

◆ **stand by 1** v/i (not take action) rester là sans rien faire; (be ready) se tenir prêt **2** v/t person soutenir; decision s'en tenir à

◆ **stand down** (withdraw) se retirer

◆ **stand for** (tolerate) supporter; (represent) représenter

◆ **stand out** be visible ressortir

◆ **stand up 1** v/i se lever **2** v/t F poser un lapin à

◆ **stand up for** défendre

◆ **stand up to** (face) tenir tête à

standard ['stændərd] **1** adj procedure etc normal; **~ practice** pratique f courante **2** n (level) niveau m; moral critère m; TECH norme f; **standardize** normaliser; **standard of living** niveau m de vie

'standby fly en stand-by;

standing *in society* position f
sociale; *(repute)* réputation f;
standoffish distant; **stand-
point** point m de vue; **standstill: be at a ~** être paralysé;
bring to a ~ paralyser
staple[1] ['steɪpl] n *foodstuff*
aliment m de base
staple[2] ['steɪpl] **1** n *fastener*
agrafe f **2** v/t agrafer
stapler ['steɪplər] agrafeuse f
star [stɑːr] **1** n *in sky* étoile f;
fig also vedette f **2** v/t *of movie* avoir comme vedette(s);
starboard de tribord
stare [ster]: **~ into space** regarder dans le vide; *it's rude
to ~* ce n'est pas poli de fixer
les gens
stark [stɑːrk] **1** adj *landscape,
color* austère; *reminder, contrast etc* brutal **2** adv: **~ naked**
complètement nu
starry ['stɑːrɪ] *night* étoilé;
Stars and Stripes bannière
f étoilée
start [stɑːrt] **1** n début m **2** v/i
commencer; *of engine, car*
démarrer; **~ing from tomorrow** à partir de demain **3** v/t
commencer; *engine, car* mettre en marche; *business* monter; *starter of meal* entrée f;
of car démarreur m
startle ['stɑːrtl] effrayer; **star-
tling** surprenant
starvation [stɑːrˈveɪʃn] inani-
tion f; **starve** souffrir de la
faim; *I'm starving* F je meurs
de faim F

state[1] [steɪt] **1** n *(condition,
country, part of country)* état
m; **the States** les États-Unis
mpl **2** adj *capital, police etc*
d'état; *banquet, occasion
etc* officiel
state[2] [steɪt] v/t déclarer;
name and address décliner
'State Department Département m d'État (américain);
statement *to police* déclaration f; *(announcement)* communiqué m; *(bank ~)* relevé
m de compte; **state of emergency** état m d'urgence;
state-of-the-art de pointe;
statesman homme m d'État
static *(electricity)* ['stætɪk]
électricité f statique
station ['steɪʃn] **1** n RAIL gare
f; *of subway,* RAD station f; TV
chaîne f **2** v/t *guard etc* placer; **stationary** immobile
stationery ['steɪʃənrɪ] papeterie f
'station wagon break m
statistical [stəˈtɪstɪkl] statistique; **statistically** statistique-
ment; **statistician** statisti-
cien(ne) m(f); **statistics** *science* statistique f *figures* sta-
tistiques fpl
statue ['stætʃuː] statue f; **Statue of Liberty** Statue f de la
Liberté
status ['steɪtəs] statut m;
(prestige) prestige m; **status
symbol** signe m extérieur
de richesse
statute ['stætʃuːt] loi f

staunch [stɔ:ntʃ] *supporter* fervent

stay [steɪ] **1** *n* séjour *m* **2** *v/i* rester; *~ in a hotel* descendre dans un hôtel; *~ right there!* tenez-vous là!

♦ **stay behind** rester; *in school* rester après la classe

♦ **stay up** (*not go to bed*) rester debout

steadily ['stedɪlɪ] *improve etc* de façon régulière; steady **1** *adj* ferme; *voice* posé; (*regular*) régulier; (*continuous*) continu **2** *adv:* **be going ~** *of couple* sortir ensemble **3** *v/t person* soutenir; *voice* raffermir

steak [steɪk] bifteck *m*

steal [sti:l] **1** *v/t* voler **2** *v/i* (*be a thief*) voler; *~ in/out* entrer/sortir à pas feutrés

stealthy ['stelθɪ] furtif

steam [sti:m] **1** *n* vapeur *f* **2** *v/t food* cuire à la vapeur; steamed up F fou de rage; steamer *for cooking* cuiseur *m* à vapeur

steel [sti:l] **1** *adj* (*made of ~*) en acier **2** *n* acier *m*; steelworker ouvrier(-ière) *m(f)* de l'industrie sidérurgique

steep¹ [sti:p] *adj hill etc* raide; F *prices* excessif

steep² [sti:p] *v/t* (*soak*) faire tremper

steer¹ [stɪr] *n animal* bœuf *m*

steer² [stɪr] *v/t* diriger

steering ['stɪrɪŋ] MOT direction *f*; steering wheel volant

m

stem¹ [stem] *n of plant* tige *f*; *of glass* pied *m*; *of word* racine *f*

stem² [stem] *v/t* (*block*) enrayer

stench [stentʃ] odeur *f* nauséabonde

stencil ['stensɪl] **1** *n* pochoir *m*; *pattern* peinture *f* au pochoir **2** *v/t pattern* peindre au pochoir

step [step] **1** *n* (*pace*) pas *m*; (*stair*) marche *f*; (*measure*) mesure *f* **2** *v/i:* *~ forward/back* faire un pas en avant/en arrière

♦ **step down** *from post etc* se retirer

♦ **step up** (*increase*) augmenter

'stepbrother demi-frère *m*; stepdaughter belle-fille *f*; stepfather beau-père *m*; stepladder escabeau *m*; stepmother belle-mère *f*; stepsister demi-sœur *f*; stepson beau-fils *m*

stereo ['sterɪoʊ] (*sound system*) chaîne *f* stéréo; stereotype stéréotype *m*

sterile ['sterəl] stérile; sterilize stériliser

sterling ['stɜːrlɪŋ] FIN sterling *m*

stern¹ [stɜːrn] *adj* sévère

stern² [stɜːrn] *n* NAUT arrière *m*

sternly ['stɜːrnlɪ] sévèrement

steroids ['sterɔɪdz] stéroïdes

mpl

stew [stuː] ragoût *m*

steward ['stuːərd] *on plane, ship* steward *m*; *at demonstration, meeting* membre *m* du service d'ordre; **stewardess** *on plane, ship* hôtesse *f*

stick¹ [stɪk] *n* morceau *m* de bois; *of policeman* bâton *m*; *(walking* ~*)* canne *f*

stick² [stɪk] *v/t with adhesive* coller **(to** à); F *(put)* mettre *f* *v/i (jam)* se coincer; *(adhere)* adhérer

♦ **stick by** F ne pas abandonner

♦ **stick to** *(adhere to)* coller à; F *(keep to)* s'en tenir à; F *(follow)* suivre

♦ **stick up for** F défendre

sticker ['stɪkər] autocollant *m*; **stick-in-the-mud** F encroûté(e) *m(f)*; **sticky** gluant; *label* collant

stiff [stɪf] *brush, cardboard, mixture etc* dur; *muscle, body* raide; *in manner* guindé; *drink* bien tassé; *competition* acharné; *fine* sévère; **stiffness** *of muscles* raideur *f*; *in manner* aspect *m* guindé

stifle ['staɪfl] étouffer; **stifling** étouffant

stigma ['stɪgmə] honte *f*

still¹ [stɪl] **1** *adj* calme **2** *adv*: **keep** ~**!** reste tranquille!; **stand** ~**!** ne bouge pas!

still² [stɪl] *adv (yet)* encore, toujours; *(nevertheless)* quand même

'stillborn: **be** ~ être mort à sa naissance; **still life** nature *f* morte

stilted ['stɪltɪd] guindé

stimulant ['stɪmjulant] stimulant *m*; **stimulate** stimuler; **stimulating** stimulant; **stimulation** stimulation *f*; **stimulus** *(incentive)* stimulation *f*

sting [stɪŋ] **1** *n from bee, jellyfish* piqûre *f* **2** *v/t & v/i* piquer; **stinging** *criticism* blessant

stink [stɪŋk] **1** *n (bad smell)* puanteur *f*; F *(fuss)* grabuge *m* F **2** *v/i (smell bad)* puer; F *(be very bad)* être nul

stipulate ['stɪpjuleɪt] stipuler; **stipulation** condition *f*; *of will, contract* stipulation *f*

stir [stɜːr] **1** *v/t* remuer **2** *v/i of sleeping person* bouger; **stirring** *music, speech* émouvant

stitch [stɪtʃ] **1** *n* point *m*; ~**es** MED points *mpl* de suture **2** *v/t (sew)* coudre; **stitching** *(stitches)* couture *f*

stock [stɑːk] **1** *n (reserve)* réserves *fpl*; COM *of store* stock *m*; *animals* bétail *m*; FIN *actions fpl*; *for soup etc* bouillon *m*; **be in/out of** ~ être en stock/épuisé **2** *v/t* COM avoir (en stock)

'stockbreeder éleveur *m*; **stockbroker** agent *m* de change; **stock exchange** bourse *f*; **stockholder** actionnaire *m/f*; **stockist** revendeur *m*; **stock market**

marché *m* boursier; **stockpile 1** *n* of food, weapons stocks *mpl* de réserve **2** *v/t* faire des stocks de

stocky ['stɑːkɪ] trapu

stodgy ['stɑːdʒɪ] food bourratif

stoical ['stəʊɪkl] stoïque; **stoicism** stoïcisme *m*

stomach ['stʌmək] **1** *n* (*insides*) estomac *m*; (*abdomen*) ventre *m* **2** *v/t* (*tolerate*) supporter

stone [stəʊn] pierre *f*; (*pebble*) caillou *m*; **stoned** F *on drugs* défoncé F

stool [stuːl] *seat* tabouret *m*

stoop[1] [stuːp] *v/i* (*bend down*) se pencher

stoop[2] [stuːp] *n* (*porch*) perron *m*

stop [stɑːp] **1** *n* for train, bus arrêt *m* **2** *v/t* arrêter, (*prevent*) empêcher; *check* faire opposition à; **~ doing sth** arrêter de faire qch **3** *v/i* s'arrêter

◆ **stop over** faire escale

'stopgap bouche-trou *m*; **stoplight** (*traffic light*) feu *m* rouge; (*brake light*) stop *m*; **stopover** étape *f*; **stopper** *for bottle* bouchon *m*; **stop sign** stop *m*; **stopwatch** chronomètre *m*

storage ['stɔːrɪdʒ] COM emmagasinage *m*; *in house* rangement *m*; **store 1** *n* magasin *m*; (*stock*) provision *f*; (*~house*) entrepôt *m* **2** *v/t* en-

treposer; COMPUT stocker; **storefront** devanture *f* de magasin; **storekeeper** commerçant(e) *m(f)*

storey *Br* → **story**[2]

storm [stɔːrm] *with rain, wind* tempête *f*; (*thunder~*) orage *m*; **stormy** orageux

story[1] ['stɔːrɪ] (*tale, account*, F: *lie*) histoire *f*; (*newspaper article*) article *m*

story[2] ['stɔːrɪ] *of building* étage *m*

stout [staʊt] *person* corpulent, costaud

stove [stəʊv] *for cooking* cuisinière *f*; *for heating* poêle *m*

stow [stəʊ] ranger

◆ **stow away** s'embarquer clandestinement

'stowaway passager clandestin *m*, passagère clandestine *f*

straight [streɪt] **1** *adj line, back, knees* droit; *hair* raide; (*honest, direct*) franc; (*not criminal*) honnête; *whiskey etc* sec; (*tidy*) en ordre; (*conservative*) sérieux; (*not homosexual*) hétéro F **2** *adv* (*in a straight line*) droit; (*directly, immediately*) directement; **go ~** F *of criminal* revenir dans le droit chemin; **~ ahead** tout droit; **~ away, ~ off** tout de suite; **~ out** très clairement; **~ up** *without ice* sans glace; **straighten** redresser; **straightforward** (*honest, direct*) direct; (*sim-*

ple) simple

strain[^1] [streɪn] **1** *n on rope, engine* tension *f*; *on heart* pression *f*; **suffer from ~** souffrir de tension nerveuse **2** *v/t back* se fouler; *eyes* s'abîmer; *finances* grever

strain[^2] [streɪn] *v/t vegetables* faire égoutter; *oil, fat etc* filtrer

strained [streɪnd] *relations* tendu; **strainer** *for vegetables etc* passoire *f*

strait [streɪt] détroit *m*; **strait-laced** collet monté *inv*

strange [streɪndʒ] *(odd, curious)* étrange, bizarre; *(unknown, foreign)* inconnu; **strangely** *(oddly)* bizarrement; **~ enough, ...** c'est bizarre, mais ...; **stranger** étranger(-ère) *m* (*f*); **he's a complete ~** je ne le connais pas du tout; **I'm a ~ here myself** moi non plus je ne suis pas d'ici

strangle ['stræŋgl] étrangler

strap [stræp] *of purse, shoe* lanière *f*; *of brassiere, dress* bretelle *f*; *of watch* bracelet *m*; **strapless** sans bretelles

strategic [strə'tiːdʒɪk] stratégique; **strategy** stratégie *f*

straw [strɔː] *material, for drink* paille *f*; **strawberry** fraise *f*

stray [streɪ] **1** *adj animal, bullet* perdu **2** *n animal m* errant **3** *v/i of animal* vagabonder; *of child* s'égarer; *fig: of eyes,*

thoughts errer (**to** vers)

streak [striːk] **1** *n of dirt, paint* traînée *f*; *in hair* mèche *f*; *fig: of nastiness etc* pointe *f* **2** *v/i move quickly* filer

stream [striːm] ruisseau *m*; *fig: of people* flot *m*; **streamline** *fig* rationaliser; **streamlined** *car, plane* caréné; *organization* rationalisé

street [striːt] rue *f*; **streetcar** tramway *m*; **streetlight** réverbère *m*; **street people** sans-abri *mpl*; **street value** *of drugs* prix *m* à la revente; **strength** [streŋθ] force *f*; *(strong point)* point *m* fort; **strengthen 1** *v/t body* fortifier; *bridge, currency, bonds etc* consolider **2** *v/i* se consolider

strenuous ['strenjʊəs] fatigant; **strenuously** *deny* vigoureusement

stress [stres] **1** *n (emphasis)* accent *m*; *(tension)* stress *m* **2** *v/t syllable* accentuer; *importance etc* souligner; **stressed out** F stressé F; **stressful** stressant

stretch [stretʃ] **1** *n of land, water* étendue *f*; *of road* partie *f* **2** *adj fabric* extensible **3** *v/t material* tendre; *small income* tirer le maximum de; F *rules* assouplir **4** *v/i to relax muscles, to reach sth* s'étirer; *(spread)* s'étendre; **stretcher** brancard *m*

strict [strɪkt] strict; **strictly**

[^1]: strain 1
[^2]: strain 2

strictement; *it is ~ forbidden* c'est strictement défendu

stride [straɪd] **1** *n* (grand) pas *m* **2** *v/i* marcher à grandes enjambées

strident ['straɪdnt] strident; *demands* véhément

strike [straɪk] **1** *n of workers* grève *f*; *in baseball* balle *f* manquée; *of oil* découverte *f*; *be on ~* être en grève **2** *v/i of workers* faire grève; *(attack: of wild animal)* attaquer; *of killer* frapper; *of disaster* arriver; *of clock* sonner **3** *v/t also fig* frapper; *match* allumer; *oil* découvrir

◆ **strike out** *delete* rayer

strikebreaker ['straɪkbreɪkər] briseur(-euse) *m(f)* de grève; **striker** *(person on strike)* gréviste *m/f*; *in soccer* buteur *m*; **striking** *(marked, eye-catching)* frappant

string [strɪŋ] ficelle *f*; *of violin, tennis racket* corde *f*; **stringed instrument** instrument *m* à cordes

stringent ['strɪndʒənt] rigoureux

strip [strɪp] **1** *n* bande *f*; *(comic ~)* bande *f* dessinée **2** *v/t (remove)* enlever; *(undress)* déshabiller **3** *v/i (undress)* se déshabiller; *of stripper* faire du strip-tease; **strip club** boîte *f* de strip-tease

stripe [straɪp] rayure *f*; MIL galon *m*; **striped** rayé

stripper ['strɪpər] strip-tea-seuse *f*; *male ~* strip-teaser *m*; **striptease** strip-tease *m*

stroke [stroʊk] **1** *n* MED attaque *f*; *when painting* coup *m* de pinceau; *style of swimming* nage *f* **2** *v/t* caresser

stroll [stroʊl] **1** *n* balade *f* **2** *v/i* flâner; **stroller** *for baby* poussette *f*

strong [strɔːŋ] fort; *structure* solide; *candidate* sérieux; *support, supporter* vigoureux; **strongly** fortement; **strong-minded:** *be ~* avoir de la volonté; **strong point** point *m* fort; **strongroom** chambre *f* forte; **strong-willed** qui sait ce qu'il/elle veut

structural ['strʌktʃərl] *damage* de structure; *fault, problems* de construction; **structure 1** *n (something built)* construction *f*; *of novel, poem etc* structure *f* **2** *v/t* structurer

struggle ['strʌgl] **1** *n* lutte *f* **2** *v/i with a person* se battre; *~ to do sth* avoir du mal à faire qch

strut [strʌt] se pavaner

stub [stʌb] *of cigarette* mégot *m*; *of check, ticket* souche *f*

stubborn ['stʌbərn] *person, refusal etc* entêté; *defense* farouche

stubby ['stʌbɪ] boudiné

stuck [stʌk] F: *be ~ on s.o.* être fou de qn

student ['stu:dnt] *at high school* élève *m/f*; *at college, university* étudiant(e) *m(f)*

studio ['stu:dɪəʊ] studio *m*; *of artist* atelier *m*

studious ['stu:dɪəs] studieux; **study 1** *n room* bureau *m*; *(learning)* études *fpl*; *(investigation)* étude *f* **2** *v/t & v/i* étudier

stuff [stʌf] **1** *n (things)* trucs *mpl*; *substance, powder etc* truc *m*; *(belongings)* affaires *fpl* **2** *v/t turkey* farcir; **~ sth into sth** fourrer qch dans qch; **stuffing** *for turkey* farce *f*; *in chair, toy* rembourrage *m*; **stuffy** *room* mal aéré; *person* vieux jeu *inv*

stumble ['stʌmbl] trébucher; **stumbling block** pierre *f* d'achoppement

stump [stʌmp] **1** *n of tree* souche *f* **2** *v/t*: **I'm ~ed** je le colle F

stun [stʌn] étourdir; *animal* assommer; *fig (shock)* abasourdir; *stunning (amazing)* stupéfiant; *(very beautiful)* épatant

stunt [stʌnt] *for publicity* coup *m* de publicité; *in movie* cascade *f*; **stuntman** *in movie* cascadeur *m*

stupefy ['stu:pɪfaɪ] stupéfier

stupendous [stu:'pendəs] prodigieux

stupid ['stu:pɪd] stupide; **stupidity** stupidité *f*

sturdy ['stɜ:rdɪ] robuste

stutter ['stʌtər] bégayer

style [staɪl] *(method, manner)* style *m*; *(fashion)* mode *f*; *(fashionable elegance)* classe *f*; **stylish** qui a de la classe; **stylist** *(hair ~)* styliste *m/f*

subcommittee ['sʌbkəmɪtɪ] sous-comité *m*

subconscious [sʌb'kɑ:nʃəs] subconscient; **subconsciously** subconsciemment

subcontract [sʌbkən'trækt] sous-traiter; **subcontractor** sous-traitant *m*

subdivide [sʌbdɪ'vaɪd] sous-diviser

subdue [səb'du:] contenir

subheading ['sʌbhedɪŋ] sous-titre *m*

subhuman [sʌb'hju:mən] sous-humain

subject 1 ['sʌbdʒɪkt] *n of country*, GRAM, *(topic)* sujet *m*; *(branch of learning)* matière *f* **2** ['sʌbdʒɪkt] *adj*: **be ~ to** être sujet à **3** [səb'dʒekt] *v/t* soumettre (**to** à); **subjective** subjectif

sublet ['sʌblet] sous-louer

submachine gun [sʌbmə-'ʃi:ŋgʌn] mitraillette *f*

submarine ['sʌbməri:n] sous-marin *m*

submission [səb'mɪʃn] *(surrender)*, *to committee etc* soumission *f*; **submissive** soumis; **submit 1** *v/t plan* soumettre **2** *v/i* se soumettre

subordinate [sə'bɔ:rdɪnət] **1** *adj position* subalterne **2** *n* subordonné(e) *m(f)*

subpoena [sə'pi:nə] LAW **1** *n*
assignation *f* **2** *v/t person* assigner à comparaître
♦ **subscribe to** [səb'skraɪb]
magazine etc s'abonner à;
theory souscrire à
subscriber [səb'skraɪbər] *to
magazine* abonné(e) *m(f)*;
subscription abonnement
m
subsequent ['sʌbsɪkwənt]
ultérieur
subside [səb'saɪd] *of waters*
baisser; *of winds* se calmer;
of building s'affaisser; *of
fears* s'apaiser
subsidiary [səb'sɪdɪrɪ] filiale
f
subsidize ['sʌbsɪdaɪz] subventionner; **subsidy** subvention *f*
substance ['sʌbstəns] substance *f*
substandard [sʌb'stændərd]
de qualité inférieure
substantial [səb'stænʃl] considérable; *meal* consistant;
substantially (*considerably*)
considérablement; (*in essence*) de manière générale
substantive [səb'stæntɪv]
réel
substitute ['sʌbstɪtuːt] **1** *n*
substitut *m* (**for** de); SP rem-
plaçant(e) *m(f)* (**for** de) **2**
v/t remplacer; **~ X for Y** remplacer Y par X; **substitution**
remplacement *m*
subtitle ['sʌbtaɪtl] sous-titre
m

subtle ['sʌtl] subtil
subtract [səb'trækt] soustraire
suburb ['sʌbɜːrb] banlieue *f*;
the **~s** la banlieue; **suburban** typique de la banlieue;
attitudes etc de banlieusards
subversive [səb'vɜːrsɪv] **1**
adj subversif **2** *n* personne *f*
subversive
subway ['sʌbweɪ] métro *m*
succeed [sək'siːd] **1** *v/i* réussir; *to throne* succéder à; **~ in
doing sth** réussir à faire qch
2 *v/t* (*come after*) succéder à;
success réussite *f*; **be a ~**
avoir du succès; **successful**
person qui a réussi; *talks, operation* réussi; **be ~ in doing
sth** réussir à faire qch; **suc-
cessfully** avec succès; **suc-
cessive** successif; **on three
~ days** trois jours de suite;
successor successeur *m*
succinct [sək'sɪŋkt] succinct
succumb [sə'kʌm] (*give in*)
succomber
such [sʌtʃ] **1** *adj*: **~ a** (*so much
of a*) un tel, une telle; **it was
~ a surprise** c'était une telle
surprise; (*of that kind*): **~ as**
tel/telle que; **there is no ~
word as ...** le mot ... n'existe
pas **2** *adv* tellement; **~ an
easy question** une question
tellement facile
suck [sʌk] **1** *v/t candy etc* sucer **2** *v/i* P: **it ~s** c'est merdi-
que P; **sucker** F *person*
niais(e) *m(f)*; F (*lollipop*) su-

cette f; **suction** succion f

sudden ['sʌdn] soudain; **suddenly** tout à coup, soudain

sue [su:] poursuivre en justice

suede [sweɪd] daim m

suffer ['sʌfər] **1** v/i souffrir **2** v/t experience subir; **suffering** souffrance f

sufficient [sə'fɪʃnt] suffisant; **not ~ funds** pas assez d'argent; **sufficiently** suffisamment

suffocate ['sʌfəkeɪt] **1** v/i s'étouffer **2** v/t étouffer; **suffocation** étouffement m

sugar ['ʃʊgər] **1** n sucre m **2** v/t sucrer

suggest [sə'dʒest] suggérer; **suggestion** suggestion f

suicide ['su:ɪsaɪd] suicide m

suit [su:t] **1** n for man costume m; for woman tailleur m; in cards couleur f **2** v/t of clothes, color aller à; **suitable** approprié, convenable; **suitably** convenablement; **suitcase** valise f

suite [swi:t] of rooms suite f; furniture salon m trois pièces; MUS suite m

sulk [sʌlk] bouder; **sulky** bouderie

sullen ['sʌlən] maussade

sultry ['sʌltrɪ] climate lourd; sexually sulfureux

sum [sʌm] (total, amount) somme f; in arithmetic calcul m

◆ **sum up** **1** v/t (summarize) résumer; (assess) se faire

une idée de **2** v/i LAW résumer les débats

summarize ['sʌməraɪz] résumer; **summary** résumé m

summer ['sʌmər] été f

summit ['sʌmɪt] also POL sommet m

summon ['sʌmən] staff, meeting convoquer; **summons** LAW assignation f (à comparaître)

sun [sʌn] soleil m; **sunbathe** prendre un bain de soleil; **sunbed** lit m à ultraviolets; **sunblock** écran m solaire; **sunburn** coup m de soleil; **sunburnt**: **be ~** avoir des coups de soleil; **Sunday** dimanche m; **sunglasses** lunettes fpl de soleil; **sunny** ensoleillé; disposition gai; **it's ~** il y a du soleil; **sunrise** lever m du soleil; **sunset** coucher m du soleil; **sunshade** handheld ombrelle f; over table parasol m; **sunshine** soleil m; **sunstroke** insolation f; **suntan** bronzage m; **get a ~** bronzer

super ['su:pər] **1** adj F super inv F **2** n (janitor) concierge m/f

superb [sʊ'pɜ:rb] excellent

superficial [su:pər'fɪʃl] superficiel

superfluous [sʊ'pɜ:rfluəs] superflu

superintendent [su:pərɪn-'tendənt] of apartment block concierge m/f

superior [suːˈpɪrɪər] **1** adj supérieur **2** n in organization supérieur m

superlative [suːˈpɜːrlətɪv] **1** adj (superb) excellent **2** n GRAM superlatif m

'supermarket supermarché m

'superpower POL superpuissance f

supersonic [suːpərˈsaːnɪk] supersonique

superstition [suːpərˈstɪʃn] superstition f; **superstitious** superstitieux

supervise [ˈsuːpərvaɪz] children, activities etc surveiller; workers superviser; **supervisor** at work superviseur m

supper [ˈsʌpər] dîner m

supplement [ˈsʌplɪmənt] (extra payment) supplément m

supplier [səˈplaɪr] COM fournisseur-euse) m(f); **supply 1** n of electricity, water etc alimentation f (**of** en); **~ and demand** l'offre et la demande; **supplies** of food provisions fpl **2** v/t goods fournir

support [səˈpɔːrt] **1** n for structure support m; (backing) soutien m **2** v/t structure supporter; financially entretenir; (back) soutenir; **supporter** of politician, football etc team supporter(-trice) m(f); of theory partisan(e) m(f); **supportive** attitude de soutien; **be very ~ of s.o.** beaucoup soutenir qn

suppose [səˈpouz] (imagine) supposer; **be ~d to do sth** (be meant to, said to) être censé faire qch; **supposing ...** (et) si ...; supposedly apparemment

suppress [səˈpres] réprimer; **suppression** répression f

supremacy [suːˈpreməsɪ] suprématie f; **supreme** suprême; **Supreme Court** Cour f suprême

surcharge [ˈsɜːrtʃɑːrdʒ] surcharge f

sure [ʃʊr] **1** adj sûr; **make ~ that ...** s'assurer que ... **2** adv: **~ enough** en effet; **it ~ is hot today** F il fait vraiment chaud aujourd'hui; **~!** F mais oui, bien sûr!; **surety** for loan garant(e) m(f)

surf [sɜːrf] **1** n on sea écume f **2** v/t the Net surfer sur

surface [ˈsɜːrfɪs] **1** n surface f **2** v/i from water faire surface; (appear) refaire surface; **surface mail** courrier m par voie terrestre ou maritime

'surfboard planche f de surf; **surfer** surfeur(-euse) m(f); **surfing** surf m; **go ~** aller faire du surf

surge [sɜːrdʒ] n in electric current surtension f; in demand etc poussée f

surgeon [ˈsɜːrdʒən] chirurgien m(f); **surgery** chirurgie f; surgical chirurgical; **surgically** remove par opération chirurgicale

surly [ˈsɜːrlɪ] revêche

surmount [sər'maʊnt] *difficulties* surmonter

surname ['sɜːneɪm] nom *m* de famille

surpass [sər'pæs] dépasser

surplus ['sɜːpləs] **1** *n* surplus *m* **2** *adj* en surplus

surprise [sər'praɪz] **1** *n* surprise *f* **2** *v/t* étonner; **be/look ~d** être/avoir l'air surpris; **surprising** étonnant; **surprisingly** étonnamment

surrender [sə'rendər] **1** *v/i* of *army* se rendre **2** *v/t weapons etc* rendre **3** *n* capitulation *f*; (*handing in*) reddition *f*

surrogate mother ['sʌrəgət] mère *f* porteuse

surround [sə'raʊnd] **1** *v/t* entourer **2** *n of picture etc* bordure *f*; **surrounding** environnant; **surroundings** environs *mpl*; *setting* cadre *m*

survey 1 ['sɜːveɪ] *n of modern literature etc* étude *f*; *Br of building* inspection *f*; (*poll*) sondage *m* **2** [sər'veɪ] *v/t* (*look at*) contempler; *Br building* inspecter; **surveyor** *Br* expert *m*

survival [sər'vaɪvl] survie *f*; **survive 1** *v/i* survivre **2** *v/t accident*, (*outlive*) survivre à; **survivor** survivant(e) *m(f)*

suspect 1 ['sʌspekt] *n* suspect(e) *m(f)* **2** [sə'spekt] *v/t person* soupçonner; (*suppose*) croire; **suspected murderer** soupçonné; *cause*, *heart attack etc* présumé

suspend [sə'spend] (*hang*), *from office* suspendre; **suspenders** *for pants* bretelles *fpl*; *Br* porte-jarretelles *m*

suspense [sə'spens] suspense *m*; **suspension** *in vehicle*, *from duty* suspension *f*

suspicion [sə'spɪʃn] soupçon *m*; **suspicious** (*causing suspicion*) suspect; (*feeling suspicion*) méfiant; **be ~ of s.o.** se méfier de qn; **suspiciously** *behave* de manière suspecte; *ask* avec méfiance

sustain [sə'steɪn] soutenir; **sustainable** durable

SUV [esjuː'viː] (= *sports utility vehicle*) véhicule *m* utilitaire sport

swab [swɑːb] tampon *m*

swallow[1] ['swɑːloʊ] *v/t & v/i* avaler

swallow[2] ['swɑːloʊ] *n bird* hirondelle *f*

swamp [swɑːmp] **1** *n* marécage *m* **2** *v/t*: **be ~ed** with être submergé de; **swampy** marécageux

swap [swɑːp] échanger (**for** contre)

swarm [swɔːrm] **1** *n of bees* essaim *m* **2** *v/i*: **the town was ~ing with ...** la ville grouillait de ...

swarthy ['swɔːrðɪ] basané

swat [swɑːt] *insect* écraser

sway [sweɪ] **1** *n* (*influence*, *power*) emprise *f* **2** *v/i in wind* se balancer; *because drunk*, *ill* tituber

swear [swer] 1 v/i (*use swear-word*) jurer; ~ **at s.o.** injurier qn 2 v/t LAW, (*promise*) jurer
◆ swear in *witnesses etc* faire prêter serment à
'swearword juron *m*

sweat [swet] 1 *n* sueur *f* 2 v/i transpirer, suer; sweat band bandeau *m* en éponge; sweater pull *m*; sweatshirt sweat(-shirt) *m*; sweaty plein de sueur

sweep [swi:p] 1 v/t *floor, leaves* balayer 2 *n* (*long curve*) courbe *f*; sweeping *statement* hâtif; *changes* radical

sweet [swi:t] *taste, tea* sucré; F (*kind*) gentil; F (*cute*) mignon; sweetcorn maïs *m*; sweeten sucrer; sweetheart amoureux(-euse) *m(f)*

swell [swel] 1 v/i *of wound, limb* enfler 2 *adj* F (*good*) super F *inv* 3 *n of the sea* houle *f*; swelling MED enflure *f*

swerve [swɜ:rv] *of driver, car* s'écarter brusquement

swift [swift] rapide

swim [swim] 1 v/i nager 2 *n* baignade *f*; **go for a ~** aller se baigner; swimmer nageur(-euse) *m(f)*; swimming natation *f*; swimming pool piscine *f*; swimsuit maillot *m* de bain

swindle ['swindl] 1 *n* escroquerie *f* 2 v/t escroquer; ~ **s.o. out of sth** escroquer qch à qn

swing [swiŋ] 1 *n* oscillation *f*; *for child* balançoire *f*; ~ **to the Democrats** revirement *m* d'opinion en faveur des démocrates 2 v/t *object in hand, hips* balancer 3 v/i se balancer; (*turn*) tourner; *of public opinion etc* virer

Swiss [swis] 1 *adj* suisse 2 *n person* Suisse *m/f*; **the ~** les Suisses *mpl*

switch [switʃ] 1 *n for light* bouton *m*; (*change*) changement *m* 2 v/t (*change*) changer de 3 v/i (*change*) passer
◆ switch off *lights, engine, PC* éteindre; *engine* arrêter
◆ switch on *lights, engine, PC* allumer; *engine* démarrer

Switzerland ['switsərlənd] Suisse *f*

swivel ['swivl] pivoter

swollen ['swoulən] *stomach* ballonné; *ankles, face* enflé

syllabus ['siləbəs] programme *m*

symbol ['simbl] symbole *m*; symbolic symbolique; symbolism symbolisme *m*; symbolist symboliste *m/f*; symbolize symboliser

symmetrical [si'metrikl] symétrique; symmetry symétrie

sympathetic [simpə'θetik] (*showing pity*) compatissant; (*understanding*) compréhensif
◆ sympathize with ['simpə-

θaɪz] *person* compatir avec; *views* avoir des sympathies pour
sympathizer ['sɪmpəθaɪzər] POL sympathisant(e) *m(f)*; **sympathy** (*pity*) compassion *f*; (*understanding*) compréhension (**for** de)
symphony ['sɪmfənɪ] symphonie *f*
symptom ['sɪmptəm] MED, *fig* symptôme *m*
synchronize ['sɪŋkrənaɪz] synchroniser
synonym ['sɪnənɪm] synonyme *m*; **synonymous** synonyme
synthesizer ['sɪnθəsaɪzər]

MUS synthétiseur *m*; **synthetic** synthétique
syphilis ['sɪfɪlɪs] syphilis *f*
Syria ['sɪrɪə] Syrie *f*; **Syrian 1** *adj* syrien **2** *n* Syrien(ne) *m(f)*
syringe [sɪ'rɪndʒ] seringue *f*
syrup ['sɪrəp] sirop *m*
system ['sɪstəm] système *m*; (*orderliness*) ordre *m*; (*computer*) ordinateur *m*; **systematic** systématique; **systematically** systématiquement
systems analyst COMPUT analyste-programmeur(-euse) *m(f)*

T

table ['teɪbl] table *f*; *of figures* tableau *m*; **tablecloth** nappe *f*; **table lamp** petite lampe *f*; **table of contents** table *f* des matières; **tablespoon** cuillère *f* à soupe
tablet ['tæblɪt] MED comprimé *m*
tabloid ['tæblɔɪd] *newspaper* journal *m* à sensation
taboo [tə'buː] tabou *inv in feminine*
tacit ['tæsɪt] tacite
tack [tæk] **1** *n* nail clou *m* **2** *v/t in sewing* bâtir **3** *v/i of yacht* louvoyer
tackle ['tækl] **1** *n* (*equipment*) attirail *m*; SP tacle *m*; *in rug-*

by plaquage *m* **2** *v/t* SP tacler; *in rugby* plaquer; *problem* s'attaquer à; (*confront*) confronter; *physically* s'opposer à
tacky ['tækɪ] *paint, glue* collant; F (*cheap, poor quality*) minable F
tact [tækt] tact *m*; **tactful** diplomate; **tactfully** avec tact
tactical ['tæktɪkl] tactique; **tactics** tactique *f*
tactless ['tæktlɪs] qui manque de tact, peu délicat
tag [tæg] (*label*) étiquette *f*
tail [teɪl] queue *f*; **tail light** feu *m* arrière
tailor ['teɪlər] tailleur *m*; **tai-**

lor-made *also fig* fait sur mesure

'tail pipe *of car* tuyau *m*
d'échappement

take [teik] prendre; *(transport,
accompany)* amener; *subject
at school, photograph, photocopy, stroll* faire; *exam* passer; *(endure)* supporter; *(require: courage etc)* demander; **how long will it ~ you
to ...?** combien de temps
est-ce que tu vas mettre pour
...?

◆ **take after** ressembler à

◆ **take away** *object* enlever;
pain faire disparaître; MATH
soustraire (**from** de)

◆ **take back** *object* rapporter;
person to a place ramener;
she wouldn't take him back
husband elle ne voulait pas
qu'il revienne

◆ **take down** *from shelf* enlever; *scaffolding* démonter;
pants baisser; *(write down)*
noter

◆ **take in** *(take indoors)* rentrer; *(give accommodation
to)* héberger; *(make nar-
rower)* reprendre; *(deceive)*
duper; *(include)* inclure

◆ **take off** *v/t clothes, hat*
enlever; *10% etc* faire une
réduction de; *(mimic)* imiter
2 *v/i of airplane* décoller;
(become popular) réussir

◆ **take on** *job* accepter; *staff*
embaucher

◆ **take out** *from bag, pocket*

sortir (**from** de); *tooth, word
from text* enlever; *money
from bank* retirer; *to dinner,
theater etc* emmener; *insurance policy* souscrire à

◆ **take over 1** *v/t company etc*
reprendre **2** *v/i* POL arriver au
pouvoir; *of new director*
prendre ses fonctions; *(do
sth in s.o.'s place)* prendre
la relève

◆ **take up** *carpet etc* enlever;
(carry up) monter; *dress etc*
raccourcir; *judo, Spanish
etc* se mettre à; *new job* commencer; *space, time* prendre;
offer accepter

'takeoff *of airplane* décollage
m; *(impersonation)* imitation
f; **takeover** COM rachat *m*;
takeover bid offre *f* publique
d'achat, OPA *f*; **takings** recette *f*

tale [teil] histoire *f*

talent ['tælənt] talent *m*; talented doué; talent scout dé-
nicheur(-euse) *m(f)* de ta-
lents

talk [tɔːk] **1** *v/t & v/i* parler; ~
business parler affaires **2** *n
(conversation)* conversation
f; *(lecture)* exposé *m*; ~**s**
pourparlers *mpl*

◆ **talk back** répondre

talkative ['tɔːkətɪv] bavard;
talk show talk-show *m*

tall [tɔːl] grand

tally ['tælɪ] **1** *n* compte *m* **2** *v/i*
correspondre; *of stories* con-
corder

tame [teɪm] apprivoisé; *not wild* pas sauvage; *joke etc* fade

◆ **tamper with** ['tæmpər] toucher à

tampon ['tæmpɑːn] tampon *m*

tan [tæn] **1** *n from sun* bronzage; *color* marron *m* clair **2** *v/i in sun* bronzer **3** *v/t leather* tanner

tangent ['tændʒənt] MATH tangente *f*

tangible ['tændʒɪbl] tangible

tangle ['tæŋgl] enchevêtrement *m*

tango ['tæŋgou] tango *m*

tank [tæŋk] MOT, *for water* réservoir *m*; *for fish* aquarium *m*; MIL char *m*; *for skin diver* bonbonne *f* d'oxygène; tanker (*oil* ~) pétrolier *m*; *truck* camion-citerne *m*

tanned [tænd] bronzé

tantalizing ['tæntəlaɪzɪŋ] alléchant

tantrum ['tæntrəm] caprice *m*

tap [tæp] **1** *n Br (faucet)* robinet *m* **2** *v/t (knock)* taper; *phone* mettre sur écoute

tape [teɪp] **1** *n for recording* bande *f*; *recording* cassette *f*; *sticky* ruban *m* adhésif **2** *v/t conversation etc* enregistrer; *with sticky tape* scotcher; tape deck platine *f* cassettes; tape drive COMPUT lecteur *m* de bandes; tape measure mètre *m* ruban

taper ['teɪpər] *of stick* s'effi-

ler; *of column, pant legs* se rétrécir

'tape recorder magnétophone *m*; tape recording enregistrement *m*

tar [tɑːr] goudron *m*

tardy ['tɑːrdɪ] tardif

target ['tɑːrgɪt] **1** *n in shooting* cible *f*; *fig* objectif *m* **2** *v/t market* cibler

'target audience public *m* cible; target date date *f* visée; target market marché *m* cible

tariff ['tærɪf] (*customs* ~) taxe *f*; (*prices*) tarif *m*

tarmac ['tɑːrmæk] *at airport* tarmac *m*

tarnish ['tɑːrnɪʃ] ternir

tarpaulin [tɑːr'pɒːlɪn] bâche *f*

tart [tɑːrt] tarte *f*

task [tæsk] tâche *f*; task force commission *f*; MIL corps *m* expéditionnaire

taste [teɪst] **1** *n* goût *m* **2** *v/t* goûter; (*perceive taste of*) sentir; *try, fig* goûter à **3** *v/i*: **it ~s like ...** ça a (un) goût de ...; tasteful de bon goût; tastefully avec goût; tasteless *food* fade; *remark, décor* de mauvais goût; tasting *of wine* dégustation *f*; tasty délicieux

tattered ['tætərd] en lambeaux

tattoo [tə'tuː] tatouage *m*

taunt [tɒːnt] **1** *n* raillerie *f* **2** *v/t* se moquer de

taut [tɒːt] tendu

tax [tæks] **1** *n on income* impôt *m*; *on goods, services* taxe *f* **2** *v/t income* imposer; *goods, services* taxer; **taxable income** revenu *m* imposable; **taxation** *act* imposition *f*; (*taxes*) charges *fpl* fiscales; **tax bracket** fourchette *f* d'impôts; **tax-deductible** déductible des impôts; **tax evasion** fraude *f* fiscale; **tax-free** hors taxe; **tax haven** paradis *m* fiscal

taxi ['tæksɪ] taxi *m*; **taxi driver** chauffeur *m* de taxi

taxing ['tæksɪŋ] exténuant

'**taxi stand**, *Br* '**taxi rank** station *f* de taxis

'**taxpayer** contribuable *m/f*; **tax return** déclaration *f* d'impôts; **tax year** année *f* fiscale

TB [tiː'biː] (= *tuberculosis*) tuberculose *f*

tea [tiː] *drink* thé *m*; **teabag** sachet *m* de thé

teach [tiːtʃ] enseigner; *person* enseigner à; **teacher** professeur *m/f*; *in elementary school* instituteur(-trice) *m(f)*; **teaching** *profession* enseignement *m*

'**teacup** tasse *f* à thé

teak [tiːk] tek *m*

team [tiːm] équipe *f*; **team spirit** esprit *m* d'équipe; **teamster** camionneur(-euse) *m(f)*; **teamwork** travail *m* d'équipe

teapot ['tiːpɑːt] théière *f*

tear[1] [ter] **1** *n in cloth etc* dé-chirure *f* **2** *v/t paper, cloth* déchirer **3** *v/i* (*run fast, drive fast*): **she tore down the street** elle a descendu la rue en trombe

◆ **tear down** *poster* arracher; *building* démolir

◆ **tear out** *page* arracher

◆ **tear up** déchirer; *contract etc* annuler

tear[2] [tɪr] *n in eye* larme *f*; **be in ∼s** être en larmes; **tearful** *look* plein de larmes; **tear gas** gaz *m* lacrymogène

tease [tiːz] taquiner

'**teaspoon** cuillère *f* à café

technical ['teknɪkl] technique; **technically** (*strictly speaking*) en théorie; **technician** technicien(ne) *m(f)*; **technique** technique *f*

technological [teknəˈlɑːdʒɪkl] technologique; **technology** technologie *f*; **technophobia** technophobie *f*

teddy bear ['tedɪber] ours *m* en peluche

tedious ['tiːdɪəs] ennuyeux

tee [tiː] *in golf* tee *m*

teenage ['tiːneɪdʒ] *fashion* pour adolescents; **teenager** adolescent(e) *m(f)*

teens [tiːnz] adolescence *f*

teeny ['tiːnɪ] F tout petit

teeth [tiːθ] *pl* → **tooth**

teethe [tiːð] faire ses dents

telecommunications [telɪkəmjuːnɪ'keɪʃnz] télécommunications *fpl*

telegraph pole ['telɪgræf-

pɔʊl] *Br* poteau *m* télégra-
phique
telepathic [telɪˈpæθɪk] télépa-
thique; **telepathy** télépathie
f
telephone [ˈtelɪfəʊn] **1** *n* téléphone *m* **2** *v/t person* téléphoner à **3** *v/i* téléphoner;
telephone book annuaire
m; **telephone booth** cabine
f téléphonique; **telephone
call** appel *m* téléphonique;
telephone conversation
conversation *f* téléphonique;
telephone directory annuaire *m*; **telephone number** numéro *m* de téléphone
telephoto lens [telɪˈfəʊtəʊ-
lenz] téléobjectif *m*
telesales [ˈtelɪseɪlz] télévente
f
telescope [ˈtelɪskəʊp] télescope *m*
televise [ˈtelɪvaɪz] téléviser
television [ˈtelɪvɪʒn] *also set*
télévision *f*; **on ~** à la télévision; **television program**, *Br*
television programme
émission *f* télévisée; **television studio** studio *m* de télévision
tell [tel] **1** *v/t story* raconter; *lie*
dire; *I can't ~ the difference*
je n'arrive pas à faire la différence; *~ s.o. sth* dire qch à
qn; *~ s.o. to do sth* dire à qn
de faire qch **2** *v/i* (*have effect*)
se faire sentir; **teller** *in bank*
guichetier(-ière) *m(f)*; **tell-
ing off**: *get a ~* se faire re-

monter les bretelles F; **telltale 1** *adj signs* révélateur **2**
n rapporteur(-euse) *m(f)*
temp [temp] **1** *n employee* intérimaire *m/f* **2** *v/i* faire de
l'intérim
temper [ˈtempər] (*bad ~*)
mauvaise humeur *f*; *lose
one's ~* se mettre en colère
temperament [ˈtemprəmənt]
tempérament *m*; **tempera-
mental** (*moody*) capricieux
temperate [ˈtempərət] tempé-
ré
temperature [ˈtemprətʃər]
température *f*
temple¹ [ˈtempl] REL temple
m
temple² [ˈtempl] ANAT tempe *f*
tempo [ˈtempəʊ] MUS tempo
m
temporarily [tempəˈrerɪlɪ]
temporairement; **temporary**
temporaire
tempt [tempt] tenter; **temptation** tentation *f*; **tempting**
tentant
ten [ten] dix
tenacious [tɪˈneɪʃəs] tenace;
tenacity ténacité *f*
tenant [ˈtenənt] locataire *m/f*
tend¹ [tend] *v/t lawn* entretenir; *sheep* garder; *the sick*
soigner
tend² [tend] *v/i*: *~ to do sth*
avoir tendance à faire qch
tendency [ˈtendənsɪ] tendance *f*
tender¹ [ˈtendər] *adj* (*sore*)
sensible; (*affectionate*), *steak*

tendre

tender² ['tendər] *n* COM offre *f*

tenderness ['tendənɪs] *of kiss etc* tendresse *f*; *of steak* tendreté *f*

tendon ['tendən] tendon *m*

tennis ['tenɪs] tennis *m*; **tennis ball** balle *f* de tennis; **tennis court** court *m* de tennis; **tennis player** joueur(-euse) *m(f)* de tennis

tenor ['tenər] MUS ténor *m*

tense¹ [tens] *n* GRAM temps *m*

tense² [tens] *adj* tendu

tension ['tenʃn] tension *f*

tent [tent] tente *f*

tentative ['tentətɪv] *smile, steps* hésitant; *conclusion, offer* provisoire

tenth [tenθ] dixième

tepid ['tepɪd] *also fig* tiède

term [tɜːrm] (*period, word*) terme *m*; *Br* EDU trimestre *m*; (*condition*) condition *f*; **be on good/bad ~s with s.o.** être en bons/mauvais termes avec qn; **in the long/short ~** à long/court terme

terminal ['tɜːrmɪnl] **1** *n at airport* aérogare *m*; *for buses* terminus *m*; *for containers,* COMPUT terminal *m*; ELEC borne *f* **2** *adj illness* incurable; **terminally: ~ ill** en phase terminale; **terminate 1** *v/t* mettre fin à; *pregnancy* interrompre **2** *v/i* se terminer; **termination** *of contract* résiliation *f*; *in pregnancy* interrup-

tion *f* volontaire de grossesse

terminus ['tɜːrmɪnəs] terminus *m*

terrace ['terəs] terrasse *f*

terrain [te'reɪn] terrain *m*

terrible ['terəbl] horrible, affreux; **terribly** (*very*) très

terrific [tə'rɪfɪk] génial; **terrifically** (*very*) extrêmement, vachement F

terrify ['terɪfaɪ] terrifier; **terrifying** terrifiant

territorial [terə'tɔːrɪəl] territorial; **territory** territoire *m*; *fig* domaine *m*

terror ['terər] terreur *f*; **terrorism** terrorisme *m*; **terrorist** terroriste *m/f*; **terrorist attack** attentat *m* terroriste; **terrorize** terroriser

terse [tɜːrs] laconique

test [test] **1** *n scientific, technical test m*; *academic, for driving* examen *m* **2** *v/t* tester, mettre à l'épreuve; **test-drive** *car* essayer

testicle ['testɪkl] testicule *m*

testify ['testɪfaɪ] LAW témoigner

testimony ['testɪmənɪ] LAW témoignage *m*

testy ['testɪ] irritable

tetanus ['tetənəs] tétanos *m*

text [tekst] **1** *n* texte *m*; *message* texto *m* **2** *v/t* envoyer un texto à; **textbook** manuel *m*; **text-message** texto *m*, SMS *m*

textile ['tekstaɪl] textile *m*

texture ['tekstʃər] texture *f*

than [ðæn] que; *with numbers* de; **faster ~ me** plus rapide que moi

thank [θæŋk] remercier; **~ you** merci; **no ~ you** (non) merci; **thankful** reconnaissant; **thankfully** (*luckily*) heureusement; **thankless task** ingrat; **thanks** remerciements *mpl*; **~!** merci!; **~ to** grâce à; **Thanksgiving (Day)** jour *m* de l'action de grâces, Thanksgiving *m*

that [ðæt] **1** *adj* ce, cette; *masculine before vowel* cet; **~ one** celui-là, celle-là **2** *pron* cela, ça; **give me ~** donne-moi ça; **~'s tea** c'est du thé; **what is ~?** qu'est-ce que c'est que ça?; **who is ~?** qui est-ce? **3** *rel pron* que; **the car ~ you see** la voiture que vous voyez **4** *adv* (*so*) aussi; **~ expensive** aussi cher **5** *conj* que; **I think ~ ...** je pense que ...

thaw [θɔː] *of snow* fondre; *of frozen food* se décongeler

the [ðə] le, la; *pl* les; **to the station/theater** à la gare/au théâtre; **~ more I try** plus j'essaie

theater, *Br* theatre ['θɪətər] théâtre *m*; theatrical *also fig* théâtral

theft [θeft] vol *m*

their [ðer] leur; *pl* leurs; (*his or her*) son, sa; *pl* ses; **theirs** le leur, les leurs; **it's ~** c'est à eux/elles

them [ðem] *object* les; *indirect object* leur; *with prep* eux, elles; **I know ~** je les connais; **I gave ~ a dollar** je leur ai donné un dollar; **this is for ~** c'est pour eux/elles; **who?** **- ~** qui? - eux/elles

theme [θiːm] thème *m*; **theme park** parc *m* à thème

themselves [ðem'selvz] eux-mêmes, elles-mêmes; *reflexive* se; *after prep* eux, elles; **they gave ~ a holiday** ils se sont offerts des vacances

then [ðen] (*at that time*) à l'époque; (*after that*) ensuite; *deducing* alors; **by ~** alors

theoretical [θɪə'retɪkl] théorique; **theoretically** en théorie; **theory** théorie *f*

therapeutic [θerə'pjuːtɪk] thérapeutique; **therapist** thérapeute *m/f*; **therapy** thérapie *f*

there [ðer] là; **over √down ~** là-bas; **~ is/are ...** il y a ...; **is/are ~ ...?** est-ce qu'il y a...?, y a-t-il ...?; **~ is/are not ...** il n'y a pas ...; **~ you are** voilà; **~ and back** aller et retour; **~ he is!** le voilà!; **~, ~!** allons, allons; **we went ~ yesterday** nous y sommes allés hier; **thereabouts: $500 or ~** environ 500 $; **therefore** donc

thermometer [θər'mɑːmɪtər] thermomètre *m*

thermos flask ['θɜːrməsflæsk] thermos *m*

these

these [ðiːz] **1** *adj* ces **2** *pron* ceux-ci, celles-ci

thesis ['θiːsɪs] thèse *f*

they [ðeɪ] ils, elles; (*he or she*) il; **there ~ are** les voilà; **~ say that ...** on dit que ...

thick [θɪk] épais; F (*stupid*) lourd; **it's 3 cm ~** ça fait 3 cm d'épaisseur; **thicken** *sauce* épaissir; **thick-skinned** *fig* qui a la peau dure

thief [θiːf] voleur(-euse) *m(f)*

thigh [θaɪ] cuisse *f*

thin [θɪn] *material* léger, fin; *layer* mince; *person* maigre; *line* fin; *soup* liquide

thing [θɪŋ] chose *f*; **~s** (*belongings*) affaires *fpl*

think [θɪŋk] penser; **I ~ so** je pense que oui; **I don't ~ so** je ne pense pas; **I'll ~ about it** *offer* je vais y réfléchir

◆ **think over** réfléchir à

◆ **think through** bien examiner

◆ **think up** *plan* concevoir

'think tank comité *m* d'experts

thin-skinned ['θɪnskɪnd] *fig* susceptible

third [θɜːrd] **1** *adj* troisième **2** *n* troisième *m/f*; **thirdly** troisièmement; **third-party** tiers *m*; **third-party insurance** *Br* assurance *f* au tiers; **Third World** Tiers-Monde *m*

thirst [θɜːrst] soif *f*; **thirsty** assoiffé; **be ~** avoir soif

thirteen [θɜːr'tiːn] treize; thir-teenth treizième; **thirtieth** trentième; **thirty** trente

this [ðɪs] **1** *adj* ce, cette; *masculine before vowel* cet; **~ one** celui-ci, celle-ci **2** *pron* cela, ça; **~ is good** c'est bien; **~ is ...** c'est ...; *introducing s.o.* je vous présente ... **3** *adv*: **~ high** haut comme ça

thorn [θɔːrn] épine *f*; **thorny** *also fig* épineux

thorough ['θɜːrou] *search, knowledge* approfondi; *person* méticuleux; **thorough-bred** *horse* pur-sang *m*; **thoroughly** complètement; *clean, search for, know* à fond

those [ðouz] **1** *adj* ces **2** *pron* ceux-là, celles-là

though [ðou] **1** *conj* (*although*) bien que (+*subj*), quoique (+*subj*); **as ~** comme si **2** *adv* pourtant

thought [θɔːt] pensée *f*; **thoughtful** pensif; *book* profond; (*considerate*) attentionné; **thoughtless** inconsidéré

thousand ['θauznd] mille *m*; **~s of** des milliers *mpl* de; **thousandth 1** *adj* millième **2** *n* millième *m/f*

thrash [θræʃ] rouer de coups; *sp* battre à plates coutures

◆ **thrash out** *solution* parvenir à

thrashing volée *f* de coups; **get a ~** *sp* se faire battre à plates coutures

thread [θred] **1** *n* fil *m*; *of screw* filetage *m* **2** *v/t* *needle, beads* enfiler; **threadbare** usé jusqu'à la corde

threat [θret] menace *f*; **threaten** menacer; **threatening** menaçant

three [θri:] trois; **three-quarters** les trois-quarts *mpl*

threshold ['θreʃhould] *of house, new era* seuil *m*

thrifty ['θrɪftɪ] économe

thrill [θrɪl] **1** *n* frisson *m* **2** *v/t*: **be** ~**ed** être ravi; **thriller** thriller *m*; **thrilling** palpitant

thrive [θraɪv] *of plants* bien pousser; *of business* prospérer

throat [θrout] gorge *f*; **throat lozenge** pastille *f* pour la gorge

throb [θrɑːb] **1** *n of heart* pulsation *f*; *of music* vibration *f* **2** *v/i of heart* battre fort; *of music* vibrer

throne [θroun] trône *m*

throttle ['θrɑːtl] **1** *n on motorbike, boat* papillon *m* des gaz **2** *v/t* (*strangle*) étrangler

through [θruː] **1** *prep* ◇ (*across*) à travers; **go** ~ **the city** traverser la ville ◇ (*during*) pendant; **all** ~ **the night** toute la nuit; **Monday** ~ **Friday** du lundi au vendredi (inclus)
◇ (*by means of*) par **2** *adv*: **wet** ~ mouillé jusqu'aux os **3** *adj*: **be** ~ (*have arrived: of news etc*) être parvenu; **we're**

~ **of couple** c'est fini entre nous; **be** ~ **with s.o./sth** en avoir fini avec qn/qch; **throughout 1** *prep* au long de, pendant tout(e) **2** *adv* (*in all parts*) partout

throw [θrou] **1** *v/t* jeter, lancer; *of horse* désarçonner; (*disconcert*) déconcerter; *party* organiser **2** *n* jet *m*; **it's your** ~ c'est à toi de lancer

◆ **throw away** jeter

◆ **throw out** *old things* jeter; *from bar, home* jeter dehors, mettre à la porte; *from country* expulser; *plan* rejeter

◆ **throw up 1** *v/t ball* jeter en l'air **2** *v/i* (*vomit*) vomir

throw-away ['θrouəweɪ] (*disposable*) jetable; *remark* en l'air; **throw-in** SP remise *f* en jeu

thru [θruː] → **through**

thrust [θrʌst] (*push hard*) enfoncer

thud [θʌd] bruit *m* sourd

thug [θʌg] brute *f*

thumb [θʌm] **1** *n* pouce *m* **2** *v/t*: ~ **a ride** faire de l'auto-stop; **thumbtack** punaise *f*

thunder ['θʌndər] tonnerre *m*; **thunderous** *applause* tonitruant; **thunderstorm** orage *m*; **thunderstruck** abasourdi; **thundery** *weather* orageux

Thursday ['θɜːrzdeɪ] jeudi *m*

thus [ðʌs] ainsi

thwart [θwɔːrt] contrarier

tick [tɪk] **1** *n of clock* tic-tac *m*;

Br (*checkmark*) coche *f* **2** *v/i* faire tic-tac

ticket ['tɪkɪt] *for bus, museum* ticket *m; for train, airplane, theater, concert, lottery* billet *m; for speeding, illegal parking* P.V. *m;* **ticket machine** distributeur *m* de billets; **ticket office** billetterie *f*

ticking ['tɪkɪŋ] *noise* tic-tac *m*

tickle ['tɪkl] chatouiller

tidal wave ['taɪdlweɪv] raz--de-marée *m*

tide [taɪd] marée *f*

tidiness ['taɪdɪnɪs] ordre *m;* **tidy** *person, habits* ordonné; *room, house, desk* en ordre

◆ **tidy up 1** *v/t room, shelves* ranger; **tidy o.s. up** remettre de l'ordre dans sa tenue **2** *v/i* ranger

tie [taɪ] **1** *n* (*necktie*) cravate *f;* SP (*even result*) match *m* à égalité; **he doesn't have any ~s** il n'a aucune attache **2** *v/t laces* nouer; *knot* faire; *hands* lier **3** *v/i* SP *of teams* faire match nul; *of runner* finir ex æquo

◆ **tie down** attacher; *fig* (*restrict*) restreindre

◆ **tie up** *hair* attacher; *person* ligoter; *boat* amarrer

tier [tɪr] *of hierarchy* niveau *m; of seats* gradin *m*

tight [taɪt] **1** *adj clothes, knot, screw* serré; *shoes* trop petit; (*properly shut*) bien fermé; *not leaving much time* juste; *security* strict; F (*drunk*)

bourré F **2** *adv hold* fort; *shut* bien; *tighten control, security* renforcer; *screw* serrer; (*make tighter*) resserrer; **tight-fisted** radin; **tightly** *adv →* **tight** *adv;* **tightrope** corde *f* raide; **tights** *Br* collant *m*

tile [taɪl] *on floor, wall* carreau *m; on roof* tuile *f*

till¹ [tɪl] *→ until*

till² [tɪl] (*cash register*) caisse *f*

tilt [tɪlt] pencher

timber ['tɪmbər] bois *m*

time [taɪm] **1** *n* temps *m;* (*occasion*) fois *f;* **have a good ~** bien s'amuser; **what's the ~?** quelle heure est-il?; **the first ~** la première fois; **all the ~** pendant tout ce temps; **at the same ~** speak, reply etc, (*however*) en même temps; **in ~** à temps; **on ~** à l'heure **2** *v/t* chronométrer; **time bomb** bombe *f* à retardement; **time difference** décalage *m* horaire; **time-lag** laps *m* de temps; **time limit** limite *f* dans le temps; **timely** opportun; **time out** SP temps *m* mort; **timer** *device* minuteur *m;* **timesaving** économie *f* de temps; **timescale** *of project* durée *f;* **time switch** minuterie *f;* **time zone** fuseau *m* horaire

timid ['tɪmɪd] timide

tin [tɪn] *metal* étain *m;* **tinfoil** papier *m* aluminium

tinge [tɪndʒ] soupçon *m*

tingle ['tɪŋgl] picoter

tinkle ['tɪŋkl] *of bell* tintement *m*

tinsel ['tɪnsl] guirlandes *fpl* de Noël

tint [tɪnt] **1** *n of color* teinte *f; for hair* couleur *f* **2** *v/t:* ~ **one's hair** se faire une coloration; **tinted** *glasses* teinté; *paper* de couleur pastel

tiny ['taɪnɪ] minuscule

tip¹ [tɪp] *n (end)* bout *m*

tip² [tɪp] **1** *n advice* conseil *m; money* pourboire *m* **2** *v/t waiter etc* donner un pourboire à

◆ **tip off** informer

'tip-off renseignement *m,* tuyau *m* F

tipped [tɪpt] *cigarettes* à bout filtre

tippy-toe ['tɪpɪtou]: **on** ~ sur la pointe des pieds

tipsy ['tɪpsɪ] éméché

tire¹ ['taɪr] *n* pneu *m*

tire² ['taɪr] **1** *v/t* fatiguer **2** *v/i* se fatiguer

tired ['taɪrd] fatigué; **tiredness** fatigue *f;* **tireless** *efforts* infatigable; **tiresome** *(annoying)* fatigant; **tiring** fatigant

tissue ['tɪʃuː] ANAT tissu *m; handkerchief* mouchoir *m* en papier; **tissue paper** papier *m* de soie

title ['taɪtl] *of novel, person etc* titre *m; LAW* titre *m* de propriét é *(to* de); **titleholder** SP tenant(e) *m(f)* du titre

to [tuː] **1** *prep* à; ~ *Japan* au Japon; ~ *Chicago* à Chicago; ~ *my place* chez moi; ~ *the north of* au nord de; *give sth* ~ *s.o.* donner qch à qn **2** *with verbs:* ~ *speak,* ~ *shout* parler, crier; *learn* ~ *drive* apprendre à conduire; *too heavy* ~ *carry* trop lourd à porter **3** *adv:* ~ *and fro* walk, pace de long en large

toast [toust] **1** *n for eating* pain *m* grillé; *when drinking* toast *m; propose a* ~ *to s.o.* porter un toast à qn **2** *v/t when drinking* porter un toast à

toaster grille-pain *m inv*

tobacco [tə'bækou] tabac *m*

today [tə'deɪ] aujourd'hui

toddler ['tɒdlər] jeune enfant *m*

to-do [tə'duː] F remue-ménage *m*

toe [tou] orteil *m; of sock, shoe* bout *m; toenail* ongle *m* de pied

together [tə'geðər] ensemble; *(at the same time)* en même temps

toilet ['tɔɪlɪt] toilettes *fpl;* **toilet paper** papier *m* hygiénique; **toiletries** articles *mpl* de toilette

token ['toukən] *sign* témoignage *m; Br (gift* ~*)* bon *m* d'achat; *instead of coin* jeton *m*

tolerable ['tɑːlərəbl] *pain etc* tolérable; *(quite good)* ac-

ceptable; **tolerance** tolérance *f*; **tolerant** tolérant; **tolerate** tolérer

toll[1] [toul] *v/i* of bell sonner

toll[2] [toul] *n* (*deaths*) bilan *m*

toll[3] [toul] *n* for bridge, road
péage *m*

'toll booth poste *m* de péage;
toll-free TELEC gratuit; **~
number** numéro *m* vert

tomato [təˈmeɪtoʊ] tomate *f*;
tomato ketchup ketchup *m*

tomb [tuːm] tombe *f*; **tomb-
stone** pierre *f* tombale

tomcat [ˈtɑːmkæt] matou *m*

tomorrow [təˈmɔːroʊ] demain; **the day after ~**
après-demain; **~ morning**
demain matin

ton [tʌn] tonne *f* courte (=*907
kg*)

tone [toun] of color, conversation ton *m*; of musical instrument timbre *m*; of neighborhood classe *f*; **~ of voice** ton
m; **toner** toner *m*

tongue [tʌŋ] langue *f*

tonic [ˈtɑːnɪk] MED fortifiant
m; **tonic (water)** Schwep-
pes® *m*, tonic *m*

tonight [təˈnaɪt] ce soir; *sleep*
cette nuit

too [tuː] (*also*) aussi; (*excessively*) trop; **me ~** moi aussi;
~ much rice trop de riz

tool [tuːl] outil *m*

tooth [tuːθ] dent *f*; **toothache**
mal *m* de dents; **toothbrush**
brosse *f* à dents; **toothpaste**
dentifrice *m*; **toothpick** cure-
dents *m*

top [tɑːp] **1** *n* also clothing
haut *m*; (*lid: of bottle etc*)
bouchon *m*; of pen capuchon
m; of the class, league pre-
mier(-ère) *m(f)*; MOT: **~ gear**
quatrième *f*/cinquième *f*;
on ~ of sur; **be at the ~ of** être
en haut de; **be at the ~ of**
league être premier de; **get
to the ~** of company, mountain etc arriver au sommet **2**
adj branches du haut; *floor*
dernier; *player etc* meilleur;
speed maximum; *note* le plus
élevé; **~ official** haut fonctionnaire *m*

topic [ˈtɑːpɪk] sujet *m*; **topical**
d'actualité

topless [ˈtɑːplɪs] aux seins
nus; **topmost** branch le plus
haut; *floor* dernier; **topping**
on pizza garniture *f*

topple [ˈtɑːpl] **1** *v/i* s'écrouler
2 *v/t* government renverser

top 'secret top secret *inv*

topsy-turvy [tɑːpsɪˈtɜːrvɪ]
sens dessus dessous

torment 1 [ˈtɔːrment] *n* tourment *m* **2** [tɔːrˈment] *v/t* person, animal harceler

tornado [tɔːrˈneɪdoʊ] tornade
f

torpedo [tɔːrˈpiːdoʊ] **1** *n* torpille *f* **2** *v/t* also fig torpiller

torrent [ˈtɑːrənt] also fig torrent *m*

torture [ˈtɔːrtʃər] **1** *n* torture *f*
2 *v/t* torturer

toss [tɑːs] **1** *v/t* ball lancer;

rider désarçonner; *salad* remuer

total ['toutl] **1** *adj* total; *disaster* complet; *idiot* fini; **he's a ~ stranger** c'est un parfait inconnu **2** *n* total *m*; **totalitarian** totalitaire; **totally** totalement

totter ['tɑːtər] tituber

touch [tʌtʃ] **1** *n sense* toucher *m*; **lose ~ with s.o.** perdre contact avec qn; **in ~** SP en touche **2** *v/t also emotionally* toucher; *exhibits etc* toucher à **3** *v/i of two things* se toucher

◆ **touch down** *of airplane* atterrir; SP faire un touché-en-but

'**touchdown** *of airplane* atterrissage *m*; SP touché-en-but; **touching** touchant; **touchline** SP ligne *f* de touche; **touch screen** écran *m* tactile; **touchy** *person* susceptible

tough [tʌf] *person, material* résistant; *meat, question, exam, punishment* dur

tour [tur] **1** *n visite f; as part of package* circuit *m* (**of** dans); *of band etc* tournée *f* **2** *v/t area* visiter **3** *v/i of tourist* faire du tourisme; *of band* être en tournée; **tour guide** accompagnateur(-trice) *m(f)*; **tourism** tourisme *m*; **tourist** touriste *m/f*; **tourist industry** industrie *f* touristique; **tourist information office** office *m* de tourisme

tournament ['turnəmənt] tournoi *m*

'**tour operator** tour-opérateur *m*, voyagiste *m*

tow [tou] remorquer

◆ **tow away** *car* emmener à la fourrière

toward [tɔːrd] vers; *with attitude, feelings etc* envers

towel ['tauəl] serviette *f*

tower ['tauər] tour *f*

town [taun] ville *f*; **town center**, *Br* **town centre** centre-ville *m*; **town council** conseil *m* municipal; **town hall** hôtel *m* de ville

toxic ['tɑːksɪk] toxique; **toxin** toxine *f*

toy [tɔɪ] jouet *m*

trace [treɪs] **1** *n of substance* trace *f* **2** *v/t (find)* retrouver; *draw* tracer

track [træk] *path, (racecourse)* piste *f*; *motor racing* circuit *m*; *on record, CD* morceau *m*; RAIL voie *f* (ferrée); **~ 10** RAIL voie 10; **keep ~ of sth** suivre qch

◆ **track down** *person* retrouver; *criminal* dépister; *object* dénicher

tracksuit *Br* survêtement *m*

tractor ['træktər] tracteur *m*

trade [treɪd] **1** *n* commerce *m*; *(profession, craft)* métier *m* **2** *v/i (do business)* faire du commerce **3** *v/t (exchange)* échanger (**for** contre); **trade fair** foire *f* commerciale;

trademark marque f de commerce; **trade mission** mission f commerciale; **trader** commerçant(e) m(f)
tradition [trəˈdɪʃn] tradition f; **traditional** traditionnel; **traditionally** traditionnellement
traffic [ˈtræfɪk] circulation f; *at airport, in drugs* trafic m
♦ **traffic in** *drugs* faire du trafic de
'**traffic circle** rond-point m; **traffic cop** F agent m de la circulation; **traffic jam** embouteillage m; **traffic light** feux mpl de signalisation; **traffic sign** panneau m de signalisation
tragedy [ˈtrædʒədɪ] tragédie f; **tragic** tragique
trail [treɪl] **1** n (path) sentier m; *of blood* traînée f **2** v/t (follow) suivre à la trace; (tow) remorquer **3** v/i (lag behind) traîner; **trailer** *pulled by vehicle* remorque f; *of movie* bande-annonce f
train[1] [treɪn] n train m
train[2] [treɪn] **1** v/t entraîner; *dog* dresser; *employee* former **2** v/i *of team, athlete* s'entraîner; *of teacher etc* faire sa formation
trainee stagiaire m/f; **trainer** SP entraîneur(-euse) m(f); *of dog* dresseur(-euse) m(f); **~s** Br: *shoes* tennis mpl; **training** *of new staff* for-

mation f; SP entraînement m
'**train station** gare f
traitor [ˈtreɪtər] traître m, traîtresse f
♦ **trample on** piétiner
trampoline [ˈtræmpəlɪn] trampoline m
tranquil [ˈtræŋkwɪl] tranquille; Br **tranquility** tranquillité f; **tranquilizer**, Br **tranquillizer** tranquillisant m
transaction [trænˈzækʃn] *of business* conduite f; *piece of business* transaction f
transatlantic [trænzətˈlæntɪk] transatlantique
transcript [ˈtrænskrɪpt] transcription f
transfer **1** [trænsˈfɜːr] v/t transférer **2** [trænsˈfɜːr] v/i *when traveling* changer; *in job* être muté (**to** à) **3** [ˈtrænsfɜːr] n transfert m; **transferable** *ticket* transférable; **transfer fee** *for sportsman* prix m de transfert
transform [trænsˈfɔːrm] transformer; **transformation** transformation f; **transformer** ELEC transformateur m
transfusion [trænsˈfjuːʒn] transfusion f
transit [ˈtrænzɪt]: **in ~** en transit; **transition** transition f; **transitional** de transition; **transit lounge** *at airport* salle f de transit; **transit pas-**

senger passager(-ère) *m(f)*
en transit

translate [trænsˈleɪt] traduire; **translation** traduction *f*;
translator traducteur(-trice)
m(f)

transmission [trænzˈmɪʃn]
TV, AUT transmission *f*; **transmit** *news, program* diffuser;
disease transmettre; **transmitter** RAD, TV émetteur *m*

transparency
[trænsˈpærənsɪ] PHOT diapositive *f*; **transparent** transparent; (*obvious*) évident

transplant MED 1
[ˈtrænsplænt] transplantation *n f*; *organ transplanted*
transplant *m* 2 [trænsˈplænt]
v/t transplanter

transport 1 [ˈtrænspɔːrt] *n*
transport *m* 2 [trænsˈpɔːrt]
v/t transporter; **transportation** *of goods, people* transport *m*

transvestite [trænsˈvestaɪt]
travesti *m*

trap [træp] **1** *n also fig* piège *m*
2 *v/t also fig* piéger; **trappings** *of power* signes extérieurs *mpl*

trash [træʃ] (*garbage*) ordures *fpl*; F *goods etc* camelote *f* F;
fig: person vermine *f*; **trash can** poubelle *f*; **trashy** *goods*
de pacotille; *novel* de bas étage

traumatic [trɑʊˈmætɪk] traumatisant; **traumatize** traumatiser

travel [ˈtrævl] **1** *n* voyages *mpl*
2 *v/i* voyager **3** *v/t miles* parcourir; **travel agency** agence *f* de voyages; **travel agent**
agent *m* de voyages; **traveler**,
Br **traveller** voyageur(-euse)
m(f); **traveler's check**, *Br*
traveller's cheque chèque--voyage *m*; **travel expenses**
frais *mpl* de déplacement;
travel insurance assurance--voyage *f*

trawler [ˈtrɔːlər] chalutier *m*

tray [treɪ] *for food, photocopier* plateau *m*; *to go in oven*
plaque *f*

treacherous [ˈtretʃərəs] traître; **treachery** traîtrise *f*

tread [tred] **1** *n* pas *m*; *of staircase* dessus *m* des marches;
of tire bande *f* de roulement
2 *v/i* marcher

treason [ˈtriːzn] trahison *f*

treasure [ˈtreʒər] **1** *n* trésor *m*
2 *v/t gift etc* chérir; **treasurer**
trésorier(-ière) *m(f)*; **Treasury Department** ministère
m des Finances

treat [triːt] **1** *n* plaisir *m*; **it's my ~** (*I'm paying*) c'est moi
qui paie **2** *v/t* traiter; **~ s.o.
to sth** offrir qch à qn; **treatment** traitement *m*

treaty [ˈtriːtɪ] traité *m*

treble [ˈtrebl] **1** *adv*: **~ the
price** le triple du prix **2** *v/i*
tripler

tree [triː] arbre *m*

tremble [ˈtrembl] trembler

tremendous [trɪˈmendəs]

(*very good*) formidable; (*enormous*) énorme; **tremendously** (*very*) extrêmement; (*a lot*) énormément

tremor ['tremər] of earth secousse f (sismique)

trench [trentʃ] tranchée f

trend [trend] tendance f; (*fashion*) mode f; **trendy** branché

trespass ['trespæs] entrer sans autorisation; *no ~ing* défense d'entrer; **trespasser** *personne qui viole la propriété d'une autre*

trial ['traɪəl] LAW procès m; of equipment essai m; *be on ~* LAW passer en justice

triangle ['traɪæŋgl] triangle m; **triangular** triangulaire

tribe [traɪb] tribu f

tribunal [traɪ'bjuːnl] tribunal m

tributary ['trɪbjətərɪ] of river affluent m

trick [trɪk] **1** n to deceive tour m; (*knack*) truc m **2** v/t rouler; **trickery** tromperie f

trickle ['trɪkl] **1** n filet m; fig tout petit peu m **2** v/i couler goutte à goutte

tricky ['trɪkɪ] (*difficult*) délicat

trifling ['traɪflɪŋ] insignifiant

trigger ['trɪgər] on gun détente f

◆ **trigger off** déclencher

trim [trɪm] **1** adj (*neat*) bien entretenu; *figure* svelte **2** v/t *hair* couper un peu; *hedge* tailler; *costs* réduire; (*decorate: dress*) garnir **3** n cut taille f

trinket ['trɪŋkɪt] babiole f

trip [trɪp] **1** n (*journey*) voyage m; (*outing*) excursion f **2** v/i (*stumble*) trébucher **3** v/t (*make fall*) faire un croche-pied à

◆ **trip up** v/t (*make fall*) faire un croche-pied à; (*cause to go wrong*) faire trébucher **2** v/i (*stumble*) trébucher; (*make a mistake*) faire erreur

triple ['trɪpl] → **treble**

trite [traɪt] banal

triumph ['traɪʌmf] triomphe m

trivial ['trɪvɪəl] insignifiant; **triviality** banalité f

trolley ['trɒlɪ] (*streetcar*) tramway m

troops [truːps] troupes fpl

trophy ['troʊfɪ] trophée m

tropic ['trɒpɪk] GEOG tropique m; **tropical** tropical; **tropics** tropiques mpl

trot [trɒt] trotter

trouble ['trʌbl] **1** n (*difficulties*) problèmes mpl; (*inconvenience*) dérangement m; (*disturbance*) affrontements mpl; *get into ~* s'attirer des ennuis **2** v/t (*worry*) inquiéter; (*bother, disturb*) déranger; *of back, liver etc* faire souffrir; **troublemaker** fauteur(-trice) m(f) de troubles; **troubleshooting** dépannage m; **troublesome** pénible

trousers ['traʊzərz] *Br* pantalon *m*

trout [traʊt] truite *f*

truant ['truːənt] : **play ~** faire l'école buissonnière

truce [truːs] trêve *f*

truck [trʌk] camion *m*; **truck driver** camionneur(-euse) *m(f)*; **truck stop** routier *m*

trudge [trʌdʒ] **1** *v/i* se traîner **2** *n* marche *f* pénible

true [truː] vrai; *friend, American* véritable; **come ~** of *hopes, dream* se réaliser; **truly** vraiment; **Yours ~** je vous prie d'agréer mes sentiments distingués

trumpet ['trʌmpɪt] trompette *f*

trunk [trʌŋk] *of tree, body* tronc *m*; *of elephant* trompe *f*; *(large suitcase)* malle *f*; *of car* coffre *m*

trust [trʌst] **1** *n* confiance *f*; FIN fidéicommis *m* **2** *v/t* faire confiance à; **trusted** éprouvé; **trustee** fidéicommissaire *m/f*; **trusting, trustful** confiant; **trustworthy** fiable

truth [truːθ] vérité *f*; **truthful** honnête

try [traɪ] **1** *v/t & v/i* essayer; LAW juger; **~ to do sth** essayer de faire qch; **you must ~ harder** tu dois faire plus d'efforts **2** *n* rugby essai *m*; **trying** *(annoying)* éprouvant

T-shirt ['tiːʃɜːrt] tee-shirt *m*

tub [tʌb] *(bath)* baignoire *f* for *liquid* bac *m*; for *yoghurt* pot *m*; **tubby** boulot

tube [tuːb] *(pipe)* tuyau *m*; *of toothpaste* tube *m*; **tubeless** *tire* sans chambre à air

Tuesday ['tuːzdeɪ] mardi *m*

tuft [tʌft] touffe *f*

tug [tʌg] **1** *n* NAUT remorqueur *m* **2** *v/t* tirer

tuition [tuː'ɪʃn] cours *mpl*

tumble ['tʌmbl] tomber; **tumbledown** qui tombe en ruines; **tumbler** for *drink* verre *m*; *in circus* acrobate *m/f*

tummy ['tʌmɪ] F ventre *m*; **tummy ache** mal *m* de ventre

tumor, *Br* **tumour** tumeur *f*

tumult ['tuːmʌlt] tumulte *m*; **tumultuous** tumultueux

tuna ['tuːnə] thon *m*

tune [tuːn] **1** *n* air *m* **2** *v/t instrument* accorder
◆ **tune up 1** *v/i of orchestra* s'accorder **2** *v/t engine* régler

tuneful ['tuːnfl] harmonieux; **tune-up** *of engine* règlement *m*

tunnel ['tʌnl] tunnel *m*

turbine ['tɜːrbaɪn] turbine *f*

turbulence ['tɜːrbjələns] *in air travel* turbulences *fpl*; **turbulent** agité

turf [tɜːrf] gazon *m*; *piece* motte *f* de gazon

turkey ['tɜːrkɪ] dinde *f*

turmoil ['tɜːrmɔɪl] confusion *f*

turn [tɜːrn] **1** *n (rotation)* tour *m*; *in road* virage *m*; *in vaudeville* numéro *m*; **take ~s doing sth** faire qch à tour

de rôle; **it's my** ~ c'est à moi **2**
v/t wheel tourner; ~ **the corner** tourner au coin de la rue
3 *v/i of driver, car, wheel*
tourner; *of person* se retourner; **it has ~ed cold** le temps
s'est refroidi

◆ **turn around 1** *v/t object*
tourner; *company* remettre
sur pied; COM *order* traiter
2 *v/i* se retourner; *with a
car* faire demi-tour

◆ **turn away 1** *v/t (send away)*
renvoyer **2** *v/i (walk away)*
s'en aller; *(look away)* détourner le regard

◆ **turn back 1** *v/t edges, sheets*
replier **2** *v/i of walkers, in
course of action* faire demi-
-tour

◆ **turn down** *offer* rejeter;
volume, heating baisser; *edge*
replier

◆ **turn off 1** *v/t TV, heater*
éteindre; *faucet* fermer; *engine* arrêter **2** *v/i of car, driver* tourner; *of machine*
s'éteindre

◆ **turn on 1** *v/t TV, heater* allumer; *faucet* ouvrir; *engine*
mettre en marche; F *sexually*
exciter **2** *v/i of machine* s'allumer

◆ **turn over 1** *v/i in bed* se retourner; *of vehicle* se renverser **2** *v/t (put upside down)*
page tourner; FIN
avoir un chiffre d'affaires de

◆ **turn up 1** *v/t collar* remonter; *volume* augmenter; *heat-*

ing monter **2** *v/i (arrive)* arriver, se pointer F

turning ['tɜːnɪŋ] *in road* virage *m*; **turning point** tournant
m; **turnout** *at game etc* nombre *m* de spectateurs; **turnover** FIN chiffre *m* d'affaires;
turnpike autoroute *f*
payante; **turn signal** MOT clignotant *m*

turquoise ['tɜːrkwɔɪz] turquoise

turtle ['tɜːrtl] tortue *f* de mer;
turtleneck sweater pull *m* à
col cheminée

tusk [tʌsk] défense *f*

tutor ['tuːtər] *Br: at university*
professeur *m/f*; *(private)* ~
professeur *m* particulier

tuxedo [tʌk'siːdoʊ] smoking
m

TV [tiː'viː] télé *f*; **on** ~ à la télé;
TV dinner plateau-repas *m*;
TV guide guide *m* de télé;
TV program, *Br* **TV programme** programme *m* télé

twang [twæŋ] **1** *n in voice* accent *m* nasillard **2** *v/t guitar
string* pincer

tweezers ['twiːzərz] pince *f* à
épiler

twelfth [twelfθ] douzième;
twelve douze

twentieth ['twentɪɪθ] vingtième; **twenty** vingt

twice [twaɪs] deux fois; ~ **as
much** deux fois plus

twig [twɪg] brindille *f*

twilight ['twaɪlaɪt] crépuscule
m

twin [twɪn] jumeau *m*, jumelle *f*; **twin beds** lits *mpl* jumeaux

twinge [twɪndʒ] *of pain* élancement *m*

twinkle ['twɪŋkl] scintiller

'**twin room** chambre *f* à lits jumeaux

twirl [twɜːrl] **1** *v/t* faire tourbillonner; *mustache* tortiller **2** *f of cream etc* spirale *f*

twist [twɪst] **1** *v/t* tordre; ~ **one's ankle** se tordre la cheville **2** *v/i of road* faire des méandres; *of river* faire des lacets **3** *n in rope* entortillement *m*; *in road* lacet *m*; *in plot* dénouement *m* inattendu; **twisty** *road* qui fait des lacets

twitch [twɪtʃ] *nervous* tic *m*

twitter ['twɪtər] *of birds* gazouiller

two [tuː] deux; **the ~ of them** les deux

tycoon [taɪ'kuːn] magnat *m*

type [taɪp] **1** *n* (*sort*) type *m* **2** *v/i* (*use a keyboard*) taper **3** *v/t with a typewriter* taper à la machine

typhoon [taɪ'fuːn] typhon *m*

typhus ['taɪfəs] typhus *m*

typical ['tɪpɪkl] typique; **that's ~ of you!** c'est bien de vous!; **typically** typiquement

typist ['taɪpɪst] dactylo *m/f*

tyrannical [tɪ'rænɪkl] tyrannique; **tyrannize** tyranniser; **tyranny** tyrannie *f*; **tyrant** tyran *m*

tyre *Br* → **tire**[1]

U

ugly ['ʌɡlɪ] laid

UK [juː'keɪ] (= **United Kingdom**) R.-U. *m* (= Royaume-Uni)

ulcer ['ʌlsər] ulcère *m*

ultimate ['ʌltɪmət] (*best, definitive*) meilleur possible; (*final*) final; (*fundamental*) fondamental; **ultimately** (*in the end*) en fin de compte

ultimatum [ʌltɪ'meɪtəm] ultimatum *m*

ultrasound ['ʌltrəsaʊnd] MED ultrason *m*

ultraviolet [ʌltrə'vaɪələt] ul-

traviolet

umbrella [ʌm'brelə] parapluie *m*

umpire ['ʌmpaɪr] arbitre *m/f*

UN [juː'en] (= **United Nations**) O.N.U. *f* (= Organisation des Nations unies)

unable [ʌn'eɪbl]: **be ~ to do sth** *not know how to* ne pas savoir faire qch; *not be in a position to* ne pas pouvoir faire qch

unacceptable [ʌnək'septəbl] inacceptable

unaccountable [ʌnə-

'kaʊntəbl] inexplicable

un-American [ʌnə'merɪkən] (*not fitting*) antiaméricain

unanimous [juːˈnænɪməs] *verdict* unanime; **unanimously** à l'unanimité

unapproachable [ʌnə-'prəʊtʃəbl] *person* d'un abord difficile

unarmed [ʌn'ɑːrmd] *person* non armé

unassuming [ʌnə'suːmɪŋ] modeste

unattached [ʌnə'tætʃt] *without a partner* sans attaches

unattended [ʌnə'tendɪd] laissé sans surveillance

unauthorized [ʌn'ɔːθəraɪzd] non autorisé

unavoidable [ʌnə'vɔɪdəbl] inévitable

unbalanced [ʌn'bælənst] *also* PSYCH déséquilibré

unbearable [ʌn'berəbl] insupportable

unbeatable [ʌn'biːtəbl] imbattable

unbeaten [ʌn'biːtn] *team* invaincu

unbelievable [ʌnbɪ'liːvəbl] *also* F incroyable

unbias(s)ed [ʌn'baɪəst] impartial

unblock [ʌn'blɑːk] *pipe* déboucher

unbreakable [ʌn'breɪkəbl] incassable

unbutton [ʌn'bʌtn] déboutonner

uncanny [ʌn'kæni] étrange,

mystérieux

unceasing [ʌn'siːsɪŋ] incessant

uncertain [ʌn'sɜːrtn] incertain; **uncertainty** *of the future* caractère *m* incertain; *there is still ~ about* des incertitudes demeurent quant à …

uncle ['ʌŋkl] oncle *m*

uncomfortable [ʌn'kʌmftəbl] inconfortable

uncommon [ʌn'kɑːmən] inhabituel

uncompromising [ʌn'kɑːmprəmaɪzɪŋ] intransigeant

unconditional [ʌnkən'dɪʃnl] sans conditions

unconscious [ʌn'kɑːnʃəs] MED, PSYCH inconscient

uncontrollable [ʌnkən-'trəʊləbl] incontrôlable

unconventional [ʌnkən-'venʃnl] non conventionnel

uncooperative [ʌnkoʊ-'ɑːpərətɪv] peu coopératif

uncover [ʌn'kʌvər] découvrir

undamaged [ʌn'dæmɪdʒd] intact

undecided [ʌndɪ'saɪdɪd] *question* laissé en suspens; *be ~ about* être indécis à propos de

undeniable [ʌndɪ'naɪəbl] indéniable

under ['ʌndər] sous; (*less than*) moins de; *it is ~ investigation* cela fait l'objet d'une enquête

'under'carriage train *m* d'atterrissage

'under'cover clandestin; ~ **agent** agent *m* secret

under'cut COM: ~ *the competition* vendre moins cher que la concurrence

under'done *meat* pas trop cuit; *pej* pas assez cuit

under'estimate sous-estimer

under'fed mal nourri

under'go subir

under'graduate *Br* étudiant(e) (de D.E.U.G. ou de licence)

'underground **1** *adj* souterrain; POL clandestin **2** *adv* *work* sous terre

under'hand (*devious*) sournois

under'line *text* souligner

under'lying sous-jacent

under'mine saper

underneath [ʌndər'niːθ] **1** *prep* sous **2** *adv* dessous

'underpants slip *m*

'underpass *for pedestrians* passage *m* souterrain

underprivileged [ʌndər'prɪvɪlɪdʒd] défavorisé

under'rate sous-estimer

understaffed [ʌndər'stæft] en manque de personnel

under'stand comprendre; **understandable** compréhensible; **understandably** naturellement; **understanding 1** *adj person* compréhensif **2** *n* compréhension *f*;

(*agreement*) accord *m*

under'take *task* entreprendre; ~ *to do sth* (*agree to*) s'engager à faire qch; **undertaking** (*enterprise*) entreprise *f*; (*promise*) engagement *m*

under'value sous-estimer

'underwear sous-vêtements *mpl*

'underworld *criminal* monde *m* du crime organisé

under'write FIN souscrire

undeserved [ʌndɪ'zɜːrvd] non mérité

undesirable [ʌndɪ'zaɪrəbl] indésirable

undisputed [ʌndɪ'spjuːtɪd] *champion* incontestable

undo [ʌn'duː] défaire

undoubtedly [ʌn'daʊtɪdlɪ] à n'en pas douter

undress [ʌn'dres] **1** *v/t* déshabiller; *get ~ed* se déshabiller **2** *v/i* se déshabiller

undue [ʌn'duː] excessif; unduly (*excessively*) excessivement

unearth [ʌn'ɜːrθ] *also fig* terrer

uneasy [ʌn'iːzɪ] *relationship*, *peace* incertain vouloir signer cela

uneatable [ʌn'iːtəbl] immangeable

uneconomic [ʌnɪːkə'nɑːmɪk] pas rentable

uneducated [ʌn'edʒəkeɪtɪd] sans instruction

unemployed [ʌnɪm'plɔɪd] **1** *adj* au chômage **2** *npl*: *the*

~ les chômeurs(-euses); **unemployment** chômage *m*

unequal [ʌnˈiːkwəl] inégal

unerring [ʌnˈɜːrɪŋ] *judgment, instinct* infaillible

uneven [ʌnˈiːvn] *surface, ground* irrégulier

uneventful [ʌnɪˈventfl] *day, journey* sans événement

unexpected [ʌnɪkˈspektɪd] inattendu; **unexpectedly** inopinément

unfair [ʌnˈfer] injuste

unfaithful [ʌnˈfeɪθfl] *husband, wife* infidèle; **be ~ to s.o.** tromper qn

unfamiliar [ʌnfəˈmɪljər] peu familier

unfasten [ʌnˈfæsn] *belt* défaire

unfavorable [ʌnˈfeɪvərəbl] défavorable

unfinished [ʌnˈfɪnɪʃt] inachevé

unfold [ʌnˈfoʊld] **1** *v/t letter* déplier; *arms* ouvrir **2** *v/i of story etc* se dérouler; *of view* se déployer

unforeseen [ʌnfɔːrˈsiːn] imprévu

unforgettable [ʌnfərˈgetəbl] inoubliable

unforgivable [ʌnfərˈgɪvəbl] impardonnable

unfortunate [ʌnˈfɔːrtʃənət] malheureux; **unfortunately** malheureusement

unfounded [ʌnˈfaʊndɪd] non fondé

unfriendly [ʌnˈfrendlɪ] *per-son, welcome, hotel* froid

ungrateful [ʌnˈgreɪtfl] ingrat

unhappiness [ʌnˈhæpɪnɪs] chagrin *m*; **unhappy** malheureux; *customers etc* mécontent (**with** de)

unharmed [ʌnˈhɑːrmd] indemne

unhealthy [ʌnˈhelθɪ] *person* en mauvaise santé; *food, atmosphere* malsain; *economy* qui se porte mal

unheard-of [ʌnˈhɜːrdəv]: **be ~** ne s'être jamais vu

unhygienic [ʌnhaɪˈdʒiːnɪk] insalubre

unification [juːnɪfɪˈkeɪʃn] unification *f*

uniform [ˈjuːnɪfɔːrm] **1** *n* uniforme *m* **2** *adj* uniforme

unify [ˈjuːnɪfaɪ] unifier

unilateral [juːnɪˈlætərəl] unilatéral

unimaginable [ʌnɪˈmædʒɪnəbl] inimaginable

unimaginative [ʌnɪˈmædʒɪnətɪv] qui manque d'imagination

unimportant [ʌnɪmˈpɔːrtənt] sans importance

uninhabitable [ʌnɪnˈhæbɪtəbl] inhabitable; **uninhabited** inhabitée

unintentional [ʌnɪnˈtenʃnl] non intentionnel; **unintentionally** sans le vouloir

uninteresting [ʌnˈɪntrəstɪŋ] inintéressant

uninterrupted [ʌnɪntəˈrʌptɪd] ininterrompu

unproductive

union ['juːnjən] POL union *f*; (*labor* ~) syndicat *m*

unique [juːˈniːk] unique

unit ['juːnɪt] unité *f*

unite [juːˈnaɪt] **1** *v/t* unir **2** *v/i* s'unir; **united** uni; *efforts* conjoint; **United Kingdom** Royaume-Uni *m*; **United Nations** Nations Unies *fpl*

United States (of A'merica) États-Unis *mpl* (d'Amérique)

unity ['juːnətɪ] unité *f*

universal [juːnɪˈvɜːrsl] universel; **universe** univers *m*

university [juːnɪˈvɜːrsətɪ] université *f*

unjust [ʌnˈdʒʌst] injuste

unkind [ʌnˈkaɪnd] méchant, désagréable

unknown [ʌnˈnoʊn] inconnu

unleaded [ʌnˈledɪd] *gas* sans plomb

unless [ənˈles] à moins que (+*subj*)

unlikely [ʌnˈlaɪklɪ] improbable

unlimited [ʌnˈlɪmɪtɪd] illimité

unload [ʌnˈloʊd] décharger

unlock [ʌnˈlɑːk] ouvrir

unluckily [ʌnˈlʌkɪlɪ] malheureusement; **unlucky** *day* de malchance; *choice* malheureux; *person* malchanceux; *that was so* ~ *for you* tu n'as vraiment pas eu de chance!

unmanned [ʌnˈmænd] *space-craft* sans équipage

unmarried [ʌnˈmærɪd] non marié

unmistakable [ʌnmɪˈsteɪkəbl] reconnaissable entre mille

unnatural [ʌnˈnætʃrəl] contre-nature

unnecessary [ʌnˈnesəserɪ] non nécessaire

unnerving [ʌnˈnɜːrvɪŋ] déstabilisant

unobtainable [ʌnəbˈteɪnəbl] *goods* qu'on ne peut se procurer; TELEC hors service

unobtrusive [ʌnəbˈtruːsɪv] discret

unoccupied [ʌnˈɑːkjʊpaɪd] (*empty*) vide; *position* vacant; *person* désœuvré

unofficial [ʌnəˈfɪʃl] non officiel; **unofficially** non officiellement

unorthodox [ʌnˈɔːrθədɑːks] peu orthodoxe

unpack [ʌnˈpæk] **1** *v/t case* défaire **2** *v/i* défaire sa valise

unpaid [ʌnˈpeɪd] *work* non rémunéré

unpleasant [ʌnˈpleznt] désagréable

unplug [ʌnˈplʌg] *TV, computer* débrancher

unpopular [ʌnˈpɑːpjələr] impopulaire

unprecedented [ʌnˈpresɪdentɪd] sans précédent

unpredictable [ʌnprɪˈdɪktəbl] imprévisible

unpretentious [ʌnprɪˈtenʃəs] modeste

unproductive [ʌnprəˈdʌktɪv]

meeting, discussion, land improductif

unprofessional [ʌnprə'feʃnl] non professionnel; *workmanship* peu professionnel

unprofitable [ʌn'prɑːfɪtəbl] non profitable

unprovoked [ʌnprə'vəʊkt] *attack* non provoqué

unqualified [ʌn'kwɑːlɪfaɪd] non qualifié

unquestionably [ʌn'kwestʃnəblɪ] sans aucun doute; **unquestioning** *attitude* aveugle

unreadable [ʌn'riːdəbl] *book* illisible

unrealistic [ʌnrɪə'lɪstɪk] irréaliste

unreasonable [ʌn'riːznəbl] déraisonnable

unrelated [ʌnrɪ'leɪtɪd] sans relation (**to** avec)

unrelenting [ʌnrɪ'lentɪŋ] incessant

unreliable [ʌnrɪ'laɪəbl] pas fiable

unrest [ʌn'rest] agitation *f*

unrestrained [ʌnrɪ'streɪnd] *emotions* non contenu

unroll [ʌn'rəʊl] *carpet* dérouler

unruly [ʌn'ruːlɪ] indiscipliné

unsanitary [ʌn'sænɪterɪ] *conditions, drains* insalubre

unsatisfactory [ʌnsætɪs'fæktərɪ] insatisfaisant; (*unacceptable*) inacceptable

unscathed [ʌn'skeɪðd] (*not injured*) indemne; (*not damaged*) intact

unscrew [ʌn'skruː] *sth screwed on* dévisser; *top* décapsuler

unscrupulous [ʌn'skruːpjələs] peu scrupuleux

unselfish [ʌn'selfɪʃ] désintéressé

unsettled [ʌn'setld] incertain; *lifestyle* instable; *bills* non réglé; *issue* non décidé

unshaven [ʌn'ʃeɪvn] mal rasé

unskilled [ʌn'skɪld] *worker* non qualifié

unsophisticated [ʌnsə'fɪstɪkeɪtɪd] peu sophistiqué

unstable [ʌn'steɪbl] instable

unsteady [ʌn'stedɪ] *on feet* chancelant; *ladder* branlant

unsuccessful [ʌnsək'sesfl] *attempt* infructueux; *writer* qui n'a pas de succès; *candidate, marriage* malheureux; **unsuccessfully** sans succès

unsuitable [ʌn'suːtəbl] inapproprié

unswerving [ʌn'swɜːrvɪŋ] *loyalty* inébranlable

unthinkable [ʌn'θɪŋkəbl] impensable

untidy [ʌn'taɪdɪ] en désordre

untie [ʌn'taɪ] *knot* défaire; *prisoner, hands* détacher

until [ən'tɪl] **1** *prep* jusqu'à; *from Monday ~ Friday* de lundi à vendredi; *not ~ Friday* pas avant vendredi **2** *conj* jusqu'à ce que; *can you wait ~ I'm ready?* est-ce que vous pouvez attendre que je sois prêt?

untiring [ʌnˈtaɪrɪŋ] *efforts* infatigable

untold [ʌnˈtəʊld] *riches, suffering* inouï; *story* inédit

untrue [ʌnˈtruː] faux

unused [ʌnˈjuːzd] *goods* non utilisé

unusual [ʌnˈjuːʒl] inhabituel; (*strange*) bizarre; **unusually** anormalement, exceptionnellement

unveil [ʌnˈveɪl] *statue etc* dévoiler

unwell [ʌnˈwel] malade

unwilling [ʌnˈwɪlɪŋ]: *be ~ to do* refuser de faire; **unwillingly** à contre-cœur

unwind [ʌnˈwaɪnd] **1** *v/t tape* dérouler **2** *v/i* of *tape, story* se dérouler; (*relax*) se détendre

unwise [ʌnˈwaɪz] malavisé

unwrap [ʌnˈræp] déballer

unzip [ʌnˈzɪp] *dress etc* descendre la fermeture-éclair de; COMPUT décompresser

up [ʌp] **1** *adv*: *~ in the sky/on the roof* dans le ciel/sur le toit; *~ here* ici; *~ there* là-haut; *be ~ (out of bed)* être debout; *of sun* être levé; *of temperature* avoir augmenté; (*have expired*) être expiré; *what's ~?* F qu'est-ce qu'il y a?; *~ to 1989* jusqu'à 1989; *he came ~ to me* il s'est approché de moi; *what are you ~ to these days?* qu'est-ce que tu fais en ce

moment?; *be ~ to something (bad)* être sur un mauvais coup; *I don't feel ~ to it* je ne m'en sens pas le courage; *it's ~ to you* c'est toi qui décides; *it's ~ to them to solve it* c'est à eux de le résoudre **2** *prep*: *further ~ the mountain* un peu plus haut sur la montagne; *they ran ~ the street* ils ont remonté la rue en courant; *we traveled ~ to Paris* nous sommes montés à Paris **3** *n*: *~s and downs* hauts *mpl* et bas

'upbringing éducation *f*

up'date *file* mettre à jour

up'grade moderniser; *ticket* surclasser

upheaval [ʌpˈhiːvl] bouleversement *m*

up'hold *rights* maintenir

'upkeep maintien *m*

'upload COMPUT transférer

up'market Br *restaurant, hotel* chic; *product* haut de gamme

upon [əˈpɑːn] → **on**

upper [ˈʌpər] supérieur

'upright 1 *adj citizen* droit **2** *adv sit* (bien) droit; **upright piano** piano *f* droit

'uprising soulèvement *m*

'uproar vacarme *m*; *fig* protestations *fpl*

up'set 1 *v/t* renverser; *emotionally* contrarier **2** *adj emotionally* contrarié, vexé; **upsetting** contrariant

upside 'down à l'envers; *car* renversé

up'stairs 1 *adv* en haut; ~ *from us* au-dessus de chez nous 2 *adj room* d'en haut

up'stream en remontant le courant

up'tight F (*nervous*) tendu; (*inhibited*) coincé

up-to-'date à jour

'upturn *in economy* reprise *f*

upward ['ʌpwəd]: *move sth* ~ élever qch; ~ *of 100* au-delà de 100

uranium [juˈreɪnɪəm] uranium *m*

urban ['ɜːbən] urbain

urge [ɜːdʒ] 1 *n* (forte) envie *f* 2 *v/t*: ~ *s.o. to do sth* encourager qn à faire qch; **urgency** urgence *f*; **urgent** urgent

urinate ['jʊərəneɪt] uriner; **urine** urine *f*

US [juːˈes] (= *United States*) USA *mpl*

us [ʌs] nous

USA [juːesˈeɪ] (= *United States of America*) USA *mpl*

usage ['juːzɪdʒ] usage *m*

use 1 [juːz] *v/t also pej: person* utiliser 2 [juːs] *n* utilisation *f*; *it's no ~ waiting* ce n'est pas la peine d'attendre
◆ **use up** épuiser

used¹ [juːzd] *car etc* d'occasion

used² [juːst]: *be ~ to* être habitué à; *get ~ to* s'habituer à

used³ [juːst]: *I ~ to work there* je travaillais là-bas avant; *I ~ to know him well* je l'ai bien connu autrefois

useful ['juːsfʊl] utile; **usefulness** utilité *f*; **useless** inutile; F (*no good*) nul F; **user** *of product* utilisateur(-trice) *m(f)*; **user-friendly** facile à utiliser; COMPUT convivial

usual ['juːʒl] habituel; *as ~* comme d'habitude; **usually** d'habitude

utensil [juːˈtensl] ustensile *m*

utilize ['juːtɪlaɪz] utiliser

utter ['ʌtə] 1 *adj* total 2 *v/t sound* prononcer; **utterly** totalement

V

vacant ['veɪkənt] *building* inoccupé; *look* vide, absent; *Br: position* vacant; **vacantly** *stare* d'un air absent; **vacate** *room* libérer

vacation [veɪˈkeɪʃn] vacances *fpl*; *be on ~* être en vacances

vaccinate ['væksɪneɪt] vacciner; **vaccination** vaccination *f*; **vaccine** vaccin *m*

vacuum ['vækjuːm] 1 *n* vide *m* 2 *v/t floors* passer l'aspirateur sur

vagrant ['veɪgrənt] vagabond *m*

vague [veɪg] vague; **vaguely**

vaguement

vain [veɪn] **1** *adj person* vaniteux; *hope* vain **2** *n*: **in ~** en vain

valiant ['væljənt] vaillant

valid ['vælɪd] valable; **validate** *with official stamp* valider; *theory* confirmer; **validity** validité *f*; *of argument* justesse *f*; *of claim* bien-fondé *m*

valley ['vælɪ] vallée *f*

valuable ['væljubl] **1** *adj* de valeur; *colleague, help, advice* précieux **2** *npl*: **~s** objets *mpl* de valeur; **valuation** estimation *f*, expertise *f*; **value 1** *n* valeur *f* **2** *v/t* tenir à, attacher un grand prix à

valve [vælv] soupape *f*, valve *f*; *in heart* valvule *f*

van [væn] *small* camionnette *f*; *large* fourgon *m*

vandal ['vændl] vandale *m*; **vandalism** vandalisme *m*; **vandalize** vandaliser

vanilla [və'nɪlə] **1** *n* vanille *f* **2** *adj* à la vanille

vanish ['vænɪʃ] disparaître; *of clouds, sadness* se dissiper

vanity ['vænətɪ] *of person* vanité *f*

vapor ['veɪpər] vapeur *f*; **vaporize** *of atomic bomb, explosion* vaporiser; **vapour** *Br* → **vapor**

variable ['verɪəbl] **1** *adj* variable; *moods* changeant **2** *n* MATH, COMPUT variable *f*; *variant* variante *f*; **variation** variation *f*; *varied* varié; *variety* variété *f*; *various (several)* divers, plusieurs; *(different)* divers, différent

varnish ['vɑːrnɪʃ] **1** *n* vernis *m* **2** *v/t* vernir

vary ['verɪ] varier; *it varies* ça dépend

vase [veɪz] vase *m*

vast [væst] vaste; *improvement* considérable; *vastly improve etc* considérablement; *different* complètement

Vatican ['vætɪkən]: *the ~* le Vatican

vault¹ [vɔːlt] *n in roof* voûte *f*; **~s** *of bank* salle *f* des coffres

vault² [vɔːlt] **1** *n* SP saut *m* **2** *v/t beam etc* sauter

VCR [viːsiːˈɑːr] (= *video cassette recorder*) magnétoscope *m*

veal [viːl] veau *m*

veer [vɪr] virer; *of wind* tourner

vegetable ['vedʒtəbl] légume *m*; **vegetarian 1** *n* végétarien(ne) *m(f)* **2** *adj* végétarien; **vegetation** végétation *f*

vehement ['viːəmənt] véhément

vehicle ['viːɪkl] véhicule *m*

veil [veɪl] voile *m*

vein [veɪn] ANAT veine *f*

velocity [vɪˈlɑːsətɪ] vélocité *f*

velvet ['velvɪt] velours *m*

vendetta [venˈdetə] vendetta *f*

vending machine ['vendɪŋ]

distributeur *m* automatique;
vendor LAW vendeur(-euse)
m(f)

veneer [vəˈnɪr] placage *m; of politeness* vernis *m*

venerable [ˈvenərəbl] vénérable; **veneration** vénération *f*

venereal disease [vəˈnɪriəl] M.S.T. *f*, maladie *f* sexuellement transmissible

venetian blind [vəˈniːʃn] store *m* vénitien

venom [ˈvenəm] venin *m*

ventilate [ˈventɪleɪt] ventiler; **ventilation** ventilation *f*; **ventilator** ventilateur *m*; MED respirateur *m*

venture [ˈventʃər] **1** *n (undertaking)* entreprise *f*; COM tentative *f* **2** *v/i* s'aventurer

venue [ˈvenjuː] *for meeting, concert etc* lieu *m; hall also* salle *f*

veranda [vəˈrændə] véranda *f*

verb [vɜːrb] verbe *m*; **verbal** *(spoken)* oral, verbal; **verbally** oralement, verbalement

verdict [ˈvɜːrdɪkt] LAW verdict *m; (opinion, judgment)* avis *m*, jugement *m*

verge [vɜːrdʒ] *of road* accotement *m*, bas-côté *m; **be on the ~ of ...** être au bord de ...

verification [verɪfɪˈkeɪʃn] *(check)* vérification *f*; **verify** *(check)* vérifier, contrôler; *(confirm)* confirmer

vermin [ˈvɜːrmɪn] *(insects)* vermine *f*, parasites *mpl*; *(rats etc)* animaux *mpl* nuisibles

vermouth [vərˈmuːθ] vermouth *m*

versatile [ˈvɜːrsətəl] *person* plein de ressources, polyvalent; *piece of equipment* multiusages; **versatility** *of person* adaptabilité *f*, polyvalence *f; of piece of equipment* souplesse *f* d'emploi

verse [vɜːrs] *(poetry)* vers *mpl*, poésie *f; of poem* strophe *f; of song* couplet *m*

version [ˈvɜːrʃn] version *f*

versus [ˈvɜːrsəs] contre

vertical [ˈvɜːrtɪkl] vertical

vertigo [ˈvɜːrtɪɡoʊ] vertige *m*

very [ˈveri] **1** *adv* très; *was it cold? – not ~* faisait-il froid? – non, pas tellement; *the ~ best* le meilleur **2** *adj* même; *at that ~ moment* à cet instant même, à ce moment précis; *that's the ~ thing I need* c'est exactement ce dont j'ai besoin

vessel [ˈvesl] NAUT bateau *m*, navire *m*

vest [vest] gilet *m* Br: *undershirt* maillot *m* (de corps)

vestige [ˈvestɪdʒ] vestige *m; fig* once *f*

vet¹ [vet] *n (veterinarian)* vétérinaire *m/f*, véto *m/f* F

vet² [vet] *v/t applicants etc* examiner

vet³ [vet] *n* MIL F ancien combattant *m*

veteran [ˈvetərən] **1** *n* vétéran *m* **2** *adj (old)* antique; *(old* *and experienced)* aguerri, chevronné

veterinarian [vetərə'neriən] vétérinaire *m/f*

veto ['vi:tou] **1** *n* veto *m inv* **2** *v/t* opposer son veto à

via ['vaiə] par

viable ['vaiəbl] viable

vibrate [vai'breit] vibrer; **vibration** vibration *f*

vice[1] [vais] *n* vice *m*

vice[2] [vais] *Br* → **vise**

vice 'president vice-président *m*

vice versa [vais'vɜ:rsə] vice versa

vicious ['viʃəs] vicieux; *dog* méchant; *person, temper* cruel; *attack* brutal; **viciously** brutalement

victim ['viktim] victime *f*; **victimize** persécuter

victorious [vik'tɔ:riəs] victorieux; **victory** victoire *f*

video ['vidiou] **1** *n* vidéo *f*; *actual object* cassette *f* vidéo **2** *v/t* enregistrer; **video camera** caméra *f* vidéo; **video cassette** cassette *f* vidéo; **video recorder** magnétoscope *m*; **videotape** bande *f* vidéo

vie [vai] rivaliser

Vietnam [viet'næm] Vietnam *m*; **Vietnamese 1** *adj* vietnamien **2** *n* Vietnamien(ne) *m(f)*; *language* vietnamien *m*

view [vju:] **1** *n* **a** vue *f*; *(assessment, opinion)* opinion *f*, avis

m; **in ~ of** compte tenu de, étant donné **2** *v/t* considérer, envisager **3** *v/i (watch TV)* regarder la télévision; **viewer** TV téléspectateur(-trice) *m(f)*; **viewpoint** point *m* de vue

vigor ['vigər] vigueur *f*; **vigorous** vigoureux; **vigorously** vigoureusement; **vigour** *Br* → **vigor**

village ['vilidʒ] village *m*; **villager** villageois(e) *m(f)*

villain ['vilən] escroc *m*; *in drama* méchant *m*

vindicate ['vindikeit] *(prove correct)* confirmer, justifier; *(prove innocent)* innocenter

vindictive [vin'diktiv] vindicatif

vine [vain] vigne *f*

vinegar ['vinigər] vinaigre *m*

vineyard ['vinjɑ:rd] vignoble *m*

vintage ['vintidʒ] **1** *n of wine* millésime *m* **2** *adj (classic)* classique

violate ['vaiəleit] violer; **violation** violation *f*; *(traffic ~)* infraction *f* au code de la route

violence ['vaiələns] violence *f*; **violent** violent

violin [vaiə'lin] violon *m*; **violinist** violoniste *m/f*

VIP [vi:ai'pi:] (= *very important person*) V.I.P. *m*

viral ['vairəl] viral

virgin ['vɜ:rdʒin] vierge *f*;

male puceau *m* F; **virginity** virginité *f*

virile ['vɪrəl] viril; **virility** virilité *f*

virtual ['vɜːrtʃʊəl] quasi-; **virtually** (*almost*) pratiquement, presque

virtue ['vɜːrtʃuː] vertu *f*; **virtuous** vertueux

virus ['vaɪrəs] virus *m*

visa ['viːzə] visa *m*

vise [vaɪz] étau *m*

visibility [vɪzə'bɪlətɪ] visibilité *f*; **visible** visible

vision ['vɪʒn] (*eyesight*) vue *f*; REL vision *f*

visit ['vɪzɪt] **1** *n* visite *f*; (*stay*) séjour *m* **2** *v/t* rendre visite à; *doctor, dentist* aller voir; *city, country* aller à/en; *castle, museum* visiter; *website* consulter; **visitor** (*guest*) invité *m*; (*tourist*) visiteur *m*

visor ['vaɪzər] visière *f*

visual ['vɪʒʊəl] visuel; **visualize** (*imagine*) (s')imaginer; (*foresee*) envisager, prévoir; **visually** visuellement

vital ['vaɪtl] (*essential*) vital, essentiel; **vitality** vitalité *f*; **vitally**: ~ *important* d'une importance capitale

vitamin ['vaɪtəmɪn] vitamine *f*; **vitamin pill** comprimé *m* de vitamines

vivacious [vɪ'veɪʃəs] plein de vivacité, vif; **vivacity** vivacité *f*

vivid ['vɪvɪd] vif; *description* vivant; **vividly** vivement; *re-*

member clairement; *describe* de façon vivante

V-neck ['viːnek] col *m* en V

vocabulary [vou'kæbjʊlərɪ] vocabulaire *m*; (*list of words*) glossaire *m*

vocal ['voukl] vocal; **vocalist** MUS chanteur(-euse) *m(f)*

vocation [və'keɪʃn] vocation *f*; **vocational** *guidance* professionnel

vodka ['vɑːdkə] vodka *f*

vogue [voug] vogue *f*; *be in* ~ être en vogue

voice [vɔɪs] **1** *n* voix *f* **2** *v/t* *opinions* exprimer; **voicemail** messagerie *f* vocale

volcano [vɑːl'keɪnou] volcan *m*

volley ['vɑːlɪ] volée *f*

volt [voult] volt *m*; **voltage** tension *f*

volume ['vɑːljəm] volume *m*

voluntarily [vɑːlən'terɪlɪ] de son plein gré, volontairement; **voluntary** volontaire; *work* bénévole; **volunteer** **1** *n* volontaire *m/f*; (*unpaid worker*) bénévole *m/f* **2** *v/i* se porter volontaire

vomit ['vɑːmɪt] **1** *n* vomi *m*, vomissure *f* **2** *v/i* vomir

voracious [və'reɪʃəs] vorace; *reader* avide

vote [vout] **1** *n* vote *m* **2** *v/i* POL voter (*for* pour; *against* contre); **voter** POL électeur *m*; **voting** POL vote *m*

◆ **vouch for** [vautʃ] *truth, person* se porter garant de

vow [vaʊ] **1** *n* vœu *m*, serment *m* **2** *v/t*: **~ to do** jurer de faire
vowel [vaʊl] voyelle *f*
voyage ['vɔɪɪdʒ] voyage *m*

vulgar ['vʌlgər] vulgaire
vulnerable ['vʌlnərəbl] vulnérable
vulture ['vʌltʃər] vautour *m*

W

waddle ['wɑːdl] se dandiner
wade [weɪd] patauger
wafer ['weɪfər] (*cookie*) gaufrette *f*; REL hostie *f*
waffle ['wɑːfl] **to eat** gaufre *f*
wag [wæg] remuer
wages ['weɪdʒɪz] salaire *m*
waggle ['wægl] remuer
wail [weɪl] hurler
waist [weɪst] taille *f*
wait [weɪt] **1** *n* attente *f* **2** *v/i* attendre
◆ **wait for** attendre
◆ **wait on** (*serve*) servir
◆ **wait up**: *don't wait up (for me)* ne m'attends pas pour aller te coucher
waiter ['weɪtər] serveur *m*; **~!** garçon!; **waiting list** liste *f* d'attente; **waiting room** salle *f* d'attente; **waitress** serveuse *f*
waive [weɪv] renoncer à
wake [weɪk] **1** *v/i*: **~ (up)** se réveiller **2** *v/t person* réveiller
walk [wɔːk] **1** *n* marche *f*; (*path*) allée *f*; **go for a ~** aller se promener **2** *v/i* marcher; *as opposed to driving* aller à pied; (*hike*) faire de la marche **3** *v/t dog* promener
◆ **walk out** *of spouse* prendre

la porte; *from theater etc* partir; (*go on strike*) se mettre en grève
walker ['wɔːkər] (*hiker*) randonneur/-euse *m(f)*; *for baby* trotte-bébé *m*; *for old person* déambulateur *m*; **walking** (*hiking*) randonnée *f*; **walkout** (*strike*) grève *f*; **walkover** (*easy win*) victoire *f* facile
wall [wɔːl] mur *m*
wallet ['wɑːlɪt] (*billfold*) portefeuille *m*
'wallpaper **1** *n: also* COMPUT papier *m* peint **2** *v/t* tapisser; **wall-to-wall carpet** moquette *f*
waltz [wɔːlts] valse *f*
wan [wɑːn] *face* pâlot
wander ['wɑːndər] (*roam*) errer; (*stray*) s'égarer
wangle ['wæŋgl] F réussir à obtenir (par une combine)
want [wɑːnt] **1** *n*: **for ~ of** par manque de, faute de **2** *v/t* vouloir; (*need*) avoir besoin de; **~ to do sth** vouloir faire qch; **I ~ to stay here** je veux rester ici; **she ~s you to go back** elle veut que tu reviennes (*subj*) **3** *v/i*: **~ for nothing**

ne manquer de rien; **wanted by** *police* recherché

war [wɔːr] guerre *f*; *fig* lutte *f*

ward [wɔːrd] *in hospital* salle *f*; *child* pupille *m/f*

◆ **ward off** éviter

warden ['wɔːrdn] *of prison* gardien (ne) *m(f)*; *Br*: *of hostel* directeur (-trice) *m(f)*

'**wardrobe** *for clothes* armoire *f*; (*clothes*) garde-robe *f*

warehouse ['werhaus] entrepôt *m*

'**warfare** guerre *f*; **warhead** ogive *f*

warily ['werɪlɪ] avec méfiance

warm [wɔːrm] chaud; *welcome, smile* chaleureux

◆ **warm up 1** *v/t* réchauffer **2** *v/i* se réchauffer; *of athlete etc* s'échauffer

warmly ['wɔːrmlɪ] chaudement; *welcome, smile* chaleureusement; **warmth** *also fig* chaleur *f*; **warm-up** *SP* échauffement *m*

warn [wɔːrn] prévenir; **warning** avertissement *m*

warp [wɔːrp] *of wood* gauchir; **warped** *fig* tordu

warrant ['wɔːrənt] **1** *n* mandat *m* **2** *v/t* justifier; **warranty** garantie *f*

warrior ['wɔːrɪər] guerrier (-ière) *m(f)*

wart [wɔːrt] verrue *f*

wary ['werɪ] méfiant; **be ~ of** se méfier de

wash [wɑːʃ] **1** *n*: **have a ~** se laver **2** *v/t clothes, dishes* laver **3** *v/i* se laver

◆ **wash up** (*wash one's hands and face*) se débarbouiller

washable ['wɑːʃəbl] lavable; **washbasin, washbowl** lavabo *m*; **washcloth** gant *m* de toilette; **washed out** (*tired*) usé; **washer** *for faucet etc* rondelle *f*; **washing** lessive *f*; **do the ~** faire la lessive; **washing machine** machine *f* à laver; **washroom** toilettes *fpl*

wasp [wɑːsp] guêpe *f*

waste [weɪst] **1** *n* gaspillage *m*; *from industrial process* déchets *mpl*; **it's a ~ of time/money** c'est une perte de temps/d'argent **2** *adj* non utilisé **3** *v/t* gaspiller; **waste basket** corbeille *f* à papier; **waste disposal (unit)** broyeur *m* d'ordures; **wasteful** gaspilleur; **wasteland** désert *m*; **wastepaper** papier(s) *m(pl)* (jeté(s)) à la poubelle)

watch [wɑːtʃ] **1** *n timepiece* montre *f*; **keep ~** monter la garde **2** *v/t* (*look after*) surveiller **3** *v/i* regarder; **watchful** vigilant

water ['wɔːtər] **1** *n* eau *f* **2** *v/t plant* arroser **3** *v/i*: **my mouth is ~ing** j'ai l'eau à la bouche; **watercolor**, *Br* **watercolour** aquarelle *f*; **watered down** *fig* atténué; **waterfall** chute *f* d'eau; **waterline** ligne *f* de flottaison; **waterlogged** détrempé; *boat* plein d'eau; **watermelon** pastèque *f*; **waterproof** imperméable; **waterside** bord *m* de l'eau; **waterskiing** ski *m* nautique; **watertight** *compartment* étanche; *fig*: *alibi* parfait; **waterway** voie *f* d'eau; **watery** *soup* trop clair; *coffee* trop léger

watt [wɑːt] watt *m*

wave¹ [weɪv] *n* in sea vague *f*

wave² [weɪv] **1** *n* of hand signe *m* **2** *v/i* with hand saluer; of flag flotter **3** *v/t* flag etc agiter

'**wavelength** RAD longueur *f* d'onde; *be on the same ~ fig* être sur la même longueur d'onde

waver ['weɪvər] hésiter

wavy ['weɪvɪ] ondulé

wax [wæks] cire *f*

way [weɪ] (*method, manner*) façon *f*; (*route*) chemin *m* (**to** de); *this~* (*like this*) comme ça; (*in this direction*) par ici; *by the~* (*incidentally*) au fait; *in a~* (*in certain respects*) d'une certaine façon; *lose one's~* se perdre; *be in the~* (*be an obstruction*) gêner le passage; (*disturb*) gêner; *no~!* pas question!; **way in** entrée *f*; **way of life** mode *m* de vie; **way out** sortie *f*; *fig* issue *f*

we [wiː] nous

weak [wiːk] faible; *tea, coffee* léger; **weaken 1** *v/t* affaiblir

2 *v/i* s'affaiblir; *in negotiation etc* faiblir; **weakness** faiblesse *f*

wealth [welθ] richesse *f*; **wealthy** riche

weapon ['wepən] arme *f*

wear [wer] **1** *n*: *~* (*and tear*) usure *f* **2** *v/t* (*have on*) porter; (*damage*) user **3** *v/i* (*wear out*) s'user; *~ well* (*last*) faire bon usage

◆ **wear down** user

◆ **wear off** of effect se dissiper

◆ **wear out 1** *v/t* (*tire*) épuiser; *shoes, carpet* user **2** *v/i* of shoes, carpet s'user

wearily ['wɪrɪlɪ] avec lassitude; **weary** las

weather ['weðər] **1** *n* temps *m* **2** *v/t* *crisis* survivre à; **weather-beaten** hâlé; **weather forecast** prévisions météorologiques *fpl*, météo *f*; **weatherman** présentateur *m* météo

weave [wiːv] **1** *v/t* *cloth* tisser **2** *v/i* of cyclist se faufiler

web [web] of spider toile *f*; *the ~* COMPUT le Web; **web page** page *f* de Web; **web site** site *m* Web

wedding ['wedɪŋ] mariage *m*; **wedding anniversary** anniversaire *m* de mariage; **wedding day** jour *m* de mariage; **wedding dress** robe *f* de mariée; **wedding ring** alliance *f*

wedge [wedʒ] to hold sth in

place cale *f; of cheese etc* morceau *m*

Wednesday ['wenzdeɪ] mercredi *m*

weed [wiːd] **1** *n* mauvaise herbe *f* **2** *v/t* désherber; **weedkiller** herbicide *f;* **weedy** *f* chétif

week [wiːk] semaine *f; a ~ tomorrow* demain en huit; **weekday** jour *m* de la semaine; **weekend** week-end *m; on the ~* this one le week--end; *every one* le week-end; **weekly 1** *adj* hebdomadaire **2** *n magazine* hebdomadaire *m* **3** *adv be published* toutes les semaines; *be paid* à la semaine

weep [wiːp] pleurer

wee-wee ['wiːwiː] F pipi *m* F; *do a ~* faire pipi

weigh [weɪ] peser

◆ **weigh up** *(assess)* juger

weight [weɪt] poids *m;* **weightlessness** apesanteur *f;* **weightlifter** haltérophile *m/f;* **weightlifting** haltérophilie *f;* **weighty** *fig (important)* sérieux

weir [wɪr] barrage *m*

weird [wɪrd] bizarre; **weirdo** F cinglé(e) *m(f)* F

welcome ['welkəm] **1** *adj* bienvenu; *you're ~!* je vous en prie! **2** *n* accueil *m* **3** *v/t* accueillir; *fig: news, announcement* se réjouir de; *opportunity* saisir

weld [weld] souder

welfare ['welfer] bien-être *m; financial assistance* sécurité *f* sociale; *be on ~* toucher les allocations; **welfare check** chèque *m* d'allocations; **welfare state** État *m* providence; **welfare worker** assistant social *m,* assistante sociale *f*

well[1] [wel] *n for water, oil* puits *m*

well[2] [wel] **1** *adv* bien; *~ done!* bien!; *as ~ (too)* aussi; *as ~ as (in addition to)* en plus de; *very ~ acknowledging order* entendu; *reluctantly agreeing* très bien; *~, ~! surprise* tiens, tiens!; *~ ... uncertainty, thinking* eh bien … **2** *adj: be ~* aller bien; **well-balanced** équilibré; **well-behaved** bien élevé; **well-being** bien-être *m;* **well-done** *meat* bien cuit; **well-dressed** bien habillé; **well-earned** bien mérité; **well-heeled** F cossu; **well-informed** bien informé; **well-known** connu; **well-meaning** plein de bonnes intentions; **well-off** riche; **well-timed** bien calculé; **well-wisher** personne *f* apportant son soutien

west [west] **1** *n* ouest *m* **2** *adj* ouest *inv; wind* d'ouest **3** *adv travel* vers l'ouest; **westerly** *wind* d'ouest; *direction* vers l'ouest; **western 1** *adj* de l'Ouest **2** *n movie* western *m;* **Westerner** occidental(e); **westernized** occidentalisé;

West Indian 1 *adj* antillais **2** *n* Antillais(e) *m(f)*; **West Indies: the ~** les Antilles *fpl*; **westward** vers l'ouest

wet [wet] mouillé; (*rainy*) humide; **wet suit** *for diving* combinaison *f* de plongée

whack [wæk] F (*blow*) coup *m*

whale [weɪl] baleine *f*

what [wɑːt] **1** *pron* ◇ : **~?** quoi?; **~ for?** (*why?*) pourquoi?; **so ~?** et alors?

◇ **~ did he say?** qu'est-ce qu'il a dit, qu'a-t-il dit?; **~ is that?** qu'est-ce que c'est?; **~ is it?** (*what do you want?*) qu'est-ce qu'il y a?

◇ *as object:* qu'est-ce que; **~ just fell off?** qu'est-ce qui vient de tomber?

◇ *relative as object* ce que; **I did ~ I could** j'ai fait ce que j'ai pu

◇ *relative as subject* ce qui; **I didn't see ~ happened** je n'ai pas vu ce qui s'est passé

◇ *suggestions:* **~ about heading home?** et si nous rentrions? **2** *adj* quel, quelle; *pl* quels, quelles; **~ color is the car?** de quelle couleur est la voiture?

whatever [wɑːtˈevər]: **~ the season** quelle que soit la saison; **~ you do** quoi que tu fasses; **ok, ~** F ok, si vous le dites

wheat [wiːt] blé *m*

wheel [wiːl] roue *f*; (*steering ~*) volant *m*; **wheelchair** fauteuil *m* roulant; **wheel clamp** *Br* sabot *m* de Denver

wheeze [wiːz] respirer péniblement

when [wen] quand; **on the day ~** le jour où; *whenever each time* chaque fois que; *regardless of when* n'importe quand

where [wer] où; **~ from?** d'où?; **~ to?** où?; **this is ~ I used to live** c'est là que j'habitais; *whereas* tandis que; **wherever 1** *conj* partout où; **sit ~ you like** assieds-toi où tu veux **2** *adv* où (donc); **~ can it be?** où peut-il bien être?

whet [wet] *appetite* aiguiser

whether [ˈweðər] (*if*) si; **you approve or not** que tu sois (*subj*) d'accord ou pas

which [wɪtʃ] **1** *adj* quel, quelle; *pl* quels, quelles **2** *pron* ◇ *interrogative* lequel, laquelle; *pl* lesquels, lesquelles; **~ are your favorites?** lesquels préférez-vous?

◇ *relative: subject* qui; *object* que; *after prep* lequel, laquelle; *pl* lesquels, lesquelles

whiff [wɪf]: **catch a ~ of** sentir

while [waɪl] **1** *conj* pendant que; (*although*) bien que (+*subj*) **2** *n*: **a long ~** longtemps; **for a ~** pendant un moment

whim [wɪm] caprice *m*

whimper [ˈwɪmpər] pleurnicher; *of animal* geindre

whine [waɪn] *of dog etc* gémir; F *(complain)* pleurnicher

whip [wɪp] **1** *n* fouet *m* **2** *v/t (beat)* fouetter; *cream* battre; F *(defeat)* battre à plates coutures

whirlpool ['wɜːrlpuːl] *in river* tourbillon *m*; *for relaxation* bain *m* à remous

whisk [wɪsk] **1** *n* fouet *m* **2** *v/t eggs* battre

whiskey ['wɪskɪ] whisky *m*

whisper ['wɪspər] chuchoter

whistle ['wɪsl] **1** *n sound* sifflement *m*; *device* sifflet *m* **2** *v/t & v/i* siffler

white [waɪt] **1** *n color, of egg* blanc *m*; *person* Blanc *m*, Blanche *f* **2** *adj* blanc; **white-collar worker** col *m* blanc; **White House** Maison *f* Blanche; **white lie** pieux mensonge *m*; **whitewash 1** *n* blanc *m* de chaux; *fig* maquillage *m* de la vérité **2** *v/t* blanchir à la chaux; **white wine** vin *m* blanc

whittle ['wɪtl] *wood* tailler au couteau

◆ **whittle down** réduire

whizzkid ['wɪzkɪd] F prodige *m*

who [huː] *interrogative* qui; *relative*: *subject* qui; *object* que; **the woman ~ you saw** la femme que tu as vue; **whoever** qui que ce soit; **~ gets the right answer** celui/celle qui trouve la bonne réponse

whole [hoʊl] **1** *adj* entier; **the ~ town** toute la ville **2** *n* tout *m*, ensemble *m*; **on the ~** dans l'ensemble; **whole-hearted** inconditionnel; **wholesale** de gros; *fig* en masse; **wholesaler** grossiste *m/f*; **wholesome** sain; **wholly** totalement

whom [huːm] *fml* qui

whore [hɔːr] putain *f*

whose [huːz] *interrogative* à qui; *relative* dont; **~ is this?** à qui c'est?; **a country ~ economy is boomimg** un pays dont l'économie prospère

why [waɪ] pourquoi

wicked ['wɪkɪd] méchant

wicker ['wɪkər] osier *m*

wicket ['wɪkɪt] *in station, bank etc* guichet *m*

wide [waɪd] *street, field* large; *experience* vaste; **be 12 foot~** faire 3 mètres et demi de large; **widely** largement; **~ known** très connu; **widen 1** *v/t* élargir **2** *v/i* s'élargir; **wide-open** grand ouvert; **wide-ranging** très portée; **widespread** répandu

widow ['wɪdoʊ] veuve *f*; **widower** veuf *m*

width [wɪdθ] largeur *f*

wield [wiːld] *weapon* manier; *power* exercer

wife [waɪf] femme *f*

wig [wɪg] perruque *f*

wiggle ['wɪgl] *tooth etc* remuer; *hips* tortiller

wild [waɪld] **1** *adj animal,
flowers* sauvage; *teenager* rebelle; *party* fou; *scheme* délirant; *applause* frénétique
wilderness ['wɪldərnɪs] désert *m*
'wildlife faune *f* et flore *f*
wilful *Br* → **willful**
will[1] [wɪl] *n* LAW testament *m*
will[2] [wɪl] *n* (*willpower*) volonté *f*
will[3] [wɪl] *v/aux: I ~ let you
know tomorrow* je vous le
dirai demain; *the car won't
start* la voiture ne veut pas
démarrer; *~ you tell her that
…?* est-ce que tu pourrais lui
dire que …?; *~ you stop
that!* veux-tu arrêter!
willful ['wɪlfl] *person, refusal*
volontaire; *willing helper*
de bonne volonté; *be ~ to
do sth* être prêt à faire
qch; **willingly** (*with pleasure*)
volontiers; **willingness** empressement *m*; **willpower** volonté *f*
willy-nilly [wɪlɪ'nɪlɪ] (*at random*) au petit bonheur la
chance
wilt [wɪlt] *of plant* se faner
wily ['waɪlɪ] rusé
wimp [wɪmp] F poule *f* mouillée
win [wɪn] **1** *n* victoire *f* **2** *v/t* &
v/i gagner; *prize* remporter
wince [wɪns] tressaillir
wind[1] [wɪnd] *n* vent *m*; (*flatulence*) gaz *m*
wind[2] [waɪnd] **1** *v/i of path,*

river serpenter **2** *v/t* enrouler
♦ **wind up 1** *v/t clock, car
window* remonter; *speech*
terminer; *affairs* conclure;
company liquider **2** *v/i* (*finish*) finir
wind-bag F moulin *m* à paroles F; **windfall** *fig* aubaine *f*
winding ['waɪndɪŋ] *path* qui
serpente
window ['wɪndoʊ] *also*
COMPUT fenêtre *f*; *of airplane,
boat* hublot *m*; *of store* vitrine *f*; *in the ~ of store* dans la
vitrine; **window seat** *on
train* place *f* côté fenêtre;
on airplane place côté hublot; **window-shop:** *go
~ping* faire du lèche-vitrines;
windowsill rebord *m* de fenêtre; **windshield**, *Br* **windscreen** pare-brise *m*; **windshield wiper** essuie-glace
m; **windsurfer** véliplanchiste
m/f; **windsurfing** planche *f* à
voile; **windy** venteux; *it's so
~* il y a tellement de vent
wine [waɪn] vin *m*; **wine cellar**
cave *f* (à vin); **wine list** carte *f*
des vins; **winery** établissement *m* viticole
wing [wɪŋ] *of bird, airplane,* SP
aile *f*; **wingspan** envergure *f*
wink [wɪŋk] *of person* cligner
des yeux
winner ['wɪnər] gagnant(e)
m(f); **winning** gagnant; **winning post** poteau *m* d'arrivée; **winnings** gains *mpl*
winter ['wɪntər] hiver *m*; **win-**

ter sports sports *mpl* d'hiver; **wintry** d'hiver

wipe [waɪp] essuyer; *tape* effacer; **wiper** ['waɪpər] → **windshield wiper**

wire ['waɪr] fil *m* de fer; *electrical* fil *m* électrique; **wireless phone** téléphone *m* sans fil; **wiring** ELEC installation *f* électrique; **wiry** *person* nerveux

wisdom ['wɪzdəm] sagesse *f*

wise [waɪz] sage; **wisecrack** F vanne *f* F; **wisely** *act* sagement

wish [wɪʃ] **1** *n* vœu *m*; **best ~es** cordialement; *for birthday, Christmas* meilleurs vœux **2** *v/t* souhaiter

◆ **wish for** vouloir

wisp [wɪsp] *of hair* mèche *f*; *of smoke* traînée *f*

wistful ['wɪstfl] nostalgique; **wistfully** avec nostalgie

wit [wɪt] *(humor)* esprit *m*; *person* homme *m*/femme *f* d'esprit

witch [wɪtʃ] sorcière *f*; **witch-hunt** *fig* chasse *f* aux sorcières

with [wɪð] avec; **~ no money** sans argent; **tired ~ waiting** fatigué d'attendre; **the woman ~ blue eyes** la femme aux yeux bleus; **I live ~ my aunt** je vis chez ma tante; **are you ~ me?** *(do you understand?)* est-ce que vous me suivez?

withdraw [wɪð'drɔː] **1** *v/t* reti-

rer **2** *v/i* se retire; **withdrawal** retrait *m*; **withdrawal symptoms** (symptômes *mpl* de) manque *m*; **withdrawn** *person* renfermé

wither ['wɪðər] se faner

withhold *information, name, payment* retenir; *consent* refuser

within *(inside)* dans; *in expressions of time* en moins de; *in expressions of distance* à moins de

without sans

withstand résister à

witness ['wɪtnɪs] **1** *n* témoin *m* **2** *v/t* être témoin de

witticism ['wɪtɪsɪzm] mot *m* d'esprit; **witty** plein d'esprit

wobble ['wɑːbl] osciller; **wobbly** bancal

wolf [wʊlf] **1** *n* loup *m* **2** *v/t*: **~ (down)** engloutir

woman ['wʊmən] femme *f*; **womanizer** coureur *m* de femmes; **womanly** féminin

womb [wuːm] utérus *m*

women ['wɪmɪn] *pl* → **woman**; **women's lib** libération *f* des femmes

wonder ['wʌndər] **1** *n* *(amazement)* émerveillement *m*; **no ~!** pas étonnant! **2** *v/i* se poser des questions; **I ~ if you could help** je me demandais si vous pouviez m'aider; **wonderful** merveilleux; **wonderfully** *(extremely)* merveilleusement

won't [woʊnt] → **will not**

wood [wʊd] bois *m*; **wooded** boisé; **wooden** (*made of wood*) en bois; **woodpecker** pic *m*; **woodwork** *parts made of wood* charpente *f*; *activity* menuiserie *f*

wool [wʊl] laine *f*; **woolen**, *Br* **woollen 1** *adj* en laine **2** *n* lainage *m*

word [wɜːrd] **1** *n* mot *m*; *of song*, (*promise*) parole *f* **2** *v/t article*, *letter* formuler; **word processor** traitement *m* de texte

work [wɜːrk] **1** *n* travail *m*; **out of ~** au chômage **2** *v/i of person* travailler; *of machine*, (*succeed*) marcher

◆ **work out 1** *v/t solution*, (*find out*) trouver; *problem* résoudre **2** *v/i at gym* s'entraîner; *of relationship etc* bien marcher

workable ['wɜːrkəbl] *solution* possible; **workaholic** F bourreau *m* de travail; **workday** (*hours of work*) journée *f* de travail; (*not weekend*) jour *m* de travail; **worker** travailleur(-euse) *m(f)*; **workforce** main-d'œuvre *f*; **work hours** heures *fpl* de travail; **working class** classe *f* ouvrière; **working-class** ouvrier; **working hours** → **work hours**; **workload** quantité *f* de travail; **workman** ouvrier *m*; **workmanlike** de professionnel; **workmanship** fabrication *f*; **work**

of art œuvre *f* d'art; **workout** séance *f* d'entraînement; **work permit** permis *m* de travail; **workshop** *also seminar* atelier *m*

world [wɜːrld] monde *m*; **world-class** de niveau mondial; **World Cup** in soccer Coupe *f* du monde; **world--famous** mondialement connu; **worldly** du monde; *person* qui a l'expérience du monde; **world record** record *m* mondial; **world war** guerre *f* mondiale; **worldwide 1** *adj* mondial **2** *adv* dans le monde entier

worn-'out *shoes*, *carpet* trop usé; *person* éreinté

worried ['wʌrid] inquiet; **worry 1** *n* souci *m* **2** *v/t* inquiéter **3** *v/i* s'inquiéter; **worrying** inquiétant

worse [wɜːrs] **1** *adj* pire **2** *adv* *play*, *perform*, *feel* plus mal; **worsen** empirer

worship ['wɜːrʃɪp] **1** *n* culte *m* **2** *v/t* God honorer; *fig*: *person*, *money* vénérer

worst [wɜːrst] **1** *adj* pire **2** *adv*: **the areas ~ affected** les régions les plus (gravement) touchées

worth [wɜːrθ]: **be ~ ...** valoir; **be ~ it** valoir la peine; **worthwhile**: **it's not ~ waiting** cela ne vaut pas la peine d'attendre

worthy ['wɜːrðɪ] *person*, *cause* digne

would [wʊd]: *I ~ help if I could* je vous aiderais si je pouvais; *~ you like to go to the movies?* est-ce que tu voudrais aller au cinéma?; *~ you tell her …?* pourriez--vous lui dire que …?

wound [wuːnd] **1** *n* blessure *f* **2** *v/t with weapon, words* blesser

wow [waʊ] *int* oh là là!

wrap [ræp] *gift* envelopper; *scarf etc* enrouler; **wrapping** emballage *m*; **wrapping paper** papier *m* d'emballage

wrath [ræθ] colère *f*

wreath [riːθ] couronne *f*

wreck [rek] **1** *n of ship* navire *m* naufragé; *of car* épave *f* **2** *v/t* détruire; **wreckage** *of ship* épave *m*; *of airplane* débris *mpl*; *of marriage, career* restes *mpl*; **wrecker** *truck* dépanneuse *f*

wrench [rentʃ] **1** *n tool* clef *f* **2** *v/t (pull)* arracher

wrestle ['resl] lutter; **wrestler** lutteur(-euse) *m(f)*; **wrestling** lutte *f*

wriggle ['rɪgl] *(squirm)* se tortiller

wrinkle ['rɪŋkl] *in skin* ride *f*; *in clothes* pli *m*

wrist [rɪst] poignet *m*; **wrist-watch** montre *f*

write [raɪt] écrire; *check* faire ◆ **write off** *debt* amortir; *car* bousiller F

writer ['raɪtər] *of letter, book, song* auteur *m/f*; *of book* écrivain *m/f*; **write-up** critique *f*

writhe [raɪð] se tordre

writing ['raɪtɪŋ] *(handwriting, script)* écriture *f*; *(words)* inscription *f*; *in ~* par écrit; **writing paper** papier *m* à lettres

wrong [rɒŋ] **1** *adj information, decision, side, number* mauvais; *answer also* faux; *be ~ of person* avoir tort; *of answer* être mauvais; *morally* être mal; *get the ~ train* se tromper de train; *what's ~?* qu'est-ce qu'il y a? **2** *adv* mal; *go ~ of person* se tromper; *of marriage, plan etc* mal tourner **3** *n* mal *m*; *injustice* injustice *f*; **wrongful** injuste; **wrongly** à tort

wry [raɪ] ironique

X, Y

xenophobia [zenoʊ'foʊbɪə] xénophobie *f*

X-ray ['eksreɪ] **1** *n* radio *f* **2** *v/t* radiographier

yacht [jɑːt] yacht *m*; **yachting** voile *f*

Yank [jæŋk] F Ricain(e) *m(f)* F

yank [jæŋk] *v/t* tirer violemment

yard¹ [jɑːrd] *of prison etc* cour f; *behind house* jardin m; *for storage* dépôt m

yard² [jɑːrd] *measurement* yard m

'yardstick point m de référence

yarn [jɑːrn] (*thread*) fil m; F (*story*) (longue) histoire f

yawn [jɔːn] **1** n bâillement m **2** v/i bâiller

year [jɪr] année; *be six ~s old* avoir six ans; *yearly* **1** *adj* annuel **2** *adv* tous les ans

yeast [jiːst] levure f

yell [jel] **1** n hurlement m **2** v/t & v/i hurler

yellow [ˈjeloʊ] jaune

yelp [jelp] **1** n *of animal* jappement m; *of person* glapissement m **2** v/i *of animal* japper; *of person* glapir

yes [jes] oui; *after* **1** *negative question* si; *yes man pej* béni-oui-oui m F

yesterday [ˈjestərdeɪ] hier; *the day before ~* avant-hier

yet [jet] **1** *adv*: *the best ~* le meilleur jusqu'ici; *as ~* pour le moment; *have you finished ~?* as-tu (déjà) fini?; *he hasn't arrived ~* il n'est pas encore arrivé; *~ bigger* encore plus grand **2** *conj* (*however*) néanmoins

yield [jiːld] **1** n *from crops, investment etc* rendement m **2** v/t *fruit, good harvest* produire; *interest* rapporter **3** v/i (*give way*) céder; AUT céder

la priorité

yoga [ˈjoʊgə] yoga m

yoghurt [ˈjoʊgərt] yaourt m

yolk [joʊk] jaune m (d'œuf)

you [juː] ◇ *familiar singular*: *subject* tu; *object* te; *before vowel* t'; *after prep* toi; *he knows ~* il te connaît; *for ~* pour toi

◇ *polite singular, familiar plural and polite plural, all uses* vous

◇ *indefinite* on; *~ never know* on ne sait jamais

young [jʌŋ] jeune; *youngster* jeune m/f; *child* petit(e) m(f)

your [jʊr] *familiar* ton, ta; *pl* tes; *polite* votre; *pl familiar and polite* vos

yours [jʊrz] *familiar* le tien, la tienne; *pl* les tiens, les tiennes; *polite* le/la vôtre; *pl* les vôtres; *a friend of ~* un(e) de tes ami(e)s; un(e) de vos ami(e)s; *~ at end of letter* bien amicalement

your'self *familiar* toi-même; *polite* vous-même; *reflexive* te; *polite* se; *after prep* toi; *polite* vous; *did you hurt ~?* est-ce que tu t'es fait mal/ est-ce que vous vous êtes fait mal?

your'selves vous-mêmes; *reflexive* vous; *after prep* vous; *did you hurt ~?* est-ce que vous vous êtes fait mal?

youth [juːθ] jeunesse f; (*young man*) jeune homme m; (*young people*) jeunes

mpl; **youth club** centre *m*
pour les jeunes; **youthful** juvénile

yuppie ['jʌpɪ] F yuppie *m/f*

Z

zap [zæp] F COMPUT (*delete*) effacer; (*kill*) éliminer; (*hit*)
donner un coup à; (*send*) envoyer vite fait

zeal [ziːl] zèle *m*

zero ['zɪrou] zéro *m*

zest [zest] *enjoyment* enthousiasme *m*

zigzag ['zɪgzæg] **1** *n* zigzag *m*
2 *v/i* zigzaguer

zilch [zɪltʃ] F que dalle F

zip ['zɪp] *Br* fermeture *f* éclair
◆ **zip up** *dress, jacket* remonter la fermeture éclair de;

COMPUT compresser

'zip code code *m* postal; **zipper** fermeture *f* éclair

zit [zɪt] F *on face* bouton *m*

zone [zoun] zone *f*

zonked [zɑːŋkt] P (*exhausted*)
crevé F

zoo [zuː] jardin *m* zoologique

zoology [zuː'ɑːlədʒɪ] zoologie *f*

'zoom lens zoom *m*

zucchini [zuː'kiːnɪ] courgette
f

Verbes irréguliers anglais

Vous trouverez ci-après les trois formes principales de chaque
verbe : l'infinitif, le prétérit et le participe passé.

arise - arose - arisen

awake - awoke - awoken,
awaked

be (am, is, are) - was (were)
- been

bear - bore - borne

beat - beat - beaten

become - became - become

begin - began - begun

bend - bent - bent

bet - bet, betted - bet, betted

bid - bid - bid

bind - bound - bound

bite - bit - bitten

bleed - bled - bled

blow - blew - blown

break - broke - broken

breed - bred - bred

bring - brought - brought

broadcast - broadcast -
broadcast

build - built - built

burn - burnt, burned -
burnt, burned

burst - burst - burst

buy - bought - bought

cast - cast - cast

catch - caught - caught

choose - chose - chosen

cling - clung - clung

come - came - come

cost (*v/i*) - cost - cost

creep - crept - crept

cut - cut - cut

deal - dealt - dealt

dig - dug - dug

dive - dived, dove [doʊv]
(1) - dived

do - did - done

draw - drew - drawn

dream - dreamt, dreamed -
dreamt, dreamed

drink - drank - drunk

drive - drove - driven

eat - ate - eaten

fall - fell - fallen

feed - fed - fed

feel - felt - felt

fight - fought - fought

find - found - found

flee - fled - fled

fling - flung - flung

fly - flew - flown

forbid - forbad(e) -
forbidden

forecast - forecast(ed) -
forecast(ed)

forget - forgot - forgotten

forgive - forgave - forgiven

freeze - froze - frozen

get - got - got, gotten (2)

give - gave - given

go – went – gone
grind – ground – ground
grow – grew – grown
hang – hung, hanged – hung, hanged (3)
have – had – had
hear – heard – heard
hide – hid – hidden
hit – hit – hit
hold – held – held
hurt – hurt – hurt
keep – kept – kept
kneel – knelt, kneeled – knelt, kneeled
know – knew – known
lay – laid – laid
lead – led – led
lean – leaned, leant – leaned, leant (4)
leap – leaped, leapt – leaped, leapt (4)
learn – learned, learnt – learned, learnt (4)
leave – left – left
lend – lent – lent
let – let – let
lie – lay – lain
light – lighted, lit – lighted, lit
lose – lost – lost
make – made – made
mean – meant – meant
meet – met – met
mow – mowed – mowed, mown

pay – paid – paid
plead – pleaded, pled – pleaded, pled (5)
prove – proved – proved, proven
put – put – put
quit – quit(ted) – quit(ted)
read – read [red] – read [red]
ride – rode – ridden
ring – rang – rung
rise – rose – risen
run – ran – run
saw – sawed – sawn, sawed
say – said – said
see – saw – seen
seek – sought – sought
sell – sold – sold
send – sent – sent
set – set – set
sew – sewed – sewed, sewn
shake – shook – shaken
shed – shed – shed
shine – shone – shone
shit – shit(ted), shat – shit(ted), shat
shoot – shot – shot
show – showed – shown
shrink – shrank – shrunk
shut – shut – shut
sing – sang – sung
sink – sank – sunk
sit – sat – sat
slay – slew – slain
sleep – slept – slept
slide – slid – slid

sling – slung – slung
slit – slit – slit
smell – smelt, smelled – smelt, smelled
sow – sowed – sown, sowed
speak – spoke – spoken
speed – sped, speeded – sped, speeded
spell – spelt, spelled – spelt, spelled (4)
spend – spent – spent
spill – spilt, spilled – spilt, spilled
spin – spun – spun
spit – spat – spat
split – split – split
spoil – spoiled, spoilt – spoiled, spoilt
spread – spread – spread
spring – sprang, sprung – sprung
stand – stood – stood
steal – stole – stolen
stick – stuck – stuck
sting – stung – stung
stink – stunk, stank – stunk

stride – strode – stridden
strike – struck – struck
swear – swore – sworn
sweep – swept – swept
swell – swelled – swollen
swim – swam – swum
swing – swung – swung
take – took – taken
teach – taught – taught
tear – tore – torn
tell – told – told
think – thought – thought
thrive – throve – thriven, thrived (6)
throw – threw – thrown
thrust – thrust – thrust
tread – trod – trodden
wake – woke, waked – woken, waked
wear – wore – worn
weave – wove – woven (7)
weep – wept – wept
win – won – won
wind – wound – wound
write – wrote – written

(1) **dove** n'est pas utilisé en anglais britannique
(2) **gotten** n'est pas utilisé en anglais britannique
(3) **hung** pour les tableaux mais **hanged** pour les meurtriers
(4) l'anglais américain n'emploie normalement que la forme en **-ed**
(5) **pled** s'emploie en anglais américain ou écossais
(6) la forme **thrived** est plus courante
(7) mais **weaved** au sens de *se faufiler*

Numbers / Les nombres

Cardinal Numbers / Les nombres cardinaux

0	zero, *Br aussi* nought *zéro*		**14**	fourteen *quatorze*
1	one *un*		**15**	fifteen *quinze*
2	two *deux*		**16**	sixteen *seize*
3	three *trois*		**17**	seventeen *dix-sept*
4	four *quatre*		**18**	eighteen *dix-huit*
5	five *cinq*		**19**	nineteen *dix-neuf*
6	six *six*		**20**	twenty *vingt*
7	seven *sept*		**21**	twenty-one *vingt et un*
8	eight *huit*		**22**	twenty-two *vingt-deux*
9	nine *neuf*		**30**	thirty *trente*
10	ten *dix*		**31**	thirty-one *trente et un*
11	eleven *onze*		**40**	forty *quarante*
12	twelve *douze*		**50**	fifty *cinquante*
13	thirteen *treize*		**60**	sixty *soixante*
			70	seventy *soixante-dix*

71	seventy-one *soixante et onze*
72	seventy-two *soixante-douze*
79	seventy-nine *soixante-dix-neuf*
80	eighty *quatre-vingts*
81	eighty-one *quatre-vingt-un*
90	ninety *quatre-vingt-dix*
91	ninety-one *quatre-vingt-onze*
100	a hundred, one hundred *cent*
101	a hundred and one *cent un*
200	two hundred *deux cents*
300	three hundred *trois cents*
324	three hundred and twenty-four *trois cent vingt-quatre*
1000	a thousand, one thousand *mille*
2000	two thousand *deux mille*

1959	one thousand nine hundred and fifty-nine	
	mille neuf cent cinquante-neuf	
2000	two thousand *deux mille*	
1 000 000	a million, one million *un million*	
2 000 000	two million *deux millions*	
1 000 000 000	a billion, one billion *un milliard*	

Notes / Remarques:

i) **vingt** and **cent** take an -s when preceded by another number, except if there is another number following.

ii) If **un** is used with a following noun, then it is the only number to agree
(one man **un homme**; one woman **une femme**).

iii) 1.25 (one point two five) = 1,25 (un virgule vingt-cinq)

iv) 1,000,000 (en anglais) = 1 000 000 ou 1.000.000 (in French)

Ordinal Numbers / Les nombres ordinaux

1st	first	$1^{er}/1^{ère}$	*premier / première*
2nd	second	2^e	*deuxième*
3rd	third	3^e	*troisième*
4th	fourth	4^e	*quatrième*
5th	fifth	5^e	*cinquième*
6th	sixth	6^e	*sixième*
7th	seventh	7^e	*septième*
8th	eighth	8^e	*huitième*
9th	ninth	9^e	*neuvième*
10th	tenth	10^e	*dixième*
11th	eleventh	11^e	*onzième*
12th	twelfth	12^e	*douzième*
13th	thirteenth	13^e	*treizième*
14th	fourteenth	14^e	*quatorzième*
15th	fifteenth	15^e	*quinzième*

16th	sixteenth	16^e	*seizième*
17th	seventeenth	17^e	*dix-septième*
18th	eighteenth	18^e	*dix-huitième*
19th	nineteenth	19^e	*dix-neuvième*
20th	twentieth	20^e	*vingtième*
21st	twenty-first	21^e	*vingt et unième*
22nd	twenty-second	22^e	*vingt-deuxième*
30th	thirtieth	30^e	*trentième*
31st	thirty-first	31^e	*trente et unième*
40th	fortieth	40^e	*quarantième*
50th	fiftieth	50^e	*cinquantième*
60th	sixtieth	60^e	*soixantième*
70th	seventieth	70^e	*soixante-dixième*
71st	seventy-first	71^e	*soixante et onzième*
80th	eightieth	80^e	*quatre-vingtième*
90th	ninetieth	90^e	*quatre-vingt-dixième*
100th	hundredth	100^e	*centième*
101st	hundred and first	101^e	*cent unième*
1000th	thousandth	1000^e	*millième*
2000th	two thousandth	2000^e	*deux millième*
1,000,000th	millionth	1 000 000^e	*millionième*

Dates / Les dates

1996	nineteen ninety-six	*mille neuf cent quatre-vingt-seize*
2005	two thousand (and) five	*deux mille cinq*

November 10/11 (ten, eleven), *Br* **the 10th/11th of November**
le dix/onze novembre

March 1 (first), *Br* **the 1st of March**
le premier mars